Judenrat

THE JEWISH COUNCILS IN EASTERN EUROPE UNDER NAZI OCCUPATION

Isaiah Trunk

INTRODUCTION BY *Jacob Robinson*

Introduction to the Bison Books Edition by Steven T. Katz

University of Nebraska Press
Lincoln

© 1972 by Isaiah Trunk
Introduction to the Bison Books Edition © 1996 by the University of Nebraska
Press
Manufactured in the United States of America

⊗ The paper in this book meets the minimum requirements of American
National Standard for Information Sciences—Permanence of Paper for Printed
Library Materials, ANSI Z39.48-1984.

First Bison Books printing: 1996
Most recent printing indicated by the last digit below:
10   9   8   7   6   5   4   3   2   1

Library of Congress Cataloging-in-Publication Data
Trunk, Isaiah.
Judenrat: the Jewish councils in Eastern Europe under Nazi occupation / Isaiah
Trunk; introduction by Jacob Robinson; introduction to the Bison books edition
by Steven T. Katz.
p.   cm.
Previously published: New York: Macmillan, 1972.
Includes bibliographical references and index.
ISBN 0-8032-9428-X (pbk.: alk. paper)
1. Jewish councils—Europe, Eastern—History—20th century.   2. Jews—Europe,
Eastern—Politics and government.   3. Holocaust, Jewish (1939–1945)   I. Title.
DS135.E83T78   1996
940.53′18—dc20
95-49993   CIP

Originally published in 1972 by the Macmillan Company, New York. Reprinted
by arrangement with Scribner, An Imprint of Simon & Schuster Inc., New York.

Contents

CONTENTS

Illustrations

Introduction to the Bison Books Edition

Steven T. Katz

In the aftermath of the Holocaust, the term now universally applied to the planned and uncompromising murder of European Jewry under the Nazi regime during World War II, almost every action and reaction of those who were its perpetrators and victims has become the subject of intensive scholarly investigation and debate. Among the most important of these retrospective subjects is the vexing question of Jewry's complicity in its own destruction. To what degree did the Jews and Jewish organizations assist, however unintentionally, in the "Final Solution" and to what degree did they resist, however successfully or not, this Luciferian undertaking? Within this broad, conflicted, debate there is also a more specific question: what role did the *Judenräte*, the involuntary Jewish Councils—created by order of Reinhard Heydrich on 21 September 1939 following the conquest of Poland, and applying to every Jewish community of ten thousand or more—play in this critical situation? To what degree were they tools, witting and unwitting, of the process of extermination and to what degree did they intentionally act so as to deflect Nazi intentions and keep Jews alive? This last is a subject laden with historical and philosophical complexities and much emotional overload.

Raul Hilberg, by scholarly consensus the most distinguished historian of the Holocaust, has, in particular, leveled a very negative judgment regarding the question of Jewish resistance. Both in the first edition of his classic work, *The Destruction of European Jewry* (1960), and in his definitive three volume revised version published in 1985, Hilberg has taken the view that:

The reaction pattern of the Jews is characterized by almost complete lack of resistance. In marked contrast to German propaganda, the documentary evidence of Jewish resistance, overt or submerged, is very slight. On a European-wide scale the Jews had no resistance organization, no blueprint for armed action, no plan even for psychological warfare. They were completely unprepared. (*Destruction*, 1st ed., 662)

Hilberg attributes this pattern to Jewish history, to the experience of two thousand years of exilic existence:

If, therefore, we look at the whole Jewish reaction pattern, we notice that in its two salient features it is an attempt to avert action and, failing that, automatic compliance with orders. Why is this so? Why did the Jews act in this way? The Jews attempted to tame the Germans as one would attempt to tame a wild beast. They avoided "provocations" and complied instantly with decrees and orders. They hoped that somehow the German drive would spend itself.

This hope was founded on a two-thousand-year-old experience. In exile the Jews had always been in a minority; they had always been in danger; but they had learned that they could avert danger and survive destruction by placating and appeasing their enemies. . . .

Thus, over a period of centuries the Jews had learned that in order to survive they had to refrain from resistance. . . .

Only in 1941, 1942 and 1943 did the Jewish leadership realize that, unlike the pogroms of past centuries, the modern machine-like destruction process would engulf European Jewry. But the realization came too late. A two-thousand-year-old lesson could not be unlearned; the Jews could not make the switch. They were helpless. (666)

And as regards the specific role of the Jewish Councils, Hilberg concludes:

The traditional role of the Jewish community machinery—to educate the children in the schools, to feed the hungry in the soup kitchens, and to help the sick in its hospitals—was now supplemented by another, quite different function: the transmission of German directives and orders to the Jewish population, the use of Jewish police to enforce German will, the deliverance of Jewish property, Jewish labor, and Jewish lives to the German enemy. The Jewish councils, in the exercise of their historic function, continued until the end to make desperate attempts to alleviate the suffering and to stop the mass dying in the ghettos. But at the same time, the councils responded to German demands with automatic compliance and invoked German authority to compel the community's obedience. Thus the Jewish leadership both saved and destroyed its people—saving some Jews and destroying others, saving the Jews at one moment and destroying them at the next. Some leaders broke under this power; others became intoxicated with it.

As time passed by, the Jewish councils became increasingly impotent in their efforts to cope with the welfare portion of their task, but they made themselves felt all the more in their implementation of Nazi decrees. (146)

Still more, Hilberg is unsparing in his estimation of the behavior, the improprieties, of the leaders of the Councils:

With the growth of the destructive function of the Judenräte, many Jewish leaders felt an almost irresistible urge to look like their German masters. In March, 1940, a Nazi observer in Krakow was struck by the contrast between the poverty and filth in the Jewish quarter and the businesslike luxury of the Jewish community headquarters, which was filled with beautiful charts, comfortable leather chairs, and heavy carpets. In Warsaw the Jewish oligarchy took to wearing boots. In Łódź the ghetto "dictator" Rumkowski printed postage stamps bearing his likeness and made speeches which contained expressions such as "my children," "my factories," and "my Jews." From the inside, then, it seemed already quite clear that the Jewish leaders had become rulers, reigning and disposing over the ghetto community with a finality that was absolute. (146)*

This extreme indictment, circulated first in scholarly circles, was disseminated widely and took deep root when it was adopted by Hannah Arendt in the course of her reporting on the Eichmann trial in Jerusalem in 1963 for the *New Yorker*. (She published a series of essays for the *New Yorker* that eventually became the well-known, highly controversial book *Eichmann in Jerusalem* [1963]). Here, among the many controversial positions that she articulated, she picked up Hilberg's radical thesis on the Jewish leadership and the Jewish Councils and argued:

[Eichmann] expected—and received, to a truly extraordinary degree—their [Jewish] cooperation. This was "of course the very cornerstone" of everything he did, as it had been the very cornerstone of his activities in Vienna. Without Jewish help in administrative and policy work . . . there would have been either complete chaos or an impossibly severe drain on German manpower.

And she concludes:

To a Jew this role of the Jewish leaders in the destruction of their own people is undoubtedly the darkest chapter of the whole dark story. . . . In the matter of cooperation, there was no distinction between the highly assimilated Jewish communities of Central and Western Europe and the Yiddish-speaking masses of the East. In Amsterdam as in Warsaw, in Berlin as in Budapest, Jewish officials could be trusted to compile the lists of persons and of their property, to secure money from the deportees to defray the expenses of their deportation and extermination, to keep track of vacated apartments, to supply police forces to help seize

---

*In the new edition of *Destruction*, vol. 1, 216–19 and vol. 3, 1030–45, Hilberg essentially repeats this position without any meaningful alteration.

Jews and get them on trains, until, as a last gesture, they handed over the assets of the Jewish community in good order for final confiscation. . . . We know how the Jewish officials felt when they became instruments of murder—like captains "whose ships were about to sink and who succeeded in bringing them safe to port by casting overboard a great part of their precious cargo"; like saviors who "with a hundred victims save a thousand people, with a thousand ten thousand." The truth was even more gruesome. (117–18)

These comprehensive accusations against the *Judenräte* have stuck in the popular mind. Most people, even if only in some loose, inchoate sense, accept this picture of Jewish complicity, passivity, cowardice, and corruption in the face of their own certain death.

But are these claims fair? Are they historically accurate? Are they morally defensible? Over against this vehement negative interpretation—this litany of asserted misjudgments and failures, the sharp ethical reproach of Hilberg, Arendt, and their many disciples—stands most especially the magisterial work of Isaiah Trunk.

In *Judenrat,* and in later publications such as his introductory material to his collection of Holocaust-related testimonies, *Jewish Responses to Catastrophe* (1982), Trunk (b. 21 July 1905, Kutno, Poland; d. 28 March 1981, New York City), Chief Archivist of the YIVO Institute for Jewish Research in New York City, set himself the task of reexamining, with a more careful, nuanced, and differentiated approach, the work of the *Judenräte* that operated in the ghettos of Poland and the Baltic states. Through a meticulous reconstruction of all aspects of ghetto life—almost nothing that went on in the ghettos falls outside his purview—he sheds a far different light on the tragic circumstance in which all the Jewish leaders found themselves. What emerges as a result of his monumental efforts is a near-definitive description of the varied responses of the Jewish leadership to their common predicament: the planned, total extermination of every Jewish man, woman, and child within the Nazi sphere of political power.

What Trunk's detailed researches show is, first, the inescapability of Jewish "cooperation" with the Nazi overlord. Subjugated, separated from the general population, and ghettoized in quick order following the defeat of Poland—without help from either local Poles or the distant Allied nations—there was, ultimately, no alternative to such interaction—all Arendt-like fantasies of an anarchic Jewish response to the contrary. Second, all solutions that the Jewish Councils might have pursued or did pursue in their attempt to save Jewish lives, *given the Nazi-created situation in which they found themselves and from which there was no general escape,* involved profound moral (and practical) uncertainties and ambiguities:

[T]here is sufficient basis to support the thesis that divergent opinions [on what should be done] came to the surface and desperate soul-searching went on in many more places during the "resettlements." The learned rabbis could not arrive at a consensus of opinion. In Kaunas, Oszmiana, Sosnowiec, and Heidemühle, the rabbis decided that it was necessary to obey the German authorities, prepare the ordered lists, call the Jews to report to "selection," etc. They reasoned that the orders referred only to transfers for forced labor and not for death (as in Sosnowiec), and that through obeying the orders parts of the ghettos would be saved (as in Kaunas). On the other hand, the rabbis in Vilna categorically forbade Gens to deliver a single Jew into the hands of the Gestapo, even if this could, as he maintained, save others from death. (429)

The Jewish leadership found itself in a supreme moral dilemma from which there was no reprieve. Whatever the Councils did would have cost Jewish lives. In response, most chose, to the degree possible, to try to influence the outcome of events with an eye to *collective* Jewish survival by selecting the sick, the elderly, and the insane for the demanded deportations. Yet this, too, was morally problematic. However, in evaluating this decision, as well as all other aspects of the Jewish response to Nazi persecution, one always needs to remember that, though the Nazi program intended the total extermination of the Jewish people, this aim was not self-evident from the outset to the Jewish leadership, or to the Jewish community at large. Moreover, the purposeful confusion sown by the Nazis as to their final intentions and their policy of partial "deportations" carried on in stages reinforced the ignorance that reigned in Jewish circles. In these misunderstood circumstances the *Judenräte*, not incorrectly, believed that the moral issue(s) facing them involved not only the question of saving individual Jewish lives, of deciding who should live and who should die, but also the transcending issue of the survival of the Jewish people.

Third, the Councils, for the most part, authentically believed, given Germany's acute wartime shortage of workers, that the strategy of rescue through "work" would save at least some segment of the Jewish people until the final defeat of the Nazi regime was achieved. On this key issue Trunk concludes that the Jewish Councils "made a great mistake in believing that Nazi policy with respect to the Jews had been motivated by rational or utilitarian considerations of any kind." However,

in those times of unprecedented calamity the Jewish Councils, groping toward means to cope with the "resettlements," had no choice but to try the mass employment strategy. It should be added that wide circles of the working segments of the population shared this strategy, though perhaps under the influence of the Councils. In retrospect we find that those who remained in the ghettos perished almost to a man, having been deported to extermination camps or killed on the spot. On the other hand, a certain percentage survived from among those who, before or during the liquidation of the ghettos, were shipped to various labor or concentration camps. There is no doubt that the decisive factor in extending the lives of some of the ghettos was the measure of their contribution to the German war economy. (412–13)

The disutilitarian character of Nazi anti-Jewish policy flew in the face of the history of the world. Victimizers enslave and exploit their victims, they do not murder them solely on racial-ideological grounds. Here the uniqueness, the unprecedented nature of the *Shoah* was essential to the misunderstanding—purposely encouraged by continual Nazi misinformation, fraud, and deceit (see Trunk's important review of these Nazi efforts on 413–20)—that governed the thinking of the Jewish leadership. This leadership, having studied history, "knew" that rational considerations dictate that masters do not kill those they can exploit for gain. But this well-proven rule was now, in a quite singular way, almost totally violated as a result of the imperatives of Nazi racial doctrine. It was more important that Jews die than that they work.

Concerning the purposeful disinformation provided to the Jewish Councils, which meant that they were always working with either inadequate or incorrect information, Trunk reports at length on the particularly telling example of Adam Czerniakow, the head of the Warsaw Ghetto *Judenrat:*

On July 20, 1942, barely two days before the Gestapo men came to the office of the Jewish Council in Warsaw to dictate the order for mass "resettlement" Czerniakow noted in his diary:

> [I visited] the Gestapo at 7:30 in the morning. I inquired of Mende [in charge of Jewish affairs] how much truth there was in the rumors [about pending resettlement]. He answered that he knew nothing about it. To my question whether this was at all possible, he again answered that he knew nothing about it. I left unconvinced. I then asked his chief, *Kommissar* Boehm, who answered that this was not within his competence, that Höhnemann [a leading Gestapo man] might be in a position to give some information. I stressed that, according to rumors, the "resettlement" was to start today at 19:30 [7:30 p.m. He] answered that he would certainly have had some information if this were so. Having no recourse, I approached Scherer, the deputy chief of Department III [of the Gestapo]. He showed surprise and said that he too knew nothing. I then asked whether I might inform the [Jewish] population that there was no foundation for the alarm. [He] answered that I could do so. Everything that has been rumored is unsubstantiated gossip and groundless talk. I have [therefore] instructed [Jacob] Lejkin [commandant of the ghetto police] to inform the population accordingly through the area committees.

Czerniakow supplemented the entry by stating that when First, the chief of the economic department of the Jewish Council, inquired of the two other Security Police officials, they got very angry because of the rumors and said that an investigation would be ordered about the whole thing. A mere two days later the "resettlement" began and Czerniakow committed suicide. (414)

Moreover, and not unimportant, Trunk notes that even with all the errors and misjudgments that the Jewish leadership made,

Had the war ended earlier, a sizable number of the labor elements might have survived. Let us take the case of the Łódź Ghetto. In August 1944, when the Soviet armies had already reached the environs of Warsaw, approximately 70,000 Jews still lived in Łódź (at a distance of some 75 miles). Had the Soviet army not stopped its advance till January 1945, a large number of these 70,000 people would certainly have escaped the gas chambers of Auschwitz. (413)

Fourth, the persistent impression created by some that the Council leaders were largely self-interested and corrupt individuals is, as Trunk's multiform evidence compellingly indicates, far from true in its generality. Given the extremely sensitive nature of this issue, the absolute moral heroism of many of the *Judenräte* leaders, the diverse forms that their unambiguous resistance to Nazi demands took, often at the cost of their lives, and the barrage of abuse, some warranted, much not, that has retrospectively been cast on them, I note Trunk's judgment that:

Even prior to the advent of massive "resettlement" there were instances where Council members refused to cooperate with the Germans, sabotaged orders, or courageously interceded on behalf of the persecuted. Often they paid for these actions with their lives on the spot or were included in the very next "resettlement" transport. These acts of dedication, high spirit, and moral standards on the part of some of the ghetto leaders deserve to be remembered. (437)

And Trunk knows whereof he speaks, as the many examples of moral heroism he cites, drawn from a wide variety of Councils, confirms (437–42).

None of these many extraordinary acts appreciably retarded the murder of Eastern European Jewry. This was something essentially outside the parameters of Jewish possibility. But these numerous ethical deeds of political courage and human concern rebut the efforts of those who would lay an undifferentiated charge of unscrupulousness and moral failing against the leaders of the *Judenräte*. Some Jewish leaders did act immorally, did behave reprehensibly, did protect themselves—for a while—at the expense of others; but many, many others, who served out of a deep, selfless sense of moral obligation, acted otherwise.

Fifth, Trunk's data shows that the Jewish leadership was very active in the support of cultural and spiritual resistance to the concerted Nazi effort to dehumanize the Jewish people. This is an elemental, much undervalued aspect of Jewish resistance, of the meaning of Jewish resistance against Nazism. In a world that would deny their common humanity, their very belonging to the human family, the Jewish People, directly encouraged and supported by its leadership, retained its spiritual integrity and inherent dignity.

Sixth, though many Councils opposed acts of physical resistance, there were many Councils that actively supported various forms of such activity. Moreover, those that eschewed overt physical struggle did so not only or even primarily out of fear but rather for well-considered and prudent reasons, such as concern over the omnipresent possibility (and often reality) of massive reprisals against the Jewish population at large, even the liquidation of the entire ghetto for which they were directly responsible.

Seventh, as Trunk persuasively demonstrates, outright collaboration by the Jewish Councils with the Nazi program of mass death was rare. Trunk reminds us that non-Jewish collaboration was voluntary; this was the defining meaning of the notion of collaboration, whereas Jewish "cooperation" was "forced upon the Jews and was maintained in an atmosphere of ever-present merciless terror" (573). (Readers should reflect carefully on Trunk's concluding remarks on the difference between Jewish "cooperation" and "collaboration" in this extreme context, 570–75.)

Eighth, Trunk's massive documentation reveals that almost every generalization about the behavior of the *Judenräte* and their leadership needs to be tested against a wide array of heterogeneous, sometimes contradictory, evidence:

It seemed to me that the inductive method was the one most suited to my purpose, and I have cited as many local events in as many ghettos as possible. To a degree it is possible to find common features in the general pattern of the activities of the Councils—in their welfare policies and in the motivation of their strategy and tactics toward the Germans. I am, however, of the opinion that the entire Council phenomenon cannot be analyzed in general terms. It has to be discussed with a view toward local conditions and personalities, the activities of individual Councils and their attitudes toward the German authorities. In the final analysis we deal here with people of diverse socio-psychological backgrounds variously reacting to similar situations. The researcher has to beware of the temptation to simplify or generalize, trying to evaluate the attitudes and actions of individual Council members in given situations. (xxix–xxx)

Lastly, and above all else, Trunk's work has the merit of reminding us that, no matter what the Jewish Councils did or did not do, the fate of European Jewry was sealed. One can, with good reason, lay individual blame in many instances, and as regards the running of many Councils one might criticize the various strategems that the Jewish leadership adopted for dealing with this supremely menacing, distinctly novel situation, and one might identify the weaknesses in traditional Jewish responses to oppression that now, in this wholly new circumstance, led nowhere but to Auschwitz and Treblinka, and one might rightly identify all the illusory psychological mechanisms that Jews, individually and as a community, adopted in the midst of the "resettlements" to the Death Camps, but, in truth, all of these real failures made no substantial difference. The Jews of Europe would have died in equal (or greater) number than they did had they done none of the above, or something very different. The Nazi obsession with the extermination of European Jewry (and had they the ability, of all of world Jewry), *coupled with the reality of near total Jewish powerlessness* (an issue insufficiently stressed by both Trunk and those who hold views opposite to his), was such that the Jewish people were marked for death quite independently of their behavior under this particular evil regime. The most important evidence in support of this repercussive judgment is the murder of one to one and a half million Jews by the *Einsatzgruppen* as part of the German invasion of Russia (22 June 1941). No Jewish Councils yet existed in these newly invaded territories; no Jewish leaders made any fateful decisions affecting their communities; no consideration of traditional Jewish responses to persecution is relevant to what occurred then and there; yet all the Jews of these territories were targeted to be killed where they stood.

This combination of Nazi intentions and Jewish powerlessness is also luminously evidenced in the collective fate of the leadership of the *Judenräte*, almost all of whom, despite their temporary power and privilege, ultimately shared in the common destiny of their Jewish compatriots. Of the leaders of the Councils it is estimated that only 12 percent survived the war. Even more striking is the fate of Mordecai Chaim Rumkowski, the Elder of the Łódź Ghetto, Jacob Gens, Elder of the Vilna Ghetto, Ephraim Barash, Elder of the Białystok Ghetto, and Roman Merin, Elder of the Ghetto in Eastern Upper Silesia—four of the most "powerful" Jews in Eastern Europe—all of whom were killed by the Nazis. And then, too, there is the end of Adam Czerniakow, Elder of the largest ghetto in Europe, who took his own life when he realized that he was absolutely unable to stop the murder of the Jews of Warsaw.

SUGGESTIONS FOR FURTHER READING

Since the initial publication of *Judenrat*, scholarly research into the subject of Jewish resistance during the Nazi era in general and that of the role and actions of the Jewish Councils in particular has increased dramatically, a good deal of it inspired by Trunk's pioneering efforts. This scholarship, much of it done by Israeli scholars, has largely reinforced and extended Trunk's basic perspective.

Among the more important of such studies are: Yisrael Gutman and Cynthia J. Haft (eds.), *Patterns of Leadership in Nazi Europe, 1933–1945: Proceedings of the Third Yad Vashem International Historical Conference, April 1977* (Jerusalem, 1977); Yisrael Gutman, *The Jews of Warsaw, 1939–1943: Ghetto, Underground, Revolt* (Bloomington, 1982); Yitzchak Zuckerman, *A Surplus of Memory: Chronicle of the Warsaw Ghetto Uprising* (Berkeley, 1993); Aharon Weiss, "Le darkam shel ha-judenratim bi-drom-mizrakh Polin," *Yalkut Moreshet*, vol. 15 (October, 1972), 59–122; idem, "Le-Ha'arakhatam Shel Ha-yudenratim," *Yalkut Moreshet*, vol. 11 (November, 1969), 108–12; idem, "Defusey Hitnahagut Shel Ha-Yudenratim," *Yalkut Moreshet*, vol. 36 (1983), 39–44; idem, "Iyun Nosaf Benose Ha-Yudenratim," in Emanuel Melzer and David Engel (eds.), *On the History of the Jews in Poland* (Tel Aviv, 1976), vol. 3, 279–94; idem, "Jewish Leadership in Occupied Poland: Postures and Attitudes," in *Yad Vashem Studies on the European Jewish Catastrophe and Resistance*, vol. 12 (Jerusalem, 1977), 335–66; Alan Adelson and Robert Lapides (eds.), *Łódź Ghetto: Inside a Community Under Siege* (New York, 1989); Philip Friedman, *Roads to Extinction: Essays on the Holocaust*, edited by Ada June Friedman (New York, 1980); Emmanuel Ringelblum, *Notes From the Warsaw Ghetto* (New York, 1974); Shimon Huberband, *Kiddush Hashem: Jewish Religious and Cultural Life in Poland During the Holocaust* (New York, 1987); Lucjan Dobroszycki (ed.), *The Chronicle of the Łódź Ghetto* (New Haven, 1984); Avraham Tory, *Surviving the Holocaust: The Kovno Ghetto Diary*, edited by Martin Gilbert (Cambridge MA, 1990); Yehuda Bauer and Nathan Rotenstreich (eds.), *The Holocaust as Historical Experience* (New York, 1981); Randolph L. Braham, "The Jewish Councils: An Overview," in François Furet (ed.), *Unanswered Questions: Nazi Germany and the Genocide of the Jews* (New York, 1989), 252–74; Dina Porat, "The Jewish Councils of the Main Ghettos of Lithuania: A Comparison," *Modern Judaism*, vol. 13, no. 2 (1993), 149–63; David Cesarani, "On the Warsaw Ghetto Uprising of April 1943," *British Journal of Holocaust Education*, vol. 2, no. 1 (Great Britain, 1993), 83–93; Verena Wahlen, "Select Bibliography on Judenraete Under Nazi Rule," in *Yad Vashem Studies on the European Jewish Catastrophe and Resistance*, vol. 10 (Jerusalem, 1974), 277–94; "The Yivo Colloquium on the Judenrate During the Nazi Period," in *Yad Vashem Studies on the European Jewish Catastrophe and Resistance*, vol. 7 (Jerusalem, 1968), 189–92; Maurice Friedberg, "The Question of the Judenrate," *Commentary*, vol. 56, no. 1 (1973), 61–66; and Raul Hilberg, "The Ghetto as a Form of Government," *Annual of the American Academy of Political and Social Science*, vol. 450 (1980), 98–112.

For more on the intense controversy created by Hannah Arendt's *Eichmann in Jerusalem* see the pre-Trunk work of Jacob Robinson, *And the Crooked Shall Be Made Straight* (New York, 1965), F. A. Krummacher (ed.), *Die Kontroverse Hannah Arendt: Eichmann und die Juden* (Munich, 1964); Hannah Arendt, *The Jew as Pariah: Jewish Identity and Politics in the Modern Age*, edited by Ron H. Feldman (New York, 1978); and Dagmar Barnouw, *Hannah Arendt and the German Jewish Experience* (Baltimore, 1990). A major original document of great importance is Adam Czerniakow, *The Warsaw Diary of Adam Czerniakow*, edited by Raul Hilberg, Staron Stanislaw, and Josef Kermisz (New York, 1979). For more on Czerniakow, see Joseph L. Lichten, "Adam Czerniakow and His Times," *Polish Review*, vol. 29, nos. 1–2 (1984), 71–89; and Marian Fuks, "The problem of the Jewish Councils (Judenrat) and the work of Adam Czerniakow," [in German] *Judaica*, vol. 39, no. 4 (1983), 241–50. For further information on Isaiah Trunk, see Joseph Kermish, "Isaiah Trunk (1905–1981) In Memorian," in *Yad Vashem Studies on the European Jewish Catastrophe and Resistance*, vol. 14 (Jerusalem, 1981), 335–40.

On the issue of Jewish resistance more generally, see: Shalom Cholawski, *Soldiers from the Ghetto* (New York, 1980); Shmuel Krakowski, *The War of the Doomed: Jewish Armed Resistance in Poland, 1942–1944* (New York, 1984); Reuben Ainsztein, *Jewish Resistance in Nazi-Occupied Eastern Europe* (New York, 1974); Yuri Suhl (ed.), *They Fought Back: The Story of Jewish Resistance in Nazi Europe* (New York, 1975); Dov Levin, *Fighting Back: Lithuanian Jewry's Resistance to the Nazis, 1941–1944* (New York, 1985); and Yitzchak Zuckerman (ed.), *The Fighting Ghettos* (New York, 1971).

Preface

THIS SURVEY OF the Jewish Councils in Eastern Europe encompasses Poland (in its prewar boundaries of 1939), the Baltic countries (Lithuania, Latvia, and Estonia), and the occupied areas of the U.S.S.R. (Byelorussia and the Ukraine). Although the ultimate fate of the Jews under Nazi rule in these territories was everywhere identical, there were some local differences in the process and tempo of persecution and extermination, depending on how the principle of "local leadership" was applied and on the general lawlessness prevailing. These nuances worked for the better or for the worse and influenced both the posture of the Councils and the attitude of the German authorities. It was, therefore, felt necessary to treat the Jewish Councils according to the regional administrative units established by the occupation authorities.

The areas of persecution and extermination covered by this study are Poland, the Reichskommissariat Ostland, and the Reich kommissariat Ukraine.

Poland was partitioned into the following units:

a) The Government General, encompassing the central and southeastern parts of the country, divided into five *Distrikte*: Warsaw, Lublin, Cracow, Radom, and Distrikt Galizien (added on August 1, 1941);

b) The *Wartheland*, consisting of the entire Poznań Województwo (province), almost the entire Łódź Województwo, five counties of the Pomorze Województwo, and one county of the Warsaw Województwo;

POLISH BOUNDARIES 1914–1945

⊩●⊩●⊩ The eastern boundaries of Germany 1914	◎ ⊙ Capitals of districts
──────── The German-Polish state boundaries 1937	──────── Administrative boundaries of the districts in the incorporated former Polish territories
✠✠✠✠✠✠✠✠ German-Soviet demarcation line 1939–1941	─·─··─ District boundaries in the General-Gouvernement
─·─··─··─ Administrative boundaries between the General-Gouvernement, and Bialystok district and the Reichskommissariate Ostland and Ukraine	

Poland in 1937

● district capitals
○ county sites
• other localities
▬ state boundaries
--- district boundaries

Okrąg węglowy
1 cm = 7.5 km

c) Danzig-West Preussen (Danzig-West Prussia), including the remaining area of the Pomorze Województwo;

d) Distrikt Zichenau (Ciechanów), consisting of the five northern counties of the Warsaw Województwo;

e) Ostoberschlesien (Eastern Upper Silesia), encompassing the counties of Sosnowiec, Będzin, and Chrzanów, and parts of the counties of Zawiercie, Olkusz, and Żywiec, i.e., the western part of the Cracow Województwo and of the former Polish Upper Silesia (Zagłębie) [units *b, c, d,* and *e* were incorporated (*eingegliedert*) into the Reich];

f) Bezirk Białystok (established after the invasion of the U.S.S.R. in June 1941), which consisted of seven *Kommissariate*: Białystok, Grajewo, Grodno, Bielsk-Podlaski, Łomża, Sokółki, and Wołkowysk. The town of Białystok was a separate administrative entity. This Bezirk was attached (*angeliedert*) to the jurisdiction of the *Gauleiter* of Eastern Prussia, Erich Koch;

g) Polish Byelorussia was in part included in the Bezirk Białystok and in part in the Reichskommissariat Ostland (concerning the Pinsk area, see below, Reichskommissariat Ukraine); and

h) The Polish part of Volhynia was included in the Reichskommissariat Ukraine.

The *Reichskommissariat Ostland* consisted of the areas of the former Baltic states (including the Vilna region) and of the greater part of Byelorussia, Polish and Soviet.

The *Reichskommissariat Ukraine* encompassed the following *Generalkommissariate*: Volhynia-Podolia, Zhitomir, Kiev, Dnepropetrovsk, and the Crimea, as well as the southern part of Polish Byelorussia and the town of Pinsk. All of the conquered areas east of the Dnieper were under military administration until September 1942, when they were taken over, together with the northern parts of the Crimea, by the civil administration. (See maps, pp. x, xi.)

When war broke out in September 1939, 5,514,500 Jews inhabited these lands. The war and the ensuing resettlement policies of the German and Soviet occupiers caused an enormous fluctuation of the Jewish population. It is impossible now to follow the course or estimate the results of all these resettlements. Suffice it to say that approximately 5,100,000 Jews fell under Nazi rule after hostilities started between Germany and the U.S.S.R. on June 22, 1941.

My research encompassed 405 Jewish settlements with Jewish Councils in operation. I could not get complete information on all of them. It is my conviction, however, that even this limited material is representative, for it refers to all of the areas and to all sorts of ghettos, from the largest to the smallest ones.

Vast archival material and material in print have been utilized for this study. I am, of course, aware that a great deal of documentation still remains in inaccessible archives and in private hands. Much to my regret I was denied access to the archives of present-day Poland. But I was able to use my large personal collection of notes and summaries of documents, assembled in Poland during the years 1946–1950. I also used in the archives of Yad Vashem the microfilms of other documents now in Poland. In addition, I used the rich Holocaust collections in the YIVO Institute for Jewish Research in New York, in Yad Vashem, in the Ghetto Fighters' House (*Beth Lokhamei Hagetaot*) in Israel, the archives of the American Joint Distribution Committee and the Bund Archives in the name of Franz Kurski, both in New York. The photographs are from the picture collection of YIVO.

Of the extensive printed literature, the most important documentary publication in Poland, Israel, and America were scrutinized, as were the two Diaspora Encyclopedias (*Encyclopedia shel galuyot* and *Arim Veimahot be-Israel*), numerous memorial books, memoirs, eyewitness accounts, and studies. All are listed in the Notes.

The main archival basis of the study are the German decrees and orders, memoranda, reports and minutes of meetings, and correspondence of the Germans among themselves and with the Jewish Councils and Jewish police in Warsaw, Łódź, Cracow, Lublin, Białystok, Kaunas, Vilna, and many other localities.

Secondary material came from contemporary *reportages* and diaries, reports published abroad, and news items and articles in the Jewish underground publications and in the official German, Jewish, and Polish press.

The third category of sources are postwar reports about the Jewish Councils and the Ghetto police, memoirs and eyewitness accounts, and documentation of the court trials against surviving Council members and Ghetto police, including discussions on this subject.

The historical and documentary values of these diversified sources are not all on the same level.

The official documentation (e.g., Nazi documents or minutes of the Council meetings) needed critical evaluation as to veracity. The minutes of Councils were open for inspection by the Gestapo and could not always reveal what had actually taken place. Moreover, these sources originated in a general atmosphere of violence and intimidation, and their reliability may, therefore, be questioned. A still more cautious approach was needed in the evaluation of the secondary sources, and particularly of the material in the third group, because of a suspicion that they might have been influenced by subjective judgments of the related facts.

A fact described years after the event is inevitably liable to the inadequacy of human memory and may be influenced by what the witness has heard or read since the end of the war. These negative factors, however, should in no way disqualify any account as a source of information. The witness may, and often does, err as to the date, the name, the numbers involved, and similar formal elements of the events, as well as in its evaluation; but his reliability as to the event itself, provided he is mentally sound and honest in his approach to the testimony, is beyond doubt.

The emotional condition of the witness at the time he relates his fearful experiences may cause a certain degree of exaggeration and even distortion of his own role or the role of persons toward whom he may be favorably or unfavorably disposed. The researcher has to take this into account. On the other hand, what the witness may presently tell about his experiences and the whole era may, from the distance of time, help in his being more objective in the evaluation of events than would have been possible for him right after the liberation.

Life during the Nazi years was permeated with such severe strain that it left a deep, permanent impression on the mentality of the surviving victims. Even now they are still unable to shake off the ferocious memories. Many still have most torturing nightmares, again and again living through the ghetto and camp afflictions.

However, no conclusion should be drawn that the researcher has to accept all related facts and their evaluation without critical analysis. The reliability of the accounts is increased if and when they are confirmed by other testimonies relating to the same fact. As always in the writing of history, each source has to be juxtaposed with another one about the same event. Where this is impossible, and where there is only a single account concerning a given fact, it must be analyzed even more critically.

An important and unique source was the material derived from a questionnaire on the social background and behavior of the Council members and the Ghetto police, which the Documentary Projects had taken from 1964 to 1966, in the United States by the Projects' coworker, Jonas Turkow, and in Israel by the Yad Vashem coworker, Yitzhak Alperowicz. Some 927 completed questionnaire sheets were collected, giving certain personal information on 740 Council members and 112 Ghetto policemen in the ghettos in Poland and the Reichskommissariate Ostland and Ukraine. Ninety-nine ghettos of all sizes are discussed in the questionnaires: 41 in the Government General, 26 in Ostland, 11 in General Bezirk Volhynia-Podolia, 7 in the Wartheland, 6 in Distrikt Zichenau, 4 in Bezirk Białystok, 4 in Eastern Upper Silesia.

Fifty-seven persons are discussed in two or three questionnaires each. This is important, because the facts relating to these Council members can be compared in one or more other testimonies.

The information that we tried to obtain regarding the Council members and the Ghetto police was collected under the following headings: age; education; marital status; number of children; occupation; prewar party affiliation and position; membership in professional, economic, cultural, philanthropic, and religious societies; position in the prewar Jewish community organs and municipal offices; residence (native or refugee); position in the Council or police hierarchies; and fate. We also tried to get evaluations of the activities of the Councilmen or policemen, and it is interesting to note that a great majority of the persons polled did not limit themselves to short statements, but supplied extensive characteristics, often taking up two, three, and four legal-size pages.

The poll was taken from survivors of the ghettos where the Councilmen or policemen were active and could be observed at work, or from such other persons as were well informed of the activities and behavior of the officials. Answers to nine questionnaires were supplied by relatives (a wife, two sons, a daughter, and a brother, among others). Forty-eight sheets were filled out as follows: 12 by the former chairman of the Jewish Council in Suchowola, 6 by the former members of the Piotrków Trybunalski Council, 11 by former Council members in Prużana, 8 by former Councilmen in Horodenka, and 11 by former Councilmen in Wieruszów. In four instances former Council members filled out questionnaires about their own activities. In one case the Councilman even attached a self-characterization on two pages.

Though there is little doubt about the veracity of the personal data, and about the prewar community life of the Council members or policemen as they are described in the questionnaires, well substantiated questions may be raised about the evaluations of their activities and their characteristics, particularly where answers were supplied by persons with close connections to the Council members in question, and by the concerned persons themselves. It may be assumed that the answers in the column "Evaluation" in the questionnaires (and the attached "characterizations") are liable to be colored.

Data concerning the evaluation of the activities of each of 57 persons could be checked against information included in two or three questionnaires. Contradictory statements were received in regard to only three persons: a Councilman and chief of the labor department in Rohatyn; a Councilman in Głębokie; and the second Council chairman in Wieruszów. Mixed opinions were given about four persons. In all remaining 50 cases, the descriptions were unanimous both in their positive and negative characteristics (40 persons were positively evaluated and 10 negatively).

I am well aware that, rich as the collected material is, it is a mere sample of what could have been achieved by a still larger and wider poll. I am also cognizant of the lacunae which could not be avoided in the filled-out sheets. In the absence of the *dramatis personae* themselves, maximum effort had to be made to analyze the polled documentation. I am satisfied that the pollsters were honest and conscientious people. And as to the individuals polled, they were assured of anonymity, and there is no reason to doubt their integrity. Their integrity is shown by the fact that no answers were given to some questions, when they had insufficient, or no knowledge of the pertinent facts. A detailed analysis of some questionnaires is given in Appendix I.

The problem of the Jewish Councils has stirred up an agonizing discussion in Holocaust literature, but little research has been done by competent historians. The late Dr. Philip Friedman was the first Jewish historian who in a number of papers discussed vital aspects of the subject: see, for example, "The Messianic Complex of Chiefs of Nazi Ghettos" in *Bitsaron* (New York), Vol. 28, No. 5 (1953), pp. 29–40, and Vol. 29, Nos. 3 and 4 (1953/54), pp. 151–158, 232–239; "False Redeemers in Polish Ghettos," *Metsuda* (London), Vols. 7–8 (1954) (both of these are in Hebrew); "The Warsaw Story," *Tsukunft*, April 1950 (in Yiddish). He dealt further with the methodological problems involved in research in the Jewish Councils in *YWS*, Vol. 2 (1958), pp. 95–114.

He devoted a substantial study to the problem of the Jewish *Repräsentanz* ("representation") in Germany, Austria, and Czechoslovakia during the Nazi era ("Aspects of Jewish Communal Crisis in the Period of the Nazi Regime in Germany, Austria, and Czechoslovakia,") *Essays of Jewish Life and Thought* [New York: Columbia University Press, 1959], pp. 199–230). He also assembled considerable source material on the Jewish Councils, which was used for this book. Unfortunately he passed away on February 7, 1960, before he was able to write a comprehensive history of the Jewish Councils, a project he had been working on for many years before his untimely death.

Also Dr. Jacob Robinson delved into the phenomenon of the Jewish Councils in his *And the Crooked Shall Be Made Straight* (chapter on "Jewish Behavior in the Face of Disaster," pp. 142–220)—the Hebrew version: *Heakov Lemishor* (Jerusalem, 1965), pp. 130–198; and the French version: *La Tragédie juive sans la croix gammée* (Paris, 1968), pp. 26–76—and in the paper, "Discontinuity and Continuity in the Jewish Councils in the Nazi Era" (1967), 37 pp. (in Hebrew).

It has taken over five years to prepare this study. I have endeavored to present a well-balanced picture of the Jewish Councils in Eastern Europe, their attitude toward the Jews and their relations with the decisive factor—the German occupiers. I began research into this difficult subject fully realizing my scientific and historical responsibility. My aim was to give an objective history of the Councils, based on unbiased documentation. It was not my intention to pronounce judgment either way on these institutions, but to try to probe deep into the entire complex topic, into the internal and external factors and conditions in which the Councils had to perform, into the motivation and deeds of the Council members, and into the results of their activities.

It seemed to me that the inductive method was the one most suited to my purpose, and I have cited as many local events in as many ghettos as possible. To a degree it is possible to find common features in the general pattern of the activities of the Councils—in their welfare policies and in the motivation of their strategy and tactics toward the Germans. I am, however, of the opinion that the entire Council phenomenon cannot be analyzed in general terms.

It has to be discussed with a view toward local conditions and personalities, the activities of individual Councils and their attitudes
toward the German authorities. In the final analysis we deal here
with people of diverse socio-psychological backgrounds variously
reacting to similar situations. The researcher has to beware of the
temptation to simplify or generalize, trying to evaluate the attitudes
and actions of individual Council members in given situations. The
fragmentary character of the majority of the sources prevented me
from doing so in each separate case. Although the ghettos as a rule
were similar, if not identical, in their formal framework of repressive
restrictions and in the role they were destined to play in the "Final
Solution of the Jewish Question," they were far from homogeneous
in their internal, demographic, and economic structures. Nor were
the history and traditions of their communities similar, and neither
was their geographical position identical. All these circumstances
left their mark on the Councils.

This study deals with the emergence of the Councils; their organizational structure (decentralization and centralization, dictatorial
and collective leadership); the degree of their representative qualities (continuation with or severance from the prewar representative
bodies of the Jewish communities); their political and social composition; the fluctuation of the Councils; their activities in the fields
of the ghetto economy; welfare, hygiene, and medical help; religious
affairs; education and cultural work; their administrative and judicial functions; the Council employees; the Jewish police; relations
with other Jewish organizations and with the resistance movement;
relations with and strategy and tactics toward the German authorities; the behavior of individual Council members; and the opposition
to the Councils and the Jewish police. Treatment of the agonizing
postwar aftereffects, and of the trials of surviving Council members
and ghetto policemen, complete the book.

I have tried to survey all these questions against a background of
problems involved in the examination of the Holocaust in general.
So-called Jewish "self-government" is one of the key problems in
the history of the ghettos, one that is most complicated and highly
controversial in Jewish as well as non-Jewish postwar historiography.
To achieve an objective history of the Councils means to find the
key to internal Jewish history under Nazi rule, a field of research
that has been largely neglected or dealt with without the required
knowledge.

This book could not have been written without the help of specialized research institutions and devoted colleagues. It is therefore a pleasant duty to express my thanks to the following institutions, which granted to me access to their archives, and to the colleagues who were most helpful during the preparation of this book:

The YIVO Institute for Jewish Research in New York and its archivist, Ezekiel Lifshitz; the YIVO Library and its librarian, Miss Dina Abramovich; the Yad Vashem archives in Jerusalem and their archivist, Dr. Joseph Kermish; Miss Rachel Auerbach of the Yad Vashem Branch in Tel Aviv; Emanuel Brand of the Department for Prosecution of War Criminals at Yad Vashem; the Ghetto Fighters' House in Memory of Yitzhak Katznelson and its secretary Zvi Shner, in Israel; and the Bund Archives in Memory of Franz Kurski in New York and its archivist, Hillel Kempinski, and the archives of the American Joint Distribution Committee, and their archivist, Rose Klepfisz, both in New York.

I am indebted to my colleagues: David Bass for checking the Notes, and to him as well as to Jonas Turkow (both now in Israel) for their help in the selection of the pertinent material from the printed literature on the Holocaust; to Dr. Ada Friedman for her assistance in the selection of source material in Polish and for making available the pertinent material from the archives of her late husband, Dr. Friedman; to Henry Sachs, who has always been helpful with his expert knowledge of the history of the Third Reich; to Mrs. Cesia Bursztyn and Mrs. Miriam Levitt for their devotion and patience in typing the consecutive drafts of the manuscript.

As the first reader of the manuscript, my colleague Chaim Finkelstein offered helpful suggestions. He also translated the voluminous text from the original Yiddish into English and cooperated in the preparation of the manuscript for print. The revision of the English style was made by Dr. Dennis Flynn of Framingham, Mass., under the supervision of Dr. Jacob Robinson.

During the years of preparing this volume I profited from the friendly critique and scholarly advice of Dr. Jacob Robinson whose devotion brought my book to its present form. For this I am greatly indebted to him.

I am most thankful to my wife, Celia, for her patience and endurance in the tiresome task of proofreading.

Finally, I should like to point out that the author alone is responsible for the views expressed in this book.

This volume has been prepared in the framework of the Joint Documentary Projects of Yad Vashem and YIVO and financed by the Conference of Jewish Material Claims against Germany, now the Memorial Foundation for Jewish Culture.

I. T.

ABBREVIATIONS

ABLG—Archives of Beth Lokhamei Hagetaot al shem Yitzhak Katznelson (Archives of the Ghetto Fighters House in Memory of Yitzhak Katznelson)

ADPC—Archives of the Displaced Persons Camps in the YIVO Archives

AGV—Archives of the *Gettoverwaltung* in Łódź, at Jewish Historical Institute, Warsaw

AJHI—Archives of the Jewish Historical Institute, Warsaw

Alaynhilf—Michał Weichert, *Yidishe alaynhilf 1939-1945* (Jewish Self-Help, 1939-1945) (Tel Aviv, 1962)

AOK—*Armee-Oberkommando* (Army High Command)

BC—Berlin Collection in the Archives of the YIVO Institute, New York

Bericht Krakau—Die jüdische Gemeinde in Krakau in der Zeit vom 13.IX.1939 bis 30.IX.1940 und ihre Tätigkeit, bearbeitet durch Franz Guen (The Jewish Community in Cracow during the Period September 13, 1939, till September 30, 1940, and its Activities) (stencil)

Bericht Warschau—Bericht über die Tätigkeit des Judenrates in Warschau vom 7.X.1939 bis 31.XII.1940 (Akta R. Ż. w Warszawie No. 16, microfilm No. PNE 53-78) (Report about the Activities of the Judenrat in Warsaw from October 7, 1939, till December 31, 1940—Records of the Judenrat No. 16, microfilm No. PNE 53-78)

BGKBZN (H)—*Biuletyn Głównej Komisji Badania Zbrodni Niemieckich (Hitlerowskich) w Polsce* (Bulletin of the Main Commission for Investigation of German [Hitlerite] Crimes in Poland) (Warsaw, 1947)

BKC—*Biuletyn Kroniki Codziennej* (Bulletin of the Daily Chronicle, a mimeographed publication of the Ghetto Archives in Łódź)

Blfg—Bleter far geshikhte (Studies in History, several volumes) (Warsaw, 1948 ff.)

BWS—*Biuletyn Wydziału Statystycznego Rady Starszych* (Bulletin of the Department of Statistics of the Council of Elders)

BŻIH—*Biuletyn Żydowskiego Instytutu Historycznego* (Bulletin of the Jewish Historical Institute, Warsaw)

CEKABE—Centrala Kass Bezprocentowych (Central Office of the Free Loan Association)

Centos—Centrala Opieki nad Sierotami (Organization for Care of Orphans)

CISHO—Tsentrale Yidishe Shul-Organisatsye (Central Yiddish School Organization)

EG—Einsatzgruppe (SS detachment for special tasks)

Eksterminacja—Eksterminacja Żydów na ziemiach polskich w okresie okupacji hitlerowskiej (Extermination of the Jews in Poland during the Hitlerite Occupation) (Warsaw, 1957)

Eksterminacja—Eksterminacja Żydów na ziemiach polskich w okresie okupacji pora) (Jerusalem and Tel Aviv)

xxxiii

Encyclopaedia—Encyclopaedia shel galuyot (Encyclopaedia of the Jewish Diaspora) (Jerusalem and Tel Aviv)

FLKh—*Fun letstn Khurbn* (From the Recent Holocaust) (Munich)

FPO—Faraynikte Partizaner Organisatsye (United Partisan Organization in Vilna)

G & EPR—General and Emergency Poland Reports

GG—*Generalgouvernement* (the German name for the occupied central provinces of Poland)

G.Ż.—*Gazeta Żydowska* (The Jewish Gazette)

HIAS—Hebrew Immigrant Aid Society

HTO—*Haupttreuhandstelle-Ost* (Central Office for Confiscations in Occupied Poland)

IRC—International Red Cross

IRU—Inspekcja Ruchu Ulicznego (Control of Street Traffic)

Ishel—Irgun Shomrim le 'Ginot (Organization of Orchard Guards)

I.V.—*Innere Verwaltung* (Department of Internal Affairs)

JDC—Joint Distribution Committee

JEAS—Jewish Emigration Association (Polish branch of HIAS)

JSS—*Jüdische Soziale Selbsthilfe* in the *Generalgouvernement* (Jewish Social Welfare in the Government General)

JUS—*Jüdische Unterstützungsstelle* (Jewish relief office in Cracow)

Lodzher geto—Isaiah Trunk, *Lodzher geto, a historishe un sotsiologishe Shtudie* (The Łódź Ghetto, a Historical and Sociological Study)

Milkhome—Michał Weichert, *Zykhroynes* (Memoirs) Vol. III, *Milkhome* (The War) (Tel Aviv, 1964)

MTA—Mersik-Tamaroff Archives, microfilm in the Archives of the YIVO Institute, New York

NSV—Nazionalsozialistische Volkswohlfart (N. S. Popular Welfare)

OD—Ordnungsdienst (Jewish Order Service, i.e., ghetto police)

ORPO—Ordnungspolizei (Order police)

ORT—Obshchestvo Razpostranienia Truda (Russian) (Organization for Rehabilitation and Training)

OSTI—Ost-Industrie (name of an SS industrial enterprise)

RA—Ringelblum Archives at Jewish Historical Institute, Warsaw

RGBl—*Reichsgesetzblatt* (official Gazette of the Nazi Government)

Rocznik—*Rada Starszych, II Rocznik Statystyczny* (cited with respective number) (Council of Elders, II Statistical Yearbook)

SD—Sicherheits-Dienst (Security Service)

Shtudie—Isaiah Trunk, *Shtudie tsu der geshikhte fun jidn in varteland, 1939–1944* (Study in the History of the Jews in Wartheland, 1939–1944), *Blfg*, Vol. II (Warsaw, 1949)

SiPo—Sicherheitspolizei (Security Police)

Sprawozdanie—Rada Żydowska w Lublinie. Sprawozdanie z działalności Rady za okres od l września 1939 do 31 sierpnia 1940 (The Jewish Council in Lublin. Report of the Activities of the Council for the period September 1, 1939, till August 1940)

SS—Schutzstaffel (Reich Security Police)

Su-KC—Sutskever-Kaczerginski Collection in the Archives of the YIVO Institute, New York.

TORPOROL—Towarzystwo Popierania Rolnictwa (Society for Promotion of Agriculture among Jews)

TOZ—Towarzystwo Ochrony Zdrowia (Society to Protect the Health of Jews)

VBlGG—*Verordnungsblatt fur das Generalgouvernement* (The Gazette of Decrees for the Government General), in the Archives of the YIVO Institute, New York

Virtshaftlekhe diskriminatsyes (Economic Discriminations against Jews in Warsaw before the Establishment of the Ghetto)

VM—Vertrauungsmann (informer)

WaC—Wasser Collection in the YIVO Institute, New York

Wohnbezirk—Der jüdische Wohnberzirk in Warschau und seine Verwaltung Zahlen und Tatsachen (Warsaw, June 1942) (The Jewish Living Quarter in Warsaw and Its Management: Facts and Figures)

WVHA—Wirtschafts und Verwaltungshauptamt (SS Main Office for Economics and Management)

YaVA—Yad Vashem Archives (Archives of Yad Vashem Martyrs' and Heroes' Memorial Authority, Jerusalem)

YBLG—*Yediyot Beth Lokhamei Hagetaot* (Information bulletin of the Ghetto Fighters' House, Israel)

YIA—Archives of the YIVO Institute for Jewish Research, New York

YIVO—YIVO Institute for Jewish Research, New York

YWS—Yad Vashem Studies

Zaderecki—Tadeusz Zaderecki's manuscript (YaVA ms. o-6/2) dealing with the history of the Lwów Ghetto

ZC—Zonabend Collection in the Archives of the YIVO Institute, New York

ŻTOS—Żydowskie Towarzystwo Opieki Spotecznej (Jewish Organization for Public Care)

Introduction: Some Basic Issues
That Faced the Jewish Councils

JACOB ROBINSON

This volume by Isaiah Trunk is the first detailed analysis, in any language, of the "self-government" the Nazis imposed upon the Jews in Eastern Europe. Along with this central theme other aspects of internal Jewish life also come to light.

While the volume speaks for itself, it was felt that some interpretive remarks on the contents of the book might help the reader familiarize himself with its subject matter and the basic problems which are raised.

The first question to be discussed is the attitude of Jewish communal leaders toward joining the Councils. Two views are predominant in the sources and literature: one condemning the prewar communal leaders (and others) for accepting membership in the Councils, and the other finding no fault.

The proponents of the "noncooperation" view believe that under the circumstances and from the viewpoint of Jewish survival a "leaderless" Jewry would have been the lesser evil and that a larger percentage of Jews would have survived the Holocaust. This view proceeds on the following three assumptions: (1) having extirpated the Jews from the general administrative framework of, say, occupied Poland, the Nazis would have tolerated the existence in this territory of two million nomads while at the same time proceeding to the partial extermination of Gypsies as nomads (*umherziehende*); (2) in condition of rationing food these nomads would have been able to find shelter and survive for some thirty months (September 1939–March 1942) prior to the beginning of deportations;

(3) the Jews would have resigned themselves to such a situation without opposition.

The opposite view refers to the spontaneous emergence after the German occupation of new "committees" and to the attempts to continue the activities of the prewar Jewish communal institutions prior to Nazi initiative (as e.g., in Warsaw and Lublin) as proof of the continuing if not reinforced sense of responsibility of Jews concerned with the fate of their coreligionists. The proponents of the positive attitude also emphasize the fact that neither the leadership nor the masses did have or could have had a clear idea of the Nazi plan for the future which, as we know now, was crystallized as the Final Solution decision only in the spring of 1941 in connection with the Barbarossa operation.

A more subtle view is taken by those who differentiate between the situation in (1) German-occupied Poland, (2) the Baltic states and eastern Poland, including Eastern Galicia, which for 23 months were under Soviet occupation or influence, (3) and in the occupied territories of the U.S.S.R. prior to September 1939. The first blow of the German occupation fell on Poland. In the two other areas, despite the silence of the Soviet-controlled press, the Jews might have had an inkling of what was in store for them. They learned the hard way, prior to the establishment of any form of Jewish organization: the *Einsatzgruppen* overran all these areas bringing within a short period of time death and destruction to some one and a half million Jews. In the formerly Soviet-occupied, now Nazi-occupied, territories, hesitations to join the Council manifested themselves, an exemplified in the case of Eishishkis (in wartime Lithuania). There, in July 1941, the rabbi had to draw lots to choose members of the Council from among the reluctant community because of lack of volunteers. But even in these areas persons of high reputation like Ephraim Barash (Białystok), Dr. Elkhanan Elkes and Leon Garfunkel (Kaunas), assumed responsible positions in the respective Councils.

The situation was different in occupied portions of the U.S.S.R. In the first place there had been no Jewish communal organization in existence there for almost a quarter of a century. The reservoir of candidates for membership in Jewish Councils was thus limited. We have some information on only 15 ghettos in those territories and no general conclusion can be drawn concerning the attitude of local Jews toward joining the Councils.

The Councils started their activities in Poland as a continuation of the prewar *Gmina* ("community"). The official documents on the establishment of the Councils (the *Schnellbrief* of Reinhardt Heydrich of September 21, 1939; the ordinance of Hans Frank, governor general of the Government General, the mandates of the police chiefs of Warsaw and Łódź) charged them exclusively with matters of German concern. In fact, however, a large part of the activities of the Councils was extracurricular and traditionally Jewish (welfare, education, and religion).

It is interesting to note that the herding of Jews into ghettos did not meet with serious opposition on the part of the pre-Ghetto Councils and the Jews in general. One of the reasons for this attitude was the fear of Jews that they might be molested by the local population, either spontaneously or in outbursts instigated by the Nazis. The opposition that did exist was directed at two points: the area destined for the ghetto and the deadline for moving into the ghetto. A correspondence between Czerniakow and the Nazi authorities in Warsaw on these two aspects has been preserved.

Was it right not to oppose the establishment of the ghettos? The answer to this question by us now, using hindsight, depends on the evaluation of the probable alternative, which was concentration camps, a form of dwelling used in the case of the Soviet prisoners of war. The ghettos preserved the family, allowed for a minimum of privacy and partly—not everywhere—for some contacts with the outer world; all these advantages were missing in the camps.

Having assumed the dual responsibilities of office—traditional and Nazi-imposed—the Councils had early to face another dilemma arising from the exploitation of the labor of Jews aged twelve to sixty. Not all labor was of the same nature: there was menial work, skilled, technical work, manufacture of uniforms, construction work, precision work, and clerical work. Nor was there lack of variety as far as places of work are concerned: in and outside the ghettos, in ghetto workshops, in labor camps. The employers were municipal institutions, ghetto administration, the German army, SS business companies such as OSTI, and private German firms based in and around the ghettos. There was also a lack of complete uniformity in the question of wages, the length of working week and workday, food, housing conditions, and the type and character of guards. It should be mentioned that available manpower was everywhere (with the exception of Łódź) larger than the amount needed by the Germans.

The question is: Should the Councils have assumed responsibilities for the supply of labor or should they have left this domain to the Germans? The first reaction of members of Councils was: it is not for the representatives of the Jews to supply to the enemy labor needed for his own purposes. The Germans went about obtaining their necessary supply by organizing an indiscriminate hunt of ghetto dwellers in, for example, the Warsaw streets, complete with shooting and beating. The hunt, and the ensuing despair of the families, was witnessed by a member of the Council, leader of the Jewish-Socialist Bund, Shmuel (Artur) Zygelbojm (later, after emigration, a member of the Polish National Council in London, who committed suicide in 1943 as protest against the indifference of the world to the Holocaust). He told the Council: "We must tell the Germans that if they need labor they should turn to us and we will assign the necessary people." The dilemma was not resolved by this decision. On the contrary, the issue of forced labor became a paramount problem of equity and a test of the conscience of the Councils. The reservoir of manpower of the ghettos could provide all the labor required and more. Under these circumstances the first question raised was: Should the Council free people capable of paying ransom from the distasteful (to say the least) labor duty or not? It appears that in order to justify the emerging inequality created by the ransom policy, the majority of the Councils took the view that such discriminatory policy is morally justifiable if the ransom is used to help the laborers (whom the Germans paid niggardly or not at all), particularly if they worked in labor camps outside the ghettos. There were other factors which could and might have been taken into account in a policy of equitable supply of Jewish labor: a just turnover of labor candidates by labor days, the quality of labor required, the family relations of the laborers, chances of meeting Aryans outside and exchanging valuables for food. Whether these conditions were met in each and every ghetto is a matter of individual consideration, but the temper of the people, particularly in the larger ghettos, and the frequently heard charges of bribery in discharging the duty of labor supply does not make it seem that equitable conditions were met everywhere. Thus the solution of the question of principle only contributed to sharpening the problems of detailed implementation.

Charges concerning the ultimate ineffectiveness of the policy of "rescue through work" as a method of extending the life of the ghettos and its inmates have overshadowed the moral problem involved, a moral problem common to the Jews and to non-Jews in occupied Europe and in particular to the millions of foreign laborers in Germany employed mostly in the war effort of their enemy. The problem was a simple one: How could such service, offering considerable help to the Germans, be justified when the laborers' compatriots were engaged in a mortal fight with their employers as army regulars or *résistants*? With the Jews, the problem had a difference: the Jews had been extirpated from the economic life of the countries of their residence, and unable to create a self-sustained economy in the conditions of ghetto life; the only alternative to 100 percent unemployment lay in serving the enemy employer. West European non-Jews had still at their disposal one alternative: not to follow the call of the German authorities for work in Germany but, instead, go underground in their homeland under the protection of the sympathetic countrymen. Thus, out of 800,000 Dutchmen called up for work in Germany, 300,000 did not show up. No such possibility was at the disposal of the Jews. The lack of any articulate reflections on this moral issue either by the Jewish leadership or by the Jewish masses is the most striking proof of the hopelessness of dealing with moral problems while facing an amoral and cruel enemy.

That the "rescue-through-work"—perhaps a melancholic illustration of the folk saying "Respite of death is also life" (*Chaye shoo is oykh lebn*)—did not work in the long run does not by itself disqualify this policy. It is only by accident of military history that a considerable part of Łódź Jews did not survive. By the end of July 1944 the Red army had reached the Vistula and established a bridgehead on its western shore, south of Warsaw. The Red army did not continue its advance, but stopped some 70 miles from Łódź. Less than a month later, in August 1944, the 68,000 Jews still alive in Łódź were "resettled."

The alternatives facing the Jews were work or resistance (either through rebellion or through flight to partisan groups). As a general phenomenon rebellion started in major ghettos in 1943, at a time when the majority of the Jewish population had already been destroyed, but also at a time when France did not yet have her *Maquis* and Tito's partisans had not yet become a serious factor, and when the Councils were no longer the only voice in Nazi-oppressed Jewry. The Warsaw Ghetto revolt of April 1943 was the first direct armed confrontation of local forces with the Nazis. The revolts in the ghettos were attempts "to save the Jewish honor." In view of the high price paid in human lives it proved to be no alternative to "rescue through work," however ineffective.

The possibility of rescue and resistance by flight from ghettos to nearby woods and marshes where partisans were active (or where new partisan groups could originate) raised moral issues among the candidates for such flights, and between them and the Councils. The would-be partisans had to take into consideration that chances for fighting the Germans and rescuing themselves were not good in view of the hostility of the majority of the partisan groups and the local population. The candidates for such flights also asked themselves whether it was right to go to the woods and leave their families in the ghettos, thus breaking family ties and depriving the populace of the protection of the young? The solutions to these questions were varied.

The Councils were faced in these cases by their own dilemma: Should they enforce the imposed isolation of the ghetto under their collective responsibility or overlook such daring and "illegal" acts allowing for some furtive contact between the partisans and the ghettos? The answer depended on the evaluation of the situation at a specific moment and the likely reaction of the local satraps. Here the moral solution was largely a result of the political acumen of a given Council. Not all their previsions proved right, nor were all of their anxieties founded.

This is the place to discuss briefly the problem of the personal integrity of the members of the Councils. East European Councils (with numerous marked exceptions) are in this respect much worse off than, for example, the members of the *Joodse Raad* in Amsterdam or the *Reichsvereinigung* in Berlin. The latter two institutions came in for their share of criticism but it was always emphasized that the personal integrity of their members was never doubted. On the contrary, many Eastern European Council members were charged with various misdeeds from nepotism to the use of funds and property of the community for personal enrichment.

The critical test of the Council members' moral standards, political acumen, personal integrity, and sense of responsibility for the community came at a time when Councilmen, knowing the destination of deportees for "resettlement," did not resign their posts and frequently participated in the process of deportation to the death camps. Jewish communities had for centuries complied with demands of governments for deliveries of "replaceable goods" such as money, but they had never delivered "life itself." In this connection the following three questions arise: (1) Should the Council members have revealed to the people their knowledge of the impending disaster? (2) Should Jews have lent a hand, however reluctantly, to the selection of Jews for deportation which was equivalent to death? (3) Should Jews "voluntarily" have offered some victims for the Moloch at the price of rescuing others, which would mean nothing else than the assumption of the power to decide "Who shall live and who shall die" (*Mi le-hayim umi le-mavet*), a decision reserved in the tradition for God alone?

It is questionable whether Jews in Eastern Europe depended on the Councils for their information on impending disaster, although the appearance of a sizeable number of "volunteers" on the Umschlagplatz in Warsaw might have been proof that such was the case. In a different area, in Theresienstadt, Leo Baeck followed a policy of nonrevelation in view of his judgment that nothing could have been done to change the course of events. It was—in his view—advisable not to let victims know the truth and to spare them the agony and ultimate desperation that comes from knowledge that the end is near and there is absolutely no way out. The analogy of the behavior of doctors in hopeless cases was invoked. Such a policy left, however, the distasteful impression that—whatever the motives—it was somehow identical with the Nazi policy of deception; and it provoked charges of "collaboration."

From the viewpoint of the traditional Jews (who constituted a minority in the Councils) the answer to the questions of Council participation in deportations was long ago given by the greatest codifier of Jewish law, Maimonides. Said Maimonides: ". . . if pagans should tell them [the Jews], 'Give us one of yours and we shall kill him, otherwise we shall kill all of you,' they all should be killed and not a single Jewish soul should be delivered."

The policy of rescuing some Jews by delivering others was a classical case of applicability of the Maimonides rule. But it appears that faced with such cases two equally authoritative rabbinates gave contradictory interpretations of Maimonides. The rabbi of Kaunas (Kovno), Abraham Duber Cahana Shapiro, ruled that "if a

Jewish community . . . has been condemned to physical destruction, and there are means of rescuing part of it, the leaders of the community should have the courage to assume the responsibility, to act and rescue what is possible." By contrast the Vilna rabbinate, replying to the argument of the head of the ghetto that "by participating in the selection and delivering a small number of Jews, he is rescuing the rest from the death," took the strict view of Maimonides.

In other Councils two opposing views confronted each other in all sharpness: the contention that the selection of who shall die and who shall live should be left to the Germans, as against the contention that the Jews themselves should do it, not on a mechanically egalitarian basis but on a discriminatory qualitative basis.

The behavior of the individual members in the face of this tragic situation varied all the way from participation in the deportations to refusal, with the ensuing repression of nonparticipants and suicides.

Let us first have a look at those who did not refuse to execute the German orders even when it was clear to them that they were becoming what might have been loosely called "accomplices of the Nazis." Contemporary sources say that these Council members were motivated, among other things, by the hope for exemption from deportation for members and their families and friends. In addition the following objective considerations played a role:

1. Step by step the Nazi terror made the Councils more tractable. "In the beginning, relatively unimportant things were asked of them, replaceable things of material value like personal possessions, money, and apartments. Later, however, the personal freedom of the human being was demanded. Finally the Nazis asked for life itself" (Kasztner). This gradualism in demands, coupled with ever increasing terror, was an effective psychological device. Recalcitrant members of Councils and their families were exposed to reprisals against themselves and the community for their unwillingness to obey Nazi selection orders.

2. The demand for "life itself" came in Poland after some 30 months of attrition when the Nazi authorities had apparently changed the qualification for membership in the Council from "remaining influential personalities and rabbis" (Heydrich's *Schnellbrief*) to obedient implementors of Nazi orders. The fluctuation in the composition of the membership was to a large extent due to

Nazi intervention and resulted in a worsening of the stature of the membership in the Council, both in their moral qualities and in their sense of communal responsibility. The remaining original Council members justified their lack of refusal to participate in the selection by the argument that they would be repressed and replaced by unscrupulous persons.

3. It was also claimed that in case of failure of the *Judenrat* fully to comply with Nazi demands the Germans would do the job themselves with much more efficiency and cruelty. This indeed happened, particularly in the larger ghettos, following the mostly "unsatisfactory" results of the Council "participation."

Are these explanations sufficient for a verdict of not guilty? This is a matter for consideration in each individual case and would largely depend on how accurately the Council members assessed the possible German reactions. Perhaps the fact that among the numerous accusations of misconduct brought against surviving Jews before Courts of Honor in the DP camps, national courts, and the courts of Israel there were only few members of Councils, may throw light on the inevitable fate of the Council members. During the war at least two heads of ghettos (Rumkowski and Gens) had pledged to appear before a Jewish court after the end of the war and plead their case; but they had not survived. A special case is that of the *Joodse Raad* in The Netherlands, where members of the Council survived, the chances for hiding were much better than in Eastern Europe, and the death camps far away and unbelievable; a Jewish Court of Honor condemned them on several counts, including participation in the selection and transportation of the Jews to the East, but not for shipping them knowingly to their death. The acts of vengeance meted out by the Resistance to traitors and informers did not embrace Council members.

So much for the apologetic explanations offered by Council members. But there was another group of Council members who, having realized that not all of the victims could be saved, considered it their *duty* to make the selections themselves in the belief that the best elements of the community must be preserved for its future rehabilitation. Perhaps the most outspoken and eloquent presentation of this viewpoint was made by Reszö Kasztner: "Once again we were confronted with the most serious dilemma, the dilemma which we had been faced with throughout our work: Should we leave the selection to blind fate or should we try to influence it? . . .

We did, tried to do it. We convinced ourselves that—as sacred as every human being has always been to the Jews—we nevertheless had to strive to save at least those who all their lives had labored for the Community [*Osekim be-Tsorkhe Tsibur*] and, by the same token those women whose husbands were in the labor camps; we also had to see to it that children, especially orphans, would not be left to destruction. In brief: truly holy principles had to be employed to sustain and guide the frail human hand which, by writing down on paper the name of an unknown person, decided on his life or death. Was it grace of fate (*Gnade des Schicksals*) if, under these circumstances, we were not always able to prevail in these endeavors?"

History had given a precedent for qualitative vs. egalitarian selection in the case of the "cantonists" in the period of Czar Nicholas the First (1825–1856) when Jewish boys were forcibly inducted into the army for 25 years, and many of them were converted to the Russian-Orthodox Church. When the Community Councils (*Kahals**) in Russia were charged with the duty to submit a certain number of youths under threat of cruel personal punishment they were not faced with a choice among rich, middle class, or poor. The Czarist government released the merchants from the heavy duty. Nor had the middle class any need to ask favors from the *Kahal*: by paying the license fee for merchants they freed the children from this duty. The choice consequently was between poor and poor. The *Kahal* gave preference in releasing from this duty to the learned and brilliant (*gute kep*) boys, the future religious leaders.

We have reached now the last problem to be considered: Was the Jewish Council a positive or a negative factor in the final outcome of the Holocaust? The problem refers to the broad outcome of the Holocaust, not to the isolated individual cases of casualties charged —rightly or wrongly—to the Councils or the individual cases of rescue attributed—rightly or wrongly—to them. Did their participation or nonparticipation influence the dreadful statistics? The following facts should help in formulating an enlightened answer:

1. In large areas of Eastern Europe at least two million victims were murdered without any participation at all on the part of Jews. This refers particularly to victims of the *Einsatzgruppen* in both the initial phase of the war and during the later stages.

---

* The word *Kahal* (Community Council) was used in Russia, the word *Kehila* elsewhere.

2. In the larger ghettos in Poland and in the Baltic states where there was Jewish participation it was of importance in the initial, not in the final, stages of deportations; the later deportations, as has been indicated above, were carried out by German forces, while the Jewish police played only a secondary role.

3. With few exceptions the process of extermination was finished by early 1943, a year and a half prior to Himmler's autumn 1944 "stop extermination" order. Whatever survivors of the fatal year (spring 1942–spring 1943) remained or could have remained alive were destroyed (one may even say at a leisurely pace) during the following months.

4. Above all, the German will to destroy the Jewish people (*Vernichtungswille*) was directed with particular fury against Eastern European Jewry. The Nazi official statements are full of warnings of the dangers to Germany of East European Jewry, which is represented as the greatest source of Jewish power, a mighty stream from which Jews spread out to all corners of the world, as the reservoir for the existence and constant renewal of world Jewry. The Nazis claimed that without the addition of fresh East European Jewish blood, Jewry in the West would long ago have disappeared. It is difficult to believe that with this determination the Nazis would not have used every day and every device to implement the Final Solution to the letter.

It would appear, then, that when all factors are considered, Jewish participation or nonparticipation in the deportations had no substantial influence—one way or the other—on the final outcome of the Holocaust in Eastern Europe.

CHAPTER 1

The Official Decrees
Establishing the Jewish Councils

UTTER LAWLESSNESS and virtual anarchy prevailed in the territories under German occupation during World War II. With respect to the civil population in general and the Jews in particular, the German authorities applied no legal norms such as are commonly understood and practiced in the relations between governments and governed or in human relations in the civilized world. The Jews were just plain outlawed as soon as the Germans caught up with them in any given town, township, or hamlet that came under their rule. Unheard-of acts of terror against the Jews by the German army and police bear witness to a bloody wave of degradation, spoliation, and murder.

By their decrees the Germans endeavored to sanction *ex post facto* conditions of lawlessness and arbitrariness, thus giving a semblance of legality to their felonious acts and a legal alibi for their criminal activities. Moreover, the entire legal and administrative system the Germans introduced in the occupied territories was sheer mockery of the elementary principles for the treatment of a civilian population in an occupied country. Law was of no practical value. Each German could break the law with impunity if, in his view, it was not in accordance with German interests. We shall find additional proof of this statement in Chap. 2, where the emergence of the Councils and their transition from theory to practice will be examined.

The first decree establishing Jewish Councils of Elders in the occupied territories came in the form of an urgent circular letter (*Schnellbrief*) concerning the "Jewish Question in the Occupied

Zone," sent by Heydrich, the chief of the Security Police, to the chiefs of all task forces (*Einsatzgruppen*) operating in the conquered Polish territories. The second part of the six-part letter deals specifically with the establishment of local representative bodies of the Jewish population, and with their duties vis-à-vis the occupation authorities. This first official document about the Councils (reprinted below) already contains the design of their structure and main functions, as they were envisaged during the very first weeks of the war. Later developments greatly expanded the initial plans.

Berlin, 21 September 1939

The Chief of the Security Police
PP (II)—288/39 secret
Special Delivery Letter
To *The Chiefs of all task forces* (Einsatzgruppen) *of the Security Police.*
Concerning: The Jewish problem in the occupied zone.

I refer to the conference held in Berlin today, and again point out that the *planned joint measures* (i.e., the ultimate goal) are to be kept *strictly secret.*

Distinction must be made between

(1) the ultimate goal (which requires a prolonged period of time) and
(2) the sectors leading to fulfillment of the ultimate goal (each of which will be carried out in a short term).

The planned measures require thorough preparation both in technique and in the economic aspect.

Obviously the tasks at hand cannot be laid down in detail from here. The following instructions and directives serve at the same time for the purpose of urging chiefs of the task forces to practical consideration of problems.

. . . .

Councils of Jewish Elders

(1) In each Jewish community, a Council of Jewish Elders is to be set up which, as far as possible, is to be composed of the remaining influential personalities and rabbis. The Council is to be composed of 24 male Jews (depending on the size of the Jewish community).

It is to be made *fully responsible* (in the literal sense of the word) for the exact execution according to terms of all instructions released or yet to be released.

(2) In case of sabotage of such instructions, the Councils are to be warned of severest measures.

(3) The Jewish Councils are to take an improvised census of the Jews of their area, possibly divided into generations (according to age)—

a. up to sixteen years of age,

b. from sixteen to twenty years of age, and

c. those above and also according to the principal vocations—

and they are to report the results in the shortest possible time.

(4) The Councils of Elders are to be made aquainted with the time and date of evacuation, the evacuation possibilities, and finally the evacuation routes. They are, then, to be made personally responsible for the evacuation of the Jews from the country.

The reason to be given for the concentration of the Jews to the cities is that Jews have most decisively participated in sniper attacks and plundering.

(5) The Councils of Elders of the concentration centers are to be made responsible for the proper housing of the Jews to be brought in from the country. The concentration of Jews in the cities for general reasons of security will probably bring about orders to forbid Jews to enter certain wards of the cities altogether, and that in consideration of economic necessity they cannot, for instance, leave the ghetto, they cannot go out after a designated evening hour, etc.

(6) The Councils of Elders are also to be made responsible for the adequate maintenance of the Jews on the transport to the cities.

No scruples are to be voiced if the migrating Jews take with them all their movable possessions, as far as that is technically at all possible.

(7) Jews who do not comply with the order to move into cities are to be given a short additional period of grace when there is good reason. They are to be warned of strictest penalty if they should not comply by the appointed time.[1]

The second known decree concerning the Councils refers only to one of the occupied Polish provinces, namely, the Government General (*Generalgouvernement*) which consisted originally of four districts (Warsaw, Radom, Lublin, and Cracow) and constituted the major part of the German-occupied territories of Poland. This decree was signed by the governor general, Hans Frank, and dated November 28, 1939.

On the Establishment of Jewish Councils

In accordance with Par. 5, Section 1 of the Decree of the Führer and Reich Chancellor Concerning the Administration of the Occupied Polish Territories, dated October 12, 1939 (*Reichsgesetzblatt* I. S. 2077), I order:

Par. 1: In every community a representative body of the Jews is to be formed.

Par. 2: In communities of over 10,000 inhabitants this representative body, the Jewish Council (*Judenrat*), is to consist of 24 Jews from the local population.[2]

The Jewish Council is to be elected by the Jews in the community. If a member of the Council leaves, a new member is to be elected at once.

Par. 3: From among its members the Jewish Council will elect a chairman and his deputy.

Par. 4: 1) Following these elections—which are to take place on December 31 at the latest—the county commissioner (*Kreishauptmann*) concerned—the town commissioner (*Stadthauptmann*) in the urban counties—is to be informed of the composition of the Jewish Council.

2) The county commissioner (or town commissioner) will determine as to whether the composition of the Jewish Council should be accepted. He is authorized to change the composition if he sees fit.

Par. 5: The Jewish Council is obliged to receive, through its chairman or his deputy, the orders of German official agencies. Its responsibility will be to see to it that the orders are carried out completely and accurately. The directives which the Council may issue in the execution of German orders must be obeyed by all Jews and Jewesses.[3]

This decree was supposed to serve as a basis for the establishment of the Jewish Councils in the Government General. When the former Polish province known as Eastern Galicia fell into the hands of the advancing German army it was incorporated, as Distrikt Galizien, into the territory of the Government General in August 1941. The Jewish Councils were established there on the basis of a decree of August 7, 1941, putting Galicia under the executive authority of the Government General. Thus Frank's decree, as well as two subsequent executive orders, were extended to the new Distrikt.[4]

The responsibilities of the Jewish Councils vis-à-vis the German authorities were outlined in more general terms in Frank's decree than in Heydrich's circular letter. In the latter, two specific tasks of the Councils of Elders were mentioned: to carry out the census of the Jewish population, and to assist the German authorities in the transfer of Jews from small towns and hamlets into larger cities. Both Heydrich and Frank decreed that, under the threat of sanctions, the Councils were responsible for the conscientious and prompt execution of German orders. Only later, during a discussion of general police matters at the meeting of the occupation government at Cracow on May 30, 1940, did Frank outline succinctly the functions of the Jewish Councils: to supply Jewish forced labor, assist in the expulsions, and take care of food problems.[5]

Neither Heydrich's urgent circular letter nor Frank's decree specified which of the occupation authorities was actually entitled to issue orders to the Councils. The pertinent references are to "authorities" (*Dienststellen*) in general. However, on April 25, 1940, Frank issued the first of the two executive orders following up his decree of November 28, 1939. This order stipulated that all orders by the various organs of the occupation authorities were to be addressed to the Jews through the office of the chief of the civil administration (*Kreishauptmann*) of the appropriate county, except for matters of forced-labor duty. These, in accordance with his previous order about the forced-labor duty of the Jewish population (on October 26, 1939), were under the jurisdiction of the Higher SS and Police Leader.[6] The second executive order, dated June 7, 1940, established a similar procedure for the "county free" (*kreisfreie*) towns, i.e., the large district cities, which constituted separate administrative counties.[7]

These two executive orders met with the opposition of the Security Police apparatus of the Government General, which strove to take over all matters relating to the Jews and thus become their only competent supervisory authority. We learn about this opposition from the already mentioned discussion at the meeting of the Government General in Cracow, which took place in connection with the executive order of April 25, 1940. At this meeting, Obergruppenführer Bruno Streckenbach, the commander of the Security Police and the Security Services (*Befehlshaber der Sicherheitspolizei [SiPo] und des Sicherheitsdienstes [SD]*), suggested transferring to the SD supervision over the activities of the Jewish Councils and of the Jews in general. He argued that "the SD is for understandable reasons greatly interested in the Jewish problem, and that this was the reason why the Jewish Councils of Elders were instituted." He requested that all demands of other authorities concerning Jews be channeled through the SD. In his summary of the discussion following Streckenbach's proposal, Governor General Frank accepted the proposal in principle, but with the reservation that "pending the final implementation of the labor duty," the employment of the Jews at forced labor should be left to the local civil administration, in close cooperation with the Security Police and Security

Service.[8] It should be pointed out that the Higher SS Police Leader, Wilhelm Krüger, was in charge of the forced-labor duty of the Jews, in accordance with Frank's order of October 26, 1939 (Par. 2), and that on the basis of this order Krüger issued two executive orders dated December 11 and 12, 1939. These orders charged the Jewish Councils with registration of all native and newly arrived Jews subject to forced-labor duty (fourteen to sixty years old) and obligated them to submit weekly reports to the local mayors. The Councils were duty-bound to supply the needed tools to forced laborers.[9]

The rivalry between the police under Krüger and the civilian administration under Frank became a lasting feature of the occupation regime. As for the Jewish aspect of the rivalry, Frank endeavored to maintain at least formal supervision of Jewish forced labor under the jurisdiction of the civil administration for as long as possible. But the SS, the SiPo, and the SD increasingly gained larger authority in all Jewish problems. After Frank issued an order (*Erlass*) on June 3, 1942, putting all Jewish problems under the jurisdiction of the Higher SS and Police Leader,[10] this aspect of the rivalry came to an end. By this time the "resettlements," which were conducted by commandos of SS and SD, were already in full swing; and, although the civil administration theoretically was the competent occupation body for Jewish affairs, the Gestapo *Referent* for Jewish problems actually decided on all questions pertaining to the Jews anyway (see Chap. 11).

No special orders are known concerning the establishment of Jewish Councils in the territories of the Reichskommissariat Ostland or the Ukraine. However, in the general regulations relating to the Jews of these territories, we find mentioned such terms as "Jewish self-government" (*Jüdische Selbstverwaltung*) and "Jewish police" (*Ordnungsdienst*). Thus we read in the secret "Provisional Instructions for the Treatment of the Jews in Reichskommissariat Ostland" (*Zeitweilige Richtlinien für die Behandlung der Juden im Gebiet des Reichskommissariats Ostland*), dated August 13, 1941, that "the ghetto inmates shall conduct their internal matters themselves, under the supervision of the district or town commissar (*Kommissar*), or his authorized representative. To maintain order the Jews may be used as Order police. At most they may be given rubber canes or sticks. They are to be identified by a white armband with a yellow Star of David on the right arm."[11]

In the third version of the so-called "Brown Folder" (*Braune Mappe*) of the Eastern Operations Staff of the Army Command for Economic Affairs (*Wirtschaftsführungsstab Ost bei dem Oberkommando der Wehrmacht*), dated September 1942, part three of Section Two is entitled, "Instructions for the Treatment of the Jewish Question" (*Richtlinien für die Behandlung der Judenfrage*), and contains the following remark: "[in the previously mentioned area] the ghettos can be recognized as [a body of] Jewish self-government, and the Jewish police is to be under their control."[12]

As already mentioned, the decree of Hans Frank of November 28, 1939, referring to the establishment of Jewish Councils, dealt with the entire territory of the Government General. However, two communities were of special interest to him: Cracow, the seat of his government, and Warsaw, the capital of Poland. He ordered the evacuation of 40 to 50 thousand Jews from Cracow, because "it cannot be tolerated" that German officials should have to meet Jews wherever they go in the seat of the Government General.[13] As far as Warsaw was concerned, Frank issued an order on April 19, 1941, authorizing Governor Ludwig Fischer to nominate a commissar for the Jewish Quarter (*Kommissar für den jüdischen Wohnbezirk*). This commissar was authorized to utilize for the purposes of his activities the transfer office (*Transferstelle*), which dealt with the economic relations of the ghetto with the outside world, and with the chairman (*Obmann*) of the Jewish Council. By the same order Fischer was empowered (Par. 3) to charge the chairman of the Warsaw Jewish Council with the same tasks and the same authority within the ghetto as a Polish mayor had—placing him, however, under the jurisdiction of the commissar.[14] On the basis of this order of Hans Frank, Fischer issued two orders, both dated May 14, 1941. In the first he nominated as ghetto commissar Heinz Auerswald, a high official of the department of internal affairs of Distrikt Warsaw, and authorized him to oversee the Jewish matters of the entire Distrikt. Fischer's second order charged the *Obmann* of the Warsaw Ghetto with the functions and authority of a Polish town mayor. This was in accordance with the first three paragraphs of Frank's order of November 28, 1939, "Concerning the Administration of the Polish Communities" (*Über die Verwaltung der polnischen Gemeinden*), with the stipulation that the delineation of the functions of the *Obmann* and the mayor of Warsaw should be made by the ghetto commissar in consultation with the plenipotentiary of the governor.[15]

In Łódź, part of the "Incorporated Eastern Territories," on October 13, 1939, the town commissar, Leister, nominated Mordecai Chaim Rumkowski, a member of the prewar Jewish community council, as Elder of the Jews of the city of Łódź (*Ältester der Juden der Stadt Łódź*). This is the text of the nomination, which is in the form of an authorization (*Ausweis*):

Authorization

The Elder of the Jews in the City of Łódź, Rumkowski, has been commissioned to carry out all measures concerning the members of the Jewish race [ordered] by the German Civilian Administration of the City of Łódź.

He is personally responsible to me.

In order to perform his duties, he is authorized

1) to move about freely in the streets at any time of day or night;
2) to have access to the agencies of the German administration;
3) to select a group of associates (Council of Elders) and meet with them;
4) to make his decisions public through wall posters;
5) to inspect the Jewish labor assembly points.

Every member of the Jewish race is required to obey unconditionally all instructions given by Elder Rumkowski. Any opposition to him will be punished by me.[16]

On the next day Rumkowski got from the commissar another order, which put under his authority all institutions of the prewar Jewish community in Łódź. The administrative bodies and councils of these institutions were disbanded and reorganized, and Rumkowski was charged with exclusive responsibility for their activities, under the threat of arrest for those who would not comply. To cover the expenses incurred for the execution of his duties, Rumkowski was granted the right of taxation. The order reads as follows:

In order to enable you to carry out the commission given to you in writing on the 13th instant, in accordance with which you are personally responsible to me for the execution of all necessary measures, I decree:

All existing institutions of the Jewish community of Łódź are placed under your control or that of your appointed representatives.

All existing governing bodies, councils, officials, or similar so-called administrative authorities are to be disbanded, or dismissed, and to be re-established by you under your sole responsibility.

Persons in your community shirking such duties are to be reported to me. I will have them arrested at once.

You are authorized to impose a tax that will cover all costs arising from the execution of the measures you have been charged with.[17]

After the Jews of Łódź were forced into the ghetto in March and April of 1940, the mayor of the city of Łódź (*Oberbürgermeister der Stadt Łódź*), Schiffer, gave Rumkowski the power to organize life within the ghetto in accordance with the following order, dated April 30, 1940:

By virtue of the decree of the President of Police of April 8, 1940, all inhabitants are forbidden to leave the Ghetto effective April 30, 1940. I hold you responsible that this prohibition is strictly complied with.

By virtue of the authority invested in me by the *Regierungspräsident* on April 27, 1940, I further charge you with the execution of all measures which are now, or will in the future be, necessary for the maintenance of an orderly community life in the residential district of the Jews. In particular you have to safeguard order in the economic life, food supply, utilization of manpower, public health, and public welfare. You are authorized to take all measures and issue all directives necessary to reach this objective and to enforce them by means of the Jewish police (*Ordnungsdienst*) under your control.

I authorize you to set up registration points immediately where lists of all ghetto inhabitants are to be prepared. These lists must also show the religious and ethnic affiliation. Carbon copies of these lists are to be submitted to me weekly in quintuplicate, beginning on May 13, 1940.

All business with the German authorities will be conducted solely by you, or by a deputy to me named by you, at the administrative agency that will be established on Baluter Ring. Admission of other representatives must be applied for in advance whenever the necessity arises.

To safeguard the food supply for the ghetto population, you have the authority to confiscate and distribute all supplies on hand.

Since, in accordance with Reich legislation, all Jewish assets are considered confiscated, you have to register and secure all property of the Jews not absolutely essential to life (as, for instance, clothing, food, housing).

You are, furthermore, authorized to conscript all Jews for labor without compensation.

For all measures other than routine (*grundsätzlicher Art*) my prior written consent is required before their execution. In the case of measures that must be taken in order to ward off a sudden threat of danger, and cannot be postponed, my consent must be solicited beforehand over the telephone, or in writing after they have been ordered.

The functions and powers of the President of Police of Litzmannstadt remain unaffected by this directive.[18]

We have quoted at length these last three documents, the only ones that have come to light so far, to show how the occupation government conceived the tasks of a Jewish Council in a large Jewish community, and how it formulated its obligations toward the authorities and the ghetto inmates.

As a rule the nominations of the chairman and of the Council, or sometimes of the chairman alone, were made in writing. There were places, however, where the establishment of the Councils was made known in public notices by the local German authorities. For example, the creation of the Jewish Council of Warsaw, the largest Jewish community of Europe, was announced on October 23, 1939 by the *Polizeipräsident* of Warsaw, along with the order for a census of the Warsaw Jewish population. The order was made public in a trilingual poster (in German, Polish, and Yiddish) and emphasized that a Jewish Council was being established "for that purpose."[19] In the publicly announced order at Radom in December 1939, concerning the establishment of the "self-government of the occupied territories," the part dealing with the Jews stated that a Jewish Council was to be set up there under the direction of the Elder of the Jews (*Älteste der Juden.*)[20] The chief of the city administration in Lwów (a Ukrainian) issued an order on July 22, 1941, establishing a Jewish Council in that city. This order also came in the form of a public announcement.[21] A public announcement in Minsk (Byelorussia) let it be known that an acting chairman (*Kommissarischer Vorsitzender*) of the Jewish Council had been nominated.[22] Public notices regarding the establishment of the Jewish Councils were also issued in Siedlce, Prużana, and Góra Kalwaria,[23] to mention just a few.

A variety of nomenclature emerged when it came to designating the official names of the Councils and of the chairmen's titles. In the first known document mentioning the Councils, Heydrich's instruction to the *Einsatzgruppen* of September 21, 1939, the official name is Council of Elders (*Ältestenrat*). Hans Frank, in his decree of November 28, 1939, uses the term Jewish Council (*Judenrat*), and this became the generally accepted name throughout the Government General, though there were some exceptions. In the "Incorporated Eastern Territories," it was generally *Ältestenrat*, though there were many variations there too. In Będzin, for example, the Council was at first called the Representation of the Interests of the Jewish Community at Bendsburg [Germanization of Będzin] (*Interessenvertretung der jüdischen Kultusgemeinde in Bendsburg*), or the Executive Council of the Representation of Jewish Interests (*Vorstand der jüdischen Interessenvertretung*). In 1941 the name was changed to Council of Elders of the Jewish Religious Community at Bendsburg (*Ältestenrat der jüdischen Kultusgemeinde in Bendsburg*). By the end of 1942 we find on the letterheads of the Będzin Council the title "Council of Elders at Bendsburg" (*Ältestenrat Bendsburg*) printed under the heading "Central Office of the Jewish Councils of Elders of Eastern Upper Silesia" (*Zentrale der jüdischen Ältestenräte in Ostoberschlesien*), which was apparently adopted by all the Councils of that region to stress the organizational affiliation of the local Councils with the main office at Sosnowiec.[24] In the city of Białystok, which together with the district of Białystok (Bezirk Białystok) had been placed under the authority of Erich Koch, *Gauleiter* of East Prussia (and Reichskommissar of the Ukraine), *Judenrat* was the official name.[25] In Silesia (both Eastern Upper Silesia and the former German province of Silesia), the title was "Council of Elders of the Jewish Religious Community of . . ." (*Der Ältestenrat der jüdischen Kultusgemeinde in . . .*). The same title was used in a number of ghettos in the territory of the Government General, such as Lublin and other places.[26] However, in Cracow the Council was ordered by the Security Police to change its name from "Jewish Religious Community" (*Jüdische Kultusgemeinde*) to "Jewish Community" (*Jüdische Gemeinde*).[27] In Rzeszów the stationery of the Council carried the heading *Jüdische Gemeinde in Reichshof* (Germanization of Rzeszów).[28] In Kaunas the Council's name was changed twice. Up to August 1941 it was "Committee for the Resettlement of the Jews to Wiliampol" (*Komitee zur Umsiedlung der Juden nach Wiliampole*). After the transfer of the Kaunas Jews into the ghetto was completed, the committee was changed to the Jewish Council of Elders at Kauen (Germanization of Kaunas)-Wiliampol (*Jüdischer Ältestenrat Kauen-Wiliampol*).[29] At first the name of the Council at Vilna was "Jewish Committee of Vilna" (*Wilnaer jüdisches Komitee*),[30] but when the ghetto was established the Council's name was changed to *Ältestenrat*.[31]

The Councils of Latvia at Riga, Daugavpils, and Liepaja were also called *Ältestenrat*.

The most used official title for a Council chairman was "chairman of the Jewish Council" (*Obmann des Judenrates*) in the Government General, and "Elder of the Jews" (*Älteste der Juden*), "Jewish Elder" (*Judenälteste*), or simply "Elder" (*Älteste*) in the "Incorporated Eastern Territories." But according to his office stationery, Adam Czerniakow, chairman of the Warsaw Council, had a double title until approximately September 1941. The stationery was bilingual, and according to its German part Czerniakow was chairman of the Jewish Council and president of the Council of Elders of the Jewish religious community in Warsaw (*Obmann des Judenrates und Präsident des Ältestenrates der jüdischen Kultusgemeinde in Warschau*). After the representative body of the Vilna Ghetto was virtually reduced to a single person in the middle of July 1942, when Jacob Gens was appointed as ghetto head and chief of police, his official title was "chief of the ghetto and police in Vilna" (*Gettoversteher und Polizeichef in Wilno*), or sometimes simply (*Gettoversteher*.[32] Before that, the title of the council chairman was *Älteste der Juden*. In the occupied territories of the U.S.S.R. the Russian traditional term *starosta*,[33] usually designating a village elder or other such low-ranking official, was in use.

The official language of the Councils' titles also varied. Within the "Incorporated Eastern Territories" the Councils were named in only one language—German. But in other occupied areas the title was bilingual: throughout the Government General, in German and Polish (*Rada Żydowska* [Jewish Council] or *Rada Starszych* [Council of Elders]);[34] in the area subordinated to the Vilna district commissar (*Gebietskommissar*), in German and Lithuanian (*Vilniaus Geto Pirmininkas ir Policijos Vadas*, "Chairman of the Ghetto and Chief of the Police," or *Vilniaus Miesto Zydu Komitetas*, "Jewish Committee of the City of Vilna"). In Minsk (Byelorussia) the name of the Council, as mentioned in the Russian text of the order of the *Kreischef* of July 19, 1941, is "Jewish Council" (*Yevreyski Soviet*).[35] No information is available regarding the languages of Council titles in Latvia, Estonia, and the Reichskommissariat Ukraine.

As far as the Jews themselves were concerned, they generally used the term *Judenrat*; but *Yuden-Rat* was in use in Lublin[36] and *Yidn-rat* in Białystok. We find this rather seldom-used spelling in the minutes and announcements of the Białystok Ghetto. It was applied by the Council's secretary, a Yiddish-language purist and well-known teacher in prewar Poland, Rafal Gutman. Among the Yiddish-language documents of the Warsaw Judenrat there are some with the heading *Yidisher Rat*.[37] However, the Council of the Warsaw Ghetto was usually called *Gmina*,[38] the shortened official Polish title of the Jewish communities in Poland, a common usage before the war. (The full Polish title had been *Żydowska Gmina Wyznaniowa*— "Jewish Religious Community.") The Jews in Łódź called the *Ältestenrat* there *Beirat* ("Advisory Board"), and this title was used both in the official documents and by the people.[39]

CHAPTER 2

The Emergence of the Jewish Councils and Their Composition

THE COUNCILS CAME to life as a result of the interplay of three factors: the Jews themselves, the German authorities, and, in some areas, the indigenous authorities. It goes without saying that the will of the occupation authorities was the determining force in the establishment of a given Council and its composition (including its chairman). Under an absolute totalitarian regime it could not be otherwise. What is remarkable, however, is that it is almost impossible to discern any coordinated and consistent pattern in the emergence of the Councils.

THE JEWS THEMSELVES

The Germans found a reservoir of Jewish communal leaders already available in the Baltic states and in Soviet-occupied Poland (though not in the U.S.S.R. proper), despite a nearly two-year suspension of the activities of all traditional communal bodies by the Soviet authorities. Much more favorable in this respect was the situation in Poland, where the Germans found a well-developed network of Jewish community bodies duly elected or nominated by the prewar national government. These traditional Jewish institutions were in many cases disorganized or, at worst, had even stopped their normal activities altogether because of the war; but their members, as individuals, remained more or less in their places of residence. The entrance of the German army into any given locality spontaneously moved such individuals, traditionally active in the affairs of the community, to try to alleviate the tragic situation of oppressed Jews, engulfed in incessant abuses, forced hard labor under humiliating conditions, robberies, and killings. Interventions were attempted, relief committees were formed, and so forth. At a later period, when the civil authorities and the police organs took over from the military and began to install the Jewish Councils, those Jews who had taken it upon themselves to help their brethren in distress for the most part became the nuclei of the Councils.

Thus the Warsaw *Judenrat* consisted largely of members of the Jewish Citizens' Committee created during the first days of the siege of Warsaw, as well as of members of the former *Gmina*.[1] In Lublin, of the 14 members of the prewar Jewish Community Council executive board, 10 continued in office after the war started. In the second half of September 1939 several members of the Community Council, together with four persons from outside the Council, were co-opted to the executive board, and its membership was thus brought up to 23. Almost all of them became members of the Lublin *Judenrat* when it was established on January 5, 1940.[2] At Zamość, several members of the prewar Community Council executive board intervened with the local military commandant in order to stop abuses of the Jews. They were later nominated, together with others, to the Council of Elders.[3]

In other places, members of the Jewish service organizations created after the war broke out (variously called civic committees or relief committees) subsequently became the nuclei of the *Judenräte*. A civic committee was created in Bełchatów (Łódź area) immediately after the Germans entered the town. Under the pressure of German abuses and because of a few undesirable people who had penetrated the committee, the respectable leaders withdrew and the committee was dissolved. Some of the committee's remaining members were later nominated to the *Judenrat*.[4] Almost all the members of the relief committee of Skierniewice were nominated to the Jewish Council, and the committee's chairman became the Council's chairman.[5] The same happened in Ozorków.[6] To the Jewish Council of Będzin belonged, among others, the prewar deputy mayor of the city and a member of the Communist faction of the City Council. However, this body was active for a short time only, until the advent of the "star of the Jewish Elder, Merin"[7] (see Chap. 3).

The eastern areas of Poland also saw Jewish initiative in establishing representative bodies that were destined later to become nuclei of the *Judenräte*. For example, in Baranowicze "several people, active in community affairs before the war, under the impact of the events, were moved to establish a Jewish center." Later it became the Jewish Council.[8] A Jewish relief committee was active in Borszczów after the town was occupied by the Hungarian army, an ally of Nazi Germany. When the Germans took over the town from the Hungarians, the relief committee was transformed into a *Judenrat*, and the chairman of the committee was named *Judenälteste*.[9] After the Germans entered Kleck several persons previously active in community affairs established a committee of sorts. Later on it became the Jewish Council.[10]

In a number of places, the initiative to establish some kind of Jewish representation agreeable to the German authorities apparently came from outside the membership of the former community bodies. Thus in the town of Ostrowiec (Radom district), as soon as the Germans came, a few individuals offered to create a Jewish committee. The local commandant accepted the offer, naming the committee *Judenrat*.[11] A similar offer was accepted in Nowe Miasto.[12]

There were also places where one or two individuals became self-appointed liaison men between the Germans and the Jews prior to the establishment of the *Judenräte*, as in Kobryń, Grodno, and Bursztyn, among others.[13] In still other towns, people who had never aspired to any role in the public life of the community tried now to take over the leadership. Such for example was the case in the town of Góra Kalwaria (near Warsaw), the seat of the renowned Hasidic rabbi of Gher (the Yiddish name of the town). Here a small-time tailor actually usurped the right to represent the community. However, when the establishment of the Jewish Council was ordered in January 1940, he did not become a member, apparently not only because of the adverse attitude of the Jewish population, but also because the "*Kommandant* had finally understood that Tch. [the tailor's full name is not given in the source] was in no position to represent the Jews of Góra Kalwaria."[14]

Jews were a codetermining influence with the German authorities in the establishment of Councils at a higher organizational level. In areas where central Councils were in operation (district or county Councils), the members of the subordinate Councils were jointly nominated by the Germans and the chairmen of the respective central Councils. For example, the members of the Council at

Radomyśl (Distrikt Galizien) were jointly nominated by the local Gestapo chief and the chairman of the Mielec County Jewish Council.[15] In Eastern Upper Silesia, Moshe Merin, in his capacity as head of the *Zentrale* of the Jewish communities of that area, used to nominate or dismiss the chairmen of the local Councils of Elders on orders from his German masters or with their approval. This was what happened in Będzin, Chrzanów, and Kłobuck, all under Merin's jurisdiction (see Chap. 3).[16]

JEWISH OPPOSITION TO THE FORMATION OF THE COUNCILS

Although Jews were forced to comply with the German orders, there was open opposition within the Jewish community to cooperating in the establishment of the *Judenräte* or participating in their activities. Certain groups in Warsaw even maintained that the Council there should be boycotted altogether. A contemporary source thus formulated this extreme point of view: "No Council, no police, nothing at all; do whatever you wish, we will not cooperate. You want to catch [for forced labor]—all right, catch. You want to kill, so kill. Passive resistance. You can rule over us—maybe fate so ordained—but never will we become a willing, cooperating subject."[17] In many other ghettos similar attitudes were formulated, though the arguments may have been less extreme. Among the intelligentsia in Łódź, for example, there were professional men who on principle did not want to participate in the ghetto administration; some even forsook their professions and registered as laborers. They refused to be identified with the Rumkowski regime and to share the responsibility for his deeds.[18]

An example of the confrontation of two opposing views within the Jewish community in Lublin is given in the following eyewitness account:

. . . In the company of Mrs. Dobrzynsky [she was active in community affairs in Lublin] I met, in the fall of 1939, with the well-known attorney and Zionist Dr. Alten, who was a member of the presidium of the prewar community executive board. Among other things, he told us that the authorities had made a demand that the community executive board change its name to *Judenrat*. . . . There was no consensus of opinion on that among the members of the executive board. Some feared the heavy responsibility of dealing with the hostile Nazi authorities, whose real

Building of the Warsaw Ghetto wall.

The Warsaw Ghetto wall.

intentions were not yet known. . . . Others argued, however, that in tragic times like these there could be no excuse for deserting the people who had given them a vote of confidence before the war. They reasoned that, should they decide to withdraw, nobody could predict whom the Nazis would put in charge instead. The opinion of those unwilling to abandon the heavy burden of trust prevailed in the end. The *Judenrat* was formed with the participation of people from all factions among the Jews of Lublin.[19]

Another example of the confrontation of these opposing views was heard during the discussion held at the inaugural meeting of the *Judenrat* at Grodno on June 28, 1941. The proposal was advanced on principle not to form a body of representative Jews, since this would only make it easier for the vicious authorities to carry out their persecution of the Jewish population. The proponents of the opposite view won, claiming that the representatives were necessary because they would be in a position to alleviate the persecution.[20]

There were other instances of opposition to participating in the Councils. When Rabbi Simeon Rosowski of Ejszyszki (Vilna area) was summoned by the *"Kommandant* of the Nazi squad" and ordered to select a 12-man "Jewish Committee," he assembled the Jews of the town in the prayer house and announced the order. No one was willing to accept the "honor," and so it was decided to select the candidates by lot.[21] The problem of forming a *Judenrat* in Vilna was discussed during a dramatic meeting. Some 60 delegates of various political factions and social groups participated. At first not a single one agreed to become a member of the Council. An inter-mission was arranged, and afterward the radical decision was adopted that anyone elected would have to accept membership as if offering himself for *Kiddush Hashem* (the sanctification of the name of the Lord). Nevertheless, a number of persons still refused to accept the election. It was with extreme difficulty that the Council was formed at last and the chairman, vice chairman, and secretary elected.[22]

It happened that people who at first were doubtful about joining a *Judenrat* later changed their minds. One of the Council members in Białystok, Dov Subotnik, in a speech delivered on June 29, 1942, the anniversary of the formation of the Council, said: "None of us was willing to accept membership on the Council. I myself abstained for a few days, until I was persuaded to offer myself for the good of the people at a time when the life of the community was at stake."[23] The Council of Elders in Kaunas was established in conjunction with the establishment of the ghetto, and in fact was explicitly formed for this purpose. By the end of July 1941 the Jewish Committee in Kaunas was ordered to choose a *Judenälteste*. According to Abraham Golub, who later served as secretary of the Council of Elders, a meeting was called of 28 representatives of political parties. The meeting took place in the building of the Jewish elementary school on August 4 or 5, 1941. None of those present was willing to accept the chairmanship. The candidacy of the prominent physician Dr. Elkhanan Elkes was suggested, but he refused. However, after a passionate plea by Rabbi Jacob Moshe Shmukler, he agreed "to be the messenger of a good deed and represent the sorely tried Kaunas Jews." On August 8 the *Gebietkommissar* nominated to the Council Dr. Yephim Rabinowicz, the lawyers Jacob Goldberg and Lejb Garfunkel, Rabbi Samuel Aba Snieg, the former military chaplain, and Jacob Moshe Shmukler—the same five persons whom the Gestapo had ordered on July 8, 1941, to establish a committee for the transfer of the Kaunas Jews into the ghetto. On the same day, the Council reported to the *Gebietkommissar* that Dr. Elkhanan Elkes was elected chairman, Lejb Garfunkel vice chairman, and M. Kopelman chief of police.[24]

In case of the refusal by prominent Jewish leaders to assume membership or chairmanship of the Councils, the Germans appointed people of their own choosing. At the beginning of July 1941, the Nazis in Lwów suggested forming a Jewish Council to Professor Moses Alerhand and some other leaders in the community. Professor Alerhand, who several years before the war had been nominated chairman of the Lwów *Kehila* (Jewish Community Council), refused under various pretexts. Dr. Judah Ehrlich also refused to form the Council. Seeing that among the prominent leaders of the community they would not find people willing to accept the job, the Germans themselves nominated the *Judenrat*.[25] In Pabianice, Yitzhak Urbach refused to accept the Council chairmanship after being elected by a meeting of activists among the Jewish population; the Germans then went ahead and nominated the lawyer Shapiro as Council chairman.[26]

A peculiar situation developed in Wieliczka, a small town near Cracow. Right after the occupation the Germans shot to death several score of Jews, all males. This act of wanton cruelty intimidated the town's Jews to such a degree that none was willing to accept membership in the *Judenrat*. Only women became Council members, and a woman became chairman. This situation lasted until the end of 1941, when two people—refugees from Cracow—took over the leadership as chairman and deputy chairman of the reorganized Council.[27]

Since none of the Jews of Biłgoraj was willing to accept membership on the Jewish Council, "the Germans themselves formed it, threatening the death penalty for refusal [to accept the nomination]."[28] In Kołomyja the Gestapo nominated the former alderman, Chaim Ringelblum, as head of the *Distrikt Judenrat*. Next day, however, he went to the Gestapo chief and told him that he could not accept the nomination. Markus Horowitz was nominated instead. But shortly thereafter, in the course of the very next "resettlement action," Ringelblum and his entire family were taken away.[29] A similar series of events took place in Bereza Kartuska.[30] In the little town of Gliniany (Distrikt Galizien) there was an ingenious by-product of the grave misgivings and hesitancy to accept responsibility for the well-being of coreligionists that generally accompanied the formation of the Councils. After a great deal of persuasion, a list of 12 persons to serve on the Council was made up to present for confirmation to the Germans. However, at the request of the elected members, a committee of 30 persons was secretly chosen at the same time to form a sort of undercover consultative body for the Council, which thus secured for itself the backing and control of the community.[31]

THE GERMAN AUTHORITIES

As was frequently the habit of the Germans in regard to other anti-Jewish measures, local officials did not wait for the higher echelons of the occupation authorities to order the establishment of the Councils. They nominated or confirmed the representatives of the Jewish population on their own, even prior to Heydrich's *Schnellbrief* of September 21, 1939. As early as the first week of the war, chiefs of the *Einsatzgruppen* picked random Jews as "representatives" to perform various tasks for them. For example, the chief of *Einsatzgruppe* No. 3 (Fischer) nominated a Jewish *Kommissar* at Kempno on September 6; and the SS *Standartenführer* Damzog, commandant of *Einsatzgruppe* No. 5, on September 7 nominated two Jews in Grudziądz to serve as "representatives" of the community and gave them an order to deliver a list of the local Jewish population indicating the property they owned. He allowed exactly 14 hours for the job. Similar orders were given in Pułtusk, Raciąż, Maków, Przasnysz, Zichenau (Ciechanów), and in Mława and Łódź counties.[32] In Piotrków Trybunalski a *Judenrat* was nominated as early as September 4, immediately after the entry of the German army,[33] and in Chmielnik during the first 10 days of September.[34] In Cracow a provisional (*einstweilige*) Jewish representative body, consisting of nine members, a chairman, and a deputy chairman, was nominated by the chief of the SD in the second half of September 1939.[35]

The establishment of the Councils was usually accompanied by intimidation, humiliation, and even massacres in many communities, large and small. For example, the *Referent* of Jewish affairs in Częstochowa summoned Moshe Ash, the son of Rabbi Nahum Ash, and ordered him to present a list of Jews formerly active in community affairs. The *Referent* told him that these people would continue to deal with Jewish affairs as they had. All those on the list Ash presented were summoned to appear before the *Referent*, who severely scolded and abused them. After a long anti-Jewish harangue, he nominated six persons as members of the *Judenrat*. This took place on September 16, 1939, five days before Heydrich issued his urgent circular letter. On October 1 the Council was enlarged to 24 members, apparently in conformity with the Heydrich letter.[36]

In some smaller communities the nomination of the Council members took place after the Jews were first chased outdoors and forced to assemble in special places, as was the case in Grajewo[37] (Białystok district) and Chmielnik (in the Ukraine).[38] Elsewhere the nomination took place after the release of the Jewish population which was kept under arrest, as in Goniądz (Grodno county).[39]

This is how the Jewish Council came into being in Warsaw, as described by Shmuel Zygielbojm, the erstwhile Council member:

As the chairman of the [prewar] executive board of the Jewish community, Maurycy Mayzel . . . was absent, the Gestapo ordered the deputy chairman, Adam Czerniakow, to appear at its office. For two days he was abused and then ordered to deliver the names of rich Jews, as well as other information about the activities of Jewish organizations and individuals active in community affairs. He had to listen to anti-Semitic speeches and Nazi propaganda oratory before he was informed that he had been nominated chairman (*Obmann*) of the Jewish Community. He also received an order to present a list of 24 Jews to be nominated members of the Jewish Council and as many names of persons to serve as deputies. . . . The first meeting of the Council thus nominated took place in the middle of October in the presence of the Gestapo officer, [Gerhardt] Mende. Members were ordered to rise and remain standing while he addressed them as if they were criminals. He bluntly told them that the fate of the Jews and of the Council was in the hands of the Gestapo. The Council was forbidden to approach any other official. No arguing [about the orders issued] was allowed. He told them, "We act in accordance with the *Führerprinzip*: what the Gestapo orders has to be accomplished quickly and punctually, not in the Jewish way." He would see to it "that the Jews did everything as ordered, or else. . . ." After his speech the Council members were given identification cards issued by the Gestapo: "——— is a member of the Council of Elders of the Warsaw Jewish Religious Community and has to perform special tasks assigned by me. Signed: '*Sicherheitspolizei, Einsatzgruppe 4*' or '*Gruppenführer.*'"[40]

The first meeting of the original Council of Elders at Łódź was called on November 11, 1939. It took place in the presence of a boorish Gestapo official who was extremely ill-tempered and intimidated the Council members, threatening them with a revolver. The following morning he summoned over 20 Council members to the Gestapo office, where they were arrested. All but five perished.[41] The establishment of the Council at Tarnopol was accompanied by a mean trick which took the lives of over 60 persons, most of them intelligentsia. Mark Gotfried, a teacher, was summoned to the commandant at the beginning of July 1941 and ordered to create a *Judenrat* of at least 60 persons selected from among local intelligentsia. Gotfried assembled a group of 63 reputable citizens and went with them to the building of the former Polish Województwo (province) as ordered. How could they suspect that this was their last walk? As soon as they arrived they were met with a barrage of jeers, beaten, loaded into trucks, and taken out of town to the "dog catcher's hill." All were killed, except for Gotfried and two very old men.[42] Bloodshed in similar circumstances took place in Nowogródek on July 6 and 7, 1941. Two hundred Jews were assembled on orders from the Gestapo ostensibly to elect a Jewish Council. Fifty of them, most of them professional men, were taken away and shot in the adjacent forest.[43]

In some places rabbis were ordered to form the Councils. In Pinczów Rabbi Rapaport was ordered to select 12 persons for nomination to the *Judenrat*. He was also ordered to make a list of names of the 4,000 Jews of the town. Both orders had to be carried out overnight. At the appointed time the rabbi presented the 12 candidates and the list of Jewish residents to the SD man, who nominated the chairman and the secretary on the spot.[44]

On July 4, 1941, an automobile stopped in front of the synagogue courtyard at Żydowska [Jewish] Street in Vilna. Two Germans armed with guns emerged, entered the court, and asked for the rabbi. The town sexton, Chaim Mayer Gordon, a tall man with a gray beard, was presented to them instead. The Germans asked him whether he was the rabbi, and he answered in the negative, explaining that Rabbi Yitzhak Rubinstein was absent on a trip to the United States, and that Rabbi Chaim Oyzer Grodzenski had passed away. The Germans curtly ordered: "If this is the case, you be the rabbi. . . . You are hereby ordered to make up a group of representatives of the Jews today, and to appear with them before us tomorrow."[45] In Białystok on June 29, 1941, the day after a bloody massacre took place, the Germans called the rabbi, Dr. Gedalya Rosenman, and ordered him to establish a Jewish Council.[46] In Kaunas, too, the Germans at first ordered the well-known and respected religious leader Rabbi Abraham Duber Shapiro to form a group of Jewish representatives.[47] There were other places, as in Mława and Byteń, where rabbis were ordered to choose the members of the Councils[48] (see also above, p. 19, about the case in Ejszyszki).

In most of the cases that have come to light so far, a single person was ordered to form the Council. In addition to Warsaw and Łódź, already mentioned, this was also the case in Lublin, Radom, Grodno, Brody,[49] Łęczyca, Stolin, Płock, and Końskie, among others.[50] In the occupied Soviet territories, and particularly in Byelorussia, this was also the rule.[51] Usually the person ordered to form the Council became chairman. There were, however, cases where the chairman was elected by the Council, or where the occupation authority nominated someone else to serve as *Obmann*: either a member of the prewar Community Council or executive board or any other prewar community leader. The Germans followed this sort of policy as long as they were interested in having the *Judenräte* enjoy the confidence of the Jews. Former Jewish officials of the city government at Płock and Końskie were given the task of forming the *Judenräte* of their respective cities; in Końskie the same person was nominated as Council chairman.[52] However, in other places the procedure was different. For example, in Biała Podlaska the authorities summoned the members of the prewar Community Council executive board and ordered them collectively to form a Jewish Council.[53] In Rohatyn a similar order was given to the representatives of the community and to several refugees who were summoned for this purpose to appear before the authorities.[54] The commandant at Jaworów (Lwów district) ordered representatives of the Jews to appear before him. When nine persons reported, he immediately nominated the chairman of the Council and the chief of the Jewish militia.[55] In Lublin and Kaunas, however, the chairman of the Councils and the deputies were elected by the Councils at their first meetings. Naturally, elected members had to be confirmed by the Germans.[56] It sometimes happened, as in Słonim, that when a list of Council members was presented for confirmation the authorities ordered these members to co-opt certain other persons.[57]

The haphazardness which characterized both the bizarre formation of the Councils and the general contempt of the German authorities for the Jews can be seen in many other instances. The military commandant of Byteń accidentally met a dentist, Arbuz (his first name is not mentioned in the source), himself a refugee from the town of Suwałki, and gave him an order to deliver within two hours the names of six Jews to represent the local community in dealing with all problems concerning the Jews. A newcomer in town, the shocked dentist felt helpless. Accompanied by a native he went to the rabbi, Ben-Zion Jaffe. An urgent meeting was called, and a Council of six persons was nominated, the dentist of Suwałki among them.[58]

In Minsk (Byelorussia) a group of Jews was seized in the street, and a German officer ordered anyone who knew German to step forward. Nobody answered. After the officer repeated the order and threatened punishment, one Eli Mishkin came forward. He was nominated *Kommissarischer Vorsitzender* of the Council. The next day his nomination was officially announced on special posters in the Jewish section of the town.[59]

In another occupation area, far away from Minsk in the town of Sosnowiec (Eastern Upper Silesia), the nomination of the notorious Moshe Merin took place in somewhat similar circumstances. A large group of Jews was held incommunicado for 24 hours in the public bath and was subjected to physical tortures and moral harassment. A German officer came to inquire who among them had been a member of the prewar Community Council. The president of the executive board, Lejzerowicz, was in the group, but dared not say a word. Then Moshe Merin (some say that he was a member of the executive board) came from behind the last row and reported to the officer. Thus began his career, first as chairman of the *Judenrat* at Sosnowiec, and later as the chief (*Leiter*) of the central office of the Jewish Councils of Elders in Eastern Upper Silesia.[60]

In the town of Chmielnik (Radom district), during the first week of the occupation a German officer summoned a large number of Jews to the synagogue and, after a speech, nominated one Abraham Langwald to be *Obmann*. Langwald then approached the members of the prewar Jewish Community Council and suggested that they join the *Judenrat*. Almost all refused. With great difficulty the *Judenrat* was finally made up from among some of the people active in community affairs before the war.[61]

In December 1939 a group of Germans came to a Jew in Krasnobród (Lublin area) and ordered him to form a *Judenrat*. He summoned several distinguished local people who suggested the names of their candidates to the Germans, and thus the Council came into being.[62] In Chęciny (Kielce area), the *Judenrat* was nominated as follows: on a certain day (the exact date is not mentioned by the source), a German military patrol approached a group of Jews in the marketplace and took them all to the commandant, who told them that they were being nominated as the *Judenrat*.[63]

In places where there were two ghettos in existence, there were often two separate *Judenräte*. This, for example, was the situation in Grodno, where two separate Councils with separate chairmen operated under an *Oberobmann*, who represented both ghettos vis-à-vis the German authorities. For a short time in Vilna, until the end of October 1941, two *Judenräte* operated out of separate offices.[64] This was also the case in Drohiczyn (Pinsk area) where there was a ghetto for productive people and another for the unemployed.[65]

THE INDIGENOUS AUTHORITIES

When the Germans attacked Soviet Russia on June 22, 1941, many of the non-Jewish population in the areas occupied earlier by the

U.S.S.R. collaborated with the Nazi invaders. In order to encourage collaboration, the Nazis allowed these areas token self-governments. These administrative organs were sometimes influential in the formation of Jewish Councils and in the selection of their chairmen. Thus the members of the *Ältestenrat* in Daugavpils (Dwinsk) were jointly nominated by the German and Latvian authorities.[66] Kalendra, district chief at Vilna and a Lithuanian, told a delegation of Jews who sought, early in the occupation, to contact the German authorities about the formation of a *Judenrat* that all such problems would have to be taken up with him.[67] In Šiauliai the *Ältestenrat* was nominated by a Lithuanian, Captain Stankus, the *Referent* for Jewish affairs in the city administration.[68] The initial group of Jewish representatives in Lwów was nominated by the Ukrainian Polansky, head of the city administration.[69] In Kołomyja, the *Kreishauptmann* requested that the Ukrainian city administration make up a list of candidates for the county *Judenrat*. Upon receipt of this list, he called in the candidates and nominated the chairman.[70] The Ukrainian mayor of Bursztyn, Skulsky, confirmed the local Jewish Council, whose members had been elected at a meeting in the prayer house. At their own request he excused the rabbi and the rabbinical judge from serving on the Council.[71] The Ukrainian *Referent* for Jewish affairs in Skałat (Distrikt Galizien) gave authority to establish a group of Jewish representatives to his Jewish friend, a cattleman by occupation, with whom he had done business before the war.[72] The members of the Council in Korzec and Łuck (Volhynia) were nominated on the recommendation of the Ukrainian county administration.[73]

The power of the indigenous authorities over Jewish affairs, and particularly over the formation of the *Judenräte*, was, however, a temporary and passing phenomenon during the early period of the occupation, while the Germans were yet eager to make the Ukrainians, Lithuanians, and Latvians believe that they were being granted political independence. The understanding was: "We are turning the Jews over to you." Later these illusions were no longer sustained, and the Nazis followed their usual occupation policy by taking administrative authority over the Jews away from indigenous administrations, except for one aspect: extermination of the Jews. The Germans readily accepted help from the local populations in the "solution" of the Jewish problem; members of the indigenous auxiliary police were assigned to participate in killing Jews.

LAW AND PRACTICE IN THE FORMATION OF THE COUNCILS

The manner and the variety of means the Germans used in establishing the Jewish Councils (or Councils of Elders) reflect their reckless arbitrariness toward the millions of Jews under their rule. As we have indicated, the written law aimed only at creating some sort of a legal alibi whereby the principle of "local leadership" could cover up the bizarre and lawless acts of the local occupation authorities, military and civilian. The same nihilistic attitude prevailed later when the *Judenräte* were facing the Germans in the course of their day-to-day activities. (This will be discussed in Chap. 11.)

Contrary to the clearly stated stipulation in Frank's decree of November 28, 1939, no elections in the ordinary sense of the word took place anywhere within the Government General. The authorities exercised their own power for the most part, and arbitrarily decided on their own who should become a Council member. Paragraph 3 of the decree, which states that the *Obmann* has to be elected by the Council, also remained a dead letter, for the pertinent authorities with rare exceptions themselves nominated the *Obmann* (or *Judenälteste*) and ordered him to form the *Judenrat* and present his list of candidates for confirmation. In any case the last sentence in Paragraph 4 of Frank's decree, stipulating that local organs of the occupation authorities have the power to *order* a change in the composition of the Council (see Chap. 1), made a complete mockery of the election clause. Only a few instances have come to light so far in which certain single *groups* within the Jewish community were ordered to elect the local Council. Thus in Drohobycz the Germans called on Jewish lawyers, physicians, and industrialists in order to decide on the composition of the *Judenrat*. The notary, Dr. Rosenblat, was elected *Älteste* of the *Judenrat*, and three physicians were elected as members.[74] In the little town of Wysock (Białystok district) a *Judenrat* of 12 members was elected during a meeting at the prayer house.[75] However, the source does not mention who took the initiative to call the meeting; neither is the mode of election indicated nor how many people cast their votes. There could not have been very many. From a poorly written news item in the *Jewish Gazette* (*Gazeta Żydowska*, No. 6, July 6, 1940), published in Cracow under Gestapo censorship, it can be deduced that the town commissar of Nowy Sącz ordered "new elections" to the Council after some members left. However, it is not mentioned whether the "elections" really took place. The same paper (No. 13, March 13, 1940) announced that of the candidates suggested by various groups in Kielce, 24 were elected: 5 professional men and office employees, 5 merchants, 4 workmen, 4 artisans, 4 industrialists, and 2 refugees. It is not explained how the list of candidates was compiled or how the candidates were elected.

The stipulation in Paragraph 2 of Frank's decree, that the Council members must be local people, was not always observed either, for on many occasions the authorities nominated refugees from far away places (later we shall analyze the significance of this policy). Nor was attention paid to yet another provision in this paragraph, that in communities of more than 10,000 souls, the Council should consist of 24 members. Often the number of Councilmen was in no relation to the number of Jews in the community. Thus in Lwów, with a population of 150,000, the Council consisted of 8 members at the end of July 1941. By March 1942 the authorities increased the membership to 12.[76] On the other hand, in Skierniewice, with a Jewish population of approximately 7,000, the Council consisted of 24 members from the very start.[77] In Wadowice (Cracow district), with a population of 2,000 Jews, the Council consisted of 4 members,[78] but in Andrychów, a still smaller place in the same district with approximately 500 Jews, the Council consisted of 6 members.[79] Scores of similar cases can be cited.

MEMBERS OF THE COUNCILS:
VITAL STATISTICS AND COMMUNAL AFFILIATIONS

In discussing the personal data and communal affiliations of the Council members, we shall use for analysis information taken from the poll mentioned above in the Preface. Table I shows their personal data during the period of their service as Council members. It should be pointed out that not all the information required by the questionnaire was supplied. This is the reason why, for example, we have only 464 answers (62.7%) regarding the educational status of the 740 Council members. Much higher (on the average about 95%) is the percentage of answers concerning family status, occupation, and residence.

Over 85 percent of the Council members were in the thirty- to sixty-year age range, and almost 90 percent had families with chil-

TABLE I

		Number of Council Members Responding[a]	Percentage of Council Members Responding
1. *Age*			
Up to 30 years		41	5.7
30–60 years		610	85.3
60 and over		64	9.0
	Total	715[b]	100.0
2. *Family Status*			
Married		654	89.8
Single		74	10.2
	Total	728[c]	100.0
3. *Education*			
Elementary		76	16.4
Secondary		204	44.3
Higher		184	39.3
	Total	464[d]	100.0
4. *Occupation*			
Merchants		311	46.7
Professionals		172	25.8
Office employees and others		125	18.9
Artisans		58	8.6
	Total	666[e]	100.0
5. *Residence*			
Natives		648	92.1
Refugees		56	7.9
	Total	704[f]	100.0

[a] Total number of Council members about whom information was supplied in the questionnaires = 740.

[b] 96.5% of 740 Councilmen.

[c] 98.3% of 740 Councilmen.

[d] 62.7% of 740 Councilmen.

[e] 90% of 740 Councilmen.

[f] 95.1% of 740 Councilmen.

dren. Only 5.7 percent were younger than thirty years of age. It can be assumed that family status may have influenced the attitude and the behavior of at least some of the Council members. They might have acted differently had they not been worried about the fate of their families, particularly during the "resettlement actions."

Section 3 on education includes, among the Councilmen with elementary and secondary education, those who were educated in religious schools such as the *cheder* (elementary) or *yeshiva* (secondary). Most significant is the large number (about 40% of the answers) of Councilmen with higher education. It is possible that this came about because the authorities tried to have in the Councils people who knew the German language, and these were quite numerous among persons with higher education. On the other hand, the Jews themselves apparently tried to have in the Councils people who, if only because of their high level of education, were considered more suited to deal with the authorities. In a number of the questionnaires it is clearly indicated that the person in question became a Councilman "because he knew German well enough." This was especially common throughout Galicia, where the percentage of Jews with higher education had traditionally been higher than elsewhere in Poland. Drohobycz and Borysław are two of the towns mentioned in this respect; and in Złoczów of the 12 Councilmen 8 had the title of doctor.[80]

Regarding the occupations of Council members, it is notable that less than 9 percent were artisans, although 45.4 percent of the Jewish population gave crafts and small industry as their occupation during the census in Poland in 1931. One reason for this discrepancy may have been that there were not many artisans in the first place among the members of the prewar *Kehila* organs which, as we will see, provided the main source of recruits for the Councils. Almost 26 percent of the Council membership about whom information was given were professional men (physicians, dentists, lawyers, pharmacists, etc.). This is much higher than the percentage of professionals among all Jews in Poland according to the census of 1931. The percentage of merchants among Council members (almost 47%) is also higher than the percentage of merchants among all Polish Jews (37.9% according to the 1931 census).

Table II (p. 34) illustrates the political and communal affiliations of the Councilmen. The purpose here was to determine the extent to which the Councils mirrored the traditional political and social makeup of Jewish communities before the war, and whether there were Councilmen who continued their prewar communal leadership.

Of the 740 Councilmen included by the questionnaires, 59.5 percent were associated with various political factions before the war, and almost one-half of these (212 out of 446) occupied leading positions in their respective parties or organizations as chairmen, secretaries, treasurers, or executive members. It should be pointed out that the Jews in Eastern Europe were intensely involved in public affairs before the war and were affiliated in large numbers with political parties. The high number of Councilmen with prewar social or political affiliations accurately depicts the alertness and diversity of their social commitments before the Nazi onslaught.

Zionists of all factions constituted over two-thirds (67.1%) of the Council members. Only a little more than 21 percent were practicing Jews of the Mizrachi or Agudat Israel persuasions, though the actual number of Orthodox Jews was notably higher in the prewar Jewish communal bodies. The same can be said about the followers of the Jewish Socialist Labor Bund, whose membership in the communal bodies had been more numerous than the 6.7 percent shown in the questionnaires. Both the Communists and Folkists (the latter were mainly active among the low-income artisans and traders) played an insignificant role in the Jewish communal institutions before the war, as their percentages in the questionnaires accurately suggest.

There are valid explanations for the disparities between the numbers of Council members belonging to the religious groups and the Jewish Socialist Labor Bund, on the one hand, and, on the other, the actual numbers of these groups before the war. As Council members the Mizrachi and Agudat Israel were handicapped in dealing with the Germans by their wearing, as was customary with Orthodox Jews in Eastern Europe, the traditional garb, long beards, and sidelocks. They also had little if any secular education and were unable generally to speak German or even the local vernacular. Nevertheless, a few questionnaires indicate that Orthodox rabbis were members of the Councils, despite the hatred and contempt of the Germans for Jewish religion; and it appears from other pertinent sources that in Białystok, Włodzimierz Wołynski, Bursztyn, and Lazdijai the (at least formal) chairmen of the *Judenräte* were rabbis.[81]

As for members of the Jewish Socialist Labor Bund, by the very nature of their party they were exposed to great danger. This reason alone was enough to limit their membership in the Councils. An underground party messenger related that in scores of towns there was a widespread divergence of opinion among the party members on the question of participation in the *Judenräte*. There was no clearcut decision of the underground central body in Warsaw. It was left to the party groups themselves to act according to the prevailing local conditions.[82] It can be assumed that in many places the local party committees decided not to participate in the Councils. It should be noted, however, that in many instances the Council members were affiliated with no political party.

Regarding elected officials, Table II shows that 43 percent of these Council members about whom information was supplied were elected officials before the war, active either in the *Kehila* or in the municipal organs. Of the 317 members in this category, moreover, 41 occupied leading positions in the organs of the *Kehila*, serving as chairmen, vice chairmen, etc.; and 26 were high municipal officials serving as deputy mayors, members of city governments, etc.

It is characteristic of the extent of social commitment among the Council members that many were involved in the work of more than one institution before the war. As can be seen from section 3 of Table II, the 740 Council members included in the questionnaires were members of one or more civic bodies. Indeed we find that in Prużana, for example, one of the Council members (a refugee from Bereza Kartuska) had been active in his native town in the Society of Merchants, the small loan bank of the *Kehila*, the people's bank, and in TOZ (Society to Protect the Health of Jews)—and was also a member of the school board. He continued his lively social activities in Prużana. In Piotrków Trybunalski before the war six Councilmen were simultaneously active in the labor unions, in ORT (Organization for Rehabilitation and Training) and TOZ, and in the vocational school, and also served on the executive committee of the Yiddish school. Three of the six were also active in the small loan bank. Five members of the Włodzimierz Wołynski *Judenrat* were before the war active at the same time in the people's bank, in ORT, in TOZ, and in various philanthropic and religious societies, schools, etc. Information reflecting on the simultaneous prewar activities of the Council members in diverse communal projects is also mentioned in questionnaires relating to: Nowy Sącz, Kozienice, Końskie, Kazimierz nad Wisłą, Płock, Krzemieniec, Głębokie, Šiauliai, and in many more questionnaires.

Five Councilmen are named in the questionnaires as having occupied leading positions in the Jewish community and on the government bodies as well. According to one questionnaire, the chairman of the *Judenrat* in Zaleszczyki had been chairman of the *Kehila* there and, at the same time, deputy county chief (*starosta*).[83] It is safe to say that the number of Council members active in various

TABLE II

	Number of Council Members Responding[a]	Percentage of Council Members Responding
1. *Party Affiliation*		
Zionists		
General	206	45.9
Socialists	49	11.2
Mizrachi	44	10.0
Revisionists	44	10.0
Agudat Israel	52	11.3
Labor Bund	29	6.7
Communists	12	2.7
Folkists	10	2.2
Total	446[b]	100.0
2. *Elected Officials*[c]		
Kehila	198	62.4
City	118	37.5
Member of Parliament	1	0.1
Total	317[d]	100.0
3. *Active in Community Affairs*		
Professional and economic	337	39.7
Welfare, philanthropic	230	27.0
Cultural and educational	175	20.6
Religious	108	12.7
Total	850	100.0

[a] Total number of Council members listed in the pertinent questionnaires = 740.

[b] 59.5% of 740 Councilmen.

[c] In addition to the Council members included in this section, another was a member of the Polish Senate, the Upper Chamber of the Polish Parliament. He was also a member of the Warsaw City Government.

[d] 43% of 740 Councilmen.

capacities both in the Jewish community and in municipal affairs was much larger than is indicated in the questionnaires. It is unfortunate that on a number of questionnaire sheets the pertinent section is blank, apparently because the informant lacked sufficient information. There are, however, reliable data from other sources concerning 30 towns not included in the poll, where members of the *Judenräte* were active before the war in the *Kehila*, in welfare projects, and in party work.[84]

Thus on the basis of the data supplied by the questionnaires it is evident that the majority of the Council members occupied various positions of trust before the war, providing community leadership in diverse professional, economic, cultural, religious, and philanthropic organizations. However, we have to bear in mind that the composition of the Councils was not constant. In time, in the process of continuing fluctuation and resulting negative selection, the social and moral standards of the Councilmen fell considerably. The impact of this process is analyzed in Chap. 12.

CHAPTER 3

The Central Jewish Councils

BESIDES THE COUNCILS established within the boundaries of individual Jewish communities, the German occupation authorities created Councils of wider geographical scope. It is difficult now to trace the origins of these hierarchically layered Councils. One indication of their purpose is perhaps hinted at in an article in the *Gazeta Zydowska* (No. 17, Sept. 17, 1940), innocuously entitled "The Development of the Councils," in which it is proposed to establish central Jewish Councils for each of the four administrative districts of the Government General, and a top Council with a seat at Cracow encompassing the whole of the Government General. The article suggests that such a centralized system would "give a guarantee that orders [by the authorities] will be properly executed." Like almost all articles in the *Gazeta*, this one is signed only by initials. Whatever its origin, however, there is little doubt that it must have had prior approval by the Gestapo. It is clear that Councils encompassing large areas could make things easier for the Germans, if only for technical reasons. Besides, the idea of centralized Councils must have been appealing to the functionaries of the totalitarian Nazi state.

A central Council was established in Upper Eastern Silesia (*Ostoberschlesien*), the new administrative entity the Germans had carved out of parts of the former Cracow province (*Województwo*) and the Polish part of Silesia. At the beginning of November or December 1939, Moshe Merin, chairman of the Sosnowiec *Judenrat*, was given the task of forming new *Kehilas* or reorganizing the leadership of already functioning *Kehilas* within the *Regierungs-*

bezirk Kattowitz; in the first days of January 1940, *Die Zentrale der Ältestenräte der jüdischen Kultusgemeinden in Ostoberschlesien* was established. By March 1941 the *Zentrale* encompassed 32 communities in 10 counties of the *Regierungsbezirk*—including two city-counties: Będzin and Sosnowiec—with a Jewish population of about 100,000. The smallest community numbered 360 souls; the largest one, in Będzin, had a population of 25,171.

According to the by-laws printed in *Gazeta Żydowska*, the *Zentrale* had widespread jurisdiction over the local Councils: its manager (*Leiter*), Merin, nominated and dismissed their chairmen and members, and represented the individual Councils vis-à-vis the German authorities. In Chrzanów, for example, the *Zentrale* reorganized the Council in March 1940, changing its entire composition. Later on, however, the chairman and two members of the reorganized Council were arrested, and Merin sent his own man over to serve as chairman.[1] He acted similarly in Będzin,[2] Kłobuck,[3] and Wadowice.[4]

Local Councils were under the supervision of inspectors acting as liaison men with the *Zentrale* through nine departments (up to April 1940 there was yet another department to deal with emigration affairs). The following departments were authorized by the German authorities: a legal department to intercede on behalf of individuals and of entire communities; a welfare department to disseminate circular letters and questionnaires regarding relief, and to call meetings of the Councilmen and heads of welfare institutions to decide on relief and its distribution; a health department to coordinate medical and sanitary work, to call conferences of Jewish physicians within given counties, to provide doctors and medical facilities for small communities, and to supervise medical institutions; a food department to coordinate the distribution of food among the Jews of the Eastern Upper Silesia area, to provide provisions for the soup kitchens, and to purchase nonrationed food products from private sources for distribution to the local communities through a wholesale warehouse; a finance and budget department to supervise the financial activities of the Councils, to prepare their monthly budgetary estimates, and to check the actual disbursement of the allocated sums (this department also collected from the main trust office, Kattowitz, paid out the small relief sums due to former owners of confiscated businesses, and was authorized to try to obtain financial help from outside service organizations, such as the Joint

Distribution Committee, TOZ, the Red Cross, etc.); a labor department to organize and supervise the forced-labor duty and to punish
for not reporting or to collect a fee from those released from compulsory labor duty; there were also departments dealing with education, statistics and archives, and general administration.[5]

In December 1940 a service organization, the *Wohlfahrtsvereinigung*, was established at the Sosnowiec *Zentrale*. It was to take
over relief activities in Ostoberschlesien from the Joint Distribution
Committee (which was not allowed to function in the incorporated
provinces) and to handle requests for relief submitted by the Councils of the incorporated territories, as in Wartheland for example.
The *Wohlfahrtsvereinigung* ceased its activities in May 1941.[6]

It is doubtful whether this detailed design on paper for regulating the activities of the *Zentrale* was actually implemented in
day-to-day practice. Naturally, a great deal depended on the local
circumstances, on the personalities of the individual Council chairmen, and on the prestige they carried with the *Zentrale* and the
Germans.

Radom was the only district within the Government General
with a central Council. An *Oberjudenrat* was established after civil
administration was installed there in October 1939.[7] It encompassed
the 282,380 Jews who lived in the Radom district according to the
German census of March 1940. The chairman of this central Council
was Josef Diament, and Joachim Geiger was chief of its forced-labor
department.[8] Though not much has been uncovered about the
activities of the *Oberjudenrat*, it is known that its authority was not
as wide as that exercised by the *Zentrale* at Sosnowiec over its subordinate Councils.[9] A person well informed about the Jewish Councils in the Government General notes that "because of the title
Oberjudenrat, its chairman considered himself entitled not only to
intervene on behalf of the local Jewish Councils of the district, but
also to meddle in their internal affairs."[10] It may be assumed that
it was his task to advise concerning the orders of the authorities, to
answer the inquiries of the local Councils, etc. The *Oberjudenrat*
took over practically all activities of the local Radom Jewish Council.
Beginning on July 1, 1940, when Jewish real estate in the district
fell under the jurisdiction of the *Treuhandstelle*, the Radom *Oberjudenrat* became chief administrator (*Hauptverwalter*) of all Jewish
properties with a gross income of 200 zlotys and over. A special office
was created—the General Administration of Jewish Real Estate in

Radom—which was entitled, under the control of the *Treuhand-stelle*, to supervise owners, tenants, and janitors. Its task was to collect rent, to hire and oversee house managers, to make house repairs not exceeding 200 zlotys, and to give its opinion about requests for relief submitted to the *Treuhandstelle* by former real-estate owners. The chief administrator was authorized to deduct 4 percent from gross rents for the benefit of the Council. House managers received a fee in the amount of 4 percent of the rent actually collected.[11] In connection with the prohibition against use of public transportation by Jews (issued as far back as January 26, 1940) the governor of the Radom district issued an order that as of December 1, 1940, requests for travel permits were to be submitted first to the *Oberjudenrat*, after having been certified by local Jewish Councils.[12] For this service the *Oberjudenrat* was entitled to a fee.[13] In a circular letter "concerning the concentration of the Jews in the ghettos," issued on December 11, 1941, the governor recommended to the *Kreis-* and *Stadthauptmänner* in his district that, in order to make possible personal contacts between the local Councils and the *Oberjudenrat* at Radom, a single person in each ghetto should be designated liaison man with the *Oberjudenrat* and be given a special authorization (*Ausweis*) to travel.[14] On orders of the German authorities, the *Oberjudenrat* sent out circular letters to the local Councils, requesting data on the ages of the ghetto inmates, detailed maps of the ghettos, etc.[15] A special provincial department had to coordinate the activities of the Councils of the entire district.[16] For unknown reasons, Josef Diament together with three other members of the central Council were arrested on April 28, 1942, and sent to Auschwitz. This spelled the end of the *Oberjudenrat* in the Radom district.[17]

Łódź Ghetto, the second largest ghetto in the occupied territories of Europe, was called *Gaugetto* and considered a central ghetto in the Wartheland area.[18] Acting as the supreme boss of the entire industrial output of the ghettos in Łódź province, the Łódź Ghetto's German administration (*Gettoverwaltung*) utilized its prerogatives in a monopolistic manner and to their fullest extent. It gave orders for work and was the only body entitled to accept the finished products. It also supervised all labor camps in the Wartheland and drew a fee of 0.70 Reichsmarks per day for each Jewish laborer. As the *Judenälteste* Rumkowski became involved in the economy of the area ghettos, Łódź also became the "assembly ghetto," to which remaining Jews from all over Wartheland, a few chairmen and policemen among them (some of the latter were integrated into the ghetto administration), were transported.[19] Jews arrested by the Gestapo or the criminal police (*Kripo*) were sent to the Łódź Ghetto jail from all the ghettos in the Wartheland.[20]

The Jewish Council at Cracow had apparently also planned to become a central *Judenrat*. In a letter addressed to the Leżajsk *Kehila* on February 24, 1940, concerning the composition of the Council there, a central representation of all Jews of the Cracow district is mentioned; it would be under the leadership of "this [i.e., the Cracow] *Kehila*, to coordinate our efforts in defending the Jewish interests."[21] This letter presumably was sent out to all Jewish Councils in the district, but nothing came of the plan.

The Germans also established central county *Judenräte* over the smaller administrative units. The county *Judenrat* at Jasło (Cracow district) became a central Council by order of the *Kreishauptmann* on April 29, 1940. The Jewish Councils of the 16 towns of this county (Biecz, Bobowa, Dukla, Frysztak, Gorlice, Nowy Korczyn, Krosno, and Żmigród, among others) were put under the jurisdiction of the Jasło County *Judenrat*. According to *Gazeta Żydowska*, its task was "to intermediate between the local Councils in Jasło County and the German authorities at Jasło."[22] County *Judenräte*, presumably with similar functions as that at Jasło, were established in Chełm, Włodawa, Jędrzejów, Miechów Radomsko, Przemyśl,[23] Mielec,[24] Rawa Ruska,[25] Tarnopol,[26] Jarosław,[27] Kołomyja,[28] Czortków,[29] and possibly still more towns (Rohatyn?) in other counties. The county Council at Czortków apparently had some sort of authority to dismiss local Council members. Its *Leiter* officially announced the dismissal of the Council at Borszczów.[30]

The Jewish Councils in some of the ghettos, without official designation as central Councils, actually exercised control over the smaller ghettos established in their neighborhoods. Jacob Gens, the chief of the Vilna Ghetto, had some control over the Councils of the ghettos in Oszmiana, Święciany, Soły, and Michaliszki.[31] Shortly before the "resettlement" at Michaliszki, Gens dispatched three of his ghetto policemen, who established a *Judenrat* there.[32] The *Judenrat* at Szarkowszczyzna was under the jurisdiction of the Jewish Council at Głębokie which may have had other neighboring ghettos under its control.[33]

The chairman of the Jewish Council at Piotrków Trybunalski was also chairman of all the Councils of the entire county. On June 19, 1941, there took place under his chairmanship a conference of representatives of seven Councils of the county, including the Council of Piotrków Trybunalski.[34]

Little has yet emerged about the activities of these Councils or about the mutual relations between the county and local Councils. Almost no documentation, Jewish or otherwise, shedding light on this aspect of the Councils has been unearthed so far. But it is known that their relations were not always smooth. The chairman of the Kołomyja County Council, Markus Horowitz, dismissed Dr. Menashe Mandl, the chairman of the local Council at Kuty, and nominated someone else in his place. Dr. Mandl had refused Horowitz's demand that Kuty participate in a forced contribution imposed on the Jews of Kołomyja; he argued that Kuty had already been thoroughly robbed by both the Germans and the Ukrainians, and that, moreover, Kuty had already paid enough forced contributions.[35] The *Judenrat* in Kosów, another ghetto under the jurisdiction of the Kołomyja County Council, bore a grudge against Horowitz, resenting his arbitrary and antagonistic treatment of the remnants of the Kosów Jews driven into the Kołomyja ghetto.[36] And Nachman Blumental relates about the Czortków County Ghetto that, when it was necessary to make a collection of money to "oil" the new Nazi boss, the individual local Councils were requested to "contribute toward the expenditures of the community." Blumental notes that the interventions of the county Council with the Gestapo were mostly in conjunction with bribery, and that this led to various misdeeds: "They never knew [at the Council at Borszczów] what was really given to the Germans and what the *Judenrat* in Czortków took for its own use. . . . The relations between the two Councils became strained, full of suspicion and lack of confidence. . . . However, nothing could be done as both sides were convinced that the bribes did make [relations with the Germans] easier."[37] At least one case is known where one of the local Councils contacted the German county authorities directly, instead of acting through the appropriate central Council.[38] More such cases may have occurred. The county *Judenrat* in Rawa Ruska became entangled in a heated struggle to get rid of a certain dishonest man, a refugee from Germany, who was the first chairman of the Council. He was discharged for unknown reasons, but was later nominated as chairman of the county *Judenrat* by the Germans. In the ensuing struggle denunciations were uttered, and a Gestapo officer from Lwów became involved in the affair.[39] Probably this was not an isolated case either.

CHAPTER 4

The Organizational Structure
of the Jewish Councils

ANY DESCRIPTION of the organizational structure of the Jewish Councils and the methods of operation of their various departments must be prefaced by an examination of the nature of Jewish self-government in the ghettos and the role assigned to it by the occupation authorities. Such an examination is necessary in order to see the image of "ghetto autonomy" in its correct historical perspective; it was an image which concealed the satanic purpose of using the victim himself to assist the hangman in his work.

The Councils were conceived by the Nazis not as an instrument for organizing life in the ghettos or for strengthening the structure of the ghetto, but the opposite; as an instrument which, in their hands, would help them to realize their plans concerning the Jewish population in the occupied territories and, in particular, their extermination plan. The Councils were permitted, at most, to take care of distributing the meager supplies and maintaining a certain standard (only too low) of sanitation (for the continuous epidemics would also threaten the Nazis themselves); they were permitted to preserve "peace and order" as understood by the authorities.

The ramified Jewish organization was originally created to carry out, precisely and efficiently, all the regulations and directives of the occupation authorities. This was the definition of its role in the very first document about the Council of Elders (the "urgent letter" of Heydrich of September 21, 1939), in the regulation concerning the establishment of the Jewish Councils of November 28 of the same year, issued by Hans Frank, and in official Nazi declarations dealing with Jewish self-rule in the occupied territories.

The Councils had to serve only one purpose—to execute Nazi orders regarding the Jewish population.

Other activities undertaken by the Councils, with the consent of the authorities, in the sphere of internal ghetto life (social welfare, economic and cultural work) were performed, in fact, outside their prescribed tasks. Such other activities, which dealt with the internal requirements of the Jewish population, were sometimes accorded a certain degree of tolerance, and even of encouragement; they served the Nazi-propagated illusion that the continued existence of the ghettos was guaranteed, and also concealed the Final Solution (*Endziel*) from the Jews for as long as necessary.

The tasks of the Councils can be divided into three classes:

1. Tasks imposed by the authorities, such as conduct of the census of the Jewish population, the supply of forced labor, registration of candidates for the work camps, for deportation, etc.

2. Routine tasks in social welfare, medical care, and in the economic and cultural fields—tasks which were, in the main, a continuation of prewar communal activities.

3. New tasks made essential by the complete elimination of the Jewish population in the ghetto from governmental and municipal services, such as food supplies, the management of the ghetto dwellings, industry, health, police and judicial services, etc.

These varied duties of the Councils necessitated the growth of a ramified, administrative apparatus. The organizational structure of this apparatus expanded as the isolation of the Jewish population from the general, governmental, and municipal framework was completed.

The turning point in this development was the confinement of the Jewish population in the ghettos, an act which isolated it almost absolutely. The Nazis intended the "autonomy" of the ghettos to be absolute, to include every aspect of a self-reliant, organized, social unit.

The Nazi-created Jewish ghetto necessarily became a Jewish city *sui generis*, linked to the main city only by slender links which had to be maintained for purely technical reasons, e.g., lighting, water-supply, sewage, and limited telephone connection (up to a certain period). Generally the ghettos were cut off from the normal postal services and, in some ghettos, special post offices were opened. Suitable administrative machinery had, therefore, to be created in the ghettos to serve the needs of the Jewish population in those matters normally dealt with by the government and the municipality. It was also necessary to set up special departments to carry out the orders and directives of the authorities with regard to forced labor, collection of taxes, delivery of various materials and merchandise, of forced-labor workers, transfers, evacuations, and the like.

From the start of the occupation, the Germans excluded Jews from the benefits of social services such as pensions for war invalids, sick benefits, etc.[1] Jewish bank accounts were withheld and Jewish property confiscated;[2] forced labor duty for the Jews was ordered.[3] In many places the Jews were also excluded from the general system of food supply. As a result of all these measures, even before the ghettos had been established, Jews were faced with most urgent tasks: to provide in short order some social and medical services, if only on a minimal scale; to take care of food supply and distribution; and to search for new sources of income for countless people eliminated from the national economies and from state and community frameworks.

A particularly urgent field of activities demanding immediate attention was the necessity to provide shelter for the overflow of homeless people who had lost all their possessions as a result of the war operations. Masses of desolated, penniless refugees surged from their ruined dwelling places into the larger communities, where some sort of lodgings had to be found for them. The ranks of these unfortunates were soon augmented by the thousands of Jews whom the Germans threw out of their homes. The Germans complemented this deluge of aimlessly wandering people without any tangible means of existence by systematic spoliation of Jewish property and by relentless, random arrests for forced labor. By such measures these people's economic existence was entirely broken down.

New departments had to be established, and old ones revitalized or reorganized by the Councils, to cope with this ever increasing responsibility and with the overriding necessity to deal with the hostile authorities on a daily basis. The departments of welfare and medical care, food supply, and forced-labor duty were the earliest ones established. Later came the crucial moment when the Jews were enclosed in the ghettos, where, according to the plans of the Nazis, the "ghetto autonomy" was to be complete and self-sustaining in all sectors of community life. It then became particularly important to extend the existing administrative apparatus (which already took care of forced labor, imposed financial sanctions, and

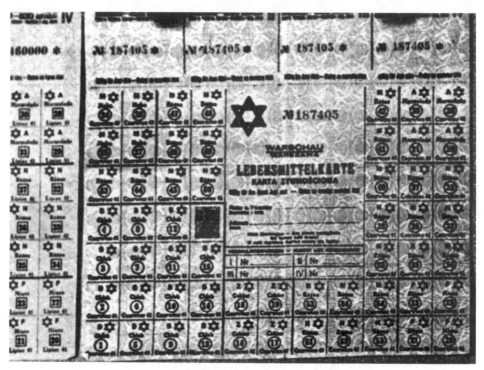

A ration card for Jews in the Warsaw Ghetto.

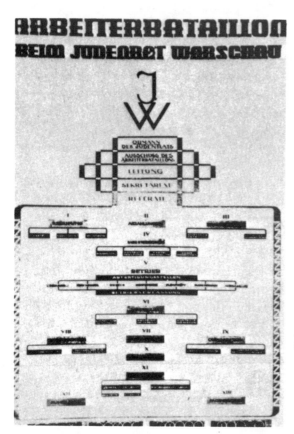

A chart of the structure of the War-saw Ghetto labor office.

The Warsaw Ghetto jail.

The central jail in the Łódź Ghetto, operated by the Jewish police. Candidates for deportation were held here before removal.

supervised deliveries of materials) to include policing of the ghetto area, management of real estate to organize the food distribution, etc.

In the three communities with the largest Jewish concentrations in occupied Poland, the departments for forced-labor duty were established even prior to the pertinent order of October 26, 1939. In Łódź, for instance, the so-called *Arbeitseinsatz* was established on October 6 or 7, 1939, even before the chief of the civil government of the *Oberkommando* of the army (AOK) ordered (on October 13) the delivery of 600 laborers on a daily basis.[4] For some unexplained reason, this order was addressed to the rabbinate. In Warsaw the labor battalion department (*Wydział Batalionu Pracy*) began its work during the second or third week of October 1939.[5] In Lublin the forced-labor department was established on October 20, 1939.[6]

As early as September 1939 a department of welfare and medical care was active as an arm of the executive board of the Jewish Religious Community at Cracow.[7] The welfare department in Łódź was established on October 15, 1939.[8] A commission for refugee relief was established in Lublin in December 1939, and a Jewish relief committee in February 1940. It should be pointed out that the refugee problem in Lublin was particularly acute: escaping from the Nazi onslaught on the western provinces of Poland, a great number of refugees was stranded in Lublin, and by September 1940 they numbered 5,633 persons.[9] Relief committees or relief commissions, as they were sometimes called, were also established in many other places during the first months of the occupation, some spontaneously, others on orders from the German authorities.

The departments of registration and vital statistics came into being quite early, in accordance with Heydrich's circular letter of September 21, 1939 (Part 2, Par. 3), which ordered the Councils to carry out a census of the Jewish population according to age. At the end of October 1939 a statistical bureau was established in Warsaw following the order to take a census of Jews residing in the Polish capital. The census took place on October 28.[10] In Lublin the registration department was established on February 22, 1940, and its first duty was to carry out the census there.[11] In Łódź a department for this purpose was established on May 9, 1940, soon after the Jews were closed up in the ghetto.[12] Prior orders during October 1939 had directed the forced labor department to carry out the registration of males eighteen to sixty years old and females twenty-two to fifty-five years old.

To take care of the deliveries of merchandise ordered by various authorities, there were established in some of the ghettos special offices, such as the acquisition office (*Beschaffungsamt*) at Lwów, the material deliveries office (*Sachleitungskomission*) at Żółkiew, etc.[13]

The "resettlement" of the Jews into the overcrowded ghettos— for the most part located in desolate, squalid, slum-ridden sections of the towns—suddenly forced upon the community leaders extremely heavy responsibilities: to move the worldly goods of thousands of dislodged families; to find the living space necessary to shelter them; to try to distribute this insufficient room among the people rendered homeless on short notice; to move dislodged institutions of public service into some new quarters; to speed up repairs of ruined buildings to create additional living space. These agonizing tasks all demanded simultaneous solution. Among the new departments that mushroomed in the ghettos, those that dealt with providing homes were necessarily among the first and most important to come into being. Initially called resettlement departments or commissions, they were renamed tenants' departments as time passed.

It was also necessary to serve in other fields. Isolated in the ghettos, robbed of personal property, forced to give up their businesses and positions of employment, and, as a rule, even compelled to surrender their homes, native Jews and refugees alike, businessmen and salaried workers, had been deprived of their livelihood and customary means of sustenance. All required immediate attention and assistance in their search for some means of support for themselves and their families. People had to start all over from scratch. Trade had to be organized, new sources of income created. Simultaneously, it was necessary to plan and bring to life a network for distribution of allotted food rations; to open schools; to make arrangements for distribution of mail (as a rule the Jews were excluded from general postal service); to establish management of real estate; and, in places like Łódź, for example, to take over servicing gas and electricity for the ghetto on behalf of the municipality. Last, but not least, when Passover approached, some of the ghettos created *ad hoc* commissions to take care of seasonal necessities, such as providing matzoth, etc.

The administrative structure of the Councils grew in stages, accretions depending on the realities of life in the ghetto, the necessity to take care of ever growing tasks for the ghetto inmates, and the heavy duties imposed by the occupation authorities. The structure of the Councils also depended on the type of the ghetto: whether life was totally regimented by a forceful bureaucratic apparatus, or some opportunities for free enterprise were left to the inmates. Added to everything else, the enormous paper work demanded by the supervisory authorities necessitated the establishment of new offices, if only to diminish the heavy work load of existing departments.

Before the Łódź Jews were confined in the ghetto, the Office of the President, or the Presidential Secretariat as it was sometimes called, directed and decided on affairs of welfare, food (supply of provisions for the ghetto institutions), forced labor, taxes, etc. In fact, only the police and the rabbinate functioned independently at that time. But when it became apparent that a single department was unable to direct the entire administration of the ghetto, it was decided, by the end of April 1940, to decentralize it. For instance, after the transfer of the Jews into the ghetto was completed, the agricultural division was established within the economic department of the ghetto administration. Its task was to lease small land parcels carved out of the few available stretches of land in the ghetto. These were to be planted with some edibles to ease the hunger of the population. In the second half of 1940, the administration of the Łódź Ghetto consisted of not fewer than 73 units arranged in 9 departments: general administration, the rabbinate and cemeteries, the police and courts, food supply, economic and finances, acquisitions (i.e., confiscations), industry, education, and welfare and medical assistance. One-half year later, by February 1941, the ghetto administration consisted of 15 major departments organized along the following lines: general administration, vital statistics, welfare, post office, food supply, economic and finances, electricity, gas, acquisitions, industry, labor, building, education, health, and police. Each of these was subdivided into smaller units.[14] After the rationing of food was introduced, a ration card division was added on January 1, 1941; and a special resettlement department was added later to take care of expulsed Jews driven into the Łódź Ghetto. (In September and October 1941, 3,082 Jews arrived from Włocławek and surrounding ghettos; and in October and November, 19,953 from Germany, Vienna, Prague, and Luxembourg.) The number of both office personnel and laborers rose accordingly: from 5,500 (6% of the ghetto population) in February 1941, to 7,316 (apart from the temporarily employed) in July 1941, and again to 12,880 (12.6% of the ghetto population) as of August 1, 1942.[15]

The administration of the Lwów Ghetto Council was organized in 22 divisions and 6 subdivisions and employed, in 1942, some 4,000 persons (4.5% of the ghetto inmates).[16]

As of January 1942 the personnel employed by the Vilna Ghetto administration numbered 1,051 persons, including the police (17.1% of all employed ghetto inmates). By September of the same year, this number climbed to 1,551, or almost 20 percent of the working population of the Vilna Ghetto. In January 1942 the employees were assigned to the following departments: health—380 persons (over 33%); technical—280 (26.6%); tenements—110 (10.5%); cultural—197 (18.7%); and food—80 (7.6%). The remaining persons worked in various other branches of the ghetto administration.

At the same time, the Vilna Ghetto police grew from 180 men in January to 266 in June 1942.[17]

In Częstochowa the number of departments increased between January and December 1940 from 14 departments with 173 employees to 21 with 676 employees, an increase in personnel of almost 400 percent. For instance, the number of employees in the forced-labor department rose from 61 to 132, in the tenant department from 3 to 28, in the welfare department from 24 to 178, and from 4 to 65 in the vital statistics department.[18] The staggering demands for forced laborers in Częstochowa and the continuing influx of refugees (3,252 arrived in 1940) to some degree account for this unusual swelling of the Council's administrative personnel.[19]

With a population of nearly half a million in the Warsaw Ghetto, the Council needed a large staff. The number of departments rose from an initial 15 in July 1940 to almost 30 in June 1942; and the number of employees from 1,741 to approximately 6,000 (including personnel working for welfare and medical institutions), an increase of almost 250 percent (before the war there were 532 employed by the *Kehila*). The police force grew from 1,700 at the end of 1940 to 2,000 in June 1942.[20]

The Białystok Jewish Council, at a meeting held on August 3, 1941, adopted a resolution to distribute work among 14 departments: administration, building and technical, security, labor, welfare, health, finances, sanitation, food supply, economic, housing, education, industry, and secretariat. Later on, in November 1941, three more departments were added: transportation, vital statistics, and taxes.[21] In January 1942, 1,600 persons were employed; and in July 1942 the number reached 2,201, a rise of over 28 percent.[22]

Other ghettos developed in similar fashion: there were 15 departments in the Prużana Ghetto Council,[23] 13 in Grodno,[24] 18 in Lublin,[25] 15 in Piotrków Trybunalski, and 19 in Cracow.[26]

Sometimes organizational changes took place in the structure of the existing administrative departments. Those whose tasks markedly increased were usually decentralized and subdivided into smaller units, which, in the course of time, were again reorganized or abolished altogether; in the latter case their activities were turned over to other departments. A coordinating body was sometimes established to oversee the work of offices dealing with related matters. Such structural changes were particularly evident in the Warsaw Ghetto. Thus in the winter of 1940–1941, following the fatal wave of epidemics in the ghetto, hygienic problems were taken from the jurisdiction of the department of health and welfare and transferred to the newly established health department, which, in turn, was subdivided into six divisions: sanitation, prevention and treatment of contagious diseases, medical treatment, disinfection, laundry, and refugees.[27] In the summer of 1940, the division of the labor department assigned to collect fines was abolished, and its work was taken over by the Justice Commission.[28] The units dealing with economic problems such as food supply, trade and industry, etc. were consolidated into a joint Economic Board.[29]

At the time of the mass deportations from the Łódź Ghetto to the death camps in 1942, a Resettlement Commission was active. It consisted of the chiefs of the vital statistics department, police, criminal division, the chairman of the court, and the commandant of the prison. During the final phase of the deportations, in June through August 1944, an interdepartmental commission of seven persons, for the most part managers of ghetto shops, prepared the lists of candidates for deportation.[30]

The administration of the Lublin Ghetto employed over 100 people. After being ordered by the *Stadthauptmann* to collect debts of prewar municipal taxes from the ghetto inmates on behalf of the city, the Jewish Council, at a meeting held on February 3, 1942, decided to establish two more departments (a tax collection department and an industrial department) in addition to the 18 already operating, as well as a section for delivery of the summonses of the city administration.[31]

However, there were weighty reasons other than the work load prompting the rapid growth of the ghetto apparatus. A job in the ghetto administration meant the attainment of a privileged position. Some of the ghetto inmates lacked other opportunities to earn a living; and Council employees were often better off than the rest of the ghetto inmates. But even more important was the fact that an employee of the ghetto administration was free from the curse of forced-labor duty and, at least for a time, protected against deportation. People eagerly looked for influential acquaintances and besieged Council members in search of a job. (In some instances this unfortunately led to corruption, about which we will say more in Chap. 14.) This may explain why the number of Council employees was in many ghettos in no way commensurate with the size of the population, and was dictated to a lesser degree by the work load or the new tasks imposed by the German authorities. To a large degree, however, it was warranted by a conscious intention to protect the endangered intellectual cadres of the community for as long as possible. Even less populated ghettos, such as Radom or Kołomyja, found employment for as many as 300 and 500 people respectively.[32] At a meeting of the Białystok Jewish Council on January 18, 1942, the chairman, Ephraim Barash, admitted that the number of persons employed by the Council was three times larger than needed.[33]

The process in reverse—shrinking of the structure of the Councils —usually took place after a series of consecutive "resettlements," deportations or whatever other terms the Germans furtively used to describe sending Jews off to their deaths. As a ghetto became depopulated, the authorities transformed it into either a labor camp or a concentration camp or a *Restgetto*. The number of the Council departments was then greatly reduced. In Lublin the *Restgetto* was established in an adjacent locality known as Majdan Tatarski ("the Tartar Field"). The ghetto inmates numbered 4,000 remnants of the approximately 42,000 Jews who had lived in the ghetto prior to the deportations. The activities of the Council were conducted by the 12 surviving Council members, and the number of employees was reduced to 38 from the 118 previously employed.[34] On April 4, 1942, the new Council formed two commissions with the morbid tasks of taking care of the worldly goods and of the food left by the "resettled" people.

After the "action" in Šiauliai on November 5, 1943, against children up to ten years and old or sick people (over 1,000 Jews were deported), the ghetto was transformed into a concentration camp. The Jewish Council was abolished (two of the Councilmen had been included in the "resettlement action"), and instead a two-man leadership of the camp was established. One of the two was the former Council chairman, Mendel Leybowitz, and the other was the newly nominated chief of the *Arbeitseinsatz*, Georg Pariser.[35] Similarly in Kaunas, after the ghetto was changed to a concentration camp, its leadership was reduced to four members.

In the town of Chmielnik, in the Ukraine, a massacre took place on January 8, 1942. When it was over, the chief of the gendarmes nominated a *starosta* in place of the former four-man Council, all of whom had perished during the "action." This *starosta* functioned until March 1943, the date of the final liquidation of the Jews of Chmielnik.[36]

The role individual departments played in the affairs of the ghetto and their authority over the inmates depended on the generally inconstant and insecure conditions of the ghettos, on the one hand, and, on the other, on the nature and extent of the German demands and orders. As a result, certain departments were at times more important than others. Everything greatly depended on the pressure of unexpected and spontaneously arising circumstances.

Usually one or more Councilmen supervised the work of one, two, three, or even more departments. In Częstochowa, however, a single Councilman with the assistance of a secretary was responsible for the work of the entire ghetto administration. His title was Chief of Organization. In the Vilna Ghetto, each of the five members of the Council was responsible for the work of several departments, subdepartments and institutions. The chairman of the Council himself supervised seven departments (bookkeeping, ghetto police, statistics, library and reading hall, bureau of addresses, general administration, and economy); another Council member was in charge of the department of supplies and the department of child care; a third directed the technical and tenement departments; a fourth the labor office and shop department; and a fifth Councilman headed the health department. Thus five members took care of all 14 departments. This situation lasted until the collective leadership was put to an end in the Vilna Ghetto, and Jacob Gens was nominated ghetto chief in July 1942.[37]

There was no uniform policy in the Warsaw Ghetto with respect to the supervision of departments. Some were supervised by a single Council member, others were collectively directed by a commission. Chiefs of the departments (who were none of them Council members) were appointed to direct everyday activities under supervision of Councilmen or commissions who, in turn, were responsible to the chairman, Adam Czerniakow. Some of the Councilmen were thus active in more than one department. For instance, one of them, H. Rosen, supervised the labor department and, in addition, was active in the fuel department, in the commission for winter relief, in the tenement department, in the economic council, and in the department for culture and arts.[38]

What were the prerogatives of the individual administrative bodies? How were responsibilities defined and mutual relations shaped among the Council chairmen, the plenary meetings of the Councils, their presidiums (where such bodies were established), and the networks of the departments? The decree of November 28, 1939, establishing the Councils in the territory of the Government General made no provisions in this respect. It thus was left to the Councils themselves to regulate problems involved in the interrelations of Council organs.[39] There is only one pertinent document preserved, the by-laws of the Lublin Jewish Council, dated February 25, 1940, which gives an insight into how the duties of the Council organs were delineated. Judging by these by-laws one may surmise that, at least at the outset, the Councils tried to act in the spirit of cooperation and mutual responsibility, the more so as their members at that time came largely from the ranks of the prewar *Kehila* or communal leadership. In the first article the by-laws stipulate that the organs of the Council are the plenary meetings of the Council, the presidium, the Control Commission, and the other commissions or departments. No particular authority is reserved for the Council chairman. On the contrary, the leadership is depicted as a collective one and consists of a presidium of five members: the chairman of the Council, two vice chairmen, and two other members, all elected by the Council. The Council reserved wide authority for itself: to approve the agenda of the plenary meetings; to vote on submitted proposals by simple majority of the members present; to confirm budget estimates and check receipts for all disbursements; to decide on taxes and on other material tribute demanded from the ghetto inmates; to accept or reject decisions taken by the presidium or other Council organs in emergency situations arising in the course of everyday activities; to elect members of the Control Commission (no presidium member could be elected to serve on this commission); and to decide on the number of departments, on personnel, and on any matters which belonged to the prerogative of the presidium, but were delegated by it to the Council for decision.

The by-laws outlined the following prerogatives for the presidium: to serve as a representative body; to execute decisions of the plenary Council meetings; to prepare the agenda of the plenary meetings; to delegate one of its members to serve on the individual commissions or departments, except the Control Commission; to manage community property; to prepare budget estimates; to decide how to sign official papers; and to delegate members of the Council to perform certain functions within the framework of its activities or without. The presidium was obligated to submit to the Council periodic reports and to supervise personnel. As to the Control Commission, its task was to check the overall activities of the Council at least once every three months, and to submit a written report on its findings.

The commissions or departments were to elect their chairmen and deputy chairmen, who would report in writing to the presidium of the Council every week. On request, oral reports or reports in writing were to be submitted to the plenary meetings of the Councils.

The obligations of the Councilmen were thus defined in the by-laws: No member was allowed to resign, nor could he refuse any task assigned to him without the knowledge and agreement of the Council. If a Councilman neglected his obligations or was otherwise disqualified by his deeds, the Council, on the suggestion of the presidium, could decide to submit a proposal to the German authorities to discharge him. The Council could decide to elect a special committee to investigate the incrimination of a member. In case a decision to discharge was referred to the authorities, the member would immediately be suspended.[40] However, it appears from the records of the Lublin Council that it did not always act in accordance with all of these regulations.

Insofar as the position of the chairman is concerned we can discern two types of Jewish Councils: (1) Councils where the chairmen ruled autocratically, and the individual members had no executive authority, with the collective Council playing the role of a sort of consultative body of little or no influence on the ghetto administration (in this type of Council, the departments were responsible solely to the *Obmann* or Elder); (2) Councils with collective leadership where all activities of the departments were duly supervised by the Council members acting singly or in commission. The Rumkowski regime in the Łódź Ghetto was an example of an autocratic ghetto,[41] as were the majority of the Councils nominated by Merin, the manager of the *Zentrale* in Eastern Upper Silesia. In Sosnowiec, for example, which was under the jurisdiction of the *Zentrale*, the Council chairman once a month called meetings of the local Council (it was called a "committee") to report to them on his activities. This policy did not last for long, however, and later he called these meetings only on rare occasions. The Council was never influential, and neither Merin nor its presidium paid much attention to it. Merin himself used it as a forum for exalted speeches, or as an instrument to play on the emotions of the ghetto inmates in promulgating his capricious wishes.[42] The Lublin Ghetto Council was an example of a Council with collective leadeship. At its meeting on February 28, 1942, it decided as a matter of principle that each department was to be supervised by a commission of three Council members.[43]

In some ghettos there emerged strong-willed Council members with pronounced organizational abilities and ambitions for authority. Soon they became the *de facto* leaders of the Councils, and the other Councilmen, the chairman included, had to take their opinions into account. Regardless, however, whether or not the chairman was the actual boss of the Council, the Germans considered him as such and exploited him as their tool, responsible for the quick completion of ordered tasks. As representatives of a totalitarian regime, the local authorities were interested in enhancing the position of the chairmen in the Councils, thus establishing one-man rule in the ghettos.

Our questionnaires record the official position of 674 Council members: 23.8 percent were chairmen and 7.3 percent vice chairmen or presidium members; 26.3 percent were heads of departments, commissions, or shops; 6 percent were judges; 5.4 percent secretaries or treasurers. Some 230 Councilmen (34.5%) had no special assignments, and only 14 (1.9%) were liaison men.

The heads of certain departments or commissions wielded a great deal of power by virtue of the services their offices had to perform. Thus, for example, the chiefs of the labor departments, in execution of the German orders, had to plan the labor schedules and compile lists of men selected for forced-labor assignments. This provided various opportunities: to send people to perform easier tasks or better-paid jobs, or to places where there might be a chance to get in touch with the local non-Jewish population and buy a little food for famished families. On occasion such department chiefs even had a chance to alleviate the orders or exempt persons from forced-labor duty for a short time. No less important was the authority of the heads of food supply departments. They were the overseers of allocated food, in charge of the quantity and quality of the ever diminishing rations. They supervised the bakeries, soup kitchens, and vegetable storages, and generally kept watch over the integrity of food distribution; they were thus given the opportunity to favor protégés at the expense of the less fortunate. The chiefs of the welfare departments also occupied extremely important positions in the ghetto hierarchy. They were responsible for the organizational set-up and for practical work in the field of social aid. Under the circumstances of indescribable poverty and hunger prevalent in the ghettos, Councilmen who decided on relief matters were in a position to ease somehow the dire need of at least some of the ghetto inmates, even if only to minute extents.

Some explanation is appropriate about the liaison men needed to maintain personal contact with the German authorities. For this contingency, often dangerous to life and limb, the Councils used men with singular qualifications such as not all of the chairmen or their deputies themselves possessed. The latter often did not even have the courage to face German officials, for the most part ill-tempered, uncharitable brutes and corrupt ones at that. To encounter the Germans on behalf of the *Judenräte*, one had to be able morally to endure and physically to deal with them. It was necessary to adapt oneself to their domineering manners and savage ways of dealing with the people at their mercy, to share in their drinking bouts, to offer gifts to "soften" their attitude, or to bargain, trying to revoke evil orders. There were ghettos with different liaison men to deal separately with the Gestapo, the gendarmes, labor and food supply officials, etc. These people operated on very thin ice, and it was not always possible to know exactly whether they acted on behalf of the ghetto inmates or indulged in covert collaboration. The peculiar tasks of the liaison men provided easy opportunities for persons with weak characters and no backbone to yield to various temptations. On the whole, they were not respected by the ghetto inmates. In our documentation we found only one reference, in the Wieruszów Ghetto, where a liaison man was not suspected of making personal profit. He enjoyed the confidence of the majority of his fellow ghetto inmates.

Some of the liaison men were Councilmen themselves; others, as in Warsaw and Kaunas, came from the ranks of the ghetto police; still others were appointed by the Germans.

The cooperation of the Council members was not always harmonious, and neither were personal relations always amicable. The minutes of some of the Councils reveal internal wrangles, conflicts, and feuds among members. Heated disagreements often occurred, personal relations were strained, mutual trust denied, accusations made. On occasion, even physical attacks took place, followed by disciplinary actions. It is safe to assume that in the nerve-wracking, precarious atmosphere that undermined the lives of the ghetto inmates and the activities of the Councils, always tense and fearful, always uncertain of the next day or hour, personal conflicts and uncontrolled outbursts of passion must have erupted more often than is generally accepted in public life under normal circumstances. The Councils had to grapple with these problems too. For instance, an extraordinary meeting of the Lublin Jewish Council was called on April 13, 1941, to consider one single question: the physical attack on Council chairman Henryk Becker by a member, Isaac Kershman, which had occurred at the meeting of the presidium held three days earlier. There is no indication in the Council minutes of the reason for the attack. The meeting ended with Kershman pleading to be forgiven. He read his written plea after it had been edited by the presidium. Kershman was suspended for a month. Another incident, this one between Kershman and the deputy chairman, Dr. Mark Alten, was placed on the agenda of the plenary Council meeting on October 4, 1941, at the request of Kershman. When Alten presided instead of the absent chairman, he requested that this item be postponed to the next meeting. However, the matter was not brought up at the meeting of October 11 either; and on October 18, Kershman withdrew his request. At a later meeting of the Council, on November 11, 1941, there was a heated discussion of the resignation submitted by presidium member Maurycy Shlaf, who had complained that not all presidium members were being informed about meetings with the authorities. Complaints were also advanced against the presidium for not preparing the agenda in advance of the plenary meetings, and there was dissension about the hirings of personnel, etc.[44] Another disciplinary act is noted in the minutes of the same Council. At its meeting held on August 11, 1942, when the ghetto had already been transferred to Majdan Tatarski, the Council censured a member, Isaak Brodt, apparently for provoking an incident with Dr. Alten, who had by then become chairman. Brodt was excluded from attending three meetings of the Council and was warned that he would be forced to resign if his attitude continued.[45]

Sometimes members were expelled for jeopardizing the good name of the Council, thus increasing the threat of additional persecution of the ghetto inmates or punishment of the Council. The Council of Elders in Šialuiai discharged a member, one Fayvel Rubinstein, for endangering the very existence of the ghetto population by taking advantage of the privilege of his office for personal gain. As a member of the Council, he could freely leave the ghetto, and he had used this privilege to trade in various illegal businesses, including traffic in foreign currency.[46]

Some of the minutes of the Białystok Jewish Council also recorded disagreements among the members, notably during the evacuation to Prużana. The attitude of Council members was not always congenial. Nevertheless Ephraim Barash, the leader of that ghetto, reassured inmates at a meeting held on the first anniversary of the nomination of the Council (June 29, 1942) that "strong harmony is prevailing among the Council members, there is no difference of opinion among them, [and] all our decisions and acts are unanimous."[47] Perhaps this was an exaggeration caused by his fervor in delivering a speech on this solemn occasion.

CHAPTER 5

The Economic Situation of the Jews and the Activities of the Jewish Councils

THE ECONOMY OF THE Jews of occupied Eastern Europe was influenced by three principal factors: the policy and practice of the authorities, the limited field of Jewish economic activities, and the economic situation of each locality. To serve their own needs, the German authorities designed for the Jews an economic framework in line with other strictly anti-Jewish plans and measures, a policy along the following lines: gradual expropriation of all Jewish property, elimination of jews from general economic life, and unmerciful exploitation of the Jewish labor force. Consequently, there is not the slightest doubt that prior to the policy of physical extermination the drive to eliminate Jews from the economy of the ever enlarging German *Lebensraum* was *the* fundamental policy for all areas under German occupation and influence. It was the set task of the German occupation authorities and their satellites to see to it that the Jews decreased in numbers by the imposition of economic measures that were designed to achieve pauperization, hunger, epidemics, and an increased death rate. Try as they did, they could not achieve these aims completely. Their intentions were to some degree frustrated, at least for a time, not only because of Jewish initiative, partly private and partly communal, but also because of the neutralizing influence of two factors: an objective factor in the size of a given ghetto's contribution to the German war economy, particularly to the army; and a subjective factor in the attitudes of some of the German ghetto overlords toward the Jews—the last vestige of humaneness in some of them, or varying degrees of corruption or moral depravity in others.

Direct Jewish influence on the scope of the ghetto economy depended on the role of the Jews in the prewar economy of a given area, on the scope of the economic initiative of given Jewish groups or individuals; and on the economic activities of a given Jewish Council (or its organs) as related to its overall strategy for rescuing and preserving Jewish life.

A third factor of purely local character was the degree to which Jews in the individual ghettos were able to sustain business contacts with gentile neighbors, and the attitudes of the latter toward the oppressed Jews. These contacts largely depended on whether a ghetto was open or sealed.

THE JEWISH ECONOMY UNDER NAZI RULE

Spoliation of All Property

In the period of the military occupation of Poland the chief of the Army *Ost* ordered on September 29, 1939, the taking over of all businesses whose owners were absent or which were inefficiently managed. As applied to the Jews, this order served as a legal pretext to install commissars as managers of the larger industrial and business enterprises, even where their owners were present.

Also in September 1939 the chiefs of the civil administration of the High Command of the army (AOK) in Poland issued orders blocking Jewish bank accounts and safe deposits. Out of blocked accounts Jews were allowed to withdraw no more than 250 zlotys a week. The total amount of money Jews were allowed to keep in cash was limited to 2,000 zlotys.

In the Government General an order of the currency department of the governor general's office on November 20, 1939, regulated currency circulation (cash and bank accounts). According to this order, banks were allowed to release no more than 500 zlotys a month out of blocked Jewish accounts. For higher amounts— needed for trade or handicrafts—a special permit from the authorities was required. The amount of cash a Jew was allowed to keep was continued at 2,000 zlotys.[1] The authorities later made some necessary adjustments of this policy in the Warsaw Ghetto. Heinz Auerswald, the commissar of the ghetto, issued an ordinance on August 1, 1941, making it known that the chief of the currency and economic department of the Government General had issued an order on June

6, 1941, canceling, with respect to the Warsaw Ghetto, both its order of November 20, 1939, and Paragraph 2 of his own order of March 1, 1940, which had limited currency circulation for the Warsaw Jews. Auerswald indicated that this had been done "in order to help the economy of Jewish artisans in the Jewish living quarters in Warsaw." Accordingly Jews were permitted to collect payments due to them in the ghetto and outside in amounts exceeding 500 zlotys a month, to keep amounts of over 2,000 zlotys in cash, and to invest amounts above 2,000 zlotys in collective artisan enterprises without control or limitations; however, in order to send money outside the ghetto it was still necessary to obtain the permission of the *Transferstelle*, the official German authority controlling economic exchange between the ghetto and the outside world. Payments in foreign currency remained forbidden.[2] It is not known whether similar adjustments were made in the other ghettos.

Further developments in the status of Jewish property came about in Goering's order of November 1, 1939, which had established the *Haupttreuhandstelle Ost* (HTO) in Berlin, with branches in Danzig, Poznań, Częstochowa, Katowice, and Cracow. In time HTO became the main organ dealing with all problems connected with expropriated Jewish and Polish property in the occupied territories. On November 15, 1939, after Frank was nominated governor general of occupied Poland, the *Treuhandstelle für das General Gouvernement* was established, with branches at the offices of the four district chiefs. The "Order concerning Confiscations" (*Beschlagnahmeordnung*), dated January 24, 1940, empowered the respective authorities to take over under *Treuhandverwaltung* or to confiscate outright all enterprises and products of industry "if this is in the public interest." Where owners were absent, all property was to be confiscated. Only personal effects were free from confiscation, provided that they were not articles of luxury and did not exceed reasonable norms.[3] Confiscated enterprises were put under the management of imposed caretakers (*Treuhänder*) nominated by the chief of the appropriate *Treuhandstelle*. This order left untouched various "legal" confiscations previously made by the army, the police, the *Waffen* SS, and organs of the SD.

Also on January 24, 1940, Frank ordered the Jews to register their property. Property not registered in time was subject to confiscation as "ownerless."[4] The term "Jewish property" was broadly interpreted. It was applied not only to property personally owned by the

Jews, but also to enterprises where only some of the partners were Jews. As a matter of fact, some local administrative authorities (for example, in Warsaw) had enforced the registration of Jewish property as early as December 18, 1939.

Finally, on September 17, 1940, Goering issued an order "Concerning the Treatment of Property of the Citizens of the Former Polish State" (*Über die Behandlung von Vermögen der Angehörigen des ehemaligen Polnischen Staates*) directing that all property of Jews be subject to immediate confiscation, except for personal belongings (clothing or home furnishings) and 1,000 Reichsmarks in cash.[5] By this single stroke of the pen the Jewish industrialist lost his factory, the Jewish merchant his business, and the Jewish owner his real estate. There were some minor differences in the application of this order between the incorporated territories and the Government General. Thus by February 1941 the *Treuhandstelle* in the Wartheland had taken under its management 216 large industries, approximately 9,000 medium-sized ones and 76,000 small ones as well as 9,120 large businesses and 112,000 small businesses. Most of these belonged to the Jews.[6] The rationalization for these sweeping measures in the incorporated areas was the idea of consolidation or liquidation of small manufacturing and artisan enterprises in the name of "economic reconstruction" of those territories.[7]

In the area of the Government General the order was initially applied to larger enterprises and Jews retained the right to manage the nonconfiscated property, except where the law prescribed otherwise—e.g., they were not allowed to trade in precious metals, jewelry, and real estate.[8] In Cracow the order was initially applied to houses carrying over 500 zlotys net rent a month.[9] However, in Warsaw an estimated 75 percent of all Jewish business and industrial enterprises were liquidated by the middle of 1940.[10]

There was no escape from loss of property, business and industry. Even selling one's business to a friendly Pole or German was no remedy, for the German courts recognized no business deals between Jews and Poles or Germans made on the eve of or shortly after the invasion. Such deals, regarded as having been made in order to camouflage (*zu Tarnungszwecken*) ownership, were pronounced void, and their objects were confiscated.[11]

By the wholesale expropriation of the Jews—whether through the *Treuhandstelle* or through outright "legal" or arbitrary confiscation—large segments of the Jewish population were left without any livelihood. Even well-to-do people became destitute, "legally" barred from receiving any income from their confiscated property or enterprises. This intention of the Germans was made crystal clear in a circular letter of the Government General *Treuhandstelle* empowering local branches to determine the amount of relief in cash to be paid to former owners, depending on the following conditions: that the person be unable to sustain himself with other sources of income; that the amount of relief not exceed 25 percent of his net earnings and not more than 250 zlotys a month; and that relief should not diminish the capital value of the property. Under these conditions it was quite easy to find pretexts for refusing requests for assistance submitted by former Jewish owners. But if these were not enough, a fourth condition stipulated that former Jewish owners of property which had been seized for the benefit of the Reich were entitled to no relief whatsoever.[12]

In a number of places, Cracow for example, the HTO at first agreed to pay former owners of apartment houses 75 percent of the net rent income. By August 1940 these payments were reduced to 50 percent.[13] In the districts of Cieszyn and Frysztak in Eastern Upper Silesia, the HTO paid relief to former owners of buildings and businesses only out of whatever cash was left after deducting for all managerial expenses.[14]

Former Jewish depositors of the Polish Post Savings Bank (*Pocztowa Kasa Oszczędności*) were paid only 10 percent of their savings, the total amount of withdrawals to not exceed 1,000 zlotys.[15] On November 18, 1940, all Jewish cooperative credit associations were liquidated by order of the Office of Bank Supervision (*Amt für Bankaufsicht*) of the Government General. They had also fallen under the order to register Jewish property (issued on January 24, 1940), and all unregistered property of the credit associations was declared "ownerless" and confiscated.[16]

The right to confiscate Jewish property was shared by Himmler (as chief of the SS and police and as *Reichskommissar* in charge of strengthening the German race [*deutsches Volkstum*]), the police organs under his command, and the "resettlement" offices; by Goering (authorized chief of the four-year plan outlined in his order of November 26, 1939), who was mainly interested in raw and semi-processed materials; and by the *Haupttreuhandstelle Ost*. All three continuously wrangled among themselves, accusing each other of trespassing.

Spoliation of property owned by Jews actually started right after the invasion, even before the various pertinent orders were issued. Like German policy on many other occasions, these formal orders were in effect no more than paper work aimed at sanctioning a *fait accompli*, creating a plausible, "legalized" basis for conditions already existing. The Germans in a very systematic way went about taking over property from the Jews as early as September and October 1939. German soldiers, policemen, officials, and even civilian persons regarded themselves as entitled to indulge in open robbery of the Jews. A few illustrations will serve: In Warsaw, Łódź, and other large and small towns, various military and police forces confiscated textile, leather, and grocery wholesale warehouses and retail shops. In some places, Ciechocinek for example, all Jewish businesses without exception were sealed off and emptied of their entire stock of merchandise.[17] Private homes were broken into, and anything that caught the fancy of the Germans was taken away.[18]

In the town of Aleksandrów Kujawski the first repressive measure against Jews took the form of an instruction giving free hand to the military to take anything they needed from the Jews without payment. The Jews were promptly robbed of all property, furniture, and home accessories.[19]

In Kutno a group of *Volksdeutsche* came on a day in February 1940 (the source is not clear about the exact day, whether the 12th or 15th) and thoroughly robbed the Jews, carrying off furniture, linen, bedding, and other household goods, ostensibly for the benefit of the German settlers brought over from the Reich. It was estimated at the time that some 70 percent of the Kutno Jews had lost their property on this one occasion.[20]

In Łódź and the surrounding area the confiscations took on such enormous proportions that high German officials—the *Regierungspräsident* (Uebelhör) and the *Polizeipräsident* (Scheffer)—found it necessary to complain openly of the "wild confiscations" perpetrated by military, civil, and party organs which, according to their findings, endangered the economy of the occupied territories.[21]

Spoliation of Jewish property continued undisturbed, however, embracing cash, merchandise, valuables, furniture, home furnishings, and even posted parcels (e.g., in the Łódź Ghetto). According to the order of October 24, 1941, issued by Koppe, the Higher SS and Police Leader in the Wartheland, furniture confiscated in the Wartheland ghettos (whose final liquidation was then already in the planning stage) was to be distributed by Nazi welfare organs among resettled Germans who had arrived from the east.[22] The *Kriminalpolizei* of the Łódź Ghetto would force Jews to relinquish the last vestiges of currency, merchandise, and valuables they had managed to conceal.[23]

Frequently imposed financial sanctions ("contributions") were another form of spoliation. They were imposed under the slightest pretext. Indeed, seldom was a Jewish community spared this sort of heavy plunder. Kidnaping hostages and calling for ransom was one more means of wanton spoliation.[24] Another form of pillage was various orders to deliver expensive merchandise to outfit the homes of numerous Germans, both official and private persons. The *Judenrat* of Częstochowa was ordered to deliver all necessities, including comfortable furniture, linen, bedding, and kitchen and table ware for the homes of all Germans and their families stationed in town, those who had already arrived from the Reich as well as those who were to come. To meet this order the *Judenrat* imposed a heavy tax on the Jews and took away from their homes not only what was necessary for the moment but much more in anticipation of the next emergency.[25] Similar plundering went on in Białystok, Łódź, Vilna, Kaunas, and many other ghettos.

There were many cases of extorting Jewish property for the private use of individual German officials. Thus we find that on July 22, 1941, Ludwig Fischer, governor of the Warsaw district, sent a request to the chairman of the Warsaw *Judenrat* to deliver "as before" for the wife of Governor General Frank, Frau Brigita Frank, "a coffee-maker to brew Turkish coffee, one lady's traveling kit, and leather boxes large enough to serve four or six people on a picnic."[26]

In the Reichskommissariat Ostland all Jewish movables and real estate were confiscated, except for home furnishings and things necessary for daily use. The Jews were allowed 20 pfennigs in cash a day (one-fifth of a Reichsmark) for each member of a family, but were not allowed more than one month in advance (i.e., 6 Reichsmarks each). As the extermination of the Jews in Ostland began simultaneously with the invasion, the vast majority of Jewish settlements there became "free of Jews" (*judenrein*) by the beginning of 1942, their property became "ownerless" anyway.[27] Total expropriation of Jewish property in Ostland, "regardless of its worth and usefulness," was announced for the first time in an order dated October 24, 1942.[28]

But the Germans in Kaunas did not wait for such a sweeping decree. Confiscation of the entire property of the Jews in Kaunas was accomplished by means of a local order issued at the end of August 1942, whereby a "cashless economy" was introduced in the ghetto. Even the Council of Elders was not permitted to keep cash in its safe, and the meager food supplies were delivered to the ghetto "free of charge."[29]

In the Reichskommissariat Ukraine, where the extermination of Jews also began simultaneously with the invasion, all Jewish property was administratively expropriated.

The "resettlement" of Jews from one area of the occupied territory to another—e.g., from the incorporated western provinces into the Government General (end of the fall of 1939 to mid-1940); from the smaller settlements in towns and villages into the central ghettos; from the ghettos in the western part of the Warsaw district into the Warsaw Ghetto (January to March 1941); and from the remnants of liquidated provincial ghettos in the Wartheland into the Łódź Ghetto (1942)—provided yet another opportunity to deprive the Jews of their property, leaving them with no means of livelihood. Almost everywhere, "resettled" Jews were forced to leave all their home furnishings. During the expulsion actions from the Wartheland into the area of the Government General, Jews were allowed no more than two pairs of underwear, one blanket, and one coat. No valuables, no jewelry, or even gold-rimmed eyeglasses were permitted. Cash allowances averaged from 20 to 200 zlotys, depending on the whim of the local official in charge.[30] Arriving at their destinations, newcomers only aggravated the misery of natives, who were faced with the problem of feeding and taking care of the unfortunate expellees.

Elimination from Business and the Professions

In pursuing their policy and practice of economic ruin for the Jewish masses, the Germans methodically drove the Jews out of all forms of economic life: trade, industry, handicrafts, and the professions. As early as October 18, 1939, the *Kommando* of the Central Border Sector (*Grenzabschnittkommando Mitte*) in Łódź issued an order forbidding Jews to trade in textiles and leather, except for odds and ends. This measure was explained as a necessary step to combat speculators. Textile factories still owned by Jews were allowed to sell their merchandise only to Jewish customers. Jewish shoe-makers were forbidden to make new shoes and could only mend old ones. They were allowed to acquire leather for this purpose only. The owners of textile and leather enterprises were ordered to take stock and submit reports to the police in Łódź and Warsaw, and to the *Landräte* and *Stadtkommissare* in other places, within two weeks.[31]

The German policy of elimination was clearly outlined in the report of the Government General of July 1940, where it was stated that "no doubt, the Jews must be eliminated from industry, import-export businesses, insurance, transportation, and warehouse management. Thought should be given, keeping a positive solution in view, to whether the Jews can now be excluded already from intermediate volume trade. However, it seems that it is still impossible to exclude them from small volume trade. The same situation is prevalent in handicrafts. Be this as it may, Jewish small traders and artisans still in business have to be concentrated in severely supervised compulsory unions."[32]

In the course of pursuing their economic aims, the Germans forbade the Jews to trade in a constantly growing number of fields. Jews dealing in machines and workbenches in Warsaw, for instance, were given one single day to sell their entire stock to "Aryan" merchants. This order was announced by the industry and trade department of the Warsaw *Judenrat* on February 7, 1941. Unsold merchandise was confiscated by the Germans.[33] The order of January 26, 1940, banning Jewish use of trains and public roads without special permission, which was later extended to all forms of transportation (on February 20, 1941), took from the Jews all possibility of undisturbed, legal trade. The number of Jewish stores permitted to continue business was substantially reduced as a result of their simply being denied the prescribed trade certificates, ostensibly because they lacked professional skill. Thus the office for economic affairs of the district chief of Cracow arbitrarily decreed how many Jewish stores and qualified merchants were allowed to function in the ghetto. All others had to discontinue business. Jewish food shops located on streets where city trams ran were also closed.[34]

The economic crusade against the Jews did not omit skilled and unskilled workers and clerks in trade and industry. As soon as the *Treuhänder* took over a business from a Jewish owner, all Jewish clerks were dismissed, and those enterprises that for any reason still remained in Jewish hands were ordered to dismiss Jewish personnel and hire *Volksdeutsche* or Poles instead.[35] By mid-1940 Jewish industrialists in Warsaw stated that they had reduced their Jewish personnel by 60 percent. A similar process for eliminating Jews began in the field of real estate in Warsaw, when buildings owned by Jews were taken over by German-appointed *Kommissare*. Not only did their owners and managers lose their means of subsistence, but so did Jewish artisans who had made a living as handymen, repairmen, or plumbers in these buildings.

According to the first paragraph of an instruction dated December 21, 1940, clarifying an order of the Governor General of the previous day concerning the introduction of labor cards in the Government General, the Jews were not to receive any labor cards. Since no person could be employed without a card,[36] it was generally taken for granted by "Aryan" owners and managers that Jews were to be dismissed immediately from their jobs, notwithstanding a clarification to the contrary received by the union of industrialists at Cracow from the Central Labor Office.[37]

All craftsmen were coerced into joining a union that was subordinated to the local artisan chamber empowered to apportion raw materials and accessories. The compulsory union of Jewish artisans in Warsaw was established on April 1, 1940. Similar unions were established in Cracow, Tarnów, Kielce, Radom, Rzeszów, and in other places. The artisans in small towns had to join unions in adjacent larger towns.[38] In theory the compulsory unions were supposed to be the only source where the Jewish artisan was allowed to get the materials he needed to function. Needless to say, in practice he received little of what he needed. For this reason the unions were actually limited to serving as self-help institutions rather than distribution centers of raw materials or trade exchanges for their members.[39]

By Paragraph 5 of Frank's order of December 16, 1939, and Paragraph 8 of the order of March 7, 1940, Jews also lost all the privileges of social security, such as disability pensions, unemployment insurance, and sick benefits. Only the right to medical help was left to Jews, though hospitalization was allowed only in exceptional cases. However, Jews had to pay all premiums to the full extent.[40]

According to the order of March 6, 1940, Jewish physicians, dentists, dental technicians, and midwives were limited to treatment of Jewish patients. On the other hand, "Aryan" doctors in the Government General were forbidden to treat Jews. Because of a scarcity of physicians, a supplementary order was issued on May 7, 1940, allowing district physicians to make exceptions to the rule for a period of one month. Jewish physicians, dentists, medical aids, and midwives in Cracow were ordered by the local Chamber of Physicians to display the Star of David outside their offices on signs measuring 10 centimeters.[41] Jewish lawyers and notaries were stricken from the rolls of lawyers and forbidden to practice law or plead in the courts. The offices of absent lawyers were taken over by *Treuhänder*, and the balances of their outstanding fees and debts were deposited in savings accounts in the currency bank.[42] The owners of offices that for a fee filled out various legal forms or petitions were ordered to close their businesses.[43]

Schools were all closed, but when schools for Polish children were reopened Jews were not admitted, and Jewish teachers lost their jobs, joining their unemployed colleagues from Jewish schools, which remained closed.

The process of full elimination from the economy, in perhaps a still more severe form, was also going on in the areas of the Reichskommissariats Ostland and Ukraine.

The final, mortal blow came when the Jews were confined in the ghettos. The economic impact of this measure was that Jews were entirely cut off from hundreds of years of economic ties to their gentile neighbors. Enforced expulsion from old homes and places of business or employment brought about considerable loss of property, even if some had been saved from robbery, systematic spoliation, and confiscations. It should be pointed out that, even before the ghettos were established, Jews in many places were forced to move from certain sections of towns on short notice—a few minutes in some instances—and were in no position to take with them more than the very bare necessities (as a rule furniture had to be left). In a number of towns, Jews could take with them no more than they were able to carry on their shoulders, all other means of transportation having been confiscated before the expulsions.

Governor General Frank's order of September 13, 1940, "Concerning restrictions of the right to live within the borders of the Government General," which served as the "legal" basis for the establishment of the closed living sections (*geschlossene Wohnbezirke*) for the Jews, stated that persons falling into this category could be forced to leave in the homes from which they were to be removed all furnishings and other effects in good order without compensation.[44]

After the Jews left, their places of business were taken over by the German authorities. When the Warsaw Ghetto was closed up on November 15, 1940, 1,700 grocery stores and 2,500 other enterprises owned by Jews remained in the "Aryan" parts of the city.[45] According to the order of the Cracow district chief on March 3, 1941, concerning the transfer into the Cracow Ghetto, Jews had to leave two-thirds of the stock in their warehouses and not move anything from their factories. Their material claims were to be treated in the general framework of the confiscation order of January 24, 1940.[46] In Łódź the order to move into the ghetto was issued on February 8, 1940. But the authorities considered that the moving tempo was too slow, and on March 6 and 7 some two hundred Jews were killed in their homes and in the streets in reprisal. After this "prodding" the Jews went into the ghetto on the run, leaving behind all their possessions.[47] For all these reasons Jews entered the ghetto entirely ruined, with extremely limited opportunities for making a living.

Forced Labor

Forced labor, ordained for the Jews from the first days of occupation, strongly influenced their lives and was pregnant with ominous consequences for their economic situation. In the beginning forced-labor duty was entirely arbitrary and, in fact, at the whim of the Germans in a given locality. However, after October 26, 1939, it was "legalized" as obligatory for the entire Jewish population between fourteen and sixty years of age. In the early period, up to the summer of 1940, forced-labor duty actually paralyzed the economy of the Jews; the "enrollment" of the laborers was achieved by brutally seizing people on the streets and in their homes, and the labor was usually accompanied by physical and mental torture. People stayed home out of fear or hid themselves in secure places. In time, the Jews themselves tried to regulate this curse. The Jewish Councils or the Councils of Elders took upon themselves the obligation to deliver a certain number of forced laborers on a daily basis to work for the civil or military authorities. For a short time this plan worked, and wild seizure diminished but never totally stopped.

The Germans paid nothing to the forced laborers. At best, where the attitude of the authorities happened to be more humane, they gave laborers a meager meal: a little soup and a slice of bread. As a rule the Councils paid the wages. In Łódź men got 1.75 Reichsmarks a day, females 1.25 Reichsmarks.[48] These wages were paid out of income derived from the fees other people paid to be exempted from forced-labor duty. In Radom the fee ranged from 2 to 10 zlotys; in Lublin from 15 to 50 zlotys and higher.[49] People willing to substitute for forced-labor duty were among the poorest, both prewar and newly created paupers. The exemption fee paid by others made it possible for them to live through the day. A high degree of poverty among Jews as early as the first months of the occupation is apparent from the fact that many people aspired to forced-labor duty despite the tortures they had to suffer. In Radom, at times, 400 out of 600 people requested for forced labor were volunteer substitutes,[50] and in Łódź 1,000 persons registered for this purpose with the Jewish labor office in the middle of December 1939.[51] Similar situations were recorded in almost all ghettos.

At the start forced labor was confined to such tasks as unloading transports, cleaning houses, and filling in ditches. Later, when economic life became less turbulent, forced labor was performed in or outside the ghettos for the benefit of various German administrative, police, and military establishments, and also for German or native private enterprises. By that time, in the second half of 1940, the workers were paid by their employers, though at very low rates. In the incorporated territories wages ranged from 10 to 40 pfennigs an hour; in the *Generalbezirk Litauen* (Ostland) and in the Białystok Ghetto Jewish forced laborers received half of their wages, the balance of their share going to the treasuries of the *Gebietskommissar* or the *Stadtkommissar*.[52] Incidentally, these wages usually amounted to from 50 percent to 80 percent of the wages paid "Aryan" workers. In the majority of ghettos in the Wartheland, except in Łódź, workers were paid at the rate of 35 percent of their earnings. The balance was transferred to the separate Jewish funds (*Judenfond*) of the local German mayors and county chiefs (*Landräte*). Ostensibly, the families of forced laborers were to be assisted out of this money deposited in the *Judenfond* (according to Paragraph 6 of *Statthalter* Greiser's order concerning Jewish labor dated August 12, 1941); in fact, however, this stipulation remained on paper. In any case the wages were so small and paid so irregularly that even in cases where the authorities magnanimously transferred to the Jewish Councils some money from the *Judenfond*, these amounts were infinitesimal and could in no way alleviate the dire need of the families in question.[53] Taking part in forced-labor duties outside the ghetto, however, provided an attractive opportunity to make contacts with the gentiles and to engage in some sort of exchange or trade (usually clothing and valuables for food) or in smuggling, which to some degree eased the economic isolation of the confined Jews. In many ghettos this desirable by-product of forced-labor duty provided the main source of livelihood.

Jews were forced to labor within the ghetto, in adjoining localities, or in far-off places in labor camps throughout the occupied territories. From the early days of the occupation, people were sent to the Altreich from certain areas of the Wartheland and Eastern Upper Silesia. In the Wartheland wages were again a mere token. According to Greiser's order of August 12, 1941, the hourly wages in the labor camps were set at 30 pfennigs. However, he issued a secret order on June 25, 1942, abolishing the payment of wages to Jewish laborers altogether.[54] In general terms, Jewish laborers in the labor camps of the Lublin area and in the Wartheland were paid the worst wages. A little better were the wages throughout the territories incorporated into East Prussia (Bezirk Zichenau) and in Eastern Upper Silesia.[55]

Since males were the main victims of deportations to the labor camps, tens of thousands of families were broken up and left without their providers. In the majority of ghettos, these families were assisted by the Councils which, in the beginning, paid them in cash (e.g., 12 Reichsmarks a month in the Łódź Ghetto) or in food stamps. As a rule, families of deported forced laborers very quickly fell into the abyss of utter penury.

The Jewish Factor

To some extent the Jews themselves were able to influence and shape their economic life in various localities and in different periods. Undercover economic activities of individuals and groups played an important role, taking on various forms. In the large cities, with long-established Jewish businesses or industrial enterprises, Jews up to a certain time had scant opportunities to make some sort of a living in an "illegal" way, taking advantage of the ineptness and corruption of managers imposed by the *Treuhandstelle*. However, even these limited opportunities stopped as soon as the Jews were confined in the ghettos and their relations with the gentile business world came to a halt.

Other aspects of the illegal economic activities of the ghettos were: undercover trade with the outside world made possible through the forced laborers, working at jobs outside the ghetto and acting as intermediary agents; cunning, intricate smuggling of food; and an undercover industry producing insufficient amounts of food products in very primitive mills, bakeries, sweet-shops, etc. These activities offered exorbitant profits for tiny groups in the ghettos. Some people soon became incredibly rich, and this development in turn contributed, at least in some ghettos, to the mushrooming of secret restaurants, coffeehouses, and nightclubs, accessible only to these *nouveaux riches*, highly contrasting their lives with the miserable existence of their malnourished fellow ghetto inmates.

However, as the overall aim of the German policy was to uproot Jews entirely from the economy of the lands under their rule, Jews were allowed to work only as long as it was profitable to the civil or military interests of the Nazis. Urged on by their vitality, traditional ingenuity, and skills, and driven by the natural will to live, Jews tried in many ghettos to adjust themselves to the anomalous, bitter conditions of their lives. This Jewish reaction to relentless oppression was a complete surprise to the Germans, who had rather expected that simple economic restrictions, continuous hunger, epidemics, and hard labor under impossible conditions would suffice to bring about the morbid results they desired.[56] Can it have been that their disappointment at the—in their view—insufficient results of slow-death policies played a role in their decision to turn to mass murder?

THE ECONOMIC ACTIVITIES OF THE COUNCILS

The Ghetto Industry

Two factors were decisive in the development of ghetto industry. One was a purely economic factor; the other appeared later and reflected the deep concern of the Councils for the physical survival of the ghetto inmates. The economic factor was rooted in the necessity to find substitute sources of income for masses of former employees in industry, trade, and crafts. These workers had lost their places of work because of war operations and subsequent spoliation of Jewish property, followed by the elimination of Jews from jobs, and finally because they were confined to the ghettos. The second factor was the determination of the Jewish Councils and the former leaders of Jewish economic life to demonstrate to the Germans that Jews were fully prepared for productive work. For the Germans came to the occupied territories with the preconceived notion that Jews were a race of parasites. The Jewish leaders in the ghettos endeavored to show them that Jewish workers, artisans, and other skilled specialists could be usefully employed in the occupation economy. The idea was to save Jews from deportation and destruction by working for the benefit of the German economy. In practice these two factors varied in their influence throughout the occupied territories. Everywhere, however, they were the driving forces behind the creation of ghetto industry, despite very limited, often primitive machinery, and almost without any raw materials available.

In some of the ghettos, as in Warsaw, Łódź, Białystok, and Sosnowiec, almost all of the merchandise manufactured was for the German war economy exclusively. In time the ghetto shops and factories in Łódź and Białystok became large industrial combines, with tens of thousands of workers, none producing much for the benefit of the ghetto inmates themselves. From the Jews' point of view, therefore, the measure of their usefulness to the Germans was the sole motivation of their tolerated existence.

On the other hand, the emergence of industry in such ghettos as Vilna, Kaunas, Šiauliai, and Lwów was dictated by the needs of the inmates themselves. But even these ghettos gradually adjusted themselves to the general tendency to harness the greatest possible number of Jewish skilled laborers and exploited Jewish human resources not only for the war machine but for personal profit of the German ghetto-masters as well.

In the final analysis, in spite of the harm to the German war effort, political and racial considerations grew uppermost and a policy of immediate physical extermination of Jews became the order of the day.

As a way of making a living, ghetto industry was negligible. The Germans paid so little for the delivered merchandise that it often was not enough to cover even the bare production expenses. Wages were trifling compared to the prices in undercover markets where some food could be acquired to appease constant hunger. For example, the German firm of Spieshafen and Braun in Heubach, specialists in ladies' corsets, paid Jewish workers in the Łódź Ghetto from 5 to 12 marks a week,[57] just enough to pay for the meager rations allowed them by the German authorities.

In addition to supplying badly needed industrial products for the German army, Jewish enterprises often served as a means for German overlords to enrich themselves by pitiless exploitation of the Jewish working population. The Nazi officials in charge of the ghetto frequently had a vested interest in an ostensibly well-functioning ghetto industry both for material reasons (as a source of grafts and "gifts") and as a means of evading service on the eastern front. Moreover, in some ghettos, with the connivance of the Germans, the workshops were used as a cover for deception by the Jewish workers, which, in a way, constituted acts of sabotage against the hated enemy.

The following example indicates that there were cases where the Jewish population profited because of a certain Jewish-German complicity. This is a report of the former chief of the Kaunas Ghetto industry:

From the purely economic point of view, the shops were a colossal fake. . . . The 4,600 workers in numerous branches of the 44 diversified shops had to show something by way of production. But there was not even token work to do. Moreover, sabotage, pure and simple, was prevalent. Under the pretext of working in the administration . . . over 1,100 persons were employed. Those working in the laundry washed linen for ghetto inmates, using German soap and detergents. . . . A good source of income was the tailor shops, where 1,200 men and women mended used military uniforms. This provided a convenient occasion to work for the benefit of the ghetto, rather than for the Germans. The garments were taken apart, dyed, and made over into civilian clothing. The activities of the other shops were likewise devoted to the good of the ghetto. . . . As far as was feasible, the workers tried to milk the German warehouses. In addition shops were used as a haven for thousands of people, men, women, old, sick, and youngsters, who, according to the German definition, were candidates for destruction as "harmful Jews" (*schädliche Juden*). The shops provided a good opportunity to present them as productive elements.[58]

In the following pages we will review the development of industrial establishments in several ghettos.

On May 13, 1940, only two weeks after the Łódź Ghetto was sealed, Rumkowski submitted a letter to the German mayor of Łódź, informing him that he had completed the registration of 14,850 skilled workers. He attached a list of over 70 articles which the ghetto was prepared to produce and asked for orders. On May 21 he further informed the mayor that he had completed an additional list of 3,345 workers and repeated his request for orders.[59]

At the request of the Jewish Council in Warsaw, the authorities gave permission, in February 1941, to establish a number of shops. Proper statistical data were submitted concerning production possibilities in different fields of industry, and available artisans and businessmen were registered.[60]

In Lwów the Council received permission to establish so-called "labor communes" of cobblers, seamstresses, and tailors.[61] Effort was also made by the Council's industry department to open shops for carpenters, plumbers, and boxmakers, and for making chemical-pharmaceutical, sanitary, and hygiene products.

The union of artisans in Cracow established in 1940 a cooperative tailor workshop with 150 members and a brush manufacturing cooperative with 70 members.[62] The makers of shoe uppers in Kielce established a cooperative for 60 skilled workers in the fall of 1940.[63] In Pabianice, in June 1940, there was established a seamstress shop with 350 workers, and in August a second such shop was added, also employing 350 people. In addition, the Pabianice labor department established cooperatives of hatmakers (40 members), a tailor shop (30 members), and later four more tailor shops.[64] Similar cooperatives for various specialties sprang up in Tarnów, Bochnia, Częstochowa, Radom, Drohobycz, Piotrków Trybunalski, Tomaszów Mazowiecki, Siedlce, and scores of other ghettos.[65] Everywhere, the initiative came usually from the Councils, the artisans, or the Jewish Self-Help (JSS), and was subject to the sanction of the German authorities. On occasion, the Germans themselves initiated workshops (a carpenter shop in Pabianice, for instance).

The emergence of an industry in the ghetto was contingent on three main conditions: the self-interest of the authorities; the accessibility of raw materials and equipment; and the availability of skilled workers. The attitude of the German authorities will be discussed in Chap. 11. As for raw materials and technical equipment for the shops, there exists a wealth of sources, indicating that the Jews solved these problems by "legal" or forbidden means and by exceptional resourcefulness. For example, a Viennese firm in Warsaw collected and bought odds and ends, metal scrap, rags, feathers, scrap paper, wastebaskets, woolens, and other collected refuse, licensing a number of Jewish warehouses and buyers to do the job. But the licensees delivered to the Germans only part of that material. Large quantities reached Jewish workshops and were made over into various items, such as brooms, wood accessories, upholstery, etc. As to genuine raw materials, they were mainly smuggled into the ghettos. And here we come to a very important aspect of ghetto life, which eluded the otherwise close surveillance of the German authorities. Notwithstanding tall ghetto walls and the strict watch of German gendarmes, Polish police, Jewish police, SS men, and other forces, ghetto inmates succeeded in maintaining contacts with the outside world. No sooner had raw materials been delivered to markets outside the ghetto than large quantities also arrived inside the ghetto by various undercover ways.[66]

In a secret report of the governor of the Warsaw district to the Government General, which covered the period June–July 1942, we read:

Despite the various control measures, extensive smuggling of raw materials and half-finished products into the [Warsaw] Ghetto is continuing. After processing, they reappear at sharply increased prices. Raw materials and half-finished articles, for the most part needed for important military purposes, are worked into merchandise [for the private market].

It is clear that no such operations were possible without the active involvement of the local German agencies whom the higher German authorities had to fight. Indeed, the governor added that "the repeated attempts by civilian and military agencies to send trucks into the Warsaw Ghetto to buy and take away from the ghetto merchandise produced there have been frustrated with all severity."[67] These measures notwithstanding, the Warsaw Ghetto and other ghettos continued to produce merchandise for the outside private "Aryan" market. The remnants of hidden stocks were used up along with raw materials smuggled in from confiscated Jewish firms managed by commissars (notably in Tomaszów Mazowiecki, Łódź, and Częstochowa). During the months of September and October 1941, 25,000 brushes were manufactured in the Warsaw Ghetto, providing livelihood for 2,000 families in some 120 workshops under the supervision of old-time Warsaw craftsmen and skilled newcomers. In addition, approximately 100 more shops were established by novices to this occupation. All this production grew from the business enterprise of a few German officers in the quartermaster corps, paid off and in partnership with the Jewish former owner of a brush factory in Cracow.[68] As of December 1940, 330 carpenter shops were working in the Warsaw Ghetto. Of these, 30 were highly equipped and mechanized.[69]

Other artisans, such as upholsterers, plumbers, and tinsmiths, were also busy, particularly during the first half of 1941, when the German war machine was making preparations for the invasion of Soviet Russia, and in the winter of 1941, when warm gloves for the military were in great demand. Refugees from Łódź, former weavers, ran small wool and cotton workshops. A refugee from Kalisz, a former toymaker, produced thousands of toys daily during the winter of 1941. He got the raw materials from German dealers. Children of six to ten years were employed in the shop.[70]

For lack of raw materials substitutes were used, such as iron pipes for military hospital beds, rabbit fur for gloves, etc. In utilizing substitutes, Jewish artisans demonstrated particular adeptness. Old prayer shawls, used clothing, linens, and bed sheets sold by impoverished ghetto inmates were dyed in secret shops and made over into new items. Out of smuggled airplane and metal scraps, aluminum utensils and pots were made, and the covers of old bookkeeping ledgers were used to manufacture luggage. Nothing was wasted; every fragment of cast-off things was used. After the ghettos in the Lublin district were liquidated in the spring and summer of 1942, Polish merchants dumped into the Warsaw Ghetto large transports of used things bought dirt cheap from the Lublin *Werterfassung*. Primitive grain mills, shops producing oil and fats, soap, knitwear and hosiery, leather goods, chemicals, and pharmaceuticals were clandestinely operating in the ghetto, using substitutes for rubber and wood to produce synthetic shoe soles, buttons, writing materials, etc.[71]

According to regulations, all import and export in the Warsaw Ghetto was supposed to be handled by the *Transferstelle* established on May 14, 1941. Jewish responsibility for all orders and deliveries had been vested in the department for industry and trade of the Jewish Council, and the *Jüdische Produktion*, representing a group of industrialists. Proportionately, however, the business of the *Transferstelle* was immeasurably smaller than the clandestine export of secretly produced merchandise which eluded it. Emanuel Ringelblum noted in his Diary that "the relation of the official transport [export] to the unofficial one resembles the ratio between the official and the actual supply of food."[72] This discrepancy was characteristic for the economy of the entire Government General, not only in the Warsaw Ghetto. The contrast was enormous everywhere.

In shops established by the Jewish Council there were employed, by the middle of July 1941, 2,136 workers (1,604 in the three tailor shops, 227 in the hat shop, 136 in the underwear shop, 104 in the saddle shop, 65 in the shoemaker shop, 81 persons employed as clerks, and a number with other assignments).[73] This influx of ghetto inmates into the shops was motivated by the illusion that they provided an opportunity to escape deportation. In July 1942 it was estimated that between 12,000 and 15,000 people were employed in their own homes or in the shops working for the "export" industry, i.e., the clandestine as well as the official one.[74] After German businessmen took over the shops during the mass deportations in the summer of 1942, they were enlarged and the number of workers temporarily increased.

Fluctuation of the worth of Warsaw Ghetto production and of payments made on account of wages in cash and food is illustrated by Table III. These figures show that in the period between January and July 1942 the production worth of the ghetto export quadrupled, with a particularly sudden increase evident during April and May, when export worth more than doubled. Between June and November 1941, the amount of wages paid rose more than threefold (from 332,836 zlotys to 1,203,405 zlotys). Characteristically, wages (in cash and food) roughly constituted 50 percent of the official export worth in May 1942 (prior to the mass deportations). In the last three months of that year, following the end of mass deportations and the drastic decrease in the ghetto population, the production fell to some 38 percent in August, to 5 percent in October, and to less than 1 percent in December (these percentages based on July 1942 production).

Mass deportations from the Warsaw Ghetto began on July 23, 1942. In August 1942 the worth of production started a rapid

TABLE III

Worth of Official Export from the Warsaw Ghetto and Payments to Workers during 1941–1942

PERIOD	WORTH OF EXPORT IN ZLOTYS	WAGES (CASH IN ZLOTYS AND FOOD)
June 1941	——	332,836
July–October 1941	——	2,160,900
November 1941	——	1,203,405
1942		
January	3,700,000[a]	——
February	4,700,000[a]	——
March	6,045,600	——
April	6,893,800	——
May	12,595,600	6,340,000[a]
June	14,458,200	——
July	15,058,558	——
August	1,900,000[a]	——
September	1,100,000	——
October	771,200[a]	2,942,000
November	159,000	2,020,000[b]
December	10,000	1,363,000

[a] In round figures. The figures for ghetto production during October–December 1942 probably were reported smaller than they were actually; for it is inconceivable that the worth of production of thousands of employed persons in the shops could have been so small.

[b] According to another source, the amount was 2,929,000 zlotys.

decline; by December 1942 it fell to 0.6 percent of what it had been five months earlier. In his secret report for August and September 1942, the Warsaw governor noted that

after the transportation [i.e., deportation to Treblinka] there cannot remain any economic life in the ghetto. . . . The textile industry is greatly damaged . . . , of the 3,500 workers in the clothing industry 3,000 were Jews. . . . In fact, production has decreased by 50 percent. . . . There can be no normal production any more until training of a sufficient number of "Aryan" workers is completed. . . . Transitory difficulties have arisen following the evacuation of the Jews employed in the armament industry. Not always has it been possible to replace them with Polish workers. The continuation of numerous ghetto shops is in question.

Concluding, the governor estimated the financial deficit following the deportations at 155,969,000 zlotys in a single segment of the ghetto economy, the real estate industry (loss of rent, damage to houses, payments for repairs, etc.).[75]

According to official figures, no more than 35,639 Jews remained in the Warsaw Ghetto after the deportations were concluded. The remaining shops were actually transformed into labor camps under the management of the SS and the police chief of the Warsaw district. Starting on September 1, 1942, any German firm employing Jewish labor had to pay to the treasury of the District SS and police chief 5 zlotys a day of which 2 zlotys were reimbursed to the shop management for the maintenance of each worker, who daily received only 500 grams of bread and coffee and one or two plates of watery soup. To sustain themselves for the heavy work load, workers had to sell the miserable remnants of their personal belongings.

But even when all work forced on the ghetto survivors was concentrated in the German shops, work for the Polish market outside the ghetto continued. Thus, for example, thousands of pairs of pants for the peasants were made over from old army trousers.[76]

The situation in the Łódź Ghetto was very different. This ghetto was tightly sealed off, and from the very beginning any connection with the "Aryan" side of the city was impossible. All endeavors by Jewish businessmen to continue trade with the outer world were of no avail. The German police and Rumkowski, along with his ghetto police, were engaged in ruthless combat against such trade and soon brought it to a full stop. Neither was there any opportunity to establish contacts with gentiles in the course of forced-labor duties outside the ghetto. Except for a limited number of fur and leather workers sent to work on the "Aryan" side (employment which, incidentally, lasted for only a very short time) ghetto inmates were not employed outside the ghetto, except when sent to labor camps.[77]

The economy of the Łódź Ghetto was based on two principles: total expropriation of all Jewish property (discussed earlier in this chapter) and labor for the benefit of the German economy in shops and factories operating within the ghetto. In this respect, the Łódź Ghetto may be considered an "exemplary ghetto" from the Nazi point of view. Here, where the Jewish Elder Chaim Rumkowski was the outspoken proponent of the "rescue through work" theory, Jewish initiative and expertise contributed to the building up of a substantial and diversified industrial complex under the harsh conditions of Nazi supervision and within a completely sealed-off ghetto. In no other ghetto was there established such colossal production machinery. Jewish energy and know-how, enhanced by necessity and Nazi terror, succeeded in building the most industrialized ghetto in all of Eastern Europe. Its full working capacity was concentrated on executing mainly orders of the *Wehrmacht*, and for this single reason the Łódź Ghetto was the last Jewish community extinguished by the Germans. It was liquidated during the last days of August 1944, after its inmates had wrangled for their lives for five long, tortured years. Rumkowski, who was the most prominent advocate of the rescue-through-work idea, was highly instrumental in building up the ghetto industry.

Discards and used things were, for the most part, the only raw materials available. The German army and a few German firms provided some raw materials and required accessories; but for the filling of orders from most German firms, the Jews themselves had to find raw materials. The German administration of the ghetto used up everything available to produce merchandise they themselves ordered or merchandise ordered by the military. Warehouses in the ghetto containing rags and used things were put at the disposal of the German *Gettoverwaltung* according to Rumkowski's order of November 2, 1940 (No. 154), which forbade, under threat of confiscation, the reprocessing of these articles. In July 1942, when large quantities of clothing, underwear, and other personal belongings were shipped to the Łódź Ghetto from liquidated provincial ghettos, three-quarters of a million kilograms of rags were deposited in ghetto warehouses.[78] Conditions were similar in the adjacent ghettos of Pabianice, Bełchatów, Sieradz, Zduńska Wola, and others which were also harnessed to work for the *Wehrmacht*.

In the Białystok Ghetto there developed a sort of mixture of the two ghetto types, Warsaw and Łódź. To some extent raw materials were procured by Jewish scrap collectors. Forty persons were employed for this purpose in March 1942. Rags for the textile factory were also smuggled in from outside the ghetto,[79] but the bulk of raw materials needed to fill the orders of the military was delivered by the German authorities. At a meeting of the Jewish Council on August 28, 1941, a speaker discussing industrial achievements stated that "all that is necessary for industrial output is gladly furnished by the authorities."[80]

As for technical equipment, the Councils endeavored at least to prevent the confiscation of whatever equipment was available in the sealed-off ghettos. Detailed material about such endeavors is extant for the Łódź Ghetto. In the section of town where the ghetto was located there were very few large-scale factories. On April 15, 1940, Rumkowski addressed a letter to the Łódź branch of the HTO in Poznań, asking that available machinery not be removed from the ghetto, or at least that he be told about planned removal in advance.[81] He succeeded only to some degree, for the confiscation of technical equipment, particularly of the more expensive type, continued. However, on October 16, 1940, at a meeting of the *Regierungspräsident's* deputy, the *Polizeipräsident,* a representative of the *Oberbürgermeister,* and other Nazi dignitaries, it was decided at the initiative of the *Regierungspräsident's* deputy and on behalf of the HTO to open all factories located in the ghetto and to allow them to use available raw materials otherwise subject to confiscation. Rumkowski was made responsible for keeping the remaining equipment in working condition.[82] But the *Treuhandstelle* did not always comply with this decision, as is evident from the chief of the German ghetto administration Hans Biebow's letter to the Łódź branch of the HTO, dated March 26, 1942, admitting that the HTO sold part of the machinery to "Aryan" firms and "loaned to the Jewish community" what was left, and consequently a substantial part of the machinery needed by shoemakers, plumbers, and tailors was purchased by the German ghetto administration.[83]

Machinery was also sent into the Łódź Ghetto by the German authorities from liquidated Jewish settlements in all of the occupied areas of Europe. In a circular letter of the Reich Finance Ministry dated March 30, 1942, concerning property left behind by deported Jews, the regional finance presidents (directors) were advised that sewing machines were to be sold to the Łódź *Gettoverwaltung* for use by the tailors in the ghetto.[84] All equipment which remained in the hands of Jewish owners was forcibly put at the disposal of the ghetto industry, and a great deal more was repaired or assembled in the ghetto shops. There were over 7,000 machines at work in the Łódź Ghetto, according to a report submitted at the end of 1942.[85] On October 26, 1940, Rumkowski announced (public notice no. 148) that ghetto inmates had a duty to lend their sewing machines, threatening that otherwise the machines would be confiscated.[86] One month later, on November 20, he announced in public notice no. 168 a similar duty to lend workbenches to equip newly established carpenter shops, again threatening that this equipment would be con-

fiscated if it was not put at the disposal of the shops.[87] The shops of
cobblers working privately were raided and their equipment confiscated in August 1942.[88] Whenever new workshops (they were
called "resorts" in the ghetto) were established, craftsmen ceded their
equipment to the shops to enable the new establishments to function.
Incidentally, a similar situation also developed in the Warsaw Ghetto.
A news item in the *Gazeta Żydowska* informed readers of tailor shops
where work was available for candidates possessing their own sewing
machines, workbenches, and electrical press irons.[89] But the problem
of equipment was less acute in Warsaw due to the fact that the
ghetto occupied part of what had been the prewar Jewish quarter.
Some equipment remained unmoved.

In the Białystok Ghetto, machinery was delivered by both the
inmates themselves (mainly sewing machines) and by the German
authorities. The Council appealed periodically to the ghetto population to report or sell equipment; but on October 20, 1941, it called
for the compulsory selling of all sewing machines. On July 22, 1942,
a request was issued for delivery of 200 sewing machines. This request, signed by the rabbinate, threatened excommunication for
those who did not comply. In a subsequent announcement, on November 11, 1942, it was stated that each sewing machine delivered
would provide work for two people in the workshops. Still another
request, this one in the form of an urgent appeal, was announced "to
save the ghetto from more danger." This was on February 17, 1943,
a few days after the February "action" was concluded.[90]

In his public speech on June 21, 1942, the acting chairman of the
Białystok Council, Ephraim Barash, said that "the German authorities deliver from German sources outside the ghetto machinery
needed to equip the factories."[91] A day before, at a meeting of the
Council, he informed members that knitting machines and equipment to make barrels had arrived in the ghetto from the outside.[92]
Still, the equipment available was not enough.[93]

There were no favorable possibilities for industry in the Vilna
Ghetto, because all workshops suffered from lack of machinery and
plant outfit. They functioned thanks to the inventiveness of the
ghetto inmates, and although they were improperly equipped, the
ghetto succeeded in establishing a technological laboratory producing
a detergent, chalk powder, and other chemical products; a "modern"
smelting plant; a large-scale mechanical laundry; a disinfection plant
to assure the maintenance of the water and sewage systems; and

factories producing complicated apparatus, vitamins, food supplies, and various other items.[94] Equipment was collected by compulsory methods. Thus delivery of sewing machines to the premises of the criminal department of the ghetto police was ordered by Jacob Gens on May 14, 1943, under the threat of severe punishment. The sewing machines had to be delivered in a single day, not later than the evening of May 15.[95]

Securing of cadres of skilled workers for labor in the ghetto shops was no problem. There was no lack of craftsmen, particularly since the workshops were limited to branches of light industry, in which Polish Jews were traditionally predominant. Over 45 percent of the Jewish population in Poland had been employed in industry and crafts, according to the census of 1931. Moreover, there was a general tendency among Polish Jews during the prewar years to change from commercial occupations to labor in industry and crafts. In such industrial centers as Warsaw, Łódź, Białystok, Vilna, and Lwów, the Councils had ready at their disposal large cadres of highly skilled workers in all fields.

To provide still more skilled labor the Councils and the JSS in the area of the Government General opened a large number of vocational courses for adults and young people. The German authorities, interested in the exploitation of Jewish skilled labor, permitted these training courses while they barely tolerated schools for the Jews. The Commission for Vocational Training of the Warsaw Ghetto Jewish Council supervised 62 training courses with 2,331 students during the second quarter of 1941. Between September 1941 and the end of June 1942, some 20,000 students, including persons who had changed their previous professions or occupations to handicrafts, got their training in these courses of occupational rehabilitation.[96] In the Łódź Ghetto the Commission for Vocational Retraining of the School Department conducted a vocational school and supplementary courses for young artisans, turning them into skilled weavers, and electrical and metal workers.[97]

We shall now attempt to analyze in more detail the activities of individual Councils in developing and supervising ghetto industry, beginning with the largest "labor ghetto" in the entire area under Nazi occupation rule: the Łódź Ghetto. In October 1940 the Central Office of the Labor Resort [Department] was established in Łódź. This department in the beginning supervised all of the work performed in the shops of the ghetto. Later on, when industry had greatly diversified and production climbed, some decentralization of supervision took place. To take care of the 15 tailor shops, a Tailor Center was established. The administrative and technical supervision of the entire ghetto industry was taken over in April 1941 by a specially created Main Vocational Commission (also known as the Vocational and Control Commission). The Central Office of the Labor Resort represented ghetto industry before the *Gettoverwaltung* and was given orders for the production of various merchandise.[98] Thus the developments which are discussed below are a direct result of the economic policies of the *Gettoverwaltung*, as relayed by the *Judenälteste*.

Starting with one tailor shop in May 1940, the number of factories, shops, and other places of work steadily increased. By August 1943, 117 factories, workshops, and warehouses were in operation. Of these, over 90 factories and workshops provided work for 73,782 men and women, 85 percent of the ghetto population.[99] In 1944, 92.8 percent were classified in the labor category. This brought about a far-reaching change in the occupational structure of the Łódź Jews, compared to their prewar situation. Suffice it to say that according to the census of 1931, 41.8 percent of the Jews in that city were employed as white-collar workers and professionals. In 1931, 27.5 percent were classified as businessmen, but they practically disappeared as an occupational group under the impact of German spoliation and oppression even before the ghetto was established. It is worthwhile to note that during the first census in the ghetto, taken on June 16, 1940, 85,036 of the 156,402 ghetto inmates (or 54%) were classified in the column "without occupation."[100] There is little doubt that for the most part these people "without occupation" were former businessmen, merchants, store clerks, and various middlemen who, for easily understandable reasons, abstained from confessing to occupations for which there was no place in the ghetto, and who were threatened with ominous abuse by the Germans.

There was also a great change in the structure of Jewish industry. The bulk of Jewish shops before the war employed only a few people on the average, seldom more than a hundred. The workshops in the ghetto were larger establishments and employed several hundred workers each. In the tailor shop at Jakuba Street, 1,200 people were employed. "The Jewish tailor . . . has never worked in such large groups," noted a contemporary observer.[101] Neither had there been in Łódź such a big factory producing furniture and other wood products as the one that operated in the ghetto during the summer of 1941, with 800 people working in its three departments. In four departments of the slipper shop, 4,500 skilled and unskilled workers were employed by the end of July 1942.[102] Looking for large orders, the ghetto industry had to organize along mass-production lines. The *Gettoverwaltung*, in its drive to increase the production of the Jewish labor force, encouraged the establishment of large enterprises facilitating strict control of the workers and their productivity. In some shops, those of tailors and shoemakers, for example, there was introduced a sort of assembly-line system. Other workshops, producing carpets, slippers, and similar wares, also employed large numbers of unskilled people: former merchants, women, old persons, youngsters, and even children, who learned the trade as they worked. At the same time, people skilled in some specialty which had no use in the ghetto tried to make themselves useful in other occupations. Thus highly qualified tailors, specialists in handmade garments, tried to adjust themselves to the awkward methods of unskilled "bunglers." When there were no orders for garments, they made shirts and fur coats for the military.[103]

The material worth of the Łódź Ghetto's production was very large. According to one of its reports, in 1941 the *Gettoverwaltung* was reimbursed in the sum of 12,881,300 Reichsmarks on account of the wages of shop workers, and 3,312,500 Reichsmarks on account of products sold, a total of 16,193,800 Reichsmarks.[104] One year later, in 1942, the respective figures read: 8,667,400 and 19,014,000, a total of 27,681,400 Reichsmarks.[105] Note that wages decreased by almost one-third, while the worth of production climbed fivefold. This alone is sufficient testimony to the degree of exploitation. Arthur Greiser, the *Statthalter* of Warthegau, testifying at his trial in Poznań in 1946, characterized the Łódź Ghetto as one of the largest industrial enterprises in the Reich.[106] And a note found in the documents of the *Gettoverwaltung* admits that, above all, the productivity of the Łódź Ghetto created an opportunity for trade in the Wartheland.[107]

The process of increasing the labor force of the ghetto filled Rumkowski and his helpers with pride. At the opening of an exhibit of products made by five labor "resorts," at the end of December 1942, one of the men in charge stressed the fact that "50,000 people were over night transformed from unemployed persons into a working element . . . bringing about great occupational rehabilitation."[108] Next Rumkowski delivered a passionate speech proclaiming: "The award [for distinguished workers] will not be in the piece of paper or some little toy they will be given, but in the proud heritage they will bequeath to future generations." He concluded in ecstasy, "Our children and children's children will proudly remember the names of all those who contributed to the creation of the most important Jewish achievement in the ghetto: the labor opportunities which granted justification to live."[109]

But such enthusiasm was found only in leaders, the great majority of whom, thanks to the authority they gained by supervising various branches of ghetto industry, became "big shots."[110] The mass of the ghetto population, and primarily the laborers, were quickly disenchanted and exhibited a changed attitude. One of the chiefs of the work resorts bluntly stated in his speech at the exhibition that "the worker who went to work did so because of his profound solidarity with the society as a whole rather than for his own benefit. . . . Only because of this attitude was it possible to work at all, and therefore to continue our existence."[111] But this positive attitude bogged down when Rumkowski applied harsh measures. A contemporary document indicates that "labor ceased to be a means of securing life for the workers since, with employment or without, they could not make a living. They could buy nothing with their wages."[112] In the main people worked only to make enough to pay for their rationed food, and even if something remained of their wages, they were unable to buy anything anyway, since wages were in no relation to the swollen prices on the black market, the only place people could go to search for additional food and avoid starvation.

To maintain production on a high level a severe labor regime was introduced, with special commissars appointed to oversee the workers. These mainly came from the ranks of the Łódź Ghetto police. In a report of one of the large tailor shops, we read that "if not for the heavy-handed commissars, unpleasant things would have happened. . . . the workers interrupted [admonitions]."[113] By the beginning of 1943, when the scarcity of labor for German army needs increased and the military became more attracted to ghetto industry, the regime in the shops became still more rigorous. Workers were subject to the most stringent control and were frisked when leaving the shops at the end of the work day. Without a special permit, no one was permitted to leave the assigned place of work. Patrols of ghetto police took care of that. At first, the working day lasted nine hours, six days a week, with a rest day at first on the Sabbath but later (beginning January 29, 1943) on Sunday. Starting on April 29, 1941, a 10-hour work day was ordered in all ghetto offices, with a 90-minute rest period.[114] In the spring of the same year, the work day was extended to 12 hours in two shifts.[115] For the most part, working conditions were very bad: little, overcrowded locations, poor sanitary conditions.[116] Hard labor in the workshops greatly contributed to the spread of sicknesses and to the deaths of thousands upon thousands of shop workers (see Chap. 7).

The economy of the Vilna Ghetto was influenced by the specific role the town played both in the overall war economy and as an important military base in the rear of the German eastern front. In Vilna and in its vicinity the Germans maintained military warehouses and repair shops full of war pillage and armor in need of repair. In other shops uniforms, underwear, and shoes were made. Vilna was an important railroad hub and airbase. The center of military building work was also located there. In contrast to Łódź and, in part, also to Warsaw, the bulk of economic activities of the Vilna Ghetto was concentrated not in the shops but in labor tasks accomplished outside the ghetto, in the so-called "labor units."

The Vilna Ghetto industry went through three phases. As mentioned above, shops in Vilna were first established to satisfy the needs of the ghetto inmates, and were planned as auxiliaries of the technical department of the Jewish Council, particularly the building section. In a report entitled, "Half a Year's Building Activities in the Vilna Ghetto," we read that it was necessary simultaneously to establish and equip shops and do the actual construction work. The most urgent tasks were to repair ruined buildings, provide homes, fix demolished bathhouses, equip disinfection establishments, and set in motion soup kitchens, schools, offices, and a theater, all at one time. In addition, care had to be taken of other tasks, such as providing ghetto inmates at least partially with technical equipment and materials.[117]

Work in shops was made possible only thanks to adroit specialists who assembled in the ghetto motors, machinery, and complicated equipment for chemical laboratories. The beginning was modest. No more than one shoemaker shop, one tailor shop, and two barber shops with a total of 31 employees were at work during the first half of 1942.[118] Soon the ghetto industry began to develop by leaps and bounds, some shops working exclusively on orders received from outside the ghetto. More light industry shops came into being, among others another tailor shop employing 15 people working at six sewing machines. In the report of the technical department for the month of August 1942, mention is made of a new industrial section, employing 62 workers making brooms and brushes, weavers, bookbinders, and carton makers. In August six new shops (tinsmith, button, plumber, carpenter, wooden shoes, and watchmaker) were added, and a chemical laboratory was opened. These shops employed a total of 180 people, in addition to clerical personnel; and their monthly turnover reached the amount of 40,053 Reichsmarks.[119] Thus in the period from January to September 1942, the number of people engaged in Vilna Ghetto industry climbed almost sixfold, from 31 to 181, and the turnover increased 16 times, from 2,465 to 40,053 Reichsmarks.

Industrial development continued. By the end of 1942 and the beginning of 1943 new shops were added with skilled specialties such as galvanizing metals, nickel coating, and orthopedic supplies. The number of workers also increased. In February 1943 there were active 12 mechanical shops, employing 161 workers, and 16 shops in various segments of light industry with 232 workers. The total turnover was 84,820 Reichsmarks during that month.[120]

With the growth of ghetto industry, the former technical department was reorganized and named Department of Ghetto Industry. According to a graph and chart dated May 18, 1943, the department worked in two sections, one for heavy and one for light industry. The latter had been subdivided into two sections in March 1943. One subsection mainly embraced the garment workshops (textiles, leather, and furs), and the second took care of technical and chemical shops, shops making precise mechanical equipment, knitting shops, ceramics shops, and barbershops.[121]

The prevalence of the need of the local market in Vilna industry is graphically illustrated by the demand from the ghetto itself.[122] A report of the Department of Ghetto Industry for February 1943 enumerated 27 orders received from outside the ghetto for a total amount of 6,336 Reichsmarks. The largest order, in the amount of 3,872 Reichsmarks, came from the Press and Propaganda Office.[123] However, in the last months of its life, almost the entire production of the ghetto was based on orders from the German authorities.

The ghetto maintained also its own very limited food industry.

A saccharine factory was in operation, producing from July to September 1942 some 9,500 boxes of saccharine of 100 tablets each; a flour mill ground 173,000 kilograms of corn; also in operation were a starch and syrup factory, using frozen potatoes and potato peels as raw materials, and a factory making marmalade and vitamin syrup out of carrots.[124]

In general the shops were not profitable and, as elsewhere, the prices paid by German clients (e.g., the *Gebietskommissar*) did not even cover bare production costs. The report of the Department of Ghetto Industry for November and December 1942 states: "Filling the order of the *Gebietskommissar* for gloves during these two months . . . brought about a deficit of 503.10 Reichsmarks. Thanks to profit from private orders [from the outside] in the amount of 273.15 Reichsmarks in December, this deficit was reduced to 229.95 Reichsmarks." The report hopefully concludes that if private orders from outside the ghetto continue at the same pace, the shop should have only a very small deficit, and perhaps even cover all expenses. In another part of the report, dealing with mixed workshops (light industry), it is stated that "with the exception of the binding and box-making shop, one cannot consider the shops commercially sound, and neither can they provide livelihood for the workers."[125] But the workshops were not meant by the Germans "to provide for the livelihood of the workers" at all. This was out of the question, if only because of excessive market prices and small wages. As one of the sources tersely commented, the shops were created simply as "a main attraction for visiting authorities who entrusted them with various orders."[126] The Jews of the ghettos entertained no illusions. They knew that the aim of the shops was "to give an excuse to justify our existence."[127]

In the Białystok Ghetto the economy was two-pronged: work in various German enterprises outside the ghetto, and work in diversified industry within the ghetto, with a preponderance of the latter, because of its greater "rescue" possibilities. On the whole, the vast network of diversified enterprises worked for the benefit of the Germans. From August 1941 until the middle of 1942, twenty factories and shops were put into operation in the Białystok Ghetto,[128] producing a wide range of items: furniture, saddles, harnesses, garments (only women were employed in the garment shops), hats, chemicals, textiles, mechanical and electrical equipment, brooms, barrels, and knitwear. Other shops, a smithy among them, were also established. Employment climbed steadily. The shops employed 1,730 workers as of March 1, 1942. In July 1942, 8,600 were employed. In April 1943, after over 10,000 persons had been deported to the death camp at Treblinka during the "February action" (February 5-12, 1943), the Jewish Council feverishly tried to expand ghetto industry to the utmost. The number of workers climbed then to 12,200 or 43.5 percent of the total ghetto population of approximately 28,000.[129]

The military ordered in large quantities. For instance, an order for 30,000 pairs of new felt boots, and for sewing leather parts on 100,000 more pairs, was given in May 1942. In August 1942 the garment shops manufactured 100,000 military hats and 40,000 pairs of gloves. The carriage shops got an order in October 1942 to deliver 30,000 carts. The total worth of the manufactured orders reached millions of Reichsmarks.[130]

In addition to industry run by the Council, the following private German enterprises were in operation in the Białystok Ghetto by the beginning of April 1943: an industrial complex, consisting of furniture, textile, and leather goods factories owned by the Nazi partyman Oscar Stepen, with a total of 1,200 workers; two textile factories with 700 workers; two garment shops with 200 workers; and two so-called military works with 130 workers, altogether 2,230. In all 14,650 persons including minors, over 50 percent of the ghetto inmates, worked in various shops for the benefit of the Germans in April 1943.[131]

Parallel to all these official industrial activities, a versatile clandestine industrial activity existed for the benefit of the inmates themselves. Flour mills and grit mills were operated by hand, shops produced soap and leather goods, knitwear, and other articles. Working in most primitive conditions and hindered by a dearth of raw materials, they produced little. Still a few hundred families managed to make some money. In the beginning the Council was indulgent. However, because these clandestine shops were reported to the Gestapo by informers, the Council was forced to close some of them and confiscate their merchandise; but this did not stop others from continuing.[132]

Right after the ghetto was established in Kaunas, the Council of Elders approached the *Stadtkommissar*, asking for permission to open workshops. An affirmative answer did not come before December 1941, ordering the opening of a public laundry. The first workshops were put in operation in January 1942. In time 40 shops were established employing 4,600 persons during the summer of 1944.[133]

In 1942 the industry department of the Jewish Council at Lwów established "labor communities," starting with shoemaker and underwear shops. Later, carpenter, plumber, metal works, hat, and paper shops were opened. All worked for the benefit of institutions active in the ghetto and for German and Polish firms and private persons as well. The "labor communities" were fashioned as production cooperatives, with members providing machinery (the labor department could not provide the necessary technical equipment) and dividing the profits among themselves. There are no figures on the number of people these cooperatives employed, nor is the scope of their production and profits known.[134]

Small ghettos also made efforts to enable impoverished inmates to find some sources of income by establishing collective artisan shops. Typical in this respect is the information supplied by one of the surviving members of the Suchowola Ghetto Council (Białystok area):

We faced the hard problem of how to find some job opportunities for the ghetto inmates. Since taxes had been abolished, the enormous expenses of the Council could be covered only by profits from various enterprises. With great effort a bakery was put into operation, securing bread for the ghetto; then a pottery was opened, using clay available in the ghetto. The products sold yielded considerable profits. A dentist's office was established in the ghetto, and, with the permission of the *Kommandantur*, a similar office was opened outside the ghetto, for the gentile population. Permission was also granted for a blacksmith shop, and the blacksmiths opened a smithy in a former stable, working as partners. The organizing of tailors, saddlemakers, carpenters, hatmakers, and other artisans followed in the same manner. But when the workshops began producing merchandise there were no buyers. The ghetto itself was unable to consume much, and it was necessary to find outside customers. We approached the authorities and soon were permitted to take orders from the outside. Jewish experts were allowed to leave the ghetto on certain days, three times a week, to accept orders from neighboring peasants. To fill these orders special permission was needed, as well as permits to take finished products out of the ghetto to sell to the gentiles. Prices were fixed by the authorities. The ghetto . . . was relieved, and life began to be normal. . . . Money for the products sold was paid to the workers on a weekly basis every Sunday. A certain percentage was deducted to cover the expenses of the ghetto.[135]

Trade in the Ghetto

The activities of the Jewish Councils with respect to trade within the ghettos depended on the general trade regulations imposed by the German authorities. The main purpose of these severe regulations was to combat free or "black" markets, though the authorities sometimes tolerated them because of the resistance of the population.[136] German measures to combat free trade in the ghettos were even more severe. The delivery of all merchandise was officially regulated and strictly rationed. Purchase and distribution were handled by the Councils on a monopolistic basis, and the Councils were responsible for strict adherence to rules and regulations. Food was sold in special shops or vegetable markets operated by clerks. In Łódź the clerks were on the Council payroll. In other ghettos, as for instance in Warsaw, storekeepers and bakers were licensed to sell groceries and bread. The Warsaw method was the more widespread one. Clerks were responsible to qualified Council departments for food received and sold in exchange for ration stamps issued to the ghetto inmates. Along with grocery shops operated under supervision of the Councils, covert or overt shops were in operation almost everywhere in the ghettos, selling food products manufactured on the premises or smuggled in from the outside. The German authorities fought the illegal trade, forcing the Councils to apply strong measures.

In the Łódź Ghetto tailor and shoemaker shops sold used and mended garments, underwear, and shoes, and newly manufactured wooden shoes. The German ghetto administration had monopolized the purchase of personal belongings from ghetto inmates, as well as valuables. A special bank was opened in the ghetto for this purpose. In fact this was nothing but another form of confiscation of Jewish property, since very little was paid to the sellers.[137] The *Gettoverwaltung* bought all these articles from the Jewish Council, paying cheaply.

The lessees of small garden plots growing some vegetables in the ghetto were entitled to sell their products to individual customers at prices announced on a daily basis by the vegetable section of the agriculture department of the Council. The lessees were allowed a 20 percent surcharge.[138] This was the only kind of trade allowed by the authorities.

Smuggling was impossible because of both severe measures applied by Rumkowski's administration and draconic punishments meted out by the authorities (the ghetto was surrounded by barbed-wire fences and the guards shot to kill anybody approaching the ghetto borders without warning). The situation within the tightly sealed-off ghetto was made still worse by the already mentioned fact that no Jewish labor was used in the labor units in the vicinity of the ghetto. There was no way for ghetto inmates to make transactions to exchange clothing or other goods for food. The price scale was determined by a single yardstick—the price of bread or its equivalent in ghetto currency. The punishment of the impoverished ghetto inmates was particularly severe for selling rationed food, and especially so for minors. Formations of female police were organized to seize and put in jail young vendors selling in the streets such "merchandise" as homemade cigarettes, candy, potato cakes, cookies, and similar edibles. Rumkowski threatened the parents of these "delinquents" with deportation. He periodically posted on the walls of the ghetto public announcements against illegal trade.[139]

Nevertheless, stark hunger was so widespread that all "legal" barriers were broken and exchange trade blossomed. It was especially common during the fall and winter of 1941–1942, when some 20,000 Jews from Germany, Austria, and Prague were "resettled" into the Łódź Ghetto. For the most part they came with considerable luggage, clothing, and some valuables; and because they were able to pay any price, ghetto prices sky-rocketed. Suffering from constant hunger, the unemployed newcomers (mostly elderly people) were forced to sell their belongings. For these there was a strong demand in the ghetto. The price of food, always in great demand, suddenly increased, resulting in inflation and devaluation of the ghetto currency. The same happened during the periods of deportation, when candidates for "resettlement," trying to buy large quantities of food, sold for very little their belongings, including household items, which would be useless in their new situations.

Rumkowski tried to combat this trade too. He threatened deportation, calling the culprits "speculators" despite the fact that many of them were selling their food rations to get a little cash. He also arrested those who milked inexperienced newcomers trying to make a killing on the black market.[140]

In the Warsaw Ghetto, trade between Jews and gentiles, who entered the ghetto by legal or illegal means, went on without interference by the Jewish Council. Business was transacted on certain streets and squares in the ghetto. Almost exclusively, the ghetto inmates offered personal belongings, mostly garments and linens, which the gentiles, for the most part clerks and workers, exchanged for cash or food.[141] Jewish laborers working at places outside the ghetto were mainly engaged in the exchange trade, and in smuggling into the ghetto.[142]

The illicit trade in smuggled merchandise, mainly food, reached considerable dimensions. It expanded with unusual ingenuity, embracing a network of smugglers, receivers, peddlers, and bribed ghetto guards. Youngsters and small children smuggled food from the "Aryan" side. Often this was the only source of edibles for their famished, sick parents and siblings.[143] The German and Polish police tried to root out smuggling activities. The struggle with the smugglers cost many human lives. It was carried out by the German and Polish police, with the Jewish *Ordnungsdienst* playing only a minor role.[144]

In the Białystok Ghetto the Jewish Council at first tolerated the endeavors of inmates to make a living by trading, and even assigned a marketplace for the conduct of "illegal" business. The winter and summer of 1942 saw lively trade in garments, leather goods, and textiles. These and other wares were exchanged for food. Small shops mushroomed, and restaurants and coffeehouses opened, selling expensive food and alcoholic drinks. Children sold cigarettes, matches, and saccharine in the streets of the ghetto. Messengers from provincial ghettos, even from far-away Warsaw, came to the Białystok Ghetto to buy "gifts" for the lords of their ghettos. Parallel to this tolerated trade, other kinds of business flourished, mainly based on smuggling; almost every necessity of life could be acquired in the ghetto at this time.

The Council's treasury derived considerable income from the fees each trader paid for a special trade certificate.[145] Soon, however, the Gestapo ordered the Council to end these business activities, particularly trade in food items they considered luxuries for ghetto inmates. At a meeting of the Council on January 18, 1942, it was decided to prohibit the sale of wheat bread and flour, meat, fish, grits, fats, and cocoa. The sale of other wares was limited to the official ghetto marketplace. Trading in the streets was also prohibited. In addition it was decided to revoke the butchers' licenses, not to license restaurants and stores facing the streets, and to combat smuggling by all means.[146] On June 9, 1942, the Council closed all restaurants and coffee and tea houses as a punishment for the illicit sale of alcoholic drinks. Later the ghetto market was abolished, notwithstanding the substantial fees it provided. Though disrupted and forbidden, trade continued from behind back doors.[147]

Ghetto shops trading in smuggled products were also opened in the Vilna Ghetto. The Jewish Council did not consider them illegal. There, too, "ghetto licenses" were needed, and trade was subject to the regulations of the sanitary and epidemiologic department. Shopkeepers had always to be on the alert in case of inspection by German officials.[148]

Summarizing, it can be concluded that the attitude of individual Councils toward illicit trade in the ghettos varied from strongly negative in Łódź to mildly permissive in most other places. It was commonly accepted as a fact of life that illicit trade was the only remedy against incessant, terrible hunger in the ghettos. The Councils tried to be lenient, and in some ghettos, such as Zamość, Šiauliai, and Lachwa, the Councils were themselves involved in illegal trade. Paying bribes, they brought food over and above the allocated rations into the famished ghettos. The money they earned from these transactions was used to cover other urgent expenses.[149] (See also Chap. 10.)

Purveyance of Provisions

Long before the ghettos were established, the Jews had been banished from the mainstream of the national economy and from the general food supply system introduced by the German authorities. The problem of securing provisions for the ghettos therefore became of necessity one of the most vital functions of the Jewish Councils. Special machinery with numerous departments and sections was necessary to acquire food and the other necessities of life; to find means to pay for the provisions; to establish distribution places for ration stamps and food; to open warehouses, bakeries, kitchens, etc. In addition a supervisory body had to be created to oversee all these activities.

Only the Councils were authorized to buy food. During the very first months of the occupation, former food wholesalers and bakers advanced money to community executives, thus creating capital funds to pay for provisions. At a later date, after the Jews were forced into ghettos, the Councils were authorized to acquire provisions from the Polish food cooperatives, or from German food supply authorities. Under conditions of strict control and regulated trade relations, rationed food for the ghettos could have been acquired only through official channels—the respective German food supply authorities of the *Stadtverwaltungen*—in exchange for special ration cards usually printed on yellow paper and bearing the Star of David.[150] Each official distribution and vegetable shop had been assigned consumers and received the appropriate amount of food. An accounting was made on the basis of the ration stamps received in exchange. Very seldom were the rations enough to satisfy even the most modest needs. Thus by order of the *Stadtkommissar* in Łódź on November 14, 1939, the Jewish community was supposed to receive 25 percent of the food rations allotted to the entire city. In practice, however, food arrived irregularly in an arbitrary manner, and even then it was sometimes confiscated.[151] The food situation in the ghettos was catastrophic at all times, and the Councils continually intervened with the authorities, calling attention to the fact that starvation would bring about the spread of epidemics. But even this suggestion did not change their attitude.

The chairman of the Jewish Council in Warsaw, Adam Czerniakow, addressed a letter to the governor of the Warsaw district on December 17, 1940, reporting that "the Jewish rations have steadily decreased since April [1940]. During all of the month of November, for instance, ghetto inmates received only 3,250 grams of bread per person, compared to 6,100 grams per person given to the 'Aryans.' Sugar, potatoes, flour, noodles, meat, marmalade, eggs, and coal were not given to the Jews at all." He added that since the ghetto had been sealed off, it had been impossible to acquire food on the free market anymore. (At this period the free market was still in existence.) He concluded by expressing the hope that the food items he had mentioned would be granted and rations increased.[152] The Lublin Jewish Council addressed a similar letter to the local authorities requesting treatment equal to that given "Aryans" in the distribution of rationed provisions by the *Stadtverwaltung*.[153]

There were times when food deliveries stopped altogether or were drastically curtailed; and this happened not only during the numerous "actions." During the year 1941 food supplies received by the Łódź Ghetto were much less than had officially been allocated to the inmates. Shortages amounted to 10,855 tons of potatoes, 503 tons of vegetables, 323 tons of marmalade, 289 tons of meat, and

258 tons of various other food products.[154] Between December 1940 and March 1941 the Warsaw Ghetto was supposed to receive 5,200 tons of flour and 517.8 tons of sugar, according to officially allocated rations. Actually, however, only 3,554 tons of flour and 236 tons of sugar were delivered by the authorities for distribution among ghetto inmates.[155] Moreover, the provisions which did arrive in the ghettos were of inferior quality, often unfit for human consumption. This was no accident, but the result of official policy. It is known, for example, that at a meeting held in Łódź on October 25, 1940, the local German authorities decided to dump in the ghetto large amounts of spoiled food.[156] In March 1942 the Warsaw Ghetto Jewish Council paid 100,000 zlotys to a sanitation enterprise for removal of some 3,000 tons of rotten potatoes previously distributed to inmates.[157] And in Łódź thousands of tons of rotten vegetables were taken from the ghetto and buried in adjacent fields in the winter of 1942.[158]

Some of the ghettos demonstrated particular inventiveness in creating substitutes for enriching their starvation diets. The distribution and purveyance department of the Vilna Ghetto established a "factory" where flour and starch were produced from dried potato peelings. Saccharine was manufactured out of sugar cystals, bicarbonate of soda, and some sweets. Soap was made out of horse bones, laundry powder out of ashes, and syrup and candy out of potatoes. Even substitutes for vitamin B were manufactured.[159] A "vegetable salad" was concocted in the Łódź Ghetto out of vegetable wastes (such as wilted leaves), the less spoiled parts of frozen potatoes, and moldy bread. Skimmed or spoiled milk, the kind usually delivered in the ghetto, was used to make curds. Both the "vegetable salad" and curds were manufactured by tens of thousands of kilograms and distributed among the working people for consumption.[160]

How did the Councils manage to pay for the provisions that were delivered? Because of the total impoverishment of the ghetto inmates the Council had no large amount of capital to work with, and payments for food deliveries could be made only out of income obtained from confiscating or "selling" property of the ghetto inmates to the Germans. Another source of income was the earnings of Jewish laborers in ghetto shops. The audacity of the German authorities went so far as to maintain that the payments they received from these two sources were not enough to cover the cost of supplying the ghetto. The Łódź *Gettoverwaltung*, in a letter addressed to the *Regierungspräsident* on September 21, 1941, maintained that "the purveyance of food products for the ghetto amounts to between 1.3 and 1.7 million Reichsmarks on the average per month," against which the *Gettoverwaltung* was compensated by the worth of the Jewish production and the value of confiscated Jewish property. Measured by the monthly wages of the four most important ghetto "resorts"—the tailor and ladies' garments, carpenter, shoemaker, and hand-weaving shops—this amounted to no more than 115,000 Reichsmarks. And the sale of [Jewish] valuables brought in no more than 100,000 Reichsmarks a month.[161]

It is obvious that the production of the ghetto inmates cannot be measured by the miserable wages, not always paid at that. As for the confiscated Jewish valuables, it may be recalled that during the first months after the sealing-off of the ghetto more than 5 million marks in cash were paid to the food account of the *Gettoverwaltung*, in addition to thousands of pieces of jewelry and furs.[162]

A similar situation existed in Warsaw. We find in a news item in the *Gazeta Żydowska* the following account of the financial situation with respect to payments for food in the Warsaw Ghetto:

> Providing food for the entire population of the Jewish Quarter is estimated at 12,600,000 zlotys a month. To somehow balance this amount, it is necessary to employ no less than 63,000 people 25 days a month at average wages of 8 zlotys a day. Only thus can the balance be achieved. . . . But up until now [July 1941] only 1 in 10 of the labor force needed to cover the cost of food has found employment.[163]

In fact, not employment but the spoliation of Jewish property constituted the basis of payments for the purveyance of food to ghetto inmates.

In some of the ghettos, particularly in the larger ones, the food supply apparatus grew to enormous proportions, employing hundreds of clerks and laborers. In March 1940 five community food shops were put into operation in the Łódź Ghetto, and by the end of 1941 the food supply department of the Council increased to such a size that it became necessary to decentralize its activities among four divisions: bread and groceries, vegetables, milk and dairy products, and meat. The bread and groceries division was in turn subdivided into several sections supervising the movement of merchandise, places of distribution, the bakeries, etc. A network embracing 45 bread and grocery shops, 16 dairy shops, and 16 meat shops was then in operation. In addition there were 4 dietetic shops for sick and other privileged persons (see Chap. 14). As of December 1941 this division employed 834 clerks and laborers. The newly established coal division (previously part of the supply department) employed 702 persons in May 1943. When it was first established in May 1940, it employed 10 persons. By the end of 1940, the kitchen division supervised 130 public kitchens and restaurants, employing some 2,500 persons. At a later date, however, during the months of May and June 1942, the number of employees sharply decreased for reasons to be explained in Chap. 15 of this study.[164] The bread and groceries division also supervised several small factories manufacturing sausages from horse meat, oil, candy, marmalade, and wood alcohol.[165] The cash turnover of the food supply department climbed, accordingly, from 42,904 Reichsmarks in February 1940 to 932,899 ghetto marks in May 1940 (the first month the ghetto had been sealed off) and to 2,770,786 ghetto marks in November of that year. For the entire year 1941, the total turnover of the division amounted to 20,502,765 ghetto marks.[166]

The Purveyance Agency in the Warsaw Ghetto developed into a colossal, almost autonomous institution, supervising all distribution places, bakeries, textile and shoemaker shops, repair shops, etc. By February 1941 it had under its supervision a network of 601 places for distribution of rationed food, 273 places for distribution of soap, and 70 bakeries. All were managed by licensed storekeepers or bakers. The agency also bought fuel, raw materials, and medicines outside the ghetto to supplement the rationed commodities. In addition to all these activities, it operated grist mills and manufactured marmalade and artificial honey.[167] In August 1941 the agency also distributed 2,661 ration stamps for shoes and 248 ration stamps for textile articles (for a population of over 450,000 in the ghetto). The agency was authorized to punish dishonest shop managers, as a rule revoking the rations of their shops.[168]

The purveyance of provisions by the food supply department in the Lwów Ghetto was directed by the economy sector (Sector 6) of the ghetto administration, serving a total of 49 distribution places, according to a public notice of the Jewish Council of January 2, 1942.[169] In Częstochowa the *Judenrat* operated 165 distribution places during 1941: 132 food shops, 32 bakeries, and 26 coal storage places.[170] In the summer of 1941, there were 7 bakeries, 12 to 15 food shops, 6 butcher shops, and 2 dairies in the Kaunas Ghetto.[171] In Šiauliai, a small ghetto, there were only two "cooperative" food stores, one in each of the two separate ghetto compounds.[172]

Nowhere in the ghettos was it possible to sustain life on the allotted rations. Not only were the normal rations infinitesimal—many ghettos, as mentioned, received no food whatsoever for long stretches of time, and large quantities of supplies unfit for human consumption were delivered. In the period from January to August 1941 only 10 percent of the calories necessary to sustain human life was made available to the Warsaw Ghetto.[173] In the Łódź Ghetto food allotted to the laborers at various periods constituted 65 percent of the minimum calorie requirement, and for the nonworking population from 46 percent to 58 percent. In the Kaunas Ghetto Jews were allotted a total of 750 calories a day.[174] The inmates of the Radom Ghetto received 1.3 kilograms of flour a month in the spring of 1941 (i.e., 4¾ grams a day).[175] In the Lublin Ghetto during the month of February 1941, 88,200 kilograms of corn flour, 8,400 kilograms of sugar, and 67,500 quarts of skimmed milk were delivered for distribution among almost 45,000 inmates.[176] Thus during the entire month less than 2 kilograms of flour, 185 grams of sugar, and 1.5 quarts of milk were allotted to each person. In numerous ghettos, small and large, people were allotted nothing more than 100 to 200 grams of bread a day, in addition to the same amount of sugar in some places;[177] no other food was allotted. With some insignificant exceptions, no fuel was allocated to the ghettos. In contrast to this stringent rationing for the Jews, a Polish gentile in Warsaw was given, during the month of May 1941, 3,500 grams of bread, 400 grams of sugar, 400 grams of wheat flour, 250 grams of grits, 250 grams of wheat bread, 5 eggs, 100 grams of meat, and unrationed marmalade.[178] Similar food rations were allotted to the Polish population throughout the Government General.

The situation in the "open" ghettos was a shade better than in those tightly sealed off, particularly in the period prior to the "resettlements." Things were better also in those ghettos where the Jewish labor force was used outside the ghettos, making possible some sort of contact with the local Polish population. Very often in such situations enterprising individuals contributed more to supplying food for the ghettos than did the meager rations allocated by the German authorities. Emaciated by these rations, worn out by hard labor, no human being could have lived on the starvation diet alone for longer than half a year or eight months at the most. Mortality in the ghettos reached disastrous proportions, but instead of increasing food allocations the authorities pressed the Councils to augment the food rations of laborers by decreasing the rations of nonworking people,[179] and the Councils had no alternative but to comply. A comprehensive program of additional food supplies was introduced in the Łódź Ghetto to improve the lot of working people. Soups were served in the shops, special kitchens were opened for workers, additional food was distributed to those working at heavy labor, etc.[180] In the Warsaw Ghetto the Purveyance Agency provided soup and bread for workers employed for the Germans at places outside the ghetto.[181] As a rule, members of the Council and its personnel, medical personnel, the ghetto police, and other selected individuals received additional food rations. In some ghettos minors and sick people were included in these favored groups. It was only human that such a policy was deeply resented by the mass of the ghetto population (see Chap. 19).

In almost all ghettos there were people whose names had to be kept off the registration lists of the inmates: people who had never registered; people who came into the ghetto illegally from other places, escaping from the camps or from other ghettos; people who had returned from hiding on the "Aryan" side; or people whose names were on the lists of people subject to "resettlement" but were saved by chance. None of these people's names could ever appear on the lists of inmates that the Councils were ordered to submit to the food supply agencies, and ration cards were of course never issued to them. Rather than leave them to their fate, however, the Councils usually somehow managed to provide rationed food for them too. Typical in this respect is the Kaunas Ghetto. After the period of "actions" in the summer of 1941, the Germans estimated that there should have remained alive at Kaunas no more than 16,000 Jews. Actually, 800 additional people remained in the ghetto. Their existence had to be concealed for fear that the Germans would promptly "correct" the situation. As no ration cards could be obtained for them, the Council had no choice other than to divide among 16,800 people the food allocated for the 16,000 persons on the submitted lists.[182]

A special situation in regard to food supply existed in labor camps into which males and females between fourteen and sixty years of age were sent outside the ghettos, sometimes in nearby places but often far from the ghettos. In any case, hunger was predominant among them. Labor camp managements refused to accept food parcels from relatives, or if parcels were accepted they were delivered only after guards had gorged themselves on the choicest morsels. Pressed by desperate families, the Councils took over responsibility for providing their fellow townsmen in the camps with food, clothing, and shoes provided by relatives or from the Councils' own warehouses. It took money and constant intercession with the authorities to get parcels accepted in the camps. In the four-month period from September to December 1940 the Warsaw Ghetto Council spent 505,700 zlotys on this service for forced laborers in various camps in the Lublin area.[183] The neighborhood ghettos in Zamość, Chełm, Hrubieszów, Tyszowce, and Biała Podlaska took care of their fellow townsmen, sending food, clothing, and medicines.[184] The same assistance was provided for townsmen in labor camps by the Councils of the ghettos in Chmielnik, Jędrzejów, Rzeszów, Sokole, Radoszyce, and Piotrków Trybunalski, among others;[185] and the Jewish Council of Częstochowa baked bread for laborers, using flour delivered for this purpose by the town's food supply office.[186]

Neither textiles nor leather were allotted to ghetto inmates by the authorities. Nor could Jews buy items of clothing sometimes sold by town shops for ration stamps. People looked very shabby in the ghettos, wearing seedy, tattered rags. The clothing of forced laborers was in utter disarray because of their work out in the open, in rain, or in freezing-cold weather. Sometimes the authorities handed over to the Councils the personal belongings left in the homes of "action" victims. These gifts were usually worn-out discards in shreds. The Germans took the better items for their own use, or sold them to the local German population (*Volksdeutsche*) or to German settlers in the occupied territories. The Councils faced a macabre dilemma in inheriting or refusing the garments of deported victims. Some decided to accept them, as the vice chairman of the Kaunas Ghetto Council put it, "because with the dire need for clothing and shoes, there was no alternative but to accept the dreadful inheritance."[187] On or about August 20, 1942, the town commissar in Kaunas informed the Council of Elders that he would deliver clothes and shoes to the working people.[188] It is not known whether he kept his promise.

By two orders of Arthur Greiser, the Wartheland *Statthalter*

(March 18 and May 1, 1942) the Łódź *Gettoverwaltung* was designated as the "heir" of the property of liquidated ghettos in that province. The first shipment arrived in the summer of 1942. The chief of the office of the *Gettoverwaltung* gave a "gift," in October 1942, to the ghetto of 15,000 suits and 5,000 winter coats for men, 10,000 kilograms of linen and hosiery, 15,000 dresses, and 5,000 ladies' coats.[189] The "gifts" were sorted out and repaired in ghetto shops, and were either sold at low prices or distributed free of charge.

Providing Living Quarters

Moving the masses of the Jewish population into the ghettos imposed upon the Jewish Councils enormous responsibilities: finding shelter, managing tenements, making habitable buildings damaged in the course of war operations, and countless other duties. Commissions to deal with all these problems on an emergency basis were urgently established in some ghettos; permanent housing departments were organized in others. People in need of roofs over their heads included natives who were forced to abandon their homes outside the ghetto borders and newcomers who had escaped or been expelled from their homes by the German authorities before the ghettos were established. According to a report of the housing department of the Częstochowa Ghetto, in 1940 for 4,722 persons (of whom only 29% were natives) 1,541 living quarters were provided. Of the remaining 61 percent, 28.6 percent came from Łódź, 9.3 percent from Cracow, and the others had escaped or been expelled from other towns.[190] Implementing their plan to establish a Lublin reservation for the Jews, the Germans forcibly concentrated a large number of refugees and expellees in Lublin and the Lublin district between the fall of 1939 and the spring of 1940. Simultaneously thousands of native Lublin Jews were forced to abandon their homes in town and in the suburb of Wieniawa. Consequently the housing department of the Commission for Refugee Assistance had to find lodgings for approximately 10,000 people in private homes and communal housing units.[191] In the fall of 1939 the Council in Cracow had to find living space for over 8,000 people in communal and private homes in the overpopulated Jewish section of the town.[192]

The Councils faced a Herculean job during the period when the ghettos were being formed. As a rule the Germans carved out as ghettos the most-run down, bleak, desolate sections of the towns, without sewers and often without electricity or sanitation. The job became even more difficult when the authorities eliminated certain streets or blocks of apartments previously assigned to the ghetto, and it consequently was necessary to squeeze still more people into still less space. Under these irritating conditions, squabbles often broke out between tenants, and the Councils had to mediate between feuding parties.

Rain or shine, the Jews were forced to move rapidly, without adequate means of transportation for their belongings, often escorted by the brutal, inconsiderate police. Amid indescribable confusion the Councils were simply not prepared to make of this chaos something orderly, unable even to find some sort of shelter for so many people in so little time and with so few available premises. Assembly centers for the homeless had to be opened, and temporary quarters were arranged in prayer houses, schools, offices, cellars, and even stables. These were still not enough to accommodate the uncountable needy. For a long time, thousands upon thousands of unfortunate families squatted in courtyards, gardens, fields, or public squares.[193] On top of all these misfortunes, many gentiles whose homes were located within the ghetto limits refused, unless heavily rewarded, to leave or to admit newcomers. In Łódź, for instance, fights took place between Polish owners and Jews assigned to move into their homes. In retaliation, some Poles destroyed furniture that Jews had been fortunate enough to bring with them into the ghetto. In Warsaw 80,000 Poles were forced by the Germans to abandon their homes because they were situated behind the ghetto walls, and 104,000 Jews from the "Aryan" side of the town were squeezed into their places—but not until they had paid off the Polish owners. Nice, comfortable homes of Jews in the "Aryan" sections had to be exchanged for run-down tenement rooms in the ghetto, and for these considerable cash had to be paid.[194] However, there were many cases where people were lucky to find bearable dwellings because of favoritism on the part of some ghetto officials or because they occupied living quarters by force.[195]

In the process of moving into the ghettos, many pieces of Jewish communal real estate—hospital buildings, orphanages, old-age homes, and schools—were left behind. Whatever had been salvaged of the movable property belonging to these institutions, after acts of outright robbery or "confiscations" by the German authorities, was carried over into the ghettos and installed in whatever places were available, a process which more often than not necessitated a great deal of costly adjustment. It was also necessary to find substitutes for equipment left behind. The reputable Jewish hospital complex in Warsaw, formerly spread over a considerable landscaped compound, had to be decentralized and its wards arranged in six separate buildings in various parts of the ghetto. The *Stadtverwaltung* forbade the transportation of the hospital's equipment, and finding replacements was quite difficult. A similar situation developed in Łódź and in Lwów.[196]

When epidemics broke out the authorities in all of the ghettos ordered the Councils to establish hospitals or to build barracks for the sick with contagious diseases. Under conditions of isolation from the outside world, where everything had to be created out of the few available materials and scarce funds within the ghettos, this was a tremendously difficult job.

The task of providing shelter also remained acute after the initial emergency had passed. It was never done satisfactorily, and it remained a constant source of painful discontent. The density of the population in the Warsaw Ghetto for instance, is best illustrated by the fact that in refugee homes between 20 and 25 people would be forced to live in a room measuring 4 by 6 meters. In the homes of natives, up to seven persons lived in one room.[197] In the Łódź Ghetto an average of less than 4 square meters per person was available in July 1942;[198] in Kaunas 2¼ square meters per person;[199] in the Lublin Ghetto five persons lived in one small room in July 1941.[200] Strangers of various backgrounds, diverse cultures, habits, traditions, and ways of life were forced to live under one roof. The extent of clashes between constantly irritated tenants sharing the same lodgings is perhaps best illustrated by the fact that the Apartment Commission of the Warsaw Ghetto included four special divisions assigned to patch up quarrels between tenants. Their work involved mediation, control and investigation of accusations; a mediation court; an appeals court; and a section dealing with the problems of subtenants.[201] A special department to deal with tenants' discords was in operation in the Kaunas Ghetto,[202] and a mediation court in the Lwów Ghetto.[203]

Remaking the ruined premises of prayer houses, schools, and warehouses into living quarters; repairing ruined tenements; building barracks for patients with contagious diseases and for people "resettled" into the ghetto from other places—these were the jobs of the building divisions or economic departments of the Councils.[204] These divisions also put up the ghetto shops. It was their task to find necessary space, adjust it to the requirements of the shops, and secure the necessary technical equipment.[205]

Whether the ghetto was confined within walls, as in Warsaw and Cracow, or within fences or barbed wire, as almost everywhere else, the building divisions of the Councils were given the task of building the walls and fences. The Councils were ordered to pay for all expenses connected with this job.[206] In places where the ghettos were arranged within two or three enclaves surrounded by "Aryan" neighborhoods (e.g., Warsaw, Łódź, and Kaunas), the Councils were ordered to build bridges joining the separate ghetto parts.[207]

The structure of the housing department in the Lwów Ghetto was especially complicated because of the nature of the ghetto topography. The department was divided into two main divisions: Division G—for most of the ghetto, located in the area beyond the railroad bridge; and Division D—the special section for artisans. These two divisions were in turn subdivided into sections (affidavits, archives and shelter certificates, vital statistics and control, executive organs, etc.). A presidium was in charge of both divisions, employing numerous clerks.[208]

The Councils hired superintendents and janitors, organized brigades of volunteer firemen and chimney sweeps. Superintendents and janitors collected rent, kept the registers of the tenants in specially designed registration books and were responsible for the sanitary conditions of the buildings.

At first rent in the Łódź Ghetto was collected by house committees elected by the tenants themselves. These committee also distributed ration cards. After November 1940 rent was collected by the superintendents under the supervision of the economic department. In the summer of 1940, 110 superintendents were employed. Janitors, who for the most part had worked on a voluntary basis or for very small wages paid by tenants, were put on the payroll of the Jewish ghetto administration in November 1940.[209]

An intricate system of house management was implemented in the Warsaw Ghetto. Before the war 6,000 buildings were owned by Jews in the Polish capital. In mid-July 1940 the *Treuhandstelle* began to take over larger buildings with considerable income. When the Jews were confined in the ghetto, buildings outside the ghetto were in the process of confiscation; and those in the ghetto were put under the surveillance of the Jewish Council, acting as an agent of the *Treuhandstelle*. The Council was empowered to recommend candidates to be authorized agents, house managers, and clerks in charge of tenant registration books, with the *Treuhandstelle* confirming or rejecting the candidates. According to the Council's report to the authorities for the period from October 1939 to December 1940, almost all of the 460 recommended house managers were confirmed, but changes had to be made in the list of 57 recommended authorized agents.[210] The Housing Commission cooperated with the municipal quartermaster's office during the resettlement into the ghetto.[211] Supervising the division of house agents, superintendents, and janitors, the Housing Commission employed approximately 2,300 persons in June 1942.[212]

Other Economic Activities

The Councils had to perform many more duties, depending on local conditions and the orders of the authorities. In January 1942 the Jewish administration of the Łódź Ghetto, on orders of the German *Gettoverwaltung*, took over the management of the ghetto department of the municipal electricity company and was paid for this service the amount of 39,000 Reichsmarks a year. The Jewish administration was responsible for collecting fees for electrical current from the ghetto consumers and for preventing cheating.[213]

In some of the ghettos the Councils ventured into animal husbandry, mainly raising cows and goats. Thus in Łódź a department was assigned to raise 100 goats, a score of cows, and some horses (for transportation purposes). In July 1941 an epidemic broke out among the goats and almost all died. When, in the same month, this department took over management of all means of transportation in the ghetto, it changed its name to Department of Cattle Breeding and Transportation. Limited tram transportation in the ghetto, when it was permitted by the authorities in May 1942, was carried out under the supervision of this same department.[214]

To ameliorate, at least in part, the constant dearth of food, some Councils made attempts at farming. In May 1940 the economic department of the Łódź Ghetto set aside for farming purposes several open spaces and orchards in the Marysin suburb. The crop was sold at a public auction in September. This was the main source of vegetables for the ghetto until the available area was reduced in February 1941. Some of the land was then partitioned into small plots and leased. In 1941 plots assigned to a family measured 200 square meters. Families of over five persons were entitled to plots of up to 400 square meters. By the beginning of April 1941, 44,000 square meters had been leased. A special consultative office for the "farmers" was opened in May 1942, and public lectures were arranged for instruction, since very few had any idea of what farming involved. Starting in June 1942 fruit trees and fruit bushes were leased at prices established by a commission of experts. Kibbutzim were also active in Marysin until Rumkowski disbanded them; and there were children's camps which, in 1941, planted 11,492 square meters with vegetables.[215]

The Council of the Białystok Ghetto encouraged planting vegetables in courtyards and other open spaces and opened an "orchard base," selling plants and seeds. Vegetables from the Council's own hothouses were sold to ghetto inmates. By April 1942 an orchard division had been put into operation by the Jewish Council. In addition to gardens existing within the ghetto limits, orchards multiplied at a steady tempo in the many empty places remaining after removal of the debris of houses that had been destroyed; these initiatives to some extent eased the miserable food supply situation. It may be added that the "orchard base" of the Białystok Ghetto was established at the initiative of Tsevi Mersyk, the secretary of the Zionist pioneer organization Hechalutz, and for the most part was staffed by youthful members of Hechalutz. During the high season, in the summer of 1942, almost 300 youngsters worked in the orchards of the Council, and their crop reached 190 tons.[216]

The orchards in the Kaunas Ghetto occupied some 62 acres along the ghetto border on the banks of the river Vilia. They were managed by the economic department of the Council. Women subject to labor duty worked in the orchards. The *Stadtkommissariat* built hothouses there which provided the German high officials with fresh vegetables all year round. There were also private orchards in operation and these too were encouraged to utilize every square inch for planting edibles. To prevent theft, the Council engaged special guards to watch the orchards day and night. Later on, this task was performed by the special youth organization *Ishel* (an acronym for the Hebrew title *Irgun Shomrim le 'Ginot*, "Organization of Orchard Guards"). This organization also conducted undercover cultural activities.[217]

The smaller ghettos also made efforts to engage inmates, particularly youngsters, in farm work. Thus the Council at the tiny town of Strzemieszyce in Upper Eastern Silesia succeeded in obtaining permission from the *Bürgermeister* to start a farm on a plot of 45 acres.[218] In a number of hamlet ghettos (in the Wartheland) the Jews expelled from their domiciles were supposed to draw their livelihood from farming. Here are some details of this "operation." The Jews from Słupce (Konin county), expelled from their homes on the night of July 17, 1940, were concentrated in 14 hamlet ghettos in the vicinity of Rzgów; in the hamlets of Zagórowo and Grodziec were concentrated the Jews from Konin, Golin, Pyzdry, Kleczewo, and Skulsk who were also driven from their homes on the night of July 17; in the 17 hamlets in the community of Kowale Pańskie-Czachulec there were concentrated, in October 1940, 4,000 families from the towns of Turek county (Tuliszków, Władysławów, Uniejów, Dobra, and Brudzew).[219] At the same time the Polish inhabitants of these hamlets had all been expelled and driven into the area of the Government General. The Councils were in charge of the agricultural activities. Having no previous experience, they asked for the advice of the central Jewish economic institutions. Thus in March 1941 the Jewish colony in Bugaj wrote to the "Society for Promotion of Agriculture among Jews" in the Warsaw Ghetto (established before the war). A letter dated April 1941, in answer to a letter received from the Society, states:

The condition of the agricultural buildings is bad. Our livestock consists of seven horses and a score of goats and fowl. We may get more horses and other animals. We intend to raise chickens and till the land. . . . Last year, before we came, corn was sown on some of the land by the peasants who lived here until they were expelled. We intend to use the remaining land for planting potatoes, vegetables, tobacco, and medical herbs which do not need rich soil.[220]

In the hamlet ghettos of the Kowale Pańskie community, Jews were supposed to make a living from agricultural labor.[221] However, all these hamlet ghettos were shortlived and were destroyed during the wave of mass murder of Jews that engulfed the Wartheland in the spring and summer of 1942.

In connection with the desperate attempts of the ghetto Jews to save themselves from starvation by attempting farming wherever possible, it should be mentioned that a few Council chairmen, notably in Warsaw and Częstochowa, helped to continue the activities of agricultural kibbutzim which had been in operation in the vicinities of these cities before the war.[222]

It goes without saying that all these improvised agricultural activities were lamentably insufficient to ease the hunger prevalent in all ghettos because of both the lack of land and equipment and the incompetence of the "farmers" who, as city dwellers, seldom if ever had had a chance to till the soil before.[223]

CHAPTER 6

Public Welfare

FACED BY ECONOMIC DISASTER for Jews at all levels, the leaders of communities and of welfare agencies had to undertake some emergency measures. The degree of affliction which had engulfed Polish Jewry can be discerned in the report of the main office of the Joint Distribution Committee in Poland discussing 13 months of its activity (September 1939–October 1940), where we read, among other things, that military operations in Poland had taken 20,000 Jewish lives [apart from Jewish soldiers in the Polish army, of whom 32,216 lost their lives]. In Warsaw alone 7,000 Jews lost their lives during the month of September 1939; the number of wounded Jews was many times greater. About 50,000 apartment houses, factories, workshops, and business establishments owned by Jews were destroyed all over the country. It is estimated that 120 Jewish settlements fell victim to military operations. In some places, 95 percent of Jewish dwellings burned down. No doubt the Jews in Warsaw suffered worst of all. The loss of Jewish property reached astronomical figures. Over 30 percent of Jewish houses, factories, stores, and workshops went up in flames. Entire sections of the city previously inhabited by Jews disappeared, including the two Jewish business centers located on or around Grzybow Square and Nalewki Street. The military operations produced colossal waves of Jewish refugees who left all their property behind, fleeing toward the larger Jewish communities, particularly Warsaw, which they believed to be more secure. This in turn resulted in the spoliation of tens of thousands of abandoned Jewish enterprises that escaped the bombs and blazes. *"It is no exaggeration to say that over 100,000*

Jewish enterprises were lost because of the military operations!
[Italicized in the Joint Distribution Committee's report.] And yet
even all this is of little import, compared to the misfortunes that
befell the Jews when military operations terminated."[1] Under the
impact of anti-Jewish measures which the occupation authorities
showered upon their hapless victims, Jews were rapidly pushed down
into an economic abyss, condemned to unavoidable destruction by
famine, sickness, and epidemics.

Along with the customary relief activities traditionally carried
out in normal times by the Jewish *Kehilas*, they were now instan-
taneously saddled with a variety of new, much more complicated, responsibilities requiring immediate solution, new forms, new
institutions, and very large sums of money. Consequently, the public
welfare program of the Councils was shaped by the necessity to
finance both traditional activities and newly established basic services dictated by the conditions of life under the rule of the Nazis.
These welfare activities were carried out by the following institutions:

1. The American organization, the Joint Distribution Committee
(JDC) which financed almost the entire relief work of the Jewish
Councils and of the organizations active in public welfare. No welfare work would have been possible were it not for the assistance
of JDC (see pp. 135-42).

2. TOZ and Centos, two institutions of prewar renown, the first
active in the field of health and hygiene, the second in caring for
orphans. Both tried to continue their activities in Warsaw and in
their other chapters throughout the country following the invasion.
After the *Judenräte* were established, the authorities closed down
all Jewish organizations, ordering that their activities be taken over
by the Councils. TOZ and Centos then continued their work either
within the general framework of appropriate Council departments
for health, children, and other public welfare activities or in conjunction with Jewish Social Welfare (JSS).

3. Jewish Social Welfare (*Jüdische Soziale Selbsthilfe* or JSS),
established in the area of the Government General by the end of
May 1940 as the official Jewish body for public welfare. As part of
the general public welfare agency in occupied Poland (*Naczelna
Rada Opiekuńcza* [*Hauptrat für Sozialen Schutz*]), which embraced
the respective public welfare agencies of Poles, Ukrainians, and
Jews) the JSS was authorized to conduct welfare activities only in

the Government General. It had no authority to act in the "incorporated areas."

4. The Jewish Councils. Although not mentioned in the governor general's order of November 28, 1939, it was possible for the Councils directly to handle public welfare projects, including medical aid. There was scarcely a Council not active in public welfare, small as it may have been. Soup kitchens were opened; and relief, food, and medical aid were given to the needy free or for a token charge.[2] But because the authorities treated the Councils as mere instruments in executing their orders, or, as tools implementing the economic exploitation of the Jews, they were, in fact, prevented from devoting all of their attention or even sufficient funds to public welfare. Nevertheless, they succeeded somewhat in softening the indescribable poverty of the ghettos.

5. Some Jewish relief organizations abroad, apart from the already mentioned Joint Distribution Committee, provided assistance in cash and materials. For the most part, these organizations were located in Switzerland. In the incorporated areas, public welfare for Jews was also subsidized sporadically by the *Reichsvereinigung der Juden in Deutschland* up to 1942.

6. In addition, self-help was organized by civic initiative, particularly during the initial period of the occupation, when pauperization was not as universal as later on, and when some Jews were still less economically victimized than the bulk of the Jewish population. This form of relief came mostly along the lines of traditional Jewish philanthropy and was extended to poor natives and refugees alike.

7. The International Red Cross in Geneva supplied food and medicines in the framework of the general relief activities of the IRC in Poland.

We shall limit our discussion here to the public welfare activities of the Councils, touching upon the work of other organizations only inasmuch as it was performed in cooperation with the Councils.

We have already mentioned in passing that the Councils were limited in their welfare work because the excessive demands for material deliveries to the Germans simply swallowed up their financial resources. Thus we read in the memorandum submitted by the Lublin Council to the *Stadthauptmann* on September 13, 1940, that, since the Council had to pay the wages of almost 1,000 forced laborers in addition to the skilled workers employed in the SS camp shops, "the Jewish Council is forced to neglect its duties as far as welfare is concerned, so that what under present circumstances is by far the most important department is idle and paralyzed."

To make more persuasive its request to be relieved of financing forced labor, the Council gave its own interpretation to the order of November 28, 1939, establishing the ghettos, arguing that "in the sense of the decree of the governor general, the *primary* [italics added] task of the Jewish Councils is to take care of the needs of the Jewish population, to provide funds for the subsistence of the poorer classes, to maintain hospitals, dispensaries, hygienic institutions, elementary schools, etc."[3] But the Lublin Council and other Councils which interpreted Frank's order in this way very soon learned its real meaning.

Naturally the occupation authorities well knew how limited the relief possibilities of the Councils were, as is attested by the letter of the *Kreishauptmann* in Busko to the *Amtschef* of the governor general in Cracow on August 11, 1941. In connection with the resettlement of 1,500 completely impoverished Jews from Radom to Busko, the *Kreishauptmann* remarked that "in view of the fact that the Councils will not be able to carry on the burden of public welfare for long, it will fall upon the general local communities and community organizations [*Gemeinden und Gemeindeverbände*]." His suggestion was that the towns that were to be "relieved" of the Jews pay a certain part of the residence tax for the benefit of the *Landkreise* which received the transports of Jews.[4] In the report for the month of August 1940, submitted by the mayor of Starachowice (Radom district) to the *Amtschef*, it is related that during the action "enlisting" the Jews for forced labor, the local *Arbeitsamt* dragged 130 married men with large families out of their homes. The Council was unable to sustain these families, so that general public welfare agencies had to take care of them.[5]

We shall now try to analyze the available reports of the public welfare activities of some of the Councils in various areas of the occupied territories. In the frequently mentioned report of the Lublin Council, we read that the department of public welfare took care of the following activities and institutions: relief for refugees and expellees, relief for the native needy Jews, child care, public health, a hospital (it had belonged to the Jewish community before the war),[6] an orphanage, and an old-age home. The relief committee for the native population introduced a self-imposed taxation for

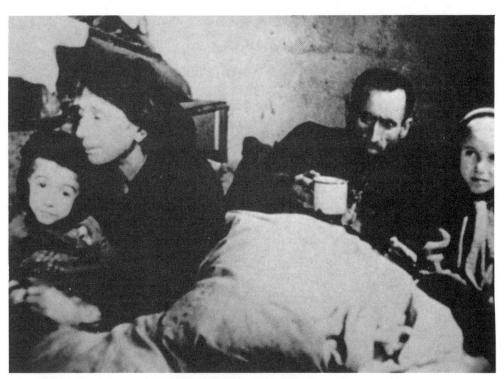

In a refugee shelter in the Warsaw Ghetto.

A public kitchen in the Łódź Ghetto.

relief. A card file of persons registering for relief was established, and special officials verified the data submitted by registrants. The town was divided into 32 districts, each serviced by a tax collector. The income from the tax amounted to 40,200 zlotys in the period from February to July 1940. A special fee of 10 groszy (pennies) for each food card issued was levied by the authorities as an additional source of income for the relief committee. On the average this fee brought in about 3,000 zlotys a month. The committee derived more or less the same amount through a 10 percent apportionment subtracted for the benefit of the committee from the fee charged for exemption from forced labor. On the average the total income of the committee amounted to 12,700 zlotys a month.

The committee initiated its activities by distributing bread and some other edibles. During the period from February to August 1940, 97,192 kilograms of bread, 5,222 kilograms of flour, 5,252 kilograms of grits, 4,100 kilograms of potatoes, 609.1 kilograms of oil, and 1,000 liters of milk were distributed in addition to other food and soap. After the rationing of food was introduced, the committee was authorized to distribute special food stamps honored at the municipal food distribution places. The committee also distributed clothing collected from the population or provided by the JDC. During the winter of 1940, clothing collections from the population produced 1,006 garments and underwear. In all, 1,441 pieces were distributed. The relief committee assisted 3,200 families (10,200 souls) during the month of August 1940, equivalent to one-third of the entire Jewish population in Lublin.

During the bombardment of the town in September, two of the child-care institutions of Centos were demolished. Because of military operations and the ensuing influx of large groups of refugees and expellees, it was necessary to take care of many orphans as well as children who had lost their parents during their peregrinations from place to place. Centos was able to renew its activities in the first days of January 1940, acting as a department of child care of the *Judenrat*. Three kitchens were opened where the children were fed three times a day. When the general financial situation of the Council deteriorated, the children received only two meals a day. The number of children fed rose from 258 in February to 2,063 in September 1940. Of the approximately 500 refugee children, 220 were orphans. Up to September 1, 1940, the kitchens distributed 309,687 meals (2,064 in February; 57,638 in August).

Before being placed on the rolls for kitchen feeding the children were given a medical examination. Deficient children were sent over to TOZ for medical assistance, and those with contagious diseases were isolated. During May and June 1940, the children were given injections against typhus. The report notes that the clothes of the children were very poor. The main office of Centos in Warsaw was able to contribute only 38,650 zlotys for child care in Lublin during the entire period from February to July 1940, despite their promise that the subsidy would amount to 25,000 zlotys a month. Later on, even this limited financial contribution from Warsaw was reduced. Centos in Lublin also received some food from JDC and from the International Red Cross in Geneva.

The orphanage and the old-age home (both located in an antiquated building erected in 1862) maintained 72 orphans and a few elderly men and women. This institution was subsidized by the *Judenrat*, jointly with the municipal government, in the amount of 15,000 zlotys a year. In addition, there were some donations from private sources. The orphanage had a deficit of 25,000 zlotys as of September 11, 1940.[7]

By order of the authorities, over 10,000 persons for whom no living quarters could be found within the small area assigned to the Lublin Ghetto were expelled to various small localities in the Lublin district. They became charges of the Jewish Council and were supplied with some cash before they wandered off to their assigned places. The financially pressed Council could not assist them and appealed to the ghetto inmates for donations. The minutes of the Council's meeting held on March 16, 1941, note that no more than 1,500 zlotys could be allotted to these expelled persons out of Council funds. However, the Council delegated three doctors to practice in the localities assigned as places of residence. A substantial amount to help them (some 14,000 zlotys) came from Jewish Social Welfare in Cracow.[8]

The report of the Cracow Ghetto Council of Elders gives the following information concerning its public welfare work.

On or before September 20, 1939, the Council opened two soup kitchens; by March 1940 there already were five kitchens in operation. During the period covered by the report (September 1939 to September 1940), the kitchens distributed 3,427,554 meals (44,400 in October 1939; 541,185 in March 1940). Two asylums for the homeless were established for 1,500 persons. During the mass influx of refugees and expellees from Łódź, Kalisz, and other places, it was necessary to open two more asylums and, on orders from the authorities, to place the remaining homeless ones in some 40 prayer houses closed down since September 1939. Over 8,000 persons found refuge in these asylums and in private homes.

At the same time the Council was faced with the task of providing food and medical care for approximately 6,000 Jews detained as civilian prisoners in the Bonarka camp, near Cracow. After this camp was abolished, 2,000 prisoners were transferred to the camp in Kobierzyn (also near Cracow). In time, the number of prisoners there climbed to 3,700, for whom the Council provided food and medical aid.

In addition to supporting a number of institutions established after the invasion, the Council inherited from the prewar Jewish community a hospital, two orphanages (one for 123 children with a staff of 8, and another for 23 orphaned sons of artisans), and an old-age home. The subsidy for these three institutions amounted to 26,420 zlotys during the report period. Their overall budget amounted to 155,065 zlotys and the ensuing deficit was covered by private donations.

The Council also gave cash assistance to prewar public welfare recipients and to unemployed refugees and expellees. Pensions were paid to the prewar government officials and to invalids excluded by the occupation authorities from social security benefits. In all, the expenses for public welfare amounted to:

578,000 zlotys (for assistance in cash)
528,000 zlotys (for other public welfare projects)
802,012 zlotys (for expellees from Cracow between
                May and September 1940)
_____
Total 1,908,012 zlotys

This amounted to 45.6 percent of the 4,184,000 zlotys expended by the Council of Elders of Cracow during the budget period from September 1939 to September 1940.[9] Expenses for medical assistance will be separately discussed (see Chap. 7).

Relief work in the Częstochowa Ghetto was conducted by the Council's department of public welfare. In the summer of 1940 it maintained six soup kitchens distributing meals free of charge to working people, to the poor, and also to the intelligentsia at one of the kitchens. On an average, they distributed 5,300 meals daily. The department also maintained an old-age home and an orphanage, and distributed cash to native poor and newcomers, spending 90,000 zlotys for this purpose during 1940. To get the necessary funds, the Council periodically addressed appeals to the ghetto inmates and conducted special cash collections under such slogans as "Holiday Action," "Winter Help Action," etc.[10]

Public welfare in Łódź encompassed a wide variety of activities. On March 5, 1940, Rumkowski submitted to the security authorities a list of institutions whose maintenance he had previously been ordered to take over. He enumerated three hospitals, two clinics, an emergency medical aid station, a kitchen for the poor, five orphanages, and a home for infants. He also included the following institutions whose activities were in part financed by his administration: a home for the aged, three asylums for the homeless, another soup kitchen, a school for the deaf and mute, and a home for cripples.[11]

Care for the poverty-stricken became the first responsibility of Rumkowski's administration. The department of public welfare took over the management of the two soup kitchens already in existence, distributing from 500 meals a day in October 1939 to 18,060 meals a day in September 1940. From November 1939 to September 1940, when the department was abolished, it served an average of 7,825 meals a day, taking care of more than 5 percent of the entire Jewish population. The meals were not popular with the population, because of the poor quality of the soups. More important was the relief in cash and in raw food staples. It fluctuated to between 5 and 6 zlotys, depending on the need of the recipient. Cash and food provisions amounting in value to 343,682 Reichsmarks were given to 52,058 persons during the period the department was in operation.

In the last days of September 1940 mass hunger demonstrations took place in Łódź because of the severe financial crisis of the ghetto. A new relief department was established which doled out cash on a monthly basis according to the following scale: adults— 9 marks; children up to fourteen years of age—7 marks; persons over sixty years—10 marks. However, all were expected to work whenever called. The dole was changed several times, until in the winter of 1941–1942 the sum of 12 ghetto marks was decided upon for every recipient regardless of age. This was so little that, at times, it was not enough to pay even for the hunger rations that fluctuated in value between 5 and 12 marks during various periods of time.

The first phase of relief action, from September till October 20, 1940, reached 124,773 persons, 79 percent of the entire ghetto population. It cost 1,077,176 ghetto marks. By the time the twelfth installment was distributed in September 1941, the number of relief recipients fell to 58,000, or 48 percent of the ghetto inmates, and cost 535,165 marks. Up to September 1941, the relief department spent approximately 10,400,000 marks. The decrease in relief recipients came as a result of the elimination of certain categories of people who earned some money—artisans for instance, and workers who had found employment in ghetto industry. Other people refused relief assistance after being called on to perform hard physical work without any remuneration.

One of the orphanages financed by the ghetto administration maintained 390 children, and one of the two homes for the aged was reserved for the aged among 19,953 expellees from Germany, Vienna, and Prague, of whom 14 percent were over sixty-five years old. A total of 1,178 elderly men and women were placed in this home at various times up to July 1942.

In the part of the ghetto located in the suburb of Marysin, a summer camp for children four to seven years old was established in the summer of 1940. Children of school age were also maintained there, and in time it became a year-round establishment. By the end of July 1941, 1,573 children (4% of them orphans) were placed there. The camp employed 33 teachers, 43 nurses, and 55 technical employees, in addition to 3 doctors, 10 medical and hygiene nurses, and 13 assistants in training. In all, 217 persons were employed. It cost 562,269 marks to cover the expenses of the camp during the year from September 1940 to September 1941. For a time, in the summers of 1940 and 1941, there was also a day camp in operation for children from four to seven years old.[12]

A contemporary document describes the public welfare activities in the area of Eastern Upper Silesia, where, in 26 of the 32 communities in existence, there were in operation 27 soup kitchens, where 350,000 dinners were distributed to 13,915 persons on a monthly basis.[13] In two or three communities, orphanages were in operation, taking care of 115 children; in 9 communities, milk and other nourishing food was given to 970 infants; in 13 (or 17) communities, special nourishment stations distributed food to 555 children from four to eight years old, each child receiving two meals a day; in 5 communities 460 children received a meal once a day; in 4 larger communities, old age homes took care of a total of 270 persons.

Relief in cash was distributed to 3,503 native families and 1,244 newcomers, the needy persons constituting approximately 25 percent of the Jewish population in the area. In addition, special collections were arranged, such as for winter relief, Passover, etc. These actions helped 40,000 persons, or 40 percent of the entire Jewish population. The monthly expenditures for public welfare in the budgets of 21 communities amounted to 85,000 Reichsmarks, between 9 and 40 percent of their total expenses (an average of 27%). The largest welfare expenditure was for the soup kitchens (33%), followed by cash relief (32.5%) and homes for the aged and orphanages (34.5%).[14]

We shall now turn to other occupied areas. The following quotation from a contemporary source concerns the welfare activities in the Kaunas Ghetto:

On March 17, 1942, the Council established a public welfare office to assist the thousands of hungry, helpless ghetto inmates. Clothing, underwear, furniture, and other things left by people killed by the Germans on October 28, 1941, were put at the disposal of the office. They were distributed among laborers who, in tatters and barefoot, dragged themselves every day in freezing weather to work at hard labor in open spaces.

The soup kitchen which was opened in April 1942 distributed up to 800 meals a day to poor laborers and other needy ghetto dwellers, free of charge or for a very minimal price. The soup was of very poor quality, but it provided the sole warm nourishment for the impoverished ghetto inmates.

The public welfare office distributed relief in cash up to August 26, 1942, when a "cashless economy" was enforced on the ghetto by the Germans. Food, wood, and medicines were also distributed, and people were assisted in finding work. On occasion, the forced laborers in the camps in the vicinity of Kaunas, where distress was particularly widespread, received some clothing and food. The home for the aged and the orphanage were initially under the management of the welfare office; later on, because of special conditions, they were turned over to the supervision of the health department.

The German authorities contributed no food, nor cash, nor clothing for the poor [except the blood-stained "inheritance" left by murdered Jews]. All that was needed was provided by the Kaunas Council of Elders.

The welfare office derived a little outside income from donations, from selling the personal belongings of the deported, and from its own enterprises, such as the bakery, for example.[15]

Welfare assistance in the Vilna Ghetto was provided by the department of welfare of the *Judenrat*, the Public Relief Committee, the Union of Writers and Artists, and the Teachers' Union. We shall limit our discussion to the activities of the *Judenrat*. During 1942 the amount of 399,246 Reichsmarks was spent by the department of welfare: 151,318 Reichsmarks during the first six months, and 247,928 during the following six months, an increase of 64 percent. During the first six months the following services were paid for in Reichsmarks: meals (lunches and dinners)—72,201; medical help—47,459; rent subsidies—23,668; cash relief—6,615; old age home—2,375; assistance in cash—32,658. In all, 7,918 persons, almost half of the entire ghetto population, had been given assistance in one form or another during this period. Services and expenditures in Reichsmarks during the second half of 1942 were as follows: 410,619 meals—89,021; relief in cash (including rent for the newly established day home and dormitory for children of the youth group *Yeladim*)—90,529; and for various other forms of relief—approximately 68,000.

The budget of the public welfare activities rose tenfold, from 7,000 Reichsmarks in January 1942 to 70,000 Reichsmarks in December. There were four soup kitchens in January and six in May 1942. The actual worth of public welfare assistance was much larger than is indicated by the figures, because the department paid according to official ghetto prices for food, medical aid, and other services, though prices on the open market were much higher. The amount spent for public relief increased still more when the department took over, in the second half of 1942, the maintenance of additional institutions, such as the dormitory of the *Yeladim*, a day home, and assistance for people engaged in forced labor in the woods. In a single month, December 1942, these new obligations swallowed up over 25 percent of the entire relief budget.[16] Expenditures for public welfare services kept growing "along with the growing pauperization of the ghetto inmates, during the second half of 1942."

The situation became even more acute later on. For the first quarter of 1943, the budget estimated expenditures at 79,450 Reichsmarks in January, at least the same amount in February (the budget for February has not been preserved), and 184,057 Reichsmarks for March, a total of 342,957 Reichsmarks, only 56,290 less than for the entire year of 1942.[17] As expenditures kept growing it was estimated that 28,000 Reichsmarks would be needed to cover expenses for food relief in January, and 34,000 Reichsmarks in March; for the child-care institutions, 16,900 Reichsmarks in January, and 27,395 in March; for winter help, 32,500 Reichsmarks for March (no expenditure of this form of help is foreseen in the January budget); and for relief to the forced laborers in the forest labor camps, 5,000 and 13,000 Reichsmarks in January and March respectively.[18] The budget estimate for April 1943 took into consideration the continuing increase of needy people, in conjunction with the arrival of additional Jews from liquidated ghettos and labor camps, bringing the increase in expenditures for relief up to the amount of 38,475 Reichsmarks.[19]

In the Białystok Ghetto, the Council faced particularly heavy and diversified obligations. On September 11, 1941, the authorities ordered the evacuation of all Białystok Jews to the town of Prużana (the total number of evacuees was actually reduced to 4,500). The first to go were the unskilled and unemployed workers, the most impoverished people in the ghetto. The Germans obligated the Council to cover not only their transportation costs, but also all expenditures incurred before and after the evacuees moved to Prużana, such as food, shelter, etc. A subsidy had to be allocated to the Prużana Jewish Council to prevent the Białystok Jews from becoming a burden on the inmates of that ghetto. The *Judenrat* spent 5,000 Reichsmarks a month (or 50,000 rubles) on this one service.[20]

To help the hard-pressed factory workers and the Council clerks (who worked without pay for long periods of time) as well as other impoverished ghetto inmates, the Council financed both existing and newly established soup kitchens, where meals were served for a small fee or even free of charge. Four public kitchens were in operation in the ghetto: one for workers and poor people with no means; one for the intelligentsia (this one established by private initiative, but later on financed by the Council) serving over 1,000 persons; one for the ghetto police, firemen, and their families; and one dietary kitchen (Matan Be'seter, "secret charity") established at the initiative of the Agudat Israel. The number of meals distributed climbed from some 3,000 in April 1942 to over 7,000 in April 1943. In addi-

tion to all these relief activities, the Council maintained an orphanage, a children's home, and a home for the aged, and doled out cash
to individuals and some food supplies to sick persons.[21]

The number of recipients of charity kept growing in all ghettos
all the time. According to data collected in the Warsaw Ghetto
during the period from May to July 1941, over 65 percent of the
inmates were served in the public kitchens managed by the city
committee of the JSS.[22] (Generally speaking, the Council of the
Warsaw Ghetto did very little welfare work; welfare was mainly
performed by the local branches of JSS, Centos, and the Jewish
Organization for Public Care known as ŻTOS). The card files of the
department of public welfare in the Częstochowa Ghetto listed
14,960 persons requesting assistance (2,169 were newcomers). This
figure represented over 40 percent of the ghetto inmates during the
year 1941.[23] A report from Radom published in the *Gazeta Żydowska*
(which can by no means be suspected of exaggerating the negative
results of the anti-Jewish occupational measures) relates that "because of changes in opportunities to earn a living, the vast majority
of the Jewish population has been excluded from economic life
and has to be supported by the community."[24] A report from the
town of Bodzentyn (Radom district) relates that of the 1,400 Jews
in that ghetto 50 percent were in need of relief.[25]

Aid to Inmates in Labor Camps

Starting in the fall of 1940, the German authorities began to send
Jews to forced labor in labor camps, most of them situated in the Lublin district, where they were maltreated in every respect: food was reduced to meager portions and living conditions were obnoxious,
since the camps were mostly arranged in desolated barracks and
stables, with no plumbing. Forced labor consisted in drying marshes,
regulating rivers, etc. On top of all this, the workers were terribly
abused by brutal overseers and camp commandants. The laborers
addressed heart-rending letters to their families, and the Councils
had to arrange some help for the camp inmates. Though the families
of the laborers tried to chip in, the bulk of the relief burden fell
to the Councils, causing a large increase in the overall expenditures
for public welfare. Expenditures for camp relief by the Warsaw
Ghetto amounted to 520,000 zlotys during the fall of 1940; the
Lublin Council spent 150,000 zlotys on this account, and the Coun-

cils of Tarnów, Radom, and Kielce spent respectively 150,000, 75,000, and 50,000 zlotys during the same period. Some Councils were ordered to build labor camps on their own account. Thus the Council in Biała Podlaska spent 200,000 zlotys for this purpose. Others (in Dębica, Mielec, and Roprzyce) were ordered to provide food, tools, utensils, and blankets for the laborers and to assist their families. The small community in Mszana Dolna was ordered to feed laborers in the camp established in Poręba Wielka.[26]

In the Łódź Ghetto relief for forced laborers deported to labor camps in the Wartheland took the form of assistance to their families. Rumkowski paid them 12 ghetto marks weekly. A total of 961,921 Reichsmarks was paid to the families of workers up to August 30, 1941, while the total sum of assistance in cash sent by workers in the camps for their families during August amounted to only 64,380 Reichsmarks.[27]

The department of public welfare in the Vilna Ghetto assisted forced laborers in the forest area turf camps in the vicinity. In the two months of September and October 1942, 14,461 marks, or 26 percent of the public welfare budget, was spent on relief for them, consisting of food, clothing, medical care, and cash. On a small scale, assistance (mainly medical care) for forced laborers continued till the end of 1943.[28]

Relief of Refugees, Expellees, and War Prisoners

We have already had occasion to mention the spontaneous migration of the civilian population after the war started, when Poles and Jews alike escaped in terror from the mechanized Nazi hordes. Extensive wandering continued after the Polish defeat, people trying to flee from those areas, incorporated into the Reich by the Germans in October 1939. The dimensions of the mass migration are best illustrated by the fact that, according to the official German population census of April 18, 1941, 1,365, or 26 percent, of the 5,239 Jews in Kutno were refugees from 75 different localities. In the small town of Zagorów (Konin district), with a Jewish population of 2,170 in 1940, 1,582, or 73 percent, were refugees. Examples from many other places in the Wartheland are available in the sources.[29]

In the Government General the situation was similar. Thus we find that in the Piotrków Trybunalski Ghetto, in July 1940, 3,762, or 45.6 percent, of the inmates were refugees.[30] There were ghettos in the Radom and Lublin districts where refugees and expellees were actually in the majority.[31]

According to the report of the Warsaw Ghetto refugee committee of December 31, 1940, there were in the Warsaw Ghetto 78,625 refugees from 73 towns (14,823 from Łódź, 6,230 from Kalisz, 2,097 from Włocławek, among others). Refugees numbered 20 percent of all the Jews registered in the ghetto at that time. During the period from January to April 1941, over 70,000 Jews from the western part of the district were driven into the Warsaw Ghetto, and by mid-1941 the refugee population rose to almost 150,000 souls, one-third of all the ghetto inmates.[32]

Following the resolution adopted at the conference held in Cracow by the Higher SS and Police Leaders of Government General and the Wartheland on November 8, 1939, the entire incorporated area was to be made *judenrein*, and Jews were to be evacuated into the southern areas of the Lublin and Warsaw districts.

Beginning in November 1939 the Germans ordered the systematic expulsion of the Jews as well as of certain categories of the Polish population from the incorporated areas of the Wartheland, Danzig-West Preussen, and Bezirk Zichenau which, for the most part, had belonged to the Polish state before the war. These people were chased mainly into small towns of the Lublin, Warsaw, and Radom districts. By March and April 1941 there were 55,245 refugees and deportees (28.5%) in the Lublin district.[33] In the Radom district in 1941 there were concentrated 67,843 refugees and expellees, constituting 20.7 percent of the Jewish population of 327,583 in this area.[34]

This pitiless displacement of vast Jewish masses and concentration in a limited number of ghettos was going on throughout all areas of the occupation.[35] The aim was, on the one hand, to speed up the pauperization of hundreds of thousands of uprooted Jewish families, and, on the other hand, to facilitate their "resettlement" at a later date. Needless to say, these unfortunate people were reduced to complete wrecks by the barbaric conditions of their expulsion; transportation in sealed boxcars, without food or water, during the severe cold of the winter of 1939–1940.[36] The expellees arrived at their destination with little or no clothing, after having been thoroughly robbed of all their belongings. This happened, for instance, to almost 10,000 Jews expelled from Płock, Bodzanów, and other places in the Zichenau district during February and March 1941.[37]

After the arrival of the refugees and expellees at their destinations, two distinct groups became conspicuous in the ghettos: natives and strangers. The latter were in desperate condition, both mentally and economically, bewildered on arrival, with no means, no food, no clothing. Only few could find lodgings with family or friends. The great majority were assigned places in community buildings, schools, prayer houses, and poorhouses. The Jewish prewar communities in the area of Lublin and Kielce, where indigence among the Jews was widespread even before the war, were now burdened with a task far beyond their means: to take care of tens of thousands of refugees and expellees, mostly women, children, and elderly people, robbed of property and belongings, dead tired after their tortured journeys. Pressed into terribly overcrowded rooms, sometimes 30 persons to a room, living in filth, suffering from illness, hunger and cold, they were condemned to early death even before the mass destruction started. Facing this unparalleled social catastrophe, the Councils tried to ease the tragic conditions, if only in a minimal way. The expulsions into the Lublin and Radom districts, and part of the Cracow district, began, as mentioned, in November 1939 with the "resettlement" of thousands of Jewish families from the incorporated western territories and from Austria, Germany, and the Protectorate of Bohemia-Moravia. This was the second of the human waves that inundated these areas, the first having been the refugees who left their homes in haste at the start of the war.

In time the largest concentrations of refugees and expellees formed in Lublin, Cracow, Częstachowa, Piotrków Trybunalski, and Warsaw, the last the largest of them all.[38]

Lublin was one of the very first refugee centers. We find that, at first, welfare assistance was not well organized and was grossly insufficient given the dire need of the refugees. A special committee for refugee aid was set up in December 1939. It started by taking a census of the refugees and expellees. The activities of the committee were split among five divisions: living quarters, food (kitchens), distribution of bread and provisions, warehouses, and medical care. The work of the division of living quarters was very complicated. Not only were there refugees to be taken care of, but those natives "evacuated" from the suburb of Wieniawa also needed roofs over their heads. Living quarters were set up in prayer houses and schools, and rooms were requisitioned in private homes. According to the report of the division, over 10,000 persons, natives and new arrivals, were placed in private homes and collective shelters up to September 1940.

There were three soup kitchens in operation, serving both the refugees and the native poor. Each meal consisted of soup and 200 grams of bread. Because of lack of flour, the distribution of bread was abolished in May 1940, and for the soup a charge of 10 groszy was leveled as of July 15, 1940. Families with children paid 30 groszy. For a large number of the consumers, even this miniscule charge was too much, and consumption in the kitchens fell by 50 percent. During the report year, a total of 603,025 servings of soup and 88,755 kilograms of bread were distributed. Clothing for the needy was collected from native Jews, and some was also received from the Joint Distribution Committee; 1,092 pairs of shoes, underwear, and garments were received from natives, and 2,351 from the JDC. As of September 1, 1940, 5,633 refugees and 2,431 native poor were listed in the card files of the committee.[39]

Former Jewish war prisoners and people "resettled" by force in Lublin and the vicinity were placed in transient camps. All needed assistance. War prisoners arrived starting in mid-February 1940; they numbered 3,224 persons (among them 112 civilian prisoners) by the end of May. A committee on care for former war prisoners and resettled Jews was established. Upon the arrival of prisoners, the German authorities put them up in a transient camp, making their release dependent on affidavits by persons willing to take care of them. Prisoners of war were obliged to leave their uniforms before departing from the camp. The committee submitted affidavits for 2,000 former prisoners of war. Of the 1,367 persons who had arrived in the camp in February, 884 were freed. The rest were ostensibly sent to a camp in Biała Podlaska, but 340 prisoners of war were shot on the way by the guards.[40] The report indicates that the remaining prisoners of war of this group in Biała Podlaska were subsequently released, as were 1,857 prisoners of war who arrived in Lublin between March and May 1940. To comply with the order that prisoners leave their military uniforms, the committee made a collection of civilian clothing; 1,500 suits, each individually addressed to a prisoner of war by his family or a friend, and 194 suits with no designated recipients were collected. Fares were paid for those who could go to stay with their families outside of Lublin. Those who had no place to go remained in Lublin, the committee providing shelter and medical care free of charge. People showed great compassion toward the prisoners of war, offering assistance in every form. By order of the presidium of the Jewish Council, the prisoners were entitled to priority treatment in getting jobs and in locating their families. By September 1940, 1,255 inquiries concerning the whereabouts of the prisoners and 1,135 inquiries about resettled German Jews from Stettin and that vicinity were answered. Among the Stettin expellees driven from their homes on February 14, 1940, there were numerous elderly and sick people who were carried in unheated railroad cars, many suffering frostbitten limbs and arriving utterly exhausted from the inhumane treatment on the trip to Lublin.[41] The relief activities in Lublin on behalf of refugees and expellees give some idea of the scope and dimension of the tasks which befell hundreds of Jewish communities in the Government General.

Another place where the refugees and expellees were concentrated in large numbers was Cracow. As was the case in Lublin, so Cracow was deluged by vast masses of refugees fleeing from their homes in the direction of the border with Hungary. Some 5,000 to 6,000 were Jews, and many chose to stay in Cracow. When, in May 1940, the expulsion of the Cracow Jews started, these refugees were the first victims. Between December 1939 and March 17, 1940, the following groups were "resettled" at Cracow: 424 families from Łódź and 308 families from Kalisz in December 1939; 100 persons freed from a transit camp in Sosnowiec in January 1940; two more transports from Łódź numbering 1,028 and 3,350 families respectively on February 17, 1940; and 580 persons, also from Łódź, on March 17, 1940. In addition, 450 war prisoners were sent to Cracow and, along with civilians from Łódź and Kalisz, were put under the care of the Jewish Council. In all, 8,000 refugees and expellees arrived in Cracow, according to official German data. The actual number exceeded these figures. Some people who had arrived during the first few weeks after the invasion had not registered with the Council of Elders, thus evading the official tabulation later on. By order of the German authorities, all these people had to be provided with shelter, food, and some clothes. By March 31, 1940, 4,386 were placed in two asylums, in prayer houses, and in private homes.[42]

The small cash assistance doled out to the "transient Jews in Cracow," as refugees and expellees were officially classified by the Council, amounted to 51,075 zlotys during 1939–1940. We may assume that together with expenditures for the soup kitchens and asylums, and for medical and child care, the total relief for this category of needy persons amounted to one-half of the 578,000 zlotys spent for relief by the Council.[43]

The exact number of refugees and expellees in Częstochowa is not known. This is because from October 1941 on, the Jewish Council was forced by order of the authorities to stop registering newcomers. To an inquiry by the office of the Government General, the *Stadthauptmann* answered on July 25, 1940, that the town was overpopulated. He noted that, as of his writing, there were registered 14,035 newcomers (refugees and forced evacuees): 6,324 Poles and 7,811 Jews. In addition there were between 4,000 and 5,000 Poles and between 12,000 and 15,000 Jews not yet registered (this number of Jews is exaggerated; it is known that the authorities tended to overestimate the numbers of Jews). It should be added that expellees and refugees, considered illegal and therefore not mentioned in the official lists, kept arriving in Częstochowa all during the time of the occupation. Thus from only one area, Bezirk Zichenau (Płock, Bodzanów), 2,330 Jews were expelled to Częstochowa during the last days of February and beginning of March, 1941, only to burden even more the overstrained budget of the Częstochowa Council. In addition to the Council's funds, a relief committee for the refugees arranged special collections in the ghetto and also received donations from the Joint Distribution Committee (for the most part donations of food). A soup kitchen for the refugees served approximately 250 meals a day.[44]

Relief for refugees and expellees was a particularly vexing burden for the small ghettos, forced to accept tens of thousands of wretched people from large ghettos like Cracow, Łódź, Lublin, and Radom. Of the many instances available, one will be cited here. Ten kilometers from Piotrków Trybunalski was located a small summer resort, Przygłów, where only a few Jewish families made their homes before the war. In a news item in the *Gazeta Żydowska* we read: "A new group of 500 'resettled' Jews from Cracow is expected in the township shortly. . . . We shall do our utmost to make life bearable for them among us." The correspondent notes that, although the community is poor, efforts are being made to open a soup kitchen to serve hot meals for the most needy, at least during the severe winter. Concluding, he appeals for assistance to the "youngest community" to have come into being as a result of the expulsions.[45]

The situation in the incorporated areas was even worse than in the Government General, because the JDC was officially forbidden to send relief to the incorporated areas, while the JSS was forbidden to work there altogether. A case in point is the Kutno Ghetto, established on June 16, 1940. Even before its establishment, the situation of the Kutno Jews was bad, and the Council of Elders urgently requested assistance from the JDC. Conditions grew still worse when typhus broke out, and the ghetto was sealed off by the end of November 1940. The Council received from the JDC two subsidies of 10,000 Reichsmarks each and a shipment of food (in August) which was distributed among 1,513 persons, mainly children. In addition 3,000 Reichsmarks came from *Reichsvereinigung der Juden in Deutschland.* This was only a drop in the sea of dire need. The questionnaire mailed by the JDC to the Council shows that relief for the month of November 1941 alone was estimated in the Council's budget at 8,564 Reichsmarks (2,784.50 for the hospital, 2,405 for bread, 2,877 for the soup kitchen, and 497.50 for cash doles). The number of persons in need of relief kept growing all the time. Thus the number of people served by the soup kitchen grew from 1,102 in August to 1,439 in November 1940, climbing to 2,340 in March 1941; and this was for a population of 6,600 souls. During the winter of 1941, the Council's deficit reached 15,000 a month.[46]

The full extent of the awesome economic situation of the Jews throughout the occupied territory of Poland is described in the report of the Joint Distribution Committee, which states that "the number of Jews in need of public relief as of this writing [end of 1940] is 1,250,000 or 70 percent [this should read 57%] of the entire Jewish population in the Government General and the incorporated areas."[47]

SUMMARY OF THE RELIEF ACTIVITIES OF THE JOINT DISTRIBUTION COMMITTEE IN OCCUPIED POLAND

As we have already mentioned, welfare work and medical aid of the Jewish Councils, TOZ, Centos, and the JSS would have been impossible without the active participation of the Joint Distribution Committee. It is, therefore, only proper to describe the relief work of the Joint Distribution Committee on behalf of the Jews in occupied Poland in more detail.

On September 14, 1939, when the Polish capital was still under the siege of the German troops, the JDC office in Warsaw called a meeting to consider relief work under war conditions. The meeting took place at the office of the JDC and resulted in the establishment of a coordination committee of the organizations active in Warsaw: Centos, TOZ, CEKABE, the committee for the relief of refugees from Nazi Germany, and others which the JDC had subsidized during its quarter of a century of activities on behalf of the Polish Jews before the war. The coordination committee immediately opened soup kitchens, teahouses, and shelters for refugees in schools and prayer houses. Assistance was given to 20,000 refugees and natives who had been made homeless when their homes burned down during bombardment.

After the military operations terminated, the JDC, as an American organization, was the only foreign body authorized to assist the Jews.[48] As soon as October 1939, the JDC established a widespread relief network for the following activities: asylums and other assistance for the incessant wave of refugees and expellees; distribution of food and clothing; measures against epidemics and other diseases; child care; aid to professionals, clergy, artisans, and laborers; individual constructive help and legal advice; emigration (as long as this was still possible); contacts with relatives abroad; and organizing self-help.[49]

Jewish Councils and relief committees spontaneously springing up at that time were entirely dependent on JDC subsidies, as were TOZ and Centos. Later on, when JSS had established a network of local relief committees and "delegations," in the second half of 1940 and during 1941, its work was also subsidized by the JDC.

This is not the place for a thorough analysis of the overall activities of the JDC for the benefit of Polish Jews during the war years. This would require a separate study. We shall here limit ourselves to a mere summary of the highlights and to discussion of the mutual relations between the JDC and the Jewish Councils.

Of the approximately 1,000 Jewish settlements in Poland before the war, 600 fell under German occupation after the invasion. Of these, some 400 were located in the Government General, and 200 were in the incorporated areas. With respect to the relief requested from the JDC, these communities fell into three categories: those able to cover 50 percent of their budgets, those able to cover only 25 percent, and those whose entire budget had to be covered by the JDC.

No sooner had war operations ended than the JDC was literally inundated by the desperate requests of local relief committees, decrying the lot of hapless Jews, particularly of refugees and expellees. All requested urgent assistance. At the same time, delegations from all over occupied Poland besieged the offices of the JDC. The financial means of the JDC in Warsaw were out of proportion to the economic disaster which befell the Polish Jews. It should be stressed, however, that even the limited financial capacity of the JDC was of the greatest import, easing the hunger and poverty of Jews in occupied Poland.

To get an idea of the scope and dimensions of the need for relief, the JDC mailed out, in March 1940, a detailed questionnaire to all Jewish Councils in both the Government General and the incorporated territories. According to initial estimates, there were functioning, as of May 1940, over 200 relief committees at the Councils, all receiving assistance from the JDC. In the Lublin district, subsidies fluctuated between 700 zlotys for a community with 70 families to 43,000 zlotys for a community with 10,000 souls. The whole district (84 communities) received 587,000 zlotys for relief work in May. In addition, local committees received a total of 204,-300 zlotys in contributions from the Jewish population. Thus the JDC covered approximately 75 percent of the budget for public welfare in the Lublin district at that time.[50]

Between March 12 and April 19, 1940, 252,000 zlotys were distributed to 78 communities in the Cracow district, the subsidies fluctuating between 200 zlotys and 30,000 zlotys, with 1,000 and 2,000 zlotys on the average.[51]

During the first half of 1940, the amount of 299,000 Reichsmarks was distributed among the 35 communities in the Wartheland and in Bezirk Zichenau, of which 100,000 zlotys went to Łódź. As has been mentioned, because of strict currency regulations the relief work of the JDC in the incorporated areas was greatly hampered. When efforts to open an office for relief of Jews in this area failed, the JDC tried to send help through the *Reichsvereinigung der Juden in Deutschland,* an effort which also encountered serious difficulties.[52]

A total of 2,361,230 zlotys was distributed for relief purposes in 240 communities, not including Warsaw, during the first half of 1940. On the average, the relief amounted to approximately 10,000 zlotys for each community during the report period, though there were small communities that received only 300 zlotys each. During the second half of 1940 the number of relief committees subsided and the amounts of individual relief sharply decreased. Only 182 committees were in operation, and the subsidies totaled 423,588 zlotys. On the average, individual subsidies amounted to only 2,355, or 75 percent less than the figures for the preceding six months. This curtailment of subsidies was due to lack of funds, a situation already apparent in May 1940. For this reason a large number of soup kitchens were closed: in April 1940 there were 70 kitchens in operation in Warsaw, but in August no more than 34. The number of meals was reduced from 1,140,893 in April to 385,924 in August 1940.[53] It should be mentioned here that the JDC was greatly hampered because transfer of dollar currency from the United States to the occupied zones was not allowed. The JDC in Poland derived its funds at that time mainly from cash deposits made by well-to-do local people who entrusted their money to the venerable American body, with the understanding that they would be reimbursed after liberation. But disbursements for relief purposes were much larger than the receipts from these deposits. On July 29, 1940, the well-known personalities Adam Czerniakow, Mair Balaban, Abram Gepner, Stanislaw Szereszewski, and one of the local JDC directors, Yitzhak Giterman, cabled the main office in New York that, because of insufficient funds, relief work had to be curtailed and soup kitchens for adults closed. Moreover, they requested an increase of $50,000 in the monthly subsidies to furnish food for children.[54] Somewhat enlarged allocations made it feasible to reopen the closed kitchens, and the number of soup portions distributed climbed to 130,000 a day by September 1940. The JDC compensated for decreased cash relief by distributing food received from abroad. For example, in October 1940 29 carloads of flour and grits arrived from the Jewish Relief Committee in Zurich, Switzerland, in addition to 790 crates of other food products (368 crates of canned milk, 217 crates of cheese, 64 crates of soup cubes).[55] The Commission for Polish Relief Inc., in the United States, also shipped a large amount of food to the JDC for distribution.[56]

Among the other activities of the JDC office in Poland, Passover relief should be mentioned. In April 1940, 97 carloads of matzoth and over half a million kilograms (3 carloads) of fats and canned meat were distributed to 560,000 persons (among them 75,000 sick and children) in 344 localities. For the Passover of 1941, relief was much smaller. It consisted of only 32,108 kilograms of matzoth bought by the JDC office in Budapest and shipped, with the help of the International Red Cross, to Warsaw.[57]

During the year 1940, the JDC paid out a total of 7,500,000 zlotys in cash. In addition, food from abroad amounted to 7,235,000 zlotys, a grand total of 14,735,000. According to another source in the same collection of documents, relief in 1940 amounted to only 9,220,000 zlotys; however, it is quite possible that this sum did not include relief in food. During the first eight months of 1941, the JDC in Poland allocated a total of 5,300,000 zlotys for relief. There is no material available concerning relief during the rest of the year. However, if relief was allocated at the same rate, we may assume that it amounted to 2,650,000 zlotys during the remaining four months of 1941, totaling approximately 8,000,000 zlotys for the entire year. However, there is no information available about relief in food and medicines received from abroad during this period. It is known that during the entire 28 months the JDC was permitted to operate in Poland (up to December 1941), it spent approximately 23,000,000 zlotys for relief.[58] According to an agreement, the JSS took over from the JDC the job of distributing JDC allocations to the local committees starting in February 1941. JDC reserved the right to check whether funds were being properly used.[59]

The poverty of the Jews confined in the ghetto became increasingly more acute, but allocations could not be increased. For lack of funds, they were in fact reduced, and welfare activities were retrenched. The JDC main office in New York allocated during the first seven months of 1942 the amount of $600,000, the equivalent of 3,000,000 zlotys according to the prewar official exchange rate for the dollar, unchanged under Nazi rule. This was much less than had been allocated in 1941. How little it meant in terms of actual need can be seen from the budget estimate of the JSS for the first six months of 1942, submitted to the European office of the JDC, at that time located in Lisbon. According to this estimate, the amount of 67,100,000 zlotys was necessary to fulfill minimal relief obligations toward impoverished, famished, and sick ghetto inmates. In the preamble, dated November 4, 1941, it was indicated that relief activities embraced 400 communities with 1,500 institutions for public welfare where 300,000 adults and 30,000 children received food. It was also indicated that even this large number of needy persons assisted did not include all the poor, although expenditures were very frugally estimated. For instance, relief for a community of 1,000 souls was estimated at no more than 700 zlotys, or 70 groszy per person per month. To make the large budget more acceptable to the main office of the JDC, the presidium of the JSS gave assurance—in compliance with JDC prewar policy in Poland—that its branches were requested to finance their activities with the help of donations from local people and that JDC subsidies were to be considered strictly as temporary, additional sources to cover the budgets.[60] This was what the JDC people abroad were told; actually the economic position of the Jews was so desperate by the end of 1941 that it was in no way possible for them to finance relief work. The budget estimate made this clear by stating that in many communities 70 percent of the ghetto inmates were in need of relief.

The JDC tried to get permission from the Government General authorities in Cracow to act as an agent between the Jews of the Government General and their relatives abroad, eager to assist their loved ones in the ghettos. These efforts failed.

The main sources of JDC receipts for relief in Poland were two-fold: loans of individuals to be repaid after the war, and "clearing" transactions of Jewish communities in Berlin, Vienna, and, to some degree, Prague. The situation with respect to loans was favorable, at least at the early stages of the occupation. Jews were not allowed to hold more than 2,000 zlotys, and instead of depositing their cash in a German bank in accordance with the official order, people preferred to make loans to the JDC. To repay these debts, the New York office of the JDC reserved $2,500,000.[61] The "clearing" transactions with the three Jewish communities mentioned were based on the emigration of Jews out of "Greater Germany." The transactions were as follows: the prospective emigrants deposited with the communities their travel expenses, and out of these amounts the JDC paid for their voyages in non-German ships. The communities exchanged part of these deposits for zlotys and transferred the money to the JDC office in Cracow to cover relief expenses on behalf of Polish Jews. With the permission of the German authorities, the secretary of *Reichsvereinigung der Juden in Deutschland*, Dr. Hirsch, and the chairman of the *Kultusgemeinde* in Vienna, Dr. Loewenhertz, regularly transferred money to the JDC office in Cracow.[62] After the emigration from Germany and occupied territories was forbidden by Himmler in October 1941 and after the United States entered World War II, emigration possibilities ceased, and the "clearing" transactions terminated with adverse results for JDC finances in Poland.

According to the sources preserved, mutual relations between the JDC and the Councils were based, on the one hand, on the wide popularity JDC enjoyed among the Councils, and, on the other hand, on its readiness to help severely persecuted Jews. There was one exception: the Łódź Ghetto, where Rumkowski reigned supreme. True to his autocratic inclinations, he requested full powers to decide on the distribution of relief funds supplied by the JDC, which it was not willing to grant. According to Merin, the chief of the Sosnowiec *Zentrale*, Rumkowski received $100,000 a month from the JDC during the summer of 1940. The money arrived from the European office of the JDC in Lisbon. This fact was *"unverbindlich"* ("unofficially") confirmed by the director of the Reichsbank in answer to an inquiry by the *Ernährungs- und Wirtschaftsstelle Getto Litzmannstadt.*[63]

After the JDC was officially forbidden to conduct relief work in the incorporated areas, the sums allocated for relief in the Łódź Ghetto and the Wartheland arrived through the "clearing" channels of the *Reichsvereinigung.* In a report of the JDC representative in Europe of January 1941, it is stated that Rumkowski got 50,000 Reichsmarks out of each "clearing" amount, and that he had already received 35,000 Reichsmarks (!) to date. Out of what the "clearing" had amounted to in October, November, and December 1940, he was to get at least 25,000 Reichsmarks.[64]

Rumkowski also suggested that with respect to relief, the JDC include the area of Eastern Upper Silesia and the Wartheland under his supervision, but the German authorities did not grant his request. Even had the Germans agreed, it is doubtful whether he would have succeeded in his ambitions, because the JDC people abroad simply did not trust him.[65]

More friendly were the JDC's relations with Merin, the boss of the Sosnowiec *Zentrale.* The JDC office, first in Warsaw and later in Cracow, utilized his good standing with the authorities. From December 1940 to the end of the summer of 1941, when it was abolished, his *Wohlfahrtsvereinigung* in Sosnowiec was the recipient of all relief funds allocated by the JDC for the area of Eastern Upper Silesia and the Wartheland. He was also instrumental in obtaining coal from Silesia for the Jewish welfare institutions in the Government General.[66] But the JDC European representatives did not much trust him. His close relations with the Germans were suspicious. In January 1941, he requested the Lisbon office of the JDC to intervene with the Portuguese government to issue him a transit visa to visit Lisbon in order personally to present his relief program. But his request was not granted, although the JDC office in Cracow cabled an expression of its support for the trip.[67]

CHAPTER 7

Medical Aid

THE PERNICIOUS CONDITIONS craftily devised by the Germans to undermine the health of the Jews resulted in the spread of epidemics and in a sharp increase in fatalities, taking a heavy toll of Jewish lives. Along with other urgent obligations, medical aid became yet another burning problem demanding the immediate attention of the Councils. However, before we discuss what remedial measures the Councils were in a position to implement, let's take a look at the various factors that contributed to the drastic deterioration of the health of the Jews.

It can be safely assumed that attrition of Jewish lives through the massive fatalities inflicted by diseases and epidemics was part and parcel of the Nazis' diabolical plan to hasten the physical destruction of the Jews. To achieve this goal, the Germans deliberately created unsanitary conditions which could not but spread contagious diseases. When this result became apparent, the Germans announced a fight against diseases while they in fact aggravated the situation. Rather than extinguishing the epidemics, their only concern was confining them to the ghettos. The outbreak of epidemics also served to spread fear among the gentiles about any contact with "Jewish disease bearers." The seeming necessity to protect the "Aryan" population from contagious diseases made a handy propaganda excuse to justify confinement of the Jews in the ghettos, while at the same time allowing the diseases to have their course and play havoc with Jewish lives.

Actually it had been the other way around: massive contagious diseases and the outbreak of epidemics came in the wake of driving the Jews into the grossly overpopulated ghettos. Moreover, the mass physical destruction of the Jews was cunningly explained by sanitary considerations, as when, on July 11, 1943, Governor General Frank explained the murder of three million Jews to a delegation of German physicians.[1]

While doing nothing to fight the diseases, the Germans interfered with the endeavors of the Councils. For instance, German sanitary authorities did not permit antityphus serum to be delivered to the ghettos of Warsaw and Kutno (among others), though the epidemics were particularly devastating there. Serum was smuggled in and became very expensive. In numerous places Jews were not permitted to buy medicines outside the ghettos but had to scrape together clandestinely from among themselves the available medicines.[2]

There is positive evidence that the authorities were fully aware what the cause of the epidemics in the ghettos really was. Governor General Frank noted in his Diary, under the date of September 9, 1941: "The chief of the [Warsaw district] office, Dr. Hummel: The danger of typhus has increased, because the resistance of the population, particularly of the youngsters, has decreased. The ghetto inmates get insufficient food. In addition, there is not enough soap, and people live in overcrowded quarters. As of today, 2,405 cases of typhoid fever were registered; the actual number, however, is much larger. The fact that the Jews have been enclosed in the ghettos is a blessing, but the ghettos have to be totally isolated."[3]

Of the momentous factors contributing to the deterioration of the health of the Jews, the following were the gravest:

1. The mass expulsions of the Jews from their domiciles in the winter of 1939–1940. Not only was the welfare of the victims undermined, but their arrival in new places of enforced residence caused the outbreak of diseases and epidemics with heavy loss of lives. To give but a few examples: In one of the shelters for expellees in the Warsaw Ghetto (at 15 Stavki Street) 207 of 673 inmates died during the period from March to July 1941, or 31 percent. Mortality swelled ninefold, from 1.55 percent in March to 13.5 percent in July. In a children's home (127 Leszno Street) 333 of 600 children died in May and June 1941. At that time, the death rate among refugees and expellees in Warsaw was five times higher than that of native Jews. They constituted 4.4 percent of the ghetto inmates, but their deaths from hunger, compared to the deaths from hunger of the total population, were 20.6 percent, five times higher.[4] The situation in the Łódź

Ghetto was similar. The death rate of native inmates rose threefold, from 5.5 per thousand during the period from October to December 1941, to 16.7 per thousand in April 1942. However, the death rate among approximately 20,000 displaced Jews from Germany, Prague, and Vienna increased over five times during the same period, from 6.7 per thousand to 37.5 per thousand.[5] In Lublin, during the year from February 1940 to March 1941, the mortality rate among Jews expelled from Stettin and Schneidemühle rose to 18.8 per thousand as compared to 2.4 per thousand among the native Jews.[6]

2. *Impossible living conditions and the crowding of large numbers of people into dilapidated lodgings.* Although these were mentioned in the preceding chapter, we shall here add a few more examples. In March 1941, the population density of Warsaw Ghetto reached 1,309 persons per hundred square meters, with an average of 7.2 persons sharing one room, compared to 3.2 persons sharing one room in the "Aryan" sections of the city. These were average figures, for as many as 20 and even 25 people sometimes shared one room six by four meters.[7] In the Łódź Ghetto 95 percent of all apartments had no sanitation service, no water facilities, no toilet facilities, no sewers. When the ghetto was closed, population density reached 68,000 persons per square kilometer, or nearly seven times higher than at the census of 1931, when 10,248 persons occupied the same area.[8]

An unusual population density was also noted in the ghettos of the Białystok area, with 3 square meters per inmate in Białystok and 2 square meters in Prużana.[9] In the small ghetto of Odrzywół (Radom district) 700 people were squeezed into a place formerly occupied by 5 families, so that between 12 and 30 people had to share one small room.[10] Population density in the ghetto of Wodzisław (Radom district) was also enormous—nearly 7 people in one room.[11] In the Lublin *Restgetto,* as many as 14 people shared small shacks often consisting of only one room.[12]

The situation in other occupied areas was similar. We find in a secret document entitled "Regulations for Treatment of the Jews in Latvia" that at most 4 square meters were to be allotted per head.[13] In the Šiauliai Ghetto, the average allotted living space was 2 square meters per head. After a number of buildings were excluded from this ghetto, an additional 270 Jews had to be forced in among the over 2,000 inmates occupying already uncommonly overcrowded quarters.[14]

In their interoffice correspondence, the Germans themselves indicated that "the apartments allotted [for the ghetto inmates] are as a rule unfit for use. . . . the tenements are so bad that 90 percent are ripe for demolition."[15]

3. *Hunger and freezing cold.* Hunger was an integral feature in the evil strategy of the occupiers against the Jews. The governor general entered in his Diary under the date of August 24, 1942, the following note: "Incidentally, I should like to state that we have condemned 1,200,000 Jews to death by hunger. Naturally the fact that [not all] Jews will die of starvation will, it is hoped, precipitate [more] anti-Jewish measures."[16] Bread, in insufficient and ever-decreasing quantities, was the main food officially allowed to enter most of the ghettos. Only on rare occasions was a trifling bit of some other staple received. The daily ration of bread allocated to an inmate of the Warsaw Ghetto was 107 grams in November 1941; but, on the average, it was no more than 83 grams a day for the whole of that year. In March 1942, 40 grams of bread were allocated, and in May 33 grams. Sugar was received in amounts fluctuating between 120 and 210 grams a month during 1941.[17] The entire amount of food received from January to August 1941 was less than 10 percent of the minimum calorie requirements necessary to sustain human life. No fats were received during all of that time. And, as already indicated in Chap. 5, the quality of the food was bad and sometimes spurious. The chemical and bacteriological institute of the health department of the Jewish Council in Warsaw stated that one-third of the food staples analyzed during the second half of 1941 was found "unsatisfactory."[18] It should be borne in mind that the majority of ghetto inmates lived on allocated food rations only. Moreover, poor people without any income whatever—a substantial segment of the population—sold their food stamps and lived exclusively on soup distributed once a day by the public kitchens. Its nourishment value fluctuated between 170 and 227 calories. Cases of cannibalism were noted in the Warsaw Ghetto: three mothers ate parts of the bodies of their babies who had died from hunger.[19] During 1941 and the first six months of 1942, 25.3 percent and 27.7 percent of the deaths in the Warsaw Ghetto were officially attributed to hunger and utter prostration respectively. The death rate from hunger edema among the refugees and expellees reached 83.1 percent of all fatalities during May and June 1941.[20]

Perpetual hunger was also the direct cause of greatly increased tuberculosis in the Warsaw Ghetto, with a sharp rise in mortality. In 1939, 387 Jews died from tuberculosis, but 754 died in 1940, and 699 in the first two months of 1941. No data are available for any later period. However, taking January and February as a yardstick, it will appear that some 3,900 persons would have died from tuberculosis during the entire year, a tenfold increase compared to 1939. In the period 1931–1933, the death rate from tuberculosis was no more than 8.3 percent of deaths among the Warsaw Jews, taking fifth place in the statistical table.[21] But in the first two months of 1941 the percentage of deaths from tuberculosis increased to 33.7 percent. Children, refugees, and expellees were among the main victims.

The situation in the Łódź Ghetto was no better. According to the estimate of the German authorities, the value of the allocated food which should have been delivered to the ghetto was estimated at 80 pfennigs a day. This was in theory. In practice, however, the ghetto inmates were put on the level of prison inmates whose daily food rations were evaluated at no more than between 30 and 40 pfennigs a day. During certain extended periods of time, the worth of food delivered to the ghetto was as low as 23 pfennigs a day. The everlasting hunger was the direct cause of a large number of various characteristic diseases such as hunger edema, scurvy, prostration, decalcification of the bones, and other illnesses, with tuberculosis taking the first place. During the two-year period from the second half of 1940 until the second half of 1942, deaths from hunger rose from 121 (or 1.8% of all deaths) to 2,811 (or 24.3%). At the same time, death from tuberculosis rose from 623 (or 9.1%) to 2,089 (or 18.9% of all deaths). In other words, deaths caused by hunger were multiplied 13 times, and deaths from tuberculosis doubled during this period.[22] Tuberculosis constituted over one-half of all infectious diseases (54.5%) in the Łódź Ghetto during the years of its existence (1940–1944), with 9.8 percent registered in the first half of 1940 and 83.3 percent in the first half of 1944.[23]

A similar situation prevailed in other occupied areas. According to the "Provisional Guidelines Regarding the Treatment of the Jews in Reichskommissariat Ostland," issued in mid-August 1941, food for the Jews in the ghettos of that area was to be allotted only insofar as the remaining population "can do without," but no more than "barely enough" to feed the ghetto inmates.[24] If one takes into consideration that the non-Jewish population in that area received very little food, one can easily imagine how little the Jews were allotted.

Freezing cold plagued the ghetto inmates. Little or no fuel was allotted to the ghettos and people themselves had to search for heating material. No wood was ever delivered to the Łódź Ghetto; only some coal dust and pressed coal waste was sometimes made available. In desperation, people took apart the remnants of demolished houses and wooden fences in Łódź, or used furniture, floor boards, doors, and stairs to heat the cold apartments. Of the 1,218 deaths that had occurred in the ghetto in January 1941, a great number came as a result of the freezing cold in homes, where children and adults were often found frozen to death.[25] In the winter of 1941, dead bodies of children lying in frozen urine were found in children's homes in the Warsaw Ghetto. Refugees and expellees were found frozen to death in their unheated shelters and in the ruins of bombed houses where beggars and homeless children sought overnight hiding places.[26]

4. *Poor sanitary conditions in the ghettos.* Courtyards were littered. Garbage was not collected for long stretches of time. Because of lack of heating materials and soap, people bathed and changed underwear less frequently. Life amid constant anguish, the unending string of misfortunes, and the torturing pangs of incessant hunger generally caused neglect of body hygiene. Lice plagued the population, particularly the refugees and expellees who, in many instances, arrived in their new places of enforced residence with no more than the shirts on their backs. In the immensely overcrowded ghettos, favorable conditions were created for the spread of diseases and epidemics. Diseases of the alimentary tract, a result of woefully inadequate diet, were another common phenomenon of the catastrophic health conditions in the ghettos. Almost all ghettos were afflicted by typhus at one time or another. Table IV (see p.149) illustrates the spread of typhus and its deadly harvest in four ghettos. As can be seen from this table, the spread of the typhus epidemic varied in the ghettos. Where the living quarters of the population were indescribably bad (e.g., Lublin, Kutno), the epidemic engulfed from 10 percent to over 14 percent of the total population, but in Warsaw and Łódź, with better sanitary conditions (hospitals, disinfectants, quarantine, etc.) the percentage was smaller. The mortality rate also varied: during the period from March to December 1941, almost

42 percent of all deaths in the Kutno Ghetto were typhus patients. In the Warsaw Ghetto deaths from typhus during the period from June 1941 to 1942 were only 3.6 percent of all deaths, and in the Łódź Ghetto, during its entire existence, the rate was still lower, 1.2 percent. It is worth noting that only 4,149 cases of typhus were registered in all of Poland in 1935 among a population of over 32 million.

The measures which the Germans applied to fight contagious diseases in fact only facilitated the spread of the epidemics. (We shall discuss this aspect of the occupiers' policy in Chap. 11.) As far as the Councils were concerned, wherever the sanitary commissions had a chance to show initiative and act without interference from the Germans, as was the case, for example, in the ghettos of Łódź and Vilna, the epidemics did not take on disastrous proportions.[27]

5. Forced labor's contribution to the rapidly increasing death rate of the Jewish population. Treated as slaves, subjected to inhuman treatment, the Jews toiled in various German places of employment, in the ghetto shops, and in the labor camps, in permanent hunger and flagrantly unsanitary conditions. The health of tens of thousands of these forced laborers was permanently undermined, causing a high number of deaths. The working conditions in the Łódź Ghetto were so severe that workers broke down at their workbenches.[28] We find in a report to Rumkowski from the health department on

TABLE IV

	Cases of Typhus[a]	Percentage of Total Number of Inmates	Percentage of Deaths in Relation to General Mortality
Warsaw (June 1941–1942)	18,579	4.6	3.6
Łódź (May 1940–July 1944)	1,355	1.2	1.2
Lublin (1941)	3,200[b]	10.0	—
Kutno (Fall 1940–December 1941)	1,000[c]	14.3	41.9

[a] These are official data, but actually the numbers were much higher. In fear of the draconic measures of the German health authorities, many cases were not reported, and patients were secretly treated at home. During the "resettlements," sick persons usually were the first victims, and this was another reason why they were not registered with the Councils.

[b] According to a reliable estimate.

[c] According to a well-founded estimate. During the period from March to December 1941, there were 663 cases of typhus.

January 8, 1941, that during three days—between the 3rd and 6th of January—172 workers had fainted at work. In a single day—January 5—113 such cases were registered.[29] In some of the shops mortality reached catastrophic dimensions. Thus in the printing shop, 28 of some 40 workers died during the year from August 1941 to July 1942.[30]

The inferno of the forced-labor camps is vividly described by one of the inspectors of the Warsaw Jewish Council who had visited the camps located in the Lublin district in 1941. A few excerpts from this macabre report follow:

> . . . In most camps, people live in old barns, mills, and "airy" sties, with no roofs and no windowpanes. They sleep on bare floor boards or on soiled straw. . . . The living places have no lights, are filthy, totally unfit to accommodate so many people. . . . In a room five by six meters, 75 people are crowded together. Lack of water makes it impossible to maintain any degree of cleanliness. . . . All kinds of vermin, and particularly lice, plague the unfortunate people. Perhaps, in two or three out of over 50 camps, it had been possible, with great effort, to make shower stalls, or a bath, or a laundry. . . . There are camps where people have no chance to change underwear or wash themselves for several months. . . . Nowhere are any measures taken to protect the health of the laborers, and no sanitary facilities are available. The physicians sent by the Jewish Council in Warsaw tried to establish sick rooms and, at best, these were located in peasant huts, without windows, without lights, without beds or bedding. . . . Even very sick patients are piled up on the straw spread over the floors. In many camps, where it was impossible to arrange even such "sick rooms" . . . the sick stay with the healthy inmates in the same rooms. . . . Diseases spread all over, with dysentery and typhus predominant. Many laborers were wounded at work, many lost their lives. . . . No medicines, no medical equipment of any kind are available. . . . Besides mortality caused by diseases, many people died from other causes [meaning the beatings of the overseers]. People who have returned from the labor camps [to the Warsaw Ghetto] have come back with ruined health, prostrated, ill, maimed, with heart disease, tuberculosis, boils. On top of all these misfortunes, those who had returned after November 1940 suffered from frostbite and rheumatism contracted while working at regulating rivers and other water conservation projects.[31]

The frequency of diseases and mortality in the numerous Jewish labor camps in the Wartheland was also very high.[32] And a witness at the *Einsatzgruppen* trial before the Nuremberg Military Tribunal had this to say about the living conditions and the high mortality rate of the Jews in occupied U.S.S.R.:

The Jews were pressed into a few fenced-in huts called The Ghetto. It was like a prison, but without guards to provide food. An unknown number of people died there, even before the *Einsatzgruppen* began the mass murder. . . . On top of this, hard labor caused the deaths of many. . . . Thousands of people tried to escape the fate of their brethren. Most of the remaining ones, if not all of them, perished from lack of food, lack of medical aid, and horrible hardship. Though these victims do not appear in reports, the *Einsatzgruppen* are as responsible for their deaths as the *Führerbefehl* is responsible for the deaths of those victims who died by shooting.[33]

The uncommonly high death rate both in numbers and in percentages in the ghettos of Warsaw, Łódź, Lublin, and Kutno is illustrated by Table V (see p.152). We see that the mortality rate in the Warsaw Ghetto kept rising continuously to August 1942 at the peak of the mass deportations. From August to October 1939 mortality jumped more than fivefold, and twelvefold by April 1942. For comparison of average mortality rates, Table V uses not absolute numbers but the mortality coefficient per 1,000 persons, thus taking into account the constantly changing numbers of ghetto inmates. There were months when the mortality greatly exceeded the average monthly figures. For instance, in Warsaw in July 1941 there were 5,550 deaths, in August there were 5,560, and in January 1942 there were 5,123. The monthly average in 1941 was 3,603 deaths, and 4,255 in the first half of 1942. Furthermore, all the statistical data reflect only deaths registered by hospitals and places of quarantine. People found dead in the streets, mainly refugees and expellees, are not counted here. In one year (1941) 846 dead bodies were found in the streets; and in the one month of March 1942, 290 dead bodies were found.

The heavy toll taken of entire families is mirrored in a survey made in the Warsaw Ghetto among 1,304 families in 1941 (the exact date is unknown). Of the 5,420 members of these families, 123 were single persons. All passed away. Of the 193 families with two members, 31 entire families (16%) died; and of the remaining 162 families, half of their members passed away. Of the 230 three-member families, 11 entire families died (4.7%), while 36 lost two

TABLE V

	Mortality	Increase over Prewar Norm of 100	Average Mortality per Thousand Persons
Warsaw, Aug. 1939	360	—	0.9
Sept.–Dec. 1939	6,560[a]	364.4	5.1 (Oct.)
Jan.–Dec. 1940	8,981	207.7	1.5 (Dec.)
Jan.–Dec. 1941	43,239	1,005.5	10.7 (Dec.)
Jan.–Aug. 1942	29,788	1,125.0	11.1 (Apr.)
Łódż, Jan.–Dec. 1938	2,340	—	10.8
May–Dec. 1940	6,851	292.3	43.3
Jan.–Dec. 1941	11,437	488.7	75.9
Jan.–Dec. 1942	18,117	773.8	159.6
Jan.–Dec. 1943	4,589	196.1	53.9
Jan.–July 1944	2,749	201.4	35.8
Lublin, Jan.–Dec. 1938	516	—	12.6
Jan.–Dec. 1940	1,224	237.2	28.3
Jan.–Dec. 1941	1,430	277.2	47.5
Jan.–Apr. 20, 1942	1,472	912.0	[b]
Kutno, Jan.–Dec. 1938	75[c]	—	10.8
Mar.–Dec. 1941	663	884.0	102.0

[a] This high figure is largely due to the bombardment of the city during the siege in September 1939.

[b] Because of the "resettlement" that had begun on March 16, 1942, it is impossible to estimate the average number of the ghetto inmates for the period from January to April 1942.

[c] According to a reliable estimate.

members each. A total of 1,696 members died among the 1,304 families questioned, including all members of 168 families (12.8%) and two-thirds or even three-quarters of the members of 205 families. Table VI (see p.153) illustrates the mortality rate of the "Aryan" population of Warsaw in 1941 compared to that of the ghetto inmates. Both are tabulated per 10,000 inhabitants. Between April and July 1941 the mortality rate was stable among the non-Jews in Warsaw, but soared almost threefold in the ghetto. In April mortality within the ghetto was almost three times higher than outside, but in June it was more than sixfold.

As for Łódż Ghetto inmates, Table V shows that their mortality started to rise sharply in 1940, reaching a peak in 1942, with a high of 159.6 deaths per 1,000 persons, or 10 times more than in 1938. The most critical period was between January and August 1942, when the average mortality rate reached 1,876 a month (19.7 per 1,000 persons in July). In 1943 the death rate fell to 53.9 per 1,000; this

TABLE VI

	Deaths per 10,000 Warsaw Ghetto Inmates	Deaths per 10,000 Warsaw "Aryans"
April 1941	55.0	18.8
May	104.0	18.8
June	118.3	18.8
July	153.8	—

was not because of improved conditions in the ghetto, but because mortality was mechanically reduced by deporting the patients in hospitals, and the aged and feeble as well, during the "September action" of 1942. The continuing process of selection of human material that had gone on during the preceding three years, with elderly and feeble people dying or being deported, was another factor in the apparent falling off of mortality. In addition, the successful fight against epidemics of typhus and typhoid fever waged by the Jewish ghetto administration during 1943 contributed to the reduction of the death rate in the ghetto. During the winter and summer of 1944, the mortality rate systematically increased, reaching a high point of 505 deaths, or 7.1 per 1,000, in July. The rise of deaths in the ghetto at that period was attributed to widespread tuberculosis. Thus even the healthy human material left in the ghetto after both natural selection and selection by the Germans was unable to endure for long.

The same thing happened in the Lublin Ghetto, where in 1941 the mortality rate was almost three times higher in absolute numbers than before the war. In relative numbers, mortality was four times higher than in prewar times.

In the Kutno Ghetto, which the Germans nicknamed *Krepierlager* ("Death Camp"), mortality during the period from March to December 1941 reached 102 per 1,000, almost tenfold compared to prewar numbers. There were months with still higher mortality. According to official German statistics there were 6,604 Jews in the Kutno Ghetto as of April 18, 1941, but only 6,015 in July. In other words, 589 Jews had died of natural causes or were killed during the three months covered by the report—a monthly average of 26.4 per 1,000, a figure which was not reported for any other ghetto.

Table VII (see p.154) is an attempt to reach some statistical conclusions concerning the mortality rate among Jews under the yoke of German occupying forces, compared to the prewar rate of 9.5 per

TABLE VII

	Average Population	Mortality in Numbers	Annual Maximal Mortality Index per 1,000	Hypothetical Mortality According to Prewar Rate	Increase of Mortality in Numbers	Percentage of the Average Population
Warsaw (Sept. 1939–Aug. 1942)	400,000	84,896	10.7	12,600	72,296	18.0
Łódz (May 1940–July 1944)	110,798	43,743	13.3	5,285	38,458	34.7
Lublin (Sept. 1939–Oct. 1942)	30,600	4,624	12.4	1,160	3,464	11.3
Kutno (March–Dec. 1941)	6,200	663	29.7	60	603	9.7
Vilna (Sept.–Dec. 1941)	17,300	517	9.3	65	452	2.5

1,000. As the table indicates, a large proportion of the ghetto inmates died as a result of conditions the Germans inflicted upon the Jews. In Łódź over one-third of the Jews died. If we consider the average percentage for the four ghettos—Warsaw, Łódź, Lublin, and Kutno (the Vilna material is too fragmentary to be taken into account)—we find that 18 percent of the ghetto inmates in the Government General and in the Wartheland died of "natural" causes, i.e., of epidemics and diseases, or were individually killed. One may reasonably infer that even had the Germans not "resettled" the Jews from the ghettos for the purpose of mass killing, they would in any case have died at a "slow" death rate in five or six years. But the Germans were impatient. They could not wait.

We turn, now, to the conditions facing the Councils in their task of securing some sort of medical aid for the Jews in their struggle to live. From the beginning of the occupation, the Jews were excluded from the general socio-medical services. The authorities demanded that Jewish patients admitted to city or district hospitals on the basis of membership in the social health insurance institutions be removed. Later, when the Jews were forced into the ghettos, Jewish hospital facilities usually remained outside the ghetto borders, and only on rare occasions could the equipment be carried over into the ghetto. The Jewish hospital in Warsaw is a case in point. It went through three phases during the occupation: before the establishment of the ghetto; up to the end of the massive "resettlement" in September 1942; and up to the final liquidation of the ghetto in May 1943.

To begin with, during the bombardment of the Polish capital in September 1939, the hospital's laundry and central heating system were destroyed by fire. The hospital was overflowing with wounded soldiers and civilians, and for lack of beds many patients were lying on the floors. There was not enough hospital linen, it was cold, and moreover the patients went hungry. Many were frostbitten.[34] With the establishment of the ghetto, the hospital was ordered to evacuate. This was a severe order, because it was known that there was no place available for the hospital's equipment and beds within the ghetto. There was no other way but to decentralize the hospital and distribute the individual departments among six buildings in various streets of the ghetto. The transfer met with considerable difficulties. For instance, the German city administration made the removal of equipment contingent on the repair of the ruined laundry and kitchen at an estimated cost of 200,000 zlotys. Another obstacle was that no machinery and no equipment nailed to the wall could be removed. This ruled out the largest and most expensive pieces. A great deal of equipment and other property was lost in the course of moving into the ghetto. The hospital arrived inside the ghetto greatly deficient in linen, blankets, and other necessities. Moreover, the buildings chosen for the hospital were unfit to serve as hospital plants. There was no gas in one, and the water facilities were damaged in another.[35] At the time of the "resettlement," the hospital was ordered to relinquish some of its buildings for use on the Umschlagplatz, the square where the Jews of the Warsaw Ghetto were assembled for transportation to the death camps. Patients sick with infectious diseases were then placed in the children's hospital and in laboratories. After the "resettlement" on September 6 and 7, 1942, when the remaining Jews in Warsaw were assembled within four streets in the so-called "kettle," the hospital was ordered to move for the third time. The staff was greatly reduced, only 200 employees receiving so-called "life certificates." The hospital was then located in a building which had formerly been used as a textile warehouse, and, naturally, had no hospital facilities. On Januray 18, 1943, the Germans carried out a bloody "action" in the hospital, killing 800 patients and over 80 of the staff.[36]

The situation in Łódź was similar. The two Jewish hospitals, the Poznański Hospital and the Sterling Gynecological Clinic, were outside the ghetto. Only the hospital for the mentally sick was located within the ghetto borders. What was left of the equipment of both hospitals after confiscation of the most valuable items had to be carried over into two former non-Jewish hospitals which were located within the ghetto. Both were dilapidated and run down. The Kehila had to pay for repairs of the new buildings and for the items that had been left in them.[37] Three hospitals were established in the ghetto, but there were still not enough to take care of the growing numbers of sick. By March 1942 five hospitals were in operation (including a children's hospital in Marysin) and in addition a gynecological clinic, five outpatient clinics, two clinics for preventive care for children, two stations for emergency aid, one dental clinic, seven pharmacies, one disinfection plant, one antituberculosis station, one electro-medical institution, and a station for insulin treatment.

This widespread hospital system was undermined immediately during the first two days of the "September action," aimed mostly against elderly and sick persons, on September 1 and 2, 1942. Patients able to endure transportation were put in trucks and carried off for destruction. Critically ill persons were killed on the spot. Three hospital buildings were transformed into shops. Only two hospitals for internal and lung diseases and two outpatient clinics remained in operation. However, a diagram of the ghetto's organizational structure as of August 1943 makes no mention of any hospitals. Only the sanitation department is shown, with three bathhouses and a disinfection plant for the use of the shops.[38]

The Jewish hospital in Częstochowa was likewise forced to relinquish its building even before the ghetto was established.[39]

With the outbreak of epidemics, the Councils had to establish hospitals on an urgent basis. This, however, involved large expenditures, and the Councils made appeals for money to the Jewish townfolk. Though aware of the threat of repressive measures by the authorities if epidemics were not effectively controlled, people were in no position to establish more than poorly equipped, improvised hospitals that for the most part were not fit to accommodate their patients. For instance, the hospital in Lublin was arranged in an unfinished building planned as a memorial to the Jewish writer I. L. Peretz. The need to take care of the numerous sick was so great that another hospital for epidemic diseases was established in an abandoned building. In Cracow, a hospital for contagious diseases was opened in a closed prayer house and in a former Jewish school.[40] In the Kutno Ghetto the hospital operated in a primitive wooden shack.[41]

A shortage of physicians greatly impeded medical care in the ghettos, particularly in the smaller ones. Many doctors had been mobilized into the Polish army and many had lost their lives in combat or fallen prisoners to the German or Soviet armies. Others had joined the refugees and fled from the smaller communities into the larger ones. The expulsions of Jews also involved medical personnel, including doctors. During the expulsion from Łódź, which took place between December 11 and 16, 1939, a number of professionals, among them physicians, were taken away.[42] Under the circumstances, it took great effort to provide medical treatment with the available medical personnel. In the *Gazeta Żydowska* one could find, in 1940, many ads placed by Councils in search of Jewish doctors. These ads often stressed that the particular community concerned had been left with not one Jewish doctor.[43] To give just one example: On September 6, 1940, the Jewish Council of the Kutno Ghetto requested the Łódź *Oberbürgermeister* to transfer two Jewish doctors from the Łódź Ghetto to Kutno Ghetto, stressing that no Jewish medical personnel was available in Kutno. The request was denied because there were not enough Jewish doctors in Łódź either.[44] The Kutno Ghetto was served by a Polish doctor, with the permission of the German authorities. Later, in 1941, when sickness caused by typhus in the Kutno Ghetto had considerably increased, the Council succeeded in getting two Jewish doctors—one from Warsaw and another from neighboring Krośniewice—to settle in the Kutno Ghetto.[45]

The ghettos suffered from lack of medicines. When the Jewish pharmacies in the Wartheland, along with all Jewish properties, were confiscated, the German *Apothekergesellschaft* (Pharmacists' Company) took over the confiscated stock. When Rumkowski tried to get back the medicines confiscated from Jewish pharmacies in Łódź, he had to reimburse the *Apothekergesellschaft* 77,000 Reichsmarks.[46] As a rule, the Councils could buy from the "Aryan" pharmaceutical firms a limited quantity of standard medicines and sanitary supplies with the permission of the authorities. Expensive medicaments were denied to the Jews. Only a limited number of pharmacies was permitted to function in the ghetto, operating under the supervision of the Councils and authorized to provide only the simplest remedies. Smuggled medicaments were very expensive and hence inaccessible to ghetto inmates. In the entire Cracow Ghetto, there was only one pharmacy in operation, owned by a Pole whose establishment happened to be located within the ghetto borders.[47]

In the beginning there were only 11 pharmacies open in the Warsaw Ghetto. In May 1941 there were 14, employing 150 druggists and 120 semiskilled and unskilled workers. By August 1941, 19 pharmacies were functioning, including one giving medicines to poor people free of charge. At times 25,000 people were served by a single pharmacy.[48] The Purveyance Office of the Council was authorized to buy medicines in the "Aryan" section of the city, using the *Transferstelle* as an intermediary agent.

Wherever sufficiently trained personnel were available, makeshift medical instruments and medicines were manufactured, and Jewish doctors demonstrated a great degree of inventiveness. In the Vilna

Ghetto, for instance, a vitamin laboratory was producing vitamin B in liquid form—a vitamin cream made from beer yeast, legally and illegally acquired from the beer brewery in the "Aryan" part of the city. Attempts were made to manufacture vitamin D. Calcium and phosphor were produced by pulverizing burned horse bones. The product was called "Ghetto Phosphate." Charcoal and a special iodine remedy were manufactured to combat the epidemic of goiter among children, along with antineuralgic, antirheumatic, and pain-killing remedies. In face of the German order forbidding pregnancy in the ghetto (an order that applied to Vilna and Kaunas Ghettos only), contraceptives (called hoods) were manufactured. The machinery shops made medical scales, sterilizing equipment, vaporizers, etc. At the same time, efforts were being made to supplement all these locally produced items by purchasing and smuggling various medicaments available outside the ghetto. Jewish laborers working in the German Red Cross and military hospitals were particularly helpful in this respect.[49]

In their efforts to improve sanitary conditions in the ghettos and the health of the inmates, the Councils were also greatly concerned to evade the draconic measures taken against the Jews by the Germans after the outbreak of an epidemic. The Nazi methods of "fighting" infectious diseases were well known and were feared not less than the epidemics themselves.

Health departments and sanitary commissions were active in almost all ghettos, operating under various names. The Hospital Office and the Office of Sanitary Activities were in operation in Warsaw until the health department of the *Judenrat* was established in January 1940. All health activities were concentrated in this department, except the collection of the hospital tax, which remained under the supervision of the Hospital Office. The health department established six health centers staffed by specialists in hygiene care and sanitary personnel. Chief physicians were in charge. The department supervised the activities of the two hospitals (operating, as already mentioned, in six separate buildings), three outpatient clinics, a sanitary commission of physicians, eight disinfection units (as of September 1941), four bathhouses, three places of quarantine, and various institutions of public welfare.[50] The Council allocated enormous amounts for medical care: 3,059,000 zlotys was spent in 1940, 28.6 percent of the entire Council budget in that year. Only 541,000 zlotys were collected through the hospital tax, so that the budget deficit of the health department amounted to 2,518,000 zlotys in that single year. Medical care and sanitary work swallowed up increasingly larger sums. During the budget year of April 1941–March 1942, the expenses of the health department rose to the sum of 5,700,000 zlotys (in round figures) or 21.3 percent of the entire Council budget.[51] All these expenses notwithstanding, the health department was able to improve neither the health nor the sanitary conditions in the Warsaw Ghetto. The main reason for this failure was the hostile attitude of the authorities.

This is how Dr. Stein, the director of the hospital located on Stawki Street, described the situation there: "The Jewish hospital is, in fact a hospital no more. It is not even a lazar-house, because the patients are given no medical help for lack of proper medicines. Food . . . is simply a fiction. . . . No more than 700 calories a day . . . not even enough to sustain the body. . . . Patients unable to buy food get hunger edema and quickly die . . . quite an unusual occurrence in hospital practice."[52]

During the epidemic, all wards, except surgical and gynecological, were given over to those sick with typhus; yet there were not enough beds to admit the patients. Two and sometimes three persons were put in one bed; others lay in the hospital courtyard for days, waiting for a bed. There were not enough linen and blankets, and in the unheated wards the patients shivered with cold. A high mortality rate speeded up the hospital's turnover, reaching 24.9 percent of the patients in June 1941, when, out of 1,419 patients admitted, 346 died.

In another hospital, the Bauman-Berson Hospital for children, the situation was no better. Here is an excerpt from notes made by a nurse:

I am on duty from 3 to 11. . . . Two and three children sick with measles are [put] in one bed. . . . Their heads are shaven, covered with scabs . . . lice all over. . . . Other children are waiting in the reception room. I have no beds, no underwear, no blankets, no linen. I call up the chief on the phone . . . her answer is terse: place a third child in every bed with only two patients, that's all. . . . It is very cold in the wards. They cling to each other under the blankets. They are shaking from fever. . . . A child with hunger edema is lying in the hall. It moves its lips begging for a piece of bread. . . . I try to feed it, but he cannot swallow food any more. He whispers: "A piece of bread" once more and falls into an eternal sleep.[53]

A contemporary source maintains that, unfortunately, the inefficiency of the hospital personnel enhanced the hardships of the patients and wrought havoc in the hospital's organization. Preferential treatment of friends, misappropriation, and even thievery were noted. A group of physicians (headed by Dr. Munwes) and communal leaders, appealed to the Council chairman, probably in the second half of 1941, to clear up the situation.[54]

The health department of the Łódź Ghetto was headed by two supervisors: one medical and one administrative. Until September 1942, 170 doctors were employed in the ghetto hospitals, along with a large number of nurses, clerks, and laborers. Twelve doctors were brought down from the Warsaw Ghetto, in addition to doctors who had arrived among Jews deported from Western Europe in October–November 1941. All worked as employees of the Jewish ghetto administration, receiving a monthly salary and a nominal fee from the patients for house calls. However, the doctors usually requested more substantial payment for house calls. As employees of the health department they were under its orders and faced possible loss of their right to practice medicine and a prison term of up to three months for insubordination. The physicians were authorized to exempt sick people from forced-labor duty and to allocate additional food rations. At first they could do so at their own discretion; however, starting on July 6, 1940, their orders required confirmation by the health department.

Here are some statistics to illustrate the work of the hospitals and clinics for preventive medicine in the Łódź Ghetto. In May 1940 there were only 227 beds in the ghetto hospitals, but in March 1942 the number of beds reached 2,100. The five hospitals in the ghetto admitted a total of 11,981 patients during 1941. The hospital of contagious diseases admitted 7,301 patients in 1942 (during the "September action" of that year many patients, as I mentioned, were "resettled"), and 3,476 in 1943. In the second half of 1940, when the ghetto population numbered 157,000, there were 122,841 visits to the clinics and 48,568 house calls. In 1941 there were 242,000 outpatient visits to the clinics and 65,390 house calls, increases of about 100 percent and almost 33 percent respectively. (On the average, the ghetto inmates numbered 153,000 persons in that year.) Despite all efforts, it was impossible to root out typhus completely, and the epidemic flared up from time to time.[55]

The health department in Cracow was established at a meeting of Jewish physicians that took place in February 1940, called at the order of the commandant of the Security Police and the SD, and held in the *Kehila* building under the chairmanship of Dr. Moritz Haber, a Council member. The department embraced the following activities: medical and hygiene supervision of over 50 various communal shelters; disinfection of the inmates and unsanitary living quarters, for which the *Stadtkommandant* put a mobile disinfection unit at the disposal of the Council; systematic sanitary control of the buildings in the so-called Jewish living section of the town. According to a preserved report, the sanitary control took place twice a month, accommodating 30,000 ghetto inmates in some 1,000 buildings with 10,000 apartments. A medical check of candidates for labor duty was also performed by the department.

In the beginning the health department administered the work of 156 physicians (89 males and 67 females) and 110 aides (hospital watchmen, nurses, pharmacists, laboratory assistants, and others). Later, as many voluntarily left town or were deported, only 110 physicians and 76 aides remained. Many worked without remuneration. Only 5 of 13 chief physicians and 2 of 20 doctors were paid by the *Kehila*. Nine male nurses (out of 11), 4 female nurses (out of 17), and 4 clerks (out of 8) also worked on a nonsalaried basis.

The health department also supervised the Jewish hospital, which contained nine medical departments, an outpatient clinic, two chemical laboratories, a radiology institute, and a checkup station for forced laborers. By order of the authorities, a department of contagious diseases was added.

The hospital had 100 beds as of January 1940, and admitted 1,828 patients during the report period (September 1939–August 1940). The outpatient clinic and the laboratories treated 47,716 cases. No contagious diseases of any kind were noted up to July 1940. By the end of September 1940, 36 patients with contagious diseases had been admitted. The small number of cases of contagious disease among a population of almost 80,000 (as of the end of 1939) was the direct result of effective sanitary and medical measures adopted by the health department.

The expenditures of the hospital amounted to 253,583 zlotys during the report period, as against an income of 253,611 zlotys, of which 70,866 zlotys came from the Council and the balance from voluntary donations. The department of contagious diseases spent 5,256 zlotys out of an income of 5,777 zlotys, of which the Council contributed 905 zlotys; the balance was voluntarily contributed by the Jews themselves.

After the first wave of expulsions was concluded, the shelters for refugees and expellees were abolished, and the elderly and patients with chronic diseases were placed in a home especially adapted for this purpose by the Jewish Council. During the summer of 1940 from 50 to 60 patients were maintained there on a monthly basis, serviced by 16 doctors and aides.[56]

The activities of the health department in the Vilna Ghetto were quite diversified and intensive. For prophylactic purposes, the department extended its activities to public welfare for children, and it employed more people than any of the other branches of the Council. In January 1942, 380 people were employed by the department or almost one-third of all employees. The activities of the department involved preventive epidemiology, medical treatment, and child care, with special institutions for each of these services.

The section of preventive epidemiology had under its management two hygiene stations, where, up to August 1942, 91,000 persons were given a bath and had their clothes disinfected; a laundry, which washed 12,370 kilograms of underwear belonging to individual ghetto inmates or delivered by various institutions; and injection stations, which, starting in March 1942, gave 16,353 injections against typhoid fever and para-typhus A and B to some 6,000 persons. (The figures in this report are as of August 1942 unless otherwise indicated.) Beginning in the second half of December 1941, the disinfection chamber treated 87,000 kilograms of underwear and disinfected 620 apartments.

The sanitary and epidemiology section, with 4 district doctors and 7 nurses, had under its supervision 1,216 apartments, 71 courtyards, and 154 public and private enterprises, and made 84,000 inspections during the 10 months it had been in operation by August 1942. To enforce personal hygiene, so hard to keep up under the outrageous conditions of life in the ghetto, the Jewish Council ordered, on August 1, 1942, that bread cards be issued only to persons who presented certificates proving that they had taken baths. Courses of popular lectures on hygiene and preventive medicine were often arranged in the ghetto hall and in the labor units, where advice was given on how to protect oneself from contracting contagious diseases. Seven doctors participated in the first course on popular medicine in September 1942.[57] The section also opened six teahouses which, starting in October 1941, distributed to the ghetto inmates at a nominal price 487,000 liters of boiled drinking water and 44,000 liters of hot water for cleaning purposes.

The sanitation office was put into operation right after the ghetto was established. It collected over 4,000 tons (some 10,000 carts) of garbage, debris, and other refuse. It also disinfected the refuse dumps in the ghetto, jointly with the cleansing brigade. The latter employed 14 people, mainly engaged in cleaning the premises of public institutions. Beginning in October 1941, the brigade washed 2,500 floors and cleaned 133 halls, 200 soiled premises, etc. Also in operation was a separate brigade to fight vermin.

The medical treatment section encompassed the hospital, the clinic, the pharmacy, and the antiscabies station. When the Council took over the hospital on July 18, 1941, it had 160 beds in 3 departments employing 140 persons. By August 1942 the number of beds increased to 237 in 10 departments with 164 employees including 26 physicians, 36 nurses, 44 sanitary aides, and 17 pharmacists.[58] (The activities of the hospital are illustrated by the figures quoted in note 58.)

Because of the outbreak of scabies among school children and deportees to the labor camps, an antiscabies center was put into operation for a time. Up to 2,000 children were treated, beginning in the last days of June 1942. By August 1942 scabies in the ghetto was almost quashed. However, at the end of the month, when people returned from the labor camps, the number of scabies patients again increased considerably.

Child care in the ghetto was conducted in the following institutions: (1) A consultation station was opened in October 1941 and treated 5,714 children on the premises and 1,277 in their homes during the same month. (2) A dairy kitchen (also opened in October 1941) operated intermittently, distributing milk, dairy products, and other edibles hard to come by in the ghetto. Up to 1,600 children were taken care of by August 1942. (3) A regular children's kitchen was opened on October 5, 1941. It started by distributing 250 to 300 meals a day, reaching 1,000 meals a day by August 1942. It was stressed in the pertinent report that "a new kitchen is being constructed which will make possible the distribution of 1,200 meals a day," and that "for some 200 children, the soup they receive in the kitchen is their only daily nourishment."[59] (4) Also in October 1941, a children's home for 60 boys and girls was established. First to be admitted were homeless children, lost or abandoned after the first "actions" in the fall of 1941. Some were later picked up by parents or relatives. A contemporary report states:

The children's health was very poor: all suffered from lice, hunger, and frostbite with wounds and rashes all over their bodies and scabies on their scalps. As a result, many died, particularly infants with whooping cough. . . . On the whole their health has now improved. They have no more lice; frostbite is cured, and scalps are clean. The younger children have gained weight; the older ones do not lose weight any more. Their nourishment meets minimum calorie requirements. The children are fed four times a day.

To enforce general sanitary supervision over the ghetto, a special sanitary and epidemiological police force was formed. The strict application of its hygiene measures was enhanced by heavy cash fines or imprisonment in the ghetto jail.[60]

Summarizing the activities of the health department of the Vilna Ghetto Jewish Council, it can be stated that the high standard of its performance, the high degree of its devotion to public interests, and its professional expertise protected the ghetto inmates from the outbreak of severe epidemics, which decimated such ghettos as Warsaw and Łódź. Such diseases as scrofula among children in the winter of 1942–1943, or typhus in May–June 1943 (after the influx of Jews driven in from the neighboring ghettos of Oszmiana and Swięciany) were soon quashed thanks to the quick and energetic administering of preventive injections, regular observation of suspicious patients, disinfection, etc.[61]

When the German authorities in Białystok carved out the ghetto area, the Jewish hospital, the clinic, and the Jewish pharmacies remained outside the ghetto. At the first meeting of the Council, on August 2, 1941, it was decided to establish two departments to deal with problems of health and hygiene and to open a pharmacy. Two weeks later, there were already in operation a general disease hospital (in the building of the TOZ), a clinic for outpatients (including a dental office), a gynecological clinic, and a hospital for contagious diseases.[62] To equip the hospitals a collection of beds, bedding, underwear, and other hospital necessities was taken up from among the ghetto inmates. After a little time, three pharmacies were in operation. Apparently the Council bought stocks of medicine from the owners of the closed Jewish pharmacies outside the ghetto.[63] The three new pharmacies operated under the Council's management with the former owners working as clerks. An emergency medical aid station was in operation at the clinic.[64]

The sanitary and epidemiological department of the Council took great pains to keep the overpopulated ghetto clean. Mobile brigades made up of a doctor and a sanitary inspector were established, charged with the task of "keeping clean the courtyards, the living quarters, and the inmates."[65] Periodically "weeks of sprucing up" were proclaimed, as, for instance, during the week of February 21 to 28, 1942;[66] and public appeals were made stressing the need to preserve cleanliness.[67] Those who did not comply with the sanitary orders were punished with cash fines or jail.[68] A disinfection chamber was established at one of the two bathhouses,[69] and children were inoculated against diphtheria,[70] typhus, and dysentery.[71]

No large-scale epidemics broke out in the Białystok Ghetto. At a meeting of the chiefs of the Council's departments held on August 20, 1941, the chief of the health department reported that no new cases of typhus had been registered, and only one case of scarlet fever.[72] The prophylactic measures taken by the sanitary and epidemiological department were visibly successful in preventing the spread of diseases.[73]

But the ghetto inmates suffered from tuberculosis. At a meeting of the Council held on May 2, 1942, the chief of the health department reported that tuberculosis had increased in terrifying proportions, causing a fourfold mortality, compared to the previous report period.[74] At the same time, diphtheria among children had greatly increased, presenting the danger of an epidemic.[75] The Council could do nothing against tuberculosis, which was primarily the result of the exceedingly bad food situation. On the other hand, the fight against diphtheria was successful, thanks to an intensive inoculation campaign by the health department.

To train personnel for the greatly increased sanitary and medical tasks, the Councils in some ghettos launched training courses. Before the war in Poland, Jews were seldom admitted to the public sanitary services in the government or municipal institutions, resulting in a lack of trained sanitation personnel.

Epidemic typhus broke out in Warsaw during the first months of the occupation, and disinfection units were formed in the winter of 1940. Six disinfection units were in operation by April 1940, and 12 by September 1941. It is doubtful whether their personnel were well-trained. To prepare qualified sanitary aides, 50 Jews were admitted to the disinfection courses of the Polish State Hygiene Institute. Their training took 12 days, from October 28 to November 9, 1939. Instruction was given by Polish doctors, Jews having been barred from the faculty. The German chief of the health department in Warsaw, Dr. Richter, was present during the final exams.[76]

At the height of the typhus epidemic (June–August 1941), every person applying for work with the disinfection units was accepted, the candidates taking a three-week training course conducted by the health department of the Council. Until September 1941 the personnel of the disinfection units consisted of Jews and Poles, but at the intercession of the Council's commissar for epidemic diseases, the Poles were dismissed. They were brutal in their attitudes, and they pressed for bribes. It should be added, however, that the Jewish members of the units were not free from similar corruption.[77]

In the summer of 1940, the Jewish Council of Cracow opened a training course for hygiene personnel. Some 63 lectures were delivered on the theory of hygiene, and a five-day course in practical work was conducted on the premises of the Jewish hospital.[78]

Training courses for hygiene personnel were also conducted in the Lublin Ghetto where sanitary and health conditions were most deplorable. The area of the ghetto was small, with practically no sewers and very few open spaces. People lived crowded together. The close air in the rooms was stifling, and, because of lack of toilet facilities and garbage containers, people threw refuse and human waste out into the courtyards.[79] In addition, insufficient food rations kept the ghetto inmates hungry all the time. (For instance, in February 1942 Jews in the ghetto were allotted no more than 225 calories of food per day.) The ghetto became a breeding place for diseases and epidemics.[80]

The Jewish community hospital in Lublin played the role of a central Jewish hospital for the entire district. It contained five departments, a section for infectious diseases, radiology and electrotherapeutical departments, an analytical laboratory, and a pharmacy. The personnel, as of September 1940, consisted of 80 employees, including 17 physicians and 17 nurses. During the report year (September 1939 to September 1940) the hospital admitted 2,107 patients of whom almost 53 percent came from outside Lublin. Expenses amounted to 216,546 zlotys (13.4% of the budget), causing a substantial deficit, particularly on account of the newly arrived out of town patients (see Chap. 10). An additional expense was the money the Council was ordered to pay to equip the epidemic department of the city hospital. The Council paid 15,325 zlotys, in addition to supplying bedding, mattresses, and various other pieces of hospital equipment.[81]

When typhus grew to epidemic proportions in 1941, the authorities ordered the establishment of a hospital for contagious diseases. Only 350 patients could be accommodated, insufficient by far for all those sick with typhus, since 581 persons fell ill in that month alone. In December additional hospital facilities for 150 patients were set up. Isolation quarters for 330 patients were arranged in a prayer house.[82]

The authorities "fought" the epidemic with makeshift and purely police measures. By their order, the buildings where typhus had been registered were put under strict quarantine. In September 1941, when the quarantine was first ordered, 130 of 348 buildings in the ghetto were shut off. There were times when almost half the buildings in the ghetto were under quarantine, effectively condemning the tenants to death from hunger. It is stated in a report for July 1941 that it was impossible to deliver food to people trapped in the quarantined buildings. But the Council did not leave these people to die of hunger.[83] As it was technically quite difficult to achieve complete isolation of the quarantined people, the authorities ordered formation of a "health service" with the express duty of keeping the quarantined buildings entirely isolated. The "health service" was established in July 1941, with 325 employees who volunteered for this duty. By September, however, there remained on duty only some 240 of them. The "health service" was unable to keep a full half of the ghetto population isolated, and the Council ordered that on the walls of buildings where no guards could be placed for lack of manpower, special announcements be posted, warning the inhabitants of severe punishment for walking out.[84] In time, more buildings displayed warnings than had guards posted. All efforts to change this obstinate rule and to limit the quarantine to the homes of the sick (as was the practice in Warsaw after the sanitary reform in April 1941) were to no avail. That this measure was quite ineffectual can be seen from the single fact that, in August 1941, 27 of 78 quarantined buildings were ruled shut off for the second time and two others for the third time.[85]

Along with the quarantine, the Germans ordered a strict disinfection. By order of the authorities, the Council established a disinfection and delousing station. A special expert from Warsaw was imposed on the Council by the authorities. He had a staff of 140 specially trained disinfectors and 50 employees from the sanitary police. The Council was also ordered to acquire a truck for transportation of typhus patients.[86]

To cover the ever greater expenses incurred in the course of wrestling with the epidemic, the Council levied a voluntary contribution in the amount of between 2 and 20 zlotys. In addition, a hospital tax of between 2 and 10 zlotys was decided on at the meeting of the Council held on September 20, 1941.[87] Still this was far from enough.[88] Searching for new income sources, the Council decided, at its meeting of October 19, 1941, to request permission of the authorities to charge, during one month only, 50 groszy for each ration card, and to make a collection of cash or valuables and use this money for the establishment of another hospital for contagious diseases. Finally, at the meeting of December 6, 1941, it was decided to levy a surcharge tax of 50 percent of the *Kehila* tax, allowing taxpayers to deduct amounts donated during the previous collection for the new epidemic hospital.[89] However, because of the utter pauperization of the ghetto inmates, all these fiscal measures could not produce enough money.

We have purposely described the Lublin situation in more detail so as to give an idea of the enormous tasks and difficulties the Councils generally faced fighting epidemics under the pressures of the diseases themselves and the terror of the authorities. The situation was even worse in the smaller ghettos, where no Jewish hospitals existed before the war, Jewish physicians were always scarce, and sanitary facilities had to be organized with most limited means. This is what a Jewish physician in Brzeziny (Łódź district) relates:

I am the only Jewish doctor in the ghetto. The medical aide, Kleinert, the nurses Tushinsky and Rosenberg, and the midwife, Buki, are my only assistants. The pharmacy is under the management of Mr. Abramowicz and Miss Mizes. As Jewish patients are not admitted to the hospital outside the ghetto, our task it to establish a small hospital with 25 beds. A house has been given to us. . . . Ladies go around from home to home collecting underwear, beds, dishes, and other things for the hospital. All of us work hard, and, so far, we have no patients. At first I was given permission from the Germans to send the critical cases for surgery to the Łódź Ghetto. Later on, this was no longer allowed. I lost a patient in need of a critical abdomen operation because I could not transfer him to Łódź.[90]

In an eyewitness account regarding the Prużana Ghetto we find the following description:

The Council was authorized to send its doctors free of charge to the homes of poor patients unable to pay, but not all could be treated outside the hospital. All needed hospital treatment. The hospital was the only place where Jews could get medicine. No pharmacies were in operation in the ghetto, and the personnel of the hospital pharmacy used medicines that were smuggled in for a high price. A group of dedicated doctors and nurses worked miracles [in the hospital]. . . . Prużana shared the lot of other ghettos in regard to epidemics. . . . They broke out at a time when all ghettos in the neighborhood were already liquidated, and Prużana was the only one remaining in the area. When the doctors diagnosed some patients sick with typhus, it was necessary to keep this a secret from the Germans lest they might use it as a pretext to liquidate the entire ghetto.[91] The medical personnel arranged a secret emergency isolation ward for the typhus patients in the hospital. The epidemic passed, without anyone in the ghetto even knowing what had taken place. Thus panic was prevented.[92]

The newly created hospital for infectious diseases (mainly typhus) in Mława (Zichenau district) treated 40 patients, with only a single nurse available. According to information of an eyewitness, the hospital served sick Poles from outside the ghetto where the epidemic had also broken out. In contrast to Lublin, the hospital fees for the Polish patients were paid. Despite its primitive equipment, the hospital functioned very well and was praised by German doctors from Königsberg visiting Mława to investigate the efficiency of the antiepidemic measures. The local authorities delivered clothing for the patients and food over and above the rations allotted for the ghetto— probably because "Aryans" were among the patients.

Some 50 outpatients were treated daily in the clinic. Mainly, these were people who had come back sick from forced-labor duty. Injections against typhus were also given. To take care of the cleanliness of the ghetto, a sanitary commission was established which disinfected the homes of the sick.[93]

In conclusion it should be stated that enormous energy and money were invested in sanitary and medical activities in the ghettos amid a constant, nightmarish fear of diseases and epidemics, resulting from the horrible conditions the German authorities imposed upon the Jews.

CHAPTER 8

Administrative, Judicial, and Police Duties

IN IMPLEMENTING forced-labor duty and pursuing their extermination plans and actions against the Jews, the Germans were eager to have up-to-date information on the ages and occupations of ghetto inmates. They therefore ordered the Councils to take over registration of the Jewish population, to make all sorts of censuses, and to analyze the collected data. These administrative tasks were given to the Councils along with various other administrative, judicial, and police duties, usually performed by governmental or municipal organs.

ADMINISTRATIVE TASKS

To record the demographic structure and movement of the ghetto inmates, the Councils (as already indicated in Chap. 4) established departments specially charged with organizing various card files, such as files of native Jews and newcomers, refugees and expellees, those temporarily residing outside the ghetto, those subject to forced labor, etc. The departments were authorized to issue birth, death, and wedding certificates, identification cards, certificates of poverty, etc.[1] The certificates of vital statistics issued by the Council became valid only after they were sent over to and confirmed by the city departments of vital statistics.[2] Some of the departments were charged with still other tasks. In conjunction with the order of January 20, 1940, enforcing the registration of all Jewish assets, the registration department of the Lublin Jewish Council was given the task of collecting the property declarations of the Jews.[3] In Cracow the registration department was charged with distributing armbands with the Jewish star.[4] As a matter of routine, these departments located persons sought by the German authorities, the Red Cross, the Jewish Councils, etc. Tenant books held by the house superintendents also were under the control of the registration departments. Where Poles were forced to move from their residences located in areas allocated to the ghettos, the registration departments remained in touch with the local governments for the purpose of handing over the tenant books of the affected non-Jewish buildings to the Jewish superintendents.[5]

Travel was prohibited for the Jews, and the authorities strictly controlled the movements of refugees and expellees who, as we have seen, inundated occupied Poland. According to the forced-labor orders, each Jew was obligated to register with the local Jewish Council upon his arrival in a new place. The Council was, in turn, obligated to report in writing to the local mayor the list of newcomers at the beginning of every week.[6] To receive a permit for railroad travel or travel by any other means, a Jew had to receive a certificate from the local Jewish Council stating the purpose of the planned trip. In many ghettos this was one of the functions of the registration departments. The registration department of the Warsaw Jewish Council, for instance, issued seventeen such certificates during the week beginning April 16, 1940.[7] The same department accepted requests from applicants for permits to leave the ghetto to obtain the issued travel permits.[8] A special office for Railroad Travel Permits was established in September 1940. An office for Travel Affairs also was in operation in Cracow. The victims of the then current "voluntary" mass expulsion were required to obtain travel certificates, and the office issued 19,103 collective certificates for 42,425 family members during the period between June 6 and September 19, 1940.[9] In the Radom district, requests for travel permits from the entire district had to be submitted to the district Jewish Council (*Oberjudenrat*) (see Chap. 3).

During the time of the "resettlements," the departments faced the difficult and grave task of preparing for the authorities lists of ghetto inmates arranged by age, sex, occupation, etc. Individual Councils each acted differently under these tragic circumstances. (A detailed discussion of this subject will be found in Chap. 16.)

Vital statistics in the ghettos were handled by departments whose titles varied from the German *Standesamt* to the Polish *Wydział stanu cywilnego* or *Urząd metrykalny*, etc. In Łódź, the offices of vital statistics and registration in fact formed one single department of registration and statistics.[10] At first permission was given only for an office of death certificates; later the department was allowed to establish two more offices: for birth and marriage certificates and for identification documents.[11] The department was obliged to submit periodic reports on birth and mortality in the ghetto to the local authorities. In Lwów, a certificate of the circumcision rite issued by the *mohel*, indicating the Jewish name given to the infant, had to be attached to the birth certificate so that the authorities were informed of each Jewish boy born.[12]

Statistical departments in a number of ghettos (Warsaw, Łódź, and Cracow, for instance) were established in conjunction with required censuses of the Jewish population. The collected information had to be analyzed by age, sex, and occupation. In addition the authorities often demanded various other statistical data which had to be delivered by a prescribed date. In the ghettos mentioned, as well as in Vilna, Kaunas, Częstochowa, and possibly in some others, the statistical departments carried out research on their own. In Warsaw, under the chairmanship of Council member Josef Jaszuński, the department performed demographic and economic statistical research along with reports concerning the activities of the Council itself, and periodically the Council published its surveys in bulletins.[13]

In the Łódź Ghetto the statistical office covered almost all fields of the ghetto administration. It was subdivided into a number of divisions: demography, occupations, health, welfare, food supplies, courts, security, etc. The department operated its own graphic and photographic laboratory, where 44 persons were employed in May 1944. All departments of the ghetto administration were ordered to submit reports and statistical data. The statistical office prepared statistical yearbooks and anniversary albums, portraying the activities of the various branches of the ghetto administration.[14]

The vital statistics department in the Cracow Ghetto compiled statistical tables about the influx of newcomers, the occupational structure of the ghetto, welfare activities, diseases, and periodic reports on the overall activities of the Council. One such report, for the period from September 1939 to September 1940, is preserved (stenciled on 134 pages). In the Częstochowa Ghetto vital statistics and general statistics were jointly collected by one department, which issued three bulletins of a professionally compiled *Statistical Year-book* for the year 1940. The bulletins contain 400 pages.[15] The statistical office of the Vilna Ghetto received material from all Council departments and compiled its statistical reports on a monthly, quarterly, and semiannual basis.[16] All these miraculously preserved materials represent first-class sources for research on the catastrophe.

The administrative tasks of the Councils and the police (for more on the ghetto police, see Chap. 18) also included issuing diverse identification documents to the entire ghetto population or to parts of it. It is not known whether all Councils were authorized to perform this task. The relevant sources refer only to a few ghettos. For instance, the district Jewish Council in Radom issued passports (*Personalausweise*) with photos of the bearer. They bore the stamp of the Council's vital statistics department and the Star of David on the first page.[17] The ghetto representative and police chief in the Vilna Ghetto also issued *Personalausweise* during 1943. A note in the passport stated that it was valid outside the ghetto when accompanied by the labor booklet of the bearer. The issuing of food cards was also entered in the passport. The police of the Vilna Ghetto were authorized to issue so-called *Passierscheine*, which entitled the bearer to move in the ghetto area after the curfew hour, but not later than 12 midnight (curfew in the ghetto was at 8:00 P.M.). During the period of the deportations for killing in Ponary (in the fall of 1941), only bearers of the so-called "Yellow Certificates," the laborers and skilled workers, were protected from the massacres. The ghetto police were authorized to issue special pink "Family Certificates" (*Familienmitgliedsausweis*) for the families of bearers of the Yellow Certificates. Another, rather limited, category to whom the Council was authorized to issue special pink "Protection Certificates" was the experts needed in the ghetto who were not included in the ranks of the other protected categories.[18]

After the establishment of the Warsaw Ghetto, the Jewish Council was authorized to issue passes to a limited number of people who had to attend to business affairs outside the ghetto walls. The forms for these persons were delivered and stamped by the German authorities. After a time, these authorizations were greatly restricted and finally canceled altogether. The Council also issued certificates to building superintendents, janitors, and other personnel, hoping

The Warsaw Ghetto streetcar. Jews were forbidden to use the public trolleys.

to protect them against raids for forced-labor duty, but these certificates were not always honored by the "catchers."[19]

The Councils' labor departments were authorized to issue labor cards or labor booklets to the forced laborers showing their days of work. As a rule, these cards (or books) had to be confirmed by the German employers.

The labor departments were also entitled to issue certificates stating that the bearers had been freed from labor duty for certain specified periods of time. We have a certificate of the Siedlce Jewish Council, dated October 26, 1940, stating that a certain town inhabitant had returned from the labor camp in Cieszanów (Lublin district) and had been exempted from labor duty until November 30 of that year. The reason for the exemption is not given.

Another type of labor card (*Aufschubkarte*) is also extant. It was issued for instance by the Będzin Council of Elders on August 17, 1941, with the annotation that temporary exemption from forced labor for the bearer of the card was in conformity with the decision of a medical commission.[20]

Among the preserved personal documents handled by the Councils, there are also the *Ausweiskarte* ("identification cards") of the Będzin Council of Elders. These were to be presented at its mail collection office by persons receiving (or shipping) mail. One of the cards is dated August 17, 1941.[21]

In the Łódź Ghetto the system of issuing personal documents was particularly involved. Before the ghetto was closed, each ghetto inmate received his identification card together with an armband. The identification cards were canceled by the end of 1940 and ordered to be exchanged for new ones with photos.[22] At the obligatory registration after change of address, each person received a new registration card at the registration office. As mentioned above, divisions of the vital statistics department (birth, mortality, and weddings and divorces) were authorized to issue certificates honored by the German authorities. Copies were forwarded to the municipal *Standesamt*.[23] Numerous workshops issued labor cards to their own workers, entitling them to move about in the ghetto after the curfew hour.[24] The cards were helpful during the raids which occurred frequently in the ghetto. The greatly enlarged food-providing departments also issued various cards and certificates to the ghetto inhabitants,[25] and the ghetto police issued certificates entitling policemen to move about undisturbed in the ghetto.[26]

Apparently the Councils were designated as the places where all sorts of official documents had to be submitted after they were invalidated. One example: the *Hauptmann* in Lublin county ordered that all canceled documents issued to the Jews in Biskupice were to be delivered to the Lublin Jewish Council under threat of heavy penalties.[27]

MAIL SERVICE

The post office or mail department was another vital organ of the Jewish Councils. It was the only official channel linking the isolated ghettos with the outer world. Not everywhere, however, did the authorities permit a post office in the ghetto. The Białystok Ghetto, for instance, was denied this privilege; but many much smaller ghettos (as, for instance, Prużana), though located in the same district, were given permission.[28] It is hard to say what motivated the Nazi bureaucrats.

Taking over mail services was a gradual process. Even before ghettoization, the use of the post offices had been denied to individual Jews, and their incoming mail had been delivered in bulk to the Councils for distribution. As early as January 1940 the Jewish Council of Lublin was ordered to take over this task. In mid-February, the Council's post office was authorized to accept packages for parcel post and to sell stamps. These functions continued till September 1940, when a special post office (No. 4) was opened in the city for outgoing Jewish mail. The Council's post office distributed incoming mail and sold stamps and mail forms as before.[29] After the ghetto was established in March 1941 the Council took over the entire mail service.

In Łódź the local post office stopped delivering mail to Jews in February 1940. The *Judenpost* ("Jewish mail") was delivered to the *Kehila* building where it was sorted out by streets and houses, the addressees personally picking up their mail. In the ghetto, closed on May 1, 1940, the delivery and collection of mail was accomplished along the line of an agreement reached between Rumkowski and the representative of the German post service. By December 1940 the mail department in the ghetto employed 139 people: 62 clerks, 50 letter carriers, and 27 messengers.[30]

Until enclosed in the ghetto, the Jews of Warsaw had access to the general post offices in town. They were, however, ordered to use only one window, forming a line on the left. Starting on December 1, 1940, after the ghetto was sealed off on November 15, an agreement was reached with the German postal service: the ghetto post office would deliver to the inmates parcels forwarded by the German post office. The same procedure was applied to general mail, starting on December 23. After January 15, 1941, the Jewish Council took over the entire postal service in the ghetto. Two post offices were in operation in the ghetto. During the initial stage of postal activities, 63 of the 94 employees were letter carriers.[31]

The agreement regarding mail service for the Jews of the Warsaw Ghetto was concluded between the chairman of the Jewish Council, Adam Czerniakow, and the director of Post Office No. C-I in Warsaw on January 15, 1941. Among other things, it stated that the Council would handle all outgoing and incoming mail, using persons authorized for this work (*Postemfangbeauftragte*); that the German post office would arrange a special exchange office (*Postaustauschstelle*); and that the Jewish Council would pay for the maintenance of this office while making a cash accounting on a daily basis. With small differences, this agreement was incorporated into the order regulating mail service in the ghettos in the entire area of the Government General. The Councils in the Government General were entitled to a 25 percent surcharge on postage.[32]

The Jewish post office in the Warsaw Ghetto charged one zloty for regular parcel post and one-half zloty for a food parcel. Part of this fee went to compensate the German post office and to cover the cost of mail storage in the ghetto.[33]

The postal stamp on outgoing mail included the word *Judenrat*, along with the name of the town and the date. Outgoing Jewish mail in Cracow bore the German inscription *Ausgeliefert durch den Judenrat* (Delivered by the Jewish Council) and a three-line stamped inscription in Yiddish, *Yidische Gemeinde/Kroke/postfarkershtele* (Jewish Community/Cracow/post office) followed by the date.[34] In Radom outgoing mail was stamped *Der Postbeauftragte des Ober-Ältestenrates der jüdischen Bevölkerung in Radom* ("Authorized for mail service by the district Jewish Council in Radom").[35] In Warsaw, as in other places, each outgoing telegram had to be certified by the Jewish Council.[36]

The fee for mail service to which the Councils were entitled was a source of income but also of discontent, particularly as some rates, in Warsaw for instance, at a certain period amounted to a surcharge of 100 percent over the official rate.[37] It is related about the Żelechów Ghetto that "seeing that so many parcels are being sent to Warsaw, the Council has made them a source of income," imposing new fees.[38] The mail department in the Lublin Ghetto deposited 18,850 zlotys in the treasury of the Council as "income" for the period from January to September 1940.[39]

In some ghettos part of the income from mail surcharges was used to subsidize the Jewish Social Welfare (JSS). In the town of Janów Lubelski, the *Kreishauptmann* authorized the local branch of the JSS to take over the Jewish post service. Following this example, the central office of the *Bevölkerungswesen und Fürsorge* department in Cracow suggested that the presidium of the JSS take over the post office service in other places, but the presidium did not accept the offer "on principle."[40]

Mail exchange between the ghettos and the outer world was often disrupted. Sometimes, as in Łódź for instance, there was a complete stoppage of mail services.[41] As a rule, mail was not delivered, or was greatly curtailed during "resettlement" actions.

Stoppage of parcel post was a particularly frequent piece of chicanery. For a time, starting on January 1, 1941, no parcels from abroad were delivered in the Warsaw Ghetto.[42] On November 21, 1941, the director of the general post office in Cracow ordered that, starting December 1, no parcels would be accepted from the Jews in the Government General, ostensibly for sanitary reasons.[43] This order was not fully effective in some places—in Warsaw, for example —where parcels would arrive from the provinces, apparently shipped by "Aryan" friends.

The German post offices would sometimes confiscate parcels addressed to Jews. In the Łódź Ghetto this was the practice almost until the end of the ghetto's existence. The authorities treated the parcels as smuggled merchandise, and Rumkowski considered that parcels from outside gave the receivers a certain independence, running counter to his plan for making the ghetto a labor camp where all inmates would be toiling to earn a living.

THE GHETTO COURTS

The court departments, or legal departments, were a peculiarity of the so-called "ghetto self-government." Excluded from the jurisdiction of the general courts in civil matters, the Jews had to establish a separate judicial apparatus. As the only Jewish public body recognized by the authorities, the Councils were, from the beginning, asked to pass judgment in cases of litigation. At first, mediation panels were established to deal with litigation between tenants and subtenants growing out of the abnormal living conditions in the ghetto. This was done, for instance, in Żyrardów, Cracow, Lublin, and Łowicz among other places.[44] Right after the ghetto was established in Warsaw, the Jewish Council asked the authorities for permission to establish a mediation panel to consider litigation involving living quarters. By January 1941 there was also a mediation appeal panel.[45] A mediation panel for tenants was established in Lwów.[46] The mediation panel in Cracow was organizationally connected with the office for legal assistance, which was very busy assisting poverty-stricken people during the mass expulsion of Jews in the first half of 1940.

Another factor that made the establishment of the courts necessary was the complex of problems arising out of forced-labor duty, breeding discord between those subject to labor and those in charge of the painful task of enforcing this severe duty. On October 24, 1941, the Council of Elders of the Kaunas Ghetto established a labor emergency court "for the purpose of publicly condemning persons willfully dodging the duty of forced labor and thus endangering the entire community."[47] As can be seen from the organizational chart of the Council of Elders, the criminal department in Częstochowa was organizationally linked with the department of forced labor, a clear indication that its main task was to consider cases of people trying to dodge the severe duty.

In certain places, courts were established by public initiative. At a meeting of Jewish lawyers in Częstochowa held on December 26, 1939, a decision was taken to establish a mediation panel. By the end of 1940, the panel had a staff of 35 people, of whom 23 were lawyers.[48]

A "judicial panel" was established in the Vilna Ghetto on February 28, 1942, to give legal advice and provide representation in court for the inmates. It consisted of 38 members: lawyers, bar applicants, and law students without previous court experience.[49]

The legal and police investigation departments in some ghettos were actually the nuclei of the courts. Thus, until a court was established in the Łódź Ghetto in June 1940, the investigation division of the ghetto police was the only judicial body there.[50] Even later, when the ghetto courts were already in operation, the right to pronounce judgment on misdemeanors was reserved for the ghetto police.

The structure of the courts was not uniform everywhere. In Łódź, for instance, in July 1941 the court consisted of 10 judges in three divisions: criminal, civil, and attorney general. A single judge officiated in the lower court and three judges in the court of appeals, which considered only cases where the sentences exceeded 50 Reichsmarks or two weeks in prison. In more important cases, the chairman of the court could order that the trial in the lower court be held before three judges.[51]

The legal department of the Białystock Ghetto was authorized to try civil cases between inmates and financial litigation between individuals and the Council's departments. Disciplinary cases involving ghetto employees were tried by the Council presidium.[52] At a meeting of the Jewish Council on May 31, 1942, it was decided to establish a permanent criminal court, consisting of a panel of 15 judges confirmed by the Council: 6 Council members, 6 representatives of the ghetto inmates, and 3 members of the legal profession. The chairman was elected by the entire panel, and he, jointly with the chairman of the Council, designated in each case the trial judges who, in turn, elected the presiding judge.[53]

Some of the ghettos had special courts. For instance, in March 1941 in Łódź, Rumkowski created an emergency court with two panels consisting of a judge and two assisting judges each of whom he personally nominated. The trials were conducted without previous investigation and in the absence of either prosecution or defense. In May Rumkowski vested in one of his closest associates the office of High Investigating Judge in charge of the activities of the clerks and laborers in the ghetto offices and shops. Rumkowski reserved for himself the right to punish the guilty. On July 1 he abolished the emergency court altogether and personally took over its functions.[54]

Because of specific local conditions, the Kaunas Ghetto court developed in stages. Its nucleus was the labor emergency court, which the Jewish Council decided, on November 28, 1941, to transform into a regular court. It was, however, abolished on July 7, 1942, by the order of the Nazi Security Service (SD). The Council then transferred the court's functions to the criminal chamber of the ghetto police, and the police commandant acted as its chairman. The decisions of the chamber had to have his approval; he could also reject them. One year later, the criminal chamber was reorganized and operated independently of the police commandant, who remained only nominal chairman. At the same time, the Council established an appeal commission whose decision was final.[55]

The court in the Vilna Ghetto had a lower court and a court of appeals. The lower court consisted of the chairman and five members. The court of appeals consisted of the chairman, three members, and a secretary.[56]

In the Łódź, Kaunas, and Vilna Ghettos, the Council chairman had the right to grant amnesty in all or in certain criminal cases.[57] Thus Rumkowski granted a partial amnesty on the occasion of the Jewish New Year and Hanukkah in 1941, and on the eve of Passover in 1943.[58]

The ghetto courts which were organized by professional jurists used the laws and court procedures of their respective countries. For instance, the Kaunas Ghetto court "applied the laws of the former Lithuanian Republic insofar as they were not contrary to the specific conditions of the ghetto, the demands of the authorities, and the orders of the chairman of the Council of Elders."[59] In the Łódź[60] and Białystok[61] Ghettos, the courts used the Polish criminal code, but in Šiauliai, the court applied the traditional Jewish laws whenever possible.[62]

In some of the ghettos, the courts introduced their own rules of procedure. The Criminal Statute of the Vilna Ghetto of February 5, 1943, consisted of 141 paragraphs. The Code of Procedure dated July–August 1942 contained 11 paragraphs.[63] The Code of Criminal Procedure in the Łódź Ghetto stated in its first paragraph that "all acts are punishable which are against the commonly recognized principles of the criminal code, the orders of the German authorities in the ghetto, and the orders of the Council chairman."[64] At the meeting held on December 19, 1942, the Jewish Council of the Siauliai Ghetto decided on rules for limiting property rights including confiscation without compensation, and the law of inheritance and guardianship.[65]

The ghetto courts passed judgment in criminal cases in the ghetto, except for those offenses the German authorities reserved for their own jurisdiction, such as acts committed against the anti-Jewish orders and political activities (listening to the radio, joining the underground, etc.). These offenses were reserved for the German *Sondergerichte* ("special courts"). People arrested by the German police or convicted by the *Sondergerichte* were in some ghettos kept in the ghetto jail. In some areas of occupation explicit orders were issued not to keep Jewish prisoners in the general prisons. In the instructions regarding criminal punishment for the Jews (*Strafverfolgung von Juden*) issued by the Higher State prosecutor in the Wartheland on August 30, 1941, it was clearly stated that Jews were not to be put in German jails for the following, quite surprising, reason: "Besides, sending a Jew into a German penitentiary will not mean harm to him, since in this institution he will find better conditions than in the Jewish ghettos. Given the mentality of the Jews, it may just be that such a Jew will have been looking for a way to get into a German penitentiary."[66]

Jews convicted by the German courts were put in the two prisons of the Łódź Ghetto at the disposal of the Gestapo or *Kripo*.[67] People arrested by the Polish police in Warsaw were put in the ghetto jail, as were persons sentenced for breaking German orders.[68] For the most part, the guilt of these "criminals," among them many children, was that they had been caught on the "Aryan" side.

Despite the pressure by the German authorities for severe punishments, including death sentences, the ghetto courts passed judgment with great consideration.

In Kaunas the labor emergency court had at its disposal the following six kinds of penalties: deprivation of food ration cards for a certain period of time, confiscation of assets, eviction from apartment, arrest for a period not exceeding one month, publication of the sentence, and turning the offender over to the German authorities. For the last penalty, the concurrence of the Council chairman was necessary.[69]

The emergency courts in Łódź, or Rumkowski himself, usually sentenced people to forced labor with prisoners' food rations, for a term ranging from one to six months. The convict was not jailed, but worked for the ghetto without wages, nine hours a day. When he did not report to work on time or behaved improperly, the convict was put in jail and his sentence was extended beyond its original term.[70] The Vilna Ghetto court passed sentences of imprisonment for from 24 hours to 6 weeks, imprisonment on probation, cash fines of up to 100 Reichsmarks, or admonitions. It seems that minor offenders were placed in the custody of guardians.[71]

Where no court was established in the ghetto, jails were set up at the police headquarters. People were jailed on orders of the Councils or the German authorities for not reporting for labor duty, for not contributing to Nazi-imposed exactions or for not paying taxes, for stealing, for offenses against Council members, for resisting the ghetto police, etc.[72]

After demands by the German authorities, Rumkowski requested that the judges in the Łódź Ghetto pass death sentences on dangerous criminals. A number of the judges and prosecutors refused and were dismissed; Rumkowski ordered that they were not to be given any other jobs, but thanks to their courageous stand, the problem of passing death sentences in the ghetto courts was quashed.[73]

Very few cases of death sentences by ghetto courts have come to light so far. In Vilna, on June 4, 1942, five Jews were sentenced to death by hanging for robbery and murder of two ghetto inmates. A sixth person was condemned to death by hanging for assault on a ghetto policeman on duty. The sentences were executed by the ghetto police.[74]

It quite often happened that persons sentenced to death by the Germans were brought over into the ghetto for execution. On December 3, 1942, three young women were hanged in the prison of the Łódź Ghetto for escaping from a forced-labor camp. Another execution by hanging took place in the Łódź Ghetto in April 1943. A man had strangled a thirteen-year-old girl and stolen four food ration cards. He was sentenced to death, and the execution was carried out by a Jewish executioner and his helpers.[75] In some ghettos the Councils and the ghetto police were ordered to assist during public executions of Jewish "offenders" carried out by the German police, as was the case in Zduńska Wola on March 3, in Bełchatów and Poddębice (both near Łódź) on March 10, 1942,[76] and in other places.

The police activities of the Jewish Councils, carried out by the ghetto police, and the mutual relations of these two organs will be discussed in Chap. 18.

CHAPTER 9

Religion, Education, and
Other Cultural Activities

DURING THE YEARS BETWEEN the wars, the *Kehilas* of Poland conducted no regular cultural activities. The Polish law of 1927 dealing with Jewish communities limited their activities to religious tasks including religious education and welfare work. Religious concerns were particularly predominant in the smaller communities, where the orthodox Agudat Israel was in control, emphasizing exclusively the maintenance of *Talmud Toras* (elementary religious schools) for the children of the Jewish poor. At most, compromises were sometimes worked out between different factions in these communities, and small subsidies were allocated to cultural and other secular organizations.

In the territories of the Soviet Union (in its prewar boundaries) no organized *Kehilas* existed at the time of the German invasion. In the new territories which the Soviet Union occupied following the Molotov–Ribbentrop pact of August 1939 (i.e., Lithuania, Latvia, and the Polish areas of Western Byelorussia and Western Ukraine), the *Kehilas* were formally abolished during the first weeks of the Soviet occupation, but actually continued their strictly religious activities, such as ritual slaughter, ritual food, and worship in synagogues.

Inasmuch as the Jewish Councils were the only body the German authorities organized to deal with matters concerning the Jews, cultural activities in the ghettos also had to be performed under the auspices of the Councils. For instance, according to a special order published on September 11, 1940, only the Councils had the right to open schools or conduct vocational courses of any kind. However, public enthusiasm manifested in the Jewish Cultural Organization was the moving spirit of the entire cultural activity of the Warsaw Ghetto, as we shall see later in this chapter. We shall see, however, that with some exceptions the educational and cultural activities of the Councils were very limited, because of both the inimical attitude of the German authorities and the specific conditions of life in the ghettos.

RELIGION

Because of the hostile attitude of occupation authorities toward Jewish religion (e.g., one of the first anti-Jewish decrees in occupied Poland forbade ritual slaughter[1]), the Councils met with great obstacles in caring for the religious needs of their communities. In accordance with the Nazi conception of Jews as a race, the Councils, unlike the prewar *Kehilas,* could not act as religious bodies. Thus, for instance, the Cracow community was ordered, in September 1939, to change its prewar title in German from *Jüdische Kultusgemeinde* to *Jüdische Gemeinde.*[2] The Councils had to represent all Jews, racially pure or racially mixed, their religion notwithstanding. In the semiofficial interpretation of the decree of November 28, 1939, concerning the Jewish Councils (printed in the *Gazeta Żydowska,* no. 30, November 1, 1940) we read:

> In accordance with the decree, the Jewish community should be defined as a Jewish collective living within the boundaries of a political community. Who is a Jew, and who belongs to the Jewish community, are questions decided by the order of July 24, 1940, where the definition of a 'Jew' is outlined. The *Kehilas* are no longer religious unions, but national or racial communities; and, therefore, care for the religious needs of their members is not their exclusive responsibility.

Taking the position that the Polish law of October 14, 1927, was not formally abolished, the Jewish Councils maintained that care for religious needs was also part of their task.

The Councils, particularly in the smaller ghettos, apparently were of the opinion that it was preferable not to establish separate departments for religious affairs within the ghetto administrations. Only two large ghettos (Łódź and Warsaw) are at present known to have had officially active rabbinical executives (*Vaadei Harabanim*).

In Lwów, religious affairs were taken care of by a Council depart-ment called the Cultural Office. The one religious activity the authorities welcomed was that of the burial society (*Hevra Kadisha*).

However, the German authorities did not uniformly apply their policy, and much apparently depended on the attitudes of local officials. In many ghettos the Germans from the start demanded that Jews report to work on the Sabbath and even during high holy days. In Łódź the authorities ordered that all Jewish businesses stay open on Yom Kippur 1939.[3] In Cracow the Council was forced to announce that on the first day of Rosh Hashanah (October 3, 1940) Jews were to report to work as usual and to keep their shops open during the second day of the holiday and on Yom Kippur under threat of severe punishment.[4] Apparently, pious Jews did not report for work during the high holy days despite the threatened punishment, or they left work to worship individually or in the synagogues during work hours. We learn about this defiance from a warning issued by the Lublin Jewish Council on September 20, 1940 (Announce-ment No. 184) directed against the taking of unauthorized leave from places of work on the two days of Rosh Hashanah and on Yom Kippur.[5] The Council of Elders in Šiauliai was forced on the very day of Yom Kippur, September 21, 1942, to order the Jews to report for work.[6]

In this respect the situation in the Łódź Ghetto was a little better. According to Rumkowski's announcement (No. 134) issued on the eve of Yom Kippur 1940, the high holy day, which fell on a Sabbath in that year, was to be a day of rest as were all the following Sabbath days.[7] According to two circular letters of the Jewish ghetto ad-ministration, dated September 30 and October 15, 1941, both Rosh Hashanah and Sukkot were to be days off in offices and shops.[8] This was not tolerated by the authorities for long, and subsequently Jews were forced to work on Rosh Hashanah, Yom Kippur, and other holidays. Sabbath as a day of rest was also abolished under pressure from the *Gettoverwaltung*. On October 17, 1941, Biebow suggested to the Gestapo that the day of rest in the Łódź Ghetto should be changed from Saturday to Sunday, indicating that the fact that ghetto inmates took their day off on Saturday, while the officials of the *Gettoverwaltung* rested on Sunday, interfered with his activities as overseer of the ghetto and with the proper execution of control functions. The result of this situation was that German officials sometimes had to work on Sunday. Moreover, Sabbath interfered with the unloading of merchandise when it arrived on that day.[9] The Gestapo gladly accepted Biebow's suggestion. Before September 1942, the day of rest was to a certain degree designated by shop managers, so that in some places in the ghetto there was no work on the Sabbath, and Rumkowski permitted the assignment to these places of people eager to observe the Sabbath.[10] In practice people chose to rest either on the Sabbath or on Sunday, until Sunday was officially decreed the day of rest on January 29, 1943. This decree, however, was not strictly enforced.[11]

After the ghetto had been established in Warsaw the Jewish Council asked the authorities to make the Sabbath the day of rest, since economic contacts with the "Aryan" part of the town had been severed anyway. The authorities granted this request, and until the Jews were enclosed in the ghetto the Council's offices and all public institutions were closed both on the Sabbath and on Sunday. On April 15, 1941, the *Gazeta Żydowska* printed Czernaikow's order designating the Sabbath, Rosh Hashanah, Yom Kippur, Sukkot (four days), Passover (four days), and Shavuot (two days) as the official days of rest in the ghetto, in accordance with Frank's decree of March 4, 1941, which permitted Jews to hold religious services in private homes, synagogues, and houses of study during these holidays. Based on this decree, the local supervisory authorities in Warsaw permitted the Council to open three prayer houses on March 17, 1941, and during Shavuot of 1941 services were held in the synagogue at Tłomackie Street. It was pointed out, however, that the order did not apply to labor duties performed by Jews on orders of the *Transferstelle*, or to other work which had to be performed urgently on the Sabbath.[12] New Year's day and important Catholic holidays were also rest days. It may be added that, before Frank's decree was issued, religious services in Warsaw were held secretly in private conventicles. No other permits for Jews to conduct religious services within the occupied territories of Eastern Europe are so far known.

In the Vilna Ghetto the Sabbath was the generally accepted day of rest except for two Council departments—public welfare and Nazi-imposed taxes—where the day of rest was Sunday, "for the convenience of the ghetto inmates."[13]

The matter of attending public worship was not uniformly regulated throughout the occupied territories. Thus in Łódź, during the high holy days of 1940, people could attend the services with the

Rumkowski officiates at a wedding in the Łódź Ghetto after the rabbis were deported in September 1942.

The post office in the Łódź Ghetto.

permission of the city authorities. German army officers even attended the Kol Nidrei services, held in a movie theater where a prayer house had been established. The officers behaved correctly. People prayed in many places, even in the open;[14] to establish a private prayer house Rumkowski's permission was needed.[15] Later, however, communal prayers could be held only in secret.[16] In Sosnowiec the authorities permitted communal prayers during Rosh Hashanah 1940. They were held in the old-age home.[17] In Warsaw the authorities officially forbade communal prayers on January 26, 1940, ostensibly because of the danger of spreading epidemics.[18] Under the date December 19, 1939, Czerniakow made a note in his Diary that all prayer houses had been closed. According to the next day's entry, on December 20 he was ordered to close all schools and prayer houses. In the last entry dealing with this matter he noted, on January 5, 1940, that the ritual bathhouse had also been closed.[19] Many prayer houses had been closed on Jewish initiative even earlier, and their premises used as shelters for refugees.

In many cities, where synagogues and houses of study were burned down by the Nazis during the first months of the occupation,[20] or where former prayer houses were outside the ghetto borders, private services were held in secret. These secret services were held despite the danger of discovery by the Germans, with the consequence that the praying Jews would be subject to mockery, chased out into the street wearing their prayer shawls, and forced to do filthy and denigrating chores.[21] Even after Frank's decree of March 4, 1941, the Jews feared to assemble in large numbers for communal prayers because of the danger of "visits" by SS men, who enjoyed making fun of the religious sentiments of the Jews. Pious Jews, therefore, continued to pray singly or in small groups. As for the other occupied areas, in Ostland, for instance, German Jews who were driven into the Riga Ghetto established their own prayer house (the *Köln Shul*), where public services were conducted on the Sabbath and high holy days—a privilege denied the native Jews of Riga, whose prayer houses had been closed long before, and who therefore worshiped in private homes (at Rabbi Zak's, for instance).[22]

After Eastern Galicia had been incorporated into the Government General as Distrikt Galizien, communal prayers were forbidden in Lwów. People prayed in secret, and praying Jews when discovered were driven to jail never to return.[23]

The Councils made efforts to secure minimal quantities of matzoth for the Jews. For Passover 1941 the inmates of the Łódź Ghetto received 2½ kilograms of matzoth per person, charged against their regular bread cards.[24] (During Passover 1940, ration cards had not yet been introduced in the Łódź Ghetto, and it was therefore possible to procure matzoth on one's own initiative.) Matzoth were baked with corn flour (not wheat flour as is required by religious law).

After an intercession with the authorities, the Lublin Jewish Council got an allocation of 100,000 kilograms of wheat flour for Passover 1940, for the price of 100,000 zlotys. A special commission of 11 members was elected to deal with the distribution of matzoth. Two kilograms were allocated per person. The price was 3 zlotys for one kilogram, but the better-off people paid a surcharge, which made it possible to distribute matzoth to 13,000 poor persons free of charge or at a reduced price. In all, some 90,347 kilograms of matzoth were sold or given away, and no Jews were left without matzoth, according to the report of the commission. The deficit of 12,000 zlotys was covered by the treasury of the Jewish Council.[25] In the Warsaw Ghetto, too, matzoth were available for Passover 1941, instead of the rationed bread.[26] For Passover 1940 a large quantity of matzoth was distributed in occupied Poland by the JDC. A lesser quantity was distributed for Passover 1941 (see p.138).

Reports exist from some other ghettos where the Councils succeeded, during the first years of the occupation, in securing small quantities of matzoth which served as a symbol rather than actual food to satisfy hunger.[27]

In a large number of ghettos dietary laws were observed in some of the special soup kitchens opened by the Councils, either on their own initiative or at the requests of orthodox people.[28]

We do not know much about the activities of the rabbis, who were subordinated to the Councils and had to act within the framework of their departments and as their functionaries. In the Łódź Ghetto religious life was officially regulated by the "Committee of Rabbis" at the office of the "Jewish Elder." It consisted of 15 rabbis. After the arrival of Jews deported from Germany in December 1941, the committee was enlarged to 19 members (4 rabbis from among the deported German Jews were co-opted to the executive). The members of the "Committee of Rabbis" were employed in the ghetto administration, and by the end of 1941 each was receiving a salary of 250 zlotys a month. They were limited, in performing marriages, to people with appropriate certificates issued by the ghetto office of vital statistics, but they were autonomous in all other religious matters. They judged in matters of religion, pronounced judgments in cases of litigation between ghetto inmates in accordance with the Jewish law, etc. There was a single official *mohel*, and one assistant, which testifies to the low birth rate in the ghetto.[29] To avoid falling into the category of the unemployed, cantors, ritual slaughterers, and sextons either registered as workers in the ghetto shops or worked in the burial department.[30] During the "September action" of 1942 against children up to ten years old and the elderly and sick, the majority of the rabbis were deported. Rumkowski then abolished the "Committee of Rabbis" and personally took over the function of performing marriage rites.[31]

The German authorities did not formally recognize marriages in the ghettos, and new wives continued to be called by their premarital family names. Only in the appropriate column of the identification documents of a couple was it indicated that they were married. The authorities recognized marriages only to the extent that children were given the family names of their fathers. Divorces were granted by a divorce bureau at the department of vital statistics. It consisted of a judge and two rabbis. The parties appeared in person, and the proceedings were either in secret or in open session.[32]

When the ghetto was established in Warsaw, it became necessary to redistrict the rabbinical circuits or regions. By February 1941, the ghetto was divided into regions under the jurisdiction of 16 rabbis, members of the prewar Warsaw rabbinate (some of whom conducted the religious affairs of two, three, and even four circuits). In addition to purely religious matters, the rabbis were also in charge of the books where all births, marriages, and deaths were officially registered.[33] On the basis of these books, the vital statistics department of the Jewish Council issued the pertinent formal certificates.[34]

During the summer deportations of 1942, most of the rabbis were killed on the spot or sent to Treblinka, and, since the Jewish population had been decimated too, the rabbinate was abolished. Only three or four rabbis remained alive, and all but one of them perished in the "actions" of 1943.

The prewar Jewish community organization in Lwów was abolished by the Soviet occupation authorities in 1939–1940, and the rabbinate formally stopped its activities. Of the two chief rabbis, Dr. Levi Freund and Dr. Lewin, the former died in April 1940, and the latter was killed in jail on July 2, 1941. The first chairman of the Jewish Council reorganized the rabbinate into a department for cultural affairs, as mentioned. It consisted of rabbis and their assistants in Lwów who had survived the July pogroms and of refugee rabbis, such as Dr. Kalman Chamajdes, the rabbi of Kattowitz. But Jewish religious life could not be restored. The abolition of ritual slaughter, formally decreed in all four districts of the Government General, was extended to the area of the incorporated Distrikt Galizien. The rabbinate worked in constant fear, afraid even to issue formal marriage certificates lest these betray its existence, which was not sanctioned by the authorities. The problem of divorces was particularly painful, mainly involving "Aryan" women who had converted to Judaism before marrying their Jewish spouses. By obtaining divorces from their husbands, they could avoid for themselves and their children moving into the ghetto and wearing the Jewish star. For the most part, Jewish husbands insisted that their wives and children rescue themselves in this manner.

After the "deportation actions" in June–July 1943, when almost all rabbis perished, the department of cultural affairs was no longer in existence.[35]

Objective conditions induced insurmountable difficulties for the Jews in the observance of religious laws and restrictions. It was impossible to find a compromise between the strict ritual requirements and the severe hardships of ghetto reality. Such religious fundamentals as dietary laws, Sabbath rest, and unleavened bread for Passover could not be strictly observed in the ghettos. The scarce documentation of the activities of the rabbis' committee in the Łódź Ghetto, for instance, shows how the rabbis wrestled to find alternatives.[36] The hard conditions of life in the ghetto forced the rabbis to be lenient. Thus women in confinement were allowed to consume nonkosher meat, as were the sick and "those who are rapidly losing strength" and had explicitly been ordered by their doctors to eat nonkosher meat. Such a judgment was issued on February 27, 1941, and bears the signatures of all 15 members of the committee.[37]

Though usually banned for use on Passover, peas and beans were allowed by the rabbinate of the Warsaw Ghetto for consumption during the Passover of 1941, because it was feared that there would not be enough matzoth.[38] Among the permissive Responsa of a Kaunas rabbi were such items as: the consumption during Passover of food staples normally suspected of being nonkosher for the holiday, the cooking of food for forced laborers on the Sabbath, the use of garments of killed ghetto inmates, and the performance of abortions if the women involved were in danger of death sentences, because of the German order prohibiting the pregnancy of Jewish women. The rabbi made only one exception, forbidding the use of "Aryan" papers for rescue purposes, which he considered contrary to the basic rabbinical law of "perish rather than deviate."[39] No documentation has been preserved reflecting the attitude of the rabbis in other ghettos toward this agonizing dilemma: how to find a suitable compromise between the requirements of the rabbinical law and the stark realities of life in the ghetto. It may be assumed that in not a few ghettos they acted as the rabbis in Warsaw, Łódź, and Kaunas had.

The traditional garments of the Orthodox Jews in Eastern Europe, the kaftan, and the observance of restrictions against shaving beards and cutting off sidelocks also fell victim to ghetto life. In the Łódź Ghetto, apparently on order of the German authorities, Rumkowski combated the long kaftans and the beards and the sidelocks. Their prominence in the ghetto was diminished anyway, because bearded Jews in kaftans were more conspicuous and were more often caught for forced-labor duty than were others. Rumkowski, in an article printed in the *Geto-tsaytung*, ordered all men up to fifty years of age to wear short jackets, except rabbis and holders of rabbinical diplomas. Only on rare occasions did he issue special permits for wearing the long kaftans.[40] However, this was not the end of it. In a speech delivered on June 1, 1942, he warned not only against wearing the traditional garb but also against beards, and he announced that beards had to disappear from the ghetto within eight days.[41] A circular letter displayed in all places of work warned that those who would not cut off their beards would be dismissed from work, and that only shaved people would be admitted to the shops. On June 13, 1942, the ghetto police made "raids on beards" and dragged people to barbershops by force where they were shaved and their sidelocks cut off.[42] (This was an ironic repetition of occurrences during the reigns of the Czars Nicholas I and Alexander II, except that this time the raids were carried out by the Jews themselves on orders of an alien authority.) There is also information from other ghettos where the authorities ordered the Councils to make sure that the workers shaved off their beards.[43] The Council in Bochnia, for example, announced, at the end of April 1941, that Jews were not permitted to wear sidelocks.[44]

Converts constituted a particularly painful problem in the ghettos. For instance, in the transports of Central European Jews deported to the Łódź Ghetto in 1941, there were some 250 Catholics and Protestants who had personally converted or had been converted as children by their parents. They had no relations with the Jewish people whatsoever, and they felt entirely alienated in a completely strange environment where they were brutally forced to dwell. There was a total separation between them and the other inmates of the ghetto. They were organized in a "Christian Union," established a place for religious services, but when, at a meeting between Rumkowski and the representatives of these Central European deportees, a request was made that their children receive instruction in Christian religion and that a separate cemetery be opened for them, it was rejected on the grounds that even in schools for Jewish children (which were still permitted at that time) no instruction in Jewish religion was allowed[45] (more on religious education appears later in this chapter).

In the Warsaw Ghetto the religious services of the Christian Jews were conducted in a church within the boundaries of the ghetto by a converted priest.[46] In the Riga *Reichsgetto* German Jews of the Catholic religion congregated in the home of their Elder, who performed the priestly functions.[47]

EDUCATION

In accordance with plans to make Poland a sort of colonial backward land for the Greater German Reich, Nazi education policy aimed at downgrading public education to the lowest level. The Germans permitted only the education they considered an artisan, laborer, or farmer to need. Only elementary and vocational schools were therefore allowed. The same "educational" principle was applied against the Jews, except that in respect to Jewish children it was used even more relentlessly and with greater chicanery, as illustrated by examples taken from various ghettos in different areas.

In Warsaw the beginning of the 1939–1940 school year, which traditionally should have started on September 1, coincided with the day the war broke out, and the schools did not open. After the siege of Warsaw came to an end in the last days of September, the teachers of the state schools for Jewish children endeavored to reopen the schools. But during the bombardment, many school buildings had been demolished or burned down, or school equipment had been stolen. Other buildings and equipment were later confiscated by the occupying authorities. On October 8, 1939, the High Command of the German occupying forces in Poland issued an order permitting the opening of all schools that had been in operation before the war. Some of the Jewish schools, taking advantage of the order, were opened after repairs to the school plants had been made by teachers and students. But by the end of November the civil authorities, having taken the administration of occupied Poland from the military, ordered the Jewish schools closed, ostensibly because of the danger that they might facilitate the spread of contagious diseases. The last Jewish school was closed on December 4.[48] At the same time, the authorities permitted the non-Jewish public schools to open, providing that Jewish teachers and Jewish students were excluded. This policy was followed throughout the occupied territories.[49]

Representatives of unemployed teachers, including the teaching personnel of all types of prewar Jewish schools (except the state schools), tried to move the Jewish Council, Centos, and other organizations to establish clandestine schools under the guise of child care. According to a memorandum submitted to the Warsaw Jewish Council by the teachers' representatives, there were in Warsaw 50,000 to 60,000 children between five and twelve years old in September 1939, and thousands of them were exposed to the demoralizing effects of roaming the streets.[50] In the meantime, unofficial instruction was undertaken for a few hours a day in the many soup kitchens for children opened by Centos, and thousands of children made use of this opportunity.

On September 11, 1940, Frank's order (dated August 31, 1940), "Uber das jüdische Schulwesen im Generalgouvernement" appeared, which authorized the Jewish Councils, and only the Councils, to open public and vocational schools, with the status of private schools (Paragraphs 1 and 2) and to take care of proper professional preparation for the teachers (Para. 2, sect. 3). Paragraph 3 ruled that schools for Jews were compulsory and were established on the basis of the Polish education law. In Paragraph 4 it was indicated that any confiscated Jewish property necessary for the schools could be put at the disposal of the Councils, with the consent of the proper authorities. Two or more Councils in small communities could be consolidated by the *Distriktchef* to open joint Jewish schools (Para. 5). The German authorities would supervise the Jewish schools (Para. 7). This was a general order, but actually to open a school each Council had to ask permission from the local authority (Para. 8).[51] However, the phrasing of the last paragraph opened the door for every kind of chicanery, and even permitted the local authorities to forbid the opening of Jewish schools altogether. Moreover, the late date of the announcement, 11 days after the beginning of the school year for non-Jewish schools, was a clear indication of the Nazi intention that no Jewish school be open on the day all other schools opened in Poland.

As soon as the order was announced, the Warsaw Jewish Council established a school commission including representatives of the pre-war Jewish school organizations, but because German sanitary authorities took the stand that opening Jewish schools might enhance the spread of typhus, the preparatory work of this commission was discontinued.[52] It is typical of the Nazi administration's perfidy that, just at that time, in the summer and fall of 1940, the incidence of both typhus and typhoid fever (which had broken out among the Jewish population in Warsaw in the fall of 1939) had greatly decreased. In December 1939 there were 540 cases of typhus but only 10 cases a month in the summer of 1940. Similarly cases of typhoid fever fell from 407 in April to 18 in August 1940.[53] The threat of infectious diseases (*Seuchengefahr*) was expedient as an argument used by the Germans against any relaxation of anti-Jewish measures, even in spite of their own orders.

In January 1941 the Council again tried to get permission to open schools, but to no avail.[54] Only in April of that year did the authorities say that they would allow the opening of a number of public schools, beginning with 5,000 children. The School Commission again came to life.[55] A general educational plan was worked out based on data submitted by prewar school organizations and leaders in the field of education, providing for six types of schools. A list of teachers and school supervisors was also made.[56] The plan was submitted to the German authorities, and there it died. The Jewish Council interceded, trying to get permission to open not only the schools but courses for teachers, which had officially been permitted

a year earlier.[57] Finally 16 schools were opened during September
and October 1941, under the auspices of the following prewar Jewish
school organizations: Central Yiddish School Organization (CISHO)
—3 schools; the Hebrew school organization *Tarbut*—3 schools;
Shulkult—1 school; the religious schools *Beth Yacov, Horev,* and
Yavneh—5 schools in all; and 4 schools with instruction in the
Polish language.[58] In all, up to 10,000 children were enrolled in
these ghetto schools, no more than 20 percent of all Jewish children
of school age in Warsaw.[59] The programs of the schools were planned
for the first three years of instruction, though some went as far as the
fourth and even the fifth grades.

The children under the care of the various institutions of Centos
also received some sort of elementary education. By December 1,
1941, Centos extended its assistance to 25,648 children in institutions
and feeding stations (16 dormitories, 5 part-time dormitories, 25
children's kitchens, 8 educational clubs, 24 children's clubs in
refugee homes, 14 homes with part-time educational personnel, etc.).
On February 5, 1942, the kitchens for children and the educational
clubs employed 319 persons, including 85 male and female ed-
ucators.[60]

Some instruction was given to children in the so-called "nooks"
organized by house committees and by tenants. Children of one or
more buildings spent some time under the supervision of professional
or nonprofessional "guides" and "assistants," members of the Zionist
Pioneer organization, the youth organizations of the Jewish Labor
Bund (*Tsukunft* and *Skif*), etc.[61]

The terrible economic conditions of the Warsaw Ghetto, and
particularly of the almost 150,000 refugees, made it very hard, if not
impossible, to conduct any planned, normal educational work. One
of the inspectors of the children's feeding stations in her report of
January 1942 describes the condition there as follows: "Freezing
cold weather, the lack of shoes and clothing, and the unheated or
insufficiently heated premises of the asylums, together with the
minimal nourishment value of the meals, all contributed to the low
frequency [in the feeding stations]. . . . No instruction in drawing
or working in clay is given. . . . no educational work whatsoever is
conducted in many of the children's kitchens."[62]

Terrible privations notwithstanding, the intellectual level of such
schooling as was available was high. Children in the ghettos matured

early and displayed great eagerness for knowledge; for the schools or "nooks" were the only bright spot in the otherwise sad life of the ghetto children.

Secondary education, which was prohibited altogether, remained outside the framework of the educational activities of the Councils. What secondary education existed was based on clandestine private or public efforts for the benefit of small groups of children, a method also used by the Poles. These groups, mainly of from 6 to 20 students, were organized by teachers in their homes or in the homes of students. Some programs were on the level of the prewar *Gymnasia* (except for a few technical subjects), and, according to a report by a group of teachers, approximately 20 percent of the former *Gymnasium* students attended. Several hundred such groups were active in 1941. A number of these groups were organized by school organizations that conducted legally operating elementary schools.[63] Secondary schools encompassing the program of the prewar Hebrew *Gymnasium* were clandestinely operated by Tarbuth and Dror. The Tarbuth *Gymnasium* was in existence until June 1942. It had three classes and six teachers with several scores of students. Diplomas were issued to the students on graduation.[64] The Dror *Gymnasium*, opened in August 1940 with only 7 children, had 120 students under the tutelage of 13 teachers for the school year of 1941.[65]

Permission to open vocational courses (issued to the Jewish Council by the German city chief in August 1940) was secretly used for giving general schooling and higher technical education to the students, although it was issued on the explicit condition that the courses be strictly technical.

The Commission for Training of Artisans (later renamed Commission for Vocational Training) in the Warsaw Ghetto consisted of members of the Jewish Council and representatives of the ORT, and it was responsible to the German authorities. By June 30, 1941, 24 courses for 832 boys, 24 courses for 818 girls, and 16 coeducational courses with 681 students of both sexes were in operation, involving a total of 2,331 students. By the end of April 1941, four courses on a higher level of vocational training were opened for those who graduated from lower-level courses and for artisans skilled in their specialties. Because of hard, insecure conditions, fluctuation of the student body was high, and absenteeism was always on the rise.

In time vocational courses on the lyceum or nearly college level were established with extensive programs such as the nurses' school with 250 students who worked professionally at the Jewish hospital. This was the single, normally functioning educational institution in the ghetto, with a two-year curriculum. A pharmaceutical course, a practical course in applied chemistry (with 50 students each), and a course in graphics were also opened.[66]

Tremendous obstacles and extreme dangers notwithstanding, two clandestine courses on the college level, a medical course and a course in technology, were established in the the ghetto. In addition there were legalized courses for teachers. Former Jewish (or converted) professors of Warsaw University and other colleges trained the students. On a particularly high level were the medical courses headed by the internationally known Professor Ludwik Hirszfeld. At various times from 180 to 250 students attended.[67]

The permit for instituting teachers' courses was based on Paragraph 2 of the above-mentioned order of August 31, 1940, which referred to the schooling of teachers for the Council's schools. Permission was given subject to the condition that no subjects in humanities would be included in the curriculum, except those relating to Judaism. But, as happened with other phases of ghetto education, this restriction was not observed either, and instruction in general pedagogy, philosophy, psychology, and similar general studies was included in the teachers' curriculum. The instructors were former professors of the Judaistic Institute and of the State Seminary for Jewish religious teachers in Warsaw.[68]

Other courses in the ghetto were motivated by practical considerations and in order to create within rubble-covered areas some green spots, "lungs for the ghetto." Agricultural and gardening courses were established by the prewar Society for the Promotion of Agriculture, known as TOPOROL (the initials of the society's name in Polish) and by ORT. Lectures in botany, chemistry, and other basic sciences were also given. The half-year report of TOPOROL stated that 324 persons attended agricultural courses, and 267 students attended short-term courses in agricultural training. TOPOROL's courses were based on a prewar program, and they aimed at "retraining and making productive the Jewish population, a problem of life and the future."[69]

To return to the tactics of the Nazi authorities in regard to Jewish schools, it should be noted that delaying tactics and the creation of difficulties were a common practice in the various districts. Radom is a good example. The *Gazeta Żydowska* of the end of March 1941 tells that all preparations for opening one school had already been made (2,000 children had registered), but permission from the authorities had yet to come. Six months later, on August 18, 1941, a news item from Radom stated "that the school is still at the stage of a project," apparently because of lack of the formal permit. Also in Zamość and Lwów the Councils could not get permits for schools despite numerous interventions.[70] And in an article in the issue of *Gazeta Żydowska* of January 17, 1941, it is stated that "because of local reasons the authorities delayed the opening of schools in various towns." The "local reasons" probably meant the intensive ghettoization process going on in the fall and winter of 1940–1941.

Generally speaking, educational data are available about only a small number of ghettos in the Government General where the Councils took advantage of the decree of August 31, 1940, and successfully approached the local authorities with requests for permits to open schools. In a number of cases this initiative came from teachers. For instance, on the initiative of the teachers in Lublin, where there were some 100 local and refugee teachers, a four-grade school with 100 students was opened during the first weeks of the occupation. A prewar Tarbuth school with a reduced number of students and teachers and a private elementary school were reopened, but the children did not rejoice for long. In mid-November 1939, when the Polish secondary schools were closed, these Jewish schools were also closed. All efforts by a small group of devoted teachers to obtain permission to reopen the schools again met with great obstacles in the constantly tense, paralyzing mood of the city, which was at that time slated to become the center of the "Lublin Jewish reservation." In March 1941, when a possibility of reopening the schools appeared (the German school supervisor had given permission), the mass expulsion of Jews began to undermine life in the ghetto. Later on, when conditions became somewhat "stabilized," there was no place left suitable for a school within the extremely overcrowded ghetto. Courses in Yiddish and Hebrew, which the Council had established with the permission of the authorities, could not meet the need for education. Of more importance were secret classes organized by teachers, each attended by some 10 children. The teachers worked as conspirators, in constant suspense and danger of being discovered by the Germans, "visiting" the Jewish homes. As one of the teachers wrote in his memoirs:

> With trembling hearts, the classes were conducted under severe strain and constant fear. . . . [We were] constantly on the alert, trying to detect from a distance the yelling of approaching SS men, raiding Jewish homes. We were always ready to remove all traces at an instant. Text-books and notebooks vanished, children pretended to be playing games, and teachers acted like customers, trying on a jacket in the house of a tailor, or shoes at a shoemaker's.[71]

The Jewish Council at Rzeszów opened its school on October 27, 1940.[72] In Cracow, after extensive efforts, the authorities permitted the reopening of Jewish private schools at the end of September 1940; (when war broke out there had been 6,400 Jewish students in all types of schools).[73] In Jasło (Cracow district) a seven-grade school was opened in December 1940;[74] in Kazimierz nad Wisłą, a four-grade school was opened on December 1, 1940;[75] in Opatów a six-grade school with 302 children opened;[76] likewise schools were opened in Radom, Gorlice, and Międzyrzec.[77] Schools may also have been opened in a number of other ghettos in the Government General about which no information has been preserved. There is documentation available concerning the efforts by various Councils to open schools, as in Jędrzejów and Bochnia, for instance.[78] However, it is not known how successful these endeavors were. Schools that were opened in the summer or early fall of 1940 finished their school year almost normally with graduation exercises. In Cracow and Jasło these graduation exercises were carried out in conjunction with a Herzl-Bialik Memorial program. In Cracow, from July 18 to July 20, 1941, objects made by the school-children were exhibited.[79]

In various ghettos, the authorities used to close the schools under various pretexts, though they had previously been permitted to open. Thus the school in Gorlice was closed in January 1942 "because of the epidemic"—the same false pretext that had already been used in Warsaw.[80] In the Kaunas Ghetto the public schools in the two parts of the ghetto, both opened on the initiative of teachers in December 1941, were closed by order of the authorities at the end of August 1942.[81]

One of the greatest technical difficulties in establishing schools

was that of finding proper premises, because former school buildings were for the most part located outside the ghetto borders. Thus,
for instance, in Kazimierz nad Wisłą the school was in the "Old
Shul" (synagogue), the single large building in the ghetto. In Radom
only three rooms of the Old Talmud Tora could be sufficiently
repaired, and the school had to function in three shifts from 8:00
A.M. to 5:30 P.M. Amid the horrible conditions of life in the Kutno
Krepierlager, there was established by communal effort a small, new
school building; but the outbreak of typhus prevented the opening
of the school, which was converted into a hospital instead.[82]

Another difficulty was the language of textbooks and of teachers.
Though the language of school instruction was left open in the
general decree, local authorities demanded that all instruction be
in either Yiddish or Hebrew. In Radom the authorities requested
that instruction be exclusively in Yiddish. Before the war, only a
small percentage of Jewish children attended the Yiddish schools of
CISHO and the Hebrew schools of Tarbuth. The majority attended
state schools for Jewish children, with Polish as the language of instruction. For these children, the sudden switch to Yiddish or
Hebrew from Polish was very difficult. Children from various types
of schools were now congregated in the same classes, and it was
not easy to find a schooling language common to all. Some of the
schools (e.g., Cracow and Jasło) which were initially opened with
Polish as the instructional language were ordered to switch to
Hebrew; in other schools, both the Yiddish and the Hebrew languages were used.

Many Jewish bookstores had been ruined in the course of the
hostilities, and those which had survived were closed and their books
confiscated by the Germans.[83] To get textbooks it was necessary first
to get a special permit from the authorities, which, as was the case
in Warsaw, sometimes released confiscated textbooks (see p.220).
Usually the textbooks were collected among the pupils themselves.

The problem of teachers was also acute. A considerable number
of Jewish teachers, particularly in schools sponsored by private
organizations, were active in political or cultural organizations and
had fled to the east with the mass of refugees. As a result there was
a scarcity of teaching personnel, particularly in the small ghettos,
and especially of teachers able to teach in either Yiddish or Hebrew.
As already mentioned, the decree of August 31, 1940, authorized the
opening of training courses for teachers, and these were opened in

a number of places—in Warsaw, Radom, and Łódź for instance. In Łódź the curriculum included Yiddish language and literature, folklore, school songs, and history of the Jewish school system, which in fact was merely a camouflage for the forbidden instruction in Jewish history.[84]

In a number of ghettos, where the Councils did not try or were in no position to open schools by themselves, or where the authorities did not give the necessary permission, some schooling was set up in the children's homes, orphanages, and feeding places established by the JSS, Centos, and TOZ. Thus in Częstochowa TOZ turned its feeding places into children's clubs, where a little schooling was provided along with food. Professional teachers (some 200 prewar teachers remained in town) took care of the approximately 2,000 children in the clubs. Sometimes secret children's shows took place which "provided some festiveness in their dreadful lives."[85]

It was easier to get permission to open vocational courses, since the Germans saw in them a source of future cadres of "the Jewish labor force." Such courses proliferated in many ghettos, established by the Councils or by the local relief committees affiliated with the JSS. Nevertheless, despite the obvious usefulness of vocational courses for their own purposes, the Germans made difficulties. On March 9, 1942, the main office of the *Innere Verwaltung, Bevölkerungswesen und Fürsorge* sent a circular letter to the four district chiefs in Warsaw, Cracow, Radom, and Lublin directing them no longer to issue to the Jewish Councils or the JSS committees permission to establish artisan and agricultural courses for Jewish youngsters. No explanation for this order was given.[86]

In a number of cities in Poland—in Warsaw, Piotrków Trybunalski, and Częstochowa, for example—some Jewish vocational schools had existed before the war. These had been ruined during the military operations, and their machinery and equipment had been confiscated or simply plundered. It was therefore a hard task to try and find new equipment for the school shops. For a time in Częstochowa the students worked as apprentices in the ghetto shops, but this proved unsatisfactory, and great effort was made to find some machines and tools for practical instruction. In the beginning of December 1940 the authorities gave permission to open carpentry and plumbing courses for men, and a seamstress course for women. The courses for men started on March 16, 1941, with 46 students. The seamstress course started in the first half of June of the same year, with 37 students. Instruction lasted four months. The courses were closed for unknown reasons, after graduation of the first group of students.[87]

In Rzeszów, in December 1940, there were vocational training courses for girls and supplementary courses for boys fourteen to sixteen years of age. Carpentry, electrical work, graphics, and interior decoration were taught. The students got practical experience working in the ghetto shops. A sanitary course for nurses was also begun.[88] Vocational courses were opened in a large number of ghettos throughout the occupied territories in Eastern Europe.[89]

The vocational courses were often used for clandestine teaching of some general subjects. As it was hard to distinguish between purely technical and theoretical subjects, it was possible to teach, under camouflage, subjects which the authorities could not control. Like the elementary schools, these vocational courses gave the students an opportunity to escape the dreary ghetto atmosphere, even if only for a few hours.

The history of the vocational school in Kaunas and its role in ghetto life is a good illustration. A group of devoted ORT teachers and instructors succeeded in opening a vocational school for forty students with the help of the Council. A large part of the tools for the school were smuggled in by the instructors and artisans from German labor sites outside the ghetto, despite searches at the ghetto gates and in disregard of the danger to their own lives and the lives of their families. Because of people's anxiety about protecting the children by making them "productive" (thus securing for them the right to live in the ghetto) the number of students steadily grew, and by February 1944, when the ghetto had been transformed into a concentration camp, 480 had been enrolled. This school, as mentioned above, had been closed on August 26, 1942, together with the two elementary schools; but in November of that year, the Council succeeded in convincing a new ghetto chief that the vocational school was needed to develop the ghetto industry, and it was reopened. The older children from the closed elementary schools were transferred to the vocational school, which had three departments for boys (plumbing, carpentry, and tinsmithing), two departments for girls (seamstress and handicraft), and a garden department with practical work in the ghetto hothouses and in gardens. There was a separate curriculum for children up to thirteen years old (Hebrew, Yiddish, natural sciences, and history); older ones were also given instruction in theoretical technology and mechanics. Later on, a department of applied art was added for the most able girls, who worked under the guidance of a woman artist, studying history of art, theory of colors, and how to make art objects. Within the walls of the vocational school there was also established a seminary for the particularly gifted students, who received special training.

The vocational school was the center of cultural activities in the ghetto and, in fact, became the house of cultural activities for the inmates. Lectures in literature were delivered there, a choir with 100 singers was established, as well as a lending library and a drama circle. In July 1943 the students produced a show in conjunction with an exhibition of art works produced by the children. *The Kabbalists*, a drama by I. L. Peretz, was performed several times. Each time the German "actions" took away new victims, the remaining teachers and students renewed their classes with a remarkable tenacity. For camouflage purposes, the school was incorporated into the ghetto shops after the "children's action" which took place at the end of March 1944. In this form the school existed up to the final liquidation of the Kaunas concentration camp in July.[90]

In two large ghettos, Łódź and Vilna, the Councils carried out particularly intensive educational programs with no apparent opposition from the authorities. In the Łódź Ghetto, which belonged to the Polish territories incorporated into the Reich in October 1939, the German authorities tried to bring public life, schools included, back to normal as soon as possible. When the war broke out there had been in Łódź 31 public schools for Jewish children with 17,902 students, 12 *cheders* with 1,452 children, 10 Jewish high schools with 1,861 students, and attached to these high schools 10 elementary schools with 1,112 students—a total of 63 schools with 22,327 students.[91] On October 18, 1939, the Łódź *Kommissar* ordered Rumkowski to dismiss all Polish teachers in the public schools for Jewish children and to pay them severance pay. At the same time Jewish teachers in the general schools were also dismissed, but received no severance pay.[92] On October 25 the *Kommissar* authorized Rumkowski to take over the supervision of the Jewish schools and to finance them by imposing a tax on the Jews.

Beginning in October 1939 the schools were administered by a school committee of six members. It was later renamed "School Council," and its membership constantly changed with the flight of the Jews from the town up until the closing of the ghetto in May

1940. In September 1941 the leadership of the school department consisted of three persons: a chairman and two inspectors.

The formal opening of the Jewish schools was on September 11, 1939, but they could not operate in a normal way because eight large school buildings mainly used for the high schools were requisitioned by the authorities, because a large number of teachers left town or were caught for forced labor, and because it was generally unsafe for Jews to appear in the streets. Because of the lack of appropriate premises, classes operated in two or even three shifts. Of the 31 former Jewish public school buildings, only 8 remained within the ghetto borders. The classrooms were overcrowded, with 90 students per class in the high schools. On December 18, 1939, classes were closed and were reopened only after the forcible removal of the Jews into the ghetto was concluded at the beginning of March 1940. Because of the long interruption, the first school year was extended up to September and the Jewish high-holy-day period was designated as vacation time. During the first school year 10,462 students registered in the elementary schools, 508 in the two high schools (with 125 students registered in the lyceum), and 56 in the vocational school.[93] This made a total of 11,151 students, a decrease of over 50 percent by comparison to the prewar figures. The actual number of students in the classes was even smaller. For instance, in May 1940 there were only 7,366 students present, or one-third of the prewar school population. This large, fluctuating absenteeism in the schools was partly caused by the severe economic plight of the ghetto inmates, which forced the children to search for income to ease the poverty of their families. Other contributing factors were the insecure situation in the streets because of murderous "actions" (the Nazi sentries frequently shot into the ghetto at random, killing innocent passersby), and the epidemics which broke out in May 1940. During the second and last school year, which started on October 29, 1940, absenteeism in the classes decreased; 45 schools were opened—40 elementary schools (including 4 religious schools and 2 schools for retarded and deaf, mute children), 2 kindergartens, 2 high schools with lyceum classes, and 1 vocational school. On the average, 10,300 students a month attended classes (in January 1941, 14,944 students).[94] In July 1941, 482 teachers were employed in all these schools: 295 females and 187 males.[95]

Under pressure from the authorities, the schools' curriculum was changed from the prewar Polish school program, and, on Rumkowski's initiative, an extensive program of Jewish subjects was introduced (Yiddish, Hebrew, Bible, and Jewish history) with Yiddish as the language of instruction. During the first school year the teachers taught in their accustomed language. Since the majority of the teachers (319 out of 482) came from the Polish state schools for Jewish children, they were not prepared for the change to instruction in Yiddish. As mentioned above, special courses in Yiddish were opened to train them. On May 15, 1941, a "Seminary for Yiddish Knowledge" was opened, operating in four shifts. It was in existence until the end of September 1941.[96]

Some schooling was also conducted in children's institutions in Marysin—in a convalescent home, some day camps, an orphanage, and a religious school, As of July 31, of 1,512 Marysin children of school age, 1,250 received some education. Two high schools and a vocational school in the center of the ghetto were closed on Rumkowski's orders in January 1941 and were moved to Marysin, situated at the ghetto outskirts apparently because the authorities did not like to see Jewish children attending high schools. Some other schools were also closed in February 1941, after the authorities had reduced the ghetto area, and it became necessary to find shelter for 7,000 displaced people.[97]

On the initiative of the chiefs of the registration and vital statistics departments of the ghetto administration, "higher lyceum courses" were established in August 1940, commonly called *Wszechnica* (short for "free university" in Polish). The courses were meant to become the nucleus of a college. These courses were planned with 10 departments (mathematics, physics, chemistry, biology, psychology, philosophy, education, philology, Judaistic subjects, and technical subjects) and a faculty of 30 teachers. During the initial registration, 318 students enrolled, all high school graduates or former college students. By September 20, 1940, 27 lectures on different subjects had been delivered wth an average of 250 students attending classes. Rumkowski gave oral permission to open the higher lyceum courses, but ordered them closed shortly thereafter. Apparently hope lingered on that they would be permitted after all, for new registration took place and 116 enrolled. It is worth noting that over three-quarters of the registered students were unemployed, a figure testifying to the economic situation of young Jewish intelligentsia in the ghetto.[98]

As elsewhere, the Łódź schools struggled with technical obstacles: lack of textbooks (particularly in Yiddish), lack of fuel in the winter (the ghetto received only enough coal to heat factories and shops), unpreparedness of teachers to teach in Yiddish, etc. Teachers mimeographed texts they composed themselves and made plans to publish textbooks, but the whole school system in the ghetto came to an abrupt end in October 1941, when school premises had to be given up to make shelters for almost 20,000 deported Central European Jews who arrived over a period of time starting on October 17.[99]

Even earlier, hundreds of children had to drop out of schools to work in the workshops. In March 1941 the school department established a retraining commission with the job of providing vocational training for teenagers to enable them to join in the economic efforts of the ghetto. A one-year vocational high school with extension training courses for young artisans was opened. The retraining process was intensified in the winter and spring of 1942, when the first deportations from the ghetto were in progress. By August 1942, 13,861 youngsters and even children eight to ten years old (13.7% of the then current ghetto population) were working in the shops.[100]

In some of the shops the working children and youngsters attended special courses (in Yiddish and arithmetic) in addition to vocational training.[101] In other shops there were day-care shelters supervised by nurses for little children of parents employed in the shops. In a number of other ghetto shops even where there was no systematic curriculum some schooling was clandestinely provided for children by former teachers working in the shops as laborers because the schools were closed. Some schooling had continued in Marysin, but by the end of July 1942 Rumkowski was ordered by the Germans to stop all classes and talks to children.[102]

In Vilna, on the third day after the Jews had been confined in the ghetto, a group of teachers had the initiative to open a school. The Jewish Council designated a few ramshackle premises which the teachers with their pupils energetically cleaned up and rebuilt. In a memoir written about the Vilna Ghetto, the hard work of preparing the school premises is described thus:

In their mutual desire to rebuild the school system, teachers and students became one family. They carried away the rubble, the rocks, and bricks out of the ruins. . . . They yanked a door or a single board from one ruined place and carried it to another one, together with part of a window from a third place, trying to put together out of these discards something resembling a room. . . . Teachers and students chopped wood for fires to heat up the rooms because people were freezing during the severe winter cold. No school benches were available at first, and the pupils sat on dirty floors huddled together. . . . Benches appeared at a later date. . . . Classes were terribly overcrowded, and pupils standing and leaning against the walls supported their notebooks against the backs of others in front of them. This was how the schools operated during the first ghetto winter.[103]

The registration in the ghetto showed that there were over 2,700 children five to fourteen years old.[104] During the first school year (1941–1942) two elementary schools and some high school courses were in operation, with the high school program operating in a building where a third elementary school also operated starting on October 25, 1942. In addition, a school for from 50 to 80 children was opened outside the ghetto, in the labor block of Kaylis.

The following figures illustrate the development of the schools during the year 1942: between January and December the number of classes rose from 9 to 40; the number of teachers increased from 23 to 72; and the average daily student attendance increased from 390 to 1,405. The overcrowding of the premises also improved: while 50 to 75 children were crammed into an average class during the first half of 1942, the number was only 40 during the second half of that year. By the end of October, at the time the third elementary school was opened, the number of children in all schools and institutions of child care rose to 1,800, or two-thirds of all children of school age.[105]

The elementary schools also operated kindergartens for preschool children.[106] In addition, some schooling was conducted in asylums for 130 boys and girls in April 1942, and in the so-called Transportation Brigade *Yeladim* where some 80 children and youngsters had to carry heavy loads all day long.[107]

Still, hundreds of children remained outside the schools, compulsory education notwithstanding. For the most part, these were children excused from school because "they are carrying out important economic functions at home." A certain number of orphans who had to maintain themselves also were excused.[108]

In March 1943, the ghetto school system received a severe blow. A number of school buildings had to be relinquished to provide shelters for Jews sent in from liquidated ghettos and camps. Classes had to be combined, and teaching was also conducted in the afternoon.[109]

In its humanistic and Jewish aspects, the curriculum followed the best traditions of the brilliant prewar Jewish school system in Vilna, the teachers demonstrating their enthusiasm and utter devotion to the schools and the children.[110] The curriculum was based on a compromise reached among the proponents of the diverse ideologies active in the ghetto. According to a report of January 1943, the curriculum covered the following subjects: Yiddish (which was the instructional language), Hebrew, arithmetic, basic sciences, geography, and Jewish and general history. In addition, from July 1942 physics, Latin, and German were taught as high school courses.[111] This curriculum was quite extensive, going much further than the official program for the Council schools in the Government General, where schools feared to include openly in their curricula such subjects as history and geography (see above, p.205).

The teaching of religion was introduced in August 1942, after the rabbis interceded with the ghetto chief. It was not an obligatory subject.[112] It is characteristic of the secular tendencies prevalent in the cultural department (which supervised the schools among other things) that it suggested to the ghetto chief that the teaching of religion be excluded from the curriculum. But this suggestion was not accepted.[113]

The teachers were organized in a union which conducted cultural activities for members and took care of their material necessities. At times additional food allocations from the ghetto chief were received by the teachers, whose economic situation was very bad.

Younger students gathered in children's clubs where diversified activities were conducted in sections for literature, drama, handiwork, painting, history, and geography. Games were played in a separate section.[114] The older students were organized in a youth club beginning on July 18, 1942, where activities took place in circles for history, literature, mathematics, philosophy, folklore, and drama. The club was quite resourceful, giving its own shows and participating in public shows with recitals, choir singing, and plays. In March 1943 the historical circle organized a play, *The Public Trial of Flavius*, with clear hints about the ghetto chief, Jacob Gens. The literature circle organized a Yehoash evening in conjunction with an exposition of the works of that distinguished poet.[115] It also published a wall newspaper (a typed or handwritten newssheet displayed on a building wall) entitled *Behind Walls—Yet Young*. The shows given by school youngsters on various occasions (Hanukkah, Purim, etc.) were inspiring and moving events in the lives of many ghetto inmates, always gravely concerned about the dangers hanging over the younger generation. The last public school function took place late in the spring of 1943.

In addition to the general school network, there was in the ghetto a special religious school system which was established on the initiative of Orthodox parents striving to secure a traditional religious education for their children. Two clandestine religious schools were in operation, a sort of elementary school called *Yeshiva Ktana* ("Elementary Yeshiva"), legalized by the ghetto chief in December 1942, and a *yeshiva* named for the then late Rabbi Chaim Oyzer Grodzenski. Both *yeshivoth* were located in prayer houses,[116] and teaching was so arranged that pupils could also attend the general schools. Some 200 students attended the *yeshivoth*, which periodically conducted public examinations with invited guests reviewing the progress of the students. After these examinations, a traditional meal would be served.[117]

A sort of higher technical school, training locksmiths and electricians, was also in operation with the aim of supplying artisans for ghetto industry in a hurry.

The schools were in operation almost to the very last days of the ghetto at the end of September 1943. Because of deportations to Estonia during mid-September 1943, the number of teachers decreased to 35 from 60. At the same time, the number of students, according to the same source, fell from 1,500 to 900.[118] The majority of these perished in Ponary, in the course of the liquidation of the ghetto (September 23, 1943), or were deported to concentration camps where almost all died in suffering and misery.

As far as other ghettos in the Lithuanian *Generalbezirk* are concerned, there is information available about Kaunas (already described above) and Šiauliai. In the Šiauliai Ghetto the school was not opened until June 15, 1943. It was located in two prayer houses in both parts of the ghetto (Traku and Kavkaz). At the opening, 200 students were divided in 7 groups. By the end of the month, 360 were enrolled under 7 teachers. The school operated in two shifts, from 8:00 A.M. to 4:00 P.M. and from 4:00 P.M. to 9:00 P.M. Unfortunately it was not in operation for long. At the beginning of October 1943 it was closed by the authorities, the older children joining the labor force, the younger ones usually remaining without care when parents left to work for 12 hours a day. Children from ten to thirteen years of age themselves went to work, "to show how useful they are for the ghetto." It was decided not to establish a kindergarten because it would be dangerous "if children and a children's home should be found in the ghetto."[119] The "action" against children on November 5, 1943, removed from the ghetto all children up to the age of thirteen years.

Regarding the Bezirk Białystok, information has been preserved about Białystok, capital of the Bezirk. The Jewish Council of Białystok received permission from the authorities in August 1941 to open the schools in the ghetto. A school commission was established within the framework of the cultural department, and registration of school children and teachers was carried out.[120] The first two classes were put in operation at the beginning of October 1941, and further classes opened during the following four months, including a regular elementary school with a seven-year curriculum. Some 1,600 students attended the school in 39 classes, some of them parallel, distributed in 3 shifts.[121] Another school opened on November 10, 1941, with some 500 children. The first school, located in the building of the prewar CISHO high school, was secular and coeducational. In the second school, boys and girls were taught in separate classes and according to the traditional religious curriculum.[122]

Along with this official school network, some kindergarten teachers supervised groups of smaller children in their own homes, for the schools of the Jewish Council could not accommodate all children of school age. In addition, many parents were afraid to send their children to the Council's schools because of the sudden "actions"; they preferred that teachers tutor their children at their homes. The cultural department, however, requested that they all register, threatening to forbid this type of schooling.[123]

The second school year began on August 18, 1942. It did not last long,[124] for, at the beginning of November, the entire Bezirk Białystok (except Białystok itself, Prużana, and Grodno) was engulfed by a wave of destruction that put an end to the entire school system. The Białystok Ghetto lived in fear of imminent liquidation, and in such an atmosphere no schools could operate.

To summarize, wherever schools could function they operated along the following lines:

1. The diverse educational policies that had characterized communal life in Eastern Europe, and particularly in Poland, disappeared almost everywhere in the ghettos after the Councils took over, formally or actually, the activities of the cultural sector, as was the case in Vilna, Łódź, and Białystok, for example. A more or less uniform school system was established in these ghettos, with Jewish cultural and political essentials (Yiddish, Hebrew, religion, and Eretz Israel) stressed in the curriculum according to the ideological affiliation of each school supervisor or individual teacher. However, the schools operated within the general framework of a uniform curriculum. Of all the larger ghettos studied, only the Warsaw Ghetto school system remained divided along the lines of diverse ideological programs.

2. Jewish subjects were central in the school programs on principle. Yiddish became the language of instruction in the Łódź Ghetto's uniform school system (in practice, however, because of lack of textbooks and teachers with sufficient knowledge of the language, this principle could not be adhered to strictly). In Vilna, Kaunas, and Białystok, with a long tradition of Yiddish and Hebrew schools, Yiddish was as a matter of course the instructional language.

3. The main advantage, however, was not the schooling itself, which was handicapped because of extreme poverty at home and lack of facilities, textbooks, equipment, and fuel in the winter. More important was the spiritual support the schools provided for the children, sheltering them from the demoralizing influence of ghetto life, and giving psychological aid and joy that were so rare in the ghettos. The schools also provided a cultural atmosphere for the ghetto inmates in general.[125]

OTHER CULTURAL ACTIVITIES

Cultural activities in the ghettos were not of immediate concern to the occupation authorities, though they did not explicitly forbid Jewish cultural activities below high school and college levels. It is possible that the authorities may have actually wanted to allow cheap amusements for the grumbling population, as was the case in other occupied countries. With respect to the Poles, it is known that the *Propagandaamt* supported smutty "art" on the stage and in obscene, illustrated magazines as a means of blunting the natural urge to resistance. With respect to the Jews, an additional purpose could have been to create an illusion of stability in the ghettos, as places where the Jews could develop their own cultural life within the general framework of "Jewish autonomy." Also the authorities must have considered that cultural activities could not possibly change or influence the vile plans they had in store for the Jews.

In a memorandum of the *Rassenpolitischesamt* of the Nazi Party, "Concerning the treatment of the Population of the Polish Territories from the Racial and Political Points of View," completed on November 25, 1939, we read: "Jewish political groups should be forbidden along with Polish ones. But Jewish cultural societies might be more tolerated than Polish ones. Jews may certainly be allowed more freedom in this respect than Poles, for the Jews have no such real political power as have the Poles. . . ."[126] It is also possible that the occupation authorities desired to masquerade as the enlightened government of a *Kulturvolk* which did not oppose legitimate cultural activities. However, wherever the authorities found out that cultural activities were a cover for political work, they instantly and severely retaliated. For instance, in the Warsaw Ghetto on the night of April 18, 1942, the Gestapo dragged from their homes several scores of underground workers active in the cultural affairs of the Ghetto and shot them in the streets.

As in other fields of ghetto life, the cultural policy of the Nazis with respect to the Jews was not uniform and depended on "the principle of local leadership." A few examples illustrate this point:

1. While in the Warsaw Ghetto, the authorities permitted, or at least tolerated, Jewish schools with Polish as the language of instruction (see above, p. 199), the *Hauptmann* of Błonie-Sochachev county (in the same district) addressed a letter on January 14, 1941, to the private Jewish school in Grodzisk, a small town in the Warsaw vicinity, stating that permission was being given to open Jewish elementary schools on the condition that instruction would be given in Yiddish or Hebrew. He based this condition on the order of the chief of the Warsaw district of December 27, 1940. As already mentioned, the permit for a school in Radom was given on the condition that all subjects would be taught exclusively in Yiddish. In Jasło (Cracow district), as we have already mentioned, the authorities

forced a switch to Hebrew as the language of instruction, permitting the teaching of Polish only as a supplementary language.[127]

2. In the Łódź Ghetto the authorities permitted the opening of two Jewish high schools, including lyceum classes, but, as far as can be ascertained, nowhere else were high schools tolerated in the ghetto, and schooling on this level was generally clandestine except in the Vilna Ghetto.

3. In Warsaw, Łódź, and in other ghettos in the Wartheland and the Government General, the selling or reading of German or Polish newspapers was strictly forbidden. Only two newspapers were allowed to the Jews in the entire occupation territory: the *Geto-tsaytung* in Łódź (Yiddish) and the *Gazeta Żydowska* in Cracow (Polish). Other newspapers were smuggled in and read in secret, though the reading room of the library of the Vilna Ghetto openly subscribed to a local Polish newspaper and a German one in 1943.[128] According to a single, unchecked news item, two Jews were hanged in the Zelwa Ghetto (Wartheland) for reading forbidden newspapers.[129]

4. Contrary to the practice in Warsaw, Łódź, and Vilna, where the authorities tolerated Jewish theater (see below, p. 224), the *Hauptmann* of Częstochowa refused a request of the Jewish Council on July 5, 1941, to permit a Jewish theater.[130]

5. In the Warsaw Ghetto, the authorities prohibited the Jewish orchestra to play music of "Aryan" composers, but no such restriction was ordered in the Łódź and Vilna Ghettos (see pp. 223, 227).

As for the internal factors which shaped the cultural life of the ghettos, they are to be considered within the framework of certain sociological and moral phenomena. In many ghettos, particularly the larger ones, one can find, on the one hand, an intensive urge for cultural and aesthetic impressions and renewed interest in the Jewish cultural past, and, on the other hand, a strengthening of assimilationist tendencies. Contemporary reports from Vilna, Warsaw, and other ghettos stress a prevailing "yearning for a Jewish book," and for Jewish music and theater on the part of a large segment of the ghetto inmates.[131] On the one hand, people longed to escape from the reality of ghetto life—"to get intoxicated with a book"—as a means of psychological compensation, a reaction against the Nazis' dehumanizing methods and the feeling of inferiority they tried to press upon the Jews in the ghettos. On the other hand, this phenomenon also manifested a deep and earnest desire to get to know the literature and the history of the people's sufferings, to search for an answer to the "Jewish question" and to find consolation for their current misery. This desire was especially evident among youths oriented toward national problems.

The fact that substantial numbers of assimilationists and converted Jews were forced to live in the ghettos prompted the emergence of an assimilationist mood among other ghetto inmates. In some of the ghettos—Warsaw, for instance—the assimilationists gained considerable influence by getting leading positions in the administrative offices of the Jewish Council, in its institutions, or in the ghetto police. It was easy for them to explain the negative aspects of ghetto life as distinctive features of Jewish folk-life in general. Their former indifference to things Jewish turned to contempt and animosity toward the Jewish masses and their culture.

Their desperate fate gave the less ethnically and religiously conscious segments of the ghetto inmates an impulse to escape from their unfortunate coreligionists. In a situation where being a Jew bristled with enormous dangers, conditions were particularly fertile for the emergence of a sort of "ethnic mimicry." The widespread fantasy about escaping to the "Aryan" side, where one could endure only if his appearance was unmistakably non-Jewish, was also a significant assimilationist factor.

It is characteristic of the mood in some ghettos that influential writers and leaders of cultural life in the Warsaw Ghetto feared a mass movement among the Jews to convert to Christianity after the war as a sort of protection against an insecure future.[132] In some ghettos (i.e., Warsaw and Lwów) there actually were frequent cases of apostasy for material reasons, due to the fact that the Catholic charity organization Caritas took care of the converts.[133]

As for the prospects and possibilities for creative cultural work in the ghettos, some Jewish intellectuals maintained up to a certain time that the ghettos created conditions favorable to cultural activities;[134] others, however, were of the opinion that no cultural creativity could exist in the ghettos.[135] Opposing opinions notwithstanding, it can be stated that cultural activities in the ghettos played an important role.

On the one hand, the aim of these cultural activities was to make the Jewish consciousness of the ghetto inmates, particularly the young generation, immune against the evil effects of ghetto life, creating some moral support in the atmosphere of naked, often brutal, materialism prevalent in numerous ghettos. On the other hand, the cultural activities gave the ghetto Jews strength to withstand the attempts at dehumanization and moral denigration of the Jews by the Nazis. It was a clearcut case of spiritual resistance.

As a rule, cultural life in the ghettos emerged on the initiative of prewar cultural institutions and political groups with a long history of experience in this field among the Jews. For legal reasons, however, the official stamp of the Jewish Councils was necessary for all cultural activities. Along with welfare, cultural work created a field of activities that enabled some groups outside the Councils to work for the benefit of the ghetto inmates. Both kinds of activities were closely associated with the Jewish Welfare organization and, in fact, served as a means of providing funds for the pertinent relief committees and welfare institutions.

Cultural activities depended to a large degree on the vitality and intensity of the prewar cultural inheritance of a given ghetto. The Vilna Ghetto is a good example. Of all the ghettos, cultural manifestations in the Vilna Ghetto were the most intense, engulfing the ghetto inmates of all walks of life, and comprising an important part of the official tasks of the Council. A historian of the Vilna Ghetto writes that "as the Vilna Jewish community was for years known as 'the Jerusalem of Lithuania,' so the Vilna Ghetto in respect to its cultural life deserves to be called 'the Jerusalem of the Ghettos,' because it was a symbol of Jewish spiritual resistance under the Nazi regime."[136]

Reading the uncommonly rich documentation of cultural activities in the Vilna Ghetto, one is often tempted not to believe that such colorful, almost "normal" cultural work took place in a ghetto where remnants of a decimated community were concentrated, constantly in danger of destruction. The work of the cultural department of the Council was performed by a number of divisions: schools, library and reading room, theater (stage, orchestra, Yiddish and Hebrew choirs), archives, statistical office, museum, folklore, sports, music school, and bookshop. The department also published *Geto-yedies* ("Ghetto News").[137]

The numerous intellectuals with Jewish orientation were of great help in fostering diversified cultural life in the ghetto. Writers, teachers, and cultural leaders who had fled to Vilna from other Jewish centers (e.g., Warsaw and Kaunas) in the fall and winter of 1939, and in the summer of 1941, increased the forces of the native intelligentsia. These refugees from Warsaw and Kaunas took over important positions.[138]

Little material on the cultural activities of the Councils in the smaller ghettos has been preserved in the sources. It is clear that these Councils were entirely absorbed in dealing with the immediate emergencies of daily life in the ghetto, and had no time or energy left for cultural activities. This was particularly evident in those ghettos where almost everyone active in the cultural life of the community before the war had been carried away by waves of refugees during the initial period of the occupation, landing in areas occupied by the Soviets. Many towns in central and western Poland lost their active cultural leaders and teachers.[139] Typical is the situation reported by an inmate of the Łęczyca Ghetto (population 3,000) in the Wartheland: "No school exists, no cultural activities can be arranged. Mothers have tried to teach their children a little . . . but no collective effort could be undertaken to establish a school."[140]

The following paragraphs deal with the activities of the Councils of a few of the larger ghettos in three cultural fields:

LIBRARIES

Right at the start of the occupation of Poland, all Jewish bookshops and libraries were closed and their books carried away. Among others, the well-known Judaica Library of the Warsaw Great Synagogue at Tłomackie Street was confiscated in October 1939, as were the Strashun Library and the YIVO Library in Vilna during the winter of 1942.

The Jewish Council in Warsaw tried to get permission to open a lending library and bookshops, and the German chief caretaker of the confiscated Jewish bookshops and libraries permitted the transferring from the "Aryan" side into the ghetto of Yiddish and Hebrew books and books necessary for religious study.[141] Soon a number of bookshops and lending libraries were opened in the ghetto, but in January 1942, after they had been in operation for some six months, they were closed on orders of the authorities.[142] Undercover portable lending libraries then appeared, delivering books to the homes of readers. The Centos established a portable library for children in its institutions.[143]

The popular library *Mefitsei Haskalah* was the first cultural institution to open in the Vilna Ghetto, lending books as early as the fourth day after ghettoization. The cultural department of the Jewish Council operated this library, along with all other cultural institutions. In September 1941 the Council took a decision to place in the library all books left in former Jewish homes now outside the ghetto, and house superintendents were ordered to hand these books over to authorized persons. In March 1943 the ghetto chief, Jacob Gens, ordered the delivery to the library of all books that still remained in private homes, except textbooks and prayer books.[144] Jewish laborers who worked outside the ghetto, the so-called "outer commandos," often smuggled in books they had found in abandoned Jewish homes. The Jewish employees of the *Einsatzstab Rosenberg*, who worked in the confiscated building of the YIVO sorting out books and periodicals taken from libraries in Vilna and nearby provinces, were particularly busy smuggling books into the ghetto.[145]

The library had 93,463 books and volumes of magazines as of January 1942, with 3,864 subscribers as of August 1942, when there were only 17,000 inmates in the ghetto.[146] The library also assisted in forming small book collections in the neighboring labor camps and in some provincial ghettos (Oszmiana, for example) which were under the supervision of the Vilna Ghetto chief.[147]

The library maintained a reading room used by from 100 to 206 visitors a day during the period from July 1942 to March 1943.[148] On the initiative of the library management, a bookshop was opened selling, according to a report for August 1942, 198 books in that month. A total of 7,281 books were in stock at that time.[149]

Of all the prewar Jewish private and public libraries in Łódź, only one library remained in operation. At the beginning of 1944, it had in stock 7,500 books with some 4,000 subscribers. All other Jewish libraries had been confiscated during the winter of 1939–1940 by the Łódź *Nebenstelle* of the *Propagandaamt* in the Wartheland. A few small lending libraries did remain in private homes, attracting readers by putting out small signs. As a rule, the authorities tolerated these small libraries, but they too were not allowed to keep German military works or books that were forbidden in the Reich. The political parties also maintained their own illegal libraries.[150] With the advent of deportations, heaps of books remained in the homes of the deportees and were later sold as pulp or used for various other purposes. On the initiative of the chief of the registration department of the Jewish Council, who had previously received permission from the economic department, the janitors and house superintendents were ordered to check sealed apartments, attics, and basements, collect all the books they might find, and deliver them to the registration department. Thus some 30,000 books were assembled in three rooms of the basement of the department during 1942 and the first half of 1943. All were sorted and catalogued. The rich book collection of Rabbi Traystman of Łódź was in this library, as were several scores of Torah scrolls, phylacteries, prayer shawls, and other religious objects. Out of this collection, several hundred books were chosen to supplement several small portable libraries serving young readers in institutions for children.[151]

THEATER AND MUSIC

The war caused widespread unemployment among the hundreds of Jewish actors, musicians, painters, and graphic artists. Their numbers swelled still further when "non-Aryan" actors previously working on the Polish stage were driven into the ghettos. Their economic situation was precarious. Jewish actors in Warsaw began to entertain at private gatherings, collecting donations from those present. After a time, places of entertainment and theaters were licensed in the ghetto with the help of partners having connections with "them." The number of such entertainment places grew steadily, causing a bigger demand for artistic talent. We read in the *Gazeta Żydowska* of June 17, 1941: "The demand for artists is big. . . . Each coffeehouse, each bar and restaurant . . . advertises its own rich program of sensational attractions. . . . Lately, small gardens have sprung up, such as the 'Idyll,' the 'Bagatelle,' the 'Garden of the Artists,' etc." According to Ringelblum, there were, in April 1941, 61 entertainment places in the ghetto.[152]

The artistic merits of all these establishments were very low indeed. In order to raise their level and protect the professional interests of the performers, a Central Show Commission was established at the JSS in September 1940, on the initiative of a group of cultural activists. Some 267 professional artists and 150 musicians were registered up to the end of September 1941, and these were given permission to perform in public. Up to October 1941 the commission arranged 1,814 shows, including 8 symphonic concerts. The first concert took place on November 6, 1940.[153] String quartets and chamber music were also offered. Several choirs performed in the ghetto: two folk choruses, two popular song groups, the choir *Shir* ("Song"), the Choir of the Great Synagogue, and children's choirs.[154] But the Show Commission could not find work for all musicians, and some worked in private places of entertainment or in backyards as street bands. It is worthwhile to cite here a few excerpts from a contemporary document describing the situation of a large number of the musicians in the Warsaw Ghetto:

> Musicians of renown have found work in [newly] opened places [of entertainment]. . . . The musicians from Łódź work . . . for whatever donations the patrons dole out. . . . They go hungry if they don't get alms. . . . Other musicians have organized small groups wandering from backyard to backyard as long as the weather is warm. Sometimes they make some money, but often they make nothing. During the winter they could not work at all. Some could be seen with their fiddles in the streets, freezing and begging.[155]

There even was a licensed street orchestra under the leadership of a popular conductor. Some artists found work in the Centos institutions, and recognition is due to them for the high level of aesthetic education in the ghetto schools where high-quality shows were produced, distinguished by their artistic, musical, and choreographic features, and by lovely stage settings, as was noted in the memoirs of the above-mentioned school inspector.[156]

Five professional theater companies played in the Warsaw Ghetto (two performed in Yiddish and three in Polish), having obtained licenses through people with connections with "them." The Show Commission lacked authority over the theaters. There were always enough people currently making money among the ghetto inmates— smugglers, shop owners, all sorts of wheeler-dealers, and others— ready to enjoy cheap entertainment. They constituted a steady audience for the various shows and theaters catering to their tastes. Two theaters, both performing in Polish, played on a higher artistic level for the intelligentsia.[157]

A puppet theater from Łódź also performed, and a puppet theater for children was established by Centos to play for children under its care. Several ballet studios with separate schools for rhythmics and dance were also opened in the ghetto.[158] Shows and concerts continued until the summer deportations.

By order of the *Kommissar für den jüdischen Wohnbezirk*, dated April 8, 1942, all works by "Aryan" authors and composers were removed from the repertories of the orchestra and theaters, as already mentioned. For insubordination, the symphony orchestra was forbidden to perform for two months (April–June 1942). The orchestra never resumed its work, for by June the ghetto was already shaken by rumors of the impending disaster.[159]

Probably at the request of the authorities, the Jewish Council tried to control the theaters and all other entertainment in the ghetto, first through its art and cultural department (which incidentally was not active at all) and later, after April 1942, through its entertainment division. In an announcement published in *Gazeta Żydowska* in April 1942, it is stated that the entertainment division has taken over the task of enhancing the artistic level of shows, and that all places of entertainment must be registered with the Council and all programs submitted to the entertainment division for approval by the supervisory authorities. Because the entertainment commission at the JSS actually competed with the entertainment division of the Council, Czerniakow tried to merge it with the division; but he was unsuccessful and finally dismissed the JSS commission altogether. However, the commission did not give in and continued its activities until the start of the mass deportations in July 1942,[160] when the entire program of cultural activities came to an end.

As in Warsaw, Częstochowa, and other ghettos, cultural activities in the Łódź Ghetto developed thanks to public initiative. A Jewish Cultural Society was established in October 1940, with the task of opening a library, a folk university, Yiddish courses for adults and teachers, a drama circle, concerts, etc. The prewar *Hazomir* Society renewed its work, choruses were organized, a symphony orchestra was established, etc. However, Rumkowski, who understood only too well that his absolute reign in the ghetto would not be complete unless he also controlled cultural activities, abolished the independent cultural institutions. It is conceivable that he acted on instructions from the authorities. Through him the Nazis controlled all that happened in the ghetto, and they tolerated no activities not under the control of Rumkowski or his men. Whatever the reason, it is a fact that all cultural work in the ghetto after February 1941 was under the official supervision of Rumkowski's administration.

On March 1, 1941, the House of Culture was inaugurated and remained under the management of the chief of the labor office. It is not known whether there was a separate cultural division at that time in the labor office; if there was it does not appear in the list of divisions of that office.

Two kinds of entertainment were offered at the House of Culture: symphonic concerts with participating soloists and revues presented by the theater studio "Avangard."

There were in the ghetto local showmen, in addition to the highly talented musicians, singers, and stage actors who arrived among the Jews deported from Central Europe. On orders of Rumkowski, all newcomers were registered by the House of Culture, and up to December 6, 1941, 60 musicians, singers, and actors and 10 painters registered. Many found employment in their fields.

The symphony orchestra averaged 10 concerts a month in 1941, but played only 4 times a month in 1942. Revues were presented two or three times a week. Some 70,000 people attended concerts, shows, and performances of high school choruses in 1941 (starting in March). All shows were under the strict surveillance of Rumkowski. He often used the House of Culture as a forum to deliver speeches.

Some of the painters and sculptors found employment painting scenery for the revues; other worked in the graphics division of the department of statistics and in the so-called scientific division, whose job it was to carve burlesque figures of Eastern European Jews and design exhibits of Jewish life for the museum of the *Gettoverwaltung.* A special room in the House of Culture was designated for the use of painters and sculptors, and food stamps were promised free of charge to those working there.

After the authorities confiscated all musical instruments in January 1944, the symphony orchestra was dismantled. The revues were also discontinued.[161]

During the first killing actions in Vilna, 20 stage actors and 7 of the technical personnel of the Jewish theater were murdered in Ponary.[162] The remaining actors and technical workers decided to establish a theater in the ghetto. But political groups called meetings and the labor parties decided to boycott the theater. It was even proposed to storm the theater because people were afraid that the shows would desecrate the mourning of the thousands of victims. The culture department of the Council was also opposed to the idea. But the plan to start a theater in the ghetto was backed by the ghetto police and their chief. As late as April 17, 1942, the chief of the ghetto police asked in a letter that the culture department not resist the opening of the theater in the small former municipal hall.[163] On opening day, hundreds of handbills framed in black were distributed in the ghetto hall with the following text: "One does not present shows in cemeteries." The premiere, on January 18, 1942, took place in a solemn mood resulting from the carefully selected program. For the most part, only policemen, officials, and members of the Council and their families attended the first show. The second show, a week later (on the 25th), was attended by the German and Lithuanian officials directly involved in killing actions. A contemporary chronicler in the Vilna Ghetto writes with exasperation that "thus the chief murderers in all actions were suitably entertained . . . [among them] one of the greatest sadists of the *Ypatinga* [the Lithuanian special police]." In time inhibitions against the theater in the ghetto disappeared, and people patronized it.[164] Whatever profits accrued were given to the public help committee.

The theatrical division in the cultural department supervised the work of the stage actors, musicians, singers, and the two choruses (one Yiddish and one Hebrew). The theater company consisted of some 20 actors, the orchestra had 30 musicians, the Yiddish chorus had 80 singers, and the Hebrew one had 75. The orchestra played symphonic music, light music, and jazz.[165] For the most part, the shows were diversified: a classical repertoire was given together with plays on contemporary ghetto topics, often spiked with bitter jests—the ghetto brand of wit—a sort of laughter with tears; it was, after all, the function of the theater to make the patrons forget the ghetto and their abominable lives there for a few hours. This was accomplished: "People spared no efforts to get tickets."[166]

There were times when the theater was in operation every day or every second day. Sixteen shows, three performances of the choruses, two symphonic concerts, and a concert of the music school, a total of 22 performances, were given in October 1942; 18 in December; and 25 in January 1943.[167] In March 1943 six or seven entertainments of all sorts were offered every Sunday, with 2,000 people attending.[168]

According to Dworzecki, the theater gave 120 shows in 1942 with 38,000 people attending.

The symphony orchestra, which performed its fifth program in March 1943, played undisturbed, two or three times a month, compositions by "Aryan" composers.[169]

In addition to the two choruses already mentioned, liturgical choral music was presented by a religious chorus. Its first concert took place on Hanukkah, in December 1942.[170] In June or July 1942 a music school was opened under the direction of two prominent Vilna conductors. Some 95 students were enrolled as of August 1942. They gave their own concerts and also participated in various other cultural engagements in the ghetto.[171]

For the forced laborers outside the ghetto who could not attend cultural events given during weekdays, special "workers' shows" were arranged on Sundays. The program usually consisted of a lecture on a literary subject or socio-medical problem, followed by recitals and performances by stage actors or student and youth clubs.[172]

The Jewish Council also subsidized the union of writers and artists, the congregating place of the intellectual elite of the ghetto who had survived the various "Ponary actions" in the fall of 1941. The union was the moving spirit stimulating cultural life in the ghetto. It often arranged lectures on literature, concerts, "literary matinees," etc.[173] To support its members' finances and morale, the union arranged literary and art contests under the sponsorship of the ghetto chief, who himself nominated the jury members or approved the candidates suggested by the contest jury. He also financed the awards.[174]

MUSEUMS, ARCHIVES, AND PUBLICATIONS

The cultural department of the Vilna Jewish Council assisted in the establishment of a ghetto museum. Here were assembled works of art, books of secular and religious content, Torah scrolls, and other religious objects that "were scattered in the abandoned, desolated homes in the ghetto." Among others, the archives of the Zionist organization in Vilna were put there, along with the library and archives of the late Rabbi Chaim Oyzer Grodzenski, the minute books of the various societies and prayer houses, etc. In the cellars of the ghetto library, and in various hiding places, precious documents and museum objects from the YIVO were hidden, smuggled in by Jewish employees in the *Einsatzstab Rosenberg*.[175]

The ghetto archives, working within the general framework of the cultural department, assembled all official and nonofficial documentation pertaining to the ghetto: orders of the Jewish Council (later of the ghetto chief); orders of the ghetto police; reports of the individual departments, shops, and factories; reports of the statistical departments; eyewitness reports of escapees from Ponary and from the liquidated ghettos; etc. Manuscripts of writers, memoirists, and scientists were also hidden there. The archives functioned quite openly as a division of the cultural department.[176]

The archives of the Łódź Ghetto formally performed the functions of the ghetto registry. Actually, however, it was busy as the documentation center of the ghetto. The archivists, among them deported intellectuals from Berlin, Vienna, and Prague, wrote monographs and reportage on all aspects of ghetto life. In the first months of 1944, they even compiled an encyclopedia of the Łódź Ghetto, intended to furnish resourceful and well-documented information on affairs and persons in the ghetto.

Starting on January 12, 1941, the archives published a house bulletin (on a daily, weekly, and monthly basis) in Polish and German (in German only since 1943). It continued until July 1944, and is one of the most important sources of our knowledge about the Łódź Ghetto and its history.[177]

The *Geto-tsaytung* in Łódź, which was published and sponsored by Rumkowski and the Gestapo, contained in its 18 issues published from March to September 1941, announcements of the ghetto administration, reports, reportage on the workings of departments of the ghetto administration, and sentences of the ghetto court. For the most part it glorified Rumkowski and his great achievements for the benefit of the ghetto. Each issue contained four pages (40 by 26 centimeters).

The agricultural department published a "Guide for the Part-time Gardener." It contained gardening information for the uninformed ghetto farmers, who leased land from the department and who seldom, if ever, had had anything to do with working the soil before. Three mimeographed issues appeared from June 5 to June 19, 1942, and one issue on July 2, 1943. How many were published altogether is not known.[178]

The Jewish Council in Lwów published *Mitteilungen des Juden-*

rates in Lemberg für die jüdische Gemeinde. It printed the announcements and instructions of the individual departments, the ghetto police, the Jewish Council, and the JSS, along with the orders of the Nazi authorities. Three issues were published during the period from January to March 1942, each containing eight small pages (29 by 21 centimeters). It also contained legal advice for individual inquirers. The editor responsible was Stanisław Matfus. It seems that publication was terminated after the third issue.[179]

The research work and publication activities of the statistical departments in Warsaw, Łódź, Vilna, Kaunas, and Częstochowa Ghettos have already been discussed in Chap. 8.

By order of the authorities, a department for conservation and buildings was established by the Cracow Jewish Council, charged with the task, among others, of taking care of the conservation of the historical monuments (synagogues, cemeteries, *pinkosim* [record books of various societies and of the *Kehilas*], and religious objects) of Cracow, one of the oldest Jewish communities in Poland. It was suggested that the Council establish a museum of Jewish religious art at the Jewish Council.[180] Nothing is known about the activities of this department which, in fact, was not established to care for Jewish cultural heritages but to provide historical and cultural material for the Nazi institutes of *Judenkunde.*

Along with the final liquidation of the ghetto in March 1943, the ancient synagogues in Cracow and the cemetery were left to wanton pillage and decay, and whatever might have remained after the confiscation by the *Einsatzstab Rosenberg* was, for the most part, ruined.[181]

With few exceptions this was also the fate of all Jewish monuments, community archives, and museums throughout Eastern Europe. Almost all synagogues, prayer houses, and cemeteries were maliciously destroyed. The museum collections, such as the Mathias Berson Museum of the Warsaw Jewish community was closed by the authorities on March 12, 1940, and when it was later reopened in the presence of a German professor from Tübingen on June 6, no objects were found there. They had disappeared together with the glass display cases. The Goldstein collection of the Lwów Jewish community, the precious archival collection of the Cracow Jewish community, the rich Gieldzinsky collection of religious objects of the Danzig Jewish community, and other collections were all confiscated and carried away to Germany.[182]

CHAPTER 10

The Finances of the Jewish Councils

As HAS BEEN SHOWN IN previous chapters, the Jewish Councils were active both in financing and executing orders imposed by the Germans (cash contributions exacted by various authorities; deliveries of goods; wages for Jewish forced laborers; building ghetto walls, barbed wire fences, etc.) and in meeting the needs of ghetto inmates in the fields of welfare, medical aid, elementary schools and vocational training; in the organization and maintenance of a widespread administrative, police, and court apparatus; and in the establishment and maintenance of ghetto shops, etc. To finance this diversified activity the Councils needed large sums of money, which had to come from somewhere.

At the outset of the occupation, the treasuries of the Jewish communities were for the most part empty, as a result of war operations and robberies by military or police authorities. In addition, many Councils were in debt for the unpaid salaries of community functionaries. When the war broke out, many communities were unable to pay salaries not only for the then past month (August) but, in many cases, for previous months still outstanding. In the introduction to the already mentioned report of the Warsaw Jewish Council it is stated that "the day the Council was established it was already one million zlotys in debt for unpaid salaries and deliveries."[1] And the Cracow Jewish Council, in its report mentioned above, stated in connection with relief activity that "it was not an easy task, taking into consideration that the newly established Jewish representative body found an almost empty treasury, with large debts and large tasks to boot."[2] In Lublin the debts of the community amounted to 200,000 zlotys as of September 1, 1939.[3] A similar lack of finances existed in Łódź.[4]

In addition, community treasuries were emptied by "visiting" German officials. Thus in Warsaw during a meeting of the Jewish Citizens' Committee at the community building on October 4, 1939, the Gestapo men opened the safe and took 97,000 zlotys, all that was there.[5]

A big obstacle for the financial activities of the Councils was the legal limit on the amount of cash Jews were allowed to handle (see Chap. 5, pp. 62–63). No distinction was made between private persons and community executives or agents of social welfare institutions.

After a time the authorities found out that this restriction was impractical. Thus, for instance, the *Stadtkommissar* in Łódź, in a letter to Rumkowski on October 16, 1939, stated that to make it possible for him to execute the orders he had received three days earlier (October 14), he had been given permission personally to withdraw from the banks as much cash as might be necessary for this purpose. The letter noted that this permission was contrary to the order of the civil administration (September 18, 1939) concerning cash payments to and disbursements by Jews, but that it had been approved by the chief of the civil administration in Łódź and a representative of the German state bank.[6]

No such order revoking the limitation on cash disbursements by Jewish Councils in the area of the Government General has been uncovered so far, except for the Warsaw Ghetto. But the authorities, in fact, tolerated exceptions for the Councils, because they would otherwise have been in no position to function.[7]

The Councils had to apply various measures to create a financial basis for their activities. Efforts were made to obtain permission to borrow money through Jewish and non-Jewish credit establishments; to release the blocked prewar accounts of Jewish communities, private institutions, and individuals for the benefit of the Councils; to get the imposed *Treuhänder* ("caretakers") of confiscated Jewish properties to pay to the Councils the community taxes that legitimate owners used to pay, etc. For the most part, these efforts either were unsuccessful or had very limited results.

Only one case is known (in Piotrków Trybunalski) where the authorities, at the initiative of the Council, permitted the *Treuhänder* of the six largest industrial enterprises formerly belonging to Jews to turn over 22,000 zlotys to the Jewish Council. This took place on March 4, 1940, in connection with the enormous expenditures (150,000 zlotys) the Council incurred while building three barracks on orders from the authorities. The Piotrków Trybunalski *Bürgermeister* cynically noted that the sum allowed, a minute part of the confiscated Jewish property, should be treated as "Jewish voluntary self-help action."[8]

The most important source of income in the ghettos came from various taxes and fees levied by the Councils. We shall discuss these later in this chapter. Now, however, we shall analyze the other sources of income.

LOANS

In April 1940 the Warsaw Jewish Council succeeded in obtaining a loan of 200,000 zlotys from the Warsaw branch of the Łódź Deposit Bank (this had been a Jewish bank before the war). The private bank of D. M. Shereshewski in Warsaw also gave the Council a loan of an unspecified amount. In addition the Council negotiated loans with two other banks in Warsaw.[9]

The *Statistical Bulletin* (No. 3, June 2, 1940) carried an item that the Council had received permission to make a loan of 100,000 zlotys in one of the Warsaw financial establishments against a mortgage on the Council's real estate. Permission had come from the "plenipotentiary of the Warsaw Governor."[10] In August 1940, the loan from the Deposit Bank was, credited to the account of the Jewish National Fund and Keren Hayesod, in the same bank.[11] The Council also borrowed money from the Joint Distribution Committee and various other Jewish organizations.[12]

In Łódź, too, the Council tried to get a loan during the first few weeks of the occupation under the pledge of the prewar Polish state securities it held.[13] Rumkowski also got loans in the form of advanced payments by wholesalers and bankers on account of flour and other food staples he bought from non-Jewish firms.[14]

In August and September 1940 the economic crisis in the Łódź Ghetto reached its highest point. An epidemic of dysentery, constant hunger, and mass unemployment created a situation without solution, particularly since Rumkowski had been deprived of the right

Both ends of the bridge over the "Aryan" street in the Łódź Ghetto.

to buy food for the ghetto on credit from non-Jewish firms. Despite the fact that the amount of confiscated Jewish assets and cash reached many millions of Reichsmarks, the German *Gettoverwaltung* was of the opinion that this amount was not enough to pay for the ghetto's food. Therefore, the *Gettoverwaltung* approached the *Regierungspräsident*, Friedrich Übelhoer, suggesting that he make available to the ghetto 3 million Reichsmarks of which 2 million were to cover outstanding debts for deliveries and 1 million were to be kept in reserve.

On October 21, 1940, the *Warenhandelsgesellschaft* in Łódź replied that it was ready to give the 3 million Reichsmarks loan for six months at 4½ percent interest; two days later Rumkowski received information that credit had been opened for this amount and on these conditions. The *Gettoverwaltung* had no illusions as to whether or not Rumkowski would be able to repay the loan with interest in such a short time, and expressed its doubts in a confirmation letter of October 23 to the *Warenhandelsgesellschaft*, suggesting that the loan be better considered a formality.[15] It also should be stated that the *Warenhandelsgesellschaft* (which consisted of representatives of the *Regierungspräsident*, the German city administration, the Chamber of Trade and Industry, and the German Society for Wholesale and Retail Trade) was established as a joint depository for textiles and other goods confiscated from the Jews. It became the branch of the HTO in Łódź. It goes without saying that the actual source of the 3 million Reichsmarks was the much larger amount of cash and goods confiscated from the Jews, and that the loan was repaid many times over in the form of Jewish assets fallen into the hands of the Germans.

The Lublin Jewish Council requested that the *Stadthauptmann* support its efforts to obtain a loan from local credit establishments.[16] It is not known whether these efforts succeeded.

RELEASE OF BLOCKED JEWISH ACCOUNTS

In another effort to find funds, the Councils sought the release of Jewish accounts blocked in the banks.

Thus the Warsaw Jewish Council got permission to borrow two amounts, 300,000 zlotys and at another time 100,000 zlotys, from the blocked Emigration Fund which had been accumulated through individual deposits in the community treasury to cover planned emigration expenses.[17]

In addition, the Council endeavored to release the blocked account of the Pension Fund of the community employees in the former Polish state bank *Gospodarstwa Krajowego* (Bank of the State Economy)[18] and to transfer the blocked accounts belonging to former residents of the incorporated territories who had fled to Warsaw.[19] The Council also tried to get permission to cover its financial needs out of the blocked accounts of individuals.[20] Some success was achieved in this respect, as can be seen, for instance, from the notice in the *Statistical Bulletin* (No. 12, January 1941) that the Council and the German Emission Bank in Warsaw had reached an agreement according to which the Council would act as agent between the bank and the Jewish owners of blocked accounts. The Council would be paid the amounts that the Jews were allowed to draw from the banks against original receipts of the owners. The Council would be entitled to a fee of 2 pro mill.[21]

In the Łódź Ghetto, Rumkowski obtained general permission from the Łódź branch of the HTO to draw cash, on a weekly basis, from the blocked accounts of Jewish organizations and individuals in five Łódź banks. But the banks made this procedure very difficult for him, refusing to recognize the general authorization and requesting a new permit from the *Treuhandstelle* each time.[22] Soon the *Treuhandstelle* canceled the permit altogether, maintaining that "the Jews have enough cash at their disposal."[23]

PARTICIPATION IN GENERAL TAX REVENUES

Some of the Councils tried to get proportionated refunds on account of the communal taxes the Jews continued to pay without getting any benefits in return. In its memorandum to the German supervisory authority on July 29, 1940, the Lublin Jewish Council asked for intervention with the town administration in order to get some funds for its welfare activities, pointing out that the Jewish population represented 40 percent of all Lublin inhabitants, paying substantial amounts for the benefit of the town treasury.[24]

In the summer of 1940 the Warsaw Ghetto Council asked the plenipotentiary of the governor to allocate a stable monthly subsidy out of taxes collected by the city (which the Jews paid along with all other city dwellers) to cover welfare expenses.[25] The request was not granted. From the above-mentioned report for the period October 7, 1939, to December 31, 1940, we learn that the Council again repeated its request for a subsidy from the city administration out of taxes contributed by the Jews, to help finance at least part of the welfare activities that the Council had taken over from the city administration.[26] This request was not granted either, nor was the request that the JSS receive part of the income derived from the surcharge on street-car tickets paid by Jewish passengers.[27]

Only one instance is known where a Council received a certain amount to cover its budget: in the report of the Council of Elders in Cracow there is included the sum of 50,000 zlotys received from the office of the *Stadthauptmann* that was allocated for welfare and education.[28] Of an entirely different nature was another subsidy, this one in the amount of 660,000 zlotys, to cover part of the expenses of the Council in connection with the mass expulsion of the Jews from Cracow.[29] For the noble goal of making the capital of the Government General "free of Jews," the German authorities in Cracow readily paid the Jews money which (as was the case with the "loan" in Łódź, for instance) was not lent at German expense, but plundered from the Jews anyway.

Thus we see that in almost all cases efforts made to get back at least a small part of communal or individual assets taken from the Jews by the Germans had no success; nor did efforts to share in some of the taxes the Jews were ordered to pay without any benefits in return. Therefore, despite the increasingly deteriorating economic situation of the ghettos, the Councils were forced to tax ghetto inmates to raise cash for their budgets.

TAXES AND FEES

In their general orders about the Jewish Councils, Heydrich and Frank did not mention that they were given the right to impose taxes on the Jews.[30] Only one general order, the one dealing with Jewish postal service (dated December 24, 1941) and issued by the chief of the German Post Office in the Government General, granted the Councils the right to a surcharge on the general postal rates.[31] However, the right of taxation is mentioned in orders and instructions issued by local occupation authorities.

On October 14, 1939, the *Stadtkommissar* in Łódź ordered Rumkowski to disband Jewish social institutions and their executives. At the same time he permitted the imposition of a tax on the Jews "to cover expenses in connection with the execution of the measures delegated to him."[32] In Warsaw on December 13, 1939, the German authorities confirmed the so-called *Kultussteuer*—actually the right to collect the prewar community tax;[33] the authorities also confirmed a tax statute for the Council on June 26, 1940. The Council's tax statute of June 26, 1940, contained 20 paragraphs and gave it the right to collect a permanent fee for monthly food cards at a rate decided by the Council; a "special tax" levied on a yearly basis against still prosperous individuals, including nonpermanent residents owning businesses or real estate in Warsaw; and in extraordinary cases an additional surcharge to be collected from persons in the "special tax" category. The yardstick for the last two taxes was the amount of income and the standard of living of the taxpayer.[34] Paragraph 3 of the statute stated that the *Treuhand* managers were obligated to pay the imposed taxes to the Jewish Council. However, this never happened. All Czerniakow's efforts to bring about the actual implementation of this provision were to no avail. They simply defied this provision, apparently with the tacit agreements of the authorities.

Also unsuccessful were the committee's efforts to finance the welfare activities of the Council by getting the right to impose a 4 percent tax on real estate, by increasing by 100 percent the fees for trade and industry licenses, and by getting a proper share of municipal income derived from additional fees for street-car tickets, gas and electricity, and from the "residence tax." With the exception of the last one, all other taxes were refused.[35]

Apart from officially introduced or approved taxes, the Warsaw Jewish Council also collected a variety of other taxes and fees which were tacitly tolerated by the authorities. They were not very interested in protecting the Jews from the heavy burden of taxes levied by the Councils. Up to the time the ghetto was established, Jews paid a community tax, a hospital tax, a 1 zloty a month fee for food rationing cards (when cards were distributed on a bi-monthly basis the fee was 2 zlotys), and an "extraordinary tribute," which was, according to the tax statute, to be paid by prosperous taxpayers.[36]

Taxes multiplied after the ghetto was established. Thus "lucky" people who had always resided in the area that became the ghetto (and, therefore, did not have to move out into new dwellings) were taxed to finance the moving expenses of people who had to move into the ghetto compound from homes situated outside the borders, in the "Aryan" part of the city.[37] Even Jewish tenants whose names appeared on lists which had to be placed on the walls of each building were taxed from 50 groszy to 1 zloty each. To cover the expenditures necessary to fight the typhus epidemic, a fee of 50 groszy was charged for each room occupied.[38]

The registration department of the Council charged a fee of 1 zloty for each Jewish newcomer. In addition, each of these people twelve to sixty years of age who was liable for forced-labor duty was charged a 1½-zloty "handling fee." If such a person submitted a request for a medical examination he was charged 5 zlotys. For incoming mail, delivered in bulk to the Council for distribution among the ghetto newcomers, the addressees were charged a fee of 30 or 50 groszy. Requests for information about the whereabouts of missing persons were also taxed.[39]

In the winter of 1941 the Council's chairman, Adam Czerniakow, announced that because of the very bad economic situation prevalent in the ghetto (the soup kitchens were closed because of lack of funds) he had introduced a special tax to finance welfare work.[40] In February 1942 one more tax was announced: each prescription filled in the Council-managed pharmacies (no private pharmacies were in operation in the ghetto) was taxed 40 percent of the price paid for the medicine, for the benefit of the Council's treasury.[41] Workers in the Council's workshops paid a 5 percent income tax.[42] An indirect tax was the fee for burial plots. But even this did not yet complete the financial burden on the Jewish population. On October 18, 1940, the German authorities ordered a consumption tax which the owners of restaurants and coffeehouses were obligated to collect from customers for the benefit of the JSS.[43] People also gave regular donations on a voluntary basis to the JSS, the TOZ, the ŻTOS, and to the house committees that took care of poor tenants.[44]

In Vilna the *Gebietskommissar* ordered (date unknown) each employed Jew to pay a tax of 10 percent of his gross wages (not later than three days after payday) for the benefit of the Jewish Council.[45] These taxes were not the only financial burdens of the ghetto inmates. There were also taxes on tickets to cultural events, various administrative fees, and, in addition, voluntary contributions made to the civic relief committee.

In Radom the Council introduced a tax for a newly established school. Only the few well-to-do parents paid tuition.[46]

In Łódź Rumkowski, by the authority given to him on October 14, 1939, renewed the collection of the community tax. Only the better-situated people, who were afraid that their property would be taken from them anyway, gladly paid the tax. After the ghetto was established, taxes on wages and other income were introduced along with a head tax. The tax on wages amounted to 1.25 percent on wages up to 104 ghetto marks a month and up to 9.45 percent on wages up to 500 ghetto marks a month. Contrary to the situation in Warsaw, rent was paid to the treasury of the Jewish ghetto administration. Included in the rent was a city tenement tax.[47] As elsewhere, various fees were also charged for diverse administrative services, such as for registration cards, for personal documents, for the "resettlement department" during the move into the ghetto, for sanitary or health services, etc.

In Lublin the Jewish population twice paid "extraordinary payments" (a total of 692,220 zlotys during the first war year) in addition to the regular community tax and fees for such things as post office maintenance, birth certificates, wedding certificates, etc.[48] After the destruction of the Lublin ghetto and the establishment of the *Restgetto*, a monthly tax in the amount of 2 zlotys minimum was introduced to establish a fund to cover the budget of a very primitive hospital opened for the large number of sick inmates.[49]

Hospital taxes were also paid in other ghettos—Płońsk, for instance.[50]

In Cracow there were two kinds of community taxes: a regular tax and an "extraordinary Jewish community tax." During the report year September 1939 to September 1940, the regular community tax amounted to 73,120 zlotys and the extraordinary community tax brought in 788,082 zlotys. Because of the sharp decrease in the number of ghetto inmates (in November 1939 there were 68,000 Jews in Cracow; in August 1940 there remained only 45,000 Jews),[51] both taxes brought in only 7,203 zlotys in September 1940. On September 26, 1940, there was introduced a new "special tax" of 10 zlotys paid by each person of either sex twenty-one years of age or over.[52]

In Białystok the Jews paid the following taxes for the benefit of the Jewish Council: (1) an individual tax on property or wages; the rates are not indicated in the source but it may be assumed that they were based on the prewar community tax;[53] (2) a rent tax, according to the size and character of the apartment, whether a private home or a business;[54] (3) a sanitary tax of 3.5 rubles (35 pfennigs) a month on each inmate for such services as snow removal from the streets and collection of refuse;[55] (4) a tax on trade and industry licenses, presumably geared to the size of the business;[56] (5) a 5-pfennig surcharge on each kilogram of bread;[57] (6) a milk tax equivalent to the price of a half-liter of milk to be paid by the owner of a cow or horse in addition to a separate tax for the right to possess an animal;[58] (7) a surcharge of up to 20 percent of the fee charged for water and electricity by the city.[59] In addition, the Council deducted 1 percent from all bills for its purchases in or out of the ghetto.[60]

Persons authorized by the Councils to sell to the ghetto inmates their allocated food and fuel paid a special charge for the benefit of the Councils. In Lublin, for instance, the initial charge for the license to sell coal was 100 zlotys, but it was increased to 300 zlotys on May 25, 1940.[61]

Besides taxes for the benefit of Jewish Councils, the Jews were obligated to pay various state and communal taxes which the Councils were ordered to collect. Thus in Warsaw the Council collected the head tax of 5 zlotys per head imposed on the entire population in the Government General by the occupation authorities.[62]

In spring of 1941 the Warsaw Council established an office for bank accounts. Its purpose was twofold: to collect from Jews, for the benefit of "Aryan" banks, prewar financial obligations such as loans, interest, and notes, and to collect for Jews permissible amounts of cash from their blocked accounts in "Aryan" banks. The office charged a fee for its services.[63]

The Jewish Council of Elders in Zawiercie was obligated to collect a head tax amounting to 10 Reichsmarks per person in 1940.[64] In Białystok it was 6 marks (60 rubles).[65] The Białystok Council was also responsible for the apartment tax collected in the ghetto[66] and for the fee charged for water and electricity (as was the case in Łódź).

The occupation authorities also demanded that the Jewish Councils send reminders for unpaid prewar taxes according to lists submitted by the financial agencies. Thus in Warsaw the supervising authorities ordered that the Council collect unpaid state taxes in amounts of over 1,000 zlotys. According to a news item in the bulletin of the statistical department of June 2, 1940, the finance department sent out 5,021 reminders.[67]

In Lublin the Council was requested by the *Stadthauptmann*, at the end of January or beginning of February 1942 to collect city taxes for the *Stadtverwaltung*.[68]

In Zamość, the Council carried out various services in connection with taxes and trade licenses on behalf of Jews in pertinent government offices.[69]

City taxes in Warsaw were collected by city officials who got special permits to enter the ghetto, but in Łódź Jews were freed from the obligation to pay city taxes after August 1, 1940 (retroactive to April 1), except for an apartment tax, which, as already mentioned, was deposited in the city treasury by the Jewish ghetto administration.[70]

The rates of the direct Jewish community tax were determined by commissions of the financial departments of the Councils. The task of the commissions was hard, particularly because of the profound changes that had taken place in the economic and social structure of the Jews (see Chap. 15). Prewar evidence concerning the finances of an individual could not, therefore, be considered a yardstick for taxation in the ghetto. It was also difficult to ascertain a person's current financial situation due to the fact that, first, life in the ghetto was unstable, and, second, considerable segments of the ghetto inmates were frequently forced to make a living by illegal and undercover means. Representatives of professional groups and area house committees were, therefore, invited to take part, together with members of the financial departments of the Councils, in the commissions to assess taxes. In Warsaw, for instance, the hospital tax was assessed in collaboration with the house committees. The department responsible for the hospital tax sent lists of tenants, with the projected tax amounts for each, to the house committees. The lists were discussed at joint meetings of the representatives of house or area committees who then returned the lists to the department with their own suggested assessments. From the available material it is not clear whether their findings were binding on the Council or were treated as advisory recommendations.[71] The departments also called meetings of large numbers of representatives of the house committees. Some 219 representatives participated in one of these meetings held in May 1940.

The assessing commissions did not always take into consideration the actual economic situation of the taxpayer, for it was not always possible to establish his financial status. Often they had to rely on prewar assessments. Thus the financial commissions in the Warsaw Ghetto decided, in January 1941, that the taxes for real estate be levied at the prewar rates.[72] In the Lublin *Restgetto* the assessment commission was entitled to take as a yardstick "the external indications of the way of life of the taxpayer." The same commission was also empowered to cancel unpaid taxes. The minimal quarterly tax amount was set at 45 zlotys.[73] In the Vilna Ghetto the tax commission at the department of finances levied the Council tax "based on the net income of the taxpayer."[74]

Taxpayers were given the right to appeal. In the Majdan Tatarski Ghetto the taxpayer had the right to appeal to the Appeals Commission within seven days, according to the regulations adopted at the meeting of July 1, 1942. However, he had to pay 20 percent of the assessed tax and a stamp tax ranging from 2 to 10 zlotys, according to the tax amount. The Appeals Commission consisted of the presidium members of the Council and two members of the Commission of Finances, none of whom took part in assessing the tax rate of the appellant. Their decision on appeal was final.[75] In Vilna the appellant had to pay at least half of the assessed tax.[76] In Warsaw a "Special Commission" used to make deals with the taxpayers, coming to terms for payment of their taxes. Members of the commission tried to locate delinquent taxpayers and make them pay overdue taxes.[77]

A specific "voluntary" tax that occupied an important position in the income structure of the Councils was the fee charged for exemption from forced-labor duty. It was collected in almost all communities and ghettos. As already mentioned in previous chapters, right from the start of the occupation and later by the order of October 26, 1939, the Germans imposed the duty of forced labor on all Jewish men fourteen to sixty years of age. (In the Wartheland the first order dealing with forced labor was issued by the *Polizeipräsident* in Łódź on October 5, 1939.) It was customary to exempt, for a price, people who, for various reasons such as bad health, occupation, etc., did not want or were unable to fulfill this hard, often dangerous duty. This "ransom money" was used to pay those Jewish forced laborers for whom it was the only source of income. The amounts varied according to local conditions and the hardships involved in the hard labor.

In Warsaw the "ransom money" varied between 60 and 100 zlotys on a monthly basis, depending on the financial abilities of the exempted persons. They received, from the Council's labor department, certificates testifying that they had fulfilled their labor duty obligations for the then current month.[78] According to one version, the daily ransom fee in Zamość was 2 zlotys. According to another version, it was 4 zlotys a day.[79]

But in the majority of communities, there was no set rate for "ransom money." It was charged solely on the basis of the financial ability of the exempted person, as was the practice in Cracow, for example.[80] Similarly in Lublin, during the month of May 1940, "ransom money" rates were between 15 and 50 zlotys and over. During this one month 2,977 men were released from forced-labor duty, and 2,949 paid a total of 63,755 zlotys. Some 28 persons paid over 50 zlotys each. In Lublin (and in many other places where females were also subject to forced-labor duty, in accord with the orders of the local authorities, although the duty of forced labor applied, in accordance with the central executive order of December 12, 1939, only to males[81]) "ransom money" varied from as little as 50 groszy to 30 zlotys on a daily basis; only a very few women paid up to 60 zlotys a month.[82]

Apart from these income sources, some of the Councils tried to enlarge their incomes by obtaining cash and valuables from the ghetto inmates to cover their ever increasing regular expenses and to meet special purposes. A reliable witness familiar with the conditions in the Sosnowiec Ghetto supplied the following information: each new disaster was a vast source of income for Merin. He was provided with "gold mines" by the *Arbeitseinsatz* and the "resettlements." People simply groveled in front of the windows at the treasury department and begged to have their money accepted for exemption from the current disaster. Merin did not scruple to apply high-pressure methods. Based on the promise made by the *Sonderbeauftragten für den fremdvölkischen Arbeitseinsatz* in Kattowitz to release 100 persons from the camps, he requested the (for that time) enormous amount of 15,000 zlotys for the release of each inmate. Wives of husbands maltreated in the camps for two years sold their belongings to set their husbands free. Thousands were paid, but in the end none came back and money was never refunded.[83]

ANALYSIS OF THE BUDGETS OF THE COUNCILS

We shall now review the hard-pressed financial situation of the Jewish Councils as illustrated by their budgets. The financial affairs of the Councils were the province of the administrative supervising authorities. A letter from the Warsaw district chief, dated April 26, 1940, and addressed to Adam Czerniakow, stressed that the Council was subordinate to the district chief exclusively in all matters of money. All kinds of money requests by other German offices without exception would have to be submitted to the district chief prior to payment.[84] Czerniakow had earlier received assurances that the Council would be able to conduct its affairs in accordance with a budget approved by the supervisory authorities in advance. Whenever the Council faced additional financial demands by German agencies, it could make these expenditures, provided it had enough financial resources to cover them. The letter once more stressed that no financial payments to other German authorities were permitted and concluded by assuring Czerniakow that the authorities would share in the Council's expenses in paying Jewish laborers in German labor places.[85] It can be assumed that similar letters were forwarded to Councils elsewhere.

Unfortunately these promises were only on paper. The Councils struggled with deficit budgets, usually covering their deficits by levying new taxes and fees and forcing deliveries of goods. It is necessary to mention that a large part of the Council's income was appropriated by the supervising authorities in the form of various redemptions in cash and other payments as well as deliveries in goods. In addition the Councils were ordered to pay enormous amounts in wages to forced laborers toiling for the benefit of the German military, police, and civil authorities. And the Councils constantly had to satisfy all kinds of demands to remodel and equip German office premises, casinos, and private apartments for various functionaries, as well as to provide expensive gifts, etc.[86] In dealing with a ghetto, each functionary considered himself entitled to be rewarded by its Council. On the other hand, the Councils themselves implemented an intricate system of bribes in an effort to try and "soften the hearts" of the ghetto bosses or to win favors for the ghetto inmates from the "good Germans" (see Chap. 16). This, in turn, enhanced the pauperization of the Jews. In view of all this, the assurance that the Council would be able to operate a rational, well-balanced budget sounds like sheer mockery.

Wanton extortions from the Jews by all occupation authorities and their functionaries were among the heaviest financial burdens of the Jewish Councils throughout their existence. The Councils were relentlessly requested to give, starting with heavy contributions in cash, gold, silver, and valuable objects in almost all Jewish communities. A few examples follow.

In Warsaw two penal contributions (in November 1939 and in January 1940) amounted to 400,000 zlotys;[87] in Słonim 2 million rubles, 5 kilograms of gold, and an unknown quantity of diamonds were delivered on November 8, 1941;[88] in Lwów the Jews were ordered to pay 20 million rubles;[89] in Vilna 5 million rubles, 1 kilogram of gold, and 1 kilogram of silver;[90] in Białystok 6 kilograms of gold and 2½ million rubles (initially, the Germans demanded 25 kilograms of gold and 5 million rubles)[91] the medium-sized community of Włocławek had to pay three cash contributions totalling 550,000 zlotys in October 1939. No cash remained to pay a third contribution, so people submitted jewelry, silver, candlesticks, etc.[92]

The Lublin Jewish community executive body (later the Council) paid the amount of 1,232,306 zlotys in the period from September 1939 to September 1940, of which 250,000 zlotys was paid in cash, 47,232 zlotys in goods, 591,872 zlotys in wages to forced laborers, and 343,202 zlotys for maintenance of artisans' shops working for the authorities. Thus 75 percent of the Council's entire income (or 1,617,780 zlotys) was used for the benefit of various German authorities.[93]

In Warsaw during the first six months of 1940 the direct "services" of the Council for the benefit of the supervising authorities amounted to 414,533 zlotys: 100,000 zlotys cash contributions; 83,000 to build the ghetto walls; and 231,583 for an unknown purpose (the pertinent document is stained with ink). Indirect "services" such as payments for forced laborers amounted to 424,583 zlotys. Thus a total of 1,839,116 zlotys, or almost 40 percent was paid on various German orders out of 4,623,295 zlotys in income during this period.[94]

The demand to pay wages to Jewish forced laborers was particularly burdensome. Neither Frank's decree of October 26, 1939, ordering forced-labor duty for the Jews, nor the two implementing orders of December 11 and 12, 1939, provided for payment of wages by employers.[95] Thus the Councils, already obligated to deliver Jewish laborers free of charge, had then to pay them at least minimal wages. As late as July 5, 1940, a circular letter of the labor department of the Government General (No. II 5317/40), addressed to the chiefs of the district labor departments, anticipated payment of wages (in the amount of 80% of wages paid Polish workers) only to Jewish laborers not subject to the forced-labor decree and employed on the basis of "free labor relations."[96] This rule was later somewhat softened for reasons of expediency.

When the Jews were forced to toil in the labor camps, as at first in the Lublin district in the fall of 1940, they were paid token wages, ostensibly as assistance for their families left without providers.[97] This new policy, dictated by the necessity physically to sustain the Jewish labor force, met with resistance by local functionaries. Thus, for example, the Częstochowa *Stadthauptmann* stated in his report for the month of August 1940, submitted to the government in Cracow, "that the new Jewish policy [i.e., the instruction that Jewish forced laborers should not work gratis in the future but are to be paid 80 percent of the wages of the Poles] has everywhere met with obstacles and refutations." Particularly he could not conceive that the Jewish Councils had no money left to pay forced laborers. In his opinion it was not so, at least not as far as Częstochowa was concerned, and he had therefore suggested that the new policy be implemented in accordance with local conditions. He himself accordingly disregarded the ordered change in the policy.[98] As a result of such attitudes, the Jewish Councils continued spending enormous amounts of money on wages to forced laborers. Even in places where the order was implemented, the wages were so small that the Council had to supplement them in various forms (additional food, clothing, medical care, cash) distributed among the workers' families.

Not least among the burdens was the necessity of financing social welfare and medical care for impoverished ghetto inmates, as we shall see.

For the first four months of 1940 the Warsaw Jewish Council spent a total of 2,684,000 zlotys (in round figures), of which the more important expenditures were: 962,000 zlotys for hospitals; 816,000 for wages for forced laborers; 238,000 for the registration of the Jewish population; 184,000 for welfare and medical care; and 179,-000 for personnel wages—a total of 2,379,000 zlotys. Income for the same period amounted to no more than 1,912,000 zlotys, of which the more important sources were: 639,000 zlotys from burial plots; 388,000 in fees for exemption from forced labor; 216,000 in registration fees; 261,000 from a "labor battalion tax"; 206,000 from a community tax; 175,000 in refunds for welfare services rendered—a total of 1,885,000 zlotys. Thus wages for forced laborers amounted to over 30 percent, and expenses for welfare, medical aid, and hospitals to 42.5 percent of all expenditures. To cover the incurred deficit of 772,000 zlotys, the Council, after prolonged interventions, got permission from the authorities to borrow 663,000 zlotys (the source of the loan is not given; apparently it came from the already mentioned banks), in addition to 85,000 zlotys from the Emigration Fund and 24,000 zlotys from the Pension Fund for community functionaries (see above, pp. 234–35).

The *Statistical Bulletin* commented: "It appears that the deficit of the community reached 300,000 zlotys a month. Taking into consideration that the Jewish population is already paying 250,000 zlotys a month, as taxes in cash alone, we may conclude that it will be impossible to cover the community expenses by further taxation." The compiler of the report suggests two remedies: a monthly subsidy from the city administration, at least for the hospitals (before the war, the budget of the Jewish hospital had been covered by the city treasury) and the payment of wages to Jewish employees by their German employers.[99]

The entire budget of the Warsaw Jewish community for the year 1940 amounted to 10,680,000 zlotys (in round figures) and was spent largely as follows: 3,811,000 zlotys for wages for forced laborers; 3,059,000 for hospitals; 920,000 for welfare; and 113,000 for vocational courses. The amount spent for the wages of personnel is unspecified. The income, a total of 5,719,000 zlotys, was derived from the following sources: 1,193,000 zlotys from burials; 2,603,000 from fees for exemption from forced-labor duty; 634,000 from a community tax; 541,000 from a hospital tax; 423,000 in registration fees; and 325,000 in fees for food cards (starting in July 1940).

The upkeep of the labor battalion (i.e., wages paid to forced laborers, the labor camps included) swallowed up 37 percent of all expenditures, and the cost of welfare and medical aid 37.3 percent. Thus these two items alone took up over two-thirds of the entire budget. The unpaid salaries for functionaries and the wages for forced laborers amounted to 2,175,000 zlotys, of which the unpaid wages for the labor battalion alone reached the amount of 1 million zlotys. The total deficit, in 1940, came to almost 5 million zlotys, or 2 million zlotys more than the sum of the entire prewar budget, even taking into consideration the devaluation of the zloty.[100] Incidentally, when speaking about the prewar budgets of Jewish communities one should bear in mind that the considerable income the communities derived from ritual slaughter fees before the war was eliminated when the Germans banned ritual slaughter.

During the last year of its existence, the Council improved its financial position. This happened, first, because of additional income through participation in collected city taxes and, second, because the Council was freed from the necessity of paying forced laborers after the principle of paying their Jewish workers was adopted by the authorities and the German employers.

The budget for the year from April 1, 1941 to March 31, 1942 amounted to 26,860,000 zlotys in receipts and 25,260,000 zlotys in reimbursements. The sum of 3,950,000 zlotys is credited on account of participation in taxes received from the Warsaw city administration. There is also credited the sum of 3,150,000 received "from the *Arbeiteinsatz*." Thus a total of 7,100,000 zlotys, or 28 percent of the Council's receipts, came from outside sources. The income from the *Arbeiteinsatz*, i.e., from fees paid for exemption from forced labor, was only 650,000 zlotys less than the Council's total expenses for this purpose (3,760,000 zlotys on a yearly basis; 54,166 on a monthly basis). Prior to this year things were quite different: for the first six months of 1940, the difference between income and expenditures on account of forced labor amounted to 630,000 zlotys, or 105,000 zlotys a month in excess of the income.

Another reason for financial improvement was the rising receipts from taxes. As mentioned, the total income from the six most important taxes and fees in 1940 amounted to 5,719,000 zlotys, some 476,000 zlotys on the average on a monthly basis. In the budget year 1941–1942, the income from taxes and fees reached the sum of 17,050,000 zlotys, or 1,421,000 on a monthly basis, a threefold increase.[101] The increased income came mostly from indirect taxation. In the budget for that period, the direct and indirect taxes are not separately presented. We have only the total amount of 10,500,000 zlotys. Another source, however, indicates that in 1941 the Council's entire income from two direct taxes (community tax and hospital tax) was 1,705,000 zlotys (805,000 zlotys and 900,000 zlotys respectively). But 4,567,000 zlotys was realized from such indirect taxes, paid by rich and poor in equal amounts, as the fee of 2 zlotys charged for each food card issued for a two-month period.[102] (The tax policy of the Warsaw Ghetto Council will be discussed at length in Chap. 15.)

During the budget year September 1939–September 1940, the Cracow Council of Elders had the following income: 73,121 zlotys from the normal community tax; 788,082 from an extraordinary tax; 897,651 in fees charged for exemption from forced-labor duty; 556,702 from donations for assistance to the expelled Cracow Jews; 176,000 from the JDC; 660,000 from the city administration to cover part of the expenses incurred during the expulsion; 50,000 also from the city administration for welfare and education expenses—a total of 3,201,156 zlotys. In addition, mention is made of income from various other sources such as fees for burials and public baths, amounts paid on account of Jewish laborers by German employers, and charity donations by individuals (these amounts are unspecified). In all, the treasury of the Council received 4,215,794 zlotys; thus the unspecified income amounted to 1,014,238 zlotys.

The expenses for this period were as follows: 287,909 zlotys in salaries for the Council's personnel; 578,001 in direct cash assistance; 528,080 for welfare expenses; 802,012 to cover expulsion expenses; 1,080,649 for wages for forced laborers; and 108,065 for administrative expenses connected with payment of wages for forced laborers (10%)—a total of 3,384,716 zlotys. In all, the Council treasury paid out 4,184,722 zlotys during this period. It therefore follows that the unspecified expenses amounted to 800,006 zlotys.[103] Thus the surplus amounted to 31,072 zlotys.

If, however, we are to judge by the treasury statement for the last budget month of that period, September 1940, it appears that a reversal of the situation by then had occurred, since the deficit in that one month reached 129,286 zlotys. The report stresses the point that the large deficit is a result of intensified expulsions necessitating larger expenses.

Table VIII (see p.250) analyzes a few monthly budgets in the period between December 1939 and March 1940 to show the profound changes that took place in the Cracow Jewish community.[104] The analysis clearly indicates the following features:

1. income from the community tax constantly diminished, a clear sign of the pauperization of the Jews;

TABLE VIII

CRACOW JEWISH COUNCIL
MONTHLY BUDGETS
DECEMBER 1939–MARCH 1940
(IN ZLOTYS)

	DECEMBER 1939		JANUARY 1940		FEBRUARY 1940		MARCH 1940	
	INCOME	EXPENSES	INCOME	EXPENSES	INCOME	EXPENSES	INCOME	EXPENSES
Normal community tax	7,867		8,639					
Extraordinary community tax	120,427		105,269		67,731			
Exemption from forced-labor duty	24,268		81,205		87,769			
Burials	10,791		17,497		15,454			
Sale of armbands	14,446		4,058					
Clinic and hospital fees					11,102			
JDC subsidy			52,000[a]				100,000	
City subsidy for welfare							33,663	
Apartments department		4,362				12,076		
Wages for forced laborers		61,142		102,032		135,671		
Welfare		50,851		54,256		52,892		62,210
Soup kitchens		17,090		19,945		28,354		86,000
Wages for personnel and administrative expenses		15,500		16,475		18,119		
Retired and fired community functionaries		9,420		12,340		13,620		

[a] JDC documents, File No. 355, p. 121.

2. income from the fee charged for exemption from forced-labor duty kept increasing, testifying to the heavy burden of this obligation from which people tried to be exempted no matter how much this cost;

3. income from the fee charged for burials was on the steady increase, an objective yardstick for the continuous increase of the death rate among the Jews;

4. a sign of the worsening of health conditions among the Jews was the fact that, in February 1940, there was an income of 11,000 zlotys from fees charged in the clinics and hospitals, while income from this source had earlier been at a minimum;

5. wages for forced laborers doubled between December 1939 and February 1940;

6. there was a steady increase of expenditures for welfare and medical help and assistance for retired community functionaries who had lost their pension rights by Frank's order of December 9, 1939[105] (a partially preserved budget covering these expenditures shows that the deficit on this account was limited to only 14,747 zlotys thanks to a subsidy received from the JDC in the amount of 100,000 zlotys in March 1940 and the payment of 33,663 zlotys out of a total of 50,000 by the *Stadtverwaltung* during the same month);[106]

7. wages for community functionaries kept rising with the increase of personnel;

8. because of the increased influx of refugees and expellees (for instance, on December 10, 1940, a new group of 500 expellees arrived from Łódź) and the necessity to find shelter for them, expenditures by the apartments department rose considerably;

9. a momentary, specific source of income from selling armbands the Jews were ordered to wear.

When the mass expulsions of Cracow Jews began in May 1940, the Councils faced a new and quite heavy task of providing some money for the poor on their tortuous way into the unknown future. The situation was somewhat eased because the authorities advanced some funds for that purpose (660,000 zlotys), but expenses ran much higher. For the period from May to September 1940 alone, the Council spent the amount of 802,012 zlotys to assist expellees.[107]

As for Łódź, we have at our disposal the budget of receipts and reimbursements for the first seven months of 1940. It shows a debit and credit of 8,361,302 Reichsmarks (or ghetto mark receipts), but a deficit of 241,056 Reichsmarks (or ghetto mark receipts) for food.[108] The largest receipts came from the following sources: 1,396,859 from sale of food; 378,712 from the community tax; 321,531 from other taxes, rent, and various fees; 38,068 from burial fees; 56,755 from fees for exemption from forced-labor duty; 124,789 from clinic and hospital fees; 134,448 from mail service; 1,412,588 from the currency bank, in exchange for submitted Reichsmarks and 177,500 ghetto mark receipts from the same currency bank; and 50,000 from the *Reichsvereinigung der Juden in Deutschland*. The largest income category was the exchange of the Reichsmarks for "ghetto mark receipts," which actually was another form of spoliation of the Jews.

The largest expenses were as follows: 1,626,626 for food; 596,054 for welfare; 575,151 for medical aid; 461,856 for wages for personnel and police; 200,963 for wages for forced laborers; 86,206 for wages for workers in the ghetto shops and public works; 140,530 for schools and education; and 222,566 for the economic department.[109]

As has already been mentioned in Chap. 5, confiscation of Jewish property was, along with exploitation of the unpaid or meagerly paid Jewish labor force, one of the main sources of refunding the cost of minimal food supplies allotted to the ghetto inmates by the German ghetto administration. All taxes and fees amounted to no more than some 10 percent of all income.

As for expenditures, welfare and medical aid counted for 52 percent of the entire expense, and this percentage kept rising. Up to September 1941 the assistance department (known as the welfare department until September 1941) paid out in cash and food the equivalent of 10,713,600 in ghetto mark receipts.[110]

Enlightening from various points of view is the budget of the Lublin Jewish Council (community executive body until January 1940) for the first war year up to September 1940. Its total income was 1,617,780 zlotys with the following main receipts: 692,220 from two extraordinary taxes; 124,520 from the community tax; 650,596 in fees charged men and women for exemption from forced-labor duty; 75,000 from burials; 23,880 from mail service; 20,232 from individual donations.

The disbursements amounted to 1,619,439 zlotys: 1,232,300 paid for the "services" for the authorities (see above pp.245-46); 108,718 for social welfare; 143,165 for wages for personnel; 21,426 for administrative costs; 10,713 paid for a new burial plot; and 90,507 for various other expenses.[111]

The community budget received only 7.6 percent of the normal community tax, while the extraordinary tax amounted to 42.7 percent of the total income and another 40 percent came from the fee charged for exemption from forced-labor duty. Thus over four-fifths of the entire revenue (82.7%) came from the extraordinary sources created by new circumstances.

We have already indicated that over 75 percent of the expenditures covered various payments exacted by the authorities, such as contributions in cash, wages for laborers, maintenance of shops working for the authorities, etc. This was not all. In a memorial of the Council to the *Stadthauptmann* on July 29, 1940, there were mentioned also other "services," such as deliveries of furniture and household goods for 200,000 zlotys, in addition to 107,076 zlotys for still other expenses, and 2 kilograms of gold and 17.5 kilograms of silver collected for the benefit of the authorities (these figures are for only 10 months of the report period). In other words, the Germans deprived the Council of almost its entire income, in addition to the gold and silver directly collected from the Jewish population.

The memorandum states that the costs of "services" imposed upon the Jewish population in Lublin during the 10-month period were seven to eight times more than the amount of community tax of any prewar year, and this is apart from extorted individual "services" and "deliveries" (i.e., property seized from individuals by various authorities). The Council complains that for this reason "the most substantial tasks could not be accomplished." Also for this reason, only 6 percent of the expenditures was spent on welfare at a time when the economic situation of the local Jews and of the 7,000 refugees had reached catastrophic proportions. To ease their hardship, the Lublin Jewish Council suggested, as did the Council in Warsaw, that it be freed from the obligation of paying wages to forced laborers and other Jewish workers employed by the authorities. In exchange the Council offered to deliver 250 workers daily who would be paid by the Council's treasury. In addition, the Council requested that the city administration contribute toward the costs of welfare for the Jews in Lublin, who constituted 40 percent of the city's population and who paid full taxes to the city treasury.

What were the results of all these efforts by the Lublin Jewish Council to rescue themselves from financial catastrophe? The crisis was somewhat eased after the order issued to the Council by the Lublin governor, Ernst Zörner, to make no further payments to the

SS camp on Lipowa Street (established in January 1940), to make no payments to third parties in general, and not to pay overdue claims. The *Stadthauptmann*, Fritz Sauermann, informed the Council of this order in a letter dated February 17, 1941, making the entire Council responsible for compliance. If a demand came from whatever office, the Council was obligated to clear it immediately with the governor.[112] It does not appear from the documents at our disposal whether the Council was granted its request that the city participate in welfare expenses, as was the case in Warsaw.

In Białystok, too, the demands of payments imposed by the Nazi authorities and the deliveries of goods swallowed the major portion of the Council's income, forcing it to introduce heavy financial burdens on the ghetto inmates. At a meeting held on August 28, 1941, the chief of the financial department reported to the Council that, in order to pay the debts, 1.5 million rubles would be necessary (apparently on a monthly basis), and this at a time when the income from taxes and rent brought (in March 1942) no more than half a million rubles. Earlier, these most important income sources had brought probably even less.

At a later meeting of the Council, on March 22, 1942, the same official stated that although spending greatly surpassed income, expenditures could not be reduced, "since they mostly stem from the necessity of meeting deliveries for the authorities." Relief could come from either imposing a new tax on the ghetto inmates or not paying for goods the Council acquired from them to satisfy the demands of the authorities.[113]

As elsewhere, the Council in Piotrków Trybunalski faced the hard task of satisfying the demands and extortions of the supervising authorities. Beginning on December 2, 1939, the Jewish Council was ordered to deliver 1,000 men for forced labor each day, and to pay their wages. The Council was ordered at the same time to build, within 10 days, a large barrack for Jews who had lost their homes as a result of bombardment during the war operations, and to deliver the building materials for two more barracks and the renovation of a burned-down factory, etc. In addition, the constant demands for delivery of furniture, bedding, and other household goods, and three cash contributions exacting a total of 390,000 zlotys greatly afflicted the Jews. On January 26, 1940, the *Stadtkommissar* ordered that all leather and textiles from Jewish stores be deposited in the community offices and that a list of this merchandise be delivered by February 3. The goods were then confiscated. This systematic spoliation financially exhausted the Jews, and the Council submitted several memoranda to the *Stadtkommissar,* boldly portraying the desperate situation of the Jews and requesting that they be spared in the future.

Along with its task of alleviating the condition of hard-pressed local Jews, the Council also faced the task of trying to help thousands of refugees and expellees who flooded Piotrków Trybunalski in the fall and winter of 1939–1940. Widespread welfare and medical aid were initiated: kitchens for adults and children, a milk distribution station for babies, shelters, clinics (the prewar Jewish hospital had been confiscated), child care, refugee care, etc.

The Council's expenditures rapidly increased from 22,611 zlotys in November and December 1939 to 106,352 zlotys in February 1940. The largest expenditures were: 13,835 zlotys for wages for forced laborers; 34,021 for building the barracks; 24,202 for fuel; 10,940 for medical aid; 5,530 for assistance to refugees; 9,795 to establish two more kitchens; 5,400 for poor wives of reserve soldiers in the Polish army and unemployed intelligentsia; and 1,600 for poor artisans to pay fees for their licenses. When the expenditures for building barracks and for fuel terminated, expenses decreased by 55,657 zlotys, but in August they again sharply increased and reached the sum of 84,100, including expenses incurred with the transportation of Jews to the Lublin labor camps and with renewed waves of refugees from Cracow.

The impoverished Jews were in no position to sustain such large expenditures. In the early period their main source of revenue came from subsidies of the JDC, TOZ, and Centos. In November and December 1939 the Council got 14,000 zlotys from the JDC, 2,000 from TOZ, and 1,750 from Centos. In February the subsidies from the JDC and the TOZ totaled 30,000 and 5,000 zlotys respectively (no money was received from Centos). In time the subsidies were substantially reduced. Thus in September 1940 only 2,000 zlotys came from the JDC and 800 from Centos, though the Council's relief committee spent 67,740 zlotys during that month. To some degree, reduced cash assistance was supplemented by food staples such as matzoth, flour, fats, canned meat, sugar, and condensed milk that the JDC was able to provide for the ghettos, Piotrków Trybunalski included. But all this was only a drop in the ocean of poverty, and the Council's deficit grew steadily. In February 1940 its total income was 39,986 zlotys, of which 35,000 came from the JDC and the TOZ, while expenditures, as mentioned, amounted to 106,-352 zlotys. In this one month alone the Council ended with a deficit of 66,366 zlotys in addition to the considerable deficit that had accumulated during five previous months. Determining the total deficit during this entire five-month period is a matter of guesswork. As of September 1940 it amounted to 134,700 zlotys, while the budget for that month estimated an additional deficit of 40,000 zlotys (income 50,000 zlotys, expenses 90,000 zlotys).[114]

The finances of a small ghetto in the Wartheland are reflected in data regarding the Pabianice Ghetto (population 8,500 in 1941) found among documents concerning the investigation against the Council of Elders in that town in 1942 (see Chap. 11). Various reports about the Council's financial and economic activities have been preserved for the month of September 1941. According to these reports, the Council of Elders got an income of 53,343 Reichsmarks during that month, and its total expenses amounted to 44,605 Reichsmarks—a surplus of 8,738 Reichsmarks. Income was derived from the following sources (listed in Reichsmarks): 4,322 from fees, rent, etc.; 554 from taxes; 3,258 from welfare (including 450 from the *Reichsvereinigung*); 2,884 from the health department (including 2,515 from the sale of medicines); 23 from burials; 14,121 in profits from the sale of food; 28,181 from labor (including 23,366 in wages reimbursed by German employers); and 3,379 deducted from wages paid in eight ghetto labor shops—a total of 53,343. Expenditures for the same month were listed as follows in Reichsmarks: 5,453 for administrative expenses (including 4,008 for salaries); 8,595 for welfare (including 2,462 for the hospital), 80 for the cemetery; 4,850 for families of deportees to labor camps; and 23,136 for wages to laborers—a total of 44,605.[115]

The Council's main sources of income in the month of September were the 15 percent handling charges deducted from the miserable wages (3,379 Reichsmarks) German employers paid Jewish workers[116] and some profit from the sale of medicaments and food for ghetto inmates. Incidentally this was one of the charges of the prosecution in the trial against the Council.[117] The traditional prewar incomes of the Jewish communities, the community tax and fees charged for graves, fell to the very minimum and amounted to only 577 Reichsmarks, or a little over 1 percent of the total.

If this budget for the month of September 1941 is indicative, it mirrors profound socio-economic changes within the Jewish population of smaller settlements after two years of Nazi occupation.

The policy of finding sources of income in Pabianice by surcharging the prices of allocated food was commonly implemented. In Zamość, for instance, it was practiced on a much larger scale. The Council bribed the Germans in charge of food allocation for the ghetto and got more food than should have been apportioned to the ghetto inmates. (The food distribution lists contained two and three times as many Jews as were actually present in the ghetto and labor camps.) The surplus was sold at higher prices and the profits went into the Council's treasury to cover both its normal expenditures of 30,000 zlotys a month and extraordinary ones mentioned above (see above, p. 99).[118]

We lack information about the budgets of most of the ghettos. Only figures pertaining to some of the income and reimbursements were preserved, shedding some light on their financial situations. In Tarnów expenditures for welfare and medical aid for the local population and refugees amounted to 52,491 zlotys in April 1940, of which the soup kitchen cost 15,840 zlotys. In the pertinent report it has been stressed that the Council took a loan, figuring that it would be repaid with financial assistance from the JDC.[119]

The expenditures of the Kalisz Council of Elders from February 1 to March 15, 1940, amounted to 30,249 zlotys,[120] and for the Kutno Council approximately 800 Reichsmarks on a daily basis during 1940. With an income of only 300 Reichsmarks a day, the monthly deficit there was 15,000 Reichsmarks, on the average.[121] The average expenditures of the Jewish Council in Lowicz in 1940 amounted to 3,000 zlotys a month. Income was negligible.[122]

In Šiauliai the Council decided, at a meeting held on May 3, 1943, that in view of its steadily growing deficit all expenditures should be limited to bare necessities. A budget estimate for the month of May was adopted, with expenditures of 35,000 Reichsmarks and a more or less certain income of 31,000 Reichsmarks (because of the fluctuation of the ghetto population, no permanent income could be estimated, while the expenditures were almost always higher than budgeted), of which 17,250 Reichsmarks were to be realized from the sale of food left in the food cooperative in order to cover the anticipated deficit of June.[123]

The small communities in the incorporated areas were assisted with small amounts by the *Reichsvereinigung.* Thus the Kutno

Council got 3,000 Reichsmarks by the end of November 1940. The Councils of Kalisz and Żychlin got 1,500 and 500 Reichsmarks respectively.[124] And even as late as September 1941 we find 450 Reichsmarks in the budget of the Pabianice Council debited as a subsidy from the *Reichsvereinigung*. In the main, the Councils based their hopes of covering incurred deficits on cash, food, and medicines coming from the JDC (for more on this see Chap. 6).

In view of the widespread, ever growing poverty among the Jews, this assistance was insufficient by far. The situation became still worse after the United States entered the war in December 1941, and the activities of the JDC were officially terminated.

The assistance provided by the JSS was insufficient, limited to the area of the Government General, and was still further curtailed when the JDC stopped its activities. The feeble ghetto was then left to its own meager resources, which could not last for long.

The Jewish Councils and
the Occupation Authorities

WE SHALL ENDEAVOR now to assess the complex problem of mutual relations between the German authorities and the Jewish Councils in the occupied territories of Eastern Europe. But first it is necessary to take a look at the Germans' reason for establishing the Councils, to analyze the power struggle within the authorities themselves and the way they treated the Councils, to review the nature of day-to-day relations, the extent of German control, and lastly, to examine the actual involvement of authorities at all levels in the liquidation of the Jews. Some of these topics have already been discussed in Chap. 1; here, however, they are considered in more detail, in light of actual occupational practices, which were more important than the orders themselves.

THE REASON FOR ESTABLISHING THE COUNCILS

According to official Nazi documentation, the Jewish Councils in Eastern Europe were given the task of assisting Nazi organs to accomplish German plans for the Jews, as were the analogous Jewish "self-governing" organs established in Central and West Europe (*Reichsvereinigung der Juden in Deutschland, Israelitische Kultusgemeinde in Wien, Jüdische Kultusgemeinde in Prag,* and other community bodies throughout occupied Europe). As early as April 1933, the word *Judenrat* ("Jewish Council") was used in a draft of a law concerning Jews. Already the *Judenrat* was envisaged as a compulsory organization of Jews in Germany functioning to carry out orders of the authorities.[1]

With respect to Poland, this task is outlined in Heydrich's *Schnellbrief* to the chiefs of the *Einsatzgruppen* dated September 21, 1939, already mentioned in Chap. 1. In the text, and in the attached diagram of the so-called Madagascar Project of the Reich Security Police (SD),[2] the Jewish organs mentioned were given the role of *Hilfstellen* in realizing this chimerical plan, which was soon to be abandoned. Thus we read in the pertinent chapter ("The Organization of Emigration from *Altreich, Sudetten Deutschland* and the Western Territories of Poland Newly Incorporated into the Reich") that the inspectors of the SD and the Security Police were responsible for executing the order, and their offices, until then subordinated, were converted into executive organs. To help the police in their task, these offices were to use the county unions of Jewish communities or local unions of the *Reichsvereinigung der Juden in Deutschland* and in the incorporated areas, the Jewish Councils, respectively (p. 8). In the paragraph dealing with the area of the Government General it is stated: "The preparation [for the Madagascar Plan] is to be accomplished by the Jewish Councils themselves to the widest extent [*weitestgehend*]" (p. 9). In the organizational table attached to the Plan, "Jewish organizations, Jewish communities, or Jewish communes" are indicated as organs (*Hilfstellen*) helping to realize the Plan.[3] Later when the German government abandoned the Madagascar Plan and, in the spring of 1941, decided to launch the *Endlösung*, the Final Solution of the Jewish question, the establishment of the Jewish Councils in the occupied Soviet territories was considered, among other measures, as a basis (*Grundlage*) for this gruesome undertaking. We read about it in a report (No. 9), dated June 26, 1942, sent from the occupied Soviet territories to the chief of the Security Police and SD:

In order to get initial control over the Jews, regardless of whatever measures may be taken later, Jewish Councils of Elders have been appointed which are responsible to the Security Police and Security Service for the conduct of their fellow Jews (*Rassengenossen*). Moreover, the registration and concentration of the Jews in ghettos have been started. . . . With these measures, the foundations for the final solution of the European Jewish problem—planned for a later time—have been laid in the territory of Byelorussia (*Weissruthenien*). . . .[4]

Local SS and police organs apparently considered that the establishment of the Jewish Councils was one of the preconditions for the implementation of the Final Solution.

Another reason for the establishment of the Councils was a scheme to divert the hostility of persecuted Jews from the German authorities to the Councils as the actual executors of Nazi persecution orders, thus enabling the Nazis to remain in the background. They admitted it themselves. Heinz Auerswald, the *Kommissar* of the Warsaw Ghetto, wrote to the deputy of the plenipotentiary of the governor general in Berlin, Dr. von Medeazza, in a letter dated November 24, 1941, that "when deficiencies appear, the Jewish population directs its protests against the Jewish management in the first place, and not against the German authorities."[5]

The same idea is expressed in a German document concerning the Łódź Ghetto. The *Kriminalkommissariat* in the ghetto, in his monthly report (dated June 23, 1942) submitted to the inspector of the German Security Police and SD, made the following characteristic remarks:

Aside from the chronic hatred by the ghetto population for all that is German, the working Jews are disgusted, as before, with their leaders in the ghetto because of insufficient deliveries of food. . . . Actually, the Jew hates the Germans less than his "race brothers" who reign over him and of whom he would gladly be rid. In time, this attitude has changed to burning hatred against the governing Jewish circles without exception, and particularly against the Jewish Elder. It is absolutely impossible to make a Jew kill another Jew; but in this case he would not stop short were he not afraid of the German authorities.

It is superfluous to note that the Nazi official did not comprehend that the commandment, "Thou shalt not kill," is older than fear of the German authorities. In another report of the *Kriminalkommissariat* (dated July 28, 1942) the hatred of the ghetto inmates toward the ghetto administration is again mentioned.[6] Thus it is clear that the establishment of the Councils with widespread apparatus served the Germans well as a lightning rod against accumulated resentment, hatred, and discord among the ghetto inmates.

Of course, for the outside world, Nazi propaganda presented the aims and tasks of the Councils in a different light. Fictitious Jewish "self-government" in the occupied territories was skillfully exploited for camouflage and deception. A high German official in the German Propaganda Ministry and in the Government General, *Freiherr* Max du Prel, notes in his book:

In order to put the Jewish loafers to useful work at last, the governor general, Reich Minister Dr. Frank, issued a decree on November 28, 1939, in accordance with which Jewish Councils were formed in all places with a population of over 10,000. The Jewish Council is the representative of Jewish interests (*Interessenvertretung der Juden*) and also the agency (*Instanz*) which the German authorities contact whenever Jewish communities are to carry out special orders.

. . . We urgently suggest to hate-mongering foreign journalists, who so often babble about alleged barbaric persecutions of the Jews in the German East, to see for themselves, on the spot, the generosity of the German administration in allowing the Jews their own way of life. In their own organizations, with their own Jewish resources, a sort of autonomous administrative system has been established, which safeguards the interests of the Jews within the limits of the possible.

We Germans do not care for the Jews; we know the part played by international Jewry in bringing about the developments of the last few years. This does not change the fact that, in the area under German control, we give Jews the opportunity to participate in the solution of the Jewish problem, or, rather, to create the conditions which in the long run will make it possible to solve the problem once and for all, not only in the interests of the world but also in the interests of the Jews themselves.[7]

The governor general, Hans Frank, also wrote in an article published by the *Krakauer Zeitung* (No. 171, July 21, 1940) and entitled "The Double Task of the German Government General" that "in each community they [the Jews] have a separate representation, the so called *Judenrat*, whose task is to take care of the life necessities of the Jewish segment of the population." We shall see later how much truth there was in Prel's statement that "the *Judenrat* represents the interests of the Jews," and we shall see what chance the Councils really got for "cooperation in solving the Jewish question . . . in the interests of the Jews themselves . . . ," and what chance they got "to take care of the life necessities of the Jewish segment of the population."

Chaim Rumkowski (left) and the chief of the German ghetto administration, Hans Biebow.

A visit of the Gestapo to the Warsaw *Judenrat*.

THE RIVALRY BETWEEN THE ADMINISTRATIVE
AND POLICE ORGANS

In Chap. 1 we stressed the evolution of the power struggle of the
Nazis with respect to the Jewish Councils, a struggle that fostered
discords and clashes between administrative organs and the police.
A well-informed student of the occupation years in Poland writes
on this subject:

Apart from centrifugal forces active within the civilian administration
of the Government General due to personal and organizational division
(*Zersplitterung*), the inconsistency of the policies in the Government
General, which soon developed into a chronic state of affairs, was, above
all, a result of the duplicated and conflicting functions of the *Wehrmacht*,
[civilian] administration, and police, whose authorities or arrogated
powers were, almost without interruption, in competition with each
other.[8]

Based on authority he had been given by Hitler, Governor General Frank considered himself the sole, pivotal seat of the occupational regime in this part of Poland, where he alone was entitled to
issue laws and orders. But Himmler, who concentrated in his hand
the colossal police machine of the Reich, also aimed at securing all
authority in the Government General for himself, the SS, and the
other police organs, above Frank's prerogatives. A similar jurisdictional wrangle between Frank and Himmler developed with respect
to Jewish problems.

On November 1, 1939, Himmler decreed that SS men and police
leaders in the Government General would function as advisers to
the district chiefs in problems relating to police, but would be independent of them. Under this decree, the police were duty-bound
to execute the instructions of district chiefs only insofar as they did
not contradict the orders of Krüger, the Higher SS and Police Leader
in the Government General, to whom they were subordinated.[9]

This was clearly in conflict with Frank's insistence that he was
the supreme authority. The jurisdictional squabble between Frank
and Himmler began with the controversy over who was invested
with the right to confiscate "enemy property." Frank had endeavored
to make himself independent of the HTO, the central office for
confiscations in the occupied Polish territories, and to keep confiscations under the exclusive authority of the government in Cracow.

Frank was partially successful. At a conference in Karinhall on February 12, 1940, under Goering's chairmanship, it was decided that the governor general would supervise the confiscated property of the Polish state, and that the HTO would not operate in the area of the Government General.[10] Frank established his own *Haupttreuhandstelle* in Cracow, with chapters in the districts. At the beginning this organ also embraced whatever Jewish confiscated property had not already been taken away during earlier confiscations by Himmler's police organs. However, with the start of mass deportations in March 1942, assets of the victims were taken over by deportation commandos of the SS, those acting under the code name of *Einsatz Reinhard* and those on duty in the destruction camps under the management of the SS and the police.

To counteract SS and police activities in this field, Frank issued an order to establish a *Referat für Judenangelegenheiten* in the department for internal affairs (I.V.). In turn, the department issued an order on March 2, 1940, in which it said among other things:

The "Jewish Affairs" desk, Section Population Matters, has been raised to the status of an independent Section in [the Department of] Internal Administration, Population Matters, and Public Welfare. The new Jewish Affairs Section is concerned with (*untersteht*): (*a*) registration of Jews and decisions about who is a Jew; (*b*) Jewish Councils of Elders; (*c*) Jewish legislation; and (*d*) work on current Jewish matters.[11]

In a special letter, district chiefs were instructed to establish an independent Jewish *Referat* within their administrative apparatus. After the order of March 2 was issued, the interior department in Cracow forwarded a letter to the Lublin district chief, Ernst Zörner, requesting reports on the establishment of Jewish Councils in the counties and on difficulties, if any, in handling Jewish affairs. A similar circular letter must also have been sent out to the other three district chiefs. On March 23 the interior department forwarded to the district chiefs another circular letter for distribution among the county chiefs and town mayors specifying their rights vis-à-vis the Jewish Councils. They were also told that there would soon be issued a general order authorizing them to issue orders to the Jews. As we know, such an implementing order for Frank's order concerning the Jewish Councils was issued on April 25, 1940 (see Chap. 1).

On April 6 Dr. Heinrich Gotong, the newly appointed *Referent* for Jewish affairs in the department of *Bevölkerungswesen und Fürsorge* in Cracow, a subdivision in the interior department, informed all four district chiefs in the Government General that he had taken over the *Referat*. At the same time, he forwarded a detailed circular letter, outlining government policy in regard to the Jews and instructing them to carry out various statistical studies in connection with the planned concentration of Jews in a special area of the Government General (the "Lublin Reservation").[12] Compulsory labor duty, however, had been excluded from the competence of the district chiefs. The police and the SS thus retained their right to demand forced laborers from the Jewish Councils.

The implementing order of April 25, 1940, had no application in the larger cities which, with their massive concentrations of Jewish population, were considered as separate counties. Apparently this omission was a temporary compromise with police authorities until Frank issued his second implementing order on June 7, 1940, which extended also to the chiefs of the town counties (i.e., cities organized as separate administrative units) the same prerogatives with respect to the Jewish Councils mentioned in the order of April 25.

But the SS and police organs in the Government General, with Himmler's support, did not stop their efforts to secure authority for themselves over the Jewish population. These efforts were particularly evident in the Lublin district, where SS and Police Leader Odilo Globocnik, future chief of the murderous *Kommando Einsatz Reinhard*, was in command. It is worthwhile to discuss in some detail this struggle that led to open strife between the leading administrative and police organs in the Government General.

As already mentioned, Frank's order of October 26, 1939, authorized Krüger, the Higher SS and Police Leader, to manage the forced-labor duty of the Jews. Later Krüger issued two implementing orders, on December 11 and 12, 1939, authorizing the police to carry out the labor duty order. However, the SS and police organs were in charge of Jewish compulsory labor for a short time, up to mid-1940. Because of a general lack of workmen in the Government General, it was necessary to involve all skilled workers among the Jews in general production, which was under the supervision of the economic sector of the civil administration. This new development in the economic policies of the occupation authorities was resisted by Krüger, who feared that taking away from police supervision the right to exploit Jewish labor might diminish police influence and power within the occupational machinery.

As already mentioned in Chap. 1, at a meeting called by Frank on May 31, 1940, Bruno Streckenbach, the commander of the Security Police in the Government General, endeavored to force the adoption of the principle that only the Security Police were entitled to oversee Jewish Councils and, through them, the Jewish population. However, the governor of the Lublin district, Zörner, was of the opposite opinion, maintaining that local administrative organs, thoroughly acquainted with local conditions, were better equipped to gear the Jews into the production force, with the help of the Councils. Ludwig Fischer, the Warsaw district chief, was of the same opinion; and Frank, in his concluding remarks, joined them, stressing that the civilian administration should have the sole responsibility for exploiting the Jewish labor force in cooperation with the police (see Chap. 1).

This controversy between representatives of the occupation authorities about how to employ Jews "with normal labor relations" came to the surface once more during meetings with Frank that took place on June 6 and 7, 1940. At that time Krüger agreed that it had become necessary to employ Jews in the "free economy" (i.e., outside the framework of forced-labor duty) and that this function should be turned over to the chief of the labor department in Cracow for supervision.

But this was not enough for the civilian administration. On July 5, the labor department distributed a circular letter to the labor offices of all four districts, informing them that not only Jewish labor "through free labor exchange," but *also Jewish forced labor* had been turned over to the labor department of the Government General and its subordinate labor offices. The circular stressed at the outset that this decision had been mutually agreed upon by the governor general and the Higher SS and Police Leader.

Before this circular letter had been sent, when Krüger's partial capitulation at the June conference became known, the Lublin governor tried to convince Globocnik to submit to the new regulations in a broader interpretation that would give exclusive competence over Jewish labor to the civilian administration. But the negotiations with Globocnik were fruitless, since he had no intention of giving up his jurisdiction in this matter. One month after transferral to the administrative authorities of all employment of Jews in the economy, Hofbauer, the *Referent* for Jewish problems in the General Staff of the SS and police, demanded that the chief of the labor office in the Lublin district deliver, at once, 3,000 Jewish laborers for the labor camp in Bełżec. A week later, he demanded an additional 500 laborers, indicating that by August 1940, 30,000 Jews would be employed at the border fortification works under the surveillance of the SS. Hans Damrau, the office chief of the Lublin district, discussed this matter with Frank and was informed that Hofbauer would no longer supervise the Jewish *Referat*, that the supervision of Jewish labor would be taken away from the SS and the police, and that only the labor offices of the civilian administration would be in charge of supervision. The police would be used only in cases when force had to be applied and only at the request of the labor offices. Frank also informed Damrau that Jewish labor from the Cracow district, and not from the Lublin district, would be used for building border fortifications. But Globocnik, certain of the backing of Himmler and his mighty SS apparatus, was not ready to give in. Without the knowledge of the local labor offices, he ordered the carrying out of raids on the Jewish population in the Lublin district to secure enough workers for SS labor camps then being established. Raids by the police took place on the nights of August 13-14, 1940 and December 11-12, 1941; and despite Globocnik's promise given to the chief of the Lublin labor department, even persons with certificates testifying that they were employed by the Germans were picked up. In a number of places the labor offices and the county chiefs were not even informed in advance that a raid was imminent, again contrary to the promise Globocnik had given to the chief of the Lublin labor office. It came out later that Globocnik had issued a secret order to local commandants of the SS and police questioning the right and competence of the labor department in the employment of Jews for forced labor. Similar police raids took place in Lublin on the night of October 20-21, and in the Radzyn county on the night of November 14-15, 1940. Globocnik established a Jewish labor camp on his own in Lublin, for example, where he assembled released Jewish war prisoners who had arrived there between December 1940 and February 1941. He forced the Lublin Jewish Council to pay for maintenance, medical treatment, and other expenditures on behalf of the laborers. Without first consulting the Radzyn *Landrat,* he issued orders to establish a Jewish labor camp near Parczów (Radzyn county) and imposed the duty of maintaining the laborers and assisting their families on the Parczów Jewish Council.

Antagonism between the chiefs of the civilian administrative organs and the police authorities in the Lublin district was not limited to exploitation of Jewish labor. On March 12, 1941, Governor Zörner established, within the department of *Bevölkerungswesen und Fürsorge* in the district administration, a special *Referat* for Jewish affairs and all problems pertaining to Jews. Globocnik immediately reacted in a letter to Zörner on March 14, stating that all Jewish affairs were within the jurisdiction of the police. The newly appointed *Referent,* Richard Türk, intervened in person in Cracow (as did Zörner by letter) asserting that indisputably there must be close cooperation between civilian administrators and police; the competence of the police, however, should be limited to the execution of orders issued by administrative organs. Cracow agreed, and on May 13, 1941, the chief of the Lublin district administration informed Globocnik that Jewish matters of a principal and political nature would be handled by the civilian administration in consultation with the police. Still Globocnik was not impressed. Two days later, on May 15, he answered the district chief that he had received no communication from Krüger canceling his prerogatives in Jewish matters. At the same time he let him know that at Heydrich's request a special member of Globocnik's staff had been designated to handle Jewish affairs on behalf of the Security Police and SD, and that all questions of principle or of a political nature should be cleared with this man. The intention was perfectly clear: to stress that on Heydrich's order there was in operation in his office a *Referat* for Jewish affairs authorized to deal with the *Judenwesen* complex, a pre-eminent *political* interest of the occupation authorities.[13]

Behind this apparent jurisdictional wrangle was a hidden scheme to monopolize exploitation of the Jewish labor force and Jewish confiscated property. The SS built a colossal economic empire in the occupied Eastern territories which embraced numerous industrial and agricultural enterprises where scores of thousands of Jewish laborers and specialists were put to work. The SS also tried to take over confiscated Jewish assets. The civilian administration begrudged these encroachments, maintaining that the economic expansion of the SS encroached on their own prerogatives, interfering with their economic tasks in the occupied territories.

Taking into consideration the Nazi occupation system that generally provided no legally regulated norms vis-à-vis the civil population (particularly with regard to Jews), the Lublin case should not be treated as a single or an exceptional one, but as typical of the Nazi attitude toward the Jews. Actually the Jews were governed by a chaotic polyarchic system, according to the pointed expression of Dr. Jacob Robinson, where the areas of jurisdiction of the various authority organs were not strictly outlined, each one considering itself entitled to rule over the Jewish population. As part of the general population of the occupied territories, the Jews, along with non-Jews, were supposed to be under the control of the civilian administration. But because of the pre-eminence given the Jewish question in the overall Nazi program, the Party and the police organs (SS, SD, and Security Police) gained dominant authority in the planning and carrying out of anti-Jewish measures. In the stark, practical reality of the Government General and the occupied Soviet Union, the police authorities were the decisive factor in all that was relevant to the Jews, and the *Referent* for Jewish affairs in the local Gestapo was the official in charge of the practical execution of policies adopted by the higher occupation authorities.

Pesach Kaplan, former secretary of the Białystok Jewish Council, writes about the polyarchic system as practiced in that ghetto:

Relations with the authorities were difficult, because of the chaos within the hierarchy of occupation organs. There was no single authority within the German military, civilian, or police administration, but a mass of diverse organs, each one maintaining that it was pre-eminent and, consequently, making arbitrary draconic demands. Often they worked at cross-purposes and contradicted each other, so that one did not know whom to obey. This situation, however, bristled with mortal danger, since the demands of the authorities were accompanied by threats to shoot half or all of the Jewish Council, or a few hundred Jews, or 300 Jews. . . . For a time, it was hoped that after the German civilian *Gettoverwaltung* had been designated the single organ the Jews were allowed to approach, the situation would become consolidated. To avoid misunderstandings, the *Verwaltung* issued to the Jewish Council a certificate of safe conduct stamped with the official German seal to the effect that no authority other than the *Gettoverwaltung* was entitled to confiscate anything or make demands of any nature. The certificate was displayed under a glass cover on the desk of the Council's chairman, Ephraim Barash. This helped somewhat, but the number of order-givers was large and their orders had to be satisfied.[14]

The so-called Jewish Committee and later the Jewish Council in Kaunas took orders from the (probably Lithuanian) *Stadtverwaltung*, from the German *Stadtkommissar*, from the commandant of the Security Police and Security Service, from the labor office, and from some other offices of the occupation authorities. From August 7, 1941, to December 7, 1942, there were recorded 54 orders from these offices in the minutes of the Jewish Committee and the Jewish Council. Even the German ghetto watchmen considered themselves entitled to issue orders to the Council. A letter addressed to the Jewish Council, dated September 1941, outlines in great detail how Jews are to greet a German official. The letter ends with this admonition: "I call your attention once more [to the order] that the heads of all males in the ghetto must be covered at all times."[15]

In the Łódź Ghetto jurisdictional strife was apparently eased by leaving to the Gestapo decisions of a political nature and to the *Gettoverwaltung* decisions of an economic nature. However, this applied only in theory. From a news item where this jurisdictional division is announced, we learn that the *Gettoverwaltung* had inquired of the Gestapo concerning delivery to the ghetto of wheat flour to bake matzoth, and that the suggestion was rejected because flour was a "scarce commodity."[16] The Gestapo in Łódź actually controlled food deliveries in the ghetto, and the *Gettoverwaltung* was obligated to report to it about the food situation.[17]

The Gestapo in Łódź actually had authority over all matters concerning the ghetto administration from the very beginning. Such must have been the pattern all over the incorporated territories, where occupation policies were much more stringent than in the Government General, and the Gestapo, with its appartus of terror, was the main organ of authority. This naturally reflected on the situation of the Jews too. Rumkowski was well aware of all this, and used to approach the Gestapo as the source of authoritative instructions to other occupying organs. Thus he complained to the Gestapo, on November 24, 1939, that German places of employment were demanding that he pay Jewish laborers their wages, although they were supposed to work without compensation, according to the order calling for forced-labor duty. This, he maintained, "may interfere with the normal labor procedure" and bring about a "colossal strain upon the community's finances." He therefore asked the Gestapo to make it clear to pertinent government offices that they had acted in error.[18] But the Gestapo had other ideas in this as in other matters, and Rumkowski was forced to pay small wages to the forced laborers.[19]

All his announcements had to be censored by the Gestapo, and he had to submit four copies of the *Geto-tsaytung* in a German translation for approval by the Gestapo prior to publication.[20] The Gestapo often removed from the ghetto offices for scrutiny all correspondence and documents.[21] The entire correspondence with Jewish communities in the Reich or with relatives of Jews deported into the ghetto went through Gestapo channels.[22] Criminal and penal matters in the ghetto were subjected to strict Gestapo supervision. On orders of the Gestapo, Rumkowski put certain persons into the ghetto jail or released them. Both local Jews in Łódź and persons from other ghettos sentenced by the German courts were kept in the Łódź Ghetto jail. When the Gestapo arrested Poles in the neighboring *Polenjugendverwahrungslager*, they were also put in the Łódź Ghetto jail. The Gestapo requested information from Rumkowski about certain ghetto inmates and also gave him directives on the deportation of certain individuals, etc.[23] In general the Gestapo was informed of everything that happened in the ghetto (see above, p. 271). The *Gettoverwaltung*, too, was obligated to submit reports to the Gestapo on a monthly basis.

Each of the organs considering itself entitled to meddle in Jewish matters watched carefully to ensure that no other authority encroached on it. Thus on April 30, 1940, Rumkowski got a notice from the *Oberbürgermeister*, who stated that he was the only authority dealing with matters relevant to the Jewish living quarters, except for police matters. He referred to the order of the Łódź *Regierungspräsident* of April 27, and declared that any demands of third parties for "services" had to be cleared by him.[24] Similar oral instructions to accept no orders from any other authority were received by Czerniakow from Ludwig Leist, the *Bevolmächtige vom Distriktchef für die Stadt Warschau*, in his capacity as the direct supervising authority over the Jewish Council (entry of December 30, 1940). The Lublin labor office informed the Jewish Council on September 12, 1941, that in case any of the branches of the district administration requested statistical data about the ghetto, the request should be referred to the labor office, which was exclusively entitled to handle such information.[25] We have already mentioned the certificate of safe conduct of the Białystok *Gettoverwaltung* issued to the Jewish Council there.

The system of multiple authority organs supervising the Jews in the Warsaw Ghetto was particularly confused both before and after the ghetto was established. During the first weeks of the occupation, the *Einsatzkommando* SS under *Hauptsturmführer* Rudolf Batz was the sole authority over the Jewish population. It was Batz who had ordered Czerniakow to establish the *Judenrat,* and he had informed the Council, at a crucial meeting called in the beginning of November 1939, that the ghetto was to be established on short notice. Moreover it was Batz who forbade the Council to approach any other authority. After a successful intervention with the commander of the German garrison in Warsaw resulted in the temporary cancelation of Batz's order, he disappeared from the horizon. When the German civilian administration was established at the end of October 1939, Waldemar Schön, the chief of the resettlement section, became involved in Jewish affairs. After the ghetto was established in Warsaw, his title was *Kommissar für den jüdischen Wohnbezirk.* On March 15, 1941, he was dismissed and, in mid-May, replaced by another official of the district administration—the lawyer Heinz Auerswald, about whom we will say more later on in this chapter. Together with Schön (and, later, with Auerswald), Ludwig Leist considered himself sole authority over the *Judenrat.*

The *Transferstelle* at the resettlement section (established in December 1940) constituted a third authority over the ghetto. Theoretically, the *Transferstelle* should have been concerned only with economic problems. Actually, however, its ambitious chief, Max Bischof, meddled in other affairs relevant to the ghetto and the Council, as we shall see later. In fact, however, both Auerswald and the *Transferstelle* were subordinated to the Gestapo, the dominant authority over Jewish affairs. An entry in Czerniakow's Diary of November 21, 1941, cites a statement by Stabenow, one of the high officials of the SD, that it is possible that his organization might take over the administration of the ghetto. Reading Czerniakow's Diary, one is simply overwhelmed by the large number of diverse offices—administrative, economic, SS, police, and military—which

Czerniakow, alone or in company with other members of the Council or the commandant of the ghetto police, had to approach with all kinds of problems.

All these offices distrusted each other, suspecting trespassing and corruption. Thus at the request of the Łódź Gestapo, the *Gettoverwaltung* and its chief, Hans Biebow, were under surveillance (*Überwachung*) by the *Forschungstelle A* of the air ministry, and their telephone conversations were tapped (starting in January 1941). This request for wiretapping was prompted by the waste (*Verschleuderung*) of property, gold, silver, etc. It was discussed in detail at a meeting of the Gestapo on March 2, 1942, where Veygand, one of the Gestapo bosses, requested that the *Überwachung* of the *Gettoverwaltung* be extended because of continuing corruption. He accused "almost all organs of the government," hypocritically complaining that for this reason the Gestapo men could not keep company with the officials of other offices and were therefore forced to rely on information gained by wiretapping. He requested that the *Überwachung* be extended to cover all affairs in the ghetto including those of the ghetto chief, Hans Biebow. Rumkowski's administration was also subjected to tapping of their telephone conversations.[26] Hepner, the chief of the *Bevölkerungswesen* in the *Statthalterei* Wartheland, writes in a letter addressed to Adolf Eichmann dated July 16, 1941, that

it seems to me that Übelhoer [the *Regierungspräsident* of the Łódź "Regency"] does not wish to liquidate the Łódź Ghetto because it gives him a chance to make a lot of money. As an example, I cite the fact that the labor department in the *Statthalterei* paid out of a special fund 6 Reichsmarks for each working Jew, though the expense to maintain a Jew was no more than 80 pfennigs.[27]

It is therefore understandable that Hans Biebow felt very uncomfortable when he got information in April 1944 about impending control of the books of the *Gettoverwaltung* from 1941 on by the Poznań branch of the Reich's Controller's Chamber (*Rechnungshof*) in Berlin. In a discussion with the *Oberregierungsrat*, Rauschauer, of the *Statthalterei* in Poznań (wiretapped on April 17), Biebow complained about control of the books; his interlocutor replied that the "*Rechnungshof* should not be permitted to investigate the ghetto in detail."[28]

It often happened that various authorities issued contradictory orders, or that one office refused to honor the order of another one. For instance, on October 16, 1940, Leist's order establishing the Warsaw Ghetto was announced, outlining the borders of the ghetto in great detail. But on October 19 the German radio in Warsaw broadcast that some of the streets mentioned in this order would be excluded from the ghetto area. This was confirmed in a news item printed in the *Warschauer Zeitung* on October 20. The next day, when Czerniakow submitted a memorandum inquiring about the change of ghetto borders, Leist told him that he had no information about it. We may assume that he did not lie, for he was one of the very few more or less decent German officials in the district administration. After Czerniakow showed him the news item in the *Warschauer Zeitung*, he phoned the *Distriktamt* and was informed that the new ghetto borders had been outlined by an order of Governor Fischer. The only thing that Czerniakow gained was a two-week extension of the date for moving into the ghetto, from November 1 to November 15.[29] Furthermore, according to Leist's order, Jews were permitted to keep business establishments outside the ghetto boundaries until further notice. Nevertheless, on November 16, the police sealed off all Jewish businesses, and Jewish owners were not permitted to enter.[30]

Under the date December 4, 1940, Czerniakow entered an item in his Diary to the effect that Herschelmann ("of the food office") had refused to honor a letter from the resettlement section and did not allow anything to be brought into the ghetto except the December flour allocation for the institutions of the Council—and the bakers were not given passes to buy flour in town.

One reason for contradictory orders and constant feuding among the Germans was the practice of granting some sort of economic privileges or jobs to Jewish confidence men. When one administrative coterie gave some job or concession to its confidence men, a competing office tried to sabotage the favor. For example: the brothers Kon and Heller got from their German protectors a concession for horse-drawn buses in the Warsaw Ghetto, but Auerswald, the ghetto *Kommissar*, made difficulties with the route. Boehm, one of their protectors and a Gestapoman, had therefore suggested that Czerniakow intervene with the *Kommissar*. Auerswald in turn told him that for certain reasons he was not going to support people whom the Gestapo patronized.[31] However, the Gestapo won in the end.

When some German office wanted to deny a request submitted by the Jews, it simply stated that it lacked authority to grant it. When Czerniakow, during his visit to Auerswald on June 3, 1942, asked for permission to arrange a "religious academy," the answer was that this would be a prerogative of the Gestapo; but Karl Brandt, the Gestapoman with whom Czerniakow dealt, told him that it was within Auerswald's jurisdiction to give the permit.[32]

The domineering position of the SS and the police over the Jews became particularly strong during the period of mass deportations to the annihilation camps. In Frank's decree of June 3, 1942, where he outlined in detail the authority of Krüger as Higher SS and Police Leader (Hitler had elevated Krüger on May 7, 1942, to the rank of secretary of state for security affairs in the area of the Government General), all matters pertaining to the Jews were included (see Chap. 1). All police matters were transferred to Krüger. It was quite "logical" that at a time when deportation actions were in full swing the fate of the Jews should be placed in the hands of the police, along with the exploitation of the labor of survivors. This last matter was finally determined in a circular letter dated June 25, 1942, from Frauendorfer, chief of the main labor office in Cracow, addressed to all labor departments and labor offices in the Government General. The letter ruled that Jews may be employed only in agreement with the local Gestapo and police chief; that the labor offices are forbidden to intermediate in securing Jewish workers or to transport Jewish workers from one county to another; and that only the police are authorized to exploit the Jewish labor force, particularly insofar as it contributes to the war industry.[33]

Despite these clearcut instructions, relations between the higher officials of the administrative and police occupation authorities in the Government General were not peaceful for long. Friction continued, culminating in a request to resign on the part of Frank, a request which Hitler did not accept, and finally in the resignation of Krüger in November 1943.[34] Only during the period of the Final Solution was there full agreement and close cooperation, except for one thing: who should inherit the property of murdered Jews. In the mass deportations that started in the Government General in March 1942, both organs fully cooperated with only a few exceptions (see below, p.310).

THE ENORMITY OF GERMAN CONTROL

The German authorities put all phases of human life in the occupied areas under surveillance. It goes without saying that the Jews were controlled much more strictly than the other elements of the population. Even philanthropy was closely controlled. In Lublin, for instance, at the beginning of 1940 the representative of the *Nationalsozialistische Volkswohlfart* (NSV) summoned a member of the Jewish community executive body (there was as yet no Council established there) to be instructed on how to carry out a winter relief drive for needy Jews. Among other things he ordered that the candidate chosen to manage the drive be recommended to him for approval and that each week (on Friday) he be given a detailed report on the progress of the drive.[35] This was also the case in Warsaw (see a letter by the *Stadtpräsident* Dr. Dengel, addressed to Czerniakow and dated January 23, 1940).[36]

The Jewish Councils were obligated to submit periodic reports on a weekly, bi-weekly, or monthly basis. The reports were to be written in great detail, as can be seen, for instance, from the letter addressed to the Vilna Jewish Council by the *Gebietskommissar* on October 1, 1942, prescribing that each month, not later than the 28th, a report be submitted containing the following data: (1) a list of working Jews by sexes and a list of their employers: army, civilian administration, or private enterprises; (2) the scope and worth of the production of ghetto shops broken down according to individual employers, the Jewish ghetto administration included, with an indication whether the shops were operated with the *Gebietskommissar*'s permission; (3) the number and movement of the population and the reasons for changes taking place during the report period; (4) the food situation; (5) a list of measures applied by the ghetto administration within the ghetto; (6) the activities and the size of the ghetto police; (7) sundry events in the ghetto; and (8) the income and expenditures of the ghetto administration.[37]

The Warsaw Jewish Council used to submit weekly reports to the *Bevolmächtigte vom Distriktchef für die Stadt Warschau*. Report No. 32 for the week November 22–28, 1940, is a good example of the diverse problems covered: (1) general observations: a short enumeration of the problems the chairman discussed with the Nazi authorities in person and of other problems submitted in writing

(22 items in all); (2) activities of the labor office: the daily sheet of work days for forced laborers, listing the number of people sent to labor camps (including the delegates of the individual "battalions" and the functionaries of the ghetto police), the number of those who came back, and those who fell sick; (3) activities of the ghetto police, including the number of sentries and patrols within and without the ghetto; (4) retraining courses for artisans; (5) the health department: the number of patients in the hospital (kinds of illness, number of patients in quarantine), the number of sanitary inspections and disinfections, the number of visits in the ambulatories; (6) welfare, including data of the orphanage, asylum for chronically sick persons, home for prisoners of war, allocations of additional food, linen, clothing, etc.; (7) cemetery: the number of funerals; (8) finances: mainly about the payment of taxes; (9) management: care of the walls and fences around the ghetto, arrangement of offices for the German authorities, parcel post, renovation, and topographical plans; (10) registration: the number of newly arrived Jews, the number of new registrations, the office of addresses of the ghetto inmates, the number of identification cards and passes issued; (11) control: the number of financial audits of departments performed within the ghetto administration and its institutions; and (12) statistics.

The following appendices were attached to this report: (a) prices of vital food in the ghetto and in the city; (b) report of the compulsory union of Jewish artisans; (c) report of the activities of the JSS, Warsaw branch, for the second decade of November; (d) seven tables showing the movement of diseases and the number of patients, convalescents, and quarantined. The report contains 18 typewritten pages, including appendices.[38] And so it went week after week. As we have already mentioned, other authorities requested reports on their own. Thus we find in report No. 37 that the *Transferstelle* requested and received information on the number of pets in the ghetto, the quantities of food and fuel stored in the ghetto, a topographic study of the area, the number of houses and apartments in the ghetto, as well as "correlative tables" of Jews listed by occupation, sex, and age, with particular attention to artisans. As the number of departments multiplied and the scope of activities increased, so the dimensions of the reports submitted also kept growing.

Excessive *Berichtserstatung* (submitting of reports) developed in the Łódź Ghetto. At various times Rumkowski had to submit reports to the German *Gettoverwaltung* on a weekly, bi-weekly, and monthly basis. In addition, the Gestapo and *Statthalterei* in Poznań received reports each month. The individual departments in the ghetto administration, particularly the economic departments, were ordered to submit their own reports. The reports of the economic department had to be very detailed. For instance, the general report for July 1941 contained the following data: (1) quantity of food and other staples; (2) kinds of delivered merchandise produced in the ghetto by individual shops and factories; (3) confiscations; (4) special events; and (5) general description of the situation in the ghetto. The individual production reports (bi-weekly, starting in January 1944) contained data about the number of workers, the average number of absentees, lost labor hours, turnover of materials, wages, current merchandise orders, and estimates of time needed to carry out the orders.

More often yet, almost every day, reports had to be submitted by the health department indicating the kinds of diseases, the incidence of mortality, and the causes of deaths in the ghetto. It is characteristic that on March 5, 1942, Biebow forbade Rumkowski to list hunger and hunger edema as a cause of death. Should such cases occur, he admonished Rumkowski, undernourishment should be given as the cause of death. After the date of March 7, 1943, even this inconspicuous diagnosis disappeared from Rumkowski's reports[39]—this at a time when thousands were dying from hunger.

One cannot easily imagine the mass of paper work which the Councils had to perform to satisfy all German organs of the occupation. This great bulk of paper alone may explain the numerous personnel the Councils had to employ. In addition, the Councils in the large ghettos, such as Warsaw, Łódź, Lwów, and others, needed trained statisticians to prepare elaborate demographic, economic, and medico-sanitary diagrams to be submitted to the authorities on a regular basis.

The preparation of all these reports consumed much time, especially since it was not always possible or advisable to give correct data on the actual situation in the ghetto. Strenuous efforts were made and great ingenuity applied to keep the reports as accurate as possible, and at the same time to prevent any harm to the ghetto. For example, it was important to conceal from the Germans the extent of epidemics in order to shield sick inmates against the draconic measures the Germans applied to suppress contagious diseases. Similarly no mention of certain events (resistance, smuggling, etc.) which might have endangered the ghetto could have been made in the reports. The composition of the reports was an agonizing procedure in which decisions had to be made on what to include, what to omit, and how to formulate each item.

In addition to written reports the Councils were often summoned to give verbal information (the passion of the Nazi bureaucrats to hold their grip on life in the ghetto was never satisfied) or to answer some questions. From the entries in Czerniakow's Diary it appears that he went almost daily to various Nazi offices either by command or on his own initiative to intervene on behalf of the Council. On a weekly basis, he would routinely visit the Gestapo in company with the chief of the ghetto police to report or to get orders.

The *Judenälteste* were sometimes accused of sabotaging the instructions of the authorities, of not always acting in accordance with orders, or even of acting against them. One of those accused was Rumkowski himself. For the meeting in the Łódź Gestapo headquarters scheduled on June 11, 1942, an official of the *Gettoverwaltung* prepared an indictment against Rumkowski, accusing him of responsibility for the bad food situation in the ghetto and for lowering production, because he tried with promises of better food to induce skilled workers to volunteer for railroad work in Poznań, employing young children as substitutes for them. The indictment cited the fact that of the 280 persons chosen for transportation to Poznań, 145 were skilled workers. Actually these were mainly Jewish workers from the liquidated ghettos in Bełchatów and Zelwa who had been driven into the Łódź Ghetto. Most of them reported for railroad work in the Poznań area between June 8 and 15, 1942, hoping to escape the terrible food situation in the Łódź Ghetto.[40] In addition Rumkowski was charged in this indictment with nominating as chief of a new shop someone other than the person explicitly recommended for the job by the *Gettoverwaltung*; with printing his orders in Yiddish as well as German despite a prohibition to print anything except in the German language because of a scarcity of paper; and with establishing (without informing the *Gettoverwaltung*) a hospital for the mentally ill in the ghetto with 450 incurable patients—a great burden, particularly since there was not enough space to open new shops.[41] It is not known whether the meeting took place or what its consequences were for Rumkowski.

In the Łódź archival collections there is also preserved some correspondence concerning the following case: in April 1944 Biebow discharged officials employed by Rumkowski in his ghetto administration and dispatched them to build barracks. Several days later Rumkowski called a few of these men back to work in the ghetto. Biebow hastened to send him a letter indicating that Rumkowski was mistaken in thinking that he was the sole boss of the Jewish labor force, since, by the authority granted to him by the *Oberbürgermeister*, he, Biebow, was the supervisor of the activities of the Jewish ghetto administration at all times.[42] Similar incidents in other ghettos are unknown, so far.

SPECIAL ORGANS OF SUPERVISION AND CONTROL

In the organizational structure of the occupation administration there were special organs whose business it was to give orders to the Jewish Councils executing the decrees of the authorities and filling their demands for material goods. These organs were also charged with supervision of the Councils. In some large ghettos (i.e., Łódź, Warsaw, and Białystok) they were particularly overgrown, with a network of main offices, divisions, and subdivisions, all staffed with a vast number of officials.

The *Gettoverwaltung* in Łódź was established in October 1940 (until then, after the ghetto was sealed on May 1, 1940, the office in the municipal administration dealing with Jewish matters was called *Ernährungs- und Wirtschaftsstelle-Getto*) and consisted of four main departments: labor, utilization of goods, finances, and acquisitions, with 74 subdivisions, storage places, and its own railroad loading station.

The labor department was in charge of the ghetto shops (textiles, wood, leather, metal), the prices of goods produced, and the wages of workers.

The department of utilization of goods maintained control over gold and silver objects, precious stones, furs, home furnishings, and crystal objects that were confiscated outright from the Jews or "bought" in special places established for this purpose by Rumkowski. The department sold these goods wholesale or retail to German occupation officials. It also supervised the transportation of raw materials to ghetto shops and of finished products to the army and private firms. The transportation of enormous quantities of merchandise confiscated in the ghetto to special storage places in the building of the *Gettoverwaltung* was also a task of this department.[43]

The department of financial administration carried out the work of general bookkeeping and was in charge of the main treasury and records of confiscated currency, delivered raw materials, and finished products. Cash assistance for ghetto inmates received from sources outside the ghetto was also under the supervision of the finance department.

The purchasing department managed the special railroad station and food allocation for the ghetto, including the distribution of food and the loading and unloading of merchandise at the Bałut Market (which, in fact, was the place [*Verbindungsbüro*] where business exchange between the ghetto, the *Gettoverwaltung*, and the railroad station was carried out).

The *Gettoverwaltung* was headed by an *Amtsleiter* with two deputies, each in charge of two departments. Only Hans Biebow was entitled to negotiate both with the occupation authorities and with the Jewish Elder. Biebow was responsible for the work of the *Gettoverwaltung*.[44] He was subordinated to the *Oberbürgermeister*. The stationery of the *Gettoverwaltung* bore the heading *"Der Oberbürgermeister."* The number of its employees fluctuated at various periods. In August 1941, 167 were employed; but in December 1942, following the September deportations of 1942, only 92 persons were employed.[45] At the time of its liquidation in August 1944, 400 persons (including laborers) were employed.[46] Incidentally the *Verbindungsbüro* at the Bałut Market employed some Jews. Because of suspicion that Jews and Germans had established close contacts, all 60 Jewish female employees were discharged in July 1943. According to one commentator, this was ordered to prevent *Rassenschande*.[47]

The Jews themselves were ordered to cover the budget of the *Gettoverwaltung* and to pay the salaries of its personnel as well as all other administrative expenses. For this purpose an Overhead Fund was created by taxing all food allocations and other necessities delivered to the ghetto at 15 percent (*Regiekosten*), in addition to a 3 percent special tax (*Sondersteuer*). These taxes greatly exceeded the actual expenses of the *Gettoverwaltung*, and the city made large profits. For instance, both taxes provided the *Gettoverwaltung* with an income of 1,498,966 Reichsmarks in the period between May 1 and December 31, 1941, while all expenses to maintain personnel and payments for other purposes totaled only 322,258 Reichsmarks during the same time. Thus the net profit came as indicated in the document to a total of 988,617 Reichsmarks (actually the net profit was 1,176,708 Reichsmarks).[48]

However, the income from these taxes shrank considerably as a result of mass deportations which involved 55,000 people (over one-third of the ghetto inmates) in the period from January 16 to May 15, 1942, and food and other articles imported into the ghetto were proportionally reduced. In a memorandum addressed to Biebow, Genewein, the chief of the finance department, indicated that the time was near when taxes would not suffice to cover the expenses of the *Gettoverwaltung*. He therefore suggested that the 15 percent tax be extended to all merchandise imported into the ghetto without exception (since June 4, 1942, only food had been taxed), that the wages paid by the ghetto shops be taxed, and that the expenses of maintaining the personnel of the *Gettoverwaltung* be paid by the Jewish ghetto administration only.[49] The fate of this memorandum is unknown.

Relations between the German *Gettoverwaltung* and the Jewish administration in the economic field were formal and businesslike. Some of the economic departments of the *Gettoverwaltung* were similar to the departmental divisions of the economic sectors of Rumkowski's own administration (textiles, leather, etc.). The *Gettoverwaltung*'s bookkeeping was reconciled with the ghetto's bookkeeping, and financial statements were exchanged on a monthly basis. Rumkowski's correspondence addressed to German occupation authorities went through the channels of the *Gettoverwaltung* which delivered it to the proper addressees. His correspondence with the *Gettoverwaltung* itself was very diversified in scope and dimension. We shall mention only a few subjects: bills for food deliveries to the ghetto; bills for fuel, medicine, and raw materials for the production of various articles; wages, including wages for forced labor in the camps; confiscated goods and currency; completed assignments; money received for inmates through the post office to be deposited in the ghetto's bank account; individual confirmations of receipt of cash from abroad or return of bank checks received from Germany and neutral countries for persons deported in the meantime; lists of ghetto inmates about whom the *Gettoverwaltung* had received inquiries; orders of the central authorities; cash transfers through the channels of the *Gettoverwaltung*; financial obligations of Rumkowski's administration; fines of ghetto inmates for violations committed outside the ghetto in other occupied areas; forced return to the ghetto of Jewish children hidden outside the ghetto as "Aryans" or whose "Jewish race" had been determined by the German *Rassenamt*; and many more.[50]

While discussing the Łódź *Gettoverwaltung*, it is appropriate to say a few words about the *Amtsleiter*, Hans Biebow himself. Before the war, Biebow had been a well-to-do merchant in Bremen, one of the largest coffee merchants in Germany, conducting his business under the firm name "Julius Biebow, Streithorst & Co." On May 1, 1940, the day the Łódź Ghetto was closed, he was nominated chief of the *Ernährungs- und Wirtschaftsstelle-Getto*. He was a member of the Nazi Party, and references in his personal Party file indicate that according to the opinion of his comrades, "there are no political reservations against party comrade Hans Biebow." According to observations of a former inmate well versed in the affairs of the ghetto, "Biebow was a very smart fellow, an experienced, crafty wholesaler, who knew how to exploit the ghetto for his own purposes. Because of his widespread connections, he succeeded in prolonging the life of the ghetto. . . . He was the sole boss over the ghetto and could do, and actually did, whatever struck his fancy." Personally interested in the development of the ghetto industry, he tried to improve food conditions for the inmates, and in his memoranda to the Gestapo and the *Oberbürgermeister* complained that the very poor nourishment of Jewish workers was bound to undermine the ghetto shop production for the benefit of the military.

Biebow carried out his exploitation of the ghetto without salary (*ehrenamtlich*), but he drew personal profit under the pretext of "buying" goods. For example, he paid 200 Reichsmarks for a fur coat which a German fur expert appraised at 1,200 Reichsmarks. He bought a diamond ring for his wife, paying a token price. A list of items he bought from November 1940 to March 11, 1943, consists of 60 separate columns, from kitchen utensils to a diamond ring of 41/804 carats (for which he paid only 2,500 Reichsmarks). In time, he gained the reputation of being such an excellent ghetto administrator that the German military commander in France tried to have him transferred to serve as his own expert, but the Łódź *Oberbürgermeister* refused to release him. According to the statement of

Veygand, Heydrich intended to nominate Biebow as commandant of Theresienstadt Ghetto. Small wonder that the Führer himself gave him a medal, the *Luftschutzehrenzeichen*, second class.

The rich merchant from Bremen displayed no lack of Nazi brutality and cynicism. He was very active during the deportations from the Łódź Ghetto and even participated in the deportation from neighboring Zduńska Wola on August 24–25, 1942, shooting Jews driven to the cemetery (as already mentioned, he personally shot the Council chairman, Dr. Lemberg). In August 1944, when the ghetto was already in process of final liquidation, Biebow visited the ghetto shops, delivering speeches to the effect that it was in the best interests of the Jewish workers themselves to leave the ghetto. During the *Gettoaufräumung* ("sweeping of the ghetto") which took place from October 1944 to January 1945, Biebow played a sadistic role, raping girls in the women's camps and torturing seized men. In the beginning of January 1945 he gave orders to dig eight large pits in which to bury (after shooting them) the survivors of the *Aufräumung*. Because of the success of the swift offensive of the Soviet armies, who liberated Łódź on January 19, the execution of these inmates was never carried out. Some survivors of the Łódź Ghetto later recognized Biebow in Germany. He was brought to trial before a Polish court in Łódź, sentenced to death, and executed. During the trial he defended himself by arguing that he tried to improve the food situation in the ghetto.[51]

The Łódź *Gettoverwaltung* became a model for the occupation authorities in their endeavor to organize mutual relations in other large ghettos. Thus a delegation of 15 high-ranking officials of the Warsaw district, headed by Governor Fischer, visited Łódź on September 13, 1940, "to get information from responsible *Referenten* about their experiences" in administering the ghetto. A gala dinner was given in honor of the guests, and a gathering of the *Referenten* from Warsaw and Łódź was arranged.[52] A similar organ, also called *Gettoverwaltung*, was established in Białystok in March 1942.[53] It is noteworthy that officials of the Białystok *Stadtkommissariat* were sent to Łódź in February 1942, to learn on the spot the organizational and operational methods of the Łódź *Gettoverwaltung*. There is evidence that the organizational structure of the Białystok *Gettoverwaltung* resembled that of Łódź, except that it was smaller, proportionate to the relative dimensions and importance of this ghetto in supplying the German war machine. The Łódź *Gettoverwaltung* suggested that the Białystok *Stadtkommissar* issue ghetto currency, as was the practice in Łódź;[54] but this suggestion was not accepted. By the end of October and the beginning of November 1942, killing actions against Jews started throughout the Bezirk Białystok, and all matters pertaining to Jews were transferred to the police and the SD, as had happened in the Government General. The *Referent* from the IV B office (Church and Jewish Affairs) of the local Gestapo was nominated head of the *Gettoverwaltung*, so that in fact the Gestapo was given full authority over the *Gettoverwaltung*.[55] The same happened in Łódź, where the chief of the local Gestapo, Dr. Otto Bradfisch, was nominated in mid-1942 as the temporary *Oberbürgermeister* and thus took over supervision of the activities of the *Gettoverwaltung*.

In Bielsko the *Inspektorat für jüdische Gemeinden in Bielitz* was apparently the competent German authority over Jewish Councils in all of Upper Silesia. Thus, when in October 1941 the Jewish Council in Zator asked the Bielitz *Landrat* for permission to establish a tailor shop, an answer came from the *Inspektorat*.[56]

In some ghettos the authorities established branches of the occupational municipal offices (*Nebenstellen* or *Niederlassungen*). For example, the *Stadtverwaltung* in Częstochowa established its *Niederlassung* in the ghetto. In other ghettos, there were in operation *Nebenstellen* of the local German labor offices.[57]

The Germans established two organs to deal with Jewish affairs in the Warsaw Ghetto: the *Transferstelle* and, later on, the office of the *Kommissar für den jüdischen Wohnbezirk Warschau*. The *Transferstelle* started its activities in December 1940 when the ghetto was sealed off. It carried out economic control in the ghetto, concentrating on relations between the ghetto and the outer "Aryan" world. Until May 1941 the *Transferstelle* worked within the framework of the "resettlement section" of the Warsaw district administration. It had an advisory committee consisting of delegates from almost all departments of the district administration, the police, and the SD. Its first head was Alexander Palfinger, a former German official of the Łódź *Gettoverwaltung*, clearly an efficient expert in ghetto matters.

The work of the *Transferstelle* embraced the following activities: merchandise and food for the ghetto; Jewish laborers for tasks within and outside the ghetto; mediation in economic relations between the ghetto inmates and people on the "Aryan" side; affairs of the

Treuhandstelle; supervision of loading and storage places; and supervision of individual business establishments.[58]

The procedures for economic relations previously implemented by Waldemar Schön, chief of the resettlement section, and by the *Transferstelle*, headed by Alexander Palfinger, were unacceptable to the central economic authorities in the Government General. Palfinger was a stanch admirer of the system practiced in the Łódź Ghetto: absolute economic isolation, total confiscation of property, and strict suppression of Jewish private initiative in any form. Walter Emmerich, chief of the economic department in Cracow, stressed during a meeting in Warsaw on January 20, 1940 that Schön and his assistants lacked sufficient experience in economic matters, and that his methods would inevitably stifle and paralyze the economy of the ghetto. On his initiative, in March 1941, a committee of experts from the *Reichskuratorium für Wirschaftlichkeit* in Cracow prepared an exhaustive report of 53 pages entitled: "Die Wirtschaftsbilanz des jüdischen Wohnbezirks in Warschau." The report came up with the following recommendations: that the basic food supply in the ghetto ought to be lower than necessary to sustain life; that workshops ought to be established as soon as possible; the economic isolation of the ghetto should be eased and some branches of Jewish industry permitted to accept orders directly from clients outside the ghetto; orders for ghetto production should come not through the *Transferstelle*, which should not act as a business establishment, but directly from the German firms; manufacture and trade should be set in motion and financed by the Jews themselves; and, for this purpose, special Jewish economic organizations should be established. In his evaluation of the report, Palfinger argued that the authors had a "capitalistic approach" to the ghetto. But at a meeting with Fischer, held on April 19, 1941, new methods of administering the Warsaw Ghetto were adopted in line with Emmerich's recommendations. Palfinger could no longer retain leadership and was replaced by Max Bischof.[59]

During April and May 1941 the organizational structure of the *Transferstelle* was changed following the establishment of the office of *Kommissar* for the Jewish *Wohnbezirk*. The order of Governor General Frank of April 19, 1941 provided that a *Kommissar* for the ghetto be nominated and that he also take over supervision of the *Transferstelle*, with the district chief deciding the terms of his authority.[60] Fischer issued the pertinent order (No. 41/22) on May

14, 1941. This order outlined the activities of the *Transferstelle* and the principle of its subordination to the ghetto *Kommissar*.[61] According to this order and subsequent guidelines, for instance, that of July 7, 1942, all contracts concluded with the ghetto by any German authority had first to be confirmed by the *Kommissar* or the *Transferstelle*.[62]

After the ambitious and energetic Max Bischof took over the *Transferstelle* on May 15, 1941, its activities greatly expanded, and, according to an organizational table dated July 1, 1942, its sphere encompassed the following areas: permits to enter or leave the ghetto; imports of goods necessary for industrial purposes; price controls; trade with the ghetto and payment for manufactured goods; economic expansion (establishment of production enterprises, planning the execution of orders received from outside the ghetto, finding premises for shops, production apparatus, and raw materials); administration (bookkeeping, control, and manufacturing enterprises of the *Transferstelle* itself); and movement of goods into and out of the ghetto.[63] Some 120 persons were employed by the *Transferstelle* under the management of Bischof and his deputy, Dr. Ulrich Rathie.[64]

A report dated March 10, 1941, by the governor of the Warsaw district to the Government General in Cracow formulated the manifold functions of the *Transferstelle* as follows: on the basis of a *Bedarfsmeldung* ("request notice") submitted by the Jewish Council (and after prepayment by the Council of the approximate worth of the goods requested), the goods were to be delivered on the account of the *Transferstelle* and unloaded at the Umschlagplatz ("unloading square") especially established for this purpose on the border of the ghetto and supervised by German officials. (A similar procedure was practiced in the Łódź Ghetto and in some other large ghettos.) The report further indicated that the *Transferstelle* would also act as an intermediary organ in relations between the ghetto and the "Aryan" world, by taking orders for ghetto industry from customers outside the ghetto.[65]

The transportation of food, raw materials, and merchandise in and out of the Warsaw Ghetto through the *Transferstelle* constituted only a small part of the ghetto's economic turnover with the outer world. The *Transferstelle* itself was forced to admit this quite unpleasant fact by issuing special "economic regulations." In a draft of a circular letter to all transport firms dealing with the ghetto (dated March 1, 1941) it is stated that "recent experiment has shown that professional transport firms are mainly responsible for the illegal import of goods into the ghetto." The *Transferstelle* demanded a stop to imports and exports to and from the ghetto and the strict adherence to prescribed procedures.[66]

Strict control of the illegal exchange of goods was made difficult by the fact that "Aryan" factories (some were owned by Poles) were still, for a time, in operation inside the ghetto. This provided a good opportunity for the exchange of raw materials and finished products as well as food, always a coveted commodity in the ghetto. Illegal contracts were also maintained through Polish municipal aides who came to collect taxes and fees for gas and electricity, and through Polish policemen either on patrol duty in the streets bordering the ghetto walls or coming into the ghetto on official business. Counter-measures by the Germans succeeded in curtailing the dimensions of these contacts, but were powerless to stop them altogether. Even as late as July 1942 the *Transferstelle* stated in its monthly report that the difficult problem of controlling imports and exports in the ghetto would be solved "by itself," now that the ghetto had been entirely isolated by Auerswald's order, and also because of the progress of resettlement (the report is dated August 15, 1942), which was getting rid of large numbers of traders and manufacturers dealing in smuggled food or illegal raw materials and goods.[67]

We have already mentioned (see Chap. 5) the report of the Warsaw governor, Dr. Fischer, for the period of June and July 1942, in which he stated that civilian and military economic agencies were dispatching trucks into the Warsaw Ghetto to carry out goods bought there at black-market prices.

Contrary to what happened in Łódź, the Nazi authorities in Warsaw failed to cut off all economic exchange between the ghetto and the outer world. A detailed analysis of the socio-economic structure and the attitude of the German authorities in both ghettos would probably explain why this was so, but such an analysis falls beyond the scope of this book.

As mentioned above, the *Transferstelle* was under the jurisdiction of the *Kommissar für den jüdischen Wohnbezirk*, but, as often happened in Nazi administrations in the occupied territories, the chiefs of both offices repeatedly disagreed on the limits of their authority. Max Bischof, the director of the *Transferstelle*, sought to absorb the economic department in the office of the ghetto *Kommissar*, maintaining that it was unnecessary to nominate another official for that job.

The *Kommissar* argued that it was improper for the *Transferstelle*, which was subordinate to him, to control the economic department of his office. But the ambitious Bischof was not deterred. There is a note in the official papers signed by the ghetto *Kommissar* on July 15, 1941, that the director of the *Transferstelle* had tried to win high officials of the district over to his view. At a meeting held in the district economic department on July 2, the opinion was expressed that economic affairs in the ghetto should be supervised by Bischof as the man directly responsible for them. It is clear that the economic department in the district administration endeavored through the *Transferstelle* to secure the upper hand in economic activities in the ghetto by eliminating the authority of the ghetto *Kommissar* over this sector.[68]

Control over the economy of the ghetto by the *Transferstelle* was carried out in practice by enforcing travel permits for people and transportation of goods. Without permits, no legal exchange of goods between the ghetto and the outside world was allowed. Whoever wished to invest capital in the ghetto, or to import merchandise or any other resources, had to secure a written permit from the *Transferstelle*. In fact, however, people traded with the ghetto without official authorization. This is explained in the report of the *Transferstelle* for December 1941 as a result of the fact that the entire price structure of the Government General had been shattered and that, therefore, merchants preferred to deal directly with the ghetto to avoid making deals in writing under the control of the *Transferstelle*.[69]

To enforce control over trade between the ghetto and the outside world, a system of "cashless exchange" was introduced by using credit checks from the Warsaw emission bank. In the beginning the *Transferstelle* placed a 15 percent surcharge on imported goods and merchandise, which, naturally, raised prices in the ghetto compared to those outside. A 10 percent tax was deducted from the wages of shop workers.[70] Later this fee was reduced.

For a time the *Transferstelle* acted as an entrepreneur, accepting orders for goods manufactured in the ghetto. There was a separate division within the administration department called "home industry," but the report for December 1941 (dated January 1942) indicates that, with a few exceptions, the *Transferstelle* had abandoned its own business enterprises, leaving it to German firms to fill orders already accepted. Its two garment experts were absorbed into the firm of "Walter K. Toebbens." The closeness of business relations between the *Transferstelle* and certain German firms is illustrated by the fact that two representatives of the Toebbens firm were "honorary" members of the *Transferstelle*. However, when the *Transferstelle* relinquished its own business sector, the two "honorary" representatives of the Toebbens firm were dismissed "in order that relations with the private business sector of the German *Firmengemeinschaft* be established on a uniform and clear basis."[71]

As chief of the *Transferstelle*, Bischof tried to increase the already large production potential of the ghetto by making it an industrial stronghold in the Government General. He discussed the insufficient food allocations for ghetto workers in his reports, requesting that they be enlarged; made publicity for the industrial potential of the ghetto in the Reich press; and tried to ease currency regulations on orders for goods coming from the Reich, in order to hamper the exploitation schemes of certain German and Polish firms.[72] In the statistical tables attached to his reports, he stressed the ever increasing value of the goods exported from the ghetto and the steady rise of wages for labor. Thus the table for the year 1941 attached to the January 1942 report shows that the worth of goods exported from the ghetto by the *Transferstelle* rose from 1,700 zlotys in February to 5,214,000 in November 1941, and that exported goods and wages amounted to 20,055,000 zlotys for the entire year 1941.[73] Preparing material for a meeting of the government (with Frank's participation) to take place in mid-October 1941, he requested that Czerniakow make ready photos showing the shops in operation.[74] He also helped the Jewish Council to get telephones installed, suggested that Czerniakow establish a cooperative bank in the ghetto, was interested to know whether there were financial experts among the Council's members, etc.

Bischof was interested in economic problems and claimed that the Council should be active only as an economic body. He suggested that the supply department be separated from the rest of the Jewish ghetto administration.[75] Characteristically he ordered the "economic council" of the *Judenrat* to call a meeting to be held on the premises of the supply department and not in the *Judenrat*'s building. Czerniakow was to be invited as a "guest" (Czerniakow's expression). He felt slighted and told Bischof that he would not attend.[76] Because of Bischof's attitude, relations between him and Czerniakow deteriorated. Criticizing Palfinger's policies during his first meeting with Bischof, Czerniakow often talked about the necessity to "clear the air" within the *Transferstelle* (banish Jewish middlemen and other measures), expecting that Bischof would show enough stamina to do it. But as can be seen from Czerniakow's Diary, their relations became strained. Czerniakow shared Auerswald's point of view in his struggle with Bischof. When Bischof reproached him that he did not cooperate in the confiscation of posted parcels over 3 kilograms in weight addressed to Jews and containing leather, flour, or fats, Czerniakow replied that he had already discussed this matter with Auerswald;[77] and when the *Transferstelle* recommended that someone intermediate in the delivery of goods to the supply department, he noted in his Diary that he would inquire about this of "his supervising authority" (meaning Auerswald).[78]

That Bischof was interested in only the economic aspects of the ghetto can be seen in the fact that he reproached Czerniakow, in the presence of representatives of the supply department (Abraham Gepner and Abraham Sztolcman), complaining that the heavy penalties (including prison terms) imposed repeatedly by Czerniakow on tardy taxpayers were detrimental to the finances of the ghetto. There is a note in Auerswald's papers, dated March 4, 1942, that Bischof intended to call a meeting of the supply department, with Czerniakow's participation, in order to make him change his strict application of penalties.[79] Bischof had no understanding of the political and social aspects of ghetto realities. In the course of his very first meeting with Governor Fischer, on April 30, 1941, he said that he did not consider himself competent to handle the political or administrative aspects of the *Transferstelle*'s work.[80]

Objectively Bischof's endeavors to enhance production potential in the ghetto went in the direction of creating conditions warranting its existence in the opinion of the German authorities. Once, in a conversation with Czerniakow, he casually remarked that "Warsaw is a temporary asylum for the Jews" (Diary entry, October 4, 1941). As a quite experienced bureaucrat, his aim was to make sure that the ghetto would be in a position to produce its maximum, not by the application of ineffective slave labor, but on more or less rational economic bases that would secure proper profits for the *Transferstelle*. The fanatical attitude of the Nazis toward the Jews apparently was alien to him. This probably was the cause of animosity toward him in SS circles. A certain SS *Hauptsturmführer* Reinhold denounced him before the governor, charging that for a time he rented rooms in the apartment of a woman who, as was later discovered, was a converted Jewess; that his best friends were ghetto inmates; that he freely gave passes to German women to enter the ghetto for treatment by Jewish doctors; and similar "crimes." Auerswald summoned Bischof, who denied all these allegations.[81]

The *Transferstelle* was closed in December 1942, when its activities ended for all practical purposes, after the mass deportations in the summer of 1942. A report by Governor Fischer for October and November 1942, states that "the current economic exchanges between the ghetto and the 'Aryan' outside world are exclusively regulated by the SS and Police Leader."[82] As was the case in the other *Restgettos* the police authorities took over the supervision of surviving Jews in the Warsaw Ghetto, and the *Transferstelle* was not needed any more. A week after the conclusion of the mass deportations, in a letter dated September 28, 1942, the ghetto *Kommissar* informed Bischof that since the Jewish *Wohnbezirk* would be dismantled by December 31, 1942, at the latest, the activities of the *Transferstelle* would be limited to liquidation matters and his office would be closed as of January 1, 1943. He also told Bischof that their agreement of June 15 would be terminated as of this date.[83]

Prior to his nomination as *Kommissar*, Heinz Auerswald served in the interior department of the Warsaw district administration. Already in this capacity he was involved in ghetto affairs. In light of his own statements in writing, Auerswald was a successfully indoctrinated Nazi functionary who strictly abided by popular National Socialist slogans about the Jews.[84] He visualized the "solution" of the Jewish question after the war in the form of Jewish reservations and considered the ghettos as only their forerunners, temporary measures which by no means gave the desired radical answer to the problems of complete isolation of the Jewish population.[85] Personally he could not stand the Jews and had complained to Czerniakow that visiting Council officials stood too close when they talked to him (Diary entry, April 22, 1942). He was a strong supporter of isolation of the Jews within the ghetto, justifying this position with the Nazi argument that isolation would help stop the spread of epidemics by the filthy Jews. He cited as evidence the fact that in Warsaw, where the ghetto had been more or less shut off, typhus among the "Aryan" population had not exceeded 10 percent of all cases during a long stretch of time, while in the eastern parts of the district, where no such strict isolation of the Jews had yet been enforced, the rate of typhus among the "Aryans" amounted to 30 percent.[86]

He devoted much of his time and energy to achieving complete isolation of the ghetto and felt unhappy that no ideally tight isolation had been achieved, despite all his strenuous efforts. It became a fixed idea with him. Twice during his tenure the ghetto borders were "corrected" (in September and November 1941 and in March 1942). When it suited his plans to attain total isolation of the Jews he even decided to include within the "corrected" ghetto borders buildings and factories which had initially been left on the "Aryan" side. Czerniakow's pleading that such "corrections" would bring about the economic ruin of thousands of families were to no avail.[87] Auerswald was unmoved by the reasoning of Dr. Hagen, the official *Amtsarzt*, that the resettlement of Jews in the southern part of the ghetto at a time when typhus had reached its highest point (2,492 new cases were registered in September 1941) was sheer madness, and that according to the opinion "of all his co-workers acquainted with prevailing local conditions and in the opinion of all experienced Polish physicians actively engaged in fighting the epidemic the 'resettlement' will inevitably end in catastrophe."[88] Moreover, Auerswald did not hesitate to recommend the death penalty for "vagabond" Jews in his biennial report dated September 26, 1941.[89] According to Ringelblum he made a proposal (or supported a proposal) to introduce the death penalty for leaving the ghetto at the meeting of the Government General in Warsaw that took place with Governor Frank during the first half of October 1941.[90] Soon this draconic punishment became a fact. On October 15 Frank issued the order, and on October 17, Auerswald announced to the shocked ghetto inmates the execution of eight Jews, among them six women, one a sixteen-year-old girl. They were all shot to death for the crime of seeking to find some food outside the ghetto walls.[91] This was the first case of shooting Jews for leaving a ghetto,[92] and there is little to doubt that Auerswald's support for this draconic measure at the meeting with Frank had stimulated its introduction.

In his attitude toward ghetto inmates he thought that only working Jews had the right to live. He could not have cared less for the fate of the others. Czerniakow noted in his Diary, under the date July 8, 1941, that Auerswald had stressed the point that Jews should report for work on a voluntary basis, otherwise the ring around the ghetto would became tighter and tighter until all the Jews would slowly die. Several months later he told Czerniakow that he was going to subdivide the ghetto inmates into three categories, and those unemployed (i.e., the majority) would get only one-half kilo (17 ounces) of bread a week.[93] This step was taken at a time when bread was almost the only food staple available to the Jews. Furthermore he was against providing food for refugees, who constituted almost a third of the ghetto inmates. According to Ringelblum, Auerswald characterized the refugees as dry leaves that must fall, and requested that all social welfare be designated for the benefit of working Jews in the ghetto. Ringelblum added that Auerswald issued an order to reduce food supplies for the soup kitchens, with the result that soup was provided only three times a week and at a higher price than before.[94]

Auerswald believed that an increase in the labor productivity of the ghetto should be stimulated not by way of increased food allocations but at the further expense of the starving population. When informed by Auerswald that the *Stachanovtsy* employed in rearranging the walls of the "corrected" ghetto borders would be given bread premiums, Czerniakow wryly noted in his Diary: "Naturally, out of the normal stock of ghetto supplies." Auerswald also demanded that the "Aryan" laborers of the "Münstermann" firm (which was given the "correction" job) receive 400 grams of bread daily out of the terribly insufficient ghetto supplies.[95]

He gave orders to send to the penal camp in Treblinka several hundred Jews who had been under arrest in the ghetto jail but had been ransomed for 1,500 fur coats and set free in March 1942 (see Chap. 10), and a group of 160 youths from among newly arrived German Jewish deportees.[96] These became the first victims of the adjacent annihilation camp of the same name when it became operational a few months later. Such were the "favors" Auerswald boasted about during a conversation with Czerniakow, adding that he had experienced great difficulties in obtaining release of the prisoners from the ghetto jail and that he would not have attempted it had he known in advance how complicated a task it was to be.[97] On May 29, 1942, Czerniakow made an entry in his diary that the *Kommissar* had ordered him to deliver 900 Jews to work at an unknown camp, as well as 240 inmates of the ghetto jail fifteen to eighteen years of age, among them 4 *previously pardoned by Frank himself*. He personally assisted in the night raid leading to deportation of 914

Jews to Bobrujsk.[98] In a word, he pretended to be the benefactor of arrested Jews and even claimed to have facilitated their release. But his role in the deportation of the released Jews to Treblinka shows clearly that, in reality, he was a typical Nazi cynic. We have already mentioned his cynical observation regarding the role of the Jewish Councils as a lightning rod for the benefit of the German occupation authorities. But perhaps his National Socialist fanaticism is best illustrated by the punishment he imposed upon the ghetto orchestra for playing the music of "Aryan" composers: he suspended the orchestra for two months.[99]

Auerswald pressed the ghetto also in financial matters. Thus we read in Czerniakow's Diary that of an amount of 700,000 zlotys which Auerswald had amassed (it is not indicated from what sources), he wanted to pay only 300,000 zlotys to the Jewish Council.[100] Moreover, he demanded that the Council provide furniture, bedding, and other home furnishings to his personnel, without ever paying one penny for the delivered goods.[101]

And yet, despite all this, a Jewish youth (he is known only by his first name, Szymek) was his "majordomus" (as Czerniakow calls him), and Auerswald told him that he was very satisfied with his work.[102]

As a narrowminded Nazi bureaucrat, Auerswald concentrated on picayune, purely formalistic matters of little relevance. Czerniakow notes with irony that once, when he came to discuss a very important financial problem of the ghetto, Auerswald talked to him at length about such "important" things as whether the ghetto policemen should wear their armbands on the left or the right arm, or that, perhaps, it was advisable that they wear two armbands, a second one in addition to the regular armband all Jews were ordered to wear. Financial problems were not discussed at all.[103]

During his first months in office, Auerswald gained his reputation in the ghetto as "a friend and a decent man." Apparently this was Czerniakow's own impression based on his initial daily contacts with the newly nominated *Kommissar*. This opinion had spread throughout the ghetto, and therefore Auerswald's role in the executions of November 17, 1940, was a grave disappointment.[104] Auerswald's relations with Czerniakow were correct, mixed with a degree of confidence and perhaps even some mutual respect. In his letter to Medeaza already mentioned, he wrote about Czerniakow: "So far, apparently, in the correct evaluation of the situation, he is working loyally." Auerswald even released Czerniakow from the obligation of wearing an armband. Czerniakow talked to Auerswald in a way that he would certainly not dare to address any other German official. Once, during a meeting with the *Kommissar*, he appealed to him as the bearer of a "historical role and responsibility."[105] During another meeting, when Auerswald complained about the difficulties he had encountered in his endeavors to free Jews from the ghetto prison, Czerniakow counseled him "to reckon only with the Almighty."[106]

As late as June 1942 Czerniakow still believed that Auerswald would have the courage to intercede on behalf of the financial interests of the ghetto.[107] In general, however, Czerniakow was skeptical about Auerswald's promises regarding interventions with the authorities for the benefit of the ghetto.[108] Auerswald's correct attitude toward Czerniakow is also evident in the fact that he gave him permission not to appear in the spurious film of the ghetto made in the *Stürmer* style for anti-Jewish propaganda purposes in May 1942.[109]

But at the crucial moment for the ghetto, the *Gettokommissar* deceived the Jewish *Obmann*. On July 18, 1942, when terrible panic had already spread in the ghetto because of persistent rumors of imminent massive deportations (which, in fact, did begin five days later) Czerniakow noted in his Diary that Auerswald, when asked about the rumors, had answered that he did not believe they were true. However, it is simply impossible to imagine that the *Gettokommissar* had no information about the impending "action" for which preparations certainly were already in full swing at the time. The *Kommissar* was no exception to the rule among Nazi officialdom in Warsaw, constantly engaging in hypocritical deceit with the Jews (see Chap. 16). His Nazi conscience apparently did not bother him at all when he was cheating the representative of a community of almost a half-million people with whom he had worked for over a year, meeting him almost daily. Czerniakow's exhortations about "historical responsibility" or "reckoning with the Almighty" proved to be in vain when the fate of the ghetto inmates was at stake.

The Jewish Council was obligated to submit to the *Kommissar* periodic reports on all its activities, and the chairman, Czerniakow, got explicit orders and directives from him. The ghetto police had to report to him on a weekly basis all cases of insubordination with respect to issued orders, criminal acts, disrespect, or resistance to the police. He also gave the police direct orders to perform certain tasks. The *Kommissar* directed economic life in the ghetto with the help of the *Transferstelle* and generally used the Jewish Council and the police to oversee the entire internal life of the ghetto.

However, he was not the absolute ruler. Other agencies, particularly the police (SS, Gestapo, etc.), only too often interfered in the affairs of the ghetto. The often capricious polyarchic system implemented by the occupation authorities was particularly evident in regard to the Jews. And for this reason Auerswald, as was typical for the Nazi administration in the occupied areas, had to wage jurisdictional fights with other administrative organs. As with the *Transferstelle* controversy mentioned above, a feud concerning Auerswald's authority over the ghetto activities of the police broke out. At a meeting held on November 8, 1941—with the participation of officials of the internal administration department in the Warsaw district, the city police director, the public prosecutor's office, the *Gettokommissar*, and a high official from his office—an agreement was reached to the effect that the *Kommissar* would be in charge of policing the ghetto. He would use his own *Sonderdienstkommandos* and the ghetto police, and, at his request, the city police director would also put at his disposal the Polish police stationed in the ghetto. Any fines imposed upon the ghetto Jews by the police director would be paid to the treasury of the *Gettokommissar*, with the understanding that every four months he would pay 10 percent of the fines to the treasury of the police director as an "administrative contribution." The same procedure was adopted regarding fines for price speculation and traffic offenses.

Along with other documents, a copy of the discussion during the meeting was sent to the SS and Police Leader in the Warsaw district who, on November 18, informed Auerswald in writing that he did not agree with the decision that the ghetto police should be subordinated to the *Kommissar*. He was of the opinion that the ghetto police should be under the express jurisdiction of the *Kommandant* of the *Schutzpolizei*. He reproached Auerswald for not having invited a representative of the district police to the meeting and ordered him to get in touch with the *Kommandant* of the *Schutzpolizei* regarding the use of police within the ghetto.[110]

The office of the *Gettokommissar* was dissolved on March 31, 1943, on the eve of the final liquidation of the Warsaw Ghetto.[111]

DEALING WITH THE GERMAN AUTHORITIES

Personal contacts with the German authorities was a particularly difficult and nerve-racking task for the Jewish Councils. The German attitude toward the Jewish Councils was as reckless as their attitude to the Jews in general. Often, the Council became the scapegoat of brutal Nazi fanatics who considered it disgusting and against their racist dignity to have any contact with Jews. Only on rare occasions were the Jews allowed seats during meetings with the Germans, not to speak of handshakes. A visit of Council members to a Nazi office was often accompanied by moral and physical torture. They were subjected to anti-Jewish tirades and scolding, and, at times, they were severely beaten or forced to perform denigrating, painful "gymnastic exercises," about which we will say more later. But contacts were unavoidable, particularly so where the Councils hoped it would be possible to wrest from the Germans some kind of concession or relief from persecution.[112]

Contacts were possible only on the level of the local authorities. Only one instance has so far come to light of a Jewish Council's intervention with a high official of the Government General in Cracow. This was when representatives of the Joint Distribution Committee and the JSS Committee in Warsaw met with Dr. Arlt, the chief of the main office of the *Bevölkerungswesen und Fürsorge* in Cracow. Dr. Michał Weichert relates that he had initially suggested that Arlt call a meeting of the chairmen of the Jewish Councils in all four district towns (Warsaw, Cracow, Lublin, and Radom); but Arlt rejected this proposal after checking with the ranking officials. Instead he agreed to meet with representatives of the Warsaw Jewish Council together with two representatives of the JDC and the JSS respectively. The meeting took place on the 27th and 28th of March 1940. Adam Czerniakow, Josef Jaszunski, Abraham Sztolcman, and Dr. Israel Milejkowski represented the Warsaw Jewish Council. Yitzhak Borenstein represented the Joint Distribution Committee, and Michał Weichert represented the JSS. At the meeting Czerniakow cited numerous cases of arbitrary acts against Jews and requested that the armband, which rendered the Jew conspicuous from a distance, be exchanged for a Star of David pin to be worn on the lapel. Concluding, he made two proposals: that personal and property security be preserved, and that the obligations and rights of the Councils be precisely outlined. The other Council members made suggestions concerning the activities of the individual departments (Jaszunski—labor; Sztolcman—industry and trade; Dr. Milejkowski—health and sanitation). Dr. Weichert notes that Arlt behaved courteously, though he often got excited and interrupted the speakers. It was the consensus of all present that although no concrete results were achieved, the mere fact that representatives of the largest Jewish community got in touch with the central civil authorities was a positive achievement and that efforts should be made to achieve similar contacts in the future. Indeed meetings with Dr. Arlt continued on a more or less weekly basis during April and May 1940, except that Jaszunski alone represented the Warsaw Jewish Council.[113] There were no known contacts between Jewish Councils and the central authorities after this date. However, representatives of the JDC and the JSS in Cracow continued to intervene with Dr. Arlt or with his deputies.[114]

In general, then, contacts were maintained only with the low-level functionaries. As a rule it was they, the *Judenreferenten* in the various offices, who summoned the Council chairmen or the chiefs of the Council departments to give orders, demand reports, threaten, reproach, etc.

In a number of areas, such as food supply, forced labor, and ghetto industry, there had developed a kind of routine in the relations between the authorities and the Jews. Thus in the Łódź Ghetto, the following cumbersome procedure was applied with regard to delivery of food and other articles of consumption. The Jewish ghetto administration had to fill out a notice of requirements (*Bedarfsmeldung*), and then, before allotted products were actually delivered to the ghetto, the German ghetto administration decided whether there would be enough left for the "Aryan" population in Łódź. The products were delivered to the loading place (*Umschlagplatz*) at the Bałut marketplace. The drivers were given delivery certificates listing the delivered articles. Piece goods were loaded on Jewish carts right at the Umschlagplatz, but heavy articles in bulk, such as coal, flour, or vegetables, were driven through the ghetto gate up to the actual ghetto border, where Jewish teamsters took over from "Aryans." Clerks of the German ghetto administration at the Bałut marketplace checked the notices of requirements and entered them in the storage book. After the notices were returned to the German ghetto administration, the respective firms would be credited with the amounts due for the goods delivered. The Jewish Council was billed for the same amount plus an administrative surcharge of 15 percent and, starting in July 1940, with an additional special tax (*Sondersteuer*) of 5 percent.[115] In other words, the prices of the goods delivered were 20 percent higher in the ghetto than in the town outside.

Orders for the manufacture of merchandise in the ghetto and for the export of manufactured goods were also directed through the hands of the German ghetto administration.[116]

We shall now try to analyze the moral climate that marked contacts between the Jewish Councils and the Nazi overseers. In the first place this moral climate was based on the degree of hatred by individual functionaries for the Jews. In general, as we have already noted elsewhere, their attitude was cynical, brutal, and denigrating. Many a *Judenreferent* used meetings with a Jewish representative to vent his hatred and sadistic inclinations. Facts are plentiful, but we shall limit ourselves to only a few cases.

In two entries Czerniakow noted the following in his Diary under the dates of November 4 and 5, 1940:

At 3:30 in the afternoon I heard in my study that the entrance door of the Jewish Council building was being pried open and that window-panes were being broken. A soldier and an officer guided by one Sacksen-hausen [a Jewish refugee from Germany who had had some squabbles with the Council's labor office] burst into the building. They beat up Popow [the chief accountant], First [chief of the economic department], Zynger, and Zylberman [?]. I phoned the Gestapo and was told to call one of the intruders to the phone. I told one of them to take the receiver, but he angrily refused and ordered me to follow him. When I came to the office of the labor battalion, the officer fell upon me and beat me so long over my head that I fell down. Then they started to kick me in the head with their heavy boots. When I picked myself up they threw me down the staircase. . . . I was dragged to the truck . . . and together with Silberstein [!] and Popow was driven to Szucha Street, and from there back to the Pawiak where we were interned. I was put in a cell in the cellar, together with five other prisoners. The cell was three steps wide and six steps long. One of the prisoners occupied the bed, the others lying on thin straw bags. One of the prisoners became sick with dysentery and relieved himself near my straw bag all night long. After a sleepless night, at six o'clock in the morning came the roll call—rise and clean up. . . , then shower and delousing. I had to dress without drying myself because I and my friends were immediately summoned to the Gestapo where our statements were taken down. I sat in the cellar waiting to be summoned before Meisinger [a high Gestapo official]. He saw me at 4:30 in the afternoon and reproached me concerning improper remarks being made about the SS, etc. In the end, all of us were released. At six o'clock, after making a statement about the beating, I was given my coat and hat. At night, three physicians and a male nurse were called to treat me [at home]. My head, arms, and legs were bandaged. I am barely able to move, but I will go to the Council tomorrow.[117]

If this could happen in the capital of Poland to the chairman of the largest Jewish community in Europe, it can easily be imagined what was likely to happen in the provinces. Here are a few facts:

In the Łódź Ghetto, Biebow, in a drunken stupor, beat up Rumkowski. Profusely bleeding, Rumkowski was taken for treatment to the hospital. The reason for this severe assault was Rumkowski's continued interest in the food problems of the ghetto, even after the German ghetto administration had taken over food supply following the September "action" of 1942. The beating took place some time in mid-October 1942, but the exact date is unknown.[118]

In Kalisz in the fall of 1939 the Germans once came to the Jewish Council and dragged nine members and an eighty-year-old physician who happened to be with the Council to their headquarters. All were forced to do "gymnastic exercises" in the courtyard and to wax and shine the floors: then all were severely beaten. On another occasion, on November 16, 1939, a group of Germans, including the German town mayor, came to the Council shouting: "No more Jews in Kalisz, no more Jewish community," and chased out everyone present, robbing them of cash and valuables. They forced open the safe and took 3,500 zlotys.[119]

In Lublin Germans in uniform forced a group of Council members to dance barefoot on a cold winter day (January 7, 1942) as punishment for not delivering fur coats and woolens on time as ordered.[120] Sometime later, they brought about 1,000 Jews from the camp at Lipowa Street and forced them, together with the members of the Council, to undress and stand naked in the snow for a quarter of an hour. The minutes of the Lublin Council also recorded the deportation to the Bełżec labor camp of six Council members who came to assist in arranging the departure of a group of Jews for forced labor.[121]

Bock, the chief civil official in Borszczów, once summoned the entire Jewish Council of the town in the early morning hours, told them to pick up brooms and shovels, and then ordered them to form a single line, drilling them like soldiers.[122]

In the Kutno Ghetto, the Gestapo *Referent* used to toy with his revolver during his meetings with the Council members, etc.[123]

These deliberate insults, arrests, denigration, and terror not only illustrate clearly the low moral level and human quality of German officialdom in the occupied territories, but also testify to the fact that these measures were implemented in order to break down the Jews spiritually and make them obedient tools in the hands of their oppressors.

Some Councils also went through the agonizing experience of being tried by German courts. There are preserved in the sources court documents of the trial of the members of the Jewish Council in Pabianice. This trial took place in the special court (*Sondergericht*) in Łódź and is of specific interest because it provides a good picture of the dangerous consequences of internal discords in the ghetto and of the corruption in some of the food agencies and German firms— corruption for which the Council was made responsible. However, it is also possible that some German functionaries or businessmen may have been involved in the case, intending to ease the tragic food situation of the starving ghetto population. It is worthwhile to discuss this case in some detail.

The *Landrat* in Pabianice had received a number of denunciations (the first one dated October 19, 1941), ostensibly in the name of "Jewish laborers." Some members of the local Jewish Council were accused of misappropriating the food allotted to the ghetto and selling it at higher prices to the detriment of poor Jewish workers. On October 23 some members of the Council were arrested. In the course of the ensuing investigation more Council members were detained; in all, 12 members were put in jail. But some were later set free, and only five, including the chairman, remained in detention. The formal accusation, based on the *Kriegswirtschaftsverordnung*, said that during a check in the storage places of the Council, comparatively large stocks of all kinds of provisions were found, and that the storage and distribution places were in great disarray. The defendants denied any guilt, indicating that the large quantities of some articles in the storage places accumulated as a result of various circumstances, such as spoiled wheat flour so full of insects that nobody wanted to buy it, and it remained in storage; or that, in some instances, the allotted food was in such insufficient quantity that it could not be distributed fairly, and it was necessary to wait for the next delivery in order to have enough to distribute to all ghetto inmates. The chairman also explained that in order to get enough funds for welfare expenses, an extra surcharge was added to the selling prices of the products, with the consent of the police chief. The arrested Council members explained the denunciation as an act of vengeance on the part of unsatisfied elements in the ghetto.

According to the statements of some witnesses, among them leading officials of the economic department and of the food office at the *Landrat* office, a German firm at Pabianice had delivered more merchandise than was allotted to the Jews. Apparently the chief of the food office himself was involved in these transactions, for it is hard to believe that they would have been possible without the necessary delivery certificates from his office. That this may have been so is, perhaps, inferrable from the fact that this Nazi dignitary left his office, or was removed from it, in the fall of 1941, and was sent as *Kommissar* to a small village. There is information available to the effect that in other ghettos (in Zamość, for instance), the German supply office was involved in the earnings from illegally increased food deliveries in the ghetto (see Chap. 10).

One can easily imagine how perplexed the ghetto became after the arrest of the Council members, the Council officials, and the police chief in the ghetto. Steps were taken to save them. Two petitions on their behalf have been preserved in the archives. Dated October 31 and November 3, 1941, one of them carried 223 signatures out of the 2,300 families registered in the ghetto. The six wives of the arrested leaders also submitted a request to set their spouses free. *Kripo* functionaries came into the ghetto, looking for evidence among the poor to use against the defendants. Sixty-two Jewish witnesses were heard and some of them made accusations. The very first summary of the investigation, dated November 8, 1941, states:

We . . . asked around if it was known that the Council of Elders had sold foodstuffs on the black market at exorbitant prices. The investigation in this respect turned up no results. . . . Also 62 Jewish workers from the ghetto were interrogated. . . . Some of these workers grumbled about food distribution in the ghetto, which they feel is insufficient and unjust. They also think that the members of the Council of Elders sell foodstuffs at high prices, putting the money into their own pockets. They are, however, unable to name even a single concrete case.

The compiler of the summary allowed for the possibility that the accusations against the Jewish police chief could have been activated by hatred of him by ghetto inmates because "he executes all the orders of local or other authorities." Concluding, the summary notes that there are no substantial points on which an accusation firm enough to stand in a criminal trial could be based. An investigation of the German delivery firm was also made, and its owner was arrested.

The documents of the investigation, filling two volumes, were forwarded to the general prosecutor of the Wartheland in Poznań, who transferred them to the chief prosecutor at the Łódź *Sondergericht* on January 19, 1942. He strongly recommended proceeding with the indictment against the five persons in view of the new *Polenstrafverordnung*,[124] which, contrary to its title, was also applied to the Jews—the chairman of the Council, Yechiel Rubinstein; the manager of the storage places, Schmelke Steinhorn; the buyer, Markus Brin; the bookkeeper, David Tenenbaum; and the Council member, Lemel Maroko—accusing them of having "removed and held back raw materials, or commodities, essential to the existence of the population, and thus [having] malevolently endangered the accommodation of its needs." The chief prosecutor suggested that the trial take place in the Łódź *Sondergericht*. Here, however, something unexpected took place. When the court trial started on June 3, 1942, the prosecutor moved to void the accusation "because judging by the material gathered in the investigation there are no grounds to assume that the defendants will be found guilty as charged."

In explaining his move in a letter dated June 13, 1942, and addressed to the Łódź *Regierungspräsident*, the chief prosecutor presented his point of view in detail. It is worthwhile to cite some of his arguments:

1. As the former chief of the food and economic office himself stated, he did not advise the Council chairman how much food had been allotted for distribution to the ghetto inmates. The allocation schedule was the responsibility of the delivery firm. However, because the proprietor had passed away in the interim, it was impossible to discover whether he had informed the Council that it had been given unallotted surplus. However, since deliveries were irregularly made, the Council often received some products in larger quantities, with the understanding that any surplus was to be used up later,

when the particular commodity was delivered in insufficient quantities or not delivered at all.

2. The Jewish Council always listed accurately in its monthly reports to the police authorities the amounts of sugar, noodles, and other commodities in storage. The Council concealed no products from the German authorities.

3. The investigation discovered no evidence that some products were put aside for the purpose of speculation.

In conclusion, the letter states that it must be assumed that the trial would end in "an unwelcome acquittal" because after the death of the owner of the delivery firm no new evidence could be unearthed against the defendants. For all these reasons the chief prosecutor decided to withdraw the accusation and to hand the defendants over to the Gestapo. He asked the *Regierungspräsident* for comments on his proposal.

The *Regierungspräsident* gave his approval, and on July 28, 1942, the chief prosecutor (*Oberstaatsanwalt*) informed the provincial attorney general (*Generalstaatsanwalt*) in Poznań that he had withdrawn the accusation, and that in agreement with the *Regierungspräsident* he had delivered the defendants (except for Markus Brin, who had died in prison on July 4) to the Gestapo.[125] In a letter of August 14, 1942, the Gestapo informed him that the defendants, on trial for war crimes, had been sent to the central prison in the ghetto where they were to be kept at the Gestapo's disposal.[126] No more information is available on the fate of the victims of the denunciation. There is valid reason to assume that the arrested Council members from Pabianice were included in the group of 21 or 22 Pabianice Jews publicly hanged in the Łódź Ghetto on September 7, 1942, in the course of the "action" against children and elderly people. (During the liquidation of the Pabianice Ghetto on May 17 and 18, 1942, 2,699 Jews had been selected and sent in three transports into the Łódź Ghetto.)[127]

Finally, notice should also be taken of the few cases when German officials treated Council members with consideration, and sometimes were even inclined to help the Jews (in other ways than by taking bribes). Czerniakow mentioned in his Diary a large number of German functionaries of various ranks with whom he had to deal, and he especially singled out the few who acted decently. On February 29, 1940, when he visited the chief of the financial department in the administration of Warsaw's German mayor, he noted in his Diary that he was offered a chair to sit on. The next day the same man advised him not to go on a certain date to the office of the Gestapo. Later, when this official told him that he expected to be transferred to Cracow, Czerniakow was very sorry and told him that he would visit him in Cracow to discuss the financial problems of the Council.[128]

We also find complimentary remarks in Czerniakow's Diary concerning Ludwig Leist. Thus he noted that during a meeting on March 21, 1940, Leist ordered an automobile for Czerniakow without charge and positively disposed of a number of vital problems concerning catching for forced labor, release of confiscated furniture, etc. Following another visit, on July 24, 1940, he noted that after reading the Council's letter regarding mistreatment of Jews at forced-labor places, Leist had told him that he would take the necessary steps.[129]

It has been said that the *Kommandant* of Borszczów, a German from Bohemia, had a positive attitude toward the Jews. He alerted them on the eves of "actions," advising them to hide themselves (some Jews even took cover in his own attic) or to run away. He even maintained contact with Jewish partisans, with the help of a Jewish employee who worked for him. It is, however, characteristic of the ambivalence and *Kadavergehorsamkeit* of the vast majority of German functionaries that the same man used to shoot Jews in the course of the "actions."[130]

Among the managers of German economic enterprises where Jews were employed within or outside the ghetto, there also were people who did not sympathize with anti-Jewish measures. They tried to help their Jewish workers and, as was the case in Białystok, were even in touch with the anti-Nazi partisan movement.[131]

It is known that the already mentioned German *Bürgermeister* in the little town of Poddębice (Wartheland) kept a secret Diary where he made sharply critical remarks about the inhuman acts of German officials of all ranks in regard to the Polish and particularly the Jewish population. He sympathized with their bitter lot and tried to help as much as he could. He befriended the local Council chairman and his wife, a dentist who treated him professionally in secret. Defying the order of the *Landrat*, he refused to deliver an additional Jew for a public hanging that the Gestapo had arranged in Poddębice on March 16, 1942 (similar hanging shows were performed in March in a number of towns in the Wartheland). He was

summoned to the Łódź Gestapo office where he was severely reproached for his friendliness toward the Jews. After he had been dismissed from his office, he was sent to the front. He survived the war,
and his Diary was published in 1961 in the series *Quellen und
Darstellungen zur Zeitgeschichte* in Stuttgart.[132] We find in this
Diary a phenomenon quite characteristic of German officialdom in
the occupied territories—namely, their lack of confidence in each
other and their fear of showing human "weakness" toward the
natives. German officials who disapproved of the inhuman policies
of the occupation regime were afraid to express criticism or to act
accordingly when in company with other officials.

In the light of such attitudes, it is clear why in Łódź Biebow issued
a circular letter on June 26, 1942 (No. 26/42) forbidding higher
officials of the German ghetto administration to discuss matters with
Rumkowski except in the presence of another official.[133]

Jews as individuals had no access to German offices. While this was
permitted at the earlier stages of occupation, it was forbidden later
on. Thus the *Kreishauptmann* in Krasnystaw (Lublin district), in
his situation report to the government in Cracow dated September
10, 1940, related that he had given orders that no Jews were to enter
the premises of the *Kreishauptmann*'s offices, because "they are always crowded with Jews who are naturally excited in connection
with moving into the ghetto." Instead all requests and wishes on
behalf of individuals were to be submitted to the Council, which
would forward them to the *Kreishauptmann* after a preliminary
investigation.[134]

RELATIONS WITH THE NON-GERMAN AUTHORITIES

The Jewish Councils also maintained relations with the non-
German authorities, such as the communal organs of the native
population in the nonincorporated territories. The ghetto, though
it was an artificially separated and isolated part of town, was actually
tied to the "other side" in such problems of daily life as food, city
taxes, fees for public utilities, and, in some places, inner transportation, etc. In all these matters, the Councils had to contact the pertinent municipal offices whose personnel were often identical to
those before the war.

In Warsaw, for instance, the Nazi-appointed Polish city administration was empowered, up to the spring of 1941, to distribute ration cards for the Jewish population, charging a fee of 2 zlotys for the benefit of the Jewish Council. According to the tax regulations of the Council, the finance organs of the Polish city administration were obligated to cash in outstanding taxes from Jewish taxpayers. The ghetto inmates paid city taxes and other fees for services provided by the city, and Polish tax collectors were entitled to enter the ghetto to collect these taxes. In January 1940 Julian Kulski, the appointed Polish mayor of Warsaw, was ordered by Dr. Dengel, the German *Stadtpräsident*, to carry out a registration of the male Jewish population from twelve to sixty years of age subject to forced-labor duty. Jointly with the Jewish Council he was made responsible for the absolute accuracy of the registration. Posters announcing this order were pasted on the walls of city buildings on February 21, 1940, along with the posters of the Jewish Council advising the Jews of the dates and places of the registration.[135] Notices to individual Jews to report for labor were delivered by Polish policemen. During the period of establishing the ghetto, the housing department of the city government was in constant communication with the Jewish Council. According to Kulski, their mutual relations were friendly. He related that when he had learned about attacks on Jews by bands of Polish youths at the end of March 1940, he had sent a letter to the German authorities requesting that they put a stop to these excesses, knowing that the Germans were the real instigators. He admitted that he was quite surprised by the quick reply that orders had been given to secure order in the city. He also stressed that his relations with Czerniakow had been friendly. Czerniakow had visited him in his office even when there were no problems to discuss, and they had talked about the general situation and the predicament of the Jews. Kulski interpreted Czerniakow's visits as his way of showing that the Jews continued to consider themselves citizens and members of the city community.[136]

For a long time in Sosnowiec, which was incorporated into the Reich, the Jews were subordinated to a Polish commissar without whose written confirmation no decision of the Jewish Council was valid. An eager bribe-taker, he exercised his authority only formally and did not interfere in the Council's affairs. Because of Merin's intervention, his office was abolished.[137]

However, there were officials among the natives who caused trouble and persecuted the Jews. They were particularly evident in the Ukrainian, Byelorussian, and Lithuanian territories. This, however, is a subject outside the limits of this survey.

THE AUTHORITIES AND THE "RESETTLEMENT ACTIONS"

As far as the top officers of the German civil authorities in the Government General were concerned—Governor General Frank, Secretary of State Josef Bühler, and *Präsident* of the Internal Affairs Department Dr. Friedrich Wilhelm Siebert—there can be no doubt that they identified themselves fully with Hitler's order about the physical destruction of the Jews in the occupied territories, and they helped to execute the order to the best of their capacities. At the meeting of his government in Cracow on December 16, 1941, when the death camp in Chełmno was already in operation, Frank stated:

With the Jews—I want to be quite frank with you—we have to finish with them anyway. The Führer once said: "If international Jewry should once more succeed in unleashing a world war, not only will the nations provoked into war have to pay with blood, but the Jew in Europe will have met his end." . . . As an old National Socialist I really must say that if the Jewish rabble in Europe should survive the war, while we would have sacrificed our best blood for the preservation of Europe, then this war would be only a partial success. As far as the Jews are concerned, I would, as a matter of principle, expect only one thing— that they will disappear. . . . But what shall be done with Jews? Do you think they will be settled in colonies in Ostland? They told us in Berlin: Why do you give us all this trouble? in Ostland or in the Reichskommissariat [Ukraine] we can't do anything with them either; liquidate them yourself. . . .[138]

At the Wannsee Conference in January 1942 Secretary of State Josef Bühler stated that he would welcome the idea of starting the Final Solution with the area of the Government General, promising the support of the civilian authorities for the security police and the SD.[139]

At the beginning of March 1942 Dr. Siebert called on all local authority organs in Lublin in a circular letter of the internal affairs department "to cooperate with the SS and Police Leader in Lublin in the execution of [resettlement] measures."¹⁴⁰ Certainly Lublin was not singled out in this respect. A similar circular letter must have been addressed to each district in the Government General. Local administrative organs cooperated hand-in-glove with the SS and police in the execution of the deportation "actions." The governors and other high officials received from the government in Cracow quite detailed instructions and information regarding the places, dates, and numbers of Jews subject to "resettlement." The governors, in turn, sent their own circular letters to the county chiefs, asking for opinions on where the "resettlements" should be executed first and inquiring how many Jews there were in the suggested towns. On May 12, 1942, such a confidential circular was sent by Zörner, the Lublin governor, to all county chiefs. He received detailed answers from them.¹⁴¹ In the town of Janów Lubelski, the county chief directly addressed the SS and Police Leader in Lublin, asking him to carry out the "resettlement" in his county, indicating the towns and the numbers of Jews to be "resettled."¹⁴² Another county chief in Puławy telephoned Türk, the chief of the population and welfare affairs subdivision in Lublin, in March 1942, requesting permission to "resettle" 1,100 Jews from the town of Wąwolnica because of the alleged shooting there of the chief of the labor office. Without giving any reason, he also requested the "resettlement" of 1,600 Jews from Kazimierz nad Wisłą.¹⁴³ As was habitual with Nazi authorities, they used camouflaged language in the documents. Thus Türk made a note on March 19, 1942, that during a conversation with Pohl (deputy to Hoefle, chief of staff of Globocnik's extermination commando *Einsatz Reinhard*) they discussed cooperation in the "resettlement" of local Jews to Russia (*sic!*) and the settlement of Jews from the Reich in their place.¹⁴⁴ Hoefle himself, talking to an unidentified functionary in the administration of the Lublin district on March 16, 1942, said, according to a note made by the latter, that "he is making ready a large camp where able-bodied Jews will be registered according to their occupations and sent to work. Jews unable to work will be sent to Bełżec, the border terminal in Zamość county." At the end of this conversation Hoefle said that "once these Jews have crossed the border, they will never return to the Government General."¹⁴⁵

That Türk was informed of what "resettlement" actually meant can be seen from his own official note of August 20, 1942, where he related that he had called on the county chiefs in Krasnystaw and

Zamość and confidentially informed them about "actions" against the Jews "already in progress and yet to come."[146] Why this piece of information should have been given confidentially is obvious.

At a meeting held by the Łódź Gestapo on April 21 or 22, 1942, Veygand, the Gestapo official, announced that all able-bodied Jews from the Wartheland would be sent to the Łódź Ghetto and that Jews from the Łódź Ghetto and the provinces who were unable to work would be sent to the so-called *Versorgungslagern* ("care-taking camps").[147] Was Veygand's impudent lie just another example of Nazi cynicism, or was it an attempt at concealing, even from his own people, the true meaning of the "resettlement" to the Chełmno annihilation camp already in progress at that time?

Moreover, it should be taken into consideration that Hitler's order about the Final Solution was a highly guarded top state secret (*Geheime Reichsache*) and every effort was made to limit the number of persons who knew about it. The personnel of the SS commandos carrying out the "*Juden-Aktionen*" (such as, for example, the *Einsatz Reinhard*) were obligated to submit statements in writing that they would keep secret the "actions" and the fate of the Jews even after they left the service.[148] Close cooperation between the civilian administrative organs and the Gestapo in the "resettlements" in Eastern Upper Silesia is evident from the minutes of a meeting of officials of the county administration, the city council, and Dreier, the Gestapo *Kommissar*, on September 29, 1942, where the gradual liquidation of the Będzin Jewish community was discussed. All present agreed that the evacuation of Jews should proceed notwithstanding the war, with the stipulation that the war economy should not be harmed.[149]

Although cooperation between the police and administrative organs in executing the "solution of the Jewish question" was generally harmonious, there sometimes occurred friction and clashes. Not always did the pertinent police organs inform the local administration about imminent "actions"; they often came unexpectedly, jarring officials' sense of proper "*Ordnung*." The administrative authorities were often dissatisfied with the raw brutality and recklessness of *Kommandos* in the course of "actions." Thus Lohse, the *Reichskommissar* in Ostland, issued orders to stop the executions in Liepaiaj "because the way they were executed cannot be justified."[150] The meaning of this laconic opinion and the attitudes of some of the officials of the civilian administration toward the "actions" can be derived from a description of the "action" in Slutzk (Byelorussia). The author is no other than Karl, the *Gebietskommissar* himself. It is worthwhile to cite some parts of his report:

On October 27, [1941,] at around 8 o'clock in the morning, there appeared an *Oberleutnant* of the police battalion in Kaunas who presented himself as the adjutant of the battalion commander of the security police. He said that the battalion had been ordered to liquidate the Jews in Slutzk in two days' time. . . . Approximately half an hour later, the battalion arrived in town. At my request we met the battalion commander at once. I told him that it was impossible to carry out the "action" without prior preparations. . . . At least he should have given a day's notice. I therefore asked him to postpone the "action" for one day; but he refused, saying that he had to execute the "action" throughout the entire county and had no more than two days reserved for Slutzk. . . . I pointed out that the liquidation of the Jews should not be carried out in an arbitrary manner . . . , and we agreed that all Jews still in Slutzk should be brought into the ghetto for selection. I had particular concern about the artisans, whose liquidation I intended to prevent. The selection would be made by two of my assistants. . . . A few hours after the "action" began, big complications occurred, for the commander did not keep his agreement, and all Jews without exception were driven out of factories and shops and deported. . . . Most of them were . . . liquidated outside the town. It took long hours before I was able to get in touch with the acting commander, a *Hauptmann*, whom I requested to stop the "action," because it was not being carried out according to my instructions. . . . The *Hauptmann* was surprised by this, stating that his orders were to free the town of all Jews without exception, as had been done in other towns. The "action" came for political reasons, and economic considerations were simply not taken into account. Still, thanks to my energetic protestations, he stopped the "action" at dusk. As far as the manner in which the "action" was carried out is concerned, I regret to say that it simply bordered on sadism. . . . With indescribable brutality by the German police and Lithuanian partisans, the Jewish people, among them also Byelorussians, were driven from their homes. Shooting was heard throughout the town, and mountains of Jewish dead lay in the streets. The Jewish people, artisans included, were brutally treated in front of the Byelorussians, who also were beaten with rubber sticks and rifle butts. . . . I and all my aides tried to save as many as was possible. In many instances I had to chase away German police functionaries and Lithuanian partisans, threatening to shoot with my revolver. My own gendarmes were also mobilized for this purpose, but in many instances they had to retreat because of random shooting which endangered their lives. The whole thing was worse than gruesome. I must also point out that in the course of the "action," the police battalion robbed not only Jewish homes but also the homes of Byelorussians. . . . As has been reported by army soldiers, watches were torn off the wrists of Jews. . . . Special storage places with Jewish valuables that had been sealed by civilian administration organs were broken into and robbed by the police. . . . I had to arrest two fully armed Lithuanian partisans caught in the act of robbing. The battalion left in the direction of Baranowicze on Tuesday night. . . . I cannot now continue the Jewish "action." First, order must be restored. . . . I have only one desire: protect me in the future from this police battalion.[151]

A functionary of the economic branch of the civilian administration in Będzin who carried out an official audit of the German factories and other enterprises using Jewish labor stressed in his report of May 12, 1943, the importance of Jewish labor for the war effort and concluded with these words:

It is in the interests of the state, the nation, and the entire military leadership to continue production at the highest capacity. Under no circumstances should it be allowed to be shattered or stopped [by removing the Jewish workers]. The productive labor force, irrespective of its ethnic origin, is necessary for the management of all factories and for all the people who are responsible for their output.[152]

This sober conclusion of a German official who "was free from any sentimental considerations and acted only because reason [thus dictated]" fell on deaf ears. Three months later, the Będzin Ghetto (at that time located in Szrodula) was liquidated.

There is also preserved source material concerning a case where Gevecke, the *Gebietskommissar*, did not permit a "resettlement action" against the Jews in Šiauliai although this had been requested by Hamann, the SS man of the *Einsatzkommando 3* in Kaunas as soon as he arrived in Šiauliai. Gevecke referred to Lohse's order to stop the execution of Jews who were employed in industry[153] (for more on this, see Chap. 16).

There was also one local functionary in the civilian administration who denounced murderous "actions" for purely humanitarian reasons. The already mentioned German mayor of Poddębice describes in his Diary the "action" there on April 14, 1942, as "a mass murder organized by the State."[154]

As has been mentioned repeatedly, the problem of confiscated Jewish property and the division of spoils between the administrative and police authorities was another source of friction. The *Einsatzkommandos* in Ostland and the Ukraine robbed their victims of cash, gold and silver objects, jewelry, and other valuables. The administrative authorities, considering themselves sole bosses over Jewish property, demanded that the *Kommandos* deliver appropriated Jewish property to the *Gebietskommissar*. But the SS *Kommandos* refused, and the robbery continued. When *Reichskommissar* Lohse got reports from his local functionaries about arbitrary confiscations by the Security Police (for example, in Šiauliai),[155] he addressed a letter to Stahlaecker, the Higher SS and Police Leader in Ostland, protesting the confiscations and requesting that he order them stopped and confiscated Jewish property turned over to the *Gebietskommissar*.[156] Apparently Stahlaecker did not comply, for in a letter dated October 20, 1941, the *Generalkommissar* in Latvia complained that he still had difficulties with SS *Kommandos* regarding confiscated Jewish goods. He suggested that Lohse give explicit orders to the police and the Security organs to comply with the orders of the *Gebietskommissars*.[157]

Similar clashes between the civilian authorities and the SS took place in the territory of the Government General. Only after protracted negotiations did Wilhelm Koppe, the Higher SS and Police Leader in the Government General (who replaced Wilhelm Krüger), make an agreement with Bühler on February 21, 1944, to turn over to the civilian authorities all Jewish movable property kept in the storage places of the SS; Frank evaluated the worth of Jewish property appropriated by the SS in the billions of zlotys. In a circular letter dated July 4, 1944, Oswald Pohl, chief of the main administration and economic department of the SS, stated that the Government General in Cracow had the right to administer Jewish real estate. Himmler, however, made the reservation that all cash derived from the sale of Jewish property must be deposited in a special bank account and used for the colonization of Germans in the territory of the Government General.[158]

In the Wartheland, Arthur Greiser, the *Statthalter*, issued two orders dated March 18 and May 1, 1942, regarding property left after "resettlements." He made the Łódź *Gettoverwaltung* the main heir. As the transportation of Jewish movable property from the liquidated ghettos to Łódź could have been difficult for technical reasons, a circular letter of the *Gettoverwaltung* dated April 20, 1942, directed that all kinds of machinery, currency, gold, silver, valuables, textile and leather merchandise, and raw materials were to be delivered directly to the *Gettoverwaltung*, but house furnishings and food should be sold where left and the cash receipts deposited with the *Gettoverwaltung* after deducting the expenses involved in the transaction.[159]

For a time, the *Haupttreuhandstelle* (HTO) and the Łódź *Gettoverwaltung* clashed in a dispute over who should get the property of murdered Jews. The Łódź *Regierungspräsident* took the side of the HTO, and a compromise was reached: confiscated Jewish goods in Łódź should be turned over to the *Gettoverwaltung*; those in the provinces to the HTO.[160] However, the agreement did not last for long. The *Gettoverwaltung* remained in fact the "legal" heir of all Jewish property in the Wartheland. Even cash and valuables that were confiscated from victims already in the Chełmno death camp were sent to the *Gettoverwaltung*. It also cashed in on claims of Jews against third persons.[161]

CHAPTER 12

The Fluctuation in the
Composition of the Councils

WE HAVE SEEN that there were continual changes in the personnel of the Jewish Councils and this was characteristic of nearly all of them. A Council seldom remained unaltered from beginning to end of its existence. Usually the opposite took place. Council members escaped, took cover, resigned, were arrested, were killed on the spot, or were deported; and others were nominated to take their places.

The reasons for this fluctuation among the Council members were twofold: an internal reason stemming from the Jews themselves, and an external one stemming from the Germans. We have already mentioned in Chap. 2 that, in the majority of known cases, Jewish communal or civic leaders were unwilling to join the Councils. Elected or nominated members were moved to accept and, once accepting, to continue in their difficult positions only out of a fear of reprisals by the Gestapo or a sense of responsibility toward defenseless coreligionists, under the illusion that as Council members they might be in a position to ease the lot of the Jews. However, Council members perceived or imagined what they could expect. Naturally there were exceptions. Some ambitious individuals tried to get nominated as Council members for egoistic reasons, believing in the power ostensibly vested in them by the Germans. These included some who tried to play the role of intermediaries between the Germans and the Jews even before the Councils had been established (see Chap. 2).

The terror inflicted on the Jews and the Councils by the Germans from the very start of the occupation (see Chap. 11) strongly influenced many Council members to relinquish the dangerous office, apprehensive of tasks the Germans might have in store for them.

There were various perilous means of avoiding membership in the Councils. Escape with or without one's family, was one of them, particularly at the early stages of occupation before the ghettos came into being. For example, we read concerning the first members of the Tarnów *Judenrat* that they

have quickly gotten the right idea about the Germans' intentions. Dr. Josef Apner, the pride of the judicial profession in Galicia, whom the Germans forced to take over the leadership of the Council, soon relinquished his position, for he understood what the Germans would be asking of him. His substitute Lenkowicz, and the Council member Waksman, escaped to Lwów right after all the prayer houses and synagogues went up in flames one day.[1]

In Szczebrzeszyn "the members of the first Council quickly relinquished their office and, for the most part, escaped to the Russian-occupied area. Another Council was then elected."[2] An eyewitness account of events in Kalisz relates that "the Jewish Council disintegrated before the expulsion in the fall of 1939. The majority of the Council members escaped."[3] The first chairmen of the original Councils in Koło,[4] Płock,[5] Przemyśl,[6] Borysław,[7] Kutno,[8] and many other places, also ran away. In Warsaw six Council members were allowed to leave Poland in the winter of 1939–1940. A seventh member escaped abroad.[9] Later, when free travel for Jews was strictly curtailed (see Chap. 5), it became very difficult to escape.

Another form of expressing unwillingness to serve on the Jewish Councils was to resign. This, however, was highly dangerous. It required a lot of courage and determination to take such a step. In the *Gazeta Żydowska* (No. 16, February 25, 1941) an answer was printed to two inquiries addressed to the "Legal Corner." The inquirers were advised that changes of Council chairmen or changes in the composition of the Councils could take place only by a decision of the *Stadt-* or *Distrikthauptmann* or by voluntary resignation. The editor cautioned, however, that this was his own personal opinion based on an interpretation of the order establishing the Jewish Councils; he did not know whether the pertinent authorities would accept this view, since the order did not specifically mention the length of tenure of members nor the procedure for changing the composition of the Councils. It is clear that in the prevailing atmosphere of constant terror "voluntary resignations" were as un-realistic an idea as were the accounts themselves in the *Gazeta Żydow-ska.*

In addition to those already discussed in Chap. 2, there were other cases of repression directed at Council members trying to resign. In Nowy Sącz a member resigned at the end of 1941 "because he was of the opinion that the Council ought to refuse to deliver Jews for the labor camps and let the Gestapo itself take whomever they wanted." Apparently at the demand of the German authorities, the ghetto police delivered him to the Gestapo. He was not seen any more.[10] A member of the Jewish Council at Kozienice (Radom district) resigned during the first weeks of the occupation and found refuge on the "Aryan" side. There were subsequent rumors that the Pole who had given him shelter killed him and buried him in a cellar. When his body was exhumed after the war, it was found that his head had been severed from his body.[11] "At first, respectable civic leaders in Krzemieniec participated in the Council. . . . After a short while, however, when they had realized its true character and tasks, they resigned."[12] A member of the Płock Jewish Council hid himself to avoid serving.[13] The first chairman of the Council at Bursztyn resigned. He had been appointed by the Ukrainian mayor, "but chose rather to work at hard labor together with all other Jews."[14] Another member gave the same mayor a suit as a gift to be released from serving on the Council.[15] In Ozierany, Council members tried to be released from membership on the local Council (although others paid large amounts for the privilege of becoming Council members").[16] The first chairmen of the Councils at Czyżów, Nowy Dwór,[17] Staszów,[18] and others also resigned.

As a rule, however, nominated Council members, fearing Gestapo reprisals, did not resign or ask to be released from service. Those who gathered enough courage to try to get permission to resign were given "friendly advice" not to do so. Adam Czerniakow notes in his Diary under the date January 26, 1940: "In view of these events [cash extortions from the Council], I have asked the SS to relieve me of the chairmanship, because I am in no position to lead the community in such abnormal times. I was advised not to do so [for his own good]."

The makeup of Councils or the hierarchy of their membership was liable to changes because of internal controversies. The attitude pre-vailing in a given Council was also a very important factor. Changes in Council memberships, dismissal of old members, and nomination of new ones were, to a certain degree, the result of struggles and divergent opinions about tactics that should be used vis-à-vis the German authorities. Sometimes the struggles degenerated into wrangles about authority, in which the Germans became involved. Thus the first chairman of the Chmielnik Jewish Council had to resign under the pressure of opposition against him within the Council and the relief committee.[19] The sources do not always supply information as to the reasons for changes in the composition of the Councils, limiting their information to the mere fact that change took place. What actually happened in many cases can only be surmised by drawing analogies to known causes of change in other places.

Changes in the personnel of the Councils in Upper Eastern Silesia were made by Moshe Merin, chief of the Union of Jewish Communities in that part of the occupied territory. He made changes in order to pack the Councils with his own people (see Chap. 3).

In Częstochowa the presidium dismissed 10 Council members for "sabotaging the Council's activities" in 1940.[20] A former member of the Bursztyn Jewish Council relates that three members, including the chairman, were removed. They were replaced by three others who had previously been sent to the *Kreisamt* in Rohatyn to deliver a cash contribution ordered by the authorities. Whether this change was initiated by the Germans or by the Jews themselves is not indicated in the pertinent account. It is possible that the success of their mission to Rohatyn (under the protection of the Ukrainian police commandant) won the approval of the *Kreischef*, who may have forced upon the Bursztyn Council the decision to co-opt them to the Council in place of three members who had been fired.[21]

For the most part the German authorities instigated changes in the personnel of the Councils. The Germans bullied the Councils in every respect; they fired, arrested, and killed chairmen and members who happened to fall into the bad graces of the authorities, refusing to become obedient tools in the execution of German atrocities or violating the arbitrary rules in other ways. No legal norms were applied in treatment of the Councils by the Germans. The principle of "local leadership" reigned supreme and without mercy. Whenever they considered it suitable to their own interests, the Germans would reduce or augment the number of Council members, disregarding their own orders concerning the number of the Council members (such as, for instance, Frank's order of November 28, 1939; see Chap. 1). In place of persons removed from the Councils, the Germans brought in people in whom they apparently had more confidence. Numerous chairmen and Council members were removed because they displeased the Germans by their independent attitudes, or because their German masters simply did not like them. It often happened that the memberships of entire Councils were replaced by hand-picked people chosen from a list of names prepared in advance. Some of the Germans' protégés were placed in top positions. In cases where they could not find people suitable for their aims within the functioning Councils, they nominated new members from outside the Councils. The degree of humaneness or the moral decline of a particular German boss should not be overlooked in this connection.

Changes in the composition of the Councils or in the hierarchy of their members occurred especially often before or during "resettlement actions," when the authorities needed the full cooperation of the Councils and the ghetto police. As a rule, when Council members and policemen were themselves caught up in the deportations, they were replaced by new, though greatly reduced, Councils and police forces.

Sources illustrating the fluctuation caused by German interference, including arrests and murders of dismissed members, are so abundant that we must limit ourselves to only a small number of illustrations pertaining to the various occupied areas.

The first Vilna Jewish Council of Ghetto No. 1 (the short-lived Ghetto No. 2 existed till the end of October 1941 and had its own Council) was established on July 4, 1941, with a membership of 10 (one resigned). On July 24 the Council received an order to increase the number of its members to 24, but at the beginning of August (the exact date is unknown), the *Gebietskommissar* ordered the Council to reduce its membership to the previous number.[22]

On September 2 Schweinenberg, a Gestapo officer, came to the Jewish Council, arrested 5 Council members and 11 other persons (mainly Council functionaries who happened to be present on the premises at the time), and sent them all to the Lukishki jail for not delivering 10 carts on time as ordered (the order had been received the previous day, but because all carts belonging to Jews had long since been confiscated, the Council had hired five carts from gentiles and sent them to the headquarters of the *Ypatinga*, which, however, had sent them back). None of these 16 persons returned from jail. Only six persons, of whom one was a Council member, were allowed to remain in the Council building after their documents had been checked. The Council actually stopped its activities.[23] When the ghetto was established, the Gestapo nominated one of the remaining Council members as head of the third Council. The new chairman co-opted three members of the second Council and one more member from outside the Council. Thus this Council was limited to only five members.[24]

In Łódź 20 or so of the 31 members of the first *Beirat* (the advisory council established during the first 10 days of October 1939), were summoned to the Gestapo office on November 7, 1939. All were arrested and deported to a penal camp not far from Łódź (a number of leaders of the Jewish Socialist Labor Party Bund, Poalei Zion Left, and other civic leaders were later deported there on November 11). Some of the *Beirat* members were shot to death or tortured, others were sent to concentration camps in Germany and perished there, and five members were sent to Cracow during the partial expulsion of Łódź Jews to certain parts of the Government General.[25] In the beginning of February, Rumkowski asked the police authorities to issue passes to members of his second Council.[26]

The first chairman of the Jewish Council at Lwów was Dr. Josef Parnas, a man in his seventies. He was a strong-willed person with a great deal of pride, descended from a noble, prosperous family, who had served as an officer in the Imperial Austrian Army. Dr. Parnas was arrested in October or November 1941, allegedly because he had refused to deliver Jewish forced laborers, and was shot in jail. The second chairman, Dr. Adolf Rotfeld, a prewar member of the executive of the Zionist organization in Eastern Galicia, died of "natural causes" in February 1942, according to pertinent sources— after only a few months in office. The third chairman, Dr. Henryk Landsberg, a well-known lawyer and prewar civic leader, was publicly hanged together with 11 Jewish policemen on the balconies of the Council building in September 1942. This was in reprisal for a Jewish butcher's resisting arrest by an SS-man, who happened to drop dead during the squabble. On the same day 175 Council functionaries were shot. Dr. Eberson was then nominated Council chairman, saying, according to a witness, "I have gladly accepted the nomination. Maybe they will shoot me soon." His gloomy prediction came true. During the "action" that took place from January

5 to 7, 1943, Dr. Eberson was shot, together with a number of other Council members, after reporting for "selection" as ordered. Other Council members hid themselves. However, according to the witness who heard him say why he accepted the nomination to head the Council, Dr. Eberson committed suicide. Some of the Council members were sent to the camp at Janowska Street.[27]

In Horodenka (Distrikt Galizien) a Jewish Council of three members was established on orders from *Kreishauptmann* Winkler. After a while a "deceitful and money-greedy SS-man" was appointed *Kreishauptmann*. He dismissed the Council and appointed a larger one. Only the chairman of the former Council was included in the new Council.[28]

The story of the Council of Elders in Bełchatów (Wartheland) is characteristic for the unceremonial, despotic manner in which the Germans governed the Councils. At first the Council there consisted of 12 members, but in March 1940, apparently on orders from the *Kommandant* of the local gendarmes, the Council was reduced to three members. It seems that after the intervention by the local German mayor on April 2, 1940, the Council was enlarged to five members. But the new Council was not of long duration. It was dismissed on October 18, 1940, and a new one was appointed. The new chairman lasted for only a few days. He was arrested on October 23 and another chairman was nominated. He functioned until July 2, 1941. The composition of the entire Council was changed on that day and a new chairman, two members of the so-called *Beirat*, and new chiefs of welfare, food, forced labor, and other departments were appointed. This Council, the sixth one, functioned only until September 24, 1941, when the German mayor again ordered a change in its composition. The chairman of the fourth, formerly dismissed, Council was appointed to head the new one. Only two *Beirat* members remained. The chiefs of the departments were also changed. It is not known how long this, the seventh, Council was allowed to function.[29] Some reasons for these repeated changes in the composition of the Bełchatów Jewish Council can be derived from the mayor's letter of October 20, 1940 (i.e., two days after the dismissal of the third Council), apparently addressed to the Council chairman, in which he and other dismissed members were accused of grumbling and agitating against the authorities. They all were warned of severe punishment if they tried to interfere with the authority of the new Council.[30] The extreme fluctuation of the

Bełchatów Jewish Council may have come also as a result of personal intrigues by some of its members who were trying to win the mayor's support for their personal aspirations.

In Końskie (Radom district) at the beginning of 1940 the Jews were ordered to elect a new Council in place of the first one.[31] The same happened in Mir,[32] Mława,[33] Kielce,[34] and in many other places.

In Jaworów (Distrikt Galizien), the chairman was changed four times,[35] in Krzemieniec three times. The first chairman in Krzemieniec, Dr. Ben-Zion Katz, was condemned to death for not delivering a second list of Jews ostensibly for labor duty (he told the Germans that he would submit a second list after the men on his first list returned). A second chairman, the lawyer Jonas Grynberg, suffered a nervous breakdown, and only the third one lived till the tragic end of the ghetto.[36]

Some of the members of the Łańcut Council (Distrikt Galizien) were arrested at the end of March 1942 during a conference called by the Gestapo at Jarosław. The majority of the Council members, expecting nothing good from the "conference," simply did not show up. According to another version, the German mayor warned one Council member, Dr. Pohorile, not to go. Eight members were therefore saved. Those who went to the "conference" were ordered to deliver 10 hostages. They refused and were arrested. Together with six other Jews seized randomly in the street, they were sent to Jarosław. All were shot in mid-July 1942. The authorities nominated a new Council, with the lawyer Rubin Nadel as its chairman.[37]

We have already indicated that before or during "resettlement actions" the authorities changed or reduced the Councils. In the Lublin Ghetto, during an extraordinary meeting on March 31, 1942 (an "action" had started there on the 17th), four SS-men came to the Council and told them, among other things, that the 24-man Council then in operation was to be reduced to 12 members. Six of the old Council, in addition to the vice chairman, one of the office functionaries, and five outsiders, were to be included in the new Council. The remaining 18 Council members were to be "resettled" in the next transport. The Council members destined for "resettlement" and who had their residence outside the ghetto (this was a rare privilege) were given a chance to go home, guarded by the Security Police, to fetch any personal belongings they might need. After that, their apartments would be sealed. The SS-men gave cynical assurances that the chairman and one member of the old

Council would take over leading positions on the Council and in the JSS in their new domicile because they had the necessary experience. The SS-men then nominated the vice chairman to be chairman of the new Council and nominated and assigned the duties of a three-member Council presidium.[38]

After the "action" in Horodenka, the *Kreishauptmann* called in Jewish representatives and, expressing his condolences for what had happened, accused the Ukrainians of requesting that the Germans decrease the number of Jews in town. He ordered the establishment of a new Council headed by Moryc Filfel, one of the "useful" Jews who had been released from among some Jews assembled in a prayer house for "resettlement."[39] In August 1942 the authorities nominated a new chairman of the Krasnobród Council (Lublin district), one month before the "resettlement action." He functioned until the ghetto was liquidated in February 1943.[40]

In Stanisławów (Distrikt Galizien) the authorities nominated new Councils after almost every "action." The first Council was nominated on July 26, 1941, immediately after the Germans had occupied the town. It was dismissed after the first slaughter, on October 12, 1941. The tenure of the second Council lasted till July 1942. All its members were then arrested and were not seen any more. Neither did the third Council last for long. In August 1942 all its members were arrested and publicly hanged. The fourth Council lasted until the liquidation of the ghetto in February 1943. Its members were shot on the 23rd of that month.[41]

Of the 24 members of the Jewish Council in Radom only 3 remained after the first "resettlement action" in mid-August 1942. The survivors were Dr. L. Fastman (who became Council chairman), Dr. N. Szenderowicz, and Dr. Żabner. Dr. Żabner and his wife committed suicide after they were arrested in the building of the criminal police. They had been accused of sending their two children over to the "Aryan" side in the course of the "resettlement." A certain Leon Yames replaced Dr. Żabner. Dr. Fastman was arrested on January 10, 1943, and sent to Auschwitz for not reporting that Dr. Dimant had come back to the ghetto from Szydlowiec (a nearby town). Ten days later, on January 20, Dr. Szenderowicz was nominated Council chairman. On May 1, 1943, the Gestapo summoned all members and functionaries of the Council, carried them away to Wolanów (near Radom), where most of them were shot. The chairman and the members who survived were sent to Auschwitz.

The commandant of the ghetto police, the lawyer Sitner, was nominated chairman of the Council for the ghetto's survivors, who were by then concentrated in a labor camp.[42]

On May 8, 1942, when the "resettlement action" to Sobibór started in Końskowola (Lublin district), several Council members were killed together with the rabbi and over 20 other Jews. For the surviving 500 local Jews (1,400 had lived in the town in October 1941), and for 1,025 Jews "resettled" from Slovakia, a new Jewish Council was established. It consisted of 11 persons: 6 local Jews and 5 from among the Slovakian deportees.[43]

In addition to the places mentioned above, Councils were completely changed or greatly reduced after liquidation "actions" in the following places: Rohatyn,[44] Siedlce (here the former vice chairman was appointed to head a new Council),[45] Baranowicze,[46] Ostróg,[47] and many other ghettos. As a rule either all (or almost all) members, or only chairmen were killed or deported in the course of "resettlement actions." In ghettos where killing the Jews was accomplished piecemeal, the Germans, if they did not murder an *entire* Council, nominated a new one in which surviving former Council members were sometimes included.

After the "residual ghettos" were transformed into labor or concentration camps, the authorities sometimes left their old Council chairmen to function as camp Elders. In the Kaunas Ghetto the number of Council members was reduced from nine to four on August 1, 1942. In the fall of 1943, when the ghetto was changed into a concentration camp, its functions were drastically curtailed, and the camp commandant, Gecke, took over its management. In April 1944 the Council was formally disbanded, and its chairman, Dr. Elkes, remained as *Lagerälteste*.[48]

After the "children's action" in Šiauliai, the Council chairman became head of the ghetto concentration camp.[49] Similar events had taken place in Piotrków Trybunalski[50] and in other ghettos.

A particularly important source for our discussion is offered by Table IX (see p.327) based on our questionnaires, illustrating the fluctuations in the composition of the Councils and the fate of its members. The figures in the questionnaires concerning the length of time individual members served on the Councils reveal that of the 724 members mentioned, 133 (over 18%) lasted no longer than six months, many of them for only a few weeks; 192 members (26.6%) served up to one year; 185 (25.6%) up to two years; and

169 (23.4%) up to three years. Only 45 (6%) stayed on for over three years; a total of 45 percent served no longer than one year. The heavy turnover of Council membership is particularly striking in the Government General and in the incorporated territories (the Wartheland and Bezirk Zichenau) where the Jewish Councils were in existence for only some three years at the most (except in the Łódź Ghetto); the ghettos in the occupied Eastern territories (Ostland, Bezirk Białystok, and Reichskommissariat Ukraine) had Jewish Councils for only some 18 months (except the ghettos in Białystok, Vilna, Riga, Šiauliai, and Kaunas).

Turning to the figures concerning the fate of individual Council members, we note that over 2.9 percent resigned, and 1.8 percent were dismissed or arrested.

It is revealed in some of the questionnaires that one reason Council members resigned was their unwillingness to join a body which, by its very nature, had to cooperate with the German authorities. Others left the Councils because of internal friction, particularly because of opposition to the policy of the Council chairman, always the decisive factor (e.g., questionnaire No. 665, concerning the town of Rohatyn). Not always was resignation a smooth course. Thus we read in questionnaire No. 290 of the prewar community chairman

TABLE IX

Fluctuation in the Composition of the Councils

Tenure		Number of Council Members	Percentage
Up to six months		133	18.4
Up to one year		192	26.6
Up to two years		185	25.6
Up to three years		169	23.4
Three years and over		45	6.0
	Totals	724	100.0
Fate of the Council Members			
Resigned		21	2.9
Dismissed or arrested		13	1.8
Killed before "resettlement actions"		182	25.5
"Resettled" or killed on the spot		383	53.2
Suicides		9	1.2
Deaths		26	3.5
Survivors		86	11.9
	Totals	720	100.0

in Kłobuck who refused to become Council chairman and, "because of this, provoked the wrath of the German authorities. He was arrested and tortured, but later released thanks to the successful intercession of the prewar Polish mayor of Kłobuck. After his release from jail, he took no further part in community activities."

A new Council was nominated in Wieruszów after the chairman of the first Council, together with a group of community leaders, was deported to the penal camp near Łódź for not being able to collect an imposed cash contribution or deliver certain ordered goods. When the deported chairman was released after paying a stiff bribe, he did not continue his work in the Council.

Not always was it possible to resign. In many instances, the authorities forced Council members to continue in office. Questionnaire No. 417 relates that the chairman of the Kleck Council, "C." (only his initial is given), "repeatedly resigned but was each time again nominated by the Germans." It seldom happened that the Germans agreed to release a chairman unwilling to cooperate and nominated another one. For more about this see Chap. 2.

The figures show that 25.5 percent of the Council members were killed prior to "resettlement actions," an aspect of their functions which has been discussed in Chapter 11. More than one-half of our sample of Council members (53.2%) perished in the extermination camps, together with other ghetto inmates, or were killed on the spot. Adding the suicides (1.2%), we see that 79.9 percent of all Council members perished while less than 12 percent survived. Compared to the number of Jewish victims in Poland, Ostland, and Reichskommissariat Ukraine (which reached between 88% and 92% of the Jewish population), this figure shows that being a Council member was no protection against sharing the fate common to all Jews in Eastern Europe. The opposite is true: over one-quarter of all Council members discussed in our questionnaires perished even before the mass destruction of the Jews started.

The original membership of the Jewish Councils (or their leaders) were often fired and new members nominated on the principle of "negative selection."[51] The moral and civic qualifications of new Council members (or of those old members who were left to continue) were not usually high. Another factor in evaluating the performance of the later Councils was the fact that for the most part they functioned in a much worsened situation on the eve or in the course of the partial or total liquidation of the ghetto, and at a time when Gestapo terror was at its most intense, having engulfed the membership of the earlier Councils. The first Council members who perished, many of whom had been respected prewar civic leaders, were replaced by people of second and third caliber, quite often without any experience in social activities. They became members of the Councils and commandants of the ghetto police, getting these appointments by chance or at the whim of a Gestapo man who believed that they would be obedient tools in his hands. At the same time, establishing a new Council after the partial liquidation of the ghetto was another means of creating illusions in the minds of survivors, making them believe that there would be no more "actions" as they were assured ("This is the last one").

Here are few examples to illustrate the foregoing observations. A well-informed survivor relates about the Grodno Jewish Council:

The decline of the Council started with the liquidation action [begun on January 18, 1943]. The Germans destroyed ghetto No. 2, which caused the liquidation of the Council. . . . The activities of ghetto No. 1 were, naturally, curtailed too. In January 1943 the Gestapo requisitioned the treasury of the financial committee and later took over the archives of the statistical department. As a result, the Council was being liquidated together with the entire ghetto. By the time of the third and last period of destruction, up to March 1943, only the department of liaison men with the Gestapo, the burial society, and parts of the food department were in operation. The presidium of the Council and its entire overgrown apparatus were of no consequence; their tasks were taken over by new people, mainly the militia authorities [the ghetto police]. It is worthwhile to note that during the last days, when only very few survivors remained, after the murder of Brawer, the Council *Obmann*, the Gestapo ordered that a new Council be established with the commandant of the Jewish militia . . . as chairman. The Gestapo intended to keep cheating the Jews by making them believe that the ghetto would continue.[52]

The evolution of the Włodzimierz Wołyński Jewish Council (Reichskommissariat Ukraine) in the direction of negative selection of its members went thus: the first chairman was Rabbi Morgensztern, who died after two months in office. The lawyer Dr. Weiler took over the chairmanship. He was arrested on the eve of Yom Kippur 1941 together with a group of 150 Jews. A small number were released, but Weiler did not return. A survivor of the ghetto relates that "he enjoyed a good opinion." The lawyer Pass took his place as chairman, and he too is described as "a decent man [who] was not active enough." According to another version, the dentist Moshe Bardach was chairman after Dr. Weiler's arrest. Bardach and his family were killed in the course of the first mass murder, which started on September 1, 1942, and officially lasted for two weeks (it is assumed that 18,000 Jews perished at that time). After that, Lejb Kudish, the head of the "small ghetto" and one of the two chiefs of the Council's labor department, became head of the ghetto. Together with one of the former Council members and the surviving secretary of the Council's labor department, he established a new Council, with the permission of the authorities.

Kudish is severely criticized in the diaries of two ghetto survivors who relate that he did not distribute all of the 500 certificates which the Germans issued to surviving artisans, but sold them instead. On the eve of the second mass murder (which started November 13, 1942) he assured the ghetto inmates that as long as he leads the Council, nothing wrong would happen; but at the same time he advised his close friends to move over into the part of the ghetto where trained specialists had been assembled. His "agents"—probably the ghetto police—helped the Ukrainian police to seek out Jews in hiding. One of the diarists adds, however, that though "Kudish administered the ghetto with a strong arm, he rescued people from jail when they were arrested for carrying something into the ghetto or for appearing in the streets without permission after curfew."

It is characteristic of the mentality of this last head of the Włodzimierz Wołyński Ghetto that during such tragic times he had the audacity to celebrate his silver wedding anniversary with luxurious feasts that lasted a whole week: "The small ghetto sent gifts and congratulations on the occasion of his 25th anniversary, people danced, and they had a good time, feasting and dancing."[53]

In the Łódź Ghetto the second *Beirat* consisted of "people estranged from the Jews who had never been interested in Jewish affairs," according to a well-informed ghetto inmate.[54] In contrast to the membership of the first *Beirat*, the majority of whom had been killed, the new members were "people without moral beliefs who blindly executed all and any orders—selfish, criminal fellows."[55] A more lenient critic stated that Rumkowski "simply made servile listeners" out of the Council.[56]

The negative moral and social evolution of Jewish representatives under Nazi rule was also evident in Eastern Upper Silesia. A few days after the Germans occupied Będzin, Benjamin Graubard was elected chairman of the Jewish community. He had been one of the leaders of the prewar Jewish Populist Party in town, active in local and public life. As much as he could, he tried to resist the orders of the Gestapo or to sabotage them to make them less harmful for the Jews. When Moshe Merin became the *Leiter* of the "Union of Jewish Communities in Eastern Upper Silesia" and Graubard refused to accept his submissive tactics with the Nazi authorities, sharp frictions developed with the result that Graubard resigned. In the summer of 1940 Merin nominated his brother to take Graubard's place. He followed his brother's policy. A respondent to the questionnaires has testified that "all the time [during his tenure] he was a devoted servant and informer [of the Gestapo]."[57]

His older brother moved him to Sosnowiec to take over the chairmanship of the local Council and nominated Chaim Mołczadzki as Council chairman in Będzin. Mołczadzki belonged to a clique of the most devoted followers of Merin's rescue scheme, a fellow with no reservations in his docility toward the authorities.[58]

In another ghetto within the same area, Chrzanów, the first Council chairman, Becalel Cukier, the prewar leader of the Zionist Orthodox Organization Mizrachi, was sent to Auschwitz for dealing with the Gestapo with self-respect and for resisting Merin's servility toward the Germans. "The Council was left helpless and chaos developed. . . ." In Cukier's place and in place of the other Council members also killed in Auschwitz, Merin sent down to Chrzanów Dr. Böhm, a member of the Sosnowiec *Zentrale*, to lead the Council. Work proceeded in Merin's spirit.[59]

According to the available sources, there was a sharp decrease in the socio-moral standards of the Councils after the resignations, escapes, "resettlements," and dismissals by the Germans of those members who were appointed to the first Councils, in Tarnów,[60] Lublin,[61] Kuty,[62] Tarnopol,[63] Kołomyja,[64] Krzemieniec,[65] Dębica,[66] Pabianice,[67] Cracow,[68] Drohobycz,[69] and in other places.

CHAPTER 13

The Councils and the
Jewish Service Organizations

THE JEWISH COUNCILS were not the only Jewish organizations active in the ghettos. We have already mentioned that, prior to the advent of the Councils, various prewar Jewish service organizations such as TOZ and Centos were in operation, though often crippled because of the war (see Chap. 2). In addition, some new relief organizations sprang up amid the changed conditions of life under Nazi rule. We have also related how the German authorities later requested that all Jewish activities be concentrated exclusively in the Jewish Councils. All other Jewish institutions had then to be disbanded.

In the incorporated territories the problem of the Jewish service organizations was in theory taken care of quite radically by the German authorities: all such bodies were simply engulfed by the law of confiscation of Jewish property, implemented actually following the decree of incorporation on October 8, 1939. However, there was some evolution evident in the way the confiscation law was put into practice. In Łódź all Jewish institutions and their executive organs were disbanded in accord with the order of the *Stadtkommissar* issued on October 14, 1939. He authorized Rumkowski to reorganize them and take over their activities under his own exclusive responsibility.[1] Rumkowski also took over their assets. At the beginning of December 1939 the *Haupttreuhandstelle-Ost* issued an order confiscating the assets not only of private persons but also of Jewish service organizations, including medical, technical, and agricultural implements, furniture, and school equipment.[2]

According to Frank's order of July 23, 1940, concerning service organizations in the Government General, all organizations and institutions, including Jewish ones, were to be disbanded and their assets confiscated for the benefit of the state treasury. A similar order regarding foundations was issued by Frank on August 1, 1940.[3]

Under the circumstances, no social welfare institution was able to continue its activities independently. The legal obstacle was overcome in some places by incorporating the activities of the disbanded organization into the Council's apparatus as part of their regular tasks in the field of welfare or medical aid. Such was the case in Lublin and Hrubieszów, for instance.[4] In other places, these services became part of the program of local chapters of the JSS. However, as was customary in the occupied territories, the interests, attitudes, and policies of various authorities criss-crossed each other not only in the various administrative areas but also within the same administrative units.

Dr. Michał Weichert, the chairman of the Jewish Social Self-Help (JSS) in the Government General (see Chap. 6), reported that following an appeal to the *Bevölkerungswesen und Fürsorge* section, the inner administration department sent out a circular letter temporarily delaying the execution of Frank's order dismantling Jewish service organizations. The presidium of the JSS had also asked that the assets of closed organizations be given over to the Jewish Social Welfare. On November 26, 1941 the JSS was informed by the *Bevölkerungswesen und Fürsorge* section that the first paragraph of its by-laws had been changed to the effect that Jewish welfare organizations were incorporated into the JSS and their assets put at the disposal of the JSS.[5]

In Warsaw, the TOZ, Centos, and the ORT were active independent of the Jewish Council and became part of the JSS when it was established there.[6] For a long time, they operated as autonomous institutions.[7] There is information available about other places (Łowicz, for instance) where Centos was not organizationally tied up with the Jewish Council and conducted activities on its own behalf, at least for a time.[8] As already mentioned, the situation was different in Lublin, Hrubieszów, and in some other ghettos.

A drastic example of the Gestapo's stopping the work of a Jewish social agency in the case of the JEAS (Jewish Emmigrant Aid Society, analogous to HIAS in the United States), which was allowed to conduct its activities up to September 1940. On February 25, 1940, the leadership of the JEAS suggested that a number of Jewish communities in occupied Poland take over the task of putting local Jews in contact with their relatives abroad (mainly in the United States) in their quest for material help and emigration. The JEAS performed this service for the Jews in Warsaw and neighboring towns. The Lublin Jewish Council accepted the suggestion and established an emigration department to deal with these tasks.[9] The Jewish Councils in Radom, Cracow, Częstochowa, Kielce, Piotrków Trybunalski, Tarnów, Rzeszów, and other towns also assisted the JEAS by collecting the addresses of persons scattered all over the country because of the war.[10] But in September 1940 Dr. Morgenstern, the head of the JEAS, was ordered by Karl Mende, the *Referent* for Jewish affairs in the Warsaw Gestapo, to stop all activities because emigration was forbidden the Jews. The activities of JEAS were then taken over by the Jewish Relief Committee and carried out in the form of help from relatives abroad. A year later Dr. Morgenstern was arrested because "he had been in correspondence with persons abroad concerning emigration matters and had used the envelopes of the JEAS for his mail. The Gestapo *Referent* for Jewish affairs threatened to send Morgenstern to a concentration camp for his insolence."[11]

The incorporation of disbanded service organizations into the Jewish Councils was not always smooth. Frictions and mutual accusations often broke out. Characteristic in this respect is the case of TOZ in Częstochowa. One of its coworkers during the occupation relates:

At the end of February 1941, Kodner, the deputy *Stadthauptmann*, summoned two TOZ representatives, Konarski and Wolberg (Kodner slapped the latter's face while he was waiting in the hall), and ordered them, in the presence of Kopinski, the chairman of the Jewish Council, immediately to stop the activities of TOZ as an independent organization and incorporate it into the Council. . . . On March 22, 1941, the presidium of the Jewish Council formally adopted a resolution to take over TOZ. On the following day the Council members Bożykowski, Kurland, and Gerichter went to the TOZ, formally took over its activities . . . , and disbanded its executive board. . . . On March 24 the TOZ published a flyer in Polish in the form of an obituary, which was distributed in large numbers among the Jews in Częstochowa and mailed to Jewish service organizations throughout Poland. This was the way TOZ announced to the Jewish public the Council's shameful act against a Jewish relief organization. . . .[12]

In this quotation from Brener's book he presents the liquidation of TOZ as an independent organization in Częstochowa as a result of a scheme perpetrated by the Council conniving with the *Stadt-hauptmann*. It is, however, likely that the Council acted because of a clearcut order from the supervising authority. The mere dates of the events (the decision of the Council to take over TOZ came only *after* one month had elapsed following the order of the deputy *Stadthauptmann*) confirms such a hypothesis.[13]

There are similar examples. In Warsaw, for instance, the *Transferstelle* repeatedly ordered (on February 21 and 28, and on March 10, 1941) that the Jewish Council incorporate the local relief committee of the JSS. The relief committee was forbidden to approach any German office or to use its name in correspondence. However, the JSS succeeded in getting this order revoked.[14]

Some other prewar Jewish organizations tried to continue their activities as institutions within the general framework of Council apparatus. Thus the Cracow chapter of the "Jewish Veterans' Union in Poland" tried to conduct its activities as the "Committee of Jewish War Veterans, Widows, and Orphans at the Jewish Council," but the Gestapo ordered it disbanded. After an intervention in Cracow, the JSS presidium was informed on September 25, 1940, that the Committee of Veterans should join the local JSS.[15]

The JSS in the area of the Government General was independent of the Councils. It had been established from May to July 1940 (see Chap. 6). At the time the JSS began its activities, the Jewish Councils had already been firmly established for a long time and were conducting some welfare activities. According to its by-laws the JSS was entitled to establish branches in county seats and, later on, also in smaller towns. During the first months of 1942 the JSS had built up a network of 412 county committees and "delegations" in smaller localities. Prior to the establishment of those offices the Councils were the only Jewish agency the JSS could approach in matters concerning relief for Jews.[16]

The mutual relations of the JSS and the Jewish Councils oscillated between close collaboration and open or concealed animosity. Some of the Councils suspected that the JSS aspired to take over their entire welfare work, thus trespassing on their own activities. They were sustained in their suspicions by the local supervising authorities, which, for reasons of their own, also regarded the JSS as an undesirable factor. (JSS was formally under the supervision of the

Abteilung Bevölkerungswesen und Fürsorge in the Department of Internal Affairs in Cracow and not under police supervision.) According to the former chairman of the JSS,

> From the very start, we had to combat two forces both of which made trouble later on: the German county chiefs and the Jewish Councils. The *Abteilung Bevölkerungswesen und Fürsorge* officially sent out the approved by-laws of all three relief organizations functioning in the occupied area [i.e., the Polish, Ukrainian, and Jewish ones] to all city and county *Hauptmänner*, some of whom prematurely ordered the Jewish Councils not to wait for the initiative of the JSS (in accordance with Paragraph 12 of the JSS by-laws) but to establish county relief committees on their own, without delay. The Council gladly accepted these orders which gave them a chance to avoid the emergence of an independent organization and to secure their control over welfare work.[17]

The presidium of the JSS reacted by sending a circular letter to the Jewish Councils in September 1940 stating that according to its by-laws only the JSS was authorized to recommend the composition of local relief committees for approval by the authorities, and that, until the establishment of local branches of the JSS, no organization was authorized to act under the name of the Jewish Social Welfare or Jewish Relief Committee.[18]

To counteract the tendency of local political administrations to take over supervision of JSS branches, the presidium interceded with the *Abteilung Bevölkerungswesen und Fürsorge* in Cracow, asking them to advise county and town *Hauptmänner* in a special circular letter that, in accordance with Paragraph 12 of the JSS by-laws, only the JSS in Cracow was authorized to designate members of its local branches. Only 18 months later, on January 20, 1942, after JSS had already been long in operation, was such a circular letter sent to the county and city chiefs. It stated that the JSS branches were organizationally independent of local Jewish Councils, which had no authority over them though the latter were obligated to finance them. The entire welfare work of the Councils was to be performed by JSS committees.[19] Naturally the Councils resented this turn of events, which removed them entirely from any participation in welfare activities. From the Jewish point of view these activities were the most important justification for the Councils' existence and helped them win some recognition in the eyes of ghetto inmates. In any event the circular letter effected no changes in practice, and the Councils continued their modest relief work. Two months later mass deportations were launched in the Government General, and all Jewish matters, as has already been mentioned, came under the jurisdiction of the police organs (see Chap. 1). Referring to the decree regarding the change in jurisdiction in Jewish matters, the SS requested that the Government disband the JSS, and on October 16, 1942, all JSS activities were officially terminated.[20] In the meantime local JSS branches faced an uncertain legal situation, for their independence from the Councils was questioned even by the local offices of the *Abteilung Bevölkerungswesen und Fürsorge*, whose representative at the office of the plenipotentiary of the district chief in Warsaw informed the chairman of the Jewish Council that he was responsible for welfare work and that the JSS city committee was subordinate to him, except for financial matters. He was also ordered to submit a list of the members of the city relief committee up to July 28, 1940.[21] We have already mentioned that the *Transferstelle* too ordered that the committee be incorporated into the Council.

According to Weichert, some of the Councils stubbornly resisted the independence of local JSS committees, as was the case in Jędrzejów and Miechów (Cracow district).[22] In Lwów, according to an item in the "Communications" of the Jewish Council, the activities of the JSS branch were limited to the organization and maintenance of soup kitchens and to location of persons with unknown addresses. All other welfare work remained in the hands of the Council.[23]

However, this wrangling was not caused simply by the formal consideration of who was to have authority over welfare work in the ghetto. What really counted most was the difference in the approaches of the two bodies to the pending tasks. Free in its day-to-day activities from Gestapo interference, the social climate prevailing in the JSS institutions was civic-oriented to a far greater extent than in the Jewish Councils, which were toiling under constant pressure, threats, and terror of the German authorities. Moreover, as a socially oriented body the JSS enjoyed the cooperation of personalities who before the war had been active in the TOZ, Centos, ORT, the interest-free loan banks, etc., and who now preferred to give their time and efforts to the JSS, which was better equipped to meet the immediate needs of the Jewish masses than were the Jewish Councils. There was yet another factor that, to a certain degree, contributed to mutual animosity between the JSS and the Councils. In Warsaw, for instance, the leaders of the JSS (Dr. Emanuel Ringelblum, Yitzhak Giterman, and others) were greatly opposed to the policies and tactics of the Council, particularly of the ghetto police.

Opposition to the welfare policies of the Council was particularly evident in the position taken by the numerous house committees which were under the organizational and ideological influence of the JSS[24] and which we will discuss more fully later. The quite openly antagonistic relations between people working for the Council and those engaged in the work of the JSS were commonly known. For instance, Czerniakow requested liquidation of the independent activities of the Central Entertainment Commission at the JSS because they crossed his own plans to concentrate responsibility for all cultural activities in the ghetto in the cultural department of the Council[25] (it is also possible that the Germans requested this). A person active in the Warsaw branch of the JSS relates that in the course of the "resettlement action" during the summer of 1942, the ghetto police, on secret orders of Józef Szerynski, their commandant, and later on Lejkin's (his successor's) orders, paid no regard to the certificates of JSS coworkers but dragged them off to the transfer place, although, according to German orders, they were not subject to "resettlement." He maintains that this was an act of vengeance.[26]

At a meeting of the Jewish Council held in Lublin on June 30, 1941, the case of two members of the local JSS branch who had publicly insulted the Council was taken up. It was decided that they should be forbidden to enter the Council building, and the branch chairman was requested to punish them and report on his action to the Council.[27]

The former chairman of the JSS presidium tried to explain the reasons for antagonism as follows:

The attitude of the majority of the Councils toward the local JSS branches was unfavorable, though actually the Councils should have been happy that there was an organization maintaining the welfare institutions or helping by giving subsidies in cash . . . , medicines, and food, thus relieving them, at least in part, of their own obligations. In reality however, the Councils could not forgive the JSS the appreciation it had won from ghetto inmates who profoundly hated the Councils. "Why should they like me?" asked the chairman of the Częstochowa Jewish Council, Lejb Kopinski, during one of my visits to that town. "I cut the fat off the rich people, I tax the middle class above their capacity to pay, I have nothing to offer to the poor—so who is going to like the

Jewish Council?" Still more pointed was the opinion of our Dr. [Elijahu] Tisch [member of the JSS presidium of Cracow] who said that the difference between the Councils and the JSS was that the Jewish Councils took away from the Jews to give to the Germans and the JSS took from the Germans to give to the Jews. The Councils used to tell our branches, "Your desire is that all evil come from us and all good from you." Small wonder that they wanted to take over our work so that both the good and the evil would come from the same hands. . . . We therefore *sharply separated* [italics added] our organization from the Jewish Councils. The origins of both bodies were different, as were their activities.[28]

We shall, however, see that the difference was not that big after all, for the objective conditions of Jewish life under the rule of the Nazis forced collaboration between the two bodies on both local and central levels, animosity notwithstanding. In the first place, cooperation stemmed from the fact that members of the Jewish Councils were also members of the presidium of the JSS and of its numerous local branches. Three members of the Warsaw Jewish Council—Joseph Jaszunski, Benjamin Zabłudowski, and Gamzu Wielikowski—were members of the JSS presidium. Marek Bieberstein, a member of the JSS presidium, was also chairman of the Cracow Jewish Council. After he was arrested in September 1940 he was replaced in the JSS presidium by Dr. Mark Alten, the vice chairman of the Lublin Council.[29] This overlap in personnel of the Councils and the JSS branches was also evident in smaller branches of the JSS, e.g., in Żyrardów, where four Council members belonged to the local JSS branch;[30] in Łańcut, where Dr. Marek Pohorile, the Council chairman, was chairman of the JSS branch for the entire county;[31] in Chełm and in Chmielnik, where three leading Council members belonged to the local JSS branch;[32] in Iwaniska (Radom district) where two Council members were representatives in the JSS branch (one of them the chairman).[33] In Częstochowa the chairman and one other member of the Jewish Council were also members of the town committee of the JSS.[34] In Radom too the chairman of the local branch of the JSS, the lawyer Abraham Salbe, was a member of the Jewish Council.[35] And it may be added that the very establishment of the JSS itself was accomplished with the active cooperation of chairman Adam Czerniakow and several other members of the Warsaw Jewish Council.[36] On January 23, 1940, Czerniakow was instructed by *Stadtpräsident* Dr. Dengel to establish in Warsaw a "Jewish

Self-Help"; Dengel also ordered that Czerniakow become its chairman and nominate a few *Sachbearbeiter* from among the Council members.[37] As already mentioned, the authorities considered Czerniakow the chairman of the JSS in Warsaw.[38] On the other hand, not all Jewish Councils were inclined to monopolize the entire welfare program. In Lublin and Radom, for instance, branches of the JSS took over social work from the respective Jewish Councils without friction.[39]

Cooperation between the Councils and the JSS branches was also expressed in their joint meetings and joint interventions with the German authorities. Even before Jewish Social Welfare had been officially established in Cracow, a conference was held on March 27 and 28, 1940, in the office of Dr. Arlt, the department chief of the *Abteilung Bevölkerungswesen und Füsorge*. A member of the city relief committee in Warsaw, a representative of the JDC, and a four-man delegation from the Warsaw Jewish Council, headed by Czerniakow, participated in the meeting.[40] And in September 1940 the JSS presidium called a conference of representatives of the Jewish Councils in Warsaw, Radom, Lublin, Częstochowa, and Cracow to discuss the results of interventions aimed at easing the hardships of Jewish forced laborers in the camps.[41] Moreover, delegates of the Jewish Councils in the various counties participated in the county conferences of JSS branches held in Busko in the summer of 1941 (the exact date is unknown) and in Chełm (from January 25 to 28, 1942).[42]

The presidium of the JSS was in touch with the Jewish Councils on a variety of problems and methods of cooperation, such as joint interventions with the authorities, preparations of lists of local Jewish prewar organizations demanded by the authorities, questionnaires (e.g., regarding children and the care of minors),[43] and statistics concerning Jewish houses put under the management of *Kommissare*, needed to support appeals by the JSS to the authorities to get some income from them to cover its welfare expenses.[44]

During the establishment of the Warsaw Ghetto, both the chairman of the Council and the JSS presidium interceded with the proper German authorities not to reduce the space of the projected ghetto and to allow the poorest people (in the suburbs) to remain in their lodgings up to April 1, 1941.[45] The JSS and the Councils often requested each other's intercession with the authorities on behalf of oppressed Jews. For instance, the JSS requested that Rumkowski obtain the release of a group of Jews from Konin county (Wartheland) sent to the camp at Osnitz in East Prussia. After their release they were to join their families expelled to Iżbica (Lublin district) in the first half of March 1941.[46] When the Jewish Council of Falenica was ordered, on October 4, 1940, to remove all children and personnel from the local children's home, it asked the JSS presidium to intervene. Dr. Wielikowski, in his role as JSS adviser at the office of the Warsaw district chief, interceded with the Government General in Cracow and obtained cancellation of the order.[47] The JSS often intervened with the authorities on behalf of the Jewish Councils to ask for larger fuel allocations, which were severely limited for the Jews.[48]

The local branches of the JSS also approached the Councils with all sorts of problems. On September 3, 1941, the branch of the JSS in Łuków requested that Rumkowski bring back into the Łódź Ghetto and take care of four minors who had been caught in the streets without their parents in the course of a deportation (perhaps in December 1939). The situation of these children was most desperate.[49]

In some of the ghettos, cooperation between the Councils and the JSS branches was very close, particularly where Council members were also members of JSS committees. At a meeting held on July 16, 1941, the Lublin Council adopted a resolution that two groups of functionaries, its own and those of the JSS committee, would in succession check buildings scheduled for disinfection.[50]

Representatives of the JSS sometimes informed the Councils of the activities of the JSS, e.g., in Lublin,[51] when Dr. Alten, the vice chairman of the Jewish Council and a member of the presidium of the JSS, reported on the activities of the presidium.[52]

The Councils subsidized JSS branches and vice versa. Thus the Lublin Jewish Council paid the following subsidies to the local JSS: 1,800 zlotys in July 1941 and 300 zlotys a week when the JSS was active in the Majdan Tatarski residual ghetto in 1942.[53] In Chełm, the Council subsidized the county JSS branch with several thousand zlotys a month. The minutes of a meeting of the JSS branches in Chełm county show that this was not the only Council to give financial support to the activities of the JSS. Thus a member of the Chełm delegation stated at the meeting that subsidies from local Councils constituted a substantial part of the income of the JSS, though he admitted that according to reports from other delegates in a large number of places there existed a harmful antagonism between the two institutions. Two more delegates, from Siedliszcze and Dubienko, stated that the Jewish Councils in these towns were doing everything in their power to help the JSS, but that the results were pitiable for lack of means at a time when the entire population was utterly impoverished.[54] On May 4, 1941, the Krasnobród Jewish Council (Lublin district), jointly with the local relief committee, addressed a request to the presidium of the JSS for immediate help to ease the disastrous situation of the local Jews, particularly those "resettled" from Zamość.[55]

As we may surmise from the above facts, the borderline between the JSS and the Jewish Councils was not sharply drawn. Their cooperation stemmed from the actual conditions of Jewish life at a given time, notwithstanding the difference in the modes of their establishment, and the aims of the German authorities with regard to their tasks. The only survivor of the Chełm conference, Dr. Elijahu Tisch, pointedly and realistically characterized the mutual relations of these organizations. Stressing the crucial necessity for cooperation between the JSS and the Councils who should appreciate "the self-sacrificing work of the . . . [JSS] which, to a large extent, releases the Jewish Councils from welfare work," he concluded each of two speeches he delivered with almost identical appeals: "You are both institutions of the Jews and must complement each other."[56]

THE HOUSE COMMITTEES

A special situation emerged in the Warsaw Jewish Council in connection with the activities of the house committees mentioned earlier. Their establishment went back to the very first days of the war, in September 1939, when they sprang up spontaneously to provide some protection against German air attacks. The original task of the house committees was to organize air raid shelters, fight fires, secure water and food for cotenants, etc. Also important was establishing some sort of liaison between dwellers of a particular building and the outer world at a time when individual persons could not go out into the streets of the besieged and bombarded city. In the beginning of October, when the battle of Warsaw had come to an end and when various newly created Jewish service organizations sprang up (the Coordination Committee of Jewish Relief Institutions and later on the JSS), the house committees were transformed, on the initiative of the historian Dr. Emanuel Ringelblum (who headed the social sector of the JSS), into self-help cells in single buildings and in entire city blocks with hundreds or thousands of tenants. By September 1940 there were close to 2,000 house committees in operation. After the ghetto was established in Warsaw some of the committees (those of buildings located outside the ghetto borders) were disbanded, and by January 1942 only 1,108 committees were functioning in the ghetto.[57]

According to the by-laws, the tasks of the house committees were: to establish soup kitchens and find sponsors for them, to provide shelters for refugees, to collect money and clothing for people deported to labor camps and for their families, to provide medical aid, and to execute the orders of the Jewish Council regarding food, welfare, and hygiene.[58] Thus the house committees performed relief tasks to satisfy local needs, and at the same time were called upon by the Council to help in executing its own various tasks. We shall here discuss only one field of their activities, their cooperation with the Council.

To execute its functions effectively, the Council depended on cooperation by the entire population. To achieve this, the Council used already functioning house committees or established new ones. For instance, to fight the spread of typhus epidemics the Council established Sanitary House Committees in the spring of 1940, to assure cleanliness in apartments and houses, making the house committees and the building superintendents jointly responsible both for hiding the sick and for maintaining sanitary conditions in the houses.[59] After the hospital tax was introduced in March 1940, the house committees were given the task of collecting it. The hospital tax department of the Jewish Council provided building superintendents with lists of tenants and the projected amount of the tax for each one (see Chap. 10). Through the channels of the JSS, the house committees received special certificates which exempted recipients from payment of the 2 zloty fee for a bread card. Up to September 19, 1940, 69,443 such certificates were distributed.[60]

The house committees were called upon to assist the Jewish Council on those occasions when it had to meet extraordinarily heavy cash demands from the authorities. For instance, in March 1940 when the Germans ordered the Council to deliver "an unheard of" quantity of furniture and underwear as well as 15 pianos, the house committees were given the job of collecting these goods from among the well-to-do tenants.[61] The house committees participated, though with little success, in the collection undertaken by Czerniakow in January 1942 to ransom Jews kept in the Jewish jail for the price of 1,500 fur coats. Over 40 of the imprisoned people faced execution after having been caught on the "Aryan" side.[62] Various departments of the Council would send circular letters and instructions on various problems to the house committees.[63]

The fact that the house committees were burdened with purely administrative or financial tasks made them into local administrative organs of the Jewish Council and caused strong resentment on their part. In a memorandum of February 10, 1942, addressed to the city relief committee of the JSS, a complaint was made that "the house committees are burdened with a number of hard jobs of a purely administrative character [and] with collecting fees and fines on behalf of various Council organs. . . . These purely administrative orders displace other activities of the house committees, and rob them of their original role as charitable institutions, detracting from the work which has been and is their primary responsibility—providing emergency assistance to cotenants."[64]

This sense of bitterness and resentment against both the Jewish Council and its organs, including the police, sometimes caused stormy protests. Thus, for instance, at a conference of the house committees called by the Jewish Council in April 1941, the chief of the labor department called upon assembled house committee members to influence the Jewish population to report for work in the labor camps. He threatened that the house committees would be made personally responsible in case the tenants of their buildings did not report. The meeting ended in an uproar. One chairman of a house committee (Leszno 2) and two other participants were arrested for insulting the ghetto police because of their behavior during night raids on persons who had not reported for work in the labor camps, but the three were immediately set free because of the protests of those present at the meeting.[65]

A former member of the central representation of the house committees notes in his memoirs that the majority of the committees were against cooperation with the Jewish Council, and all the Council's efforts to transform the committees into its instruments were met with strong resistance. He also writes that when, at a meeting of the area committee, a speaker who was a functionary of the Jewish Council tried to make his point, there broke out such a storm of protest that he ran from the meeting.[66]

Clashes between the house committees and the ghetto police took place later too. For instance, in an entry dated January 6, 1942, Czerniakow notes in his Diary that he met with a representative of the house committees to discuss the arrest by the ghetto police of a number of committee chairmen "for not executing instructions to take care of the poor population" (the details of the matter are not indicated in the entry). Following the meeting, he once more ordered the ghetto police not to arrest house committee chairmen without his permission.

Besides the house committees, there were also active in the Warsaw Ghetto so-called "sponsorships" for refugee shelters, soup kitchens, etc., composed of representatives of house committees located near given shelters for refugees and expellees or given soup kitchens.[67]

Shortly after the Łódź Ghetto was established, house committees appeared charged with the task of collecting a fee of 3 Reichsmarks from each family member. This money was used to establish a fund for the food department to acquire food staples for ghetto inmates. The house committees in Łódź also collected the monthly fee charged for maintenance of apartment houses and for paying volunteer janitors. This fee was collected up to November 1940, when the janitors were absorbed by the ghetto administration and their salaries were paid out of its budget.[68] Under the dictatorial system in the Łódź Ghetto, the house committees, with their distinctive character as social organizations, could not last for long.

House committees were also established in Częstochowa by the TOZ. These committees functioned for only a short time, collecting from tenants weekly fees for self-help.[69] There were house committees in Piotrków Trybunalski too.[70]

COMPULSORY UNIONS OF JEWISH ARTISANS

By order of the German economic authorities, Compulsory Unions of Jewish Artisans were established in a number of district and county towns, in Warsaw, Cracow, Radom, Lublin, Kielce, Rzeszów, and in some other places in the area of the Government General. Artisans in smaller towns had to join compulsory unions in the nearby district or county towns. The German order stated that the Jewish Councils were to establish these compulsory unions. *Gazeta Żydowska* (No. 41, December 10, 1940) printed a news item stressing their usefulness and the need to establish such unions in the area of the Government General "for defending the economic interests of the Jewish artisans and for their economic and technical development." This was another example of German hypocrisy toward the Jews: at a time when the Germans had already decided to curtail sharply the work of Jewish artisans, the censored *Gazeta Żydowska* was permitted to print encouraging articles about the rosy future of Jewish handicrafts in the area of the Government General.

In Warsaw the Compulsory Union of Jewish Artisans was established in April 1940 in the course of a conference held at the Jewish Council at that time. Leaders of the Jewish artisan guild and of its branches were invited. In time 16,000 master artisans and their apprentices joined the compulsory union. Master artisans paid 2 zlotys membership dues a month and were charged an additional 50 groszy for each employed worker.[71] The union's executive was nominated by the Council chairman, who also designated one of the Council members to serve on it.

In ordering compulsory unions of Jewish artisans, the Germans pursued their own economic aims by exercising strict control over Jewish labor. The officially designated task of the unions was to distribute among their members leather and other allocated raw materials which they were to receive from the general Artisan Chambers. But these allocations were so meager and so rarely distributed (every two months or, sometimes, at still longer intervals) that the unions soon became self-help agencies tending to the personal needs of their members. For instance, the artisan union in Warsaw interceded with the authorities in order to obtain the renewal of artisan identification cards and the admission of artisan representatives to hearings in the financial office regarding taxation of Jewish artisans. They also extended legal advice to members and approached the authorities through channels of the Jewish Councils in order to obtain permits for their members to leave the ghetto for business purposes, etc. But these activities of the union were officially forbidden in June 1942.[72] In agreement with the health department of the Council, the union established low-cost medical aid for members and two soup kitchens where 1,800 meals were served daily;

assigned work among the members according to their specialties; and established a self-help bank where money was loaned to pay for labor licenses or to establish workshops. Relief in cash was also given. The union interceded with the housing department of the Council to obtain space for shops and to purchase from the Council, at reduced prices, the special signs that Jewish artisans were obliged to display, etc. The union functioned up to the uprising in the Warsaw Ghetto in April 1943.

Similar activities were performed by the Compulsory Union of Jewish Artisans in Cracow (which also provided food for its members),[73] Tarnów,[74] Rzeszów,[75] Kielce,[76] Lwów,[77] and other places. Their self-help efforts made easier the tasks of the Councils and the JSS, particularly in the field of legal advice and welfare.[78]

OTHER ORGANIZATIONS

In a number of ghettos various philanthropic, professional, cultural, or religious institutions were established at the initiative of social organizations or individual persons. These organizations were active outside the Jewish Councils, though sometimes financially supported by them. Their activities relieved the Councils of some of their tasks, particularly in the field of welfare, but friction sometimes developed.

In the fall of 1941 in Vilna a social aid committee was established at the initiative of the Jewish Labor Bund Organization in the ghetto, which also directed the committee's work at first. Later, in January 1942, Zionist, Communist, nonpartisan, and religious groups joined the social aid committee. Functionaries of the ghetto Council and members of the ghetto police contributed to the fund of the social aid committee by paying 18 rubles from monthly salaries up to 450 rubles a month and as much as 50 rubles from monthly salaries up to 900 rubles. Laborers working for the Germans in so-called "units" outside the ghetto also contributed to the fund. Social events, shows, and concerts in the ghetto theater, gifts by individuals, and *yortsayt* offerings in memory of perished loved ones supplied additional income.[79]

The social aid committee distributed cash and food to the needy on a monthly basis. According to the report on welfare work in the ghetto, 5,302 persons received assistance (in cash, food, assorted clothing, plank cots in dwellings) during the first six months of 1942, amounting to a total of 75,480 Reichsmarks distributed.[80] In the second half of that year, 900 persons received assistance from the committee amounting to 90,434 Reichsmarks. This amount was accounted for as a contribution by the social aid committee to the expenses of the Jewish Council for welfare, expenses totaling 338,367 Reichsmarks.[81]

In close cooperation with the Jewish Council, the committee arranged winter and special relief drives.[82] It subsidized professional groups such as teachers, writers, artists, etc. There was also established a professional representation of people employed at various labor places, schools, theaters, medical stations, and other such institutions in the ghetto.[83]

The committee's income dwindled in the spring of 1943, when income derived from the so-called Internal Tax was taken over by the Jewish Council. This tax was deducted from salaries and was included as a surcharge in the price of tickets to various events in the ghetto. Having lost this source of income, the committee curtailed its relief activities.[84]

During the first years of the occupation, the prewar organization called *Dobroczynność* (Polish for "charity") conducted relief work in Częstochowa, maintaining an old-age home for 188 persons, an orphanage for 150 children, and a hospital. A relief committee for refugees was also active. All were financed by funds collected from among the Jewish population, from selling special badges, and by allocations from JDC.[85] The pertinent sources do not indicate whether the Council also subsidized these activities.

In May 1940 in Częstochowa, an official professional representation was established for workers, employed mainly at forced labor, whom the Germans had ordered the Council to take care of. The official name of this body was Labor Secretariat at the Labor Department of the Jewish Council. According to the treasury report of the Labor Secretariat for the period from May to December 1940, "the Secretariat had its origins in the Labor Delegation that sprang up spontaneously when forced-labor duty was introduced." The report thus describes the duties of the Labor Secretariat: "It has to take care of all labor matters, as far as they concern the labor department and all other departments of the Council, and to conduct widespread activities in all fields of labor." For this purpose, "a number of relief and loan *kassas*, medical aid, and a fund for un-employed and invalids" were established.

The Labor Secretariat derived its income from indirect taxation on bread cards and other items, which covered such administrative expenses as salaries, writing materials, etc. During the eight months of the report period, income from these taxes amounted to 9,242.55 zlotys, of which 8,200.93 zlotys was spent by the office. It is not specified for what purpose this money was paid out, but it may be assumed that 5,065 zlotys was spent to pay wages for personnel and to aid workers and others. The self-help *kassa* received 2,000 zlotys and the rest was accounted for as overhead and other expenses. An unspent balance in the amount of 1,041.62 was shown as of January 1, 1941.

The Labor Secretariat also interceded with the Jewish Council to improve the lot of the workers. The report states that it "carried out dozens of actions to increase the wages and bread allocations of the workers, 203 interventions [the figure is not sufficiently clear in the text] regarding dwellings, 96 interventions in school matters, 676 hospital interventions, and 808 interventions in various other matters."

The Secretariat gave special attention to matters concerning forced laborers in camps where it had its own representatives. Its representatives also took part in the winter drives of the Jewish Self-Help Committee. The office of the Secretariat was located in one of the rooms of the Council's labor department.[86]

According to some postwar information, not entirely clear, the Labor Secretariat changed its name to Labor Council when the ghetto was established in April 1941. It adopted the character of an independent social organization and severed its formal ties with the Council of Elders. Its membership came from the political parties: Zionists of all shades, Bund members, Communists, and people without party affiliations. The representatives were elected by the forced laborers themselves. According to the former treasurer of the labor council executive, its mutual relations with the Council of Elders became strained because of the labor council's demands to improve the lot of the forced laborers. The laborers and their families proclaimed a hunger strike in the spring of 1941, occupying the Council's office and demolishing the office fixtures (earlier the forced laborers had arranged protests in the building of the Council).

The Council of Elders accepted the laborers' requests concerning bread and wages and the labor council proceeded with its self-help work and with political and cultural activities among its members.[87]

In the Łódź Ghetto, on the joint initiative of the political parties and Rumkowski's administration, kibbutzlike farms were established in Marysin by people of similar political persuasion. There were Zionist kibbutzim, centralized in the Kibbutz Executive (*Vaad Hakibbutzim*), a kibbutz of the Bund, and a kibbutz of orthodox girls (*Benoth Poalei Agudat Israel*). All were subordinated to the agricultural department of the ghetto administration. The crop harvested was distributed for consumption among the kibbutzim, the orphanages, and the summer camps. The kibbutz people were also employed by the ghetto shops in Marysin. The kibbutzim conducted political and cultural activities.

During the summer of 1940 some 1,500 youths lived on the kibbutzim farms. Young people strove to get away from the starving ghetto and to join the kibbutzim, where life was more cheerful, with unpolluted air and better food. They could have become a dynamic, wholesome force with a positive influence in the ghetto. But because they were too independent and resisted attempts to transform them into labor battalions under police surveillance, Rumkowski, who in general abhorred any socially independent group, liquidated the kibbutzim in March 1941 (the Bund kibbutz had already been liquidated in January).[88]

For the same reason, in October 1940 Rumkowski liquidated the Jewish Cultural Organization, where members of the Bund, ORT, the Society of Friends of YIVO, writers, and artists were represented. At the same time, the *Hazomir* club was also closed.[89]

In a number of ghettos, prewar religious societies continued their activities and new ones actually sprang up with the aim of counteracting the destructive influence of the ghetto on Jewish religious life. In the Łódź Ghetto, the prewar *Bnei Horev* society promoted observance of the Sabbath, conducted a religious school, established religious study groups for children, accompanied children on their way to prayers, and took care that the numerous orphans said *Kaddish* (the prayer in memory of the dead), etc. Another religious society, *Peh Kodesh*, was established in the second half of 1940 for the specific purpose of seeing that Jews in the ghetto did not consume nonkosher food. The members of this society picketed in front of butcher shops and exhorted people standing in line not to buy the usual horse meat which had been allocated for ghetto inmates. They posted appeals at the entrances to prayer houses, etc. After a year-long losing battle against their most potent adversary, the pangs of hunger, the society disbanded during the second part of 1941. Still another society, *Shomrei Mezuzot,* was established in May 1940 to watch over the observance of the commandment regarding *mezuzot.* Not only did the society provide *mezuzot* for private homes, particularly those formerly inhabited by non-Jews, but they also placed *mezuzot* at the gates of apartment houses, in soup kitchens, courtyards, etc., causing clashes with the Jewish police. The society was liquidated in the second half of 1942 after the death of its founder.[90]

CHAPTER 14

The Personnel of the Jewish Councils

WE HAVE ALREADY MENTIONED in Chap. 4 the fact that the machinery of the Councils was abnormally large. In this chapter we will discuss the hypertrophy of the ghetto apparatus in more detail, analyzing the qualifications, social origins, education, and mentality of Council employees, all of which, naturally, were important for the proper execution of their tasks and, to a large degree, influenced their relations with the ghetto inmates. The employees of prewar Jewish communities stayed on at their jobs when the war started, except where they were affected by the waves of mass escape. In many places, however, their numbers swelled considerably. For instance, the Jewish community in Warsaw had had a staff of 532 employees before the war; it increased to over 800 at the beginning of 1940, and to 1,741 by July of the same year.[1]

The number of officials in the Jewish communities had been quite small before the war, because of both insufficient funds and limited tasks. Only a minimal number of Jews had been employed by municipal or government offices. For this reason the number of people in the Jewish communities in Poland and the Baltic states who were qualified to take over responsible positions in the Councils was not large, particularly since the tasks they faced were much more diversified than in prewar times.[2] Having little choice, the Councils were forced to engage persons who were not always fit for the tasks at hand, often not even having sufficient formal schooling. Moreover, for the most important positions in the main office, labor department, food department, etc., positions involving direct contact with the German authorities, it was necessary to speak and write German. The main sources of competent employees were from among professionals, people formerly employed by the community or by various Jewish service organizations, and students who could neither attend school nor obtain other work because of anti-Jewish measures. From these segments of the Jewish population came cadres of new functionaries for the Councils, particularly in the large and medium-sized ghettos. These people, however, suffered from a great handicap. The Jewish professional intelligentsia, except in the eastern Polish areas and the Baltic states, was for the most part culturally assimilated and alien to the Jewish masses, their needs, aspirations, and ways of life. They knew little or no Yiddish, and generally lacked understanding and sympathy for the Jewish masses and their vital needs and interests.

Thus in the Warsaw Ghetto, where officials used Polish in their contacts with the public and in interoffice correspondence, the chairman of the Council, Adam Czerniakow, apparently under pressure from Jewish survivalist elements, issued a circular letter to all departments and institutions ordering all announcements, circular letters, and displayed signs to be written in Yiddish as well as in Polish and German, the official languages. We also know of assimilationist tendencies prevalent in the Sosnowiec Jewish Council from a source relating to the Eastern Upper Silesia province.[3]

There was yet another reason why it was difficult to overcome the shortage of proper candidates for employment by the Councils. The radically changed conditions of life under a pitiless totalitarian government forced Council functionaries to deal with corrupt German officials on their own terms. Every day new situations arose, agonizing problems requiring instant solutions not always in conformity with ethical norms, to say the least. Educated people with high moral standards and with long, unblemished careers in Jewish public life were incapable of making themselves deal with the corrupt officials of the German occupation.

In general the employees of the Jewish Councils came from the ranks of young people with a background of secular education who had often severed their ties with traditional or religious ways of Jewish life. We find in leading positions, particularly in Galicia, numerous professionals, mostly jurists. Orthodox Jews were very scarce among these, for reasons indicated in Chap. 2 where we have discussed the socio-political composition of the Councils.

Another important factor determining the composition of the Council functionaries was the patronage of people deserving first consideration for available jobs. In general, the policy was to engage persons who had been active in public life before the war, though there were opinions that these unblemished, straightforward people were not necessarily qualified to work under new conditions requiring not only administrative and professional office experience but entirely new methods of dealing with the authorities. The majority of prospective employees lacked both.

Because work in the ghetto administration provided an opportunity to gain preferential treatment, patronage blossomed in certain places. See, for example, an article published in the *Gazeta Żydowska* (No. 47, December 13, 1940) by A. M. Rogowoj, one of the prewar leaders of the Orthodox Agudat Israel party. He complained that Council jobs were being given to people without any experience in civic work, and that the only reason why these persons got appointments was that they knew influential Council members or high officials of the ghetto administration who distributed patronage to their own relatives and friends. He noted that "the scope of the widespread patronage system is demonstrated by the fact that in numerous institutions [of the Council] entire families are employed." The article was widely discussed in the pages of subsequent issues of the paper. An official of the Lublin Jewish Council, the former editor of the Yiddish daily *Lubliner Togblat* complained of nepotism, and that, at a time when the majority of Council officials were suffering from poverty, those employees related to Council members lived in comfort as did their benefactors. Concluding the discussion the *Gazeta Żydowska* suggested that the practice should be adopted "of selecting officials from among the most able public workers of long standing, while also considering the requests of persons with no experience and no recommendations who can support their candidacies only by their high personal qualifications."[4]

But this objective yardstick was rarely implemented. Quite to the contrary, at a time when work for the Jewish Council could be considered a means of climbing the social ladder in the ghetto (and, later on, as a means of providing an opportunity for "rescue"), patronage and nepotism blossomed not only in Warsaw, but also in the ghettos of Łódź,[5] Złoczów,[6] Lwów,[7] Piotrków Trybunalski,[8] Białystok,[9] and other places.

In addition to all this the Warsaw Ghetto suffered from the

painful problem of converted Jews employed by the Council. Among the "racially mixed" gentiles and converted Jews confined in the Warsaw Ghetto there were many excellent specialists: jurists, engineers, physicians, and many more experts in various fields. Czerniakow's policy was not to alienate these "sinful brothers." Some were given important positions in the ghetto administration, a policy which outraged survivalist Jews even within the Council. Opinions were divided.[10] Czerniakow was, for instance, supported by Dr. Israel Milejkowski, the chairman of the health department, who noted:

My attitude toward the converted Jews with whom I have contacts is strictly businesslike. There are many experts among them and, since our only ideal at present is to survive, we need to use them for the benefit of our institutions. We have, however, to bear in mind one principal condition—and I for one always remember it—that the converted ones not be given a chance to occupy leading positions, so that they may not have a chance to become policymakers [and] leaders.[11]

On the other hand, two ghetto intellectuals who were active in social work before the war stated that "the Council befriended and gave privileged status to people who had cut off any connection with the Jews, who had prided themselves on their asemitism before the war,"[12] and that "a high ranking position [in the Council] was not infrequently occupied by a converted Jew, such as the chief of Jewish police . . . , a converted Jew and an ardent anti-Semite, Colonel Szerynski, a former Polish police inspector."[13]

In Tarnopol too a converted Jew was a high-ranking functionary (or even a member) of the Jewish Council.[14]

In some of the ghettos able, ambitious functionaries won leading positions in the Councils. Thus in the Sosnowiec *Zentrale* of the Jewish communities in Eastern Upper Silesia the secretary, Fayga Czarny, became Merin's most trusted coworker ("his brains"). She participated in meetings of his intimate coworkers when important decisions had to be made.[15] Similarly in Łódź Miss Fuchs, the female secretary of the presidium department (Rumkowski's personal office), played an important role. Together with Rumkowski she visited German offices. As an expellee from Germany, she knew the German language well.[16] In general, knowledge of German was often an asset for advancement in the ghetto administration.

As we have already mentioned, the Council functionaries enjoyed a privileged position compared to ghetto inmates, except for trained artisans, the ghetto police, etc. The Germans considered Council work as equivalent to forced-labor duty, from which Council workers were released. The proper certificate of the Council protected the bearer, though not unfailingly, from being carried away for forced labor. Thus in Piotrków Trybunalski "the Council functionaries had to perform forced-labor duties once or twice a week to pacify the Jewish population."[17] In Białystok the Council adopted a resolution on January 27, 1942, that, when necessary, every department of the ghetto administration should put 5 percent or 6 percent of its personnel at the disposal of the labor department.[18] At the time the ghettos were established and the problem of lodgings became acute, Council employees were assigned apartments for themselves and their families.[19] As a rule their food allocations were higher than those for the other ghetto inmates. For instance, in the winter of 1942 the supply department of the Warsaw Ghetto Council allocated monthly supplementary portions of bread for certain categories of ghetto inmates, such as police, laborers, patients in hospitals, inmates in welfare institutions, and Council functionaries. The supplementary portions consisted of 10 or 12 kilograms for the police and 4 kilograms for the other categories on a monthly basis. This occurred at a time when most ghetto inmates were allocated no more than two irregularly distributed kilograms of bread a month.[20] In Łódź, Kaunas, Vilna, and Piotrków Trybunalski among other places the Council employees were also given supplementary food allocations.[21]

A poll in the Warsaw Ghetto conducted in December 1941 among 10 groups of inmates showed that Council functionaries were getting the largest food allocations, 1,665 calories a day, compared to an average of 1,125 calories allocated to the general population.[22] In some of the ghettos Council employees established their own kitchens, as was the case in Warsaw, for example, where a kitchen for the ghetto functionaries was opened on June 22, 1941.[23]

Along with Council members, ghetto employees enjoyed a privileged status during the first stages of "resettlement actions." In his telegram to 15 *Leitstellen* of the Gestapo on April 22, 1942, Eichmann ordered the use of Council members and ghetto employees in the accomplishment of "resettlement actions," while they themselves were to be deported by stages, the last ones to be sent away with the last transport.[24] In the Warsaw Ghetto, the functionaries of the Council were among those exempted from the deportations that started on July 22, 1942.[25] Council functionaries were also exempted from deportation in Lublin beginning on March 17, 1942 (the first deportation to Bełżec), in Łódź (during the deportations in 1942), and in many other ghettos.[26] Yet not everywhere did service for the Council safeguard against deportation. Thus in Radom this privilege was accorded neither to Council members nor to ghetto employees during the first "resettlement action" between August 15 and 17, 1942. Only a small number of laborers was left.[27] In places where residual ghettos were established some employees were usually spared to take care of forced-labor duty, distribution of food, and sanitary problems (see Chap. 12).

As a rule Council functionaries were paid wages. In the Łódź Ghetto in January 1942 monthly wages of employees of the ghetto administration fluctuated between 84.50 ghetto marks and 500 ghetto marks.[28] In the Vilna Ghetto there were six different scales of wages, ranging from 45 Reichsmarks to 90 Reichsmarks a month. In January 1943 the minimum wages of an employee in the health department amounted to only 30 Reichsmarks a month. The maximum wage rate of 90 Reichsmarks remained unchanged.[29] After extensive deportations in Lublin in March and April 1942 there were eight categories of monthly wages paid to Council employees in the residual Majdan Tatarski Ghetto.[30] Wages in Pabianice were graded in 14 categories, from 3 zlotys to 25 zlotys a week.[31] On the average wages were very small, taking into consideration the high prices legally charged for food and other commodities. For instance, the worth of food allocated in the Łódź Ghetto in May 1942 amounted to 3.50 ghetto marks per person, which meant that a low-ranking employee with a family of four (and a salary of only 84.50 ghetto marks) had to spend 42 ghetto marks to pay for the meager allocations of food usually distributed three times a month. And there were times when food was more expensive (e.g., 7.50 ghetto marks in January 1943). Only the higher officials with larger salaries could afford to buy anything at high prices on the black market.

The Białystok Jewish Council was wary of paying regular salaries to its functionaries. At a meeting held on January 18, 1942, Barash, the acting chairman, explained that because the staff of the ghetto administration was three times larger than actually needed, it was impossible to pay regular wages. Only four categories—the inspectors in the bakeries, the building superintendents, the police, and the

teachers—were paid salaries. In addition to increased bread allocation ("bonuses"), given mostly to the bakery inspectors, teachers
were paid a monthly wage of 8 marks per teaching hour. Thus a
teacher with a minimum of three teaching hours a day made 24
marks a month. All other functionaries were paid in goods. During
the fall and winter of 1941/42, the basic salary was half a kilogram
of bread a day (in the summer of 1942 the bread portion was reduced to 375 grams). Higher-ranking functionaries, factory managers, and foremen received double bread allocations, but this privilege was abolished in November 1942 in order to create a surplus
and to attract more people to work in the ghetto factories. From
time to time Council officials received stamps entitling them to
potatoes and other inexpensive food staples in larger quantities than
those allocated to ghetto inmates at large. Only in exceptional
cases did the Council pay some cash to employees and laborers. For
instance, before Passover 1942 all department chiefs received 75
marks, employees 50 marks, and laborers 30 marks. Starting in February 1942 cash bonuses were paid on merit only to employees recommended by chiefs of departments.[32]

Because of the chronic financial crisis of the Councils, their employees were not regularly paid, a circumstance frequently deplored
by Czerniakow in his Diary.[33] The Warsaw Jewish Council was so
much behind in payment of wages that when it got a loan of 1 million zlotys (see Chap. 10), over one-third was used to pay overdue
salaries.[34] Employees often lost their salaries as a result of terrible
events that undermined the Councils' finances, as happened during
the expulsions, partial "resettlements," or similar occurrences. Thus
the Lublin Council decided, at a meeting held on April 1, 1942 (an
"action" was then in progress), not to pay employees their overdue
wages.[35]

Wages of employees constituted a substantial part of Council
budgets. In Lublin wages for the year from September 1939 to September 1940 amounted to 38 percent of the total normal expenditures (excluding cash contributions and "services" for the Germans):
143,105 zlotys out of a total of 377,131 zlotys.[36] In Cracow wages
for the Council personnel and retired former community officials
amounted to over 25 percent of normal expenses during February
1940, not counting wages paid to workers on forced-labor duty:
31,739 zlotys out of a total of 125,061 zlotys.[37] In Pabianice in Sep-

tember 1941 wages were over 22 percent of the normal expenses: 4,088 out of a total of 18,425 Reichsmarks.[38]

The Council functionaries had their representative bodies, self-help banks, etc., as for instance in Warsaw, Vilna, Lublin,[39] and probably also in other ghettos where the size of the administrative apparatus warranted.

The material situation of the average employee was not much better than that of the worker in a ghetto shop or even worse than of those laboring in the *Arbeitseinheiten* outside the ghetto. Compared to people laboring outside the ghetto, Council functionaries were disadvantaged in that they had no chance to leave the ghetto and, therefore, had no access to the gentile environment for exchanging goods or smuggling some food into the perpetually starving ghetto.

The chronic lag in payment of wages was often a cause for stormy outbursts and threats of hunger strikes by employees. Thus, for instance, the hospital employees in Warsaw threatened a hunger strike if not paid their overdue wages.[40] Clashes between the Council and the hospital employees occurred one year later. Czerniakow noted in his Diary under the date July 18, 1941:

Got a letter from Milejkowski [chairman of the health department] that he has been forcibly detained in the hospital and will not be released until overdue salaries are paid. Three delegates of the hospital employees [the names are given in the entry] came to force me to pay the overdue salaries, [but] I do not know where to get the funds. I replied that I refused to do so under terror. . . . Over 100,000 zlotys will be needed to pay them tomorrow.

When Czerniakow visited the hospital in October 1941 he was greeted with protests by the employees demanding payment of salaries. They encircled his car, preventing him from leaving the hospital premises (Diary entry of October 14).

Friction also occurred because of worsening working conditions. For instance, a strike of hospital personnel broke out in the Łódź Ghetto on December 1, 1940, following Rumkowski's demand to extend the work day beyond the usual eight hours. Opposition was put to an end by jailing the striking nurses and some of their relatives.[41] In Lublin, too, conflict broke out between the Council delegate for hospital affairs and the doctors and hospital personnel (the reason for this conflict is not given in the pertinent document). At its meeting on December 26, 1941, the Council expressed support for its delegate.[42]

The financial hardship of low- and middle-ranking personnel was a cause of spreading corruption. The hard life of the ghetto, with its constant hunger, weakened the moral standards of some of the inmates, and this, in turn, led to an increase in crime in the ghetto. Unable to sustain themselves on the miserable food allocated to them, people in the ghettos were forced to seek ways and means of providing food staples from the "black market." It was a struggle for physical survival, pure and simple. Employees with access to food distribution were under pressure of terrible temptations. A contemporary source describing conditions in the Białystok Jewish Council relates:

Certainly, the chief of the food department has to fight one of the greatest of all difficulties, expressed in the biblical saying: Thou shalt not muzzle the ox when he treadeth out the grain [Deuteronomy: 25:4]. Hungry functionaries work in the distribution centers . . . , so how can it be taken for granted that they will not try to take something before the population gets its due? But how can it be prevented? This is one of the more serious problems under the prevailing conditions of poverty and lack of food. . . .[43]

Unfortunately there were numerous instances of illegal acts performed not only to satisfy one's own hunger or the hunger of one's family, but beyond this to make a good living out of common misfortune. Both contemporary sources and postwar memoirs complain about the corruption of Council employees.

Bribes were the most widespread form of corruption. Ringelblum notes in January 1942 that, in connection with the order to deliver furs (in December 1941 and January 1942), "bribes played a large role. . . . the Council employees would [for bribes] sell certificates confirming the delivery of furs."[44] In the underground organ of the Bund, *Der Wecker*, we read that when, in January and February 1942, Sienna Street was excluded from the territory of the Warsaw Ghetto, and people had to move into the reduced ghetto area,

apartments were traded, and he who paid well got a good apartment. . . . As a matter of principle, new apartments were given to those banished from their old homes, but they were also given to Council functionaries and policemen who exchanged their old apartments for new, more comfortable ones. . . . Even for the chance to enter the housing department to talk to its employees, one had to pay a bribe of thousands of zlotys.[45]

Ringelblum noted by the end of 1942 that

The housing department is a nest of corruption of the worst type. . . . When one gets an apartment, after long tribulation and anguish without paying a bribe, one then finds out that there is no water or gas available, or that is is a walkup on the fifth floor. The house manager may change the number of the designated apartment, as was the case in the house at 18 Chlodna Street. For the right number [of the apartment] somewhere in the attic . . . an additional fee has to be paid.[46]

We read in a postwar memoir about the Warsaw Ghetto:

Each department was headed by a Council member . . . , but the real chief was the paid senior functionary. In the majority of cases this was unfortunate for the Warsaw Jews. It is perhaps possible to say a good word for some of the Council members and some of the heads of departments who acted with the best of intentions, trying to do their best; but, for the most part, the employees undermined the prestige of the institution and of the Jews in general. A band of dishonest career-seekers obnoxiously officiated, made money, and had a good time, exploiting our misfortune.[47]

During certain periods in the Łódź Ghetto frauds and swindles often occurred in the ghetto administration, particularly in the food department.[48]

A survivor of the Kołomyja Ghetto writes:

At the beginning, the Council had to supply comfortable apartments for German officials and Gestapo men. As a result, Jewish families were forced to leave their good homes. Council employees checked individual apartments, and to our shame and pain searched homes, taking anything of value. Only part of what they took was turned over to the Germans. They later sold a great deal of the valuables to Poles and Ukrainians.[49]

In a semiofficial diary written in the Šiauliai Ghetto, bitter resentment is expressed against corruption on the part of certain officials:

I.R. [a functionary of the transportation department] is one of the leeches of the ghetto, similar to those employed by the [food] cooperative. . . . Z. is also one of them. As a deliverer of meat allocations for the ghetto, he made a fortune for himself. Great effort was needed to remove him from his position. Still worse are the deliverer B., who robbed the ghetto and made thousands of marks . . . , the supervisor of bread deliveries, and a few others.[50]

In the course of a forced evacuation from the Białystok Ghetto to Prużana during September and October 1941, some Council employees were accused of accepting bribes for not including persons in the lists of candidates for evacuation.[51] The Jewish Council issued a special announcement on October 7, 1941 (No. 118), stating that

it has been rumored that in connection with the evacuation, some of the Council's employees have accepted bribes, committing criminal acts. The Council appeals to all those who fell victims, or who have any pertinent information, to inform the presidium immediately. Information can be given in writing or in person. Full secrecy is guaranteed. The victim will get back his money and most severe measures will be taken against the guilty ones.

Frauds perpetrated by some of the employees are reported from Kaunas, Lublin, Lwów, Zamość, Bełchatów, Klementów, Kopyczyńce, and other ghettos.[52]

To fight the plague of bribes some of the Councils enforced disciplinary measures on their own, or established disciplinary commissions or courts. A discipline division was established at the personnel department of the Warsaw Ghetto and, according to an item in *Gazeta Żydowska*, 108 complaints against Council employees were submitted for investigation in June 1940. Of these 45 cases were decided, and 2 cases were turned over for decision by the Council chairman. The cases of those found guilty and suspended (among them 2 cases in course of appeal) were decided in the course of 23 sessions.[53]

Disciplinary authority in the Białystok Ghetto was within the jurisdiction of the presidium of the Council. Each removal of a guilty employee or other mode of punishment was announced to the public. Removed or otherwise punished were: an employee in the labor department, a house superintendent, an inspector in a bakery, a "brigadier" of a labor unit, and nine other employees in the orchards maintained by the Council. The "brigadier" was sent to a penal camp for stealing bread from laborers working under his supervision. Two of the nine employees in the Council orchards were each sentenced to pay a fine of 500 marks or serve a prison term of one month; two others were sentenced to pay a fine of 150 marks or serve two weeks in prison. The remaining employees paid small fines or were sentenced to one or two weeks detention. They had been found guilty of stealing potatoes for themselves or of letting others steal potatoes from the supplies in the orchards.[54]

Up to the time when a disciplinary court was established in Lublin, the Jewish Council itself investigated accusations against functionaries. The Council members presented charges at a meeting of the Council, which then designated a committee of its members to investigate the case. Minutes of a case exist where a commission absolved an employee, finding that the accusation against him, submitted by two Council members, had not been substantiated.[55] Two months later, on November 9, 1940, the Council adopted a resolution establishing a disciplinary court for functionaries. It consisted of one presidium member, one Council member, and one representative of the employees. The Council members designated to act as representatives of the Council were nominated on the spot. Apparently at the request of the employees, the Council included in the court one more representative of the Self-Help Commission of the employees. Thus the disciplinary court consisted of an equal number of Council members and employees. For reasons only vaguely mentioned by the source, a conflict broke out within the disciplinary court. At a meeting held on December 12, 1940, the Self-Help Commission decided to withdraw its two representatives from the court and informed the Council of its decision in writing. The Council accepted the resignation and designated two of its own members to serve on the disciplinary court instead. It was also decided to elect a commission of five Council members to hear complaints from the representatives of the employees, and, if warranted, to conduct an investigation into "the other factors" mentioned in their letter of resignation. It is not known how the conflict was resolved. The disciplinary court did not function for long. By September 1941 a Committee for Personal Affairs is mentioned in the Council's minutes, with the prerogatives held by the former disciplinary court, i.e., to remove guilty persons from the roster of employees. Those dismissed were given the right of appeal to the Council. We find two cases mentioned in the minutes where the Council, on appeal of the employees, changed the verdict of dismissal to one of suspension for a certain term (approximately three months).[56]

A High Control Office was established in the Łódź Ghetto in November 1940. Initially, it consisted of 9 members and 13 inspectors, but, because of Rumkowski's inclination to grasp all authority, the office was disbanded in December 1942, after its composition had twice been changed. The High Control Office had the task of checking the activities of individual departments of the ghetto administration and of dismissing or even arresting employees found guilty of frauds in the performance of their official duties. In accordance with his dictatorial character, Rumkowski took over the right to punish the employees himself, as we learn, on the basis of reports by a high-ranking official of the ghetto administration, the lawyer Naftalin. Rumkowski also issued an order to the chief of the personnel department on April 16, 1941, that all dismissed functionaries be forbidden to get any other position or even work as laborers. This order, in practice, was tantamount to a sentence of death by starvation, for no opportunity to work was available in the ghetto except work supplied by the ghetto administration.[57]

It would, however, be unfair to draw a general conclusion based on the above-mentioned facts that the entire apparatus of the Councils was corrupted everywhere. Unfortunately, for the most part only negative information has been preserved about the functionaries. Corruption was the kind of scandalous news which, when revealed, became the topic of the day in the ghetto. And what was there to talk about concerning the activities of honest functionaries who devotedly performed their tasks? Little was known about them, and they were of little interest to gossip-prone ghetto inmates. To a large degree, the behavior of the employees depended on the example from above, on the attitudes and moral standing of the Council members, and on the spirit of civic responsibility they showed. There is no doubt that a considerable number of the Council functionaries were good, honest, devoted people of high integrity. Unfortunately there is little information preserved about these good men.

We find, for instance, in a diary kept in the Łódź Ghetto that "even among the big shots in the ghetto, there were people of high moral standards."[58] We know of physicians in the Łódź Ghetto (where physicians were on the payroll of the ghetto administration) who refused special food allocations for themselves for the benefit of their patients.[59] Also in the Łódź Ghetto a group of judges and public prosecutors of the ghetto court refused to apply capital punishment, despite Rumkowski's demands on orders from the German authorities. They paid dearly for their high civic spirit. Rumkowski dismissed all of them, forbidding them any other work, and thus in fact condemned them to death from hunger (see also Chap. 8).[60]

Jonas Turkow writes about some functionaries in the Warsaw Jewish Council:

There were also people who had sacrificed their own well-being for the benefit of the community. They did everything possible to cleanse the [corrupt] atmosphere. Suffice it to mention Gornstein the general secretary (later head of the school department), his follower the lawyer Zygmunt Warman, who distinguished himself in underground activities, and Nahum Remba, the chief of the Council's secretariat, nicknamed "the Conscience of the Council." Remba was the "unknown just benefactor." His high moral standards, his heroic and self-sacrificing deeds up to the very moment of his tragic death, were one uninterrupted chain of good, brave work and striving for righteousness.[61]

Ringelblum also mentioned Remba's role in the rescue of people from the Umschlagplatz in Warsaw.[62]

A functionary of the Cracow Jewish Council, Aron Markus, was deported to Auschwitz for the "crime" of assisting victims of the expulsion of Cracow Jews in 1940. Shortly thereafter it became known that he had died. He was an employee of the department of railroad travel permits. The source does not indicate what he was accused of.[63]

Hersz Tenenbaum, an official of the prewar Jewish community and later secretary of the Siedlce Jewish Council, is described as one who "saved many a Jew from the clutches of the Gestapo."[64]

Nazi reprisals directed against members of the Councils were often applied against employees too. In Warsaw 24 Council deputies were arrested in the building of the Council in November 1939 in order to obtain their agreement for the establishment of the ghetto; a number of functionaries present at the time were also arrested.[65] Among those arrested in the Vilna Jewish Council on September 12, 1941, were 5 Council members and 11 other people, for the most part employees. They were confined to the Lukiszki jail and later perished in Ponary.[66] Ringelblum noted under the date of May 11, 1941 that "in Otwock, one hundred ghetto employees were taken to labor camps because the *Kehila* [the Jewish Council] did not deliver the ordered number [of forced laborers]."[67] There are many more known cases of Council functionaries who were persecuted for the "sins" of the Councils.

As was the case with the nomination of Council members, the Germans often forced the Councils to hire people of their own choice, with the apparent intention of planting informers in the Councils or of granting favors to people who had served them well. This happened in Warsaw,[68] Kaunas, [69] Lublin,[70] and probably in a number of other ghettos from which no information is extant.

Functionaries who lost favor with the Germans or were suspected of illegal activities were severely persecuted by the Gestapo. Jacob Nisenbaum, a Council employee of Lublin, was shot to death in the street.[71] And in Tarnów a functionary of the Jewish Council was shot to death because he did not rise when a Gestapo man entered the office.[72] People employed by the Council were severely beaten in the Włodzimierz Wołynski jail,[73] etc.

The Germans were displeased by the fact that the Councils employed large numbers of people, thus depriving them of additional workers for their own purposes. Prior to the liquidation of a ghetto the Germans usually ordered the Councils to reduce their personnel. Thus Czerniakow noted in his Diary, under the date March 2, 1942, that the *Gettokommissar* had ordered him to reduce the Council's personnel by 10 percent to 20 percent.[74]

When the Łódź *Gettoverwaltung* launched preparations for the final liquidation of the Łódź Ghetto, it ordered Rumkowski to reduce his personnel. Biebow, the head of the *Gettoverwaltung*, visited various departments and shops in March 1944, made a list of employees, and simply dismissed many, ordering them to do physical work in the shops or to build barracks in Radogoszcz. Even high-ranking officials, judges, the head of the Council archives, and others were ordered to work in Radogoszcz. The largest reduction of personnel took place in the food department (food supply had for a long time been managed by the *Gettoverwaltung*). Of 2,623 employees in the soup kitchens, 677 were fired. The Vocational and Control Commission was disbanded altogether, some employees being sent to complete the contingent of 1,500 laborers ordered for work outside the ghetto.[75]

Before the "resettlement action" in Lwów in August 1942, the personal certificates of the ghetto functionaries were invalidated and the Jewish labor office was disbanded.[76] In the Vilna Ghetto, too, the personnel of the ghetto administration was reduced once more in June 1943 to provide more workers for ghetto industry.[77]

Council personnel faced a difficult moral dilemma during partial expulsions and "resettlement actions." In exchange for being exempted from the looming disasters, the Germans demanded that Council employees help in the "actions" by making lists of candidates for expulsion or deportation. This problem will be discussed at length (see Chap. 16) in connection with the role of the Councils during these fatal occurrences in the life of the ghettos.

Mutual Relations between the Jewish Councils and the Diverse Groups in the Ghettos

THE SOCIO-ECONOMIC GROUPS

WAR OPERATIONS, expropriation of Jewish property, and forced mass displacements caused an economic disaster of unprecedented dimensions for the Jewish population in the occupied areas. The disaster was accentuated after expulsions and confinement in the ghettos. Jewish merchants, industrialists, traders, and artisans lost their businesses, factories, or shops located outside the ghetto limits. They were thus cut off from Polish markets where they had been active for generations (see Chap. 5). Formerly well-to-do people were ruined, falling into an abyss of poverty. At the same time individuals and entire groups succeeded in staying on the surface with their families either by chance, by smuggling, by proving themselves useful to the occupiers, by speculation, or by achieving a favorable position in the ghetto hierarchy. These people became the *nouveaux riches* of the ghettos. Thus no complete leveling took place: chance, boldness, readiness to take risks, the ability to keep one's bearings under any circumstances—all these contributed to the appearance of unequal levels in the social status of individuals and groups among the economically impoverished ghetto inmates.

An inmate of the Łódź Ghetto noted: "The wheel of fortune turned around. The former merchant or industrialist had to bow his head in front of a nobody, a contemptible fellow, who would never have been able even to come near that respectable person before the war."[1]

Stratification by Reason of Origin

The mere designation of ghetto limits caused a division of the ghetto inmates into two distinct segments: natives and resettled Jews. People who had lived, worked, or traded inside the area that became the ghetto continued in their homes or places of work, though they had to share their homes with resettled newcomers from "Aryan" parts of town. These people also had undisturbed access to their places of business located within the limits of the ghetto, and to the merchandise they were lucky enough to hide from the Germans. Resettled Jews, however, lost not only their sources of income, but often moved into the ghetto with no more of their belongings than they were allowed to carry in their arms or transport in handcarts. This was the case in the large ghettos—Warsaw, Łódź, Vilna—and in many small places. For the most part, furniture had to be left behind because of the orders of the police (in Warsaw and Łódź) and because means of transportation had been confiscated long before the ghettos were established.

There were, however, enterprising individuals who succeeded in moving substantial parts of their property into the ghettos. The Jews in Vilna, for example, were allowed to carry into the ghetto bundles of belongings and only 300 Soviet rubles (30 marks) in cash. Gold and other valuables had to be surrendered directly before entering the ghetto. Fearing dreadful consequences (the first slaughters had already occurred in Ponary), the majority of people, for the most part middle class and professionals, complied with the order. Others, however, took a chance and carried into the ghetto food, cash, and valuables hidden in their clothes. For the most part these were coachmen, teamsters, black-market dealers, and underworld operators.

By sheer chance people were randomly assigned to the abandoned living quarters of, say, a prosperous Jew who had run away with his family or had been taken to Ponary. Others were permitted to remain in their old homes or to share apartments with relatives in the ghetto, or they were given lodgings in ruined or emptied apartments formerly occupied by the poor. Still others remained homeless or were assigned dwellings in attics, cellars, or stables. This last category, the most numerous one, destined inmates to live the life of the ghetto beggar.[2]

In Warsaw the Jews who had occupied comfortable homes, now

located in the "Aryan" section of town, were forced to exchange their apartments for one-room or two-room apartments formerly belonging to Poles, mostly janitors, poor artisans, or laborers who had lived in the ghetto area.[3]

There was also a sharp distinction in the ghettos between people who were at least lucky enough to remain in their native towns and those who were newcomers, refugees and expellees (see Chap. 6). These uprooted people, without means or relatives, fell to the very nadir of human misery and despair.[4] Mutual relations between native ghetto inmates and newcomers varied, depending on time and place. At first, as long as the material situation of the indigenous population was not yet desperate, compassion was shown and help extended to the newcomers. They were taken into private homes, given clothing, food, etc. Relief committees sprang up, and the local branches of the Jewish Social Welfare, together with the Jewish Councils, made a joint effort to establish kitchens and to distribute cash, food, clothing, etc. In time, however, the native Jews became impoverished themselves, and the old talmudic saying, "The needy of your own town come first," was frequently implemented to the detriment and resentment of people recently arrived. Wherever newcomers were concentrated in large groups they tried to establish their own relief committees, and it often happened that between these committees of newcomers and the local relief committees friction and controversies sprang up concerning the distribution of relief allocations from the JDC and the JSS.[5] Instructive in this respect are the debate and the resolutions adopted by the conference of delegates of the local branches of the JSS in Chełm county at the end of January 1942, where the delegate from Siedliszcze reported that "of the 2,100 Jews there, 800 are desolated newcomers in desperate need of assistance. The whole *shtetl* is poor. We distribute . . . bread among the needy people to the detriment of others who are thus deprived of part of their own allocations."[6] The resolution adopted speaks for itself: "As far as the resettled people are concerned, they should be treated *on an equal basis* [italics added] with permanent inhabitants . . . extending special financial and moral assistance in all fields . . . to resettled persons and to laborers. . . ."[7]

In Łódź bread allocations were not increased in the ghetto despite the arrival of approximately 20,000 deportees from Central Europe, a fact that was greatly resented and held against the newcomers.[8] An eyewitness relates that in the Krzemieniec Ghetto "there

A painting of Chaim Rumkowski, the "Eldest" of the Jews in the Łódź Ghetto. It is indicative of the tenor of the times that paintings such as this one were often done to curry favor with Rumkowski, perhaps for extra rations. Another shows Rumkowski hovering in flight over the night-darkened ghetto, angelically protecting it from harm.

Chaim Rumkowski addresses an outdoor meeting.

was terrible resentment against newcomers. They lived off indigenous Jews, took over positions (in the ghetto administration), and mutually assisted each other in competition with permanent ghetto inmates." The two successive chairmen of the ghetto Council were newcomers, constantly quarreling and causing harm to the ghetto. One of them came from Czechoslovakia, and the other had formerly been a resident of Łódź.[9]

Jews driven into the ghettos from adjacent towns and villages sometimes had representatives in the Jewish Councils. Naturally these representatives were first of all concerned with the fate of their fellow expellees, an attitude that caused conflicts with indigenous Council members.[10]

The Case of the Central European Jews

During the period 1939 to 1941 no fewer than 50,000 Jews from the Reich and the Protectorate were deported into the ghettos in Poland, Latvia, Lithuania, and Byelorussia. Sporadic deportations also took place during 1942.[11] These people constituted a special group of strangers in their imposed places of domicile, different from the so-called *Ostjuden* even in their looks. For the most part these expellees had been upper-middle-class people, merchants, industrialists, professionals, and intellectuals unable to adjust themselves to an economy where the only kind of work of value to the Germans and hence available to Jews was, at best, skilled labor. The expellees' adjustment to ghetto conditions met with hard, often insurmountable difficulties. They were profoundly disappointed on arriving in the ghettos. They had been told that they were being taken to work either in industrial towns or in agricultural colonies. But they were confined instead in an Eastern European ghetto to live in great poverty. They had not lived in ghettos before their expulsion. Their economic situation had been, in the main, bearable, and therefore the sudden change was the more shocking, leading to alienation and hate.

Language was an important divider, separating indigenous Jews from newcomers. The Central Europeans regarded Yiddish-speaking ghetto inmates as culturally inferior people and looked at them with condescension and disdain. Only those from the Protectorate (from Prague, Brno, etc.) were somehow able to adjust in the matter of language, because their language, Czech, was similar to Polish, the second official language in the ghetto. Sources dealing with both Łódź and Zamość substantiate this finding.[12]

The legalistic mentality of Jews from Germany and their apparent loyalty to the German ghetto administration contributed to mistrust of all the Jews from Central Europe. They were open to suspicion because they looked for favors from the Gestapo and because of apprehension that some of them might be undercover Gestapo agents or informers. In some of the ghettos, in Zamość and Riga for instance, the police were recruited mainly from among the expellees, which only made the ghetto inmates' animosity more acute.[13] An additional factor contributing to mutual bitterness was the large number of Catholics and Protestants of Jewish origin among the expellees (see Chap. 9).

By its very nature, the ghetto of the Hitler era was not a place prone to create solidarity or mutual understanding between two so immensely diverse groups, with misery the only link between them. Only those expellees sensitive to the Jewish catastrophe, to the obliteration of their Jewish and human philosophy, could feel the urge to rapprochement with the culture and way of life of Eastern European Jews, and to bring about a return to their ethnic roots. The majority, elderly people of long-established habits, life philosophy, and manners, were unfit for such a far-reaching transition. Almost all maintained a passive attitude toward the life and the conditions they faced in their new environment, where bitter fate now forced them to live. Instinctively, they defended themselves against identification with indigenous ghetto inmates, trying to separate themselves by all means from the "natives" in the belief that this might save them from submerging into the mass of the ghetto population. "They were not so much sorry for being dragged to Zamość, as for being equated with the Polish Jews," commented a survivor of that ghetto on the feelings of the 2,100 expellees driven there from the Reich and the Protectorate.[14] The situation became even more acute during the "resettlements" in Łódź in May 1942 and, later, from June to August 1944, when Central European Jews went obediently to the assembly places, still nourishing the illusion of eventual return to their former homes where, they hoped, conditions would be more favorable for survival.

In the Łódź and Riga Ghettos, for instance, indigenous inmates were convinced that the deportation and annihilation of large numbers of native Jews was caused by the arrival of expellees for whom living space had to be found.[15] On the other hand, the expellees from Central Europe complained that during the "resettlement actions" the Councils tried to spare the indigenous Jews to the disadvantage of newcomers. This is mentioned in a contemporary document pertaining to the "resettlement" in the Łódź Ghetto in May 1942, for the most part affecting the deportees from Central Europe.[16] In Zamość, too, the number of victims among deportees in the course of the ghetto's liquidation was much larger than the number of indigenous Jews.[17] The objective reasons for this phenomenon were twofold: a large percentage of deportees were over fifty years old (over 54% in the Łódź Ghetto), and there were fewer working people among them.[18]

Social Structure in the Ghettos

The ghetto regime brought on a deepening of socio-economic differences among the inmates. The social structure of the majority of the ghettos took the form of a pyramid with a sharply narrowing peak. Above all, at the very top, were the Jewish Council, the leading functionaries of the ghetto administration, and the police. These were the privileged groups, exempt from the curse of forced-labor duty, from deportation to the labor camps, and, as a rule, from the "resettlements" until the very end. They were also privileged in their food allocations in that they were, officially and otherwise, in a position to benefit from smuggling, secret bakeries, and illegally operating restaurants.[19]

The ghetto police were particularly well off, having adequate means (through bribes and secret dealings with ghetto sentries and smugglers) to derive additional income and to protect themselves against hunger. Their uniforms, hats, and armbands with all kinds of colors and inscriptions, along with their generally better appearance, conspicuously distinguished them from the shabby, emaciated ghetto inmates.[20] Also they lived in comparatively better homes.

In the Kutno Ghetto, established in the area of a ruined sugar mill, a small clique of Council members and ghetto functionaries, together with several prosperous families, occupied the few buildings in the ghetto. Meanwhile (in June 1940) the vast majority of inmates were left squatting outside and were later assembled in the ruins of the mill halls, tunnels, cellars, and stables. The house occupied by the ghetto elite was ridiculed as "the House of Lords" by the ghetto inmates.[21] This was the name given also to the house where Council members lived in the Pabianice Ghetto.[22] In the course of assigning apartments in the Chełm Ghetto, ". . . no consideration was given to the size of a family. . . . it all depended on the price paid for a more comfortable place."[23] The same attitude has been noted in connection with the "summer residences" occupied by Rumkowski and his associates in the Łódź suburban ghetto, Marysin, and in other ghettos as well.[24]

Individuals who became rich because of their readiness to join the ranks of smugglers, to deal with corrupt German officials, or to participate in other illegal dealings, constituted another group of economically privileged people in the ghettos. Thousands of such people lived in the Warsaw Ghetto. As Ringelblum noted in his Diary:

Even Napoleon could not solve the smuggling problem [the "continental blockade"], and the contemporary dictator will not succeed either. The amount of money involved in smuggling is very high. I was told of a company of four smugglers who made 35,000 zlotys in a single week. . . . The smugglers are lavish spenders. Easy come, easy go. The parties given by smugglers are notorious in the ghetto. . . . The smugglers come from the lowest classes: they deal in stolen goods, and they are professional thieves, former porters, pimps, underworld figures. Polish and German guests come to their parties, people of common interests and dealings.[25]

Similar facts were also reported from the ghettos of Vilna,[26] Białystok,[27] and Kaunas,[28] as well as other places. But the smugglers did not last long. As a result of the merciless war the authorities waged against smuggling, a smuggler's "career" was short-lived. It was impossible to bribe every guard; sooner or later the smuggler was shot down by German ghetto sentries or otherwise liquidated by the Gestapo.

Next in the privileged ghetto hierarchy were the employees of the ghetto administration, whose ranks increased exceedingly as compared to prewar personnel employed by the Jewish communities. To these privileged ones belonged the diverse specialists, the brigadiers of the labor units, the skilled workers in the ghetto shops or in the various German labor places outside the ghetto. Those employed by the Germans outside the ghetto took advantage of very risky opportunities to trade with non-Jews, Germans included, bringing scarce, high-priced food items into the ghettos.[29] Laborers in the ghetto shops and those employed in the ghetto administration were in a somewhat better position too. As a rule the food allocations of these groups were better. Moreover, they were sometimes spared being sent to labor camps outside these ghettos where some ghetto industries were in operation; and, in the course of the "resettlements," they were more often deported to concentration camps than to annihilation camps.

The next to lowest level on the ghetto pyramid was that of the nonworking inmates, the big mass of paupers on relief, clients of the soup kitchens and their families. They were usually the first victims of hunger, cold, sickness, forced labor, and deportations to labor camps. They were also first on the list of candidates for deportation to death.

These well-known facts are related in contemporary documents pertaining to the ghettos of Warsaw, Łódź, Lublin, Šiauliai, and many others.[30]

The establishment of more than one ghetto in a given town was a concealed form of selection for annihilation. Those placed in the worse ghetto were annihilated after a little while, and the ghetto was liquidated. In Vilna, Głębokie, Kobryń, and Nowogródek, for instance, the Germans established for the "nonuseful Jews" (i.e., aged, sick, maimed, unskilled, or otherwise unfit for labor) a special ghetto (Ghetto No. 2). All those who were not given the so-called Yellow Certificates or Blue Family Certificates distributed to specialists and their families in Vilna were placed in Ghetto No. 2. The majority of these were killed in Ponary in October 1941.[31] Along with the "nonuseful Jews" in Głębokie, artisans unable to pay the fee charged by the Jewish Council for living in the first ghetto were also confined in Ghetto No. 2, which was liquidated first.[32] In Nowogródek skilled workers and their families (some 5,000 persons) were confined in the so-called first ghetto located in the buildings of the county court; the rest of the Jews were put up in the school of the Nazareth Sisters. After selection, almost all of the inmates of the second ghetto were driven out of town and killed on December 5, 1941.[33]

There were three ghettos in Kołomyja. The first, the privileged ghetto, was occupied by Council members, employees of the ghetto administration, the ghetto police, and the ghetto elite in general. "To get a room in this aristocratic ghetto, one had to pay a wealth of money." This ghetto remained longest and was liquidated at the end of the "resettlement actions."[34]

Such were the general socio-economic conditions of life in the ghettos. A further analysis in depth, however, shows that in those ghettos where the economy was not under the rigid control of the Germans and (as in Łódź) also of the Jewish Council, and where individual inmates were still able to exercise some economic freedom, the social structure was even more complicated and diversified.

In the Warsaw Ghetto numerous socio-economic groups with hard, distinguishable lines of separation appeared in 1941. In the insecure, unstable, and often wavering conditions of ghetto life it was easy to fall suddenly from comparative comfort to a level of extreme poverty (the reverse situation seldom occurred). The following groups could have been distinguished in the Warsaw Ghetto:

a) Poor people dying of hunger, who found shelter among ruins, on staircases, or in one-room apartments, 15 to 20 people crowded together. They were insufficiently sustained by the Councils and by various service organizations. Many of them lacked even the token price of 10 groszy to pay for the soup distributed by public kitchens.

b) Peddlers of homemade candy, cigarettes, and similar wares, making from 1 to 3 zlotys a day when (in June 1941) the price of 1 kilogram of bread was 27.60 zlotys on the black market.

c) Petty smugglers, for the most part little children sneaking out of the ghetto past the sentries, through the fences and in passing trams. They smuggled food (mostly bread) into the ghettos, usually making between 2 and 5 zlotys a day.

d) Respectable unemployed people, selling their personal belongings and housewares, unwilling to degrade themselves by peddling in the streets.

e) Traders in clothing, shoes, used garments, and other second-hand things. At various times, depending on the market, they made 10, 20, or even as much as 100 and 200 zlotys a day.

f) Traders in vegetables, fuel, etc.

g) Several thousand people employed outside the ghetto, making 3 zlotys and 20 groszy for a day's work. These people, however, had an opportunity to make money by trading illegally on the "Aryan" side.

h) Formerly prosperous people who systematically sold their jewelry, expensive household pieces, garments, underwear, etc.

The following were good money-makers:

i) Former owners of big enterprises who had been lucky enough to save part of their prewar stocks or who now had the opportunity to acquire new merchandise. To the same group belonged the middlemen in large, illegal business exchanges of currency and rationed articles.

j) The wholesale smugglers of food, fuel, etc.

k) Former teachers, lawyers, physicians, and nurses who were employed mostly as functionaries by the Jewish Council and by the welfare service organizations.[35]

Summing up our discussion of this subject we may conclude that there were, in all ghettos, inmates on various rungs of the social ladder, their status depending on the amount of property they had saved, their opportunities to establish contacts outside the ghetto, their position in the ghetto hierarchy, their length of residence, their degree of displacement, etc.

There was no social peace in the ghetto because there was no equality among the inmates. Quite the opposite was true. During the entire life of the ghettos, an intense social ferment prevailed, fed by the sharp contrast between the indescribable poverty of the majority and the relative comfort of the small minority (enough bread to eat was considered a luxury in the ghettos). Some of these people were able to work their way up, exploiting the common hardship and enjoying the favors of the authorities, or committing fraud, misdemeanors, etc.

The weird, crippled structure of the ghetto notwithstanding, it represented a social cell of sorts, with a death sentence suspended over it and a "privilege," granted by the hangman, of struggling in the meantime for its bare physical existence. As already mentioned, the first victims were the economically ruined Jewish middle class, the uprooted masses of refugees, and the poor in general. The more prosperous element, by paying bribes as long as possible, strove against oppressions and resisted the effects of the destructive policies implemented against the Jews by the Germans. Until the period of the mass "resettlements," sufficient means provided a better chance for survival. Even in the course of the liquidation actions in the ghettos, people with enough means still had opportunities to seek cover on the "Aryan" side. This struggle for survival, and the privileged position of some segments of the inmates, contributed to the creation of sharp animosities among the ghetto population; for under ghetto conditions one had a chance of rescue mostly at the expense of his neighbor. Competition that would have been characteristic of a normal society took on drastically different shapes in the ghetto, where a bitter struggle for survival was going on all the time. No other civilized society up to the Hitler era had experienced a situation where discrimination resulted eventually in loss of life.

ATTITUDE OF THE COUNCILS TOWARD THE SOCIAL GROUPS IN THE GHETTOS

The objective situation in the ghettos forced the Councils, in order to execute the exorbitant material demands of the Germans, to rely on well-to-do elements to finance numerous cash contributions and "services." Furthermore, the furniture and housewares of prosperous Jews was fit for the homes of German officials, which the Councils were constantly being ordered to furnish.

The right of the Councils to release people from forced-labor duty was a source of substantial income; but, at the same time, it was also the cause of injustices perpetrated upon people of insufficient means in no position to pay for release from this insufferable duty that endangered life and limb. Bitter complaints are noted in innumerable sources against allowing the rich to ransom themselves from this calamity and against putting the entire burden upon the shoulders of the impoverished masses, especially since so-called voluntary enrollment for forced labor was usually accomplished in the course of night raids and chases after people were summoned by the Jewish police[36] to report to assembly places.

It should be borne in mind, however, that the fee charged for release from forced-labor duty was used to pay minimal wages to forced laborers who otherwise worked for nothing or for token wages at German labor places. They would simply have died from hunger without this money.[37]

During the so-called "voluntary enrollment" many people among uprooted refugees and those on relief were willing to substitute for people ready to pay for release from forced-labor duty. For instance, in memoirs pertaining to the Staszów Ghetto we read, under the date June 1942:

The Jewish Council was ordered voluntarily to deliver 100 Jews for work at the ammunition camp at Skarżysko. The Council promptly prepared a list . . . of boys and girls from among the refugees and the native poor in town. The Jewish police took those listed into custody at night, and they were sent away the next day. Before they left, they were given working clothes and a little money.[38]

The man in charge of the Jewish labor office in Jaworów "scrupulously utilized every opportunity to send helpless, sick, and poor Jews to work in the labor camps."[39] The labor distribution official of the Jewish Council in Bransk "put on his list mainly the poor, orphaned youngsters."[40] The Council in Żelechów "accepted money from the rich, but seized the poor and sent them to work at forced labor. For the most part, these unfortunates were refugees from both Warsaw and little [adjacent] towns."[41] Similar facts are monotonously repeated in scores of memorial books and by eyewitnesses.

We saw in Chap. 6 that the Councils endeavored to give clothing, food, and some cash relief to forced laborers both before their departure and in the labor camps. Often this was done under pressure from their families, but it was never enough to soften the severe grievances of the laborers against the terrible injustice committed against them.

Another aspect of Council policies was their tax policy, which generally favored indirect taxation. In the Warsaw Ghetto the finance department adopted a policy that people without income should not pay taxes. This was fine for normal times, but in the ghetto were formerly wealthy people who had saved all or part of their property in the form of foreign currency, valuables, garments, or house furnishings, and who, not having any income, still managed to live comfortably by selling their assets. Another problematic group was the successful smugglers, the clandestine manufacturers of food, articles to be exported from the ghetto, and the dealers in foreign currency. Their income was illegal and secret, and therefore they, as well as the group of formerly well-to-do ghetto inmates without visible sources of income were not liable for payment of direct taxes.

A member of the Warsaw Jewish Council, the engineer Rosen, gave the following answer in a questionnaire of *Oneg Shabat*, the clandestine Jewish archives:

This principle [that people without known sources of income should not be taxed] was perhaps right for normal times, but under present conditions we are not interested in enabling the Jews to accumulate property or prevent their assets from decreasing. . . . The right yardstick should be the present standard of living. If one eats white bread and meat, . . . takes meals in restaurants, then it makes no difference how he makes his living—by working or from income derived from selling his houses or his diamonds. He must pay taxes to [provide means] to maintain the poor. Here is an example of how the Warsaw Jews are [ostensibly] paying. In the house where I live, there live wealthy Jews who together pay 25,000 zlotys a month rent. But the same house pays [the Jewish Council] no more than 1,000 zlotys a month in taxes and various voluntary contributions, i.e., only 5 percent of their [*sic*] rent.[42]

As already mentioned, the Council charged 2 zlotys a month for each ration card. All had to pay except the very poor. In addition a registration fee was charged by the food department.[43] The Council pharmacies (no others were permitted) surcharged medicines with a 40 percent markup for the benefit of the Council (see Chap. 10). In a note in *Der Wecker* we read that "as estimated in knowledgeable circles, up to 20,000 ration cards were not taken out by the poor because they could not obtain certificates entitling them to get the card free of charge, and they nevertheless had no money to pay the fee."

The income figures in the budget of the Warsaw Jewish Council for the year 1941 clearly demonstrate the nature of its tax policy: of the total tax income of 10,500,000 zlotys the direct taxes (the community tax and the hospital tax) amounted to 1,705,000 zlotys, but income from the 2-zloty fee charged for ration cards alone brought in the sum of 4,567,000 zlotys, or 43.5 percent of the Council's total income.

A similar tax policy was implemented by the Cracow Jewish Council. A special 10-zloty tax was introduced on September 26, 1940, to be paid by every person of both sexes twenty-one years of age and older (see Chap. 10.). The Council in Lublin practiced a more equitable policy in that it resolved not to charge people on relief the fee of 1 to 3 zlotys for disinfection of homes and courtyards in the Jewish section. Thus over one-third of the ghetto inmates were released from this payment.[44]

Neither was the special taxation for welfare services in the Warsaw Ghetto based on a just principle. In an open letter written by A. M. Rogowoj, the well-known Orthodox journalist and coworker of the Council, dated September 5, 1941, we read:

If one takes a close look at what is happening in our community, one can see that we are constantly rotating in a vicious circle of social injustice. Our entire welfare system is based on injustice and wrongdoing. . . . I have already mentioned on another occasion that the policy of reducing bread rations [by 10%] for social welfare is an injustice perpetrated against the poorest. It means that the poor, swollen from hunger as they are, living in mere shelters but blessed with many children, have to give more to support our charitable institutions than do the rich. . . . It appears that this is not an exception to the rule, since our entire welfare system operates in such a way as to burden not the rich or those making a living, but the hungry, the swollen beggars, the customers of the soup kitchens.[45]

Emanuel Ringelblum expressed a similar view on the financial and tax policies of the Warsaw Jewish Council, concluding that "the Jewish poor in Warsaw bear the burden of the Council's budget."[46]

Another characteristic social policy of the Councils, this one emanating from the "rescue-through-work" idea (see Chap. 16), was the privileged position enjoyed by those ghetto inmates who were harnessed into German industry within the ghettos or employed in German labor places outside the ghettos. The Councils in many ghettos tried by every means within the limits of their meager power to improve the material and moral conditions of these workers. They were given substantial food allocations, larger rations, better living quarters, etc.[47] Increased food allocations were made possible because of supplementary allocations for the workers, seldom granted by the authorities, or—and this was a more common feature—at the expense of the nonworking population. The Councils were ordered to do this in accordance with the Nazi policy of classifying Jews by two categories: the "useful ones" (i.e., those who labored) and the "useless, harmful ones," who were robbed of parts of their food rations for the benefit of the first category.[48]

A poll conducted among 10 groups of inmates in the Warsaw Ghetto during December 1941 showed that the highest consumption of food (1,665 calories) was among Council employees, as compared with 1,407 calories consumed by independent artisans and 1,229 calories consumed by shopworkers. The average consumption of food among the ghetto inmates was 1,225 calories.[49] Supplementary monthly bread allocations for the police, employees of the Council, social institutions, patients in the hospitals, and 30,000 laborers in the Warsaw Ghetto in the winter of 1942 were already mentioned in Chap. 14. In other ghettos too (e.g., Vilna and Białystok) the police sometimes received supplementary food allocations.[50]

In the Łódź Ghetto, in accordance with Rumkowski's "rescue-through-work" idea, a sort of food pyramid emerged as a result of the German food supply policy that aimed at dividing the population into two principal segments, those working for the benefit of the Germans and those unemployed. Depending on the level occupied by a given individual, he was allocated his meager portion of food. On top were those entitled to the so-called *Beiratzuteilung* for ration cards marked with the letter "B." Here were included members of the Council of Elders and high functionaries of the Jewish ghetto administration (such as the chiefs of the departments or of the ghetto shops and factories, the masters of artisans, and instructors, and the members of the cooperative of physicians and pharmacists). All were given a supplement of various food staples— mainly meat, flour, and sugar—obtainable at four designated stores. All in all it was a rather small group of highly privileged ghetto inmates, some 1,500 persons, as of mid-May 1942.[51]

To the second privileged segment belonged the lower ghetto administration personnel, workers in the ghetto shops, laborers employed at public works, working long hours or amid bad sanitary conditions, the police, the foremen, the chimney sweeps, and the janitors. Apart from their regular food rations, they received food supplements for so-called extra food stamps, beginning in March 1942. Extra certificates marked "No. 1," affording larger allocations, were given to workers, and extra food stamps marked "No. 2," affording smaller supplements, were issued to ghetto functionaries. In addition workers in shops received one or two plates of soup daily at their places of employment, paying 25 or 30 pfennigs. By the end of May 1943 Rumkowski had established soup kitchens for certain categories of workers where so-called nourishing meals were distributed. By the end of October over 7,000 persons were being served in these kitchens, but only some 3,000 remained by the end of November 1943.

At the bottom of the food pyramid in the Łódź Ghetto were the unemployed, the most populous segment in the period from 1940 to 1942.[52]

The Germans considered unemployed inmates to be harmful

gluttons, an unnecessary burden hindering the ghetto's food supply. Auerswald, the *Kommissar* of the Warsaw Ghetto, was of the opinion that relief should be given only to those engaged in work, and he tried to influence the Jewish Council and the JSS accordingly.[53] In the report of the German criminal department of the Łódź Ghetto, dated July 28, 1942, the writer suggests improving the food allocations of working Jews "by separating them from their parasitic relatives by all means available . . . and taking over control of food allocations, for many working Jews can be found who are able to contribute greatly to the benefit of the state, but who are on the brink of starvation and are dying because of bad diet."[54]

Biebow, the *Amtsleiter* of the German *Gettoverwaltung* in Łódź, who was personally very interested in increasing the output of ghetto industry, complained in his memorandum to the Gestapo on March 4, 1942, and to the *Bürgermeister* on April 19, 1943, that, on the one hand, it was questionable whether Jewish workers were still productive and able to work, inasmuch as their health had been undermined as a result of insufficient nourishment; and on the other hand, despite the fact that the output of Jewish workers was of a higher quality than that of Poles, the latter got much better food allocations than did the Jews.[55]

Segregation of the inmates with respect to food rations was a source of great dissatisfaction in the ghettos, though it could have been argued that this inequity was necessary to preserve the existence of the ghetto through achieving greater productivity, a task of vital concern to all. This line of reasoning led consequently to a situation where the weaker elements in the ghettos—those unemployed, those in need of relief, the sick, children, and the elderly—were the first victims during expulsions, "resettlements," and other such "actions." This practice sprang from the illusory expectation that by delivering to the German death machine elements without any or with very little chance of survival, it would be possible to save the working Jews. This rationale, that it was important by all means to save working inmates who might yet have chances of survival, along with the more biologically valuable elements of the young generation and the intelligentsia, at the expense of the others—this rationale is stressed in the various preserved statements of contemporary ghetto leaders. This vital aspect of the social policy of the Councils with respect to the ghetto inmates will be discussed at length in Chap. 16.

FAVORITISM AND CORRUPTION

Along with the protection of some segments of ghetto inmates, one of the Councils' important "rescue" considerations, the sources also tell of various kinds of favors, bordering on corruption, extended to certain social groups and to individual protégés. The sources indicate that these people paid a price for favors. We shall cite only a limited number of pertinent cases.

In the Warsaw Ghetto a Council member in charge of forming the Jewish police was accused of accepting bribes of 500 zlotys for giving applicants jobs with the police.[56] Similar accusations were made in the Councils at Zawiercie[57] and Horostków (Tarnopol county).[58]

Some Councilmen in Warsaw were accused of becoming silent partners in a business favored with a license by the Council's economic department to manufacture marmalade, honey, and candy.[59]

Contemporary sources from the Łódź Ghetto strongly indicate that a system of favoritism was practiced by the Jewish ghetto administration, starting with the men at the very top. Rumkowski, for instance, took upon himself the right to issue supplementary food stamps at whim. As Tabaksblat relates, he favored certain Orthodox groups and rabbis. He considered food allocations his own domain and allowed no control over what he did.[60] Favoritism bloomed in the food supply apparatus of the ghetto, and friendship with the food department management or with the personnel of the food stores, vegetable storages, and soup kitchens was very helpful.[61]

Also mentioned in the sources are instances of bribes for release from forced-labor duty. An eyewitness account in the Zamość Ghetto states that "when people came begging to release members of their families [from work at the Bełżec labor camp], members of the Jewish Council charged from 300 to 1,000 zlotys a person. People bargained and wept, assuring Council members that they had no such sums. . . ." The eyewitness suspects that the Council members took a percentage of the money for themselves.[62]

In the above-mentioned eyewitness account concerning events in Horostków, it is related that when a transport of 160 workers was assembled at the railroad station to be sent to the labor camp in Stupki, near Podwołoczyska, "the community benefactors made a deal with those able to pay well, so that only 147 people were sent away." The eyewitness, himself one of the 147 sent away, adds that his father was able to get him released by paying a large ransom to the Council after he had stayed in the labor camp for two months.

Because of this practice of accepting ransom money with which to pay off German labor commandants, rumors inevitably circulated, particularly among those in no position to pay, to the effect that the Councils made money on such deals. Moreover, no official accounting was possible in these transactions. But even accepting as fact the suspected misdeeds, it is still questionable whether the money went into the pockets of individual Council members or was used to cover exorbitant Council expenses made to satisfy countless greedy German functionaries.

There were also complaints against the Councils for allegedly protecting some protégés against expulsion in exchange for money. In an eyewitness account of the expulsion to Sławotycze (Lublin district) in December 1939, the Radzyn Jewish Council is blamed for trading in so-called residence certificates, whose owners were entitled to remain in town. Those without such certificates had to leave.[63] It is now hard to establish who benefited from the deal. It is quite possible that the Council tried to collect a fund to cancel or ease the execution of the expulsion order.

Some Councils were blamed for protecting cronies in the course of preparing lists of payees of cash contributions imposed by the Germans. For instance, in memoirs about the Żelechów Jewish Council, it is indicated that when the ghetto was ordered to pay a contribution of 40,000 zlotys in cash, and a committee was established to collect the money, "the Council sent us [the eyewitness was a member of the committee] instructions to release their friends from payment—people who had not contributed a penny until then." The committee resigned in protest.[64] Unfortunately no indication is given why the Council ordered them to release these people from participating in the contribution.

We have already mentioned above cases where the Councils granted some people the privilege of living in the "productive parts" of the ghetto, considered more secure.

Some sources blame the Councils for releasing from deportation transports people in a position to pay gold, cash, or diamonds, substituting for them people who were not on the "resettlement" lists at all. Such accusations were made against the Jewish Councils in Zawiercie[65] and Międzyrzec.[66]

It is said that the Council in Horodenka sold labor cards during a "resettlement" action, ostensibly granting life to the purchaser. The price was 100 dollars a card (presumably meaning U.S. dollars). The eyewitness added mention of the rumor that the Council had taken all the money for its own use.[67]

CHAPTER 16

The Strategy and Tactics of the Councils toward the German Authorities

INTERVENTION AND BRIBERY

THE JEWISH COUNCILS learned quite early that they had fallen prey to a government which recognized no legal restraints with respect to the Jews. They faced an unremitting enemy whose attitude toward the Jewish population and its representatives aroused grave worry and foreboding. The problems of dealing with the sworn enemy of the Jewish people were a source of constant anxiety and heated controversy, both within the Councils and in the communities at large.

Having lived in hostile environments and been oppressed by inimical authorities, the Jews throughout the ages had not accepted persecution without attempting to find remedies. Appealing to the authorities (both subalterns and their superiors), Jewish notables had used whatever influence they could muster for the good of the community. Now, trapped by the Nazi occupiers in their hour of highest anguish, the Jews once more tried to use their traditional remedies. The Councils busily addressed petitions to the occupation authorities describing in detail, though usually in very cautious terms, the ravages that had befallen the Jews, and requesting that their bitter lot be improved. Personal interventions were made at the proper government offices (notably in Warsaw and Kaunas) in an effort to reverse such cruel measures as the establishment of the ghettos, to lessen hunger and starvation in the ghettos, to ease the tribulations of some of the population groups (i.e., refugees facing more expulsions), and to improve the lot of forced laborers maltreated by German and native overseers alike, of merchants robbed of their businesses, of artisans unable to get raw materials, or of persons arrested for no reason. One could extend the list of problems which had to be taken up with occupation authorities *ad infinitum*, for the woes were endless.

In contrast to petitions submitted at a later date, the Jewish petitions and statements of the first period of the occupation were at times daring in that they openly stated objections to and requested relief from the persecutions imposed by the Germans. Typical in this respect is the statement adopted by the Warsaw Council shortly after the Germans occupied the Polish capital. In November 1939 an underworld character (who happened to be a Jew) shot a Polish policeman to death in Warsaw. In retaliation, and in accordance with their policy of attributing collective responsibility, the German authorities decreed that a penal fine of 300,000 zlotys be made by the Jewish population. In addition they demanded that the Jewish Council name five of its members as hostages to be shot in case the fine was not paid on time. On the motion of one of its members the Council adopted a resolution to pay the fine under duress, but, at the same time, to submit in writing a statement to the Gestapo "that the Jewish population cannot and will not accept the proposition that all Jews are collectively responsible for the act of an individual Jew. The Jews bear no guilt and see no reason why they have to be [collectively] punished. We are paying the money not as a punishment, but only because we are forced to."[1]

Some other Councils were also quite outspoken in their initial approaches to the German authorities. Not only did they describe in their petitions the horrible situation of the Jews; they also stressed the causes forcefully. For example, the petition submitted on February 15, 1940 to the *Oberbürgermeister* of Piotrków Trybunalski by Zalman Tenenbaum, chairman of the Jewish Council, stated: ". . . starving people, weakened by persistent freezing weather, pressed into the strait boundaries of the ghetto, in homes without the most elementary conditions of hygiene, the mass of them wandering with continuous shipments of thousands of people [from one place to another], are liable to cause an explosion of epidemics."[2]

At later stages of persecution, under an avalanche of increasingly severe blows, the tenor of the petitions changed.

Interventions with the authorities began during the first weeks of the occupation, when the outlawing of the Jews and a wave of continuous terror forced the legitimate prewar representatives of Jewish communities (no Jewish Councils yet existed) to intercede with the German authorities throughout the occupied territory of Poland. An early example was the letter addressed by the executive of the Jewish community of Lublin on October 10, 1939, to the "Honorable *Landrat*" [county chief], in which attention was called to the oppression of the Jews of that area, and a request was made to end it. The letter mentions pogroms in the Lublin and Krasnystaw districts, mainly perpetrated by Polish criminals released from prisons after the war had begun, and the suggestion is made that military guard posts be established in these localities to prevent similar occurrences in the future. Obviously out of fear to describe them in more realistic terms, a number of acts of terror are only warily hinted at as "causing chaos and disturbing peace and order." Listed were the following incidents: soldiers had demolished a prayer house and desecrated the Holy Scrolls; soldiers had requisitioned merchandise and tools without producing orders from proper authorities; and Jews were being caught in the streets at random and used for forced labor; or, in other instances, chased from queues in front of the City Hall during the distribution of ration cards among the poor.[3] That this petition was to no avail can be seen from a later one (though it has no date, its contents indicate that it was written in approximately May 1940), in which the Jewish Council repeated complaints it had made in its first petition—that the military's requisitions continued without proper authorization and that Jews were still being caught in the streets for forced labor. In addition new complaints were made: Jews engaged in forced labor were not secure of life and limb; shops and homes and whole buildings owned by Jews were being confiscated; Jews were beaten for failing to salute German soldiers (though, the petition indicates, it had been clearly established by competent authorities that no such order had been issued); no packages or legal assistance were allowed to arrested Jews. Similar to other Jewish petitions of the period, this one also concludes with a number of requests which sound quite bold: to end the polyarchic system under which almost every local office of the government had its own official to deal with Jewish problems; and to repeal the special limitations ordered for Jews by the Security Police—such as the prohibition against lighting homes after eight o'clock in the evening (which was also the curfew hour for Jews), sealing off streets where Jews lived, etc. Moreover, the petition requested that the order prohibiting use of the railroad by Jews be revoked or at least liberalized, that Jewish lawyers be permitted to practice their profession, and, generally, that Jews be given rights equal to those of Poles.[4]

Interventions were made in the interests of the entire community or for the benefit of individuals. In the short time from August 30 to September 19, 1940, the Jewish Council in Warsaw approached the German authorities concerning 18 problems, such as canceling the requisition of the furnishings from Jewish schools, allowing Jewish coachmen to continue their trade,[5] etc. Particularly numerous petitions were submitted during the move into the ghetto (first half of November 1940), in which the Council stressed that it was simply physically impossible to move approximately 130,000 Jews out of the "Aryan" sectors of the town into the small, desolate, mostly one-room apartments of the approximately 50,000 Poles who had lived in those parts of the town assigned to the ghetto. Other petitions stressed the heavy material losses of the entire Jewish population sealed off in the ghetto, the danger of epidemics, etc. To at least four petitions submitted from October 27 to November 12, 1940, elaborate statistical tables were attached supporting the contentions of the Council.[6] All these petitions were summarily rejected.[7]

After the Warsaw Ghetto had been established, the Jewish Council submitted petitions to various government offices regarding 40 problems during the three weeks from November 22 to December 12, 1940.[8] A special department, the Field Office, was even established by the Council to deal with the German authorities in various problems, such as arrests, confiscations of food, etc.[9] On December 17, 1940, after the Warsaw Jews had been in the ghetto for over a month, Adam Czerniakow submitted a petition to the chief of the Warsaw district (resettlement division), in which he described the plight of the Jews shut off within the ghetto and asked for an increase in the meager food rations and the number of food commodities allowed the inhabitants of the ghetto. Otherwise, he warned, "the great majority of the Jewish population, which has no steady income and no assets, will not be able to satisfy even the most rudimentary necessities of life and will be condemned to death by starvation."[10] This petition also remained a voice in the wilderness.

Seldom did Jewish petitions have any success. Thus Ephraim Barash of the Białystok Ghetto, summarizing the results of the

A meeting of the Warsaw *Judenrat*.

Rabbi Feiner (holding document) and Rumkowski (to his left) at a meeting in the Łódź Ghetto.

The office of Adam Czerniakow, chairman of the Warsaw *Judenrat*.

The office of the Jewish Self-Help in the Warsaw Ghetto. Most of those pictured here are clerks.

Jewish Council's interventions at a meeting with its officials held on November 2, 1941, said:

. . . as far as it was possible, the following concessions were obtained regarding the [German] demands: 6 kilograms of gold [may be submitted] instead of 25 kilograms; 2½ million [rubles] instead of 5 million; the present borders of the ghetto [were fixed] instead of limiting the ghetto to the territory of Chanayka [a section of Białystok where the most destitute Jews had lived]. No more than 4,500 persons were evacuated to Prużana, instead of the entire Jewish population [of Białystok]. The demand for lists of Jewish professionals was rescinded. All this was achieved because of our good relations with the authorities, but not without long and hard labor.[11]

A few more places can be cited where petitions had some success, though often only for a while. Thus when the Germans were planning to establish the ghetto in Warsaw, as early as November 1939, it was possible by intervention with the military to postpone the decision;[12] in Włodzimierz Wołynski[13] and Żarki the establishment of the ghetto was also postponed;[14] and in Byteń the territory of the ghetto was enlarged.[15] In Šiauliai 31 Jews (among them 10 women) were released after successful intercession by the Council of Jewish Elders. The Jews had been accused of smuggling food into the ghetto, and their release had been achieved under the pretext that they were needed for digging turf.[16] In Warsaw 151 arrested Jews were released on March 11, 1942, in exchange for 1,500 fur coats delivered to the authorities. Among the arrested, who had all been detained in the Jewish prison, were 40 who faced death sentences because they had been seized on the "Aryan" side.[17]

At times, however, such interventions could be dangerous. For example, all members of the Jewish Council in Stołpce were arrested for interceding on behalf of an arrested Jew. The Council members were detained for 24 hours and subjected to severe beatings.[18]

The intercessions were, as a matter of course, accompanied by bribes for the officials involved. Because of the widespread corruption of the German occupation apparatus, bribery was one of the most common means of "softening the hearts" of Nazi bureaucrats and of their helpers among the natives. By dealing with the authorities, the Jewish Councils learned how insatiable they were to acquire material goods in any shape and by all means. Their greed for desirable goods of all kinds was bottomless. Seldom were any of them inaccessible to bribe. On occasion, too impatient to wait for delivery, officials went to the Council offices to pick up their bribes in person. The general policy of spoliation of the Jews implemented by German occupation authorities was so intense that the border-line was quite often indistinguishable between, on the one hand, allegedly "legally" imposed deliveries of goods and, on the other, bribes brazenly demanded by corrupted German overseers.

We have already commented on the widespread extortion prac-ticed by the Nazi bureaucracy (see Chap. 4), saying that in some of the ghettos (e.g., Lwów and Żółkiew) there were actually special offices under inconspicuous names whose task it was to find expen-sive "gifts" to satisfy the demands of German administrative and police functionaries. Some of the Councils, like the one of Skałat, maintained stocks of precious jewelry, hard liquor, rare delicacies, hard to get during the war—all for treating Nazi visitors.[19] Sim-ilarly the Council of Białystok maintained a warehouse stocked with furniture, textiles, dinnerware, and other household articles to be able, in an emergency, to give the Germans "a present."[20]

Hoping to save the lives of Jews in ghettos by satisfying the glut-tony of the Nazis for Jewish property, the Councils appealed to the ghetto population for the greatest material sacrifices to ransom their bare physical existence. These appeals brought often the desired results, for people had learned from past experience that when expulsion time came, everything would be lost anyway.

Memik Garfunkel, the former chairman of the Jewish Council of Zamość, relates in his extensive eyewitness account:

. . . The main financial worry of our Council was the necessity of cover-ing growing expenses for bribes, gifts, and other expenditures for the benefit of various dignitaries, Gestapo men of higher and lower ranks, German policemen, gendarmes, and other officials. It soon became clear that this was the only way, the only basis on which some mutual rela-tions could be established and the only possibility for obtaining relative peace. Unfortunately, the amounts necessary for this purpose kept grow-ing and reached the sum of 150,000 to 200,000 zlotys a month. . . . Most expensive proved to be the house, or rather the complex of buildings, which the Jewish laborers built as a gift for the First Company of the SS *Todtenkopf Reiter* Regiment, with materials delivered by Jewish merchants and industrialists. This alone cost one and one half million zlotys. The German County Chief Weichenheimer (a native of Stuttgart) cost us 300,000 zlotys. Enormous amounts of money, which are now hard to estimate, fell into the pockets of the Gestapo men during three years.[21]

There is a plethora of material from first sources on the subject of bribes the Germans forced the Jews to pay. We shall here limit ourselves to a few outstanding cases, in addition to those already mentioned.

One example involved the little ghetto of the township of Żarki in Radom county in the Government General. In his memoirs, printed in the Żarki Memorial Book, one of the survivors relates:

Among various measures of persecution, there was one depriving the Jews of their stores. This was a severe blow. The Jewish Council tried to rescind this order, and after paying large sums of money to the local authority in Radom . . . poor shopkeepers were permitted to continue in business. No sooner did we get rid of this disaster when another one struck us. A so-called *Selbstschutz*, consisting of *Volksdeutsche* and Poles in unifrom, was established in the township. Its members were burly people of low standing who exploited their new positions without restraint. Anyone who came across their path was severely beaten. . . . Once again the Jewish Council tried to get rid of this plague, and once again the old maxim "Money answereth all things" (Ecclesiastes 10:19) proved a remedy. The band of murderers was removed. . . . Then came the order from the authorities in Radomsko to close up and isolate the ghetto. Again the Jewish Council undertook energetic steps, and for a substantial amount of money it was possible to rescind this order too. The ghetto in Żarki was not fenced off.[22]

In the ghetto of Poczajów (Krzemieniec county) the Council had to pay a large amount of money to cancel a degrading order to deliver twenty Jewish girls, eighteen to twenty years of age, for the pleasure of soldiers in a house of shame.[23] In Radoszkowice the Council was ordered to submit a list of Jewish Communists "sympathetic to the Soviet Union" (until the German-Soviet war, this little Polish township had been occupied by the U.S.S.R.). Only "after great effort and payment of money . . . was the order canceled."[24] In Staszów a number of Jews were caught for forced labor on September 27, 1942. After the intervention of the chairman of the Council, Efraim Zynger, and, of course, after paying ransom, they were released.[25] Two Brańsk Jews escaped from a Lublin camp back to Brańsk. They were saved from almost certain death after the *Kommandant* of the Brańsk gendarmes accepted a bribe, though the camp *Kommandant* had insisted that the escapees be returned to Lublin. Three more Jews of Brańsk were also saved by the same means from the death penalty for smuggling food into other ghettos.[26] In Markuszów (Lublin district), bribes helped the Council to reduce the number of people demanded by the German employment office for forced labor in the camp at Janiszow.[27] A survivor of the Piotrków Trybunalski Ghetto relates that the chairman of that Council, not only paid a ransom in cash to prevent the confiscation of many items, but also paid bribes to quash cases threatening Jews with prison and even death sentences.[28] In Chmielnik, the Jewish Council succeeded in freeing the majority of those employed as forced laborers at the melioration works in Biała Podlaska, but not before "paying large amounts that ended up in the pockets of Hitlerites, in addition to gifts of most exquisite garments and valuables."[29]

Bribes also flowed into the pockets of all kinds of collaborators among the natives. In Baranowicze "The Council collected money to bribe the authorities among the Germans and Poles. The former Polish police commissioner, Bakhar, was in charge of housing problems on behalf of the Christian Citizens' Committee [of Baranowicze]. He readily accepted bribes, so that it was possible to avoid many measures of persecution."[30] In Grójec the Jewish Council paid off Polish overseers for treating Jewish forced laborers with consideration. The memoirist adds that "Poles gladly accepted bribes, yet they did not stop beating up [the Jews]."[31] In Łachwa, after the Council bribed a number of Byelorussian policemen and some Germans, the Jews were able to take some housewares into the ghetto from the homes where they had lived before the ghetto was established on the eve of Passover 1942.[32] In Parzewo (Wołkowysk county) "Jews could live in relative peace" thanks to bribes paid systematically first to the Polish town administrator, and, after November 1941, to the German *Kommissar* and the gendarmes. The Council also obtained permission for a number of refugees from neighboring localities to remain in the ghetto.[33]

When an office holder of the administration or the police was transferred, after having been "softened," the bribe game started all over again, and fresh efforts had to be undertaken to "soften" the new appointee.[34] Facts to this effect are known from a large number of ghettos.

The highest organs of the occupation authorities were well aware of the prevailing corruption. For instance, the Intelligence Office (*Forschungstelle A*) of the Aviation Ministry at Łódź noted on

January 22, 1941 (No. 142) that it had received instructions from the Gestapo to include in its wiretapping activities the telephones of the *Gettoverwaltung* and its chief, Hans Biebow. The reason given was that valuables confiscated or otherwise taken from the Jews had not been accounted for.*[35]

Paying bribes to the Germans was a method widely practiced by the Jewish Councils before and even in the midst of "resettlement" actions. (During final "resettlements" other means were also used, more about which below.) Unaware of Hitler's secret order for the physical extermination of the entire Jewish population, the Councils acted under the delusion that the timetable and dimensions of "resettlement" were within the competence of local authorities. Therefore they believed that, as had so often happened in the past, they would now also be able to sidetrack a current calamity by paying even larger bribes or, if necessary, by surrendering all Jewish property. Thus when news of "resettlement" in a neighboring town reached an as yet unaffected ghetto, its Council rushed to apply the tested remedy in order either to repeal the "resettlement" altogether, or at least to postpone it or reduce its scope. From extensive source materials we shall here cite only a few cases.

In the already mentioned eyewitness account of the chairman of the Jewish Council in Zamość, we find the following statement: "We soon learned what took place at the [death camp] Bełżec [at the end of March 1942]. One can imagine our fear. . . . We undertook energetic steps in all directions, still believing that the "resettlement" depended on local factors and that we might avoid the fate of the Lublin Jews."

In Lublin the "resettlement" had started on March 16, 1942.[36] What "energetic steps" meant we know from the portions of the chairman's account already cited. When rumors spread about "actions" in the neighborhood, the chairman of the Jewish Council in Mir, Eliahu Baruch Shulman, accompanied by another member of

* Widespread bribery was common not only in the ghettos, but also in the camps. Judge Hoffmann, presiding at the trial of former SS-men of Auschwitz in Frankfurt/Main between December 1964 and August 1965, stressed in his verdict that horrible corruption had been common practice in the camp. None of the personnel, from the highest ranking officer to the lowest underling, was free from having taken bribes. There was scarcely an SS man who had not made himself rich with money, foreign currency, valuables, and garments taken from the Jews brought for extermination to Auschwitz. . . . In the Auschwitz camp, one could buy everybody, everything had its price [*Judgment*, p. 55]. And Auschwitz was no exception.

the Council, went to the local chief of the gendarmes with gifts of gold watches and jewelry, hoping to postpone the catastrophe.[37] It is related that a member of the Jewish Council of Włodzimierz Wołyński, Symcha Bergman, "selected the best diamonds and gave them to the district *Kommissar* in an effort to postpone the ominous order hanging over our heads, but it was to no avail."[38]

Attempts were made to stop "actions" already started, or, at least, to ransom those Jews who could pay off the Germans. On the third day of the "resettlement" in Częstochowa (the "action" began there on September 22, 1942) those Jews who had thus far escaped deportation were assembled in the metallurgy factory. A group from the shops who paid large sums in gold and valuables were also sent to this place. "Members of the Jewish Council officiated there and took it upon themselves to mediate [between the Jews and the Germans]. They cashed in fresh ransom money for the Security Police . . . , sacks of gold, jewelry, and diamonds were given over to Council members. Yet the deceived, doomed Jews were all put into cattle cars and sent to Treblinka."[39]

The already quoted chairman of the Council of Zamość tells in his account that during the first day of the "action" on April 11, 1942, when a large crowd of Jews had already been assembled (the authorities had called for 2,500 persons) at the ordered place, "taking advantage of his [the Gestapo chief's] good mood because the 'action' was going forward with success, I slipped into his hand a diamond ring, which I had kept ready for him. He ordered them to stop the 'action' . . . . The joy of those who returned to their homes was as great as the desperation of those unfortunate ones who remained surrounded by the crowd of German guards."[40]

After the second "action" at Hrubieszów, on October 28, 1942 (the first "action" had taken place on June 2, 1942), the Jewish Council openly initiated a collection for ransoming the small number of Jews who still survived. The price was "from 50 to 200 grams of gold (14 carat) per person." Together with another person, the witness was chosen to check the quality of the pieces delivered. It is worthwhile to quote from the pertinent part of this eyewitness account: "When we came to the Jewish Council we met with the chairman, Shmuel Brand, in the presence of other members. The safe was opened, twelve gold watches with gold chains were taken out. . . . We were asked to clean the watches. . . . I and the watchmaker, Bekerman, worked all night long. . . . The guests [county officials] came in the afternoon, and the gifts were divided among them."[41]

A similar attempt at ransom took place in Będzin, in May 1943, after two "resettlement actions." "Scores of crates with silver candlesticks, candelabras, spice boxes, Hanukkah lamps, and other valuables were delivered to the Gestapo by the Jewish Council."[42] Three months later the Będzin Ghetto was liquidated. There is a somewhat vague report that the Lublin Jewish Council also tried to pay a large ransom to repeal the "resettlement." According to this report, two members of the Council and the ghetto police decided who was to pay how much toward the ransom. They collected gold and jewelry from ghetto inmates. However, a few days after the collection had started, both Council members were arrested by the Gestapo and they disappeared without a trace.[43]

For granting that Jews be allowed to go to their homes before deportation, the Council of Zarszyn (near Sanok) "gave the local Gestapo a few kilograms of gold collected from the Jews." The witness adds that the Jews "knew that death had been postponed only for a few days."[44]

It goes without saying that all this bribery failed to change the ultimate fate of the doomed Jews. Whatever success the bribes may have had was only temporary. In the last analysis bribery was only another form of spoliation of Jewish property by the Nazis. Jews themselves deliberately gave up their possessions into the hands of their oppressors in the fervent, though futile, hope that perhaps, somehow, at the very last moment, delivery might yet come. Occasionally these delaying tactics paid off and brought about some positive results, even if only for a short time.

THE "RESCUE-THROUGH-WORK" STRATEGY

We have already mentioned in Chap. 5 that industry in the ghettos was important not only for purely economic reasons, but because it also had weighty aspects in connection with the idea that the Jews could be rescued from their fate. We shall now endeavor to analyze, in more detail, "rescue-through-work" as a fundamental element in the strategy of the Councils vis-à-vis the Germans before "resettlements" and even after "resettlements" were partially completed. The practical implementation of this strategy stemmed from the assumption that the work of Jews within and outside the ghetto for the benefit of German war industry could serve as a basis for survival, or at least for a reprieve from extermination. One finds these theoretical considerations in the preserved speeches of prominent leaders in a few larger ghettos.

The most outspoken propagator of the idea that the lives of ghetto inmates could be preserved only by work was the Elder of the Łódź Ghetto, Rumkowski. On innumerable occasions, in all his public utterances both before and during the "resettlements," he untiringly repeated that the physical existence of the ghetto depended solely on labor useful to the Germans and that under no circumstances, even the most tragic ones, should the ghetto give up this justification for its continuation. In an address delivered to deportees from Central Europe on November 1, 1941, barely one month before preparations for deportations from Łódź had begun, he said, *inter alia*:

When I moved into the ghetto on April 6, 1940, I told the mayor that I was moving in the belief that this was a gold mine. When he, astonished, asked for an explanation, I told him: "I have forty thousand hands for work in the ghetto and this is my gold mine." As I began successfully to organize work, the authorities gradually began to deal with me and to count on me more and more. . . . Today there are 52 factories in the ghetto testifying to my success in creating places of employment. These factories have been visited by the highest representatives of the authorities on many occasions, and they have been amazed. They repeatedly have told me that up to now they had known of only one type of Jew—the merchant or middleman—and had never realized that Jews were capable of productive work. I shall never forget the reaction of one of the dignitaries from Berlin. Noticing a patrol of the ghetto police in the factory, he was sure that their duty was to chase people to work. I informed this gentleman that the duty of the policemen was rather to chase away the many people constantly searching for some kind of work. . . . Work provides the best publicity for the ghetto and enhances confidence in it. The multi-millions of credit [meaning the loan of 3,000,000 marks—see Chap. 10], is a clear expression of this confidence.[45]

We have already mentioned Rumkowski's emphatic speech, delivered at the opening of an exhibition of products manufactured in five shops in the ghetto at the end of December 1942 (see Chap. 5). His slogans—"Work is our currency" and "Work is our guide"—were painted in large letters over posters displayed in places of work, at production shows, and during mass rallies.[46]

Another enthusiastic preacher of "rescue-through-work" was Ephraim Barash of the Białystok Ghetto. At a mass meeting of the ghetto population, called by the Jewish Council in the *Linas Hatzedek* hall on June 21, 1942, he said:

From the political point of view, the main danger of the Białystok Ghetto is the fact that it is the largest and the most populous one [in the Białystok district]. Steps have to be taken so that our 35,000 inhabitants achieve justification [for their existence], so that we may be tolerated. We have transformed all our inhabitants into useful elements. Our security is in direct proportion to our labor productivity. We already have 20 factories in operation. Any day now, there will be opened a weaving factory, a factory making wooden lasts, a woodwork and a wheel factory. . . . You are all aware of the visits we have recently had. It is hard to enumerate them all, and I shall only mention those most important ones, on which the fate of the ghetto depended. . . . All delegations have expressed their satisfaction with our work, and we received massive orders after the last visits. The visits brought about a continuously improving attitude toward us. The very person who, from the start, was totally against us, now has become friendly. Instead of contributions, evacuations, etc., we are now given subsidies for our institutions, for the kitchens, training courses, hospitals, and also for industry. But the financial aspect [of the changed attitude] is not as important as is the friendly attitude toward us.[47]

Barash formulated the strategy of "rescue-through-work" in even more bold terms in the speech he delivered in the same hall on October 11, 1942, before invited members of the Jewish Council, the chiefs of ghetto enterprises and their assistants, house managers, police commissars, firemen, and others. According to the minutes, this is what he said on that occasion:

. . . There have recently appeared tangible menaces throughout the Białystok district,* and in the town of Białystok itself. It is imperative that we find means to postpone the danger, or at least reduce its scope. Unfortunately our Białystok has recently become the largest ghetto next to Łódź, and this is our great danger. . . . There simply have to be special justifications if we are to evade the calamity. . . . But if only

* A large-scale "resettlement action" had been launched in the Białystok district on November 2, 1942. For a time, however, the inhabitants of Białystok, Prużana, and Grodno were spared.

14,000 persons work out of a population of 35,000, even the well-disposed among those in authority may pose the question: "Where are the others?" . . . You know well where extermination starts—from those who do not work. . . . There must be an end to all nice ideas about normal times! He who is capable even of only lifting his arm has to work and thus increase the security of all. The proportion of 14,000 workers against a ghetto population of 35,000 is a menace. Even had the authorities not demanded more workers, we, on our own initiative, should have made every effort to penetrate the economy, so that a hiatus would appear and we should be missed if we were destroyed. As I have already indicated, this is what we hope for, not to wait for their compassion, particularly since we do not satisfy their continuous demands [for more workers]. One can easily imagine the consequences![48]

Still another advocate of the "rescue-through-work" strategy was Jacob Gens of the Vilna Ghetto. In a speech delivered before the brigadiers (foremen) of work units in January 1943 (the exact date is unknown), he stressed the importance of work for the continuance of the ghetto:

While working for ghetto industry or for the commandos [Germans] outside the ghetto, we have, contrary to the trite opinion that we are poor workers, shown that we are very useful and irreplaceable. Under present war conditions, work in general and work for the German army in particular is the command of the hour. . . . It is urgent that we make changes to increase the output of the workers and thus enhance the justification for our existence.[49]

In the Vilna *Geto-yedies*, there often appeared such slogans as, "Jewish woman, remember, work saves blood."[50] On September 6, 1943, when large-scale mass deportations to Estonia from the Vilna Ghetto were in full swing (they had been launched on September 1), Gens ordered the remaining inhabitants to register in order "to be able to return to normal life in the ghetto as soon as possible." He threatened that the right to bread cards and employment would be revoked for those who disobeyed.[51]

Moshe Merin, whom the Germans installed as chief of the Central Office of Jewish Communities of Upper Eastern Silesia, also considered work for the benefit of the occupation authorities a mainstay of his rescue strategy. In Będzin at the end of June 1942 he called a meeting of young people, exhorting them to report voluntarily to the German labor office (*Arbeitseinsatz*) for work in camps. He tried to convince them that their sacrifice would give the remaining Jews a chance to stay in town. He even enlisted the help of Rabbi Yitzhak Groysman. However, Merin failed. He then requested that German shop managers release some of their Jewish workers whom he intended to send to the labor camps. In the end, on orders of the plenipotentiary in charge of alien labor (*Sonderbeauftragter für fremden Arbeitseinsatz*) 500 young men, who ostensibly were called for a checkup, were actually transported to the labor camps.[52]

To what extent some of the Councils, against all odds, believed that work (in conjunction with bribes) might provide a panacea for their plight can be seen from a discussion at a meeting of the Jewish Council of Częstochowa. The meeting was called to hear a report by Nathan Eck, who had escaped from Warsaw after the mass deportations there. It should be borne in mind that, at that time, the mass "resettlements" in Lublin, Radom, Kielce, and other ghettos, as well as in the Polish capital, were already over. I quote excerpts from Eck's report, as printed in the *Yiddisher Kemfer* (No. 718, September 12, 1947):

What depressed them most was our (Eliezer Geller, a member of the Zionist youth organization Gordonia, also participated in the meeting) account of what had been happening in the shops in Warsaw—namely, that Jews had been dragged for deportation out of the shops too. As soon as I mentioned it, they looked at each other in bewilderment. I was deluged by questions. . . . I learned during the meeting that they were then engaged in building a very large shop, a factory, under the sponsorship of the German mayor himself. They very much hoped that this would contribute to the security of a substantial number of Jews.

Summarizing the discussion at the end of the meeting, Mr. Pohorile, an able lawyer, said:

It is true that the Germans have now launched mass murders of the Jews, but from all that we have heard so far, it still does not follow that this must occur everywhere. It seems that in Warsaw the Jews are not secure even while working in the shops; but from what we have now learned from the report, it follows that there is a great difference between the fate of the shop-Jews and the other Jews. While *all* the others are summarily taken away, the shops are raided only once in a while, which means that the chances of the shop-Jews are, at any rate, much better than those of the others. In view of this, we in Częstochowa must speed up the building of the shop. We have also heard here that before mass deportations started in Warsaw [i.e., July 22, 1942] a number of incidents took place signaling the imminent calamity. We must, therefore, be alert for such signals here in Częstochowa, though so far—and here he glanced at his colleagues as if to ask their consent—we have noticed nothing of this kind, praised be the Lord.

Despite the fact that the ghettos had been sealed off, the assumption that employment might make rescue possible spread from ghetto to ghetto through escapees, special emissaries, and other channels. A witness relates that the Council of the ghetto of Staszów, in search of information on how other ghettos had acted in face of looming disaster, sent out a special man "who looked like a true Aryan." He came back with the news that "there were certain German places of work for Jewish laborers who, for the time being, were in no danger of destruction. The leading Council members immediately made energetic efforts to create legalized employment places and thus save the largest possible number of Jews from their unavoidable fate."[53]

According to sources at our disposal, it can be stated that not only in large ghettos but in a great number of small ghettos there was a widely shared belief that the employment of Jews for the benefit of the Germans was an outstanding course for achieving rescue.

When people in the town of Łuków (Lublin district) complained that the Jewish Council had done nothing to prevent imminent disaster, they received the answer that "it is necessary to work. . . . it is possible that the Germans will not bother workers at employment premises, and that they will live." A frantic search for places to work ensued. People tried by giving bribes and gifts to find better, more secure German employment places.[54] It is alleged that Hendler, the chairman of the Jewish Council at Brzesko (Cracow district), advised the Jewish population on the second day of the "resettlement" to clench their teeth and continue working, since labor was the only rescue possibility available.[55] As in some other places (see Chap. 4), there were two ghettos in Drohiczyn (Pińsk district), one for unskilled or unemployed workers and one called the "productive ghetto." According to the testimony of a witness, the Jewish Council maintained that it would be unable to save the ghetto of unskilled workers, some 1,600 persons, for their fate had already been sealed.

They hoped, however, that following their intercession the other ghetto would survive the war.[56]

There were towns where the Jewish Councils, as a last resort against destruction, made efforts to establish "productive ghettos" on their own initiative, or put large contingents of workers at the disposal of the Germans, or even establish labor camps in the ghetto. A few examples follow.

Shatz, chairman of the Jewish Council in Wilejka, initiated the establishment on the festival of Purim 1942 of a ghetto for approximately 1,000 skilled workers and their families, under the supervision of the county *Kommissar*, Schmidt.[57] When the Council of Chełm felt that their ghetto was next in line for "resettlement," it put 6,000 workers at the disposal of the *Wasserwirtschaftsamt* ("Waterworks"), which had been engaged in a melioration project in the Lublin district.[58] The Council of Skałat, "after strenuous efforts and very large gifts of gold, was able to get permission from *Obersturmführer* Rebel to establish a [labor] camp for the Jews of the ghetto in Skałat."[59] The Jewish Councils of Zamość[60] and Tłuste[61] acted similarly.

The policy of employment as a rescue strategy was probably encouraged by the attitude of certain circles of the occupation authorities, notably the military, who had sometimes expressed their opposition to the rapid and total physical extermination of the Jews. Though on the whole the *Wehrmacht* and the *Einsatzgruppen* in the occupied territories of Soviet Russia cooperated in the Final Solution, this cooperation was not always smooth.[62] The intra-office correspondence of some occupation authorities in areas invaded by the Germans after June 1941 (when mass murder of the Jews began to take place concurrently with the victorious advance of the German army) indicates that the contradiction between the economic interests of the *Wehrmacht* and the political exigencies of carrying out the Final Solution appeared very early. When the Germans occupied the Ukraine and Ostland they found that Jewish artisans and skilled workers were predominant. In a number of small towns the only artisans and skilled workers were Jews. The following exchange of correspondence demonstrates the point.

The Ministry of the Occupied Eastern Territories in Berlin, in a letter to Heinrich Lohse, the *Reichskommissar* of Ostland, inquired on October 31, 1941, on what grounds he had prohibited the execution of the Jews of Liepaja. A complaint in this matter had been lodged by the Reich Security Office.[63] In his answer, dated November 15, 1941, Lohse explained that he had stopped the Liepaja executions "because the manner in which they were performed could not be justified." On his part Lohse inquired whether the liquidation should engulf all the Jews of Ostland, without regard to age, sex, or economic factors—i.e., whether skilled Jewish workers employed in the war enterprises of the *Wehrmacht* were also involved. He concluded that he, naturally, agreed that cleansing Ostland of Jews was an urgent matter, but that, in his opinion, it should be accomplished in harmony with the interests of the war economy.[64]

In accordance with this point of view, and following the request of General Bremer, chief superintendent of the army commander in Ostland, Heinrich Lohse issued on December 3, 1941, an instruction to the Higher SS and Police Leader in Riga and the commissars general in Tallin, Riga, Kaunas, and Minsk, in which he stated, among other things:

The Chief Superintendent of the *Wehrmacht* in Ostland complains that because of liquidations the military is losing skilled Jewish workers employed in armament factories and repair shops who cannot now be replaced. I urgently request that you not allow the liquidation of those Jews who work in armament factories and repair shops for the *Wehrmacht* and who, at present, cannot be replaced by the native [workers]. . . . Measures must be undertaken at once to train native substitutes. The same applies to Jewish skilled workers who, although not directly employed by the *Wehrmacht*, are engaged in work important for the war economy.[65]

When Lohse's pragmatic position became known in Berlin, he immediately received from the Ministry of Occupied Eastern Territories a clearcut instruction that, "as a matter of principle, no economic factors were to be taken into consideration in the solution of the Jewish question. Should any problems arise in the future, advice was to be requested from the Higher SS and Police Leader."[66] This meant that the orders of the Reich's Security Office would prevail.

However, the *Wehrmacht*, having in mind its economic considerations, did not give in. Characteristic in this respect is the secret report of Gentz, the Baranowicze *Kommissar*, dated February 10,

1942, addressed to the *Generalkommissar* in occupied Byelorussia, Wilhelm Kube. The Baranowicze *Kommissar* complained that local *Wehrmacht* authorities

have from the very start, used the [services of the] Jews with whom it is easier for them to communicate [in Yiddish]. . . .They have exploited their monopoly as skilled artisans and workers in industry and trade. . . . The military, in general, employ the Jews, the more so because the Council of Elders just established took over the functions of an efficiently operating labor exchange. . . . It is a fact that the *Wehrmacht* requests that Jews be spared as skilled workers, when in fact they are no more than office cleaners, housekeepers, etc. Even officers in responsible positions lack the [right] instinct for the Jewish problem.[67]

Skepticism regarding the advisability of the mass physical extermination of the Jews, including skilled labor (which, incidentally, cost the Germans next to nothing) was also expressed by the Nazi bureaucratic and military machines in the occupied territories of Poland, both in the Government General and the Wartheland. It was particularly evident in the middle of 1942, when the German war economy began to feel a pinching scarcity of reserves. The net result of the sudden mass elimination of Jewish laborers was a drastic decrease in production, which caused uneasiness among the economic and administrative authorities responsible for production output. In the secret report of the governor of Warsaw district for the period from October to November 1942, we find the information that the production of the Warsaw Ghetto fell off sharply in the textiles industry to as low as 2½ million zlotys from 44 million zlotys in July 1942 when the mass "resettlement" started. The removal of Jewish skilled workers is given as the reason.[68]

German firms working for the army were reluctant to let their Jewish workers go and tried to intercede with the SS and police in order to exempt them from "resettlements." In their secret reports, various German labor offices sounded the alarm, warned against drastic reduction of the labor crews, and requested new workers to replace "resettled" ones. Interventions followed on the part of the economic agencies of the German army directly affected by negative results of the "resettlements" for war production potential. The armament inspector of the Government General repeatedly intervened on behalf of German firms engaged in the war industry to exempt their Jewish workers. He was not successful. The army commander in the Government General therefore submitted a secret memorandum to the Army High Command, dated September 18, 1942, in which he stated: "The resettlement of the Jews, performed mainly without the knowledge of the military, has resulted in visible complications in production or delays in the delivery of urgently needed orders. . . . Continuing the speedy resettlement of the Jews may result in weakening the war potential of the Reich (*Sofortige Entfernung der Juden hätte zur Folge, dass das Kriegspotenzial des Reiches erheblich gedrückt . . . würde. . . .*).[69] Similarly, the Central Armament Office of the *Wehrmacht* in Berlin urged the *Statthalter* of the Wartheland, Arthur Greiser, in a communication dated August 15, 1942, to postpone the "resettlement" of Jewish workers in the C. Klose ammunition factories at Bełchatów and Warta (Łódź district) until substitutes were found.[70]

Another secret report, this one from the main propaganda office of the Government General to the Propaganda Ministry in Berlin, touching upon the conditions of the Galicia district, notes: "We have to accept the fact that economic activities will sink in the areas affected [by the "resettlements"]. It can be said in advance that the results will be deeply felt throughout the entire district of Galicia."[71]

It should be added that the police and various officials of the civil administration having personal contacts with the ghettos in their line of duty constituted one more segment among the occupation authorities with vested interests in the continuation of the ghettos. One such vested interest was purely materialistic. The ghetto had been a source of bribes in gold and gifts and "confiscations." But, besides the materialistic considerations, there was yet another reason, a momentous one for the Germans themselves: ghetto assignments provided a convenient excuse for avoiding the dreaded Eastern war front.

However, all warnings and interventions were to no avail. Total speedy extermination of the Jews ranked with the highest priority throughout the administrative and police apparatus as an affirmed policy to be strictly adhered to. The policy's influence on and costs for the war economy were minimized by the security organs that alleged the output of the Jews was very low compared to that of non-Jewish workers, and that the branches of industry where Jews were mainly employed, such as textiles, leather, and apparel, were of no major importance to the war economy anyway. Consequently no economic considerations were allowed to take precedence over

the realization of so impelling a political dogma as the cleansing
of Jews from all of Europe.[72] The Baranowicze *Kommissar* was not
alone in belittling the value of Jewish skilled work for the German
war effort.

In those parts of the occupied territories where Jews in sizable
numbers participated in the partisan movement, both Jewish and
general, the proponents of speedy realization of the Final Solution
had one more argument: ". . . the merits of Jewish skilled workers
. . . are in no proportion to the damage caused by Jewish support
of the partisans" (quoted from a circular letter of the commissar
general in Byelorussia, Wilhelm Kube, to all district commissars,
dated July 10, 1942).[73]

Last but not least it should be noted that the reason the SS insisted on having the final decision on the scope and dimensions of
the Final Solution was that its economic arm, the *Wirtschafts-und-
Verwaltungshauptamt* (generally known as WVHA), had schemed
to establish a strong economic combine of its own, such as OSTI
(Ost-Industrie), for example. SS had, therefore, striven to concentrate
the Jewish laborers in its industrial enterprises near or within concentration camps under its command. Thus SS aimed at becoming
the sole master of the Jewish labor force.[74]

The leaders of at least some of the Jewish Councils, men like
Barash, Gens, and Rumkowski, were aware of the "resettlement"
friction between certain economic circles of the local civil and army
authorities, on the one hand, and on the other the SS and police
organs, which followed orders from Berlin. Usually they got this
information from the "good" Germans, those who accepted bribes.
Their plans to save the ghetto population, or at least its productive
segment, were stimulated by this intelligence.

Mordecai Tenenbaum-Tamaroff, who apparently got the news
from Barash, notes in his Diary under the dates February 17 and
18, 1943:

 . . . a scandal [has broken out] in the office of the Armament Inspector
at Königsberg in connection with the [planned extermination] action.
For the time being, the ghetto is not going to be reduced. Our fate will
be decided on Friday, when General Constantin Canaris [the commander
of the SiPo and SD in Eastern Prussia] comes back. . . . Klein [chief of
the office of the Chief of the Civil Administration], our benevolent
protector, became master of the ghetto. We see in this a victory for the
more moderate circles of the Gestapo. He argues that "there will always

be time to destroy the Jews of Białystok, even on the last day. In the meantime, however, let them toil for us."[75]

That Barash had been informed about behind-the-scene wrangles concerning the fate of the Białystok Ghetto, is confirmed by the following facts. In the archives of the Jewish Council of Białystok, dug up from outside the ghetto area after the war, were included copies of certain excerpts from letters and notes of the Gestapo office at Białystok with specific references to the ghetto. Barash must have obtained them from a bribed German official or a German who could have had an interest in creating the illusion (or maybe himself believed) that the ghetto was going to last. It is worthwhile to cite some of the material. In a letter dated January 21, 1943, the town *Kommissar*, Dr. Schwendovius, who had been authorized to resettle Byelorussians into the ghetto after its liquidation, wrote to the *Oberpräsident*, Erich Koch:

. . . I have discussed with the chief of the *Treuhandstelle, Landrat* von Einsidel, the procedure for liquidating factories in the ghetto. He will attempt to prepare [a plan] in accordance with my conception as to how these factories will be put under the supervision of managers of [those] German factories where no Jews are employed. After a discussion with me, the *Kommandant* of the Security Police, Government Councillor Dr. Altenloh, also agreed that the sudden, forcible removal of the Jewish labor force from the town economy would result in great losses, particularly for important war production. The *Kommandant* is going to present his opinion to his Berlin center.

Nevertheless, two weeks later (on February 5) the "resettlement" of Jews from the Białystok Ghetto began. Over 10,000 persons were deported to an annihilation camp or shot on the spot.

Following this "resettlement action," during a meeting held at the office of the SiPo *Kommandant* on February 19, the problems involved in reducing the area of the Białystok Ghetto were discussed. Dr. Zimmermann, the *Kommandant*'s assistant, stated that "for the time being, no further resettlements are to be taken into consideration. *One may assume that the remaining 30,000 Jews will stay in the ghetto till the end of the war* [italics added]. Since we may expect that the Reich Security Office will approve this opinion of the Security Police here, we have now to contemplate the [resulting] economic factors." However, in another note dated March 20 the future of the Białystok Ghetto was being discussed in more ambiguous terms—namely, that "the local Security Police intends to let the ghetto exist to a certain extent. The final decision is up to the Reich Security Office in Berlin and is expected this month."[76] In the second half of August 1943 the Białystok Ghetto was finally liquidated and its inhabitants sent to Treblinka and Majdanek.

Rumkowski too must have had some perfidious assurances from certain officials of the German ghetto administration to the effect that the working elements, even if "resettled," were to be protected and employed elsewhere.[77] We may assume that Gens and perhaps a few ghetto leaders elsewhere were also aware of the "resettlement" controversy.

We know now that the Jewish Councils made a great mistake in believing that Nazi policy with respect to the Jews had been motivated by rational or utilitarian considerations of any kind. Now we know for sure that the difference of opinion between the *Wehrmacht* and the SS had been *only about slowing down* the tempo of the Final Solution and *not about stopping* the total physical destruction of the Jews. The army was interested solely in the exploitation of Jewish slave labor for the benefit of the German war machine until the time when replacement of Jews with non-Jewish workers from the native population would become feasible. As already indicated above, the German army as a rule readily cooperated with the *Einsatzgruppen* in carrying out the Final Solution. The *Einsatzgruppen*'s own reports on concluded "actions" testify to this point. Military detachments took part in hunting and surrounding the victims, military execution platoons were supplied, and soldiers and officers actively participated in the mass executions.[78]

Admittedly, however, in those times of unprecedented calamity the Jewish Councils, groping toward means to cope with the "resettlements," had no choice but to try the mass employment strategy. It should be added that wide circles of the working segments of the population shared this strategy, though perhaps under the influence of the Councils.[79] In retrospect we find that those who remained in the ghettos perished almost to a man, having been deported to extermination camps or killed on the spot. On the other hand, a certain percentage survived from among those who, before or during the liquidation of the ghettos, were shipped to various labor or concentration camps. There is no doubt that the decisive factor in extending the lives of some of the ghettos was the measure of their contribution to the German war economy. Thus the final liquidation of the Łódź Ghetto took place as late as the end of August 1944 (except for Theresienstadt, Łódź was the last ghetto in occupied Europe to be liquidated). Among the relatively long-lived ghettos, important for the German war economy, were those of Białystok and Vilna, which were liquidated in August and September 1943 respectively. The ghettos of Kaunas and Šiauliai, which were converted into concentration camps, were liquidated in July 1944. These few ghettos were almost the last remaining ones in occupied Eastern Europe at the time. Each of them was what the Germans called an *Arbeitsgetto* ("labor ghetto").

Had the war ended earlier, a sizable number of the labor elements might have survived. Let us take the case of the Łódź Ghetto. In August 1944, when the Soviet armies had already reached the environs of Warsaw, approximately 70,000 Jews still lived in Łódź (at a distance of some 75 miles). Had the Soviet army not stopped its advance till January 1945, a large number of these 70,000 people would certainly have escaped the gas chambers of Auschwitz.

THE GERMAN POLICY OF FRAUD AND DECEIT

What were the tactics used by the Jewish Councils vis-à-vis the ghetto population during the "resettlement actions"? What answers could they give to placate frightened people inquiring in a state of terror about the alarming news from neighboring ghettos of disaster descending upon them?

At first the Councils had no hint whatsoever what the intentions of the Germans were. At most they may have guessed intuitively that this was not a simple matter and that the "resettled" people were in danger. It simply was humanly impossible to perceive that "resettlement" meant physical destruction of the entire Jewish population, particularly since the police and the officials of the civil administration used elaborate tricks before and during the course of the "actions" to keep the Jews in the dark about their monstrous intentions. A few examples will suffice to illustrate German fraud and deceit.

On July 20, 1942, barely two days before the Gestapo men came to the office of the Jewish Council in Warsaw to dictate the order for mass "resettlement" to Adam Czerniakow, he noted in his Diary:

[I visited] the Gestapo at 7:30 in the morning. I inquired of Mende [in charge of Jewish affairs] how much truth there was in the rumors [about pending resettlement]. He answered that he knew nothing about it. To my question whether this was at all possible, he again answered that he knew nothing about it. I left unconvinced. I then asked his chief, *Kommissar* Boehm, who answered that this was not within his competence, that Höhnemann [a leading Gestapo man] might be in a position to give some information. I stressed that, according to rumors, the "resettlement" was to start today at 19:30 [7.30 P.M. He] answered that he would certainly have had some information if this were so. Having no recourse, I approached Scherer, the deputy chief of Department III [of the Gestapo]. He showed surprise and said that he too knew nothing. I then asked whether I might inform the [Jewish] population that there was no foundation for the alarm. [He] answered that I could do so. Everything that has been rumored is unsubstantiated gossip and groundless talk. I have [therefore] instructed [Jacob] Lejkin [commandant of the ghetto police] to inform the population accordingly through the area committees.

Czerniakow supplemented the entry by stating that when First, the chief of the economic department of the Jewish Council, inquired of two other Security Police officials, they got very angry because of the rumors and said that an investigation would be ordered about the whole thing. A mere two days later the "resettlement" began and Czerniakow committed suicide.

In Eastern Upper Silesia Merin got assurances from an "authorized source" that only a few transports would be "resettled" to new places, where the people, particularly those living in bad housing conditions and on relief, would have better opportunities to settle down.[80]

In the Vilna Ghetto, three weeks before the final liquidation of the ghetto, the Gestapo chief, Neugebauer, delivered a speech to the shop foremen and Council workers on August 9, 1943, reassuring them that "the Vilna Ghetto and the Jews are in no danger" and denying that there was any truth to "the ridiculous rumors spread [in the ghetto]."[81] Biebow, the chief of the Łódź *Gettoverwaltung*, told similar lies in his speeches during the first ten days of August 1944, when preparations to send the last 70,000 Jews of Łódź to Auschwitz were already in full swing.[82]

Misled by these treacheries, some of the Councils issued public statements in an effort to ease the agitation of the panicky Jewish population. Thus in Vilna, in March 1943, when the Jews were in a state of shock because of rumors that all the Jews from the neighboring camps were going to be moved into the ghetto as an initial step toward liquidation, the chairman of the council of the shop foremen at their meeting advised them in his own name and on behalf of the ghetto chief "that the rumors and suspicions of the last days are all groundless." Moreover, he assured them "that there is no danger looming over the ghetto at the present time."[83]

A day after the "resettlement action" began in the Łódź Ghetto, on January 17, 1942, Rumkowski made the following public statement:

Based on statements of the authorities, I have firm hope that the fate of the resettled people is not going to be so tragic as has commonly been feared in the ghetto. They will not be put behind wires. Farming will be their task. . . . I guarantee with my own head that the working people will be subjected to no injustice; and I am saying this not only in my own name, but my statement is based on the promises of qualified, competent persons.[84]

If this went on in the large ghettos, such as Łódź, Warsaw, Vilna, and Sosnowiec, the scope of deceit in the smaller ghettos can easily be surmised. We know that in Mińsk Mazowiecki, the *Kreishauptmann*, told the delegates of the Jewish Council that "Jews of Mińsk may rest assured they have nothing to fear." An elderly person, the *Hauptmann* enjoyed the reputation of an honest man, and his statement was taken with trust, particularly since the gendarmes and the Gestapo men ["the Black ones"] at Mińsk had constantly been bribed.[85] At Łuków the Gestapo assured the chairman of the Jewish Council, Lender, when he delivered a contribution of 10 kilograms of gold, that nothing was going to happen to the Łuków Jews and that they might peacefully continue working.[86] After a large detachment of German police descended upon Rejowiec (Lublin district), the Council, on the assurances of the authorities, calmed the people, saying that nothing wrong was going to happen to them. Only a few hours later the Council was ordered to call the Jews to report to the outskirts of the town. All assembled were taken away, except the Council chairman.[87] In Siedlce the Council passed on to the population the continuously deceitful assurances of the authorities that nothing was going to happen there, that "it was impossible to keep up a large Jewish center such as in Warsaw, but that Siedlce would be spared because of the great production ability of the Jewish population" (3,000 Jewish workers were employed there for the benefit of the Germans).[88]

On August 24, 1942, the Jews in Sarny (Volhynia) were ordered to report for registration in three days. They became frantic, and the Council decided to go to the Nazis and give the *Gebietskommissar* a bribe in gold and textiles. In his magnanimity the *Kommissar* was even willing to accept the bribe in monthly installments, which the Jews interpreted as a good omen. He also reassured the Council members that the Jews had nothing to fear as long as he was in charge. He said that if there had been any plans for action the authorities would have closed up the ghetto first of all. And that was what happened. The ghetto was closed on August 27. In a desperate last-minute attempt the Council delivered to the *Gebietskommissar* all the gold deposited in its safe. He again reassured them that no more than a registration was planned, and that all the people would remain safely in their homes. Yet the same day all were taken away and shot on the outskirts of the town.[89]

Among the members of the Councils were people who believed naïvely that some German officials were against the "resettlements" as a matter of principle, and that they were even trying to intercede with the higher authorities. An eyewitness tells that the liaison man between the Jewish Council at Łuków and the local *Arbeitsamt* reported that after the bloody "resettlement" in the town of Parczew, the chief of the *Zentrales Arbeitsamt* of Lublin, together with the deputy chief of the Gestapo and the chief of the *Arbeitsamt* at Radzyn, pounded the desks of the higher ups at the Lublin district office arguing that they wished no more such acts to happen in their labor areas. They were given promises that in the towns of Biała, Międzyrzec, Radzyn, and Łuków no actions of this kind would take place. Yikheskl Grynblat, a member of the Radzyn Council who was present, confirmed the report of the liaison man. As to the eyewitness himself, he notes that when he expressed doubts about the reliability of the report of the liaison man, David Lieberman, one of the members of the Łuków Council and a very religious man, argued that as an atheist he believed in nothing anyway.[90]

Fraud and deceit—this was the policy used not only vis-à-vis the Councils but, generally, against the ghetto population. The *Bürger-*

meister of Krośniewice (Wartheland), an elderly man, ordered the Jews to assemble at a certain place and in a speech assured them that they were going to be taken to Bessarabia. Finishing, he told them to go home and have a good night's sleep before the trip. When a woman asked whether they were not going to be sent instead to Chełmno (the "resettlement" from neighboring towns to Chełmno had started in the Wartheland on December 7, 1941, and rumors of what was taking place there had already become common), he answered categorically, "no."[91] The next morning, March 2, 1942, the Jews were sent to Chełmno.[92]

Jews were treated in a somewhat similar manner during the "resettlement" from Konin county, where close to 3,000 persons were involved. They were ordered to the village of Zagórów and assured that all would be shipped to work in the Łódź factories. In another place, in Koło, all persons assembled for "resettlement" were subjected to a medical examination, allegedly for working ability. Also, all had to pay a head tax. When the "resettlement" was already in progress, one of the deportees submitted a written request for the position of leader of the camp to which the Jews were allegedly being transported. His application was accepted.[93]

In February and March 1943, after groups of armed Jewish resisters had unexpectedly forced the Germans to interrupt liquidation of the Warsaw Ghetto (the resisters struck on January 18 and 19), the German owners of ghetto shops, with Walter Toebbens in the lead, began a drive to "peacefully" induce Jewish workers to let themselves voluntarily be transported to the labor camps of Poniatowa and Trawniki in the Lublin district. To persuade the Jews that this "resettlement" was for economic reasons, Toebbens, and not an SS man, was appointed *Übersiedlungskommissar*. His business partner, a man named Stehmann, addressed the workers in eloquent orations, describing with pathos the ideal life awaiting them in the camps. But the Organization of Jewish Fighters, in posters put up on March 14, warned Jews that the allegedly "peaceful resettlement" was nothing but another fraud. Turning polemicist, Toebbens put up his own posters, side by side with the posters of the Organization of Jewish Fighters, arguing that the camps were the only place where the workers would be able to survive until the war was over. "You should believe only your leaders of German enterprises," he exhorted them, "who, together with you, will continue to work. Take your wives and children, and we will take care of them too." This time, however, the deceit did not work. The majority of the Jewish workers did not voluntarily report. Out of 3,500 workers at the brush shop, not a single one volunteered. From then on the Organization of Jewish Fighters became a decisive factor in the ghetto and later bravely led it during the ghetto uprising which broke out in April 1943. As for other shopworkers, those who were lured by Toebbens and transported to Trawniki were all killed during the mass slaughter on November 3, 1943. Four days later, on November 7, the neighboring camp of Poniatowa was liquidated. In all, including the shopworkers who fell prey to Toebbens' treacherous promise that they would have a chance to survive the war if they listened to him, over 25,000 Jews were killed in both camps during those two days.[94]

In towns where liquidation of the Jews was accomplished in installments, the Germans reassured them after each subsequent "action" that it was the last one. To give just one example, after the first slaughter in Włodzimierz Wołyński in August 1942, a new Jewish Council was established there. The German town mayor ordered the new Council to influence Jews in hiding to return to the ghetto. He gave assurances that they would be given an opportunity to start a new life. An eyewitness, a refugee from the town of Zamość, who was himself in hiding, adds that "people went to work believing that, maybe, they would survive." For over a year they lived under this illusion. On December 12, 1943, the *Gebietskommissar* unexpectedly arrived in the ghetto. Since he usually came on rare occasions, this visit caused a great deal of anxiety. The alarmed ghetto Jews inquired of the Council chairman, who told them that "he had just come back from a meeting [with the authorities] and there was no danger looming."[95] By the end of December, the entire ghetto was "resettled."

A widespread, unscrupulous, well-planned fraud perpetrated by Wilhelm Krüger, the Higher SS and Police Leader of the Government General, took place in the area under his jurisdiction at a time when the vast majority and, in some places, all of the Jews had already been killed. On October 28 and again on November 10, 1942, he announced two orders allegedly establishing Jewish settlement areas throughout the Government General. The first order designated six settlements in the Warsaw district and eight in the Lublin district. The second order established settlements in the Radom district (4), Cracow district (5), and Galicia district (32).[96]

The intention of these orders was to create an illusion of security for those remnants who had somehow managed to survive, and to induce them to come out from hiding and move into the "haven" of the new ghettos allegedly established. In this Krüger succeeded to a certain degree. Because of the extreme hardship of hiding inside the ghetto and outside on the "Aryan" side, Jews began to move into Krüger's "new Jewish settlements." Shortly thereafter, they were summarily "resettled." Thus the "new" Siedlce Ghetto did not last even one month. The entire ghetto became *judenrein* when all the local Jews had been "resettled" on November 25, 1942.[97] The "newly established" ghetto in Piaski (Lublin district) was liquidated at the end of February or beginning of March 1943, only four months after it was named a "Jewish settlement area."[98] Of the "newly established" settlements none lasted longer than May 1943, as was the case in Warsaw, Międzyrzec, Włodawa, and Łuków. Only one, Rzeszów, vegetated until November 1943.

All this intentional fraudulence and cheating in cold blood during the Final Solution process was used by the Germans in order to soothe the panic-stricken Jews, reduce their alertness, and entirely disorient them so that to the very last minute they had no inkling of what "resettlement" really meant. The instinct of self-preservation, which prompts people to resist the thought of imminent destruction and to cling to even a spark of hope, here played into the hands of the executioners. A vast number of ghettos fell prey to this combination of circumstances. To a large degree the age-old Jewish optimism that a miracle might yet occur even at the very last moment itself contributed to the fatalistic attitudes of Council members and of the ghetto population as well,* particularly since no other

---

* How Jews felt during the process of the Final Solution can be seen in the following excerpt from the memoirs of a former inhabitant of the Buczacz Ghetto (Eastern Galicia): "Two opinions prevailed. On one hand, the fatalists made peace with their fate, reasoning that what would happen to the entire community would also be their personal lot. On the other hand, many hoped to escape destruction. These people hoped that with the help of the Almighty, or because of some miracle, they would survive until victory and their only worry was to be tenacious enough to persevere to the end. These people lived in the illusion that he who escaped an "action" had secured his life for the next few months, and that, in the meantime, deliverance might come. People hoped that the war would end, or that the Nazis would have to stop the murders under pressure from world opinion. There was no knowledge of Treblinka or Auschwitz in Buczacz, and the opinion of the majority about nearby Bełżec was that this was just another labor camp." (Yitzhak [Shikhor] Szwartz, *Buczacz Memorial Book*, 1956, p. 243.)

solution to their tragic situation was in sight. Thus we come to the problem of Council policy with respect to the Jewish resistance movement, a problem to be discussed elsewhere in this study.

THE STRATEGY OF SURRENDERING CERTAIN GROUPS DURING "RESETTLEMENT ACTIONS"

The Jewish Councils faced a particularly grave dilemma when the fateful time of the "resettlements" came. It was perhaps the most excruciating moral predicament encountered by a representative body in history.

The German authorities forced the Councils to make all the preliminary preparations for "resettlements" on their behalf: deliver data on the demography and employment of the ghetto population; prepare, in accordance with their strict guidelines, lists of suggested candidates for deportation; order the Jews to report at the places designated for "selection"; search for deportation candidates who tried to conceal themselves and deliver them in person, or order the ghetto police to find them according to lists prepared by the Councils or given to them by the authorities.

During these most awful times, the Councils realized that it was impossible to save the entire ghetto community. Though they may have reasoned that, thanks to their "rescue-through-work" strategy, the working segment of the ghetto population, the young men and women, would have a better chance of survival, they understood at the same time that people on welfare or otherwise not working had no chance at all—people like the elderly and the feeble, who faced death or illness anyway, and large families with small children as well as the children themselves. Beset by the impending ordeal, a sizable number of Councils fearfully came to the fateful conclusion that since not all the Jews could be saved, it was better to deliver to the Nazi Moloch those ghetto dwellers with little or no chance of survival in order to save others. This desperate reasoning, that in the calamity that had befallen them it was necessary as a kind of rescue strategy to sacrifice some to save others, emerged within many ghettos. We find the rationale in the sources. The chief of the Vilna Ghetto, Jacob Gens, and the chairman of the Central Council of the Jewish Communities in Upper Eastern Silesia, Moshe Merin, vividly outlined the theory in particularly drastic terms.

By the end of October 1942 an "action" took place in Oszmiana. The Vilna Ghetto police took an active part in assembling and transporting over 400 victims to this execution and, according to Dvorzhetsky, even took part in the execution itself. After the "action" Gens delivered a speech, on October 25 or 27 (the exact date is uncertain).[99] According to Zelig Kalmanovich,[100] he said:

It is true that our hands are smeared with the blood of our brethren, but we had to accept this horrible task. We are innocent before history. We shall be on the alert to preserve the remnants. Who can tell whether victims will not be demanded here [in Vilna] as they were demanded there [in Oszmiana]? We shall give only the sick and the old. We shall not give the children, they are our future. We shall not give young women. A demand has been made to deliver workers. My answer was, "We shall not give them, for we need them here ourselves."

To illustrate how recklessly the Germans had dealt with the population, Gens pointed out that they had caught some 1,000 Poles in the street and sent them to Riga for forced labor. Gens posed the question: "Who can guarantee our future?"

Mark Dvorzhetsky cites records of the speech that Gens delivered on October 27. Gens then said:

The Jewish police took no part [in the "action"] in Kiemieliszki and Bystrzyca, so all were slaughtered [there]. Jews from the surrounding towns have come now and beg for help. I could have told them that I do not wish to smear my hands and send my police to do the filthy work, but I said, "Yes, it is my duty to foul my hands." After five million have been slaughtered, it is our duty to save the strong and the young and not let sentiment overcome us. I am not sure that everyone has understood what I have said, or that people will justify our deeds after we are liberated from the ghetto, but this is what the police think: to save whomever possible, our personal emotions notwithstanding. I expect moral support from you. Evidently not many are aware of the danger that hangs over us daily of being sent to Ponary. My desire is to bring you closer to the realities of life, to make you understand life. I personally take responsibility for all that has happened. I don't want any discussion. I have called you to explain why a Jew dips his hands in blood, and that in the future, whenever we have to go, we shall go too.

Commenting on this speech, Dvorzhetsky notes that at that time opinion in the ghetto was divided. "There were those who cursed him, but, on the other hand, there were people who maintained that this was the only way to save at least a fragment of Jews."[101] Zelig Kalmanovich was among those who agreed with Gens. In connection with the events in Oszmiana he writes in his Diary:

It is horrible, perhaps the worst of all predicaments, still there is no other way. Blessed be the God of Israel, who sent us this man [Gens]. . . . The young people [the ghetto police] have accepted this dreadful duty. . . . The result: over 400 souls have perished—elderly people, the weak and ill, retarded children. However, 1,500 women and children were saved. If this had been the work of strangers, 2,000 people would have perished, God forbid.[102]

True to his announced policy Jacob Gens personally participated in the removal to Ponary of the Jews from the Vilna Ghetto in the fall of 1941. He was at the exit gate and directed the "action," deciding who was to be deported and who was to remain in the ghetto. This in fact meant to decide who was to live and who to die.

After the first series of "resettlements" in Eastern Upper Silesia, during the period from May to August 1942, Moshe Merin delivered a speech justifying his participation in the "action." According to the account of an eyewitness, this is what he said, among other things:

I knew that I would be blamed for causing the deportation of 25,000 Jews. I am even glad to hear this accusation in my own circle [of associates], and I want to show how superficial, unfounded, and foolish this reproach is. Quite to the contrary to what is said, I state that I have saved 25,000 people from resettlement. Blood would have flowed in the streets. I have information from very reliable sources that the resettlement would have engulfed 50,000 people, and our entire district would have been crushed, so that no might in the whole world would have been able to rebuild it. Respected people, active in our community life, would have been the first to go. It is easy to imagine what the lot of the remaining ones might have been. Nobody will deny that, as a general, I have won a great victory. If I have lost only 25 percent when I could have lost all, who can wish better results? Diaspora has made an asocial people of the Jews. Only we could have adopted the teaching of Maimonides,* who ordained that the entire community be sacrificed

* He meant Maimonides' ruling that "if pagans should tell them [the Jews], 'Give us one of yours and we shall kill him, otherwise we shall kill all of you,' they should all be killed and not a single Jewish soul should be delivered." (*Mishne Torah Hilkhot Yesoday Hatorah* ["The Fundamentals of the Torah"], Chap. 5, Para. 5.)

for the sake of one man. We shall all be condemned to extinction if we do not change our mentality in this respect. . . . I have never considered the interests of the individual as against the interests of the community, I always bear in mind the best interests of the community, for whom I am ready to sacrifice the individual at any time.[103]

Rumkowski was also a strong believer in this kind of rescue method. According to the report of Josef Zelkowicz, Rumkowski discussed the problem in quite bold terms. In a speech he delivered before a large assembly on the eve of an "action" against the elderly, sick, and children, on September 4, 1942, he said:

I was given an order yesterday evening to deport some 20,000 Jews out of the ghetto. [I was also told that] if I refused, "We shall do it ourselves." The question arose: Should we comply and do it, or should we leave it for others to do? We were not, however, motivated by the thought of how many would be lost, but by the consideration of how many it would be possible to save. We all, myself and my closest associates, have come to the conclusion that despite the horrible responsibility, we have to accept the evil order. I have to perform this bloody operation myself; I simply must cut off limbs to save the body! I have to take away the children, because otherwise others will also be taken, God forbid (a terrible outcry from the assembled people followed these words). . . . I did not come to console you today. And I did not come to quiet you down either, but to reveal to you the whole woeful, torturing truth. I came like a robber to rob your dearest ones from your very hearts! With all my might I strove to repeal this evil order. And as it has been impossible to rescind it, I have tried to make it milder. Only yesterday, I ordered the registration of children nine years of age, because I have endeavored to save children of at least this single age group, from nine to ten. But they did not relent, and I have succeeded only in saving the ten-year-olds. Let this be the consolation for our terrible bereavement. We have in the ghetto many persons sick with tuberculosis, whose lives are numbered in days, perhaps in weeks. I do not know— perhaps it is a satanic idea, and again perhaps it is not—but I cannot restrain myself from mentioning it. Deliver to me those sick ones and it may be possible to save the healthy ones instead. I am well aware how dear the sick are to everyone. It is particularly so among the Jewish people. But in times of disaster one has to weigh and measure who is to be saved, who can and should be saved. To my mind those are to be spared in the first place who have any chance of survival, not those who cannot survive anyway.[104]

A survivor of the Białystok Ghetto relates that "Barash, as usual, prepared a list of Jews who should be delivered [during the various 'actions']. A few hours earlier he had called the Jewish police and their commander Isaac Markus and told them that 'when one is dangerously poisoned and his arm has to be amputated to save his life, it is done.' "[105] Also Hayke Grosman, Mordecai Tenenbaum, and Rafael Reisner confirm in their writings that Barash compiled lists of candidates for the "resettlements."[106]

In other places, too, victims were delivered to the Nazi Moloch in desperate attempts to save the remainder of the Jews. In August 1942 the Gestapo at Tarnopol ordered the Jewish Council of the town of Skałat to deliver all elderly people for deportation. However, the Council "bargained for only 500 souls to be delivered on August 31, 1942." The Council and the ghetto police actively participated in rounding up the sick and the beggars. The witness notes that "some Jews were of the opinion that, if it was destined that people had to go to their deaths, it was preferable that the elderly go first! After all, they had already lived their lives. . . . such wrong, sickly ideas were prevalent among people close to the Jewish Council. They believed that they were thus helping the community."[107] The Council of Złoczów was motivated by a similar opinion that "if they went along and participated in the 'action' [it took place on August 28, 1942], it might prove beneficial . . . for only inferior elements (the sick, weak, old) would be delivered, and the young, the healthy, and the intelligentsia would be spared."[108]

A vivid description of the crushing moral dilemma that overpowered the Jewish Councils during the "resettlements" comes from the Kaunas Ghetto. On October 26, 1941, there arrived in the ghetto its newly appointed boss, the Gestapo man Rauke, who ordered the entire Jewish population, without exception, to assemble at the Democratic Square two days later. All were to bring their working papers. A check would be made, and those unable to work would be transported elsewhere. Whoever was found at home after 6 A.M. on the day of the assembly would be shot. Only the ill were exempt; however, they had to produce a certificate from a doctor. The vice chairman of the Council thus describes the anguish that tortured its members.

The Council faced problems of conscience and responsibility at the same time. . . . [There were two alternatives:] . . . either to comply, announce the Gestapo order to the ghetto inhabitants, and issue proper instructions to the Ghetto police; or openly to sabotage the order by disregarding it. The Council felt that if it followed the first alternative, part, or perhaps the majority, of the ghetto might yet be rescued at least for a time. Should however, the other alternative be chosen, heavy measures of persecution would follow against the entire ghetto, and possibly its immediate liquidation [might result].

Aware of the situation and of this burden of responsibility for the lives of thousands whom it might yet be possible to save, the Council at the same time felt the traditional Jewish optimism that, perhaps, a miracle might yet mercifully come at the last minute. These considerations influenced the Council once more not to choose the path of open sabotage against the Germans. A resolution to this effect was adopted in Kaunas after an agonizing moral struggle during a long meeting and following a night of consultation with the old Kaunas rabbi, the late Abraham Duber Shapiro. The rabbi fainted when he heard what the Council members told him. When he came to, he asked for a few hours to search the holy books for advice on how one is to act in times of such a calamity, according to Jewish ethics. In the morning, he gave the following opinion to the Jewish Council: "If a Jewish community (may God help it) has been condemned to physical destruction, and there are means of rescuing part of it, the leaders of the community should have courage and assume the responsibility to act and rescue what is possible." Of the 26,400 Jews remaining in Kaunas after three previous "actions" (on August 18, September 26, and October 4, 1941) some 9,000 persons were taken away during this "selection" on the next day. They were transported to the 9th Fort and killed.[109]

Sharp disagreements came to light in the debates of some Councils during discussions about "resettlements." We shall here cite some of these impassioned debates. Paul (Fayvel) Wiederman, quoted above (see note 103), relates that prior to the "resettlement action" in Sosnowiec, Merin, as chairman of the Central Jewish Council of the Jewish Communities of Eastern Upper Silesia, called a meeting of his associates. Also invited were the chairman and one member of the Jewish Council of Będzin, the Council members of Dąbrowa and Sosnowiec, and others, some thirty persons in all. Merin stated in his opening speech that it would again be necessary to follow the standard policy that anything the authorities demand should be done by the Jews themselves. In the course of discussion some quite contrary opinions emerged. The member of the Jewish Council of Będzin, Michael Laskier, declared himself against Merin's proposition. He said that in all Jewish history no instance had been known where a Jewish community had itself delivered thousands of victims for extermination to the enemy. He stressed that the categories of people named by the authorities for selection—namely, the sick, the maimed, and the elderly—left no doubt what could be expected. Concluding, he too referred to Maimonides' ruling and requested that the Councils not participate in the "resettlement action." Let the authorities themselves select.

A member of the Central Jewish Council and some others also talked in this vein. They warned against the danger of slipping into a moral abyss if Merin's advice were followed. However, the chairman of the Będzin Jewish Council, Chaim Mołczadzki, supported Merin's suggestion.

Merin scoffed at his critics. In his rebuttal he jeered those who maintained that Maimonides' decision was binding for all times. The times and the circumstances we live in, he said, dictate an entirely different approach. One must act as a statesman having been given the alternatives either to rid the community itself of those socially worthless elements or to leave it to strangers to perform this operation, a course which would result in the loss of the most worthy individuals. He concluded that as a serious and wise statesman he could not hesitate which path to choose.[110]

A similar disagreement occurred in Skałat. At a meeting held after the first "action" in August 1942, three of the Council's members expressed their view

that there is no alternative, but to leave events to destiny. What the Almighty ordains shall prevail; the Jews should not participate in the action. Others at the meeting maintained and even categorically requested that, as had happened during the previous action, an attempt be made to get the authorities to agree that, in the future, the Council should continue to deliver ordered contingents, thus rescuing itself, its families, and many young and useful people. . . . The Council should try, once more, to collect a large amount of money [to bribe the Gestapo]. . . . We should not deliver our own people at a time when so many beggars from other places are roaming the streets, lying in the market, and dying from hunger anyway.

Such were the arguments advanced by the Council member S——. This proposition was adopted after a stormy discussion. More than half the Councilmen voted in favor.[111]

When it was necessary to compile a list of candidates for the third "resettlement" transport from the ghetto of Włocławek into the Łódź Ghetto (at the beginning of October 1941), a sharp divergence of opinion emerged in the Jewish Council of Włocławek. Although from the pertinent document the details of the disagreement are not clear, it is a fact that the list of "candidates for resettlement" was not submitted and the German police prepared their own list, albeit with grave complications. Those selected for deportation tried to conceal themselves, but they were caught; in retaliation, the police included in the transport more people than were first ordered. A group of 182 persons was added to the approximately 750 initially scheduled to report. Moreover, a slaughter took place in the ghetto, arranged by the police.[112]

Prior to the "action" in Łuck which began on August 20, 1942, the authorities demanded a contribution from the Jewish Council in the amount of 10,000 gold rubles, half a million German marks, 1,000 cuts of textiles for men's and ladies' garments, 1,000 kilograms of leather, and, for good measure, 50 kilograms of onions and garlic, the last two items apparently intended to denigrate the Jews. In addition the Jewish Council was ordered to deliver 50 Jewish Communists. Two orientations emerged in the Council: one group, in an effort to save the Jews from "resettlement," suggested paying the contribution but refusing to deliver the 50 Communists. The other group maintained that the last demand should be rejected forthwith, and that the ghetto should prepare itself to resist the Germans if they entered the ghetto. However, the first opinion prevailed. Before they were destroyed, the Jews of Łuck surrendered all their possessions to their murderers.[113]

The Kaunas Jewish Council was not alone in seeking advice from rabbis on what to do during the "actions." It is related that Merin called a meeting of rabbis and their assistants, together with a number of persons active in welfare work at Będzin and Sosnowiec, after no volunteers had reported for the "action" scheduled in Będzin for the middle of May 1942 (during a previous "action" at the beginning of the month, some 1,000 people had volunteered, after the Jewish Council had reassured them that they were going to be

resettled in some other place). Merin asked for advice whether or
not he ought to go along with the order of the Gestapo and deliver
the Jews for transportation by force. If he obeyed, he said, there was
hope that many Jews would be saved, and there would be a chance
to select informers, thieves, immoral or sick and mentally ill persons,
and retarded children as candidates. Otherwise the Gestapo would
take people at random and what had already happened in Sosnowiec
might happen again: the most revered personalities of Sosnowiec had
been the first victims to go. He expressed his own opinion that the
decision should be in the affirmative, the demands of the Gestapo
accepted. Nevertheless he was willing to comply with the rabbinical
judgment and would wait for the verdict in the next room. After
a lengthy consultation, Rabbi Yitzhak Groysman made a statement
on behalf of his fellow rabbis present: basically Merin's suggestion
was against the fundamentals of Jewish ethics and religion, but, according to his presentation, each Jewish household in town faced a
great calamity. There was no other way, therefore, but to choose the
lesser evil. They hoped that Merin would act as his Jewish heart
dictated. In conclusion Rabbi Groysman expressed the hope that
Merin would be granted the privilege of becoming a savior and
would deliver from bondage the Jews of Eastern Upper Silesia.
Consequently both Merin and the Jewish police took an active part
in setting up the next transport of about 1,200 people to Auschwitz.[114]

Another witness also gives details of the meeting with the rabbis.
He relates that the opinion was expressed during the discussion that
Maimonides' ruling was still binding and that, therefore, the Jews
should be forbidden to busy themselves with the "resettlements."
There were others, however, who argued against the Maimonides
ruling. No consensus of opinion could be reached, but the prevailing
view was that, under the circumstances, Merin could be allowed to
take an active part in the "resettlement," particularly since the
authorities had said nothing in the order about the fate awaiting
the deportees.[115]

After the conclusion of the so-called "action" of the "Yellow
Certificates" in Vilna, the orthodox leaders of the ghetto held a
meeting. A delegation of four rabbis later warned Gens that, according to Jewish law, he had no right on his own to make the
selection and deliver the Jews to the authorities. They referred to
Maimonides' ruling, but Gens argued that because of his participa-

tion in the selection and because he had delivered a certain number of Jews, he had saved the lives of others.[116]

The colony of Heidemühle was located near the village of Kowale Pańskie, in Turek county in the Wartheland. It consisted of 16 hamlets into which the Germans herded some 4,000 Jews from the towns and hamlets of Dobra, Turek, Uniejów, Tuliszków, Władysławów, and Brudzew on the eve of Yom Kippur 1941. At the end of October 1941, the chairman of the ghetto Council, Hershel Zimnawoda, got an order from the *Landrat* of Turek to make a list of all deportees and to note their ability or disability to work. Though nobody yet knew at the time that disability meant death, the chairman asked four rabbis from among the deportees to decide how to act. The rabbis deliberated for two days, November 5 and 6. They ordained a day of fast for the inhabitants of the ghetto. People prayed, recited psalms, and blew the Shofar. At long last, in an atmosphere of suspense, they announced their decision that, according to religious law, a decree of the government is obligatory and must be obeyed. Therefore the chairman must prepare the list; everyone, however, had to be given a chance to check the list to see how he had been marked. The chairmen of expulsed communities should themselves prepare lists of the Jews from their places and present them to the chairman.[117] A similar request for the opinion of the rabbis was made in Oszmiana.[118]

Unfortunately no other tangible records can be traced in the preserved sources, but there is sufficient basis to support the thesis that divergent opinions came to the surface and desperate soul-searching went on in many more places during the "resettlements." The learned rabbis could not arrive at a consensus of opinion. In Kaunas, Oszmiana, Sosnowiec, and Heidemühle, the rabbis decided that it was necessary to obey the German authorities, prepare the ordered lists, call the Jews to report for "selection," etc. They reasoned that the orders referred only to transfers for forced labor and not for death (as in Sosnowiec), and that through obeying the orders parts of the ghettos would be saved (as in Kaunas). On the other hand, the rabbis in Vilna categorically forbade Gens to deliver a single Jew into the hands of the Gestapo, even if this could, as he maintained, save others from death.

In some of the ghettos, chairmen of Councils invited influential personalities from outside the Councils for consultation on how to act during imminent "resettlements."

When the first deportation from the Łódź Ghetto was already well advanced, Rumkowski called a meeting of ghetto intellectuals: teachers, physicians, rabbis, and high-ranking police officers. According to the preserved text of his speech, this is what he said at that time:

> The ghetto Jews keep criticizing me, asking why I did not prevent the catastrophe. It will get even worse. People will have to be deported for minor faults. The families of those already deported and those who idle in the streets [will also have to go]. Women, children, elderly people, all will be involved. . . . I cannot take upon myself so big a burden. I want you to bear witness to my warning [that work is the only salvation]. Were I not ashamed, I would have cried in front of you like a baby and begged you to help me in this disaster.

Twelve people took part in the ensuing discussion. Unfortunately the report does not tell what was said. Only one detail is mentioned. The rabbis complained that they had not been given the chance to work in the ghetto enterprises, which, so far, had protected people against "resettlement." They also requested that they be represented on the committee assigning work in the ghetto enterprises. However, Rumkowski rejected this request, denying any discrimination against pious, observant Jews.[119]

According to Jonas Turkow, when the "resettlement" from Warsaw was officially announced, the chairman of the Council, Adam Czerniakow, called an extraordinary meeting of prominent public figures, mostly associated with the Jewish Social Welfare (JSS). He stated that in case the Jews themselves did not deliver the number of people ordered (6,000 daily), the Germans would take over the "action" and the situation might become even worse. He requested that all departments of the JSS, like the Council's departments, delegate a number of coworkers to assist at the Umschlagplatz.[120]

It is worthwhile to note that one of the leaders of the Jewish resistance movement supported at one time the strategy of offering sacrifices to save the majority of the community. On February 4, 1943 (on the eve of the "action" in the Białystok Ghetto), Mordecai Tenenbaum, one of the leaders of the Jewish underground movement in occupied Poland, noted in his Diary:

> A meeting [has been called]. B [arash] gives news in brief. [In the discussion] I give my own opinion that if the "action" continues within

present norms [i.e., three transports, 2,100 each], we should not react. We shall have to sacrifice these 6,300 Jews to save the remaining 35,000. The situation at the front is such that radical changes may take place any day. If they [the Germans] extend the "action," if their behavior forces us to act or [the people in] the streets spontaneously arise to defend themselves, then we shall be forced to take over the initiative, our positive or negative resolution notwithstanding.[121]

Despite nuances in formulation of tactical problems, both Barash and Tenenbaum virtually shared the same opinion: save the majority by sacrificing a minority.

Some of the Council chairmen believed that destiny had chosen them for a historic mission of saving at least that part of the Jews who fitted into the framework of the rescue strategy they had devised. Concluding his address of January 3, 1942, to the representatives of shops, Rumkowski said: "I do hope that, with your help, I shall be able to accomplish my mission and create conditions that will make it possible for wide circles of the ghetto population and its younger generation to live through the present times secure in their lives and health."[122] He thought that "Providence would help him to accomplish this task."[123] There were people who tried to strengthen Rumkowski in his belief. On February 1, 1942, he called a meeting of delegates of approximately 20,000 deportees from Germany, Vienna, Prague, and Luxembourg. Two rabbis from Germany, quoting the Bible and the Midrash, spoke of "the historical role in the history of modern Jewry which has been granted to Rumkowski by the Almighty."[124]

Merin also believed that he had been granted the historical role of saving the Jews from complete destruction, not only in Eastern Upper Silesia, but everywhere under German rule. He entertained grandiose plans, a kind of "salvation philosophy," quite apart from work as a strategy for rescue. He dreamed of establishing a strong Jewish state, which would, as he said in his loose talk, under his leadership gain respect from all and sundry. According to Wiederman, Merin confessed to his secretary, Fanny Czarny, that he had heard an inner voice calling to him: "You, Moshe, are chosen to redeem your people out of Hitler's bondage, even as your namesake freed the Jews from the bondage of Egypt." He added that "he devotedly believed in this call."[125] In the course of Hitler's unbroken chain of victories, Rumkowski allegedly confided in his secretary that after the war, when the problem would arise of solving the Jewish question by settling the Jews somewhere on land designated by the victorious Hitler, he, Rumkowski, would be given authority over all Jews and would establish an exemplary state, for he had great influence with Arthur Greiser, the *Gauleiter* of the Wartheland, and was also known in Berlin.[126]

It is hard to judge now how much of these sickly fantasies about historic missions was pathological *mania grandiosa*,[127] encouraged by the German strategam of granting deceptive "authority" over large Jewish communities to individuals whom they kept firmly on a leash, or how much was simply rationalization of an urge for personal prestige and power dominating these two ghetto heads.[128] Perhaps both factors have to be considered.

The process of preparing lists of candidates for "resettlement" was not identical everywhere. As often happened under German rule, here too one finds a great deal of arbitrariness and inconsistent procedure. In the Łódź Ghetto, for example, candidates for "resettlement" during the first half of 1942 were chosen from lists prepared by the resettlement committee of the Jewish ghetto administration. The same procedure was followed during the first days of the 1942 "September action" against children less than ten years of age, the elderly, and the sick, when the ghetto police were still in charge. However, when the Germans took over the "resettlement" action themselves, they selected deportees out of buildings, blocks, or entire streets at random. People were snatched away who were not even in the categories of the lists submitted.[129]

The massive "resettlement action" in Warsaw from July to September 1942 was accomplished in the same arbitrary manner. Until July 29 the inhabitants of entire buildings were taken after checking their personal documents, by the ghetto police, while the SS men stayed in the background. Afterward, however, *Einsatz Reinhard* took over, using the ghetto police as helpers. During the so-called "registration" from September 6 to 12, the fate of the remaining 100,000 Jews of Warsaw depended on their being placed on lists of people entitled to "life numbers." These lists were made up by Jewish foremen and shop managers, in cooperation with the presidium members of the Jewish Council. Thus the Jews themselves had the authority to make selections according to their own criteria. Each foreman of a shop and each chief of a department or enterprise of the Council distributed "life numbers" to persons already assembled at the selection place for resettlement, calling out their names from lists. (The selection place and the selection itself had been nicknamed "the Kettle.") But the SS men in charge did not always adhere to this procedure, and selected people for deportation according to their whims. According to official figures, only about 30,000 Jews (shop workers, ghetto clerks, and policemen) remained in the much reduced ghetto area after this "selection."[130]

In other ghettos, where several "resettlements" took place in sequence, the Germans ordered the Councils to prepare lists of candidates according to their instructions. As a rule, the Jews were afterward chased from their homes and ordered to assemble at certain places, where the selection was made from the submitted lists. But it often happened that the Germans disregarded the lists and chose victims according to their own momentary whims. During the period of final liquidation of the ghettos, no lists were necessary anymore. All Jews without exception were then "resettled" or killed, mainly on the outskirts of towns. Sometimes a few persons may have been spared to clean up deserted ghettos, or a small group of young men and women would be sent to a labor camp. Slaughter, without using prepared lists, was particularly common during the mass murders in Ostland and the Ukraine in the second part of 1941 and early in 1942. In places where German authorities did not themselves assemble the Jews, the Jewish Councils were often ordered to announce to the Jews when and where to report for "resettlement."

In executing orders to submit lists of able-bodied Jews and those incapable of work, the Councils sometimes used tactics bordering on sabotage. At the beginning of January 1942 the Council at Krosno (Galicia district) got an order from the *Stadtkommissar* to submit a list of the Jewish population as of June 22, 1941. The list had to include age, occupation, and working ability for each person. The list was ready on February 10, 1942, and contained the names of 2,072 persons from 626 families. All requested data were indicated except the ability to work, which was given regarding only 531 persons. In regard to 1,499 persons, i.e., 72.5 percent of the entire Jewish population of the town, this detail was omitted, the proper space simply left blank. Apparently sensing the fate of the infirm and unwilling to take upon itself responsibility for the people involved, the Council simply gave no information as to whether they were able to work. Only 42 persons, whose infirmity was apparent (elderly or sick), were designated "unable to work."[131]

The Jewish Councils were not the only representative bodies under Nazi rule that, under duress, applied the tactics of sacrificing the weak, the undesirables, in order to save those regarded as more worthy. The incidents in Buchenwald of April 1945 are a case in point.

Benedict Kautsky, one of the members of the underground political group in the camp, had this to say about those fateful events when the SS menacingly pressed for the delivery of victims to the transports destined for annihilation:

This [underground group] sabotaged orders and put up passive resistance to the point where the use of force on the part of the SS had to be reckoned with; above all, it consciously tried to save the real political elements of all nations from the transports. This was the most difficult part of the task which burdened this group of prisoners. They had to take upon themselves the responsibility for the deaths of thousands in order to save thousands of others. They applied the law of the camp for the last time: those to be sent to the transports were the undesirables (for example, all "green" and "black" German prisoners [criminals and asocial elements]), but due to the fact that the numbers for this category were far from enough, the weakest inmates were also sent, mostly those who were candidates for death anyway. In spite of my usual doubt about [the equity] of this camp-law I couldn't this time deny its justification, because now such a basis of selection was the only right one. For the political underground this was an agonizing decision and a bitter task in which to cooperate first on this April 7, and later in the following days, in the evacuation of the camp, which constantly was replenished with newcomers from the neighboring camps. . . . just because it was evident that the majority of these unfortunates were doomed to death, it was justifiable to save thousands of healthy men through their death, . . . later it developed that even political prisoners had to be delivered into the hands of the SS. . . . People who didn't shrink from the task of sending others to death were the most active in the endeavor to save as many people as possible in the spring of 1945 [after the liberation]. How many contradictions are hidden in human nature and how impossible is it to characterize it with only one quality.

Similarly, with less soul-searching, another former prisoner of Buchenwald, Eugen Kogon related these occurrences in Buchenwald in April 1945.[132] It may be added that it is safe to conjecture that similar occurrences took place in other camps, though this is the only incident to have come to light so far.

Looking for a historical analogy to the heart-rending dilemma the Jewish Councils had to face in this fateful era, we recall the times of the despot Czar Nicholas I, from 1827 to 1856, when conscription into the Russian army was forced upon the Jews of Russia. Paragraph 8 of the law of August 26, 1827, ruled that "it is the responsibility of the Jewish community to see to it that military service for Jews, when ordered by the governor, is punctually accomplished." According to Paragraph 33, "in case the authorized functionaries [of the community] are guilty of abuses against the performance of military service, they will pay a fine [of 1,000 rubles] for each missing recruit. If they have no money, they themselves will be conscripted, but will not be included in the quota of recruits of the pertinent community." Furthermore, Paragraph 9 stated that "if the recruits and the fines are not delivered on time, the governor will take both recruits and fines by force."

This draconic law, which made hated Czarist agents out of community leaders, forced them to deliver for military service for twenty-five years even children (Par. 3 of the law stated that "the Jewish communities are to deliver recruits twelve to twenty-five years of age"). Sometimes even smaller children were snatched away from their parents. All this created an unbearable situation for community leaders: they faced the danger of themselves being drafted for hard labor in military penal battalions if they did not comply with the law.

The law of 1827 exempted from conscription rich traders, members of the "merchant guilds," officially appointed rabbis (but not their children), honor graduates of elementary and high schools or universities, licensed, skilled workers employed in factories owned by Jews, and farm laborers, all in very short supply among the Jews at that time. Thus the heavy burden of the "cantonist *gzeyra*" (evil order, as it was called by the Jews) fell upon the poor and unprivileged people. It had a profoundly demoralizing effect upon individuals and communities at large. As in the dismal era of Hitler's rule, some people searched for means to save themselves and their loved ones at the expense of others. It happened that parents kidnaped and delivered children to the authorities, substituting them for their own. Some communities even engaged professional kidnapers resembling the ghetto police of over a century later. Communities also went through a time of grim police terror. We learn from contemporary literature and from the memoirs of former "cantonists," that the community leadership themselves made some kind of selection of expendable persons. Religious scholars, young Torah students, and, generally, boys with "sharp brains," who might have been expected to produce future cadres of scholars and rabbis, were spared as far as possible. "Taking into consideration the great role piety and religious scholarship played in Jewish life of that era, this was quite natural," noted the historian of Russian Jewry, Saul Ginsburg.[133] It should be taken into consideration that for the conscripted youngsters this ultimately meant forced conversion to the Russian Orthodox faith—a fate, to the parents of these times, equal to death.

The President of the State of Israel, Mr. Zalman Shazar, has recently drawn a similar analogy. During a session of the Circle for the Study of Jewish Life in the Diaspora held at the president's residence in November 1964, Dr. Jacob Robinson delivered a paper entitled, "Discontinuity and Continuity in the Jewish Councils during the Nazi Era." In the ensuing discussion, Mr. Shazar compared the activities of Jewish community leaders in conjunction with the "cantonist evil order" and the selection of victims for the Germans by the Jewish Ghetto Councils, and speculated that the head of the Vilna community had probably reasoned as follows: If they [the Czarist authorities] take [the recruits] themselves, they will snatch children and Torah students from whose midst future sages may come; if I, however, deliver them myself, I will choose the simpletons, thus saving those who are the most promising. Concluding his remarks, Mr. Shazar added that the path which Gens took, and for which he has been condemned, may have been similar to the one his forebears chose a century before him.[134]

THE INDIVIDUAL AND COLLECTIVE BEHAVIOR
OF COUNCIL MEMBERS

We have already indicated that the behavior of individual members and the collective reactions of Councils toward the German authorities and their orders were not uniform. A great deal depended on their moral background, personal courage, and readiness to make sacrifices. Two principal—and contradictory—attitudes emerged. One of these was to go along with the authorities, even as far as participating in the "resettlement actions," but at the same time to try and mollify the ferocious measures of persecution and to save whomever possible by intercessions and bribery, and by making the Jews useful to the German war economy. The second attitude was to refuse cooperation as much as was feasible, or to confine cooperation to the very minimum, but, in any event, not to participate in "resettlements," even if this resulted in the severest punishment. There were, however, Council members who recklessly assisted the Germans in chasing victims to assembly places for "selection," even helping to expose concealed Jews. Some were anxious in this way to rescue themselves and their families and friends. Others were eager to exploit the anarchy and lawlessness of the German occupation to enrich themselves at the expense of their mortally endangered brethren. These people, the products of times without analogy, assimilated the mores of their oppressors, and, contaminated by poisoned conditions and the complete breakdown of all ethical criteria among the German authorities, slavishly collaborated—coercing, blackmailing, and informing against their fellow Jews.

The individual and collective attitudes of members and Councils in a few major ghettos have already been discussed. We shall now proceed to discuss the conduct of individual members and of Councils as a whole in the medium and small ghettos throughout the occupied territories in the East.

Refusal to Cooperate during the Pre-"Resettlement" Era

Even prior to the advent of massive "resettlement" there were instances where Council members refused to cooperate with the Germans, sabotaged orders, or courageously interceded on behalf of the persecuted. Often they paid for these actions with their lives on the spot or were included in the very next "resettlement" transport. These acts of dedication, high spirit, and moral standards on the part of some of the ghetto leaders deserve to be remembered.

The chairman of the first Jewish Council at Lwów, Dr. Joseph Parnas, was arrested in October 1941 and apparently killed shortly thereafter for refusing to comply with an order to deliver several thousand Jews, ostensibly for forced labor out of town.[135] The chairman of the first Jewish Council at Nowogródek, the lawyer Ciechanowski, and his Council members (eight persons in all) were shot, presumably in the spring of 1942. According to another source, they were executed "for refusing to cooperate with the Germans."[136] The chairman of the second Council at Nowogródek, Chaim Ajzykowicz, was shot a few months after taking office, again "for not collaborating with the German authorities."[137] For the impudence of trying to rescind the expulsion of the Jews from Cracow (which lasted from May 1940 to April 1941), the Council chairman, Marek Biberstein, was arrested together with four Council members: Dr. Wilhelm Goldblat, Bernard Leinkram, one Goldflus (his first name could not be ascertained), and Shmelke Mayer. Biberstein was sentenced to a prison term of one and a half years, and Goldflus to six months. Goldblat and Leinkram were acquitted, and the investigation against Mayer was quashed; but a short time thereafter he was sent to Auschwitz where he perished.[138]

Numerous other Council members lost their lives endeavoring to help ghetto inhabitants. Some sought to alleviate the misery of forced laborers or interceded on behalf of arrested Jews; others tried to have certain measures of persecution canceled or refused outright to comply with orders which endangered the lives of Jews. In this category belong Elisser and Lipe Mishelevski, one the chairman and the other a member of the Council at Kleck; also in this category was the second chairman of the Council at Włodzimierz Wołyński, the lawyer Dr. Pass. Elisser and Mishelevski lost their lives because they tried to get more food for the ghetto through their contacts with non-Jews outside. Together with approximately 200 Jews, they perished during the first slaughter at Kleck on October 30, 1941.[139] Dr. Pass, who had also tried to provide more food for the ghetto, was shot during the second "action" in Włodzimierz Wołyński in the fall of 1941.[140] A member of the Council there, Symcha Bergman (according to another source, he was the police chief of this ghetto), was murdered together with his entire family during September 1942 because he did not round up the required number of Jews and, moreover, tried to set free those already arrested.[141] The deputy chief of the labor department of the Jewish Council of Siedlce, Josef Sadownik, was shot by the SS-man Beckenstadt at the end of November 1942 because of his "liberal treatment" of Jewish forced laborers. He had taken the elderly and sick persons from the labor columns and sent them home.[142] A Council member at Rubieżewicze, Stołpce county (Byelorussia), Yitzhak Gurian, "was repeatedly beaten by the Germans whenever he tried to intercede on behalf of a Jew in trouble." He was deported to Nowogródek and, later, to a camp at Smolensk, where he perished.[143] In 1941 the

Germans demanded that the chairman of the Council at Sandomierz (Lublin district), Leib Goldberg, deliver within a few hours a well-to-do Jew whom they accused of concealing personal property. Although Goldberg knew where the man had been hiding, he did not betray him. When the hidden person did not report at the appointed time, the German police shot Goldberg to death on the staircase of the Council building.[144] Later on, SS men came to arrest the vice chairman of the Council, Apelbaum, for the same crime. Not finding him, they threatened to shoot 20 Jews. Apelbaum then reported to the police and was shot.[145]

The Period of "Resettlements"

1. *Reprisals against noncooperation in general.* The period of the "resettlement actions" provided the Germans with a convenient opportunity to get rid of Council members they disliked. The first chairman of the *Judenrat* at Kołomyja, Chaim Ringelblum, was deported shortly after he had informed the Germans that he could not accept the nomination. As already mentioned in Chap. 2, he and his family were included in the first "resettlement" transport from Kołomyja. The first chairman of the Jewish Council at Zawiercie (Eastern Upper Silesia), Ignatz Buchner, opposed those Council members who favored cooperation with the Germans. He also opposed their various schemes and misdeeds. His attitude evoked the wrath of the authorities, and he was arrested together with his family. All were deported to Auschwitz in the summer of 1942. His was the only entire family deported at that time.[146] The chairman of the Council at Przemyśl, Dr. Ignatz Duldig, was accused of sabotaging collection of a fine imposed on the ghetto. He and the vice chairman of the Council, Zygo Rechter, were shot in the course of the first "action" at the end of July 1942 for noncooperation in the execution of orders issued by the authorities. Under the same accusation another Council member, Samuel Meisler, was deported to the death camp at Bełżec.[147] According to Israel Tabaksblat, Hans Biebow, chief of the Łódź *Gettoverwaltung*, personally shot to death the chairman of the Jewish Council at Zduńska Wola, Dr. Jacob Lemberg. Biebow took him from a group of some 1,000 persons who had already been exempted from the "resettlement action" of August 24 and 25, 1942, and sent into the Łódź Ghetto. According to another source, Biebow took revenge on Lemberg because he had refused to

deliver 10 Jews for hanging on March 3, 1942, stating that though he had no Jews for hanging he could deliver himself and his family.[148]

Some 20 Jews from the neighboring village of Giełczyny were taken to Łomża and put in the dungeons of the Gestapo. The Jews broke the lock and, having no place to go, took refuge in the ghetto. The next morning the Gestapo ordered the chairman of the Jewish Council to deliver 40 Jews of his own choosing and threatened harsh punishment if the order was not executed. When the Jewish police refused to comply, the Gestapo "selected" the Jews themselves, including two Council members.[149]

2. *Reprisals for noncooperation during the "resettlement actions."* Council members who refused to cooperate in the course of "resettlement actions" were treated with particular severity. The vice chairman of the Council at Biłgoraj (Lublin district), Hilel Janover, and three members—Szymon Bin, Shmuel Leib Olender, and Ephraim Waksszul—were all shot on May 3, 1942, on the eve of the "resettlement" to Bełżec, for not executing an order to compile a list of candidates for deportation.[150] The chairman of the Council of the Baranowicze Ghetto, Joshua (Ovsey) Izykson, was shot, together with his secretary, Genia Men, after he rejected an order to select and deliver elderly and sick Jews and to prepare a list of such persons. Both were executed on Shushan Purim of 1942.[151] The prewar community leader and city councilman of Kałuszyn, Abraham Gamzu, who was chairman of the Jewish Council, categorically rejected a demand of the Gestapo to deliver Jews for "resettlement" (the first deportation to Treblinka took place in Kałuszyn in September 1942). He was shot at his home.[152] Another Council member who refused to compile a list of candidates for deportation was a member of the Council at Czernolice (Horodenka county), Moshe Drohobyczer, who represented the expellees of Horodenka.[153] His fate is not recorded.

The chairmen of the Councils and individual members were sometimes included in "resettlement" transports when the German authorities were not satisfied with the results of "actions." Such was the fate of the second chairman of the Cracow Ghetto, Dr. Artur Rosenzweig. He was dismissed on the spot, arrested, and with his family included in the current transport for deportation because the "resettlement" action in Cracow, which took place from June 4 to 6, 1942, "gave no satisfactory results in regard to both the number and the technique of delivery of the people to the assembly square."[154]

The chairman of the Dąbrowa Jewish Council (Eastern Upper Silesia), the lawyer Adolf Weinberg, refused to deliver a list of "resettlement" candidates or to tell where some of the endangered people were hiding. He and his entire family were deported.[155]

Some members of the Councils were executed for interceding with the authorities before the start of a "resettlement action." Such was the lot of the chairman of the Mołczadź Ghetto, one Ehrlich (a refugee from Silesia), as well as of a Council member, Leib Gilerowicz, who interceded with the *Distriktkommissar* of Baranowicze on the eve of the liquidation of the ghetto. They were tortured and killed.[156] Two members of the Council of Elders in Šiauliai, Aron Katz and Berl Kartun, tried to save children during the "children's action" on November 5, 1943. They were deported along with the young victims.[157] After the first "action" in the Włodzimierz Wołynski Ghetto had passed, the treasurer of the Jewish Council, David Halpern, came out of the bunker where he had been hiding and tried to ransom the surviving Jews (there had been a rumor that people could be ransomed to escape further "resettlements"). He was caught and killed on the spot.[158]

Council members were also killed for refusing to sign certain "resettlement" documents. In Mińsk Mazowiecki the chairman of the Council, Moshe Kramarz, refused to sign on behalf of the Council a paper which was given to him by two Gestapo men, Brandt and Handtke. Both had arrived from Warsaw where the death squad had interrupted the "action" in the ghetto for a few days "to work" in other ghettos throughout the territory of the Warsaw district. The paper stated that the Council hereby delivered the Jews of its own free will. Kramarz tore it into small pieces in front of the people and in a loud voice warned of the real meaning of the "resettlement" (which was to take place there on August 21, 1942). The Gestapo men beat him up and dragged him, three other Council members—Leon Weinberg, Meir-Sholem Briks, and Jacob Popowski—and several Jewish policemen first to a camp in the town and then to the Gestapo building, where they were shot.[159] The chairman of the Council at Złoczów, Dr. Meiblum, was shot by Engels, deputy chief of the liquidation "action" in Galicia, after he refused to sign a paper stating that the liquidation of the ghetto was necessitated by the spread of a typhus epidemic.[160]

As mentioned above, there also were Council members who during the "resettlements" refused offers by the authorities to allow them to save their lives by remaining with the remnants. There also were Council members who refused to take advantage of help offered by their non-Jewish friends outside the ghetto, choosing rather to join the community at the execution place or in the already loaded railroad cars. A member of the Jewish Council in Warsaw, Abraham Gepner, rejected an offer from Polish friends to shelter him on the "Aryan" side. He remained in the ghetto until the end.[161] There are three different sources testifying to the fact that the chairman of the Jewish Council at Rubieżewicze, Lote Eisenbud, refused the offers of a local priest and of the chief of the local Byelorussian auxiliary police to take him out of the ghetto before the liquidation action started there in July 1942. "He proudly went to his grave in the company of the rabbi and other distinguished citizens, all wearing their prayer shawls and phylacteries, carrying the Torah, and singing psalms on the way."[162]

Two Council members at Iwie (near Lida)—Shalom Zak and Bezalel Milkowski—refused to join a group of people who were among those selected to remain for the time being. They went over to those who were doomed to destruction. Their families were also included in this group. Milkowski removed the Council member's armband he was wearing and told the Germans that he did not want their "favor."[163] The Elder of the Council at Brailów (in the Ukraine), Josef Kulok, acted similarly. Though the leader of the "action" there told him to join the skilled workers who were being spared with their families, Kulok chose to go to his execution together with approximately 3,000 Jews.[164] Nor did the chairman of the Council at Siedlce, the physician Dr. Henryk Lebel, accept any "favors" when the Germans, during an "action" on August 22, 1942, gave him a chance to go into the "small ghetto" established for the remnants of the Siedlce Ghetto. He remained at his post in the hospital and was shot two days later when the hospital was closed and its patients and personnel liquidated in the backyard of the hospital.[165]

During a "resettlement" action in August 1942, the chief of the *Arbeitsamt* at Mińsk Mazowiecki offered to hide in his home a member of the Council's presidium Mordecai Josef Kirszenbaum, who was a friend of his (the reason for this unusual friendship of a German occupation official and a member of a Jewish Council is not revealed in the pertinent source). Kirszenbaum, however, refused, saying that if it was ordained that he perish, he preferred to die together with his family and in the company of Jews.[166] The chairman of the Council at Kosów Poleski, Motel Chajkin, scornfully rejected an offer by the *Stadtkommissar* to save him.[167] On German orders, a member of the Jewish Council at Łuków, David Liberman, collected money from Jews who were already assembled in the market square for "resettlement." He apparently believed that the money would ransom the Jews. Only after completing the collection did he learn that the Jews were to be shipped to Treblinka anyway. He shouted at the German supervisor of the "action": "Here is your payment for our trip, you bloody tyrant." Then he tore the money into small shreds and slapped the German's face. Ukrainian guards murdered him on the spot.[168]

There were Council functionaries who demonstrated similarly high moral standards. In a spirit of solidarity with the community and loyalty to their fellow Jews, they chose death rather than the privilege of exemption. Thus the secretary of the Council of Elders in Ozorków (Wartheland), Mania Rzepkowicz, rejected an offer of the German *Gettoleiter* to be excluded from the "resettlement" which took place there on May 22, 1942. Together with her child, she joined a group of approximately 300 children who were being transported to the death camp at Chełmno.[169]

There were Council members who preferred suicide rather than life amid the unbearable suffering and moral pressures of these loathsome times. Suicides took place not only during periods of "resettlement," when the Councils, deceived and terrorized by the authorities, were pressed into the service of the Germans to assist in preparing and executing the "actions," but also at earlier times during the occupation. Unable to stand the constant tension of deliberate humiliation and insult by the Germans, some Council members put an end to the miseries of their lawless and demeaning existences.

The case of the chairman of the Jewish Council of the Warsaw Ghetto, Adam Czerniakow, is well known. He took his life by poison on the second day of the massive deportation on July 24, 1942, when the Germans increased the daily quota of Jews to be delivered to the Umschlagplatz where people were loaded into freight cars for Treblinka. Incidentally the chief of staff of the *Einsatz Reinhard*, Hoefle, who was in charge of the Warsaw "resettlement action," had threatened to shoot Czerniakow's wife on July 23 if the "action" did not produce the desired results.[170]

Among the first suicides of Council members was that of the

chairman of the Jewish Council at Tomaszów Mazowiecki, B. Szeps. He took his life as early as the end of 1940.[171] The first chairman of the Council at Bolechów, Dr. Reifeisen, hanged himself after the *Stadtkommissar* slapped his face because the remodeling and furnishing of the house chosen for his residence had not been completed on time. "The Germans will not slap me anymore," were Dr. Reifeisen's last words.[172] His deputy Council chairman, Dr. Israel Shindler, also took his life after the first "action" at the beginning of March 1942.[173]

The member of the Równe Jewish Council, the lawyer Jacob (Leon) Sucharczuk, who had been active in communal work before the war, committed suicide in the summer of 1941. He injected a large dose of morphine following an order to deliver a large group of able-bodied Jews ostensibly for labor out of town. At a meeting of the Council, called to prepare lists of candidates, he had sharply opposed the idea of submitting any lists at all and had appealed to his fellow Council members to refuse the demand. The majority, however, decided to comply. He went home and put an end to his life.[174]

Abraham Shvetz, chairman of the Jewish Council at Międzyrzec (Volhynia district) committed suicide after the Germans ordered him to deliver 100 (according to another version, 250) young and healthy Jews, ostensibly for labor in Kiev.[175]

The chairman of the Council at Równe, Dr. Bergman, was ordered by the Germans to deliver a number of Jews for "resettlement." He told them that he could deliver only his family and himself. Shortly thereafter he committed suicide.[176]

Zvi Wider, former chairman of the ORT at Białystok (he had been active in the affairs of artisans and served as a member of the Jewish Council during the occupation), hanged himself after he learned that the Council had prepared a list of candidates for the first "resettlement" on February 5, 1943.[177]

A member of the Jewish Council at Grodno, Arye Marder, who had been in charge of the ghetto's statistical department, submitted his resignation in November 1942 when it became apparent that the Germans intended to use his statistical material to liquidate the Jews. The Council put his name on the list of candidates for the next transport. When he learned about this he committed suicide. Efforts to revive him failed. His family was deported on the next transport.[178]

When Hersh Getzel Hoichbaum, a member of the Council at

Szczebrzeszyn, learned that people sent away during "resettlements" were not heard from anymore, he told his colleagues that he did not want to be the dispatcher of fellow Jews to their deaths. He hanged himself later in the attic of his house.[179]

Shortly after the Jewish Council was established in Krzemieniec, a Council member, the lawyer Benjamin Landsberg, tried to cut his throat. He had been terribly beaten for allegedly trying to sabotage an imposed contribution and other measures of persecution. He was, however, saved.[180]

A member of the Council at Łomża, Dr. Joseph Hepner, "rather than cooperate with the Nazis," committed suicide during a "resettlement" action that lasted from the beginning of November 1942 till January 10, 1943.[181] Similarly the secretary of the Płońsk Jewish Council Sieradzki, took his life during the liquidation of the ghetto.[182]

The chairman of the Council of Kołomyja, Markus (Motel) Horowic, who as has been mentioned was a controversial figure in the ghetto, tried to take his life twice—once in November and a second time in December 1942, when only some 3,000 Jews were left in the ghetto of approximately 15,000. After his first attempt the Gestapo with much effort revived him; however, he succeeded the second time, poisoning himself together with his sister Miriam in the Council building. It is said that he left a letter stating that he "had hoped to be able to save at least part of the ghetto community, but seeing that there was not the slightest possibility, he decided to die an honorable death and be given a [customary] Jewish burial."[183]

A member of the Council of Włodzimierz Wołyński, Jacob Kogen, committed suicide together with his wife and their thirteen-year-old son on September 1, 1942, after the authorities had demanded delivery of 7,000 Jews. Kogen "did not want to decide who was to be taken away."[184]

Information is available concerning two attempted collective suicides of entire ghetto Councils. At Bereza Kartuska, when the Germans ordered that Jews report at the marketplace on October 15, 1942, "for work in Russia," the Jewish Council intuitively sensed what the real intention of the Germans was. During a meeting held on October 14, almost all of the members took their lives by hanging themselves in the room where they deliberated. Two ghetto physicians, Dr. Lichtiger and Dr. Shapiro, who were not Council members, also committed suicide in the same room together with their families.[185] Another source does not mention the physicians' suicide, but confirms that almost all of the 12 Council members took their lives. According to this source, the tragic act took place in the house of Elias Moshe Epstein.[186]

As for the Prużana Ghetto, we have the account of a survivor of the ghetto which sounds like a modern Masada epic. On November 1, 1942, after the ghetto had been surrounded by the Germans, the intelligentsia (physicians, teachers, etc.) and their families gathered in the house of the Council's vice chairman, the lawyer Velvl Shreibman. Forty-one persons including the members of the Jewish Council were present, and it was decided to commit suicide collectively by poison in order to avoid falling alive into the hands of the SS men. The decision was to poison the children first, then the women, and finally the men. The host was to be the last to take his life, so that he would be able to see that the mass suicide was accomplished without a hitch. Apparently the doses of poison were too small, for the victims only drowsed. Shreibman then heated the oven, shut off the chimney, and filled the room with fumes. At dawn people came to visit Shreibman and ask for news about the Council's decision. They saw the horrible scene and tried to revive the people. With the exception of one person, Hirsz Ilenicki, all were revived and lived until the end of the last "action" in January 1943, when they perished. Characteristically this attempt at collective suicide was resented by the ghetto community. People maintained that the intelligentsia should not have let the community down, yielding to desperation rather than serving as an example to prevent the community from a spiritual breakdown at such a crucial time.[187]

Shmuel Verble, chairman of the ghetto of Kamién Koszyraki, a little town in Volhynia, was ordered to deliver a list of names of 80 inhabitants of the ghetto. The purpose of this list was unknown to him, but when, after the delivery, he learned that the Germans were going to kill all the people on the list, he went to the local post of the gendarmes and asked to be included in the group. The Germans accepted his request. He was the last of them to be shot, in August 1941.[188]

Thus far we have analyzed the behavior *in extremis* of those Council members who gave their lives to protect the community, help individuals in danger, or protest German measures. Unfortunately lawlessness and the breakdown of all moral principles provided persons of weak character or low moral standards with opportunities for self-advancement. Driven by the ambitious pursuit of authority, honor, and profits, and with a total disregard for the welfare of the ghetto community, some Council members used the positions of pseudo-authority the Germans professed to have granted them for their own personal security and selfish advantage. It should be added that in the course of negative selections of people to serve on the Councils chosen by the German authorities, the quality and ethics of the members had generally been lowered with the result that their acts became even more damaging and degrading (see Chap. 13). Instances of moral breakdown among the Council members follow.

Members of the Złoczów Jewish Council actively participated in a "resettlement action," assisting the Germans and the Ukrainian police in hunting Jews out of their hiding places.[189]

Eyewitness accounts relate that the chairman of the Jewish Council at Głębokie, Gershon L.,

obediently executed all orders of the German authorities . . . exploited the ghetto population and enjoyed a good living . . . punished youngsters who endeavored to leave and join the partisans. . . . He used the ghetto police to assault, arrest, and terrorize the Jews. . . . He often spread alarming news: once, that it was necessary to find 10 kilograms of gold for the Germans; another time, that gold watches and other valuables were needed. Nobody ever knew for sure whether L. actually needed the jewelry to satisfy the Germans or wanted it for himself. One of the witnesses relates that L. informed the Germans that some Jews were planning to leave the ghetto to join the partisans. Because of his betrayal, two families (the daughter of Elisha Gordon, her husband and child, and the Feigel family, parents and a daughter) were shot.[190]

The physician Dr. F.S., a member of the Council and chief of the sanitation department at Baranowicze, "together with two other members, A. and B., informed, collaborated, and entertained lavishly at the expense of the starving community. . . . Dr. F.S. threatened to denounce us to the Gestapo, if we did not see to it that the local partisan group stopped its activities." One of the eyewitnesses, who was with F.S. in the camp at Kołdychevo, writes: "In company with policemen, Dr. F.S. searched out and beat up Jews who had hidden themselves with the intention of joining the partisans."[191] The Berezno Council in Volhynia did not distribute even the tiny portions of bread the Germans allowed the Jews. . . . They sold the bread . . . allocated to forced laborers in Kostopol. . . . The Council requisitioned a fur coat from one Nyse Sapoźnik, sold it, and arranged revels with the money. . . . They reasoned that since only they would survive of all the Jews in Berezno, there would be no one to testify against them, anyway. . . . The Council was paid large amounts of money for the chance to be included in the lists of skilled workers. . . . They demanded textiles and cash in gold.[192]

The pernicious activities of a number of the Council members at Zawiercie, including the second chairman, M.W., are described by an eyewitness:

He [the chairman] was rude and coarse, allowing no criticism of the activities of the Council and, particularly, of his own doings. He protected those who knew how to lick his boots. . . . During the "resettlement" of August 1943, when he received news that all Jews, except a very small group of skilled workers, would be deported to Auschwitz (and it was already known what *that* meant) he assembled 40 members of his own family and put their names on the list of skilled workers.

Of the liaison man between the Zawiercie Council and the local German authorities the following is related: "F. freely walked [in town], dealt with the Germans, flattered them to win their favors, drank and played cards with them. [However,] such a character was needed in the Council, and not many were willing to take the job." The chief of the financial department of the Zawiercie Council, I., also had a bad reputation. He was Merin's relative and therefore an influential person in the ghetto. A former resident of the Zawiercie Ghetto relates that during a "resettlement action" I. gave him a large amount of money and valuables to conceal because the Gestapo was after him. Yet another high official of the ghetto, the physician L., who was in charge of the ghetto hospital, was hated for his brutality toward patients. He would call the police to forcibly remove unwelcome patients from his office.[193]

An eyewitness relates about the vice chairman of the Siedlce Council, C., that

as soon as the Council was established, he instantly upgraded his standard of living. . . . The fact that all of a sudden large amounts of money came into his hands, and that other opportunities also came his way, simply turned his head. He believed that he had limitless powers and took advantage of his position, profiting by the general misery. He took a lion's share of the large sums of money and jewelry which were entrusted to him for safekeeping against a time of emergency when it would be necessary to pay off the Germans. He lived in comfort. The Councilmen used to go for a good time to his home.[194]

Another case of moral breakdown in the atmosphere of the Final Solution is provided in the chronicle of the Skałat Ghetto by A. Weisbrod, a former ghetto inmate:

During the so-called "wild action" on October 21 and 22, 1942, *Obersturmbannführer* Müller made a deal with the representatives of the Council and the *Kommandant* of the Ghetto police, Dr. Joseph Brif, to take an active part in the "action," solemnly proclaiming that [if they did] they and their families would be saved. . . . In the meantime, they got Müller to release Council members and their families who had already been caught in the course of the action. Their main task was to help find bunkers and other hiding places of the Jews. . . . After the bloody action . . . a band of SS men went to the Jewish Council where they had a good time. A banquet was waiting for them. . . . caterers busied themselves around the richly adorned tables and slavishly tried to satisfy the guests. Jolly laughter was heard, music played, and the guests reveled, sang, and were merry. This at a time when 2,000 persons had been driven into the synagogue and nearly suffocated from lack of air, while others were kept in the meadow by the rairoad tracks in the cold.[195]

Faced with the realities of their terrible situations, some of the Council members underwent changes of heart in their attitudes. In our poll taken among former ghetto residents is an account to this effect concerning the vice chairman of the Opoczno Jewish Council, one M.R. Since this is rather an unusual case, we quote here an extensive excerpt from Questionnaire No. 788:

No sooner was the Jewish Council established in Opoczno than R. became the informant of the Germans [he had been an informant of the Polish authorities before the war] and was appointed a member of the Council after completing a successful exchange of hostages.* He worked

---

* This event took place in the following circumstances, characteristic of the times: Three weeks after the occupation of Opoczno, the Germans arrested three well-to-do Jews as hostages to be shot, if 20,000 zlotys in ransom money was not paid within 24 hours. Their alarmed families begged that they be rescued, and R., who knew German, volunteered to intercede. He went to the local *Kommandant* of the gendarmes with the proposition that the Germans free the arrested Jews, who, as rich people, would be able to provide the amount demanded. He also promised to produce three other hostages in their place. The suggestion was accepted. The person who gave this information indicated that his father was one of the three initial hostages. He had given R. all their valuables to pay the ransom money. This case actually started R. on his career of collaboration.

hand-in-glove with the Germans . . . informing them where they would find hidden merchandise. . . . People begged him to intercede on behalf of arrested relatives. . . . He was given money to pay off the Germans, but kept a nice share for himself. Although people knew it, there was no alternative, for he was the one and only Jew who was able to deal with the Germans. The man was deep in sin . . . one could see him dining and wining in the company of the Germans, constantly offering them new gifts. . . .

In June 1942 there took place in Opoczno an event which profoundly shook the Jewish population. Twenty Jews had escaped from forced labor and, at the order of the authorities, the ghetto police seized the escapees and placed them under guard in the ghetto jail, located in one of the chambers of the prayer house. When R. intervened with the *Kommandant* of the gendarmes, he was told that all 20 would be shot. The account goes on to describe what happened then:

A sudden change came over R., as if the felon's conscience woke up. Apparently intending to vindicate himself, he went to the prayer house and, through the window, made known to those under arrest that they were in danger, hinting that they had better escape without delay. The arrested Jews broke the window, overpowered the Jewish guards, and escaped. In the morning, when the gendarmes came to take them, all they found was an empty chamber. The gendarmes then went to the Jewish Council and ordered R. and the chairman, F., to find the escaped Jews, or else. To their great surprise, R. answered that he would not deliver them, and that the Germans themselves should go and search for them. He left and disappeared. All efforts by the Germans to find R. were unsuccessful. The *Kommandant* threatened to kill 100 Jews if R. did not report. To prevent innocent people from calamity, R. voluntarily reported to the *Kommandant*. What took place then is not known. However, R.'s dead body was found in the hall of the German *Kommandatur*. Thus, the former informant died a hero's death.

CHAPTER 17

The Attitude of the Councils toward Physical Resistance

BEFORE ANALYZING Council attitudes toward physical resistance against the Germans, three aspects of the problem should be taken into account: (*a*) the objective chances for resistance; (*b*) resistance in relation to other prospects for rescue; and (*c*) the ethical positions of diverse segments of the Jewish population on the very idea of physical resistance. These matters are complicated, and we shall limit ourselves here to discussing only a few of them:

1. The situation of the Jews in the tightly sealed ghettos was such that the objective conditions for physically resisting the Nazi extermination machine with some hope of success simply did not exist.

2. The number of able-bodied males capable of fighting was continually reduced as a result of demographic changes among the ghetto inmates.

3. Because of complete isolation, it was next to impossible to get arms from the outside world, even if they had been offered.

4. There was a complete lack of arms (for instance, the Organization of Jewish Fighters in the Warsaw Ghetto was able to accumulate no more than 10 old pistols up to January 18, 1943, the day of the first attempt at armed resistance).

5. Gentile neighbors were hostile to the Jews except for certain democratic and socialist circles, parts of the liberal intelligentsia, and some of the clergy.

6. An endless mass of often conflicting German orders frustrated any plans for counteraction. The Jews in the ghettos were rendered

physically and mentally weak by constant hunger, disease, and relentless terror. These conditions brought about widespread apathy and a fatalistic attitude, rendering long-range planning impossible, as is demonstrated by events in Vilna, Białystok, and Częstochowa.[1] In addition, the perfidy of the Germans, sudden raids, roundups, and the graduated scale of extermination actions all contributed to the emergence of the illusion that the Jews who remained after each action would survive.

7. The Jewish underground movement could not rely on direct aid from any institution abroad, while the non-Jewish resistance groups systematically received arms, manpower, training, and money from their respective governments-in-exile in London. Without this support they could not exist, grow, or effectively perform.

Of the two basic forms of physical resistance, in the ghettos and in partisan units, the latter offered better prospects for rescue. Considering the chronology of the Holocaust, however, even these prospects were not too bright. It is important to bear in mind that the partisan movement in Eastern Europe, which perhaps provided a chance of rescue for small groups of escapees from the ghettos (because of the generally hostile attitude of the non-Jewish environment, purely Jewish resistance groups had very little chance of holding out), became a serious factor as late as the second half of 1942, at a time when the vast majority of Jews in the Ostland and the Ukraine had already been murdered, and when extermination in the areas of the Government General and the incorporated territories was already in full swing. Incidentally the partisan movement could have meaning only for those ghettos in Eastern Europe situated close to Soviet partisan units, the only ones which were not openly hostile to escapees from the ghettos. The other ethnic partisan groups in that area—Polish, Latvian, Lithuanian, and Ukrainian (except the very small Communist groups)—not only did not admit Jews, but fiercely combatted ghetto refugees who tried to find shelter in the woods.

These and other tragic circumstances thwarted efforts to create meaningful Jewish resistance in the ghettos. To bring the problem into historical perspective it is sufficient to compare the objective fighting possibilities of Jews enclosed in ghettos to those of the resistance movements of non-Jewish segments of the populations in the occupied territories. It is clear that the prospects for armed Jewish resistance leading to rescue were quite minimal. Only young people in good health had a chance to free themselves from the condemned ghettos and reach the partisans, after hazardous peregrinations. The large majority of ghetto inmates—mothers with children, old, sick, emaciated people—were not able to go the long, dangerous way. Not many of those who joined the so-called family camps—groups connected with purely Jewish partisan groups (of the Belsky brothers, for instance)—survived.

There also were unfavorable subjective circumstances for physical struggle. Even during these most difficult times the Jews were confident that the world was not lawless. It was unthinkable that a government in the very heart of civilized Europe, even a Nazi one, should openly hold as its main political goal the physical elimination of an entire people; and it was unthinkable that the world would let it happen. This was one of the reasons why people did not believe in the terrible truth until the very end, when it was too late to plan or undertake anything. When the hideous truth revealed itself in its full horror on the thresholds of gas chambers or on the brinks of mass graves, the victims may have pondered whether it was worthwhile to fight for life after all in a world of limitless bestiality and passive silence.[2] It should also be borne in mind that the Orthodox population of non-Soviet Eastern Europe (constituting perhaps half the inmates of the ghettos) grew up amid the age-old Jewish tradition of spiritual heroism and martyrdom in times of oppression and was therefore historically and mentally unprepared and mostly opposed to the concept of physical resistance. These people were armed with quite different weapons: prayers and faith that the Almighty would have mercy on His oppressed people—that a miracle would happen in the end.

Another factor crippling the will to armed resistance was the nightmare of collective responsibility mercilessly imposed on the occupied areas by the Nazis—the fear that innocent people would suffer because of the resistance of small groups, that for each endeavor to resist or escape from the ghetto into the woods the Nazis would inflict collective reprisals on particular families and even on the entire ghetto. This anxiety sometimes rendered helpless even the most courageous young people in the underground organizations. As long as they remained in the ghettos with their parents and siblings, their feeling of responsibility for their families was a restraining factor against joining the resistance. Only on the eve or during the course of the last liquidation actions, when the end was obviously inescapable, did groups of young people or entire families escape from ghettos in Eastern Poland and Ostland, where there was a better chance to join partisans in the adjacent woods. They often paid a high price for their courageous endeavors.

One more factor hampering organized resistance by the Jews was the deep-seated conviction prevalent among some of the ghetto inmates—particularly the workers, artisans, and experts working for the benefit of the German war machine—that they had a good chance to survive because of their work but that this chance would be destroyed by attempts at resistance. This was the fundamental tenet of the entire rescue conception of the Jewish Councils, a tenet that adversely influenced the ghetto inmates by weakening their will to resist (see Chap. 16).

The majority of ghetto inmates maintained that resistance was not a real alternative to their desperate situation. They feared that it might even speed the liquidation process by giving the Germans an excuse to implement bloody repressions. As evidence of the gap that had grown between the majority of the inmates and the underground resistance movement it is enough to cite the Witenberg case in the Vilna Ghetto in July 1943 (see below).[3]

Believers in the idea of resistance could be found only among the politically conscious inmates—mostly party-affiliated young people. But even these men quarreled among themselves because of fear for the fate of helpless ghetto inmates and of their loved ones, and also because of their inability to agree on where the armed struggle with the enemy should be undertaken. Some believed that the Jewish resistance movement bore a historical responsibility to protect the lives and honor of the oppressed Jewish masses within the ghetto walls; others maintained that, in view of extremely adverse conditions for fighting within the ghetto, the best thing to do was to leave and join the partisans. Heated and prolonged discussions went on in the Vilna, Białystok, and Warsaw Ghettos.[4]

Councils also grappled with this problem and sources testify to their dramatic, passionate discussions. One report describes the soul-searching debate of the Šiauliai Jewish Council: on February 5, 1943, the Council of Elders called a meeting of the coworkers of the ghetto administration, the ghetto court, and members of the Hechalutz organization to discuss the burning problem: whether to start immediately to resist or to wait a little longer; whether to escape to the woods or join the Lithuanian resistance movement with whom some contact had been established prior to the meeting. An evasive answer had been received from the Lithuanian underground: there were not enough arms, it would be hard for escapees to hide, etc. It became clear in the course of the discussion that only well-organized and armed young people had any chance of escaping from the ghetto into the marshlands of northeastern Lithuania, where Soviet partisans operated. Women, elderly or weak people, and children had no chance. As most of those attending the meeting were in these categories, the proposal to escape from the ghetto was rejected. The chairman, Mendel Leibowicz, suggested that the inmates be given arms to prepare for resistance within the ghetto and that the ghetto be set in flames on all sides at the critical moment, so that inmates would have a chance to escape. E. Yerushalmi, to whom we are indebted for this report, notes that apart from arms and a detailed plan, a strong will and readiness to sacrifice women and children were also needed. Those present at the meeting lacked both. This was the main reason why no underground organization was created in Šiauliai.[5]

There was a group in the Łuck Jewish Council who maintained that it would be necessary to put up armed resistance when the Germans came to take their victims from the ghetto,[6] but the majority were against it.

We may therefore conclude that, as with other problems, there was no uniform opinion among the Jewish Councils on the problem of resistance. There were Councils with an extremely negative attitude both to resistance within the ghetto and to escape from the ghetto to join the partisans in the woods. On the other hand, there were Councils that sympathized with the resistance groups and supported them morally and materially. Still others were ambivalent, wavering in their attitude. There were also Councils which actively participated in resistance during the last period of the ghettos' existence.

COUNCILS WITH A NEGATIVE ATTITUDE

It is clear from available sources that the majority of the Councils were against the idea of organized resistance. There were Councils that actively opposed underground groups and denounced them to the Germans. They were afraid that open resistance might spoil their strategy of making the ghetto inmates useful to the Germans. Collective reprisals against the ghettos after Jews had been caught with arms or waging other forms of resistance confirmed these Councils in their negative attitudes. To give only one instance of many: On July 22, 1943, members of a group of the Jewish United Partisan Organization in the Vilna Ghetto left for the Narotch Forest. Fourteen people joined them on the way. During an encounter with the Germans, some of the fighters fell. Two were taken prisoners and perished in Ponary. In retribution, the Gestapo chief, Neugebauer, ordered that the families of the escapees be delivered to him. He also ordered that the brigadiers of the labor units where the escapees had been employed be delivered together with their families. Thirty-two persons were taken from their homes in the night and brought to the prison and, later, to Ponary. Neugebauer issued an order of collective responsibility: the entire family of each escapee was to be seized. In case an escapee had no family, all the persons living with him in the same room were to be seized. If these persons were not found, all the tenants of his building were to be shot. All Jews leaving the ghetto for work were to be separated into groups of 10; if one was missing on return from work, all of his group were to be shot.[7] After this tragic event in which 32 persons were murdered, there appeared in the *Geto-yedies* the following item under the headline "Wrath and Grief" (*Tsar un tsorn*):

The responsibility for these deaths falls onto those who betrayed our ghetto community and all its serious tasks in the full knowledge that they were endangering the existence of our entire ghetto and the lives of their loved ones in the first place. They are responsible for the spilt blood.[8]

The authorities forced the Councils to fight attempts at resistance within the ghettos. Thus, for example, when two armed youngsters detained outside the Białystok Ghetto in mid-February 1942 told who gave them arms, the Jewish Council, in an announcement on February 17, promised a reward of 5,000 marks (the amount was doubled on February 18) to anyone providing information about the arms supplier.[9]

Clearly the reasoning behind the Councils' negative attitude toward resistance was that any attempt at physical resistance would accelerate the liquidation of the ghetto. Under the Nazi system of collective responsibility, every act of opposition by an individual was liable to result in collective punishment for the entire ghetto. As already indicated above, even young people most eager to join the partisans in the forest had agonizing misgivings about whether they were morally entitled to endanger the lives of the vast majority of ghetto inmates, among them their own loved ones. We shall illustrate the situation by a few examples.

One of the members of the underground in Radoszkowice related:

The town was stirred by news [of the establishment of an underground group]. The Council members tried very hard to persuade us that the plan to join the partisans should be abandoned. . . . We were warned that many Jews would be killed because of us, for the Germans would doubtless take revenge on the Jews left behind in the ghetto. The people threatened to denounce us to the Germans if we did not give up our plan. . . . they assembled in the *shul*. . . . preparations began for excommunicating the 10 who, defying the elders, intended to leave for the forest, thus endangering the lives of the others. But they lacked the stamina to excommunicate and wanted only to intimidate us.[10]

The chairman of the Lachowicze Council, Icie Zamudzik, threatened to denounce to the authorities a group of young people of the *Brith Ha Chayal* organization who were planning to escape from the ghetto. He claimed that their escape "would bring about the destruction of the remaining Jews."[11] Szatz, chairman of the Jewish Council at Kurzeniec (Vilna area), summoned the parents of young people who had joined the underground and warned that if their children did not stop their sabotaging activities, or if they escaped to the forest, he would turn the parents over to the Gestapo. Otherwise, he feared, the Germans would destroy all the Jews.[12] Another witness from Kurzeniec related how two Council members came to his and his friend's houses to induce them not to join the partisans. He added that a partisan who had returned to the ghetto from the forest threatened to shoot one of the Council members unless he stopped persecuting the group of young people. Afterward not only were the young people left undisturbed, but the Council even released them from forced-labor duty. Moreover, at the young people's request the Council agreed to send bread to a group of escapees who had hidden themselves in the adjacent camp at Kniahini. Later the group escaped to the forest and took an active part in partisan combat.[13]

Young people in the Kobryn Ghetto made plans to escape and get in touch with partisans in the adjacent woods. When news of their plans reached their parents and the Council, both tried to convince them not to seek their own deaths and to bear in mind that because of them the Germans would destroy the entire ghetto; instead, they would do better, said the parents and the Council, to start working in the labor shops, thus securing the ghetto's existence.[14]

In the Chmielnik Ghetto, when "the Jewish Council learned that a group of people was trying to get some arms, they were threatened with sanctions. The responsible citizens supported the Council in its effort to persuade these people not to engage in such irresponsible acts, which might end in great misfortune." The plan to acquire arms was dropped.[15]

Some Councils actually imposed sanctions against people in the ghetto who spread the resistance idea and who tried to make the necessary arrangements. A survivor of the Kleck Ghetto testified that after he had been in touch with peasants and heard about the activities of partisans in the forests, he, together with some of his friends, began to agitate for the idea of escaping to the forests. But the Council learned about this and warned him that he would be handed over to the Germans if he continued to spread rebellion in the ghetto. He became very angry and tried to convince the Council that this was the only remedy left to the Jews, who were certainly all going to be killed in the ghetto anyway. He was locked up in the so-called cold *shul* for the night. His children asked for his release, and he was set free with the admonition not to spread resistance among the inmates anymore, since this would only lead to disaster for the ghetto.[16] Another Kleck survivor related that, "believing the assertions of the Germans, and trying to protect parents and children, the Jewish Council took various measures to foil all these plans"— he did not describe the measures.[17]

A survivor of Nowogródek related how the Council and the ghetto police did everything in their power to prevent people from leaving the ghetto. As soon as the Jewish policemen received information about someone's planning to leave the ghetto, they imprisoned him in the cellar of the Council building, gave him a thorough beating, and left him lying on the floor. The boots of others who were scheduled to leave for special labor assignments outside the ghetto were taken away each night and returned in the morning.[18]

Other Councils tried to persuade rebellious youths that resistance could not succeed.

Moshe Merin relentlessly opposed the underground movement in Eastern Upper Silesia (Będzin and Sosnowiec). He spared no effort to stop the underground political activities of resistance groups carried out through the youth organizations Hanoar Hazioni, Hashomer Hatzair, Gordonia, Poalei Zion, and Hitachdut. These groups distributed mimeographed leaflets calling on the Jews not to listen to the Council, not to report for labor duty, etc. They even tried to conduct anti-Nazi propaganda in the German army on the eastern front. For this purpose, they put antiwar leaflets in military straw boots and in the pockets of uniforms manufactured in the ghetto. Merin, on whom the resistance had imposed their sentence of death, discovered that the mimeograph machine they used was located in the apartment of Zvi Dunski, the leader of Hashomer Hatzair in Sosnowiec. He ordered Dunski arrested along with his comrade, H. Minc. But the police did not find Dunski in his home, so Merin arrested a number of his comrades, demanding that they tell him of Dunski's whereabouts. They refused, and Merin ordered the arrest of Dunski's mother and sister. They were confined in the former orphanage in Będzin, which was being used as an assembly place for deportations. Merin did not rest until the police discovered where Dunski had taken refuge. He was finally arrested together with a friend. Two more youngsters were arrested in Będzin as suspects in underground activities (Ber Graubard and Leib Zachariasz). All four were delivered to the Gestapo and sent to the Gestapo jail in Mysłowice. Dunski smuggled out a message which revealed that Merin had signed a statement accusing all four arrested youths of Communist activities. Shortly thereafter, the Będzin Jewish Council got a letter from Merin, dated April 22, 1943, stating that according to a communication from the Gestapo, eight young boys from Będzin had been condemned to death by firing squad "for high treason." The two youngsters arrested by the Będzin Council were listed among the executed.[19]

The Jewish partisan Abraham Zaretski came into the Stołpce Ghetto in November 1942 to lead a group of Jews into the forests in the Kopuła area and join the "Zhukow" partisan group there. But the Council chairman delivered him to the Gestapo "because he feared possible consequences for the entire ghetto." Zaretski died of torture.[20] It is said about Yitzhak Kac, chairman of the last Council in Brody, that he took revenge on Jewish partisans active in the area by sending them off to labor camps when they happened to come to town.[21]

In eastern provinces offering much better possibilities of escape to the forests than were available in central districts of the Government General or the incorporated territories, the Councils sometimes called on inmates to keep watch against prospective escapees from the ghetto.

A witness testifies that in the Horochów Ghetto (near Łuck) in 1942 the Jews secretly considered their chances of leaving for the forest. Not all were ready to do so, but 1,000 people agreed. It happened on Saturday evening, September 11, 1942. As soon as the group . . . began to leave . . . Jewish policemen came running and in the name of Chairman Abel told us to return to the ghetto. They blocked the road and forced us to return to town. Their action was effective, and the majority went back. But we, a group of 235 people, did not listen to the chairman and the police and went on to the forest.[22]

In the Głębokie Ghetto

the Council, the police, and the inmates in general kept an eye on each other to prevent escapes from the ghetto. . . . At the instigation of the Council, the inmates guarded the ghetto fence so that nobody was able to escape in the dark of night. . . . It happened that one night the Council found 30 people hiding in the Jewish cemetery. They already were outside the ghetto on their way to the forest, but the Jewish police took them all back. The Council made no fuss about this incident, fearing that the Germans might learn about it.[23]

A similar event took place in the Vilna Ghetto. After the disaster of July 22, 1943 (already described), suspicion spread in the ghetto. People watched each other at work. At night, house and block commanders checked the inmates against tenant lists. Frightened female room overseers woke up their roommates at night to check in the darkness whether all were present. The police introduced special report books and checked at night whether all were present in their lodgings. M. Dvorzhetsky, to whom we are indebted for this information, notes that "the law of collective responsibility blocked the road to the forest at that period. [It was understood that, by] leaving for the forest, one endangered the life of one's family and neighbors."[24]

After the Šiauliai Council learned on September 27, 1943, what had happened in Vilna (the "action" sending Vilna Jews to Estonia had started on September 1), panic spread in the ghetto. Many people broke through the fence and escaped. The Council of Elders increased the fence guard to prevent large-scale escapes.[25]

In the Krasno Ghetto (Mołodeczno county) the Council sent two policemen to foil the escape plans of a group of inmates who were hiding in a barn.[26]

The negative attitude of the Sarny Ghetto Jewish Council toward the idea of organized resistance to "resettlement" frustrated preparations by an underground group. On August 24, 1942, the Council was ordered to assemble all surviving Jews at the ghetto gate. The ghetto inmates assembled in the Council building, and preparations started for armed resistance. Hand grenades, lye, benzine, and kerosene to burn down the town were made available. But on the fateful day of August 25 the Council secretary voiced his opposition to the resistance plan because "the summons was not for destruction but for selection of able-bodied people for work. People then let themselves be deceived and did not act. The police commandant had also ordered them to do nothing but wait until Thursday, August 25."[27]

Some Councils opposed the endeavors of Jewish partisans who took great risks coming into the ghettos to take young people into the forests. Thus the Council at Nowe Świerzno, near Stołpce, where the survivors of adjacent liquidated ghettos (Turec, Stołpce, etc.) labored in a sawmill, "took great pains not to let the inmates escape from the camp." (The camp-inmates had established contacts with Jews in the adjacent forests.) "The Council argued that as long as the sawmill was in operation, the Jews would not be hurt," but that the escape of individual laborers might bring collective punishment for the remaining ones.[28]

We also have information from the Słonim Ghetto that the idea of negotiations between the representative of the Jewish partisan group in the area of Pińsk—Soviet Army Officer Abrasza Blumowicz (he has since changed his name to Atsmon and is now serving with the Israeli army as chief of medical services)—and the local Jewish Council to take inmates out to join the partisans in the forests met with strong opposition from the Council.[29]

Even among Council members who sympathized with the young people's opinion that rescue was possible only through escape from the ghetto, responsibility for the fate of the majority of inmates left behind overweighed all other considerations. A former member of a youth group in Międryrzec (Volhynia) relates that in this little town a group was ready to escape. Knowing that the entire ghetto would be held responsible, they decided to consult the chairman, Isaiah Rubinstein, in whom they trusted, and confided their secret plan. This was Rubinstein's approximate answer: "Believe me, I too would have escaped together with you, but how can one abandon the ghetto? You may escape, but next day the Germans will kill everyone, including your families. If all could escape, I would have understood your desire. But even if you rescued yourselves, your parents and all those who remained behind in the ghetto would perish, innocent victims." The witness concluded that "people understood that the responsibility was too great, that it was a crime to risk the lives of other ghetto inmates. Those were quite weird times. One did not know what was better to do and what was not."[30] Similarly tragic decisions had to be made by other ghettos in the eastern area.

The Councils' negative attitude toward resistance was also motivated by fear that they themselves would be the first victims to pay with their lives. For instance, a survivor of the Prużana Ghetto thus formulated the reasoning of the local Council against mass escape from the ghetto: mass escape would make it impossible for the Council to negotiate with the Germans in order to revoke measures of persecution, or, at least, to save some inmates; Council members who were responsible to the Germans for the inmates' behavior would be the first to pay with their lives if a revolt took place. The ghetto inmates knew about these dangers very well.

The same survivor relates how partisans suggested to the leader of a group of laborers working in the forest that he let some of them join the partisans. The leader refused, saying that he could not endanger the lives of the Council members responsible. Though members of the ghetto resistance group were themselves among these laborers, none escaped.[31]

Thus, it is evident, as mentioned above, that the system of collective responsibility imposed by the Germans on the occupied territories not only influenced the ghetto inmates' attitude toward the idea and practical implementation of resistance, but also was a strong restraining factor for those of the ghetto inmates—for the most part young people—who were desperately trying to find ways to escape. It is noteworthy that fear of the tragic consequences of collective responsibility influenced responsible leaders of prewar political parties among the inmates of the Warsaw Ghetto. At a meeting of party representatives in April 1942 two emissaries from Vilna reported on the destruction of Jews in Lithuania and Byelorussia. The representative of the General Zionists was against preparing for a revolt. He argued that if the plot were discovered collective responsibility as imposed by the Germans would have the same tragic results in Warsaw as it had had in Vilna. By the end of July 1942, a few days after the "evacuation" from the Warsaw Ghetto began, a meeting of representatives of political parties and people engaged in social work ("the Civic Council") took place. No consensus of opinion was reached on tactics for dealing with the "resettlement action." Representatives of the Zionist-Socialist youth organizations, the Poalei Zion (Left), the Communists, and the Bund demanded that an appeal be issued to the ghetto inmates calling for active resistance. But the representatives of the bourgeois parties and the independent leaders in social work were against such a step, mainly because they were afraid of collective responsibility. Also they believed that the entire ghetto would not be destroyed, but that only the "unproductive elements" would be carried away. No concrete results were achieved at the conference.*

COUNCILS WITH A POSITIVE ATTITUDE

There were Councils that adopted a positive attitude to resistance and rescue endeavors by all those able to escape from the ghetto, dangerous consequences notwithstanding. There were individual Council members and entire Councils involved in underground activities against the Germans even before the "resettlement actions." Thus the Council at Piotrków Trybunalski was involved in the underground activities of the Bund in the area of the Government General. The Council's leading members, under the leadership of its chairman, Zalman Tenenbaum, were all active in prewar community activities. Representatives of the Bund won the majority of seats during the last community elections of 1938. In July 1941 a Polish underground courier, Marya Szczęsna, was arrested while

* A. Berman, "Ruch oporu w getcie warszawskim," BŻIH, No. 29 (1959), p. 44.

carrying illegal publications and the names of underground activists. Shortly thereafter four Council members (including the chairman) were arrested. One of them, Jacob Berliner, surrendered to the German authorities of his own will in solidarity with his arrested colleagues. They were sent to Auschwitz, and shortly afterward a telegram arrived stating that they had all died.[32]

Sholem Weiss, a member of the Council and chief of the Council's labor department in Pajęczno (Radom district), maintained regular contacts with the Polish underground movement. He helped persons to cross the border of the Czech Protectorate. Before the "resettlement" action, he took refuge in the Częstochowa Ghetto.[33]

Positive attitudes to resistance took various shapes: some Councils granted young people financial assistance, some encouraged them to organize groups for resistance when the time came to join the partisans. The highest degree of cooperation was achieved when chairmen or other leading Council members themselves actively participated in preparing and executing acts of resistance, particularly in the course of liquidations of ghettos. Here are a few examples.

Jacob Łazebnik, a member of the Lenin Jewish Council (near Pińsk), called upon the youth to organize themselves.[34] In Radomsko the Council chairman Gutgesztalt in January 1943 warned members of the Zionist Youth Organizations Hechalutz and Hashomer Hatzair not to trust German assurances that there was a possibility of their going to Palestine as part of a special exchange program. He labeled this another Gestapo trick and advised them to flee the ghetto. He himself escaped into the forest.[35]

One of the most prominent members of the Warsaw Jewish Council, Abraham Gepner, adopted a positive attitude toward the resistance movement and contributed money to buy arms.[36]

When the Sasów Jewish Council (Distrikt Galizien) got an order to deliver people for "resettlement," it warned the inmates to escape and itself escaped to the forest. When the Gestapo arrived, they found the Jewish homes empty.[37]

A witness who apparently maintained contact with a resistance group relates that Josef Korn, a member of the Mołczadź Council, came to him at night in his hiding place in the fields (afraid of arrest, he did not stay home overnight) on the eve of the slaughter and warned him of the looming danger. He suggested that young people should not sleep at home but should make preparations "in case anything happened."[38]

Elijahu Lidski, leader of the Jewish partisan group in Horodok (near Vilna), and another witness testified that Efraim Retskin, chairman of that Council, Shmaryahu Zuckerman, the vice chairman, and Nachman Swirski, the treasurer, encouraged youth to establish contact with the partisans. Moreover, when Lidski came to the Council to negotiate the escape of a large group of inmates, Retskin and Zuckerman bribed the sentries at the ghetto fence to let the people escape. Naturally they well knew the danger involved for the ghetto.[39]

A survivor of the Pilica Ghetto (Radom district) relates that when the Jewish resistance group approached the chairman of the Council (his name is left out), he revealed to them a place, where three revolvers were hidden and contributed a certain amount to buy two rifles. He allowed them also the use of the typewriter for printing of leaflets.[40]

A dilemma facing the Kaunas Council of Elders, though not restraining them from acting, is related by the former vice chairman, Lejb Garfunkel:

On the one hand, the Council was unwilling to interfere with escape to the woods or to block resistance . . . intended to rescue hundreds of people. But, on the other hand, the Council well knew the great danger involved in escaping from the ghetto. It was clear that, cautious and conspiratory measures notwithstanding, the Gestapo was bound to find out about preparations. But despite all these doubts the Council continued large-scale assistance to the escapees by some of its departments. Without this assistance not a single person could have been sent out into the forest. The Council's labor department provided forged working papers from the town labor units for all those leaving the ghetto to join the partisans. This enabled them to pass the ghetto gate in trucks driven by rescuers wearing German uniforms. . . . People scheduled for escape to the partisans got warm clothing, underwear, boots, and other apparel from the ghetto shop warehouses and medicine and bandages from the ghetto pharmacies. Arms smuggled into the ghetto were repaired in the ghetto shops.[41]

A number of Council members in the Pružana Ghetto gave clothing to inmates escaping to the forest. They also received food and cash to bribe sentries. The Council members requested only that escaping inmates not leave the ghetto in large groups. Wooden butts for firearms smuggled into the ghetto were made in the cellar of the house of Velvel Shreibman, the Council's vice chairman. He also took care of the fighting group's ammunition. With the consent of the Council a clandestine radio receiver was established in the carpenter shop and contact was maintained with those who had joined the partisans in the forest. Emissaries came in secret to the ghetto to ask the Council for assistance. On January 27, 1943, during one such visit by two (or three) armed partisans, the local Gestapo chief unexpectedly came to the Council. The partisans escaped, but in the ensuing shooting, the Council's watchman was shot to death, and some persons present, among them Council members, were wounded. The Gestapo gave the Council a short time to deliver the partisans—which naturally was impossible, for they had disappeared. The entire ghetto was soon liquidated.[42] Thanks to the Wallenrod-type characteristics of Oswald Rufeisen, a Hechalutz member, the Mir Council was able to maintin contacts with emissaries of an underground group.[43]

The Minsk (Byelorussia) Jewish Council was, in fact, an important base of the partisan movement. The town committee of the illegal Communist Party maintained close contact with the Council. The Council chairman, Eliyahu Myshkin (not himself a Communist), fully cooperated with the organizers of the Minsk underground and with those who had escaped into the forest. The chiefs of various departments—Rudicer (economic), Dulski (housing), Goldin (shops), and Srebrianski (the police commandant) also cooperated wtih the resistance. They furnished important intelligence about German intentions, provided warm clothing and shoes, found secret lodgings, and prepared false documents. Srebrianski hired as policemen numerous members of the ghetto underground. Jaffe, the new Council chairman after Myshkin was killed (he was shot during the "action" against 12,000 Jews in November 1941), continued to assist the partisans. The two secretaries of the Minsk Council labor department, Mira Strogin and Sara Levin, worked devotedly for the local underground. Thanks to all these activities by the Jewish Council, several hundred Minsk Jews were able to escape from the ghetto and join the partisans.[44]

A survivor of the Iwaniska Ghetto (Radom district) relates that the local rabbi and Council member Chaim Ikheskel Rabinowicz agreed to escape to the woods with the young people. He tried to persuade everyone that the only way to surive was to escape into the forest in order to tell the world, after the war, of the disaster that had befallen the Jewish people. "Thanks to Rabbi Rabinowicz, over 300 youths escaped to the woods on the eve of liquidation. The majority survived and were able to carry out his testament—to take revenge on the enemy." Rabbi Rabinowicz himself apparently perished in the ghetto.[45]

Jewish Councils or their individual members suspected of cooperating with the underground were mercilessly persecuted. According to a witness, Shmuel Zalcman, second chairman of the Chmielnik Jewish Council, maintained contact with underground circles, advising them on how to organize the underground in the ghetto. Zalcman was arrested because of an informer. Fastened to a horse-drawn cart, he was dragged all over town and died a horrible death.[46]

The Gestapo wanted Hirsz Lewin, the liaison man between the Kaunas Council (in whose deliberations he took part) and the resistance organization. Unable to locate him the Gestapo arrested the entire Council and a number of officials on April 4, 1943, imprisoning them in the 9th Fort. During extensive interrogation they were treated in the well-known Gestapo manner. The majority were freed after a short time, but two of the Council members (including Lejb Garfunkel) remained under arrest and were tortured for long weeks.[47]

A Ukrainian accused the Jews in the camp at Nowe Świerzno of trying to purchase firearms. He named Szlomo Szwertok, a former member and secretary of the ghetto Council. Szwertok was arrested together with another man by the gendarmes in Stołpce. Both were shot.[48]

COUNCILS WITH AMBIGUOUS ATTITUDES

It is known that the attitudes of the chiefs of two large ghettos—Białystok and Vilna—were ambivalent, dictated by tactical or personal considerations with respect to the resistance movement. They were afraid that resistance activities might hinder their carefully contrived strategies to gain time and postpone the liquidation of their ghettos for as long as possible. On the other hand, they favored the idea of physical resistance when the end came. They believed that they would know of impending doom in time to then put themselves at the disposal of the resistance.

Hayke Grossman, in her capacity as emissary of the underground movement in Białystok, met several times with Barash and later described her discussions with him on the subject of resistance. On one occasion, after she told him what had happened to Jews in Vilna, Barash remarked:

I do not believe that this will happen in Białystok. Those Germans I am acquainted with will not have the courage to do so. They do only what is ordered by Berlin. But should the danger arise they would tell me in advance. They will not carry out a Vilna-type slaughter here. They need us. Whatever may happen later, we may live in peace for the time being. I am afraid that the young people may do foolish things. You should not take upon yourselves such a responsibility. I shall always know in advance if something is going to happen.[49]

When Barash learned that underground cells in the ghetto factories were distributing secret leaflets, he took the occasion of a public meeting of ghetto inmates on August 16, 1942, to discuss, according to the minutes of the meeting, "a grave danger that had better be mentioned with great care . . . political work is being conducted in the factories. I shall not speak now about idealism. If one endangers one's head for an ideal of his own volition, we bow our heads before him. But to risk 35,000 heads is the worst type of banditry, leading to very bad results."[50] Yet he sympathized with the Białystok underground. He legalized the presence of nonresidence members of the Hechalutz, Hashomer Hatzair and members of other Zionist youth organizations in the ghetto. Their kibbutz simulated a shelter for the poor. Here young people escaping from the ghetto got passes, and the fighting organization was given money and valuables. Barash also shared intelligence with the underground.[51]

Mordecai Tenenbaum-Tamaroff, a leader of the Białystok Ghetto uprising in August 1943, was in close contact with Barash, frequently discussing timely topics with him.[52] From his notes we know that in Barash's study in the Council building at least two meetings of delegates of the interparty resistance block were held. The start of the "counterattack" and the tactics toward the planned "action" were discussed.[53] Barash was even in favor of establishing a unified organization including the Communists, who, however, made difficulties, suspecting that he was trying to establish an alibi for him-self to use after the victory of the Soviet army.[54] When the uprising broke out on August 16, 1943, Barash was not among the fighting young people. He was among the Białystok Jews who were deported to Treblinka or Majdanek.

Jacob Gens of the Vilna Ghetto also displayed a contradictory attitude toward resistance. He too maintained contacts with the United Fighting Organization (FPO). As is related by Raizl Korczak of Vilna, a former partisan herself, Gens assured the FPO that at the right moment he would take over command of the uprising in the ghetto, for as a former military man he had had more experience. He also promised to supply the necessary arms.[55] Nevertheless, be-cause of his fear of collective responsibility, he opposed escapes to the forest or storage of arms in the ghetto.[56]

Under the date June 12, 1943, Herman Kruk entered a note in his Diary concerning a search by the ghetto police for concealed arms. Shortly before that the German police had taken armed people in the ghetto into custody, and some were wounded in the course of shooting between the police and the arrested ghetto inmates. According to Kruk one of the arrested, a young boy, told Gens that he was a partisan sent to take people from the ghetto. He was set free by Gens, who reportedly told him before parting: "Go, if this is your desire, and come to our rescue when we are in danger." Kruk adds that "the youngster left this morning with farewell blessings, taking 51 people with him. A special man was assigned to watch at the exit gate and see to it that everything went smoothly."[57] M. Dvorzhetsky also relates on the word of a partisan that Gens helped the partisan movement, knew about people leav-ing for the forest, and assisted them. It was also said that he gave money to buy arms.[58]

But in June 1943, when up to 100 young people left the ghetto in secret, Gens delivered a speech in the course of a meeting of the ghetto police and said, among other things:

We face the problem whether or not to go into the forest. In my opinion it would be easier for me to leave than for all of you. Although I am a former officer [of the Lithuanian army], a former member of Brith Hachyal [a paramilitary group of the Revisionist Zionist Organiza-tion], and a policeman with no sympathies for Bolshevism, I will be gladly welcomed, for I know better than you do how to use firearms. Still I won't go. . . . For the problem is one of one man against

20,000. . . . Imagine 500 people leaving. . . . When I think of it, I put myself in Neugebauer's position. If I were in his place, I would have liquidated the entire ghetto in one blow, for one has to be a complete idiot to permit the ghetto to become a hiding place for the partisans. And Neugebauer is no idiot. He is more clever than all of us together. . . . We may all maintain that escape to the forest is for the good of the ghetto. This may be so. But my task is to guard a loyal ghetto as long as it exists, so that nobody reprimands me.[59]

Gens, who consistently and cruelly enforced his policies, betrayed the commandant of the United Partisan Organization, Yitzhak Witenberg, to the Germans. The betrayal took place at a meeting with the partisans at Gens' office. Witenberg was then arrested by a Lithuanian policeman. The partisans succeeded in liberating and concealing Witenberg after a clash with the ghetto police on July 16, 1943. Gens then instigated a revolt in the ghetto against the partisan organization.

Because of the tense situation this tragic case brought about in the ghetto, and out of fear of a clash between the inmates, Witenberg accepted a resolution adopted by the United Partisan Organization and surrendered at Gestapo headquarters, where he perished.[60] According to M. Dvorzhetsky, Gens himself was killed on September 15, 1943, by the Gestapo. He went to the Gestapo of his own will, although one of their agents warned him not to go. Gens was accused of maintaining contacts with the partisan movement and financing its activities.[61]

The chairman of the Council at Nieśwież, Megalif, who had practiced law in Warsaw before the war and had reached this little town, escaping from the Germans when war began, hesitated about what position to take on the question of resistance. He cooperated with the local fighting group, but was not trusted because of his contacts with the Germans and the Byelorussian police. He remained chairman, even after the Council was reorganized. When news spread of the "action" in the little town of Horodziej he "demanded that the Jews [in Nieśwież] stay calm and do nothing for their part." According to another version, when the authorities ordered the Jews, on July 22, 1942, to assemble at the marketplace, many people hid themselves in cellars and bunkers. Megalif did not join those preparing for armed resistance. Together with his family he took a place in the first line of the assembled column, saying, "Brothers,

I know you had no trust in me, you thought I was going to betray you. In this, my last minute, I am with you. I and my family—we are the first ones to go to our deaths."[62]

COUNCIL MEMBERS ACTIVELY PARTICIPATING
IN ARMED RESISTANCE

The sources mention instances of Council members actively taking part in acts of armed resistance against the Germans and physically resisting the "actions." One of these was Berl Łopatyn, chairman of the Council at Łachwa Ghetto (Pińsk area). Based on facts contained in four eyewitness accounts collected independently, this is what took place. On September 3, 1942, the ghetto was unexpectedly shut off by the Byelorussian militia. Next day, the SD men began chasing inmates through the ghetto gate to prepared graves nearby. The SD men entered the Council building, demanding that Dubski, a Council member, give them the list of Jews in the ghetto (probably in order to carry out a "selection"). When Dubski refused, he was shot on the spot. Before the "action" began, Łopatyn unsuccessfully tried to pay off the *Kommandant* of the SD unit. In company with a member of the underground group, he then went from house to house, telling ghetto inmates that when he sees that the end had come he would set fire to the Council building as a signal for all inmates to do the same [to their homes]. It seems that on his advice many people armed themselves with knives and axes. A large number of armed ghetto inmates waited at the assembly place for the signal. When the Council building began to burn, people put their own homes to flame. In the turmoil that broke out one of the inmates, Yitzhak Rechstein, split the head of a gendarme with his hatchet. As if on signal the crowd surged forward, trying to reach the ghetto gate. Łopatyn snatched an automatic gun from a German but did not know how to use it and began shooting at random. The German wounded him in the arm. A former soldier of the Polish army, Hajfec, snatched a gun from another German and began shooting in the direction of the German cordon, which opened fire on the Jews. The crowd, armed with knives and bottles of lye, attacked the ghetto sentries. Some escaped, taking along some arms from the watchmen. Many others escaped from the burning ghetto, but the majority perished. One eyewitness, Leon Slutski, related that of 2,000 ghetto inmates some 600 escaped, of whom only 100 or 120 remained alive and met in the forest. Łopatyn was among these, and later on he fought in the Stalin squad of the Kirow Brigade (operational area: Lida-Nowogródek). Hit by a mine, he perished on April 1, 1944.[63]

Two members of the Nieśwież Jewish Council, Yerechmiel Szklar and Jacob Klaczko, were active in the resistance group of the ghetto and took part in the uprising of July 21, 1942. Klaczko killed a Byelorussian policeman, but lost his life in battle afterward. When the Council got information about the "action" in the adjacent town of Horodziej, a meeting of the inmates was called in the *shul* one day before the slaughter. Szklar appealed to those present not to run away and leave behind unprotected elderly people, children, and the sick, but to remain to fight and to die with dignity.[64] Miss Lachewicki, the secretary of the Council, was active in the local resistance group. She escaped with her father, a Council member, a day after the slaughter. Together with other inmates of this ghetto, they joined a partisan group, took part in battles, and lived to see freedom, Klaczko and Szklar went to their deaths during battles with the ghetto sentries.[65]

The chairman of the Jewish Council at Zdzięciół (Nowogródek district), the lawyer Alter Dworetsky, was the organizer of the partisans in the ghetto. He placed trustworthy men as ghetto policemen and personally smuggled arms into the ghetto. He also supplied those escaping to the forests with cash, arms, and advice. The partisan organzation was discovered because of an act of provocation by one of the arms suppliers, himself a Soviet partisan. As a result, Szolem Fialin, a member of the undercover group, died a hero's death, and Dworetsky and his entire staff of six men were forced to escape to the Lipiczany forest on April 20, 1942. Dworetsky tried to bring about an attack on the ghetto by a joint Jewish-Russian partisan group to give the inmates a chance to escape in the course of the battle, but the Soviet partisans refused to attack the large German unit which had arrived to slaughter the Jews. A few weeks later, on May 11, 1942, Dworetsky and another organizer of the Zdzięciół resistance group, Moshe Pazulski (Israel), were treacherously shot to death by Soviet partisans of the Wachonin group. But Dworetsky's activities in the Zdzięciół Ghetto bore fruit. Right after the second slaughter, on August 6, 1942, 800 Jews who had concealed themselves in bunkers succeeded in escaping from the ghetto. They reached the Lipiczany forest where the Jewish partisan group was established with Hirsz Kaplinski as the leader. The group merged with the Soviet Orlinski detachment as the third Jewish platoon. A large number of Zdzięcioł partisans escaped death and lived until liberation. Kaplinski, however, was killed by anti-Semitic partisans in December 1942.[66]

On September 22 or 23, 1942, the vice chairman of the Jewish Council at Tuczyn (Równe district), Meir Himelfarb,[67] got an order from the district chief to assemble all Jews at the ghetto gate. The young laborers were to be carried away. He called together the inmates in the prayer house and told them to set the ghetto on fire so that the Germans would inherit nothing from the Jews. He advised the people to attack the Germans at the ghetto barbed wires and distributed bottles of kerosene to start fires with. He greatly inspired the Jews who heard him speak, and as night approached the entire ghetto was aflame. The surprised Germans and Ukrainians started shooting in the direction of the fires. Taking advantage of the general confusion, people ran in the direction of the ghetto fence, with hatchets in their hands, ready to attack. In the ensuing clash with the sentries, a great number escaped, but the pursuing Germans and Ukrainian police, assisted by the local Ukrainian population, caught some 1,500 escapees who were all subsequently killed at the Jewish cemetery.[68]

In the fall of 1942, on learning of the activities of Soviet Byelorussian partisans in the forests, a group of local young people and refugees in the Marcinkańce Ghetto (near Grodno) made plans to join the partisans. The Jewish Council was informed and helped by smuggling arms and making preparations for an uprising when the ghetto became in danger of liquidation. Money was allocated for acquiring 12 guns. It was too late. On November 2, 1942, when the Jews assembled at the ghetto gate to march to the labor places, they were informed that they would be sent to work at a new place. The ghetto was then encircled by heavy sentry detachments. Some of the Jews succeeded in leaving the ghetto secretly at dawn, others concealed themselves. When the Jews were assembled at the railroad station to be sent to the new labor places, the Council chairman, Aron Kobrowski, cried out in a loud voice: "Fellow Jews, everybody run for his life. Everything is lost!" People started running for the ghetto fence which was broken under pressure of the crowd. They attacked the watchmen with their bare fists, and 105 persons were shot on the spot. The Council chairman, his brother, and two other people succeeded in hiding themselves in a bunker. But the bunker was discovered, and those in hiding were ordered to come out. Instead, they began shooting with revolvers. Hand grenades finished off the four brave men. The ghetto inmates were chased like beasts, and little by little the majority were seized and killed. Only a small number succeeded in reaching the so-called "Russian forest" where they joined the Dawidow detachment of the partisans.[69]

Last but not least, Leibl Felhendler, chairman of the Żółkiewka Jewish Council (near Lublin) should be mentioned. He was one of the organizers and leaders of the uprising at the Sobibór death camp, which broke out on October 14, 1943. He was among those who escaped. He was killed by some partisans of the Polish secret army (Armia Krajowa, A.K.) in April 1945.[70]

CHAPTER 18

The Ghetto Police

ESTABLISHMENT, AIMS, AND FUNCTIONS

As WAS THE CASE with the Jewish Councils, the ghetto police (officially called *Ordnungsdienst*—"Order Service") was established on the initiative of the German authorities. In contrast to the Councils, a general order by a central authority regarding the establishment of the Jewish police has not yet been discovered for any occupation area. In the light of available sources, the ghetto police appear to have come into being on the initiative and orders of local administrative supervisory organs, which delegated the task of recruiting policemen to the Councils themselves. At times the authorities were apparently interested in creating the impression that the ghetto police came about on Jewish initiative. Thus the commandant of the German Security Police in Cracow suggested to the Jewish Council that the Jews ask the *Stadthauptmann* for permission to establish the ghetto police. Permission was granted and received on July 5, 1940, by the Council. A few more examples follow.

In Warsaw Czerniakow was summoned by the plenipotentiary of the district chief for the city of Warsaw on September 20, 1940, and was ordered to establish, on short notice, a Jewish Order police of 3,000 men to take over the functions of the Polish police in the projected "Jewish living quarters." The ghetto was officially sealed off on November 15, and the ghetto police started their activities at the end of the month.[1]

The ghetto police in Lwów was established on the basis of a letter from the SS and Police Leader addressed to the Jewish Council on

November 8, 1941.[2] In Łódź the German police president, on February 21, 1940, issued an order establishing the ghetto police.[3] In Radom, the establishment of the ghetto police was ordered by the administrative authority on April 1, 1941, and the ghetto was established a week later.[4] In Ozorków (Wartheland),[5] in Cracow, and in Częstochowa[6] the order to establish the ghetto police came from the respective *Bürgermeister*.

The establishment of the ghettos, which took the inmates out of the jurisdiction of the general police framework, accelerated the establishment of a separate ghetto police. In some of the orders concerning the establishment of the police this is given as a motive. Thus, for instance, the Service Instructions of the *Ordnungsdienst* in the Jewish quarters in Częstochowa, issued by the *Stadthauptmann* under the date of April 21, 1941, indicated that, following the establishment of the Jewish living quarters, the Częstochowa Jews themselves were to take care of peace and order, and that this would be the task of the *Ordnungsdienst*, which was to be equipped and maintained by the Jewish Council.[7]

The letter of the Łódź police president addressed to Rumkowski on April 17, 1940, states that "since the establishment of the ghetto has progressed to the extent that it can be sealed off on the 30th, the Jewish police has to take over immediately [the task of] guarding the safety of the ghetto enclosure." (The police order concerning the establishment of the ghetto was issued on February 8, and the order to establish the ghetto police on February 21, 1940.)[8]

In some of the ghettos the establishment of the police force went through various stages, from small units with very limited tasks to complicated police apparatus. Thus, for instance, the nucleus of the ghetto police in Częstochowa was the *Inspekcja Ruchu Ulicznege* (IRU)—Control of Street Traffic—which was established in May 1940. It was headed by a commission of six persons and consisted of 45 functionaries at the time of its establishment. It later grew to 72 functionaries. At the beginning, its task was to regulate the street traffic of the Jews, to see that they did not enter central streets, congregate in streets, or sit on benches, all of which Jews had been forbidden to do. Later they were given the tasks of patrolling 25 intersections in 20 streets with dense Jewish population, and guard duty in the 14 Council departments.[9] After the ghetto was established, IRU was called the ghetto police.

The establishment of the ghetto police in Warsaw came in conjunction with the building of fences around the Jewish quarters (*Seuchensperrgebiet*) in mid-1940. To accomplish this imposed duty, the Council established a special guard detachment, the *Instandhaltung der Mauern im Seuchengebiet*. It consisted of some 120 young men who were paid from 9 to 12 zlotys a day. They were given yellow armbands with the inscription *Posten an der Sperre zum Seuchengebiet*. This was the nucleus of the ghetto police established later.[10]

There was yet another Jewish parapolice formation in Warsaw, which was later integrated with the ghetto police. This was the *Straż Porządkowa*—the Order guard of the so-called Labor Battalions (Labor Office) at the Jewish Council. Its duty was to escort Jewish forced laborers to various German places of employment and to report their arrival for work. In addition, they kept watch on the premises of the Labor Battalion. The *Straż Porządkowa* was headed by an inspector who later became deputy commandant of the ghetto police. Two or three months after its establishment the Order guard was disbanded. Numerous guardsmen were later accepted in the ghetto police.[11]

The embryo of the future ghetto police in Kaunas was the Order group (*Ordnungsgruppe*) consisting of former soldiers and sportsmen. Their duty was to guard the Jewish Committee and its commissions in the course of moving the Jews over into the Słobodka Ghetto. It was established on August 15, 1941, to guard peace and order in the ghetto.[12]

It also happened that people not in the ghetto police were commandeered to assist the German authorities in "actions" against the Jews. Thus in the Lublin Ghetto, for instance, Jewish prisoners in the SS camp at Lipowa Street were forced to take part in the raid ordered by Globocnik during the night of December 11–12, 1941, with the aim of seizing Jews for the Majdanek camp; 320 Jews were rounded up, and 150 were sent to Majdanek.[13]

The organizational setup, the functions, and the statutes of the ghetto police had to be confirmed by the supervisory authorities.

In Warsaw the ghetto police functioned on the basis of organizational rules (*Organisationsverschriften* or *Przepisy organizacyjne*) adopted by the Council's legal department and confirmed on November 29, 1940, by the "resettlement" department of the district administration.[14] The rules consisted of 26 paragraphs divided into 6 groups: general regulations; tasks; disciplinary responsibility; suspension; rights; and regulations about uniforms.[15]

The organizational rules constituted the primary legal act, the first organizational framework to formulate the scope and limits of the activities of the ghetto police in Warsaw. Later on, however, both the functions and the organizational framework expanded, following internal "Orders of the Headquarters of the Order Police" (*Rozkazy Kierownictwa Służby Porządkowej*). These "orders" encompassed regulations pertaining to all activities—administrative, service, planning central posts and patrols, personnel matters (hiring and firing policemen, advances, commendations, punishments), etc.— and were patterned after the "Orders of the Headquarters of the Polish Police." The first "order" was issued on November 15, 1940, the day the ghetto was sealed off; the last "order" was issued by the end of 1942.[16]

Until the time of mass deportations, the actual functions of the Order police were: (1) regulating street traffic and keeping people from congregating in the streets; (2) taking care that the streets, backyards, and staircases were kept clean; (3) combating crime; (4) maintaining order in buildings, offices, and institutions of the Jewish Council.[17]

The Order police had three more tasks: to guard the walls and fences of the ghetto, and all street corners converging on the "Aryan side"; to punish people not complying with orders issued by the Council regarding taxes and cash payments for imposed contributions, forced labor, etc.; to assist in carrying out the order for forced labor of Jews, execution of this last task taking sometimes the form of night raids against prospective laborers during the period of mass shipments to forced-labor camps.

The above-mentioned Service Instructions to the ghetto police in Częstochowa contained nine parts which formulated the jurisdiction, functions, responsibility, uniforms, and ranks of the police.[18]

The development of the functions of the Kaunas Ghetto police is described as follows in a contemporary document:

At the start 60 young people were mobilized for the ghetto police. They kept order in the lines in front of food distribution places and at meetings of the commissions and the committee [later named Council of Elders]; installed inmates in their lodgings assigned by the Council's housing commission; and delivered workers to the labor assembly places. Little by little, their tasks expanded. . . . Immediately on the day after they were established the police were given the task of issuing vital statistics certificates. A little later they were charged with managing the

German and Jewish police at the exit from the Łódź Ghetto.

The Jewish police in the Warsaw Ghetto.

office of addresses of the inmates (on August 29, 1941). . . . When crime
was on the increase, especially after deportees had left their belongings
unattended, a criminal department was established on November 12,
1941, to investigate and fight crime in the ghetto. Prior to that, on May
12, 1941, a detention house had been established at the office of the
ghetto police. Another detention house, for labor dodgers, was established
on July 15, 1942. When the ghetto court was established, the police was
given the task of executing its decisions as well as the orders of all other
departments of the Council of Elders. After the court was liquidated a
criminal chamber of the police was established on July 15, 1942, which
in fact acted as a ghetto court. On order of the ghetto commandant, an
air defense service was established at the police office on July 31, 1942,
to help guard the ghetto during air raids, in cooperation with German
and Lithuanian air raid wardens. . . . The gate guard also checked
traffic in and out of the ghetto. It was the duty of the police to escort
labor columns on their way through the town to labor places, to keep
watch where necessary over labor columns sent to the provinces (to labor
camps) and to perform special duties on instructions of the authorities.
On May 8, 1943, the ghetto police took over sentry duties along the fence
of the ghetto. A special police unit was established for this purpose. At
all times the police had to be ready to perform extraordinary tasks.[19]

The sphere of activities of the ghetto police varied. Sometimes
the authorities tended to enlarge the scope of their duties, causing
the establishment of new departments (e.g., criminal and vice squads
in Warsaw); at other times their activities were reduced. Much depended on the attitude of the German official in charge.[20]

In some ghettos police platoons were organized with special duties
such as fighting epidemics. Such platoons were active in Warsaw,
Łódź, Vilna, Skierniewice, Lublin, and other places.

Within the general framework of the ghetto police in Łódź there
was a detachment called *Überfallskommando*. Its task was to quell
on the spot any demonstration that broke out in the ghetto against
Rumkowski's administration.[21] The *Sonderabteilung* ("Special
Squad") of the Łódź Ghetto police, established at the end of June
1940, enjoyed an unusually independent position. It was given the
task of confiscating merchandise, foreign currency, and valuables
(gold, silver, diamonds) from the ghetto inmates either on their
own authority, or on orders from Rumkowski, or in collaboration
with the German criminal police (*Kripo*). The *Sonderabteilung* also
carried out political intelligence work against opposition elements
and had secret agents for this purpose. Because of constant contact

The fourth precinct of the Warsaw Ghetto police.

A group of Jewish policemen of the Łódź Ghetto.

The Jewish police in the "Kaylis" camp, a branch of the Vilna Ghetto.

with all kinds of German police, the *Sonderabteilung* gained a great deal of influence in the ghetto and became quite independent of Rumkowski. Biebow made it the supreme control agency over the economy and provisioning of the ghetto, also putting it in charge of bakeries. In 1944 the *Sonderabteilung* decided such important matters as exemption from deportation, mail matters, etc.[22]

The ghetto police held jurisdiction over matters that in normal times belonged to the courts. In the majority of ghettos the police were authorized to impose sentences. It should be borne in mind that until the establishment of the ghetto courts the ghetto police was, in actual fact, the only agency entitled to punish delinquents, as was the case in Łódź, Kaunas, and other ghettos.

The limits of the administrative and criminal jurisdiction of the police were different in various ghettos. Thus in the Vilna Ghetto only the police chief himself was authorized to impose penalties on culprits handed over by the Germans to the ghetto police for violating regulations prescribed for Jews outside the ghetto. The verdict of the police was final.[23] An administrative-judiciary section and a criminal department were in operation at the Vilna Ghetto police office. The administrative-judiciary section was authorized to impose punishment for such transgressions against police regulations as leaving the ghetto without a pass, staying in town outside the ghetto without a valid pass, not wearing the Jewish badge, forging passes, using a pass made out to another person, disturbing the peace, breaking curfew or blackouts, trading in the streets, etc.[24] The punishment imposed by the police commissioners or their deputies, the chiefs of the sanitation police and—after hours—the policemen on duty, could not exceed 24 hours' detention. For not observing curfew hours or traffic regulations and for not wearing the Jewish badge, the policemen on duty were authorized to impose a fine (up to 10 Reichsmarks?). Members of the Jewish Councils were excluded from the jurisdiction of the ghetto police.[25]

Administrative-judiciary functions were also carried out by the police chiefs in Šiauliai,[26] Łódź, Częstochowa,[27] and many other places.

The ghetto police also executed punishments imposed by the Jewish Councils and ghetto courts, including death sentences on rare occasions. For instance, in the Vilna Ghetto the police hanged six persons on July 6, 1942, for the murder and robbery of two Jews. A seventh person was sentenced to death for stabbing a Jewish policeman and for informing on the Lida Jewish Council. All were sentenced by the ghetto court.[28] Sometimes the ghetto police were forced to assist in the execution of death sentences imposed on Jews by German courts. On German orders, participation of the ghetto police in public execution of Jews took place in Zduńska Wola, Brzeziny, Łęczyca, Bełchatów, Poddębice, Wieluń, Piontki, Ozorków (all between February and April 1942), Białystok (on December 31, 1943), and Łódź (where one execution was performed by a Jewish executioner and his assistants).[29] Everywhere the ghetto police were in charge of ghetto jails. They were also authorized to take measures enforcing the orders of the authorities and the Councils with respect to taxes and other obligations.

In the Warsaw Ghetto, for example, the ghetto police locked the gates of houses where tenants had been tardy in paying taxes. Thus they imposed a kind of collective responsibility on all tenants. At times they went so far as to take hostages from among the members of house committees when a tenant assigned to forced-labor duty failed to report.[30] A taxpayer who stubbornly refused to pay taxes was dragged from his home at night by the ghetto police. He was maltreated, forced to clean the streets or to move into an asylum for the homeless and made to do all kinds of degrading chores. Persons without Council labor cards or bearing cards with lapsed dates, were seized in the streets and committed to assembly places for inmates destined for labor camps, until such time as their families ransomed them. Money thus gained was used to cover the budgets of labor battalions. These methods were sharply criticized even in the *Gazeta Żydowska*.[31] For different reasons Max Bishof, chief of the *Transferstelle*, was also opposed to these measures.

In Częstochowa, Będzin, Chmielnik, Radom, and Kołomyja the ghetto police also arrested people or sealed off their homes for not paying taxes in time, for being late in paying their shares of enforced cash contributions or in delivering fur coats, furniture, and other goods. They were jailed until they paid up or delivered the items requested.[32]

In the Częstochowa Ghetto the police carried away and stored at the Council building merchandise and home furnishings from persons delinquent in their payments. The eyewitness who supplied this information stated that "some of these things were deposited at the Council by the Jewish police; the rest they kept for themselves and brazenly sold later."[33] Council members did not hesitate to ask the Germans to help collect overdue taxes and fees. Thus in Lublin the representative of the Finance Commission suggested, on May 5, 1941, that the Council try and get assistance from the authorities to collect unpaid taxes by force.[34] The Zamość Jewish Council, in a public announcement in Polish and German, revealed a list of 40 delinquent taxpayers, warning that the list would be submitted to the authorities if payments were not made by August 30, 1940. (One of the delinquents, a woman, was 3,475 zlotys in arrears.)[35] Confronted with such threats, people sold their possessions to save themselves from encounters with the Germans. The same Jewish Council warned in a public announcement on April 26, 1940, that "lists of people who inexplicably failed to report for forced-labor duty would be presented daily to the authorities for punishment."[36]

People in arrears for unpaid taxes in Będzin were handed over to the Gestapo. Gestapo-men visited the Jewish Council every Wednesday to take away groups of 10 or 12 imprisoned delinquents or others arrested for different reasons.[37] The ghetto police in the Będzin and Sosnowiec Ghettos arrested the parents of persons who had not reported for forced-labor duty in the labor camps. Their ration cards were taken away from them, they were removed from their homes, etc.[38] Similar measures against the families of people hiding from the *Arbeitseinsatz* were implemented in the Zawiercie Ghetto.[39] The Vilna *Geto-yedies* of February 27, 1943, headlined: "Last warning to 200 persons who have not reported for work—they will be handed over to the authorities"[40]

Five women and two men in the Białystok Ghetto were sentenced to long terms in a penal camp for hiding their daughters from transportation for labor duty in Wołkowysk.[41]

The ghetto police also imposed penalties for not keeping buildings and backyards clean. On December 17, 1941, the Białystok Ghetto police announced that for not keeping their backyards clean tenants would be deprived of their bread rations for a term of one month.[42]

The ghetto police were also forced to participate in "resettlement actions," about which we will have more to say later.

THE SUPERVISORY AUTHORITIES OF THE GHETTO POLICE

As in other fields, there was no uniformity in the supervision of the ghetto police by occupation authorities. Various interests, intentions, and attitudes crisscrossed, opposed each other, and competed, seeking to secure full jurisdiction over the ghetto police. There were two underlying factors—an internal Jewish one and an external one that further complicated the supervision problem: (1) formally the ghetto police were the executive arm of the Councils, to whom they were supposed to be subordinated. However, in some ghettos the police tended to become a force independent of the Councils, and, as was the case in the Vilna Ghetto, they achieved their goal.[43] (2) The Germans left some jurisdiction in dealing with the Jews to the ethnic police (*Hilfspolizei,* "auxiliary police") in the areas of the Government General, Ostland, and the Ukraine, and this, in turn, influenced the position of the Jewish police with regard to the *Hilfspolizei.*

What all the crisscrossing factors meant in day-to-day practice can be seen in the example of the Warsaw Ghetto police. As mentioned, Paragraph 4 of their organizational rules names as the controlling organs of the ghetto police the Council chairman, the Control Commission, and the commandant of the ghetto police, all internal Jewish factors. Actually, however, the ghetto police were subordinated to three centers of authority: the German authorities, the commandant of the Polish city police, and the Jewish Council. One of the bulletins of the Council's statistical department carried the information that "the legal basis of the ghetto police are the orders of the [German] authorities, of the [pertinent] commissars of the Polish police (street traffic, control of trading in the streets, guard duties), and of the Jewish Council (keeping watch within and outside the Council offices and over the property of its institutions)."[44]

According to the postwar memoirs of a former member of the leadership of the Warsaw Ghetto police, the *Kommandant* of the German *Ordnungspolizei* (ORPO), Jahrke, stated that the ghetto police had no official connection with the ORPO. He said that the ghetto police were the executive arm of the Council chairman, on the one hand, and an "organ of order" of the Polish police, on the other hand. The commandant of the Polish police had the authority to give orders to the commandant of the ghetto police and was also entitled to oversee their activities, always with the knowledge of the Council's chairman. According to the author of these memoirs, the division of authority between the ghetto police and the Polish police was such that the ghetto police took care of public order, street traffic, and sanitation matters, while the Polish police had jurisdiction over criminal offenses.[45]

We learn from another source that the ghetto police performed auxiliary services (patrols) in the precincts assigned to Polish police active in the ghetto area.[46] The leadership of the ghetto police was obligated to submit weekly reports to the commandant of the Polish police, mentioning such events as disturbances against public order, resistance to the authorities, criminal offenses, fires, etc.[47]

In May 1941, after the *Kommissar* of the Jewish *Wohnbezirk* was appointed, the problem of subordinating the Jewish police became more complicated, and a jurisdictional dispute broke out in the ranks of the occupation authorities (see Chap. 11).

In the territory of the Government General, the Polish police wielded considerable authority over the ghetto police. In Chmielnik (Kielce area), for instance, the commandant of the Polish police, at a meeting with the Jewish Council, instructed the ghetto police on their duties as a unit of the Polish auxiliary police.[48]

The hierarchy and jurisdictional relations between the ghetto police and the Polish police in Częstochowa clearly show the degree of subordination of the former to the latter. The commandant of the ghetto police was a Polish police major. The commandants of the ghetto police precincts (I and II) were Polish sergeants. The Polish commandant nominated a few Jews as liaison men between the Polish precincts and the ghetto police. With respect to jurisdictional matters it is evident that only smaller fines (up to 10 zlotys) could be imposed by the Jewish police. The Jewish police were obligated to refer more serious administrative or criminal cases to the Polish police. By the same token, disputes between Jews and non-Jews over transactions concluded before the war, or even after the ghetto had been established, were handled as a rule by the Polish police. The ghetto police made arrests of those not reporting for forced-labor duty only under supervision of Polish policemen, and Polish policemen patrolled the ghetto and made arrests of inmates on their own.[49]

It is hard to say whether relations between the ghetto police and the Polish police were shaped in ghettos all over the Government General as they were in Częstochowa. There is not enough evidence on this matter in the available sources. To a large degree, it all depended on the attitude of the German authorities. A certain measure of subordination was evident everywhere. In the territories of Ostland and the Reichskommissariat Ukraine, the jurisdiction of the local auxiliary police over the Jewish Councils and the ghetto police was even stronger (see Chap. 2).

The degree to which the ghetto police were subordinated to the Councils also varied, ranging from strict control to various degrees of independence. The role of the ghetto police, and consequently of their position in the ghetto, increased during "resettlement actions" and in the *Restgettos*, where the Councils were often dominated by the police. However, in the Kaunas Ghetto, for instance, the subordination of the ghetto police to the authority of the chairman of the Council of Elders was greatly emphasized.[50] In the Lublin Ghetto, the Council's vice chairman, Dr. Mark Alten, was also commandant of the ghetto police. Even in the *Restgetto* in Majdan Tatarski, where the commandant of the reduced ghetto police was the notorious Gestapo agent Shamay Grayer, Dr. Alten formally continued to oversee the police.[51]

In Sosnowiec and in the entire area of Eastern Upper Silesia, the ghetto police were under the administrative supervision of the chief of the *Zentrale* administration, Fajge Czarny. She acted as a kind of super-commandant of the entire ghetto police force in this occupational area.[52] The ghetto police in the Łódź Ghetto was also strictly subordinated to the chairman, Rumkowski (except, as already mentioned, the *Sonderabteilung* of the ghetto police at a later period). The correspondence of the ghetto police appeared under the letterhead: *Der Älteste der Juden, Vorstand des Ordnungsdienstes*. A similar situation prevailed in the Białystok Ghetto.

In some of the ghettos a personal union of sorts existed between the Councils and the police. On July 12, 1942, the Vilna police commandant Jacob Gens was nominated ghetto representative and police chief by the Vilna *Kommissar*, and thus became head of the Jewish Council and chief of police at the same time.[53] (In actual fact, he had wielded great authority in the ghetto even prior to his nomination.) His former deputy was appointed police commandant. In the Pabianice Ghetto the police chief was a member of the Council.[54] In Raków (Radom district) the Council chairman was also police commandant.[55]

It happened that the Councils delegated some employees to the police to perform certain urgent duties for a time. Thus the Lublin Jewish Council made a decision on March 16, 1941, probably in connection with the expulsion of 10,000 Lublin Jews to adjacent small towns, to assign 11 employees of the ghetto administration and the local JSS committee to assist the ghetto police.[56] The Warsaw Jewish Council imposed on its employees the duty of helping out in the "resettlement action." They were issued special armbands with the inscription *Aussiedlungsdienst* ("Resettlement Service").

ORGANIZATIONAL STRUCTURE

As mentioned, the ghetto police operated as a separate department in the administration of the ghettos. In Warsaw it was Department XVII, in Łódź XI, in Lwów X, in Vilna XV.[57] The establishment of the ghetto police was accomplished by the Councils, which recruited candidates for the police. In a number of ghettos, however, this was not an easy task. As was the case with the Councils, so also with the police: at least in the beginning, nobody was eager to join the ghetto police force. Eyewitnesses relate about two ghettos, Sierpce (Zichenau district) and Kalisz (Wartheland), that there were no Jewish police at all.[58]

The former Council chairman in the Zamość Ghetto relates that when at the end of 1941 the Gestapo demanded that he establish a ghetto police force he refused, explaining that such a force was unnecessary. Pressed by the Gestapo, the Council yielded.[59] In Rokitno (Volhynia) "only with difficulty were young people found who were willing to serve as policemen under the Germans."[60] It was the same in Klementów,[61] Raków,[62] Staszów,[63] and other ghettos.

Still the privileges accorded to ghetto policemen did induce young people to join Jewish police forces. Policemen were free from the cursed duty of forced labor, from paying their shares toward cash contributions imposed by the Germans, and from being sent to labor camps. And they received larger food allocations. Some individuals with a drive to govern were probably also tempted by the opportunity to rule over the inmates and at the same time make material gains by virtue of their authority. There were also socially motivated young people who made up their minds to join the ghetto police in the belief that it was their duty to help establish a force capable of protecting Jews against the molestations of Polish hooligans before the ghettos were established and from all kinds of dangers and oppressions afterward. In certain intellectual circles in the Warsaw Ghetto, for instance, the opinion was widespread that it was the duty of a responsible member of the community to serve in the ghetto police.[64]

The regulations for hiring police are known for only one ghetto—Warsaw. To qualify, a candidate had to meet the following conditions: be twenty-one to forty years of age, have a diploma from a *Gymnasium* (secondary school), be of proper height and weight, have completed military service, have an unblemished past, and be recommended by two persons. Each candidate had to pass the screening of three or four offices: the so-called small commission that collected all necessary personal documents, a medical commission, and lastly the "super scrutiny" commission, presided over by the commandant of the ghetto police (after a time, the "super scrutiny" commission was reduced to only one person, the police commandant). But even if a candidate satisfied all these commissions, his personal dossier still had to be checked by a special supervisory commission (*Aufsichts-ausschuss*, or *Komisja Nadzorcza*) of the Jewish Council which, with the help of its own trusted investigators, once more checked the integrity and qualifications of the candidate. The decision of this commission was final. The accepted candidate signed a solemn declaration (in lieu of an oath) of his unblemished past (which was later check against the registry of convicted persons at the prewar Polish Ministry of Justice), a vow of unconditional obedience, and a vow to serve without pay.[65]

We may assume that in other ghettos, particularly the medium and smaller ones, where the supply of candidates was limited, the hiring procedures were much simpler.

Of a number of ghettos we know that favoritism was prevalent, combined with nepotism and graft. Among others Warsaw,[66] Lwów,[67] Zbaraż,[68] Krasnystaw,[69] Drohobycz,[70] Zawiercie,[71] and Staszów[72] are mentioned in this connection. The German police authorities delegated or nominated their own trusted confidants to the ghetto police, and no proper credentials could be requested from them. Such was the case in Warsaw,[73] Łódź,[74] Kaunas,[75] Lwów,[76] Cracow, and Nowy Dwór,[77] among others.

SOCIAL BACKGROUND

What was the social background of the ghetto police? Had the policemen had any socio-political connections with the Jewish community? Unfortunately we have only fragmentary material at our disposal. Still what is available is relevant and enlightening.

As we have mentioned, our questionnaires refer to 112 policemen in 39 towns in different occupation areas. They contain data as to the age, education, profession, family status, domicile, party affiliations, and ultimate fate of the policemen (see Table X, p. 491. To judge by Table X, over 50 percent of the 112 policemen about whom information was supplied in the questionnaires were young people up to thirty years of age. Of the 38 policemen on whom educational data were supplied, over 30 percent had secondary or higher education (however, the small number of answers to this question—25%—permits no conclusive evaluation). Of the 73 policemen whose occupations are mentioned, 42.4 percent were former merchants, and almost 16.4 percent were artisans. The remainder were clerks, etc. (30%) or professionals (1.1%). Of the 104 whose marital status is mentioned, over 35.5 percent were single, which is explained by the comparatively young ages of policemen. Of the 105 policemen about whom pertinent information has been supplied, 15 percent were refugees or expellees. As for former party affiliations, followers of the Zionist Revisionists are in first place (45%) among the 44 policemen for whom information was given. Less than 30 percent were General Zionists. As for labor groups, one policeman was a Bundist and seven belonged to the Zionist Socialists' groups (16%). Nine of these were prewar leaders in their parties. The comparatively large number of members of the Revisionist Party in the ghetto police (which has been confirmed by other sources)[78] may be explained by the fact that the recruitees of this group came to a large degree from the rank and file of the so-called combatants (former front veterans or army reservists) who were mainly affiliated with the Revisionists. Youth divisions of the Revisionists (*Betar*, *Brith Ha Chayal*) had also received paramilitary training before the war. Therefore they were better qualified for service with the ghetto police than members of other political groups.

The small amount of data regarding party affiliation (less than 10%) testifies to the fact that a large number of the ghetto policemen belonged to no party. Their participation in prewar community activities was also small (14%).

As to their fates, a comparatively small number (7%) were killed before the start of the "resettlement actions," but over 60 percent shared the final destiny of the ghetto inmates. Over 25 percent

TABLE X

Background Data of Ghetto Policemen

	Number	Percentage
Age		
Up to 30 years	57	50.8
30 years and over	55	49.2
	112	100.0
Education		
Elementary	8	21.2
Secondary	23	60.4
Higher	7	18.4
	38	100.0
Occupation		
Merchants	31	42.4
Artisans	12	16.4
Professionals	8	1.1
Clerks	22	30.1
	73	100.0
Marital status		
Married	67	64.5
Single	37	35.5
	104	100.0
Residence		
Permanent	90	85.7
Refugee or expellee	15	14.3
	105	100.0
Party affiliation		
Bund	1	2.3
Zionist Socialist	7	16.0
General Zionist	13	29.5
Zionist Revisionist	19	43.2
Other	4	9.0
	44	100.0
Membership in organizations	16	14.0
Evaluation		
Positive	44	39.3
Negative	55	49.9
Neutral	12	10.8
	111	100.0
Fate		
Resigned	3	4.2
Killed before the deportations	5	7.0
Killed after being deported	45	63.3
Survived	18	25.5
	71	100.0

survived, whereas less than 12 percent of Council members survived.

Some of the data reflected in Table X are confirmed by other sources. Thus one source mentions that in Warsaw 10 percent of the ghetto police were professionals. Jonas Turkow indicates that a large number of lawyers, whom he lists by name, served with the ghetto police.[79] The commandant of the ghetto police and his deputy in Radom were both professionals.[80] In the ghettos of Galicia (Lwów and Drohobycz among others) a large number of professionals joined the ghetto police.[81]

On the other hand, some sources stress the fact that in certain ghettos the police included characters of doubtful morality or outright criminals. This is said about Łódź (particularly about the *Sonderabteilung*), Warsaw, Nowy Dwór (where a notorious prewar underworld character was nominated ghetto police commandant by the Germans), Międzyrzec, Chełm (where a prewar Jewish *agent provocateur* was nominated as commandant by the authorities), Bełchatów, the *Restgetto* of Lublin, and Minsk (Byelorussia)[82] (at a later period).

A considerable percentage of refugees and expellees among the ghetto police is also mentioned by other sources. Thus the commandant of the police in the Płońsk Ghetto was a newcomer in town. He arrived after the war had broken out.[83] In Chełm both the commandant and his deputy were refugees, the former from Libawna (three miles from Chełm) and the latter from Warsaw.[84] In Końskie the chief of the ghetto police was an expellee from Germany (his two brothers also served under him).[85] In Radom these positions were occupied by two newcomers: one from Memel (or Galicia) and the second from Kalisz.[86] In Falenica the commandant, his deputy, and the majority of the rank-and-file policemen were refugees (or expellees) from Łódź.[87] In Łuck neither of two commandants of the ghetto police were local residents; one came from Lublin, and the other from Sosnowiec.[88] In Słonim a newcomer from Silesia was the commandant of the ghetto police.[89] In Zamość the ghetto police were headed by a deportee from Dortmund, starting in May 1942. He arrived together with a group of Jews from Czechoslovakia and Germany.[90] The commandant and the majority of the policemen in the Strzygów Ghetto were expellees from the neighboring town of Sierpc.[91] The commandant and his helpers in the Minsk Ghetto (Byelorussia) were refugees from Poland who had arrived in the fall of 1939, etc.[92]

The fact that the Germans placed nonresidents of the community at the helm of the ghetto police was probably motivated by a desire to form a police force without close relations to the ghetto inmates. The Germans may have cherished a hope that these people would more easily be made into obedient tools to implement planned measures of persecution.

The police in the large ghettos grew into a populous police apparatus with a vast hierarchy. The ghetto police force was bound to increase as the functions of the Councils multiplied and, later on, during periods of "resettlement actions" when the Germans requested their assistance. For instance, in the Warsaw Ghetto the initial force of 1,700 policemen increased by 200 in 1941 in connection with the antiepidemic campaign. After the notorious "13" (for more on this quasi-police formation in the Warsaw Ghetto see below in this chapter) was dissolved, some 200 of its men were admitted into the ranks of the regular ghetto police. Another increase of 200 men took place in the spring of 1942, at the time when the fire brigade was established (the fire brigade was part of the ghetto police). By then the ghetto police force totaled some 2,300 men, an increase of close to 35 percent as compared to their initial numbers.[93]

A public communication (No. 38) by the Lublin Jewish Council (dated February 5, 1942) announced an increase of the ghetto police by order of the authorities who were to decide who would be hired from among those registering for the job. In view of the date of this communication (approximately one month before the start of the "resettlement") and of the fact that the Germans left to themselves the hiring of these new policemen, there is no doubt that the increase of the police force was ordered in connection with the forthcoming event.

In the Kaunas Ghetto the number of policemen increased from 60 in August 1941 to 210 a year later—two and a half times.[94] In Otwock the initial police force consisted of 30 men. Later it was doubled, numbering 100 a short time before the liquidation of the ghetto.[95] In Zamość the ghetto police started out with 10 men. After the arrival of expellees from Czechoslovakia and Germany in the spring of 1942, the police force doubled as new policemen were hired from among the newcomers.[96]

In the Łódź Ghetto also, some 100 newcomers were admitted into the police force in December 1941, all former officers in the German, Austrian, and Czechoslovak armies.[97] In the Vilna Ghetto the police force was augmented in December 1942, following expansion of the jurisdiction of the ghetto representative over a number of small adjacent ghettos.[98]

Whenever a "resettlement" was carried out in stages, the ghetto police were usually reduced after each consecutive deportation. For example, the Łódź Ghetto police dwindled from 850 men in September 1940 to 530 men in April 1943, after conclusion of the deportations to Chełmno in 1942.[99] In the Warsaw Ghetto the retrenchment process started in the course of large-scale deportations to Treblinka in the summer of 1942. Some policemen resigned, refusing to remain with the police, or unwilling to lend a hand in "resettlements," foreseeing that the police would be reduced anyway, if only because the ghetto would be greatly depopulated. When the Warsaw deportations terminated on September 21, 1942, the survivors were confined within the shrunken ghetto, and some 300 of the ghetto policemen were transformed into the so-called *Werkschutz*, whose task it was to guard German ghetto shops and blocks where Jewish laborers were confined.[100] In Lublin the ghetto police were reduced from 113 to 35 men on March 31, 1942, in the course of the "resettlement action."[101]

Like any other police force, the ghetto police had an elaborate hierarchy. It was headed by a commandant with the German title of *Leiter des O.D.* or *Chef der Gettopolizei.* One or sometimes two deputies served under him. The large ghettos were divided into police areas or precincts whose numbers used to be reduced following curtailment of the ghetto territory. The Warsaw Ghetto started out with six precincts, each headed by a *Leiter.* The Łódź Ghetto also had six police precincts, which later were reduced to five and, finally, to three or four.[102] In Lwów, the ghetto police had four precincts.[103] In Vilna there were four precincts and a special ghetto gate guard at the beginning.[104] In Kaunas the four initial precincts were reduced to three after the so-called "small ghetto" was liquidated on October 4, 1941.[105] There were four police precincts in the Białystok Ghetto.[106]

In the large and medium ghettos police operations were performed by specialized departments. The organizational setup in the Warsaw Ghetto police was as follows: general secretariat, headed by a chief and his deputy; organization and administration department, with three section chiefs; personnel department, with two section chiefs; economic department, with four sections; external service, encompassing six precincts in addition to the precinct "community" (Jewish Council) and a reserve squad; special units (central jail and anti-epidemic campaign); and the fire brigade. In addition, there were also permanent sentries, ranging from two men to squads of up to several score each. Their task was to guard the institutions and offices of the ghetto. Each precinct consisted of three platoons divided into three sections, each with its own section *Leiter*. Each platoon was headed by its own platoon *Leiter*. Each platoon had a liaison section riding bicycles and headed by a chief and a secretary. On the average a platoon numbered 50 policemen; thus each precinct had some 150 policemen at its disposal. The entire police force was headed by the *Leiter* (*Kierownik* was his title in Polish), assisted by an adjutant and a deputy.[107]

The hierarchical setup and the insignia of the Częstochowa Ghetto police were similar to those of the Warsaw Ghetto; there was the *Leiter* and his deputy, the precinct *Leiter* and their deputies, and group and section *Leiter*. The ghetto police force in 1942 numbered 250 men.[108]

By mid-1942 the police office in the Vilna Ghetto encompassed two police precincts, the ghetto gate guard, the criminal police, the arrest house, the registry, the labor police, the sanitary police, and the camp police.[109]

As already indicated, the police jurisdiction in the Łódź Ghetto was divided topographically into six precincts. One, the Bałut Ring, acted as an intermediary between the ghetto and the 6th German police precinct. The police departments were: reserve; investigation or legal department (until the ghetto court was established this was the only judicial agency in the ghetto); sanitary control; price control (abolished in January 1942); and the *Sonderabteilung* (see pp. 480, 482). The ghetto police was headed by a *Vorstand* (executive) consisting of the commandant and four section chiefs. As of April 1943 the officer corps consisted of 5 commissars, 5 subcommissars, 18 aspirants, 10 chiefs, 10 section chiefs, 50 guard-masters in charge of the sanitary service, and sentries posted at strategic places in the ghetto. In addition the ghetto police paid the salaries of nine policemen directly subordinated to the German criminal police in the ghetto. Their specific tasks were to deliver goods confiscated from Jews, to guard arrested inmates kept in the ghetto jail at the disposal of the *Kripo*, etc. A special detachment of 52 policemen guarded the shops and factories. They did not belong to the regular ghetto police force but were subordinated to the chiefs of individual labor places and to Rumkowski, the highest authority. They wore police insignia to increase their importance in the eyes of the laborers. For a time, a sort of a civilian *Hilfsordnungsdienst* ("Auxiliary Order Service") was in operation, with the task of keeping order in houses. It was, however, disbanded at the beginning of November 1940. In October 1942 a women's squad of the ghetto police was established to take care of children roaming the streets, to combat street trade, to keep order in distribution shops, etc. The women's squad was disbanded by Biebow's order of March 3, 1943. The majority of these women were absorbed by labor shops, and some were admitted into the *Sonderabtielung*.[110] Women also served in the Vilna Ghetto police.[111]

The police in the Kaunas Ghetto were set up as follows: the top men were the chief of police and his deputies, followed by the police inspector, precinct chiefs, chiefs of squads and their deputies, lower-grade police officers, and rank-and-file policemen.[112]

The ghetto police wore special hats and inscribed armbands showing their rank marks. No uniforms were issued except in Vilna during the "actions" in Oszmiana, when a group of 20 policemen were given leather coats and military hats emblazoned with the Star of David.[113] There was vast variety in this respect, if only for lack of general instructions. Apparently these matters were left to the discretion of local authorities or even of pertinent Jewish Councils. With very few exceptions (Łódź, Kaunas, and a few others), no hats, armbands, or rank insignia of ghetto policemen have been preserved. In treating this subject we have had to investigate old, sometimes blurred photos and sometimes inaccurate descriptions in sources of postwar origin. Therefore our information is at times fragmentary. The "uniforms" of the ghetto police, as already mentioned, featured hats of various shapes and colors; armbands (often rubber-stamped) of various shades and inscriptions; rank marks; and wooden or rubber clubs. In all these variations, however, the "uniforms" were distinguished by a single, constant element, the Star of David (*der Judenstern*).

The police in the Warsaw Ghetto wore dark blue hats, similar in shade to the hats of the Polish police, with a wide, light blue stripe, a metal Star of David, and the letters J.R.W. and R.Z.W. Their armbands, 12 centimeters wide, were inscribed in German and Polish, *"Der Judenrat in Warschau, Ordnungsdienst"* and *"Rada Żydowska w Warszawie, Służba Porządkowa"* ["Jewish Council in Warsaw,

Order Service"]. In addition to this armband, the ghetto police were obligated to display the regular Jewish armband. Each policeman, except high-ranking officers, displayed his service number on his armband and coat. The high-ranking officers had silver stripes on their hats. The rank insignia on the hats and armbands (placed between the two inscriptions) consisted of from one to four stars for the higher ranks, or metal buttons, also from one to four, for the lower ranks. The rank marks on the armbands were framed by a black square (for lower ranks) or by a velvet square with white stripes for higher ranks.[114]

In Radom the stripes around the hats of the ghetto police were red, the armbands yellow, with a bilingual inscription: *Jüdischer Ordnungsdienst—Służba Porządkowa*. The rank marks were the same as in the Warsaw Ghetto.[115] In Częstochowa the "uniforms" were also similar to those in Warsaw.[116] But in Chełm the ghetto police wore round, black hats, and in Siedlce their armbands were red and stamped by the local *Arbeitsamt*.[117]

In Lwów the ghetto police wore hats similar in shape to the hats of the Polish police, but distinguished by a red stripe, the inscription *Jüdischer Ordnungsdienst J.O.L. Lemberg*, and the Star of David. The armbands were red with a yellow Star of David and rubber-stamped by the German Security Police.[118] In Bolechów the hats were blue with a yellow stripe. The armband was red.[119]

We find the same variety in colors also in other occupied areas. In Łódź the hats were round and dark blue with a red stripe; the armbands were white and yellow with a Star of David in the center. The rank marks were triangular pins for the higher ranks, or metal buttons on the hats. The uniforms of the police in the ghettos of the Łódź province—in Ozorków, for instance—were similar.[120]

In the East Silesian area there was a difference between Będzin and Sosnowiec. The Będzin Ghetto police wore blue armbands with an inscription, but in Sosnowiec the armbands were yellow and bore the number of the individual policeman.[121] In a draft (*Entwurf*) of a regulation of the Jewish problem in Latvia, dated August 25, 1941, and presented to the area *Kommissare* by the *Generalkommissar*, a white armband with the *Judenstern* was envisaged for the ghetto police.[122] In fact such an armband, bearing the inscription *Getto-polizei*, was displayed by the police in the Byelorussian and Lithuanian Ghettos—for instance in Swisłocz, Vilna, Kaunas, and other ghettos.[123]

The ghetto police were armed with wooden or rubber staffs, but they were issued no firearms. It seems that the Germans did not trust the ghetto police enough to issue them firearms. In one instance in the Vilna Ghetto during the Oszmiana "action" at the end of October 1942, when the Vilna police took part in the "resettlement," they were issued firearms for the time they participated in the "action."[124]

As employees of the Councils the ghetto police usually were on the Councils' payrolls. Starting on August 1, 1942, the salaries of the ghetto police in the Lublin *Restgetto* were paid according to the following scales: the *Kommandant* received 325 zlotys a month, the officers received 225 zlotys, the subalterns received 180 zlotys, and the policemen got 150 zlotys.[125] In Pabianice, the *Kommandant* was paid 25 Reichsmarks a week; the salaries of the other police functionaries fluctuated between 10 and 15 Reichsmarks a week.[126]

However, there were ghettos where service in the police was considered an honorary duty for which no salary was paid. In the Warsaw Ghetto, for instance, where salaries were paid only to the commandant and 100 high-ranking functionaries of the disbanded *Ordnungswache* (who had been incorporated into the ghetto police), the Council budget could not absorb an additional burden of more than 20,000 zlotys a month, a sum needed to pay the salaries of the 1,700 ghetto policemen. According to a person well versed in events in that ghetto, this was the primary cause of the negative selection of candidates for the ghetto police. The prospect of work without remuneration simply did not attract well-qualified, honest people. Only dishonest ones, seeing an opportunity to make money the easy way, applied in large numbers.[127] In April 1941 a ghetto police fund (*Fundusz Służby Porządkowej*) was established. Its by-laws were approved by the *Transferstelle*. To provide the necessary money, a tax of 30 groszy was collected from each inmate in addition to a tax leveled against various business establishments in the ghetto. Up to December 1, 1941, five payments were made to the police, averaging 75 zlotys a man. A precinct chief got from 120 to 130 zlotys.[128]

CORRUPTION

Contemporary as well as postwar documentation is rich in critical observations about the corruption among the police in various ghettos. It is apparent that the ghetto police were the weakest component of so-called ghetto autonomy. Their specific functions and their daily contacts with the German authorities rendered them most vulnerable and submissive to the negative influence of life in the ghetto and of the destructive, nihilistic German morality. The personnel of the ghetto police, penetrated as it was by a number of low, asocial elements, faced difficult ethical tests which not all passed unblemished.

The precarious situation of the ghetto police as the executive organ of the occupation authority and the Councils, enforcing draconic German measures, caused a conflict between their personal affiliations and feelings and their official duties. They were burdened with the most inhuman tasks anyone ever carried out against his own brethren: to help the German enemy tighten the noose around the necks of Jewish victims.

Even in normal times a regular police force is disliked by large segments of the population; the more so the ghetto police, whose main task was to effectuate the persecutions showered upon the Jews by the authorities. The police collected cash contributions and taxes; they assisted in raiding, guarding, and escorting hungry, mentally exhausted people on their way to places of forced labor; and it was the ghetto police who often were ordered to enforce discipline in the presence of German officials. The ghetto police sentries formed the inside guard at the ghetto fences, and in the minds of the ghetto inhabitants they were identified with the German and Polish sentries outside the fences. Both the Germans and the Councils used the ghetto police to carry out confiscations of Jewish property and to combat smuggling, the only means of overcoming constant hunger in the ghettos. The Jewish police carried out raids against and arrests of inmates destined for shipment to labor camps; they executed penalites against inmates for offenses against draconic ghetto rules. Last but far from least, in the final stages of the ghettos the Jewish police were called upon to assist in "resettlement actions." In short, the ghetto police came to be identified with the inhuman cruelty of the Nazi ghetto regime.

Small wonder that they were hated by the ghetto inmates. Their defense, as recorded in numerous sources, was that they only carried out orders issued by the Germans or the Councils, and that the situation in the ghetto would have been still worse had the Germans themselves carried them out. These excuses made little impression on their unfortunate victims, particularly since the behavior of some policemen in the course of performing their duties was too often highly improper. The sources note that considerable segments of the ghetto police were morally and materially corrupted, that they enriched themselves on account of the oppressed and persecuted inmates when carrying out their assignments.

The methods the ghetto inmates used in their dealings with the Jewish police were similar to the methods of the Councils in their dealings with the Germans (see Chap. 16). Cash, jewelry, and similar valuables were used in efforts to "soften up" the ghetto policemen, to ransom people from oppressions or persecutions in connection with confiscations, raids, etc. To a certain degree, the ghetto police were in a position to make some secret exemptions for individuals, to look the other way while ostensibly combating smuggling, to erase the names of some individuals from the lists of people destined for expulsions or "resettlements," etc. For these services payments were demanded and made. The price scale depended on the importance of the favor or how serious the offense was, ranging from a bread ration card to very large amounts of cash or valuables. In the poisoned, amoral atmosphere caused in the ghetto by the foul Nazi regime, corruption was a rather normal vice, proliferating in the ghetto. But to a much larger extent than was evident among other ghetto employees (see Chap. 14), corruption spread among the ghetto policemen, who by the very nature of their activities were in a better position to demand graft for favors. Everyone in the ghetto was aware of this. It was evident in the good life led by the police, in their free spending, alcoholism, revels, sexual frivolity, etc., and it only served to deepen hatred and contempt for the police.

There was yet another type of police corruption bordering on betrayal of their own people. Nihilism and lawlessness became widespread among the ghetto police, leading to far-reaching collaboration with the Germans. Little by little, more and more policemen adopted the mores and morals of the Nazi oppressor. The Germans encouraged the demoralization of the Jewish policemen in order to make them willing tools in their hands. Open and secret German agents planted among the ghetto police were treated as a fifth column by the ghetto inmates. German offices that constantly competed for authority over the Jews established agencies of their own in many ghettos, often under cover of quasi-police forces with informants reporting on Jews. These unworthies terrorized the Councils and the ghetto inmates, infecting the regular ghetto policemen with poison of the deepest demoralization.

We shall now attempt to discuss the corruption that prevailed in various aspects of ghetto life.

Forced Labor

The most severe plague torturing the Jews until the start of the "resettlements" was the duty of forced labor. The ghetto police were called upon to apply vigorous measures in carrying out this program, including severe repression of evaders. This afforded the corrupt police a good opportunity to make large profits.

Ringelblum wrote on April 17, 1941:

People are being caught [in the Warsaw Ghetto] for work in the labor camps because the community executive did not make the requested contingent available. The Jewish and Polish police have had to seize them. Those deemed able-bodied got summonses, but did not report. Naturally they would not stay in their homes overnight, and in their places people of over fifty years of age have been seized. The Jewish and Polish police have taken advantage of the situation. Business has been good. They have demanded 100 zlotys from innocent people [for release] and ransom money has been accepted on behalf of entire houses. A real bacchanalia has taken place.[129]

After describing the brutal beating of assembled Jewish workers by German and Lithuanian police, Lejb Garfunkel makes these remarks about the behavior of the police in the Kaunas Ghetto:

As much as it hurts, it has to be mentioned that Jews at the assembly place were often beaten by their own people . . . the Jewish police and employees of the labor department. They tried to justify it, arguing that it would otherwise have been impossible to keep order at the assembly place, and that they were responsible to the Germans. It should be admitted that it was, in fact, hard to keep in line thousands of people, not always in a peaceful mood, underworld characters among them. Everyone had tried somehow to gain release from forced work at the very worst labor places. People tried to leave the lines where they waited and join groups assigned for light work or at more convenient places. At times the Jewish "bosses" thought that they had to whip people for their own good to protect them from more severe beatings by the merciless Germans, or even from much more horrible things.[130]

Severe, brutal treatment of Jewish forced laborers (arrests and beatings) often accompanied by acts of corruption (bribes for assignment to places of lighter work) are reported by eyewitnesses in Gostynin (Wartheland), Będzin, Zawiercie, Włodzimierz Wołyński, and Brańsk,[131] among many other places.

Cash Contributions, Taxes, and Confiscations

It has been reported from various ghettos that, in the course of collecting taxes and imposed contributions in cash or valuables, the ghetto police treated inmates without mercy, committed frauds, and appropriated large quantities of cash and valuables. A survivor from the Drohiczyn Ghetto complains in his memoirs that "people who had lost their possessions and ruined their health at hard labor in a short time could not forgive the Council members and the ghetto police for enriching themselves after each enforced contribution or other affliction. Every misfortune made them fatter. Jewish policemen got drunk, had a good time, and traded with the non-Jewish police."[132]

A witness reports that in the Brańsk Ghetto, "the more the Council raised the taxes, the more the Jewish police carried out confiscations of the last pieces of bedding, clothing, and whatever else they were able to lay their hands on."[133] A group of ghetto policemen in Łuków, headed by their commandant, "denounced the Jews and whipped them, thus assisting the Gestapo in forcing the Jews to surrender gold. Each new oppression became a source of income for them. They became very rich in partnership with the Germans."[134] We have already mentioned (see Chap. 10) the corrupt methods of tax collecting used in the Żelechów Ghetto.

In the course of the so-called "fur action" (the Jews in the occupied territories were ordered to deposit their furs with the Jewish Councils, to be placed at the disposal of the German authorities, or to hand them over directly to the Germans), the Jewish police outdid themselves in their eager and submissive execution of the order, as was the case in Vilna, for instance.[135]

Smuggling

Smuggling was widespread and an important factor in the corruption of the ghetto police. Serving as sentries posted to guard the ghetto gates and crosspoints leading to "Aryan" streets, the ghetto police had a good opportunity to use their position to obtain illicit income. Very often they were go-betweens for smugglers and bribed German and Polish guardsmen. It was only natural that the middlemen made a pretty penny for themselves. In the process of searching people who were passing through the gates, the ghetto police demanded a share of smuggled goods (mainly food) for themselves. Often they did this in covert partnership with German and local ethnic police. There is a great deal of material available concerning both positive and negative aspects of the role played by the Jewish police with respect to smuggling. Ringelblum noted that in the Warsaw Ghetto "the meanness of the Jewish policemen goes far enough to squeeze out of the child smugglers 20 groszy for each smuggled loaf of bread. . . ."[136] In the underground organ of the right-wing faction of Poalei Zion, *Dos Fraye Wort* (No. 1/38, May 23, 1942), a typical case is cited: "As soon as a little girl smuggler carries a few kilograms of potatoes over into the ghetto, a Jewish policeman appears to weigh the potatoes and exact his toll according to weight."

We read about the Kołomyja Ghetto police that as "each worker was forced to [engage] in smuggling because of sheer destitution, the ghetto police pressed for its share of the smuggled food, or even appropriated all of it, or was paid a ransom in cash."[137]

A survivor from the Grodno Ghetto writes: "Because of these relations [with the German ghetto guard], the Jewish police were in a position to make smuggling easier. But they did this only in order to exact a large income for themselves. The Jewish policemen are getting rich, enjoying a life of ease and plenty. With few exceptions, they are the only patrons of the expensive restaurants, and they lavishly buy food and drink at a time when hundreds of Jews are starving."[138]

According to contemporary notes of a chronicler of the Vilna Ghetto, the Jewish ghetto guards treated inmates brutally (beatings, arrests, and confiscations of smuggled goods) when searching the laborers returning from work outside the ghetto. Extortion was also noted.[139] It should be added, however, that the brutalities at the ghetto gate took place only when searches were made in the presence of German functionaries and SS men. The Jewish policemen were under stress then and tried to show the Germans how well they were performing their duties.[140]

GERMAN UNDERCOVER AGENTS IN THE GHETTO POLICE

Before analyzing the problem of the Gestapo's infiltration into the ranks of the ghetto police, it is necessary, at least in brief, to discuss the Gestapo's policy of infiltrating the ghettos in general.

It is in the nature of the police everywhere to infiltrate institutions under their control. The ghettos were no exception. The Gestapo tried to establish confidence men (*Vertrauensmänner—VM*) either within the Councils and the ghetto police or outside, often in opposition to and in competition with them. In light of the material available in the sources, it often happened that the Gestapo succeded in finding among the demoralized elements in the ghetto persons "who sold their souls to the devil" (according to Judge Halevi's phrase at the Kastner trial in Israel). These men came from various strata of the Jewish population and also from various cultural environments.

Open and secret agents, who supplied information to their German masters, were active in the ghettos. Generally speaking, the ghetto inmates knew who these people were. Some were ambitious enough to wield influence in the ghetto, to share in the leadership, and even dictate policy. Knowing who was behind them, the Councils often were helpless to resist. With the approval of their German bosses, they often took over the ghetto police, food allocations, etc. As known protégés of the authorities, they were able to do some favors, bring about the release of people from jail, reduce or cancel penalties, and so on. Parading as prominent ghetto personalities influential with the authorities, they overshadowed the Councils in the opinion of the inmates.

To increase their agents' prestige in the eyes of the ghetto inmates and, at the same time, to make the agents still more efficient, the Gestapo granted some "favors" on behalf of individual inmates at their request. Naturally there was no way to know how much of the money or valuables they received for obtaining the "favors" was used to bribe their German protectors and how much landed in their own pockets. These "favor-getting" practices made possible widespread corruption and blackmail, often in partnership with overseers. These characters were known in the ghettos, and they flourished poisonously in the demoralized atmosphere created by the German occupiers.

There were two such characters in the Kaunas Ghetto—Kaspi-Srebrowicz and B. Lipcer. They made life miserable for the Council of Elders.[141] In the Warsaw Ghetto an attempt was made to establish an octopus organization with ostensible police, economic, and philanthropic aims. For some time it was even in competition with the Council and the ghetto police, allegedly as the Office to Fight Usurers and Speculation in the Ghetto. It called itself in German, *Überwachungstelle zur Bekämpfung des Schleichenhandels und der Preiswucherei im Jüdischen Bezirk*. It was established on January 5, 1941 and had its own police force (called the "green police" because of the green stripe on their hats), prosecutor, and court. It also established departments for the following matters: administration of hundreds of buildings in the area of Leszno Street, under the management of a "special deputy of the *Treuhand* management of the houses in the ghetto"; emergency medical service, commonly called the Yellow Emergency because of the ambulance painted yellow (established on May 15, 1941); control of the display of posters in the ghetto; youth affairs; and religious matters. "The men from No. 13," as they were known after the address of their headquarters at 13 Leszno Street, who had lured into their nets well-known but politically naïve ghetto personalities, performed espionage and diversionary activities on behalf of their German benefactors. However, the Gestapo liquidated them as soon as they had accomplished their tasks in the ghetto. The history of the "13" is one more vivid illustration of the perfidy of the Germans and of the fierce rivalry among the various agencies of the occupation authorities.[142]

The Białystok Ghetto also had its evil informers. One of them, Grysza Zelkowicz, was particularly repugnant. As a protégé of the Germans in the ghetto police, he usurped for himself the role of a middleman between the authorities and the Jewish Council. He carried out various injurious schemes and informed on the Council to the Gestapo, thus endangering its very existence. He blackmailed, extorted large sums in cash and jewelry, and forced the ghetto inmates to sign false denunciations against the Council. He won over some of the Councilmen to his side and even dared to denounce the *Polizeipräsident and Polizeiinspektor* in Białystok to the Gestapo, accusing them of taking bribes from Barash. However, Barash succeeded in having Zelkowicz and his five helpers liquidated by the German Order police. After that, the ghetto police were thoroughly cleansed.[143]

Information on the presence of confidants of the Gestapo within the ghetto police and generally in the ghettos is available about Cracow,[144] Lublin,[145] Sosnowiec,[146] Łódź,[147] Piotrków Trybunalski (where the witness identified these characters as "The men from No. 13"), Grodno,[148] and many more ghettos.

THE ROLE OF THE GHETTO POLICE
IN THE "RESETTLEMENTS"

The supreme test of the ghetto police came at the time of the mass "resettlements" when, in accordance with their tasks and prescribed functions, they had to take an active part in deportations to the annihilation camps. Their participation ranged in degree from assisting SS squads and local auxiliary police to actually taking the job of collecting the victims and taking them to loading places. Not everywhere were the ghetto police given the same responsibilities. It is difficult now to find reasons for this variation, for pertinent written orders and instructions remain undiscovered. It may be assumed that orders were seldom given in writing. The authorities may have been wary of issuing written orders for "resettlements," which were ostensibly conducted as evacuations to new places of work under cover of deceptive excuses. Everything points to the conclusion that the orders were given orally.

Because of lack of proper documentaion, one can only assume that the extent of the ghetto police's involvement in "resettlements" was determined by local authorities, on the one hand, and, on the other, the degree to which individual ghetto police forces were willing to accept the abominable task. It was the intention of the authorities, in accordance with their general policy vis-à-vis the Jewish Councils, that the Jews themselves carry out "resettlements." Thus the Germans could spare their own men from the additional work-load of assembling and conveying victims, and from the psychological trauma of witnessing the bestiality and murder that went along with the "actions." Also, in cases of resistance, the direct victims of it would be the Jewish policemen instead of German guards. Not always did this "ideal" scheme work. Because of the hostility of the ghetto inmates, and because of their prevailing premonition of the acute danger inherent in the "resettlements," the

Councils and the ghetto police could not conduct the "actions" on their own.

People destined for deportation did not report at assembly places for "selections," tried to escape from the ghetto, or hid themselves within the ghetto. Brutal force had to be used. It soon became clear to the authorities that the unarmed ghetto police, which despite all its alienation from the ghetto community was still tied to it by ethnic solidarity or personal bonds, was in no position to carry out the "resettlement" all by itself. We knew that in a number of large ghettos the authorities initially tried to burden the Councils and the ghetto police with the task of carrying out the deportations, while keeping a close watch on the proceedings from a distance. But because of unsatisfactory results, the Germans, after a while, took over the job themselves.

In the secret report of the Jewish underground in the Warsaw Ghetto of November 15, 1942, already mentioned frequently in our study, we read:

At first the Germans played a negligible part in carrying out the so-called "resettlements." Trying to avoid facing the wrath of the masses, the Germans at first directed the initial stages of the action in secret. They let the Jews themselves prepare daily lists of candidates for "resettlement." . . . For a few days, the Germans took almost no part in catching the Jews . . . , acting as a concealed force ready to intervene in case contingents were not satisfactory or orders were not carried out. . . . The second phase of the "action" was launched by a combined blockade of the houses at Nalewski and Gęsia Streets on Wednesday, July 29 [the "resettlement" had begun on July 22], and was carried out under the command of the SS men.[149]

In the Łódź Ghetto, too, the Jewish police were in charge at the start of the "action" against children, the elderly, and the sick that lasted from September 5 to September 12, 1942. But because the manhunt on the first day netted few people, the German ghetto administration and the Gestapo concluded that, at this rate, the delivery of the ordered 20,000 persons would not be accomplished in time. The authorities took over the "action," and the ghetto police were given only auxiliary tasks.[150] At that time it was the prevailing opinion in the ghetto that it was preferable that the ghetto police carry out the deportations. Jewish elders like Moshe

Merin, Mordecai Chaim Rumkowski, and Jacob Gens, who generally maintained that it was to the advantage of the ghetto that Jews themselves carry out German orders, did not change their minds when it came to "resettlements." In their ghettos, and particularly in the ghettos in Eastern Upper Silesia, the police took an active part in the deportation procedures. But not only these three ghetto rulers thought thus. In a contemporary report on the "September action" of 1942 in the Łódź Ghetto, the sensitive author Josef Zelkowicz wrote:

> . . . They are taking [Jews] away. . . . The Jewish police show compassion, seizing people [strictly] as ordered: children up to ten years of age, elderly persons over sixty-five years, and sick ones who, according to the physicians' statements, have no chance to get well. The snatching is carried out by Jewish police to whom one may talk, whose consciences one may yet try to move, in front of whom one may cry and ask for consideration. . . . Taking away the victims, the policemen cry and sigh with the victims . . . talking in hoarse voices they try to console the victims, to soothe them in their desperation. A father or mother, giving away a child, believes that the baby has been handed over to Jews. The picture is quite different when others snatch away [the victims].[151]

Whatever the excuse, the fact remains that the Jewish police everywhere, to a larger or lesser degree, participated in the "deportations" and in the horrid events that went along with them. Naturally there were individuals who refused to cross the dangerous borderline. They suffered dire consequences, which we will discuss more fully later.

Tremendous coercion was applied to harness the Jewish police in the deportation "actions." The authorities told them that they and their families were exempt from the "actions." This was customary almost everywhere. The Germans slyly counted on the self-preservation instincts of the policemen, particularly acute in time of danger. As a contemporary source remarked, this promise "bought off" the policemen. In the perpetually starving ghetto, even the promise that one would not be deprived of his bread ration was sometimes enough to assure his cooperation in the deportation procedure. Such was the case in Łódź during the "September action," when bread allocations were stopped during the seven-day "action."[152] But even here the Germans deceived. The ghetto police were spared only for as long as their assistance was required. As soon as it became superfluous, the policemen went the way of all Jews. At most they were given a "privileged," separate railroad car in the transport train, as was the case in Siedlce.[153]

In the ghettos with consecutive "resettlements" the police were reduced after each "action" and those dismissed were included in the transports. At a meeting of the Lublin Jewish Council held on March 31, 1942 (the "action" had started there on March 16), the SS representative, Dr. Sturm, announced that 35 of the 113 ghetto policemen would be resettled, and that of the remaining 78, only 35 policemen would continue "in permanent service" after the "action" was terminated.[154] After the Lublin *Restgetto* was liquidated in November 1942, these "permanent" policemen were either shot on the spot, as happened to the commandants Shamay Grayer and J. Goldfarb, or deported to Majdanek.

In the Warsaw Ghetto, too, the ghetto police were promised security for themselves and their close family members, but of the police force of 2,600 men only some 300 were spared to keep order in the greatly reduced ghetto and abandoned shops. The rest were deported together with their families on the last day of deportations. The same deceitful tactics were applied in Cracow on December 14 and 15, 1943.[155]

But the illusion spread by the Germans among the ghetto police that they would be saved with their families if only they delivered their own brethren worked well and was an important factor in the "resettlement" scheme. The Jewish police went for the bait.

Severe intimidation and a state of continuous fear was another well-proved Nazi means of putting the yoke on the ghetto police in the course of the "resettlements." Even earlier the police had often to pay for "sins" committed not only by one of their own, but also by outsiders. Here are some random examples:

Of the 110 prisoners the Germans carried off from the Warsaw Ghetto jail on June 23, 1942, 10 were members of the ghetto police force. They were accused of mediating between smugglers and German gendarmes. Four were hostages for others who could not be located. All 10 were shot.[156] Twenty ghetto policemen were executed by hanging in the Lwów Ghetto at the end of April 1943, as penalty for a young Jew's resisting arrest by an SS man. The execution was carried out in public. All ghetto inmates were ordered to be present.[157] An eyewitness testified that 12 Jewish policemen were hanged in Mława because of a pair of pants found during a raid on the home of a Pole. The Pole testified that he bought the pants in the ghetto.[158]

The atmosphere of constant terror, demoralization, and lawlessness surrounding the ghetto police, along with their dealings with the corrupted German officials, undermined them morally and spiritually and conditioned them for the activities planned for them in Nazi extermination schemes. And let us not forget that, as already indicated, undesirable elements permeated the police ranks. They were predisposed to wrongdoing, belonged in the underground world of crime, had no moral scruples, and readily carried out German orders.

Last but not least, the ghetto police were influenced by the Councils' strategy of rescue through voluntary sacrifices (see Chap. 16). The police were the very instrument fit to secure its success. We have already discussed Gens's evaluation of the "historical rescue role" of the Vilna Ghetto police. Corncerning the "ideological" considerations that influenced the ghetto police in Łódź, Zelkowicz remarked:

> The Jewish policemen acted as idealists. Teeth were pulled out and limbs were chopped off bodies by Jewish hands. . . . Perhaps it was not as painful as if strangers had done it with their coarse, callous hands. . . . We heard more or less the same thing in all three speeches [by Rumkowski, Jacubson (chairman of the ghetto court), and David Warszawski (chief of the tailor shops) , all delivered at a meeting of ghetto inmates on September 4]: "We clearly were given the hint: if you do not carry out the orders yourselves, we shall do the job. . . . And it was our intention to prevent them from doing it . . . so who was there to do the job if not the ghetto police, which was bought and intoxicated and made to believe ideologically [that this was the right thing to do]?"[159]

Ringelblum wrote about the behavior of the Warsaw Ghetto police:

> The Jewish police enjoyed a bad opinion even before the start of the "resettlements." . . . But their meanness reached a pinnacle in the course of the deportations. No word of protest was issued [by the police] . . . against carrying off their own brethren to the slaughter. The police became mentally conditioned to doing this dirty work and, therefore, performed it with perfection. People are torturing themselves now, puzzling over how it was possible for Jews, the majority of whom came from the intelligentsia, to drag [in carts] children, women, elderly people, and sick ones, knowing well that they were being taken for slaughter.

There are people who maintain that each society has the police it deserves, that the malaise of helping the occupier slaughter 300,000 Jews infected the entire society and not [only] the police, which are only a mirror of the society. But there were others who, trying to survive the holocaust, maintained that the will to survive the war justified all means, even [the sacrifice of] human lives.[160]

As we have mentioned above, the ghetto police took part in "resettlement" procedures in various ways—assisting in chasing victims to assembly places for "selections," personally carrying out "selections," assisting in executions (this, however, occurred only once so far as is known). Here are a few illustrations taken from several occupation areas:

The Lublin Jewish Council announced on March 21, 1942, that the Jewish population was to report "in their own interests" to a certain street, thence to be escorted only by the functionaries of the Jewish police to assembly places.[161] The assurance that the inmates would be escorted "only" by the Jewish police was apparently intended to calm the highly disturbed people. But not all were convinced, and some did not report. The SS interfered in their customary manner. Inmates were raided in their hiding places. In the process some were shot on the spot.[162] Others were carried directly to the trains. At this stage the ghetto police were forced to find the hiding places and call on the victims to come out from hiding. SS men and local auxiliary police squads were reluctant to risk their own lives, leaving it to the ghetto police to discover the bunkers.

Diverse reactions by the ghetto police to their imposed tasks became evident from the start of the "actions" when victims were collected for "resettlement." In numerous ghettos the police were given lists of candidates for deportation that had been prepared in advance. All those located at the addresses given in the lists were directly taken to the places of assembly. In Łódź it was the ghetto jail; in Lwów the precinct premises of the ghetto police force; and in still other places the squares in front of buildings housing the Jewish Councils, etc. From there victims were sent to trains where they were taken over by German police.

Wherever some categories were exempted from current deportations, the ghetto police carried out control of personal identification cards of exempted individuals. Such individuals were placed in sealed-off houses, as was, for instance, the practice in Warsaw during the initial stages of the "action." The same procedure was applied in Lwów during the "action" of March 10, 1942.[163] Thus the corrupt members of the ghetto police got a chance to trade in human lives, as already indicated above.

We find in an eyewitness report on the Warsaw Ghetto:

. . . Right after the blockades stop for the day [after 6 o'clock] the Jewish policemen, coming home, find in front of their homes tense people waiting to plead for their relatives [taken to the Umschlagplatz]. Each one brings something, cash or valuables, to get cooperation. With eyes swollen from overflowing tears, they wait to be admitted. Although their hearts are burning with hatred toward the "blue uniform man" who may have assisted in dragging their relatives to the carts only a short time ago, people beg in subdued voices for some sort of mediation, trying not to vex the [man in] uniform. Lucky is the one from whom a deposit is accepted on a later payment. At least he cherishes some hope; but the majority go away empty-handed, for the policeman has no time for them. One of these money-takers lives in our building, and the heartbroken wailing of the relatives of deported people gathered in front of his apartment can be heard all night long.[164]

Ringelblum thus described the corruption of the ghetto policemen and their state of mind during the "resettlements":

Horrible stories are told about the [Jewish] policemen at the Umschlagplatz. For them [the victims] were not human beings but heads for which money could be extorted. Ransom could be paid in cash, diamonds, gold, etc. The price of a head ranged from 1,000 to 2,000 zlotys at the beginning, until it grew to 10,000 zlotys per head. The amount depended on a number of objective circumstances. . . . The policemen knew no mercy, even in regard to the most respected man. If he could not pay, or if there were no relatives ready to pay, he was shipped off. There were known cases when policemen demanded payment in kind—the flesh of women in addition to cash. . . . One was simply unable to comprehend the behavior of the policemen in the course of "resettlements." They had been trained to persecute those trying to hide from deportation. Already demoralized prior to the "resettlement," they were threatened that their own wives and children would be taken. The people apprehended, . . . particularly women, put up resistance. All these factors created an unbearable situation for the policemen. They went berserk, committing unspeakable acts.[165]

Ransom payments to Jewish policemen during the "resettlements" are also reported from Łódź, Lwów, Kołomyja, Lublin, Cracow, Vilna and other ghettos.[166]

We have already mentioned that in the course of "resettlements" the Jewish police were hard pressed and "worked" under conditions of terror. Each policeman in the Warsaw Ghetto was threatened that he himself and his family would be "resettled" if he did not deliver the prescribed quota of five "head" per day.[167]

Grzymek, the *Kommandant* of the Lwów *Julag** (as this ghetto was called after partial liquidation), threatened to shoot every Jewish policeman who would not deliver six "illegal" Jews each day during the March "action" of 1943.[168]

As a rule the "selection" of people rounded up was carried out by the German authorities. But there were also instances where the ghetto police both assembled the candidates for the "resettlement" and carried out the "selection." For example, Gens did this in Vilna as chief of the ghetto police, and so did Shamay Grayer in the Lublin and Majdan Tatarski Ghettos. It also often happened that the Germans ordered the Councils to deliver a certain number of Jews without indicating any specific category, thus leaving it to the Councils to select the victims. In such cases the ghetto police seized people who, in their own opinion, were proper candidates for "resettlement." This is reported from Kołomyja, Buczacz, Lwów, Dębica, Oszmiana, Skałat, and other ghettos.[169]

The ghetto police actively participated in uncovering hidden Jews in many ghettos. Familiar with the topography of the ghetto, the layout of the apartments, and the nooks where people might try to hide, the ghetto police were given the task of sniffing out Jews in hiding. No doubt a number of well-camouflaged places in Warsaw, Cracow, Vilna, Kołomyja, Buczacz, Skałat, and many other ghettos would not have been discovered otherwise.[170]

It is reported from several ghettos (e.g., Zamość, Sosnowiec, and Kołomyja), where the police were unable to locate people they were after, that other family members were taken: children, parents, wives, or siblings.[171]

To accomplish their task, the ghetto police chased Jews who, after surviving "resettlements" in other ghettos, had tried to hide

* *Judenlager.*

in a ghetto which was still in no immediate danger. Some 100 Jews survived the "resettlement" in the Legionowo Ghetto (near Warsaw) on the last day of Sukkot 1942. However, when they tried to enter the Nowy Dwór Ghetto (Zichenau district), the Jewish police arrested them and put them in the local ghetto jail to hand over to the Gestapo.[172]

The police in some large ghettos became such experienced "resettlement" experts that the Germans would send them to adjacent ghettos to help in the "action." Thus squads of the Lwów Ghetto police took part in the deportation of the inmates from ghettos in Jaworów and Złoczów in April 1943, and in a number of small ghettos in the vicinity of Lwów.[173] The Jewish police of the Sosnowiec and Będzin Ghettos were dispatched to take part in "resettlements" in small ghettos in Eastern Upper Silesia, such as in Olkusz in July 1942.[174]

A squad of Vilna Jewish policemen, some 30 strong, was issued new uniforms and dispatched to Oszmiana in October 1942, where Jews from Smorgonie, Soły, and other small ghettos in the Vilna area were assembled. They were told that their task was "to deliver certificates" to the inmates of those ghettos. They took over from the Lithuanians the task of guarding the ghetto gate. On October 23, 1942, the Jews were driven to the assembly place by the police from the Vilna Ghetto accompanied by local policemen. They "selected" 200 sick and 392 elderly people; 410 were sent off to Zielonka, some 7 or 8 kilometers from Oszmiana, in previously prepared carts. They were put to death in the presence of several Vilna Jewish policemen. According to Dvorzhetsky, the Jewish policemen took part in the actual execution.[175]

An eyewitness from the Dębica Ghetto relates that during the final "action" (on November 15, 1942) the last surviving Jews were confined in a kind of *Restgetto*, which was called *Arbeitslager*. The Jewish camp Elder ordered the ghetto police to deliver some 50 "illegal" Jews, those who had escaped and somehow made it back to the camp later on. These were detained in a room of the local Talmud Torah and killed the same night, with the help of the ghetto police ("the men of the *Ordnungsdienst* grabbed the hands of the victims and Gabler [apparently the *Lagerkommandant*] shot them").[176]

COMPASSION AMONG GHETTO POLICEMEN

We have given quite a dark picture of the ghetto police and of their activities. But this presentation would not be historically balanced if we left out facts and attitudes illustrating the other side of the coin. For there were among the ghetto police positive elements who behaved toward their persecuted brethren with compassion, assisted them in time of distress, tried to help in an emergency, and attempted to improve the lot of the victims. They paid with their lives for it, as is illustrated by a few recorded cases.

It is understandable that the background of the police was not uniform with respect to morals, education, and social responsibility. It is necessary to stress at the outset that in some ghettos, there were in the police ranks people not happy with the role and tasks assigned to them. They were also cognizant of the low moral level of the police and tried to bring about some improvement. In an entry on April 26, 1941, Ringelblum noted that a delegation of officers of the ghetto police in Warsaw had reported to the Council and stated that they did not want to continue the repulsive work of catching Jews for work in the labor camps. Some declared that they were ready to go to the camps themselves.[177]

A memorandum of this opposition group of the Warsaw Ghetto police regarding the cleansing of police ranks is also preserved. It is entitled: *Memoriał opozycyjnej grupy w łonie Służby Porządkowej w sprawie uzdrowienia stosunków na odcinku policyjnym* ("Memorandum of the Opposition Group within the Order Police concerning the Restoration of [Proper] Conditions in the Police"). Ten suggestions were submitted on reforming the police by indoctrinating social responsibility, eliminating harmful elements, and introducing strict discipline. Among others the suggestion was made to put the police on the Council's payroll.[178] No positive results were attained.

A sort of civil control over police activities was in effect in the Białystok Ghetto when the police were established there. A public announcement (No. 55) of the Security Service of the Jewish Council, dated August 16, 1941, made it known that the police could search private homes only when ordered to do so by the Jewish Security Service or by the chief of the Criminal Service. The search was to be made in the presence of the house committee, which had to sign a statement on its result. Charges of misconduct against the police were to be submitted to the headquarters of the Jewish police, through house committee channels.[179]

A few cases have been reported of policemen fired for offenses committed.

In the course of liquidating the Zelkowicz Affair (see p.505) in the Białystok Ghetto, 16 policemen were fired. Five were sent to a labor camp.[180]

The Disciplinary Commission of the Warsaw Ghetto was flooded with complaints against Jewish policemen and with investigations and trials against them. Ringelblum cites the astonishing fact that 700 of the 1,700 policemen were subjected to disciplinary trials.[181] One case of "cleansing" was used as a trick by Merin to fix on the ghetto police his own responsibility for the corruption prevailing during the "resettlement action" in August 1942. That the "cleansing" was undertaken by Merin only to calm down the inmates can be seen in the fact that only some low-grade policemen and police employees were dismissed. For the most part these were later found not guilty and were readmitted to service.[182]

Cases were also recorded where Jewish policemen resigned, unwilling to perform the tasks imposed upon them. We have already mentioned that policemen in the Warsaw Ghetto threatened to leave the force at the start of the "resettlement." Similar cases are also recorded from Złoczów, Głębokie, Zbaraż, Rohatyn (by the first commandant), and Borysław (by the first commandant, who ran away prior to the initial "action").[183] It can be assumed that such acts took place in other ghettos too, but no records have been preserved.

A contemporary chronicler of the Warsaw Ghetto related that during the summer deportations of 1942, eight policemen committed suicide, unable to endure their horrible tasks and moral stress.[184]

Cases were also recorded where members of the ghetto police refused temporary delays in their own "resettlement," preferring to share the fate of the entire community, an example being the case reported by Benjamin Orenstein about a policeman in the Otwock Ghetto.[185] An eyewitness from Kołomyja told how some Jewish policemen preferred death to participating in the murder of their brethren.[186] The same was reported about several policemen in the Ostrowiec Ghetto.[187] In some cases, the Jewish police warned Jews not to leave their hiding places. The ghetto police in Baranowicze were ordered to search all houses one by one and call on the Jews in hiding to come out, because no danger was threatening them. The policemen executed the order, but added in Hebrew: "Jews, don't!"[188]

In some contemporary and postwar reports the ghetto police are not summarily accused, and it is pointed out that some were humane.

A witness from the Kielce Ghetto reported that the conduct of the majority of the police and of the chief of police and his deputy was correct.[189] The majority of the Kobryń Ghetto police "did not assist the murderers in shedding Jewish blood and have not helped in the discovery of Jewish hiding places."[190] Five of the questionnaires collected by us, where the Kobryń Ghetto police are discussed, indicate that all except the chief behaved correctly.[191] An evaluation of the police of the Skierniewice Ghetto depicts them as "not meeting the wishes of the Germans." They were hardly active, for the chief "had lost his zest . . . after the director of the German labor office, Faste, beat him up."[192]

Pesach Kaplan, member of the Białystok Jewish Council, states in a contemporary report that during the "resettlement" which took place between February 5-12, 1943, ". . . the Jewish police . . . did not displease the ghetto inmates. On the contrary, it is stated that the policemen did their best to help their brethren as far as was possible, warned them in advance, and tried to save them, even at the risk of their own lives. No mention was made of pressing ransom money from the inmates here as was done in Warsaw. But the police were used as the arm of the murderers and could not help but obey orders."[193]

A survivor of the Radom Ghetto relates: "There were cases of great trouble caused by the Jewish policemen . . . [but] Jewish policemen also looked the other way and did not interfere in bringing food into the ghetto. There were policemen who helped condemned inmates to escape."[194]

A woman survivor of the Rohatyn Ghetto related that the Jewish police served a useful purpose there. Having been informed of the impending "action" in advance, they secretly made it known to the ghetto inmates, thus giving them ample opportunity to go into hiding.[195] The attitude of the police at the Dokszyce Ghetto (Vilna area) was similarly evaluated.[196] A former inmate of the Bolechów Ghetto wrote that "honest policemen did what they could to give water and food [to people assembled for transportation], but their possibilities were limited."[197] Memoirs of survivors from the ghettos in Kowel, Żarki, Łosice (Warsaw district), Grodno, Tarnów, Riga, and Kaunas also give positive evaluations of the behavior of individual policemen or the police as a whole.[198]

The sources record cases where individual policemen lost their lives while trying to save Jews. The cited secret report of the underground Jewish organization in the Warsaw Ghetto, dated November 15, 1942, stated that a Jewish policeman saved 70 Jews already assembled at the Umschlagplatz. He was shot to death by an SS man.[199] A Jewish policeman was shot in the same ghetto by a German gendarme when he asked the German to give back a sack of smuggled potatoes to a woman smuggler.[200] From Sokołów Podlaski and Łomża two cases are reported: in the course of "actions" in these places German gendarmes ordered Jewish policemen to search houses (to climb to the attic of a house in Łomża) for Jews in hiding. In both places policemen reported that they had found no Jews, though they well knew that Jews were hiding there. The gendarmes became suspicious and went to check for themselves. Finding that they had been cheated, they shot both policemen.[201]

A Jew from Chmielnik, who had been caught by peasants and was being taken to the German gendarmes, was rescued by two Jewish policemen. They told the peasants that the Germans had ordered them to seize all Jews and promised the peasants that the liquor due to them as a reward would be delivered to their homes. The Jewish policemen put the rescued Jew in a Jewish jail.[202]

A survivor of the ghettos in Siedlce and Otwock related that once, when he was an "illegal" inmate in the ghetto, a Polish and a Jewish policeman jointly convoyed him to his execution. On the way, the Jewish policeman wept and embraced him. Once a policeman in Siedlce secretly threw aside a banknote of 20 zlotys for him to take. When he picked up the bill and gave it back to the policeman, he refused it saying that it was not his money.[203] There were Jewish policemen who tried to atone for their behavior.

The case of the Jewish policeman in the Minsk Ghetto (Byelorussia) is characteristic of the behavior of a ghetto policeman trying to atone for his sins. M.Z., a refugee from Poland, was for two years "one of the most ill-behaved policemen in the ghetto. . . . he was callous, beat up and bullied the inmates, and performed the most despicable orders." After a time, however, he became apprehensive.

He approached the leader of the underground movement in Minsk, asked for forgiveness, and offered his services for the most dangerous tasks. In the beginning the underground was skeptical of his change of heart, fearing that he was an *agent provocateur*. After a while the committee decided to use him, but keep him under permanent surveillance. Later on, together with others, he left to join the partisans in the forest where he was arrested on charges made by one of the partisans. The underground court sentenced him to death.

The sentence caused a sharp controversy among the Jewish partisans of the "Parkhamenko Detachment." Those who came from the west, the so-called Westerners, maintained that he had been very useful during the last 10 months in the ghetto and had helped people to escape into the forest. They said that if anybody was to be shot, it was the Vlasov people in the group. . . . The people from Minsk, however, were in agreement with the court prosecutor, except for the political commissar of the group, Alter Feldman, himself a former resident of Minsk. In the end the Westerners won. M.Z. was freed and given a chance to atone for his sins with his own blood. He was sent to perform the most dangerous operations. He often volunteered for the most difficult and most dangerous tasks and, generally, behaved as an exemplary partisan. He survived and emigrated to a remote continent.[204]

THE JEWISH POLICE AND THE JEWISH RESISTANCE MOVEMENT

Composed of young, healthy men, many with prewar military training, the Jewish police were in a position to supply first-class men for the Jewish underground movement. Their privileged situation in the ghetto, their ability to be out even after curfew hours, keeping watch at the ghetto gates and in contact wih the world outside the ghetto, were potentially valuable to the underground.

As in the case of the Councils, so the ghetto police as a whole had no consistent policy with respect to the underground movement. In a number of ghettos, the leadership of the police force, or individual policemen, maintained secret contacts with the underground groups and even actively participated in their activities, helping to smuggle people into the forests, often paying with their own blood. The underground tried to plant their members among the police to

know what was going on in the ghetto administration and to find
out who informers were. There also were policemen who served as
liaison men between the underground and the Councils and other
Jewish organizations, and warned Jews of the impending "actions."
On the other hand, there were police chiefs and rank-and-file policemen who fully obeyed the orders of the authorities and relentlessly
combated the underground movement, even delivering members
to the Gestapo.

Analyzing the source material pertaining to this problem, we
find that in the ghettos of occupied eastern territories (Eastern
Poland, Lithuania, Byelorussia) cases of a positive attitude on the
part of ghetto police toward underground activities were more numerous than in central and western parts of Poland. M. Kaganowicz,
who researched the partisan movement in those parts, wrote: "As
in *many ghettos* [italics added] the Jewish police in Iwje [Lida
county] were given a chance to do underground work. Their assistance was valuable because of liaison, freedom of movement, and
watch at the ghetto gates."[205] The deputy commandant of the Iwja
Ghetto police, Leib Kalmanowicz, was authorized to serve in the
police by the underground group. A former resident of the ghetto
characterized him as "one of the finest figures in the ghetto." Later
on he joined the partisans and was killed by a Russian partisan who
hated Jews.[206]

There were two reasons for the difference in attitudes in the east
and the west. The factor that contributed to a greater quantitative
development of underground activities in the eastern ghettos compared to the western ones, namely, closer proximity to large forests
where the partisans were active, also influenced the attitude of the
police in their relations with the underground.

Another factor was that in the eastern ghettos young Jews with
prewar party affiliations and distinctive ethnic consciousness, with
some exceptions (for instance, in Vilna), joined the police more
readily than in other places. This, in turn, made much easier the
task of finding contacts with underground groups in the respective
ghettos, with the result that the police took a more positive attitude
toward the whole idea of resistance.

A. Lidowski, a member of the resistance group in the Baranowicze
Ghetto, told in his memoirs that the first meeting of the group took
place on March 17 or 18, 1942, in a building occupied by the ghetto
police. Of the police force of 22 men, 15, including the commandant,

Warszawski, were members of the underground. The police escorted people who participated in the meeting to their homes.[207] According to the contemporary memoirist Herman Kruk, the Baranowicze Ghetto police were conspicuous in the local resistance movement. This was also reported sometime in 1943 by a refugee from Warsaw, Mordechai Polanski, an inmate in the Baranowicze Ghetto. The underground was denounced to the Germans by one of their own members. The commandant, Warszawski, was severely beaten in an effort to force him to show where their firearms were hidden; but he led the Germans to some bunkers from which he himself had taken some people a few days before. Nothing was discovered there. He was shot.[208]

Josef Glazman, deputy police commandant in the Vilna Ghetto (later dismissed by Gens and appointed head of the housing department) was one of the organizers and deputy commandant of the United Partisan Organization (FPO). Because he did not obey Gens's order to leave the Vilna Ghetto he was arrested in July 1943, but his friends from the FPO freed him from the ghetto police. In company with others he left the ghetto, went into the forest, became a fighting partisan, and lost his life during a battle with the Germans. Members of the FPO were planted among the Vilna Ghetto police.[209]

Most important was the assistance given the underground movement by the Jewish police in the Kaunas Ghetto. Lejb Garfunkel wrote:

. . . The principal assistance that the partisan movement received came from the Jewish ghetto police. Several police officers, former Lithuanian army officers, took over training people to leave for the forest. . . . Secret training courses were conducted in how to use rifles and machine guns. Led by the police commandant, M. Levin, and his assistants, the policemen would keep watch near the [ghetto] gate at the time the partisans were ready to leave for the forest, removing undesirable persons [from the vicinity]. They took care that leaving the ghetto was accomplished in an orderly fashion, without a hitch. When necessary, they blew fuses, so that there was not too much light at the gate. In the end, the Jewish police had to pay a horrible price for this.[210]

Two former residents of the Kaunas Ghetto who were active in the Communist sector of the underground movement added: "Comrades planted among the ghetto police had helped to carry arms into the ghetto and assisted people in going through the ghetto gates. They kept guard over hiding places where military training was given at night. During curfew hours in the ghetto, they accompanied members of the underground on their way to perform various missions, pretending that they were convoying arrested people."[211]

But the Gestapo discovered the underground organization in the ghetto and decided to destroy it. On March 27, 1944, 140 ghetto policemen and their chief, Levin, were ordered to report at the office of the *Kommandatur*. All were taken to the 9th Fort and given the notorious Gestapo treatment. After torture, Levin was shot. Except for seven men, all the policemen passed the cruel test of the Gestapo inquisition, not telling a thing. Levin's two assistants, the officers and policemen in responsible positions, a total of 40 people, were all shot. The others were released and taken back to the ghetto, including the seven who had broken down during the torturous investigation.[212]

The Gestapo in Riga took bloody revenge against the ghetto police for their participation in anti-Nazi resistance. A group of policemen in the so-called Little Ghetto (established at the end of November 1941—after the slaughter of the Jews in Riga it was officially renamed *Kasernierungslager*) together with a number of laborers, formed a resistance cell. They built a camouflaged bunker and collected arms Jewish laborers had stolen from the so-called Powder Tower, where firearms were loaded for the eastern front. But at the end of October 1942 a group of Riga Jews was seized on the highway, carrying arms. As a result a punitive action against the ghetto was carried out which cost the lives of 100 Jews. The entire Jewish police force was also killed, either because the authorities suspected their cooperation or as an act of collective punishment.[213]

During the tenure of the police commandant Srebrianski and his deputy Blumenstok, a refugee from Warsaw in the Minsk Ghetto, the Jewish police maintained contact with the partisan organization and were instrumental in helping people leave for the forest. Some members of the underground served in the police and thus were able to warn of impending "actions," so that people could seek cover in bunkers, etc. Srebrianski was denounced to the Gestapo and shot in public, in company with members of the partisan movement. Blumenstok too was shot in the course of an "action." After that the command of the ghetto police was taken over by notorious Gestapo informers, refugees from the west.[214]

The nucleus of the underground resistance group in Stolin was organized by the Stolin Ghetto police, which thereby received moral compensation for serving with the police. As the day of the expected "resettlement" approached in the month of Elul 1942, the group decided to set the ghetto afire at the start of the "action." All was ready, but for reasons unexplained by the witness the arson was not carried out.[215]

As was related by two former inmates in the Rohatyn Ghetto, it was decided at a secret meeting in which members of the Council and the police participated to acquire firearms and facilitate escapes to the forest. A group of policemen went into the forest accompanied by several girls. They built a bunker and stored arms and food, but after a time all returned to the ghetto, hoping that they would be able to escape before the "resettlement" started. Apparently the authorities had been informed. On June 6, 1943, the German police assembled the entire Jewish militia, shot them all, mutilated their dead bodies, and hanged them in public, as a warning for others.[216]

Lejzor Stolicki, police commandant in the Lida Ghetto, greatly helped the local partisan movement. Because of his good relations with the Polish police, the watch around the ghetto was weak. Whenever people left for the forest, the Polish policemen happened to be dead drunk from vodka Stolicki had treated them to, so that the escape path was free. It was rumored in the ghetto that he also secured arms for these partisans. Cooperation between the partisans and the police commandant made it possible for a few hundred partisans to leave the ghetto. He himself had been thinking of joining the partisans, but was afraid that he would be put on trial and abandoned the idea. He probably perished in the course of the last "action" in the ghetto, after September 17, 1943.[217] There were individual Jewish policemen (for instance, Israel Belski and his comrades) who provided arms to people escaping to the forests.[218] Even in ghettos where the Jewish police persecuted the underground, there were individual policemen assisting resisters. In the Cracow Ghetto, for instance, the local Jewish police was notorious for their brutality toward the local resisters. Still there was one policeman who served as liaison man between the ghetto and resisters hidden on the "Aryan" side.[219]

Also in the Warsaw Ghetto the Organization of Jewish Fighters had its people on the police force and was therefore in a good position to fight the Gestapo agents in the ghetto. The starting day of the last "resettlement" in April 1943 was divulged by a Jewish policeman.[220]

Some Jewish policemen became fed up with their work and escaped to the partisans, as happened for instance, in the Brańsk[221] and Dołhinów Ghettos (Vilna region.)[222] Szymon Kazimierski, a former Jewish policeman in the Chmielnik Ghetto, participated in the Warsaw Ghetto uprising and lost his life in combat.[223] There is also recorded an act of individual resistance by a ghetto policeman during the "resettlement" actions: the Kobryń policeman Mordecai Berezniak attacked a German and stabbed him during the deportation from the ghetto in the month of Ab 1942. He was shot on the spot.[224]

The sources also report that the police in a considerable number of ghettos took a negative, often an aggressively hostile, attitude toward the resistance movement, persecuted their members, and even informed on them. Some did it because their way of thinking was similar to that of the Jewish Councils. For instance, the commandant of the police in the Sarny Ghetto promised to cooperate during the resistance planned in the course of the impending "resettlement." But he changed his mind, reasoning thus: "What was there to do? Escape, save ourselves leaving our wives and kids in the hands of the murderers . . . ?"[225]

We do not know whether such moral motivation was decisive in shaping the negative attitudes of ghetto police toward resistance. We have good reason to doubt it. Rather, we may assume that the Jewish police opposed the resistance groups because of purely opportunistic and egoistic reasons, for the resistance was a menace to "order and peace" in the ghettos, for which they were responsible before the authorities. Moreover, it endangered the very continuance of the ghetto which they believed they would outlast. On the other hand, the underground that called upon the Jews to resist the "resettlement" treated the police who took part in the "action" as traitors to the Jewish cause. It should be taken into consideration that there were plenty of open and secret Gestapo agents within the ghetto police whose task it was to locate nests of resisters and inform on them. The Jewish resistance movement fought these people, and many perished by the hands of underground fighters.[226]

Two antagonistic groups emerged in the ghettos, fighting each other; the resisters, on the one hand, and the police, including German agents, on the other hand. In some of the ghettos (Warsaw, Vilna, and Cracow) they fought severely.

The ghetto police sometimes blamed the ghetto underground for acts of terror committed against inmates by the Germans. Thus when the Gestapo dragged a number of underground members from their homes and killed them in the Warsaw Ghetto streets on the night of April 17–18, 1942, the ghetto police announced through house committee channels that this "action" was an isolated "punishment of people engaged in business of no concern to them."[227]

A proper illustration of the mutual relations between the ghetto police and the United Partisan Organization in the Vilna Ghetto is supplied by the events in which Yitzhak Witenberg and Josef Glazman, the commandant and deputy commandant of the FPO respectively, were involved in July 1943 (see p.470).

A continuous feud raged between the ghetto police and the underground organization in the Cracow Ghetto. A former underground member wrote in his memoirs: "It was impossible to avoid the police in the streets. They constantly kept us under surveillance and, quite naturally, were cognizant that something was going on in the ghetto. To a degree they feared us and considered it the better part of judgment to look the other way. There were times when we watched them more closely than they watched us."[228] The agents within the Cracow Ghetto police were after the resisters and informed on them. They were instrumental in uncovering the secret underground headquarters after the assassination carried out by a resistance group in the coffeehouse *Cyganeria* on December 22, 1942. Seven German officers were killed and many wounded. In connection with the "plague of traitors" the same author wrote: "The police spied on us all the time, fearing that they might be accused of helping the fighters and . . . in order to gain postponement of their own destruction." The animosity of the Jewish police toward the resisters was enhanced by the bloody repressions the Germans applied following acts of sabotage carried out in the ghetto by the underground. Thus a group of fighters in January 1943 sabotaged the railroad tracks between Cracow and Kattowitz. Many Germans were killed, and communication was interrupted for the day. In retaliation the Gestapo shot 22 Jewish laborers working for the *Ostbahn*, together with members of the Jewish Council and the police.[229]

We have already mentioned the fight ordered by Merin between the Jewish police in Eastern Upper Silesia and the underground (Chap. 17). A female member of the underground movement in Sosnowiec related in her memoirs that after she was arrested and incarcerated by the Jewish police she was interrogated in the familiar Gestapo manner. She was beaten and tortured by the police commandant Goldmintz.[230]

A Międzyrzec native, a Pole, related about the last police commandant in the ghetto there, one Lubicz, that when two young escaped inmates of that ghetto came back from the forest in search of bread for their group, he betrayed them to the gendarmes. The youths were shot.[231]

FIREMEN AND CHIMNEY SWEEPS

Because the ghettos were excluded from municipal services, it was necessary to establish special firemen and chimney sweep brigades. In the ghettos where some prewar volunteer firemen remained, as was prevalent in the east, they became the nucleus of the ghetto fire brigades (as in Kaunas). In some ghettos (e.g., Warsaw and Łódź)[232] they were subordinated to the ghetto police. Elsewhere, however, they established departments on their own and worked within the framework of the ghetto administration, as in Kaunas and Lublin.[233] The times of their establishment varied: in the Warsaw Ghetto the fire brigade of 200 men was established as late as the spring of 1942, apparently in connection with anticipated bombing by Soviet planes. On the other hand, in the Łódź Ghetto the fire and chimney sweep brigade was established soon after the ghetto was sealed off. At the beginning it was a voluntary unit, but, starting on September 1, 1941, it was included in the general budget of the ghetto administration. As of February 2, 1941, 270 permanent firemen were listed on the payroll, and 150 worked on a daily basis. There were 38 chimney sweeps.[234] Because of the numerous factories in the ghetto working for the *Wehrmacht*, the authorities were interested in maintaining an efficient and well-manned fire brigade. Their main task was to guard the ghetto factories and offices. With each reduction of the ghetto the fire brigades were also reduced, as happened in the Kaunas Ghetto, where of the initial 97 firemen only 29 remained in 1943.[235] Except for Łódź the equipment of the fire brigades was quite primitive. The authorities supplied no substantial fire-fighting machines, and when a large fire broke out the general city fire brigade was called in to help extinguish it. In the Lublin *Restgetto* each building had to provide its own fire-fighting utensils (in accord with Para. 6 of the by-laws of the fire-fighting watch, adopted by the Council at its meeting held on August 26, 1942).[236]

In addition to their customary duties, both the firemen and the chimney sweeps were called upon to serve as auxiliary police. Thus, for instance, the firemen in the Kaunas Ghetto had to transport the sick and wounded to the ghetto hospital and guard the ghetto fence. After the order was issued for Jews to deliver all their property, they were given the task of "searching wells for valuables hidden by the Jews, and thereby prevent a disaster for the ghetto should the authorities themselves discover them."[237] In the course of "resettlements" in the Łódź and Żelechów Ghettos, firemen functioned as auxiliary police at the "selections" and during transportation of the victims.[238] It is not known if they served in other ghettos in the same capacity.

CHAPTER 19

Opposition to the Jewish Councils
and the Ghetto Police

Opposition to the Jewish Councils emerged as soon as they came into being and became even stronger when, as a result of their activities, much of people's initial suspicion was confirmed. In fact, all sources, whether contemporary or of postwar origin, stress the prevailing negative, often hostile attitude of ghetto inmates toward the Jewish Councils. What were the reasons for this hostility? There were *general* causes, emerging from the very nature of the Councils almost everywhere, and *local* ones, rooted in the social and moral caliber of the Councilmen and in the attitudes of the local German authorities.

GENERAL CAUSES

1. For the ghetto inmates the Jewish Councils were the visible organs of oppression. Moreover, in the large or medium-sized ghettos, the inmates were informed of current measures of persecution by announcements over the signatures of the Council members. As a rule the Germans used the perfidious tactic of ostensibly not interfering with the way the Councils carried out orders. The real bosses, the Gestapo and SS men, seldom appeared in the filthy and vermin-infested *Judengettos*. Orders were unobtrusively issued to Council chairmen, to their deputies, or to members, or were even given by phone. Except in the course of expulsions or "resettlement actions" (i.e., during the very last tragic phases of the ghettos), the

ghetto inmates seldom encountered their actual persecutors. But their Jewish oppressors were better known to them. The objective facts clearly pointed to the Councils as instruments of the hated enemy. That the Councils had been established for this very purpose, that the Councilmen were personally responsible to the Germans for strict execution of orders, could not change the blunt facts. In the final analysis, the heavy burdens imposed on the ghetto inmates by the Council apparatus were in no way compensated for by the little good that they were able to do for the persecuted inmates. Small wonder that all the pentup hatred for the relatively remote Nazi enemy was aimed at the one visible adversary, the hated Council (see Chap. 11).

2. The second reason for a hostile attitude toward the Councils in a large number of ghettos was their social policy—unjust taxation and the implementation of forced-labor duty. We have already endeavored to analyze the greatly differentiated social structure of the ghettos and the social policy of the Councils in Chap. 15.

3. There was one more general reason for a negative attitude toward the Councils—the traditionally negative attitude toward the *Kehila* characteristic in many places before the war. For the ghetto inmates, the *Judenräte* were sort of a continuation of the unpopular prewar *Kehila* Councils. For generations the *Kehilas* were governed by representatives of the conservative and well-to-do segments of the Jewish population. By the end of the nineteenth and beginning of the twentieth century, the progressive Jewish social and national movements considered the official leadership of the Jewish communities as fortresses of obscurantism, unwilling to change the old order. They tried to bring about reforms, to change obsolete community leadership into modern Jewish self-government, but with little success. The main obstacles in reforming the *Kehilas* were the assimilatory policies of Eastern European governments interested in preserving the *Kehilas* as purely religious institutions. In this they were supported by the conservatism of the Orthodox Jewish masses and their leaders. Although radical parties before the war abandoned their policy of boycott in the *Kehilas* and took part in elections, and although some secular cultural and social institutions were subsidized by most *Kehilas*, opposition remained strong among the assimilated intelligentsia and the common people. The *Kehilas* were regarded as a sort of necessary evil. One paid the community tax and, when needed, could get vital statistics certificates. The obso-

lete, paternal, philanthropic character of the welfare activities of the *Kehilas* could not win over the Jewish masses. The Jewish Councils in the ghettos inherited this traditionally negative attitude, and it was greatly enhanced by the new role imposed by the Germans.

LOCAL CAUSES

The local reasons for hostility to the Councils depended on the attitudes of the Councilmen, their character, behavior, and methods of work. Opposition to the Councils and the ghetto police expressed itself: (1) by individual resistance to orders of the Councils, which, in turn, brought the resisters into conflict with the ghetto police ("civil disobedience"); and (2) by collective acts of opposition, variously taking the form of (*a*) spontaneous group actions to demand specific improvements in the situation or to cancel or ease measures of oppression, or of (*b*) organized opposition by social or political groups active in the underground. This form of opposition was manifested by public demonstrations, the clandestine press, etc.

We shall now analyze all these forms of opposition as they were manifested in various ghettos.

INDIVIDUAL ACTS OF RESISTANCE TO THE COUNCILS

Included in the weekly reports submitted to the *Kommissar* of the Warsaw Ghetto and the chief of the Polish police in Warsaw for the period from June 22, 1941, to July 10, 1942, are unspecified cases of "breach of public peace and order" and of "resistance against the authorities." Apparently reference is made here to cases where inmates resisted the ghetto police during raids in the course of assembling people for forced-labor duty, carrying out confiscations, combating smuggling, closing clandestine shops, collecting taxes, etc. Political acts in connection with the resistance movement are probably also included here. It is, however, hard to discern them and separate them into a specific category, though they occurred quite often and were directed against both the Councils and the ghetto police. Thus, for instance, 1,012 cases of "breach of public peace and order" and 29 cases of "resistance against the authorities" were reported in the period between November 22, 1941, and January 2, 1942, an average of 26 cases a day, taking both categories together. Starting in mid-April 1942, cases of "resistance against the authorities" visibly increased. From April to July 10, 1942, 317 such cases were registered, or 3 cases a day. This was the period preceding the mass "resettlements." During the entire report year, 2,504 cases of "breach of public peace and order" and 657 acts of "resistance," or an average of 7 cases a day were reported.[1]

The Vilna Ghetto police registered cases of "insulting and resisting the ghetto police" and "not carrying out police orders." From January to June 1942, 46 cases of the first type and 301 cases of the second were registered. We may assume that, as in Warsaw, among the 1,094 unspecified cases of "breach of order" recorded by the Vilna Ghetto police during the same period of time, there were cases of resistance and covert manifestations of "civil disobedience" against the ghetto administration and its policy.[2]

The documents of the Białystok Ghetto also record cases of resistance to the police. Thus, for instance, the Council's announcement No. 293, dated June 26, 1942, made it known that five named persons had been "indicted for insulting and resisting members of the ghetto police." Another announcement by the Council, dated August 1942, reported that a coachman had been sent to a penal camp for "physically insulting" a ghetto policeman on duty.[3] Another got six weeks' imprisonment for physically attacking a member of the presidium.[4]

In reports submitted by the Łódź Ghetto police, to Rumkowski and the German *Gettoverwaltung* there was a column headed "Resistance." A bulletin in the *Ghetto Chronicle* dated January 23, 1941, reports about "33 persons arrested for resistance." For the period from January to March 1941, 95 cases of "resistance" were reported. For the most part these were people arrested during hunger demonstrations and strikes for "agitating against the existing order in the ghetto." However, people resisting arrest for other offenses are included in this list too.[5] Reports for later periods likewise mention cases of resistance against the ghetto police.

In the majority of ghettos individual resistance was typically expressed either by nonpayment of taxes and fees (also in kind) or by evasion of forced-labor duty. In the Częstochowa Ghetto police blotter already cited (see Chap. 18) appears a substantial number of arrests of stubborn tax delinquents or people avoiding forced-labor duty. In the course of a single month, from October 26 to November

27, 1941, the ghetto police apprehended 425 inmates for nonpayment of taxes or fees. Arrest orders were issued by the Council or jointly by the Council and the chief of the first police precinct. The delinquents were taken either to the Council's finance department (apparently following the first reminder), or to the Jewish labor camp in the town, or directly to the ghetto arrest house (apparently this was done only after the second or third reminder).[6] In the period from August 20 to October 7, 1941, the ghetto police apprehended 233 persons and delivered them to the labor places by force. The apartments of 19 additional persons (who apparently were absent at the time) were emptied and sealed. In a single day, on November 23, 1941, the Council issued orders to arrest and deliver to the labor department 94 persons who had not reported for forced labor or who had not paid the release fee.[7]

Resistance was put up when the ghetto police tried to confiscate smuggled goods. On October 4, 1942, the Šiauliai Ghetto police stopped people at the ghetto gate for smuggling food. They beat up the policemen. The police of the second ghetto sector (Traku) and the Council of Elders were called upon to protect the embattled policemen. The Lithuanian police also came and fired shots in the air.[8]

In the minutes of its meetings and in public announcements the Białystok Ghetto Jewish Council often complained that people were delinquent in paying taxes, that agitators spread the idea of nonpayment, and that people prided themselves on dodging forced-labor duty. The Council would call special meetings to remind the inmates of the dangers facing the ghetto if the orders of the German authorities concerning payment of taxes and forced-labor duty were not strictly carried out.[9] Some 100 coachmen called a strike at the end of April or beginning of May 1942, protesting the mandatory registration of horses ordered by the Germans on April 25. During the registration a fee had to be paid, and a coachman tax was imposed.[10] The homes of delinquents were searched, and they were arrested by the Council.[11] All these measures were of little help. Half a year after the last general meeting on October 11, 1942, the Council chairman, Rabbi Gedalia Rosenman, at a special meeting again spoke about "the widespread bacchanalia in the ghetto manifested by disobedience of [the Council's] orders, evasion of forced-labor duty, and concealment of those called for labor, all of which cause great displeasure to the authorities."[12]

Similar cases of nonpayment of imposed cash contributions or taxes and evasion of forced labor are reported from other ghettos.[13]

It should, however, be pointed out that these acts were not always indicative of opposition to the Councils. Only too often people paid no taxes because of lack of cash. Others dodged forced labor because of inhuman working conditions, more a revolt against the Nazi oppressors than an expression of disobedience toward the Councils.

The sources preserve information on trials for resistance against the police as they tried to carry out their disagreeable duties. For instance, a woman in the Vilna Ghetto was sentenced to 18 hours' arrest in May 1942, "for insulting and resisting the police." In addition she was threatened with a trial in the ghetto court, but the case against her was quashed on the initiative of the police because of double jeopardy.[14]

Herman Kruk, the chronicler of the Vilna Ghetto, entered a note in his Diary on July 10, 1943, concerning two sentences by the ghetto court for resisting the police (he did not indicate the details). In one case a youth was sentenced "to stay for 14 nights in the ghetto jail"; in the other one, a man received a 17-day jail term.[15]

Sometimes the police themselves inflicted harsh punishments for resistance, not waiting for the sentences of the proper authorities. For instance, Ringelblum noted that the Warsaw Ghetto police clubbed a man to death in the building of the Warsaw Jewish Council for kicking a policeman.[16] Another case of a policeman beating a man to death was that of the Jewish physician Dr. Zusman. It was made public by the underground publication of the Hashomer Hatzair, *Oyfbroyz* ("Flash"), on June 7, 1942.

SPONTANEOUS COLLECTIVE OPPOSITION TO THE COUNCILS

The sources note a number of spontaneous manifestations of opposition by entire groups of inmates against the Jewish ghetto administrations.

In Łódź in March 1940, after the ghetto had come into being, Jewish war prisoners of the Polish army who had been sent back to the town of their birth assembled in a square demanding bread, work, and relief for needy veterans. Rumkowski ordered the Jewish police to chase them away. They resisted and started marching to his Secretariat in another part of the ghetto. The Germans on guard at the ghetto gates (no bridges had yet been built between the two parts of the ghetto) fired shots in the air and ordered the marchers to disperse. They refused, requesting to see Rumkowski. When he agreed to admit them they succeeded in receiving help in food and cash.

In July 1940 the situation in the ghetto was very bad because parcel post deliveries were no longer allowed. Moreover, trade with the outside world and even smuggling stopped after ghetto currency was introduced. A crowd of hungry welfare recipients who had received no assistance marched to the community building and began to demolish the premises. Rumkowski then ordered that everyone who wished should be given food stamps free of charge.[17] In the summer of 1940 tailors assaulted Rumkowski with shears and other tools, to take revenge for his orders to confiscate their sewing machines for use in newly established tailor shops.[18]

Forced-labor duty was a permanent cause of spontaneous demonstrations against the Councils. A few examples follow. In Piotrków Trybunalski a crowd assembled in front of the Council building. People cried and shouted—why did their loved ones have to carry the burden of forced-labor duty while rich people could get released for a fee? At the suggestion of the eyewitness who reported this incident in his book (himself an official of the Council), the protesters were granted the right to choose two or three delegates to take part in the Council's deliberations on how to help people who were being sent away for forced labor.[19]

A group of tailors in Council Tailor Shop No. 12 in Warsaw decided on June 6, 1941, to address a letter to Czerniakow complaining that they and their families were going hungry, since they were being paid only some watery soup for a day's work. The letter was written, but was never mailed because of fear of persecution by the Council's production department. A meeting of tailors with the representatives of the production department achieved no improvement in their lot, so they later decided to send the letter, after all. It is not known what happened to the famished tailors.[20]

Some Councils had no qualms about seeking German help when stormy demonstrations broke out against them. A group of forced laborers in Radomsko assembled in front of the Council building, asking for reductions in their work load so that they might have some time left to make a little money to maintain their families. "They started breaking the windowpanes, and the chairman phoned the Gestapo. The poor Jews with yellow patches were severely beaten up."[21]

A memorandum of the Lublin Ghetto to the authorities on July 29, 1940, states that "forced laborers are again causing disturbances among the workers in front of the offices of the Community. The premises and the furnishings are very often damaged and the members of the Jewish Council gravely insulted and even pelted with stones. To restore peace we had to call in the German police."[22] In this case the problem was wages which the Council was late in paying. Similar events took place that month when wives demonstrated about the fate of their husbands sent to labor camps. The situation became so tense that in a special announcement the Council warned on July 15, 1940, that it would take care of the laborers only after the people calmed down so that the Council would be able to work in peace. As long as the turmoil in the Council offices continued, no steps would be undertaken to change or to ease the fate of the laborers.[23] The mood did not calm down, and on October 19, 1940, the Council decided to publish an appeal against the agitators and punish those taking part in the demonstrations.[24]

ORGANIZED OPPOSITION TO THE COUNCILS

Organized opposition against the Councils was for the most part the work of political parties in the ghettos. Before discussing this we need to review the political activities of the Jews under the Nazis.

Under the profound impact of war and German occupation, surviving Jewish political activists were first of all preoccupied with the preservation of their sparse party cadres. They concentrated largely on an effort to assist destitute party members, to intercede with the Councils on their behalf, and, last but not least, to get in touch with central party committees in the capital. Soup kitchens for party members were initiated with funds received from the Councils or from party central offices. The kitchens often served as clandestine meeting places for camouflaged political or cultural activities (in Warsaw, Łódź, and Vilna, among other places).

Because travel for Jews was outlawed, contacts with the central party committees in Warsaw were severely curtailed. Channels of communication, such as they were, were made possible only thanks to the devotion and daring of liaison men, for the most part youthful messengers. The emissaries of the Joint Distribution Committee in Poland also helped as long as the JDC was permitted to conduct relief work.

One of the earliest, most complicated problems the political parties faced was developing an attitude toward the Jewish Councils (or the Councils of Elders) which the Germans established in the fall of 1939. Most acute was the problem of whether to participate, and if so in what form, in the activities of the Councils, or to oppose them from the start. This question was the subject of heated discussion on the local and central party levels. In practice the policy varied, with a wide range of nuances depending on local conditions. The Zionist groups in Będzin, for instance, had no uniform opinion. Some rejected cooperation with Merin and his institution on principle, maintaining that he was the obvious tool of the German authorities. Others considered him a lesser evil, arguing that it might prove useful to see first how he handled his tasks before deciding on a clearcut policy, and that the community should not be left without management.[25] Similar discussions were taking place in the Łódź Ghetto and in other ghettos (see Chap. 2).[26]

The forms of political activity were determined by the necessity to work clandestinely. The membership of parties was divided into small groups of five or seven members. Only proven and trustworthy persons were admitted. They usually met in the homes of comrades, or in cemeteries (in smaller ghettos) and other places considered secure. As already mentioned, the soup kitchens were also used for such purposes. In Warsaw, Cracow, Vilna, and Białystok some of the parties—the Bund, Poalei Zion, Hashomer Hatzair, and the Communists—used apartments occupied by their party comrades on the "Aryan" side to meet in secret.

In some of the large ghettos, the activities of the political parties were quite lively right after the ghettos were established. Thus Ringelblum noted on May 7, 1942:

Up to the famous Friday, April 18, [1942],[27] this could have been considered the era of the legal underground [in Warsaw]. All political parties were sort of semi-illegal. Publications mushroomed. . . . Things went so far that a certain faction issued its publication twice in a single week. Distribution was freely made, and the tracts and communications were read in offices and shops. Meetings of various political parties were held almost openly in the halls of institutions. Large public celebrations were also arranged. During one such meeting a speaker talked about active resistance to the 50 [?] people assembled. I attended a celebration arranged for 550 youths of a certain group. It was no secret who the authors of articles in the [underground] papers were. The articles were discussed and invectives exchanged, as was the habit in the good prewar years. One almost believed that everything was permitted . . . that it was all the same to the Germans what the Jews thought or did. The prevailing opinion was that they were only interested in uncovering Jewish goods, cash, and currency, and that spiritual problems were of no concern to them.[28]

According to incomplete information, approximately 50 underground publications in Yiddish, Polish, and Hebrew were issued in Warsaw between 1940 and April 1943 by almost all political parties. Literary and historical anthologies and books under titles such as *Martyrdom and Heroism, The Paris Commune* (both in Yiddish), and others were published. The incomplete list of Bund publications alone contains 13 titles with a total of 180,000 typewritten pages.[29]

In other ghettos, large and small, various underground publications were issued in diverse polygraphic forms, such as mimeographed tracts, newspapers pasted on walls, appeals, etc.[30]

We have already discussed opposition to joining the Councils by individuals and groups in Chap. 2. After the Councils had been formed there were two possible ways to express opposition to them: (*a*) criticism of the Council's activities in the underground press, in reports forwarded abroad, in appeals to the inmates, in tracts, etc.; and (*b*) street demonstrations.

Unfortunately, little material has been preserved on criticism in the underground publications. Because of Gestapo terror, their circulation was rather limited. People were afraid to keep the papers, appeals, or leaflets and destroyed them right after reading them. Those which were hidden vanished when the ghettos were destroyed. However, thanks to the Ringelblum Archives numerous copies of the illegal papers published in the Warsaw Ghetto were preserved. The underground publications of the Warsaw Ghetto were in sharp opposition to the activities of the Council and the ghetto police. The publications of the Bund took a most negative attitude. In the *Wecker* of March 15, 1942 (No. 9/33), the 40 percent surcharge on all medicines was commented on:

You won't find a similar institution in the whole wide world with the cynicism and nerve to impose a tax like this one. In the Warsaw Ghetto, where the most terrible sicknesses, such as typhus, tuberculosis, etc. are rampant, a clique of so-called "leaders" dares to impose a tax of 40 percent on each medicine a sick person must buy. The very same Councilmen who speak in public with so much sentiment about children and adults dying of illnesses are the very people who make it impossible to cure the sick. . . . The Warsaw Jewish Council has made a business out of the epidemics.

In *Dos Fraye Wort* (published instead of the *Wecker*) of May 23, 1942 (No. 1/38), in an article under the title, "To the Warsaw Jewish Council," it was said: "Corruption and rot that have eaten away at the Council from the start . . . keep increasing daily. . . . licenses and partnerships [are known of] between various Councilmen and managers of the Purveyance Agency [the Council's food supply department]. . . . The Jewish population was openly robbed of the little coal that the Germans allocated, and it was put on the black market. . . ." The same happened in the housing department, where criminal acts were committed.

In the Bund publication *Biuletyn* of July 1940 the Council is sharply criticized in two articles: "Of Jewish Life" and "The Bread Tax." In *Der Wecker* (issued in place of the *Biuletyn*) of January 18, 1942, we find an article entitled, "The Warsaw Jewish Council Buys Furs"; in the issue of February 1, 1942, appeared articles entitled, "The Leadership Mania in the Warsaw Ghetto" and "How Does Bread Disappear?"; on February 8, 1942, appeared articles entitled, "The Masses Pay and the Rich Reign" and "How They Boss Around"; and on March 15 two more articles: "One More Source of Income for the Warsaw Jewish Council" and "The Estate of the President of the Merchants' Union."

The Warsaw Ghetto police were criticized as follows in an article in *Dos Fraye Wort* of May 23, 1942: "Books will be written about their crass meanness. . . . they have learned how to chase the traders in the streets, the *rikshas*, and [they are doing it] about as well as the [Polish] police used to do [before the war]. There are brutes among them who beat up [their victims] . . . shameless blackmailers, and thieves." The ghetto police were also criticized in the Bund's Polish language publication *Za naszą i waszą wolność* ("For Our Liberty and Yours") for January and February 1942 (pp. 12–13).

Publications of other parties also criticized the ghetto police. Thus *Unzer Weg* (Poalei Zion-Socialists) of December 1941 printed an article entitled, "The Jewboys' Councils in the Provinces" (pp. 16–18). Hashomer Hatzair's *Oyfbroyz*, No. 16, June 7, 1942 (p. 8), printed an article entitled, "The *Shulchan-Aruch* ["Guidelines"] of the Jewish Police in Warsaw," in which the Service Instructions of the ghetto police, issued on May 21, 1941, were critically appraised and the above-mentioned case of Dr. Zusman (who died after he was clubbed in the head by a policeman) was described.

Jutrzenka ("The Dawn"), the clandestine organ of the Gordonia in the Warsaw Ghetto, characterized the Council on March 14, 1942, as "a tool in German hands, traitors who will yet receive their well-earned punishment."

A group of underground activists in Częstochowa, consisting of members of various political parties and people who had no party affiliations, published an underground paper called *Rasta* (the name is derived from the first syllables of *Rada Starszych*, Polish for Council of Elders), where opposition to the Council and the ghetto police was expressed. The paper printed cartoons ridiculing the Council. Two Poles helped to distribute the paper: one kept the printed copies in his home outside the ghetto, the other transported part of the edition to Warsaw and mailed it out from there.[31]

For a long time (every three or four weeks during 1941) the mimeographed, illustrated *Biuletyn fun Bund* was published in the Łódź Ghetto. It contained news items and criticized the activities of Rumkowski's administration.[32]

The Hechalutz movement in Cracow published (in 1942 and 1943) an underground paper in Polish (only the paper's title was in Hebrew): *Hechalutz Halochem* ("The Fighting Hechalutz"). Some 30 issues were published. The paper occasionally printed items critical of the Council, but more often of the ghetto police. The police in particular were labeled traitors to the Jewish people and were warned that they would be fought without mercy. In a number of ghettos (Cracow, Bochnia, Tarnów) physical confrontations with the ghetto police took place.[33]

In the already cited report of the united underground organizations in the Warsaw Ghetto of November 15, 1942, addressed to the Polish government-in-exile in London, we find sharp criticism against both the Council and the ghetto police for their behavior during the "resettlement action." The report states:

The treason of the Jewish Council in Warsaw will be remembered for generations. . . . They agreed to carry out the "resettlement," fully knowing though pretending ignorance of the actual situation. Along with the treason of the ghetto police, that of the Council will remain forever a black stigma on the honor of the Jewish ghetto authority. While branding it as such, we must stress that the Jewish ghetto authority, a creature of occupation conditions, in no way mirrors the mood of the population. The Councilmen and their advisers, these little men, careerists placed in high positions by the grace of the occupiers, were unable to face the truth. Consciously or not, they gave in to the divide-and-rule tactics of the [German] "resettlement" office. Accepting a few concessions for certain groups . . . they agreed to carry out the destruction of the [Warsaw] Jews.[34]

There is sufficient evidence to assume that in some other ghettos handwritten or hectographed underground publications (they were seldom printed) appeared in time of crisis. Published by the remnants of party activists, they expressed opposition in general to local Councils or to some of their actions or decisions.

Strikes and demonstrations constituted a third kind of organized opposition to the Councils. Unfortunately, relevant material is preserved only concerning events in the Łódź and Częstochowa Ghettos.

During the extremely bad summer months of 1940, when epidemic dysentery was particularly rampant and the population famished, mass meetings and demonstrations were held in the Łódź Ghetto, for the most part by workers who belonged to or were influenced by the prewar labor parties or trade unions. According to a secret communication of *Forschungstelle A* ("Intelligence Office A") of the German Air Force Ministry in Łódź, dated August 10, 1940, a hunger demonstration against Rumkowski took place on August 8. The alerted German police used firearms to disperse the crowd. No mention is made of casualties.[35]

The opposition was not intimidated. Twice, on August 10 and 11, hunger forced people out into the streets. The demonstration was not large on the first day, and the Jewish police easily dispersed it. But on the second day several thousand people filled the streets shouting: "We want bread, we are dying from hunger." The ghetto police could not handle the large crowd and withdrew. Rumkowski phoned the authorities, and at his request the Germans dispersed the people by shooting in the air. The demonstrators fled, but the German police followed and attacked them in their homes. Fortunately only a few people were wounded. The next day, August 12, Rumkowski issued a statement calling on the ghetto inmates to calm down. Attacking "irresponsible elements who wish to create turmoil in our lives," he promised to improve the food situation in the public kitchens. But the mood did not quiet down. Handwritten announcements were posted on walls from August 23 to 25, calling people to gather in certain streets to protest against the regime in the Łódź Ghetto.[36]

Again in September 1940 street demonstrations against Rumkowski took place. The Gestapo dispersed the crowd and apprehended "the more dangerous Jewish criminals." In mid-September an unidentified group attacked Rumkowski while he was riding in a *Droshke* ("horse-car") in the evening hours. The "main leaders" were seized by the ghetto police, and the Gestapo "rendered the agitators harmless."[37] Rumkowski felt insecure and was afraid that his prestige with the authorities might be undermined. He therefore called a meeting with representatives of the workers. He was reproached for the bloodshed in the ghetto and made some concessions. The workers and their children were given free soup; the distribution of food was carried out by delegates of the workers, who arranged for meals to be served in the party kitchens of the Bund and Poalei Zion. But by October Rumkowski apparently felt enhanced in his authority and disbanded the workers' delegations. He became tougher in December, when he forced nurses to break their strike for an eight-hour work day by arresting the strikers and their families.[38]

By January 1941 the atmosphere in the ghetto was again tense. On January 11 and 12 large demonstrations took place, people demanding more food and fuel. On occasion food carts were attacked in the ghetto and the police had to intervene, patrolling the streets all day long. But tension continued and stormy events broke out on January 23.

As already mentioned, Rumkowski revoked the right of the workers to elect shop stewards, and on January 12, 1941, he abolished the additional food rations (soup and 500 grams of bread) for workers in the shops and factories. Control over the workers was intensified, and they were not allowed to take waste wood to heat their homes any more, though because of lack of fuel in the ghetto this had been the only means to provide some cooked food for their starving families.

In desperation the carpenters decided to strike and occupy the shops. When persuasions to clear the shop were to no avail, the Jewish *Überfallkommando* was alerted, and the striking men locked themselves up in the shops. But the *Kommando* took their barricade by storm and dispersed the rebellious workers. During the scuffle several men were wounded. As a result defiance spread to other shops. It looked as though a general strike were imminent, and Rumkowski closed all shops in the ghetto on January 24. After Rumkowski announced the lockout the striking workers listed their grievances and demands in a public statement. Rumkowski called a meeting of the instructors of the closed shops and threatened them with punishment for sabotaging work. The instructors of the tailor shops then agreed to persuade the tailors to go back to work, but the strike committee of the carpenters (which perhaps also represented some other trades) called them scabs. On January 30, 1941, the strike committee's appeal appeared, calling on all workers not to return to work in the name of solidarity with their striking comrades; but the strike was already on the wane, for the carpenters were unable to go on unemployed and suffer hunger any more. Of close to 600 carpenters, 460 were at work on January 31. The next day they held a meeting and decided to call off the strike and issue a public statement, reproaching Rumkowski and his police. By February 2 all carpenters had resumed work.

A strike of gravediggers broke out for the same reasons on January 26. Some 200 men refused to work, but their work stoppage was of short duration because they were threatened with arrest.

But the opposition of the workers to the Rumkowski regime did not stop, the failure of the strike notwithstanding. As early as March 26, 1941, another street demonstration took place with the participation of a crowd of close to 700 people. People shouted against the ghetto administration, and leaflets were distributed and pasted on the walls. The police dispersed the crowd, hitting several demonstrators. Two of the policemen were wounded. At night raids were carried out against the workers, and 50 people were arrested. They were labeled "thieves, second offenders, agitators against the present order in the ghetto," and were to be sent to work in Germany.

Next, in August 1941, Rumkowski shut all kitchens administered by political parties. This was his revenge against his opposition, and especially against the labor parties whom he quite rightly suspected of initiating the street demonstrations. The last vestiges of social institutions in the ghetto thus came to an end. Earlier, in January and March 1941, the Bund collective and the Zionist kibbutzim in Marysin had been disbanded.

Opposition to Rumkowski and his corrupt regime continued and was variously manifested: resistance against the ghetto police; agitation urging people not to report to the "resettlement" transports; sabotage in the ghetto factories; the so-called soup strikes, in which workers refused to consume their soup served in the ghetto shops. At times the opposition took more intense forms, and at other times it decreased; but it was in evidence until the ghetto was liquidated in August 1944.[39]

In the Częstochowa Ghetto, too, a hunger strike and stormy clash took place between the forced laborers, led by the labor council, and the Jewish Council. In 1941 there were close to 5,000 daily workers, and from December 15, 1941 close to 8,000 on the average. They demanded an increase of bread rations (1 kilogram a day for heavy laborers) and higher wages (an increase of from 20 to 30 zlotys for a six-day work week).

One day in December 1941 people assembled in the workers' kitchen in the Maccabi Hall, announced a hunger strike, and marched to the building of the Council. They occupied offices and demolished equipment. At the suggestion of a representative of the labor council who tried to calm the storming demonstrators, a delegation was elected to negotiate with the Council. The Council's presidium requested that the demonstrators leave the building, refusing to negotiate under duress; but the workers refused. The negotiations lasted till late in the night, when the Council yielded to the demands.[40]

There was a noticeable difference between the forms of opposition in the ghettos of Warsaw and Łódź. In Warsaw the opposition never took extreme form, neither against the Council nor against the ghetto police. No street demonstrations took place and no hunger strikes occurred.

The problem of how the poor masses facing extreme impoverishment would react was of great concern to thinking people in the ghettos. Ringelblum wrote:

One of the problems of great import is the passivity of the Jewish masses, dying without a whimper. Why are they so quiet? Why are fathers, mothers, and all the children dying without protest? . . . Various excuses can be found. Intimidation by the [German] authorities is so great that people are scared to raise their heads, fearing mass terror against the hungry in case of any turbulence. This is the reason why the socially responsible remain silent, passive, so as not to cause turbulence in the ghetto. Others, having a little initiative, find some sort of accommodations. Smuggling provides a means to eke out a living for thousands of porters. . . . The shops and the orders that came from German cells provide employment for large numbers of workers and artisans. Some . . . trade in the streets. . . . The rest are passive, helpless people who are simply dying out. . . . The Jewish police have learned how to hit, to enforce order, and to send people to the labor camps, and they are one of the contributing factors that keep people in line. The dying are mainly refugees from out of town.* They feel lost in the strange environment and are incapable of seeking a way out of their predicament. The only thing left for them is to whine for a dole, to protest in their *Landsman-schaft*, to beg for a piece of bread from the institution [the relief committee] or from the house committee. . . . After a little shouting they keep quiet, become resigned, and simply wait to die, as if yearning for the moment when death will deliver them from suffering.[41]

We may assume that Ringelblum's tragic analysis of the mood prevailing among impoverished inmates in the Warsaw Ghetto was also correct with respect to the majority of the ghettos, particularly those with large numbers of refugees and expellees. However, despite the refugees and expellees so characteristic of the Warsaw Ghetto as opposed to the Łódź Ghetto, neither Gestapo terror—no less severe in Łódź than in Warsaw—nor the ghetto police—no less "diligent" than their counterparts in Warsaw—was able to restrain the desperate masses in the Łódź Ghetto from street demonstrations against Rumkowski. We may therefore conclude that Nazi terror and the Jewish police were not decisive in suppressing the will to demonstrate of the ghetto inmates in Warsaw, where the fighting tradition of the Jews was as strong as in Łódź.

To comprehend the difference in the attitudes and moods of these two ghettos, it should be remembered that opposition to the Council and its policies legitimately came to the surface in Warsaw through the various welfare institutions, cultural organizations, and the house committees. Contrary to the situation in Łódź, all these public bodies in Warsaw were able to express sharp criticism of the Jewish Council.

* By mid-1941, there were close to 150,000 refugees in Warsaw, almost one third of the entire Jewish population in town.

The Jewish Social Welfare was an opposition factor of such prestige that willy-nilly the Council had to listen. Moreover, the opposition found expression in numerous underground papers in the ghetto. Altogether, there were in the Warsaw Ghetto channels of opposition that made it less urgent to have secretly organized demonstrations when people were brought to the brink of desperation. In Łódź, however, legitimate social activities, smothered and ruthlessly persecuted by Rumkowski, went underground.

There was one more reason: in no other known ghetto was the life of the individual so trammeled and his initiative so constrained as in Łódź. Rumkowski was the sole provider of bread. All other channels of making a living were cut off; smuggling, selling private assets, and illicit trade were forbidden and suppressed. On the other hand, the average individual inmate in Warsaw, as well as in the majority of ghettos, had more room left to use his own initiative, to try and stay on the surface. He was more independent of a Council that did not decide his fate, at least not until the "resettlement actions." Consequently the individual inmate in these ghettos did not feel as much direct pressure from the ghetto administration on his daily life as was the case in Łódź. This alone was enough to allow social protest against the German oppressor, rather than against the ghetto administration; whereas in the Łódź Ghetto there was only one visible target for all social unrest—Rumkowski and his administration. This is the principal difference between the Łódź Ghetto and the other ghettos, though in those ghettos too there were sufficient local conditions to nourish social protest.

In the comparatively extensive documentation on the Vilna Ghetto there is no information available about any active, organized, mass demonstrations against the Council. The steps undertaken against Gens in connection with the affairs of Josef Glazman and Yitzhak Witenberg were carried out by the underground movement and were limited only to them. No relevant information can be found in the postwar literature either. The reasons vary: social help in the Vilna Ghetto was organized on a wide social basis and was more effective than in Warsaw, for instance. Three welfare organizations were active: the relief committee, the welfare department of the Jewish Council, and the winter relief committee. The slogan of the relief committee—"Nobody Should Go Hungry in the Ghetto"—was not an empty appeal, and mass hunger and impoverishment were not so prevalent in the Vilna Ghetto as in Warsaw and Łódź. (The same can be said about the Białystok Ghetto.) No cases of death from hunger were officially registered in the Vilna Ghetto. This quite effective welfare work apparently was instrumental in easing the tension in the ghetto.

It should also be borne in mind that the inmates who remained in the Vilna Ghetto from the end of 1941 until its final liquidation had all undergone "selection" and lived through the phase of the Ponary slaughters, and therefore had a more homogeneous social structure. For the most part, these were able-bodied laborers who had been engaged at work in German and Lithuanian labor places outside the ghetto or in the Council shops. Thus they had had an opportunity to barter goods with gentile neighbors. Except for a tiny group of rich inmates, the "nouveaux riches of the ghetto," all had more or less equal chances of survival. Thus there was less antagonism because of social inequalities or social grievances which, in the Łódź Ghetto, led to explosions and mass demonstrations against the ghetto regime. It does not mean, however, that there was no social ferment in the Vilna Ghetto. It simply found expression not in collective demonstrations against the Jewish Council, but in "civil disobedience" against the ghetto police (see p.533).

Information is preserved regarding hostile demonstrations against the Councils of Elders in two Wartheland ghettos.

In a postwar eyewitness account, an inmate described a stormy demonstration against the Kutno Ghetto Council. These are the more characteristic passages:

It happened in February 1941, at the time when typhus killed scores of people every day and the danger of [mass] deaths by hunger loomed. . . . Folks in Konstancja [a former sugar plant in the territory of the ghetto] considered [what to do]. . . . One day a big crowd gathered in front of the "House of Lords" [as the Council building was ridiculed by the inmates]. Hungry and pale, people demanded to see F. [the cashier of the Council]. He came down a few minutes later, inquiring what was the matter, but could not continue talking, for he was dragged into block No. 10, where heavy iron was stocked. He was forced to stand on an iron "stage" and people showered angry questions on him: "Where is the money? You used it to make business profits for yourself. Why is there no relief left for us? Of what use are you to us? Down with the Council of Elders! Thieves, robbers!" Screaming people attacked F. giving him no chance to answer. . . . The German authorities, called in by the ghetto police, rescued him. The crowd was dispersed.[42]

In Poddębice, a little town near Łódź, people arranged a demonstration in front of the Council building, shouting: "Give us bread and fuel!" This apparently happened in December 1940. It is not known how the demonstration ended.[43]

Jewish folklore in the ghettos evidenced animosity toward the Councils, their officials, and the ghetto police. Numerous biting satires denounced the social order in the ghettos, the heartless officials and policemen, their favoritism, moral corruption, and servility toward the German authorities. In a song entitled, "In the Kaunas Ghetto Committee," the anonymous author criticized, with a sort of gallows humor, the depravity of the ghetto authorities, favoritism, etc. Other similar songs are preserved from the Kaunas Ghetto, such as "The Gate Watch," where the anonymous writer lashed out against the corruption of Jewish guardsmen at the ghetto gates. The "Committee Man" is another bitter satire against the privileged position of the Council members. The satire "Vitamins" deals with favoritism practiced by some officials in the Vilna Ghetto, and the miserable life in the Warsaw Ghetto is depicted in the satirical song "Money, Money." It was very popular.[44] The sources of the Łódź Ghetto also preserved a number of songs and satires directed against the Rumkowski regime.[45]

The ghetto songs and satires were an important historical source for analysis of the mood of the inmates toward the Councils, which were made responsible for the social conditions prevailing in the ghettos.

CHAPTER 20

Postwar Trials of Councilmen
and Ghetto Police

POSTWAR REACTIONS to the question of the guilt or innocence of survivors who were once members of the Councils and ghetto police (individuals or organizations) are important for the overall analysis of the problem under discussion in this study. The trials and judgments of the Courts of Honor and of the courts of the State of Israel that considered cases against surviving Councilmen and policemen to a large degree help to assess their actions and motives.

No sooner had hostilities stopped than Jews at large, and the remnants assembled in displaced persons camps, began heated discussions on the extent of culpability of surviving former Councilmen and policemen, some of whom occupied leading positions among the survivors. Public opinion, as expressed in the press and literature published by the displaced persons, demanded that these people against whom accusations of collaboration with the Nazis in the persecution of their fellow Jews were made public be brought before Courts of Honor. Requests for trials came from individual survivors and their committees, such as the Central Committee of Liberated Jews in the American Zone in Germany in Munich. But some of the accused themselves requested trials in order to clear themselves of accusations they considered unjust or unfounded.

In the memorandum entitled, "Rehabilitation Will Clear the Social Atmosphere," to be found in the Archives of the Central Committee of Liberated Jews in the American Zone, we read:

> . . . During the war there was a sharp delineation between the German rulers and the Jews condemned to pain and agony. A sort of "elite"

surfaced which, under various names and for various reasons, more or less consciously put itself in a favored position between the two worlds, the torturers and the tortured. It is natural that, after liberation, Jewish society is obliged to request that the role of these "notables" of the tragic years be surveyed and judgment pronounced, as to whether they warrant a place in our society or should rather be banished from our midst.[1]

Courts of Honor under various names were established in countries where displaced persons were concentrated: in Bergen-Belsen (British Zone of occupation); in Munich (the "Court of Honor and Rehabilitation of the Union of Liberated Jews in the American Zone in Germany"); in Rome ("The Court of Honor at the Central Organization of Survivors in Italy"—*Merkaz Irgun Hapleitim Be'-Italia*). Along with these central courts there were also local courts in individual survivors' camps, as in the Landsberg Center, in Neu-Ulm (both in Germany), in Trani, and in "Adriatica" (Italy). They acted according to court procedures worked out by the legal departments of the respective central committees.[2]

The Israeli Parliament (Knesset) adopted the Nazis and Nazi Collaborators (Punishment) Law 5710/1950, promulgated in the *Sefer Ha-Khukim* No. 57 of August 9, 1950 (p. 281). Based on this law, the Israeli courts passed judgments in a number of trials against former policemen and Kapos in various camps.

THE TRIALS IN THE COURTS OF HONOR

The judges of the Courts of Honor were, for the most part, survivors of the Holocaust themselves. What was their attitude with respect to the accusations advanced against defendants during the trials? It was expressed in judgments based on the legal principle that the mere fact that a person belonged to the organs of the Jewish ghetto administration was not punishable by itself. Each case had to be judged on its own merits and on relevant evidence of specific acts charged. Thus the "Decision" of the Rehabilitation Commission of the Central Committee in Munich in the case of the Kaunas Ghetto policeman Beinish Tkach, on May 17, 1948, stated:

The ghetto inmates considered the police no good in general. However, to generalize this opinion and extend it to all policemen without exception, without an individual approach to each case, may lead to harmful injustice. In any event, lacking definite regulations, and in the absence of a decision by a higher legislative body condemning as a criminal act the mere belonging to the ghetto police or another similar body, the Rehabilitation Commission adjudicated the case of the man requesting rehabilitation *in the same manner as in all other cases* [italics added], in agreement with general principles of jurisprudence, basing judgment on concrete evidence of guilt or innocence.[3]

In the memorandum cited above, which theoretically outlined some of the regulations for the Courts of Honor, the question was also raised:

. . . Does the term "harmful activities" include membership in the Jewish Councils, membership in the Jewish police in the ghettos and camps, and the performance of functions as foremen, *Stubälteste* ("Room Elders"), etc.—i.e., mere affiliation with the institutions that to a larger or smaller extent contributed to the tragic fate of hundreds of thousands of Jews? . . . As long as this problem is not solved, the Rehabilitation Commission will continue to judge each individual case and pass each judgment strictly on the merits of the concrete acts of the accused.

It was not always clear to the courts how to evaluate the role of Jewish Councils in the course of "actions," and they avoided taking a clearcut position. The extensive nine-page judgment and explanation of the "Rehabilitation Commission" of the Central Committee in Munich (dated July 22, 1948) concerning the case of Chaim Aleksandrowicz, a former policeman in the Kaunas Ghetto, states: ". . . This is not the place to judge whether forced assistance to the Council of Elders in calling the entire population to assemble at the Democrats' Square means guilt or, perhaps, not. Certainly the Council of Elders knew that its role in the coming 'big action' was agonizing and tragic."[4]

Another principle these courts applied in passing their judgments was that "nobody is released from guilt by having merely carried out an order issued by a higher authority, according to the opinion of the Court of States [reference is apparently made here to the judgments of the Nuremberg Trials against German war criminals]."[5]

The Courts of Honor rejected defendants' arguments that they had acted under conditions of *force majeure*, reasoning that a defendant "did not have to accept his position and could have refused [to carry out] his functions," though they took into consideration that "the regime in the concentration camps forced the accused to assault other Jews in some cases."[6] It should be pointed out that there was a substantial difference between the refusal by a German to carry out an order to kill and the refusal by Jewish helpers of the Nazi murder apparatus. A German legal authority has recently pointed out that if a German policeman or soldier refused to carry out a criminal act against the civil population, he was in no danger of persecution.[7] But a Jewish ghetto or camp policeman or Kapo, if he refused to carry out an order, was, in the lawless atmosphere of the ghettos and camps, in mortal danger on the spot or soon thereafter.

As for procedural matters, the Division of War Crimes of the legal department of the Central Committee in Munich, in charge of preparing the trials, was of the opinion that an accusation by a single person was not enough to open an investigation, unless it was confirmed by other witnesses. Thus, because a former member of the Brześć Ghetto Council was accused by only one person, who could not produce any corroborating witnesses, the legal department decided to quash the case.[8] The defendant in any case, or his lawyer, had the right to appeal on the basis of new evidence or new witnesses.[9]

As a rule, the court consisted of two judges and a presiding judge, but sometimes five judges adjudicated a case. A representative of the Central Committee in Munich was also present.

The courts imposed two kinds of punishment: (1) Bans against holding any position in the organizations and institutions of the displaced persons, and dismissal from such a position if the convict held it before the trial. The sentence could also decree that the defendant was not entitled to material assistance by any Jewish relief organizations (such as the Joint Distribution Committee) or to emigration with the help of the Jewish Agency for Palestine or HIAS. As a rule, copies of sentences were given to the relevant *Landsmanschaften* and the press of the displaced persons. The most severe sentences labeled the defendant as a "traitor to the Jewish People," which entailed banishment from the Jewish community or, as happened in one recorded case, transfer of the case to the military court of the allied occupation authority.[10]

The Courts of Honor gained high moral standing. Their sentences were binding and recognized by the displaced persons community, except for one known case where an attempt was made to charge a court with lack of authority to pass judgment.

To judge by the materials at our disposal not many trials were instigated against former members of Jewish Councils. There were apparently two reasons for this. First, only an insignificant number of Councilmen survived, and second, the accusations of survivors were, for the most part, directed against Jewish policemen. Our own poll indicates that 62 percent of those questioned gave positive opinions of the activities of Jewish Councilmen, but less than 39 percent favorably evaluated the activities of policemen.

Jewish inmates of ghettos and camps started settling their accounts with the Jewish police long before liberation. Dictated by the conditions of the time, this rough justice was done with disregard for legal procedure.

Deep-seated hatred against particularly brutal or mean policemen resulted in lynching even during the war, or as soon as the victims were able to take revenge after the war ended. In the Kielce Ghetto there was a policeman, a Jewish expellee from Düsseldorf, by the name of Johann Spiegel. The Kielce memorial book notes that he and three other policemen "behaved just like the Nazis." According to one report, he was killed in Auschwitz by the Jewish camp inmates from Kielce. They had all been deported together to Auschwitz (the date is not given).[11]

The liberated inmates of the Greidetz Camp (or Faulbrück) killed the Jewish Kapo (a former ghetto policeman), Kolski.[12]

The Jewish resistance movement, too, carried out a number of death sentences against commanding officers of the Jewish police and against Jewish Gestapo agents who had particularly "distinguished" themselves as informants or in the course of "resettlement" actions.

The first shot of the Organization of Jewish Fighters in the Warsaw Ghetto, on August 20, 1942, was directed against the chief of the Ghetto police, Józef Szerynski. He was gravely wounded. Jacob Lejkin, who took over his job, was shot to death on October 29, 1942; and, one month later, on November 29, Israel First, manager of the economic department of the Jewish Council and liaison man with the Gestapo, was also killed. Following death sentences by the Organization of Jewish Fighters, six Gestapo agents, among them the notorious Dr. Alfred Nossig, were killed between February 21 and 28, 1943. One was severely wounded. He recovered and continued to serve the Germans as an informant on the "Aryan" side. He was killed by the Polish underground movement in November 1943.

The Organization of Jewish Fighters in Cracow also conducted revenge activities against the Jewish police in that ghetto and in other ghettos of the district. Jewish policemen were blacklisted, their personal data and criminal acts described, and the information distributed in hundreds of copies with requests for revenge. The blacklists were also forwarded abroad.[13]

The (DP) displaced persons' courts tried two kinds of cases: (1) those initiated by legal divisions of the Central Committee in Munich or the Organization of Liberated Jews in Italy or in the local DP camps; and (2) trials initiated by persons requesting rehabilitation proceedings. In such cases the verdict either accepted or rejected the request, without passing sentences in cases where rehabilitation had been denied.

Of the trials of former Councilmen, that of Dr. Ludwig Jaffe of the Lwów Jewish Council attracted the widest attention. It took place in Rome, from September to November 1948, before the Court of Honor of the Central Organization of the Liberated Jews in Italy.

At the first court session on August 25, the prosecutor charged Jaffe with collaboration with the Germans, extorting money from the victims of Nazi terror (bribes for assigning living quarters or for releasing people from "resettlement" during "selections" of candidates), and assisting in the "selections" of victims for "resettlement." The defendant, who did not appear in court, sent a letter requesting that his case be considered by a commission of representatives of various organizations, including the Bund. Jaffe was a member of the Bund and had been put on trial before the party court in Poland after the liberation.* Six witnesses testified for the prosecution.

The second session of the court took place on September 29. The lawyer for the defendant requested postponement of the trial be-

---

* Another trial of Dr. Jaffe before the Bund party court was held in Paris at a later date. Unfortunately I was denied access to the documents of this court, which are now in the Bund Archives in New York. According to a news item on October 1, 1948, in *Baderech*, the organ of liberated Jews in Italy, "the party court absolved Dr. Jaffe of any guilt." However, as long as the court documentation is unavailable to the researcher, this news item cannot be considered as a final statement, particularly since its author had no chance to peruse the relevant documentation but based his information on hearsay.

cause the party court of the Bund had refused to send him the documentation of Jaffe's trial. He argued that he needed the documents to call additional witnesses for the defendant. He also requested that the Court of Honor ask the chairman of the party court in Paris, Professor Libman Hersch, to make available the documentation of the party court in the Jaffe case. The Court of Honor accepted this request.

The third session was held on October 21. Nine witnesses testified in person or their statements were read in court. Only one of the 15 witnesses heard by the court testified for the defense.

The verdict in absentia was announced on November 10, 1948. Dr. Jaffe was found guilty of collaborating with the German police and the Gestapo in the Lwów Ghetto from 1941 to 1943, taking an active part in the segregation of the Lwów Jews for transportation to the death camps, and acting not in solidarity with the ghetto's interests but for his own benefit. Based on the court's evidence and on Article 16 of the court's regulations, he was forbidden to hold any official position and was denied material assistance from Jewish organizations. The court also decided to send the verdict to the relevant emigration organizations (The Jewish Agency for Palestine and HIAS) and to announce the verdict in the *Baderech*.[14]

Another trial against a former Councilman was that of Julius Zigel, a Councilman in Będzin and chief of the labor department. After the war he was employed as chief of the DP camp in Padua. According to the documentation of the Court of Honor in Rome, Zigel was sentenced for assaulting Jewish workers, lawless increase of work norms, etc. Four witnesses testified. The verdict was announced in Milan, where the case was tried by the Court of Honor on July 19, 1946. It states: "Zigel did not act properly, did not help his brethren to fight the enemy under all circumstances and by all means available. Quite to the contrary, he carried out all tasks . . . over and above his orders, beating [victims] on his own initiative. . . . Although no evidence has been produced that Zigel carried out these harmful activities for his own benefit, and although . . . he expressed his sincere remorse, his guilt had been proven."

Zigel confessed that he was, in fact, severe in his actions against Jews, but did not consider them criminal. Based on Paragraphs 8 and 59 of its regulations, the Court of Honor "condemned the actions of I. Zigel . . . as criminal and harmful to the Jewish community . . . during five and one half years," and Zigel was "forbidden to hold any position in the public life of the Jews." Copies of the verdict were to be sent to all relevant Jewish organizations in Italy.[15]

The Court of Honor of the Central Committee of Liberated Jews in the American Zone tried the case of Roman Merin, a former Councilman in Sosnowiec. He was also chief of a department in the *Zentrale* of the Councils of Elders of the Jewish Religious Communities in Eastern Upper Silesia. The trial took place in the months of March and May 1949. A number of witnesses testified, and on May 26, 1949, the court announced the verdict that the defendant had taken active part in actions aimed against the Jews, watching, along with other officials of the Jewish Council and the Jewish police, that no Jew escaped the assembly square. According to the sentence: "He was forbidden to hold any position in Jewish institutions, and the verdict should be announced in the press of the liberated Jews. Copies were forwarded to all Jewish organizations and to the local committee in Erding, where the defendant resided." The sentence also noted that "the court found this slight penalty commensurate with the extent of guilt proved." The court found unproved the charges that Merin had informed for the Germans, taken part in searching actions, and transported children out of orphanages during "resettlements."[16]

The trials against ghetto policemen were more numerous. After the liquidation of the ghettos many policemen held various positions in camps where they had been shipped together with the remnants of the ghetto inmates.

The material at our disposal, preserved in the documentation of trials or in other sources, refers to 42 trials against former ghetto policemen and/or Kapos, but includes the verdicts in only 27 of the trials. In 9 of these, the defendants were freed or rehabilitated. In 13 cases the defendants were forbidden to hold any position in Jewish public life or were condemned as traitors to the Jewish people and in 5 cases banished from the community. Requests for rehabilitation were denied with no punishment imposed in 2 cases. Three cases were quashed for various reasons (emigration of the defendant or lack of evidence). In 4 cases only the prosecution's charges remained in the files. Two of these requested that the defendant be given the supreme punishment.

The trials reveal a tragic chapter of the history of the Jewish catastrophe during the Hitler era, the active participation of Jews in the persecution of their fellow Jews in time of distress on orders of the Germans. The trials exposed deep roots of human frailty and degradation, including the perfidy of the Nazi regime in the ghettos and camps in luring their collaborators. In addition to all this, the trials also revealed high moral standards and readiness to help victims. In the poisoned ghetto environment, in constant struggle for bare physical existence, some individuals, probably predisposed by traits of character and mind, reached extreme depths of moral decline. Some without scruples became blind instruments of Nazi oppression and its murderous system, fully identifying themselves with the Nazis. There were those who tried to justify their brutalities, pleading that by carrying out measures of oppression themselves they had saved the ghetto inmates from vastly greater evils the Nazis would otherwise have been left to accomplish. They maintained that they sometimes had to act severely, even brutally, for the good of their "guilty" brethren, in order not to lose influence with their Nazi overseers and, by staying on in their positions, to try to help wherever possible.

Certainly it is not easy now to judge whether these rationalizations emerged only *post factum*, as arguments at trials. That the merciless executors of the Nazi orders surrounded themselves with small cliques of people whom they favored (mainly for a fine "consideration") is shown by the fact that seldom was there a trial without at least one witness for the defense. In the abyss of human misery, in times of social and moral decline impossible now to perceive, the lowest, most primitive forms of human reactions and motives came to the surface. The manifestly increased urge for self-preservation often took the form of a defensive-aggressive mechanism, leaving "thou" beyond the bars of ethical restraint. Moreover, the Nazis granted the ghetto police and the Kapos some "authority" which, in conditions of unlimited lawlessness, became a corrupting factor.

We shall proceed to examine a number of trials of this kind.

The Court of Honor in Munich tried a case against Mair Kiwkowicz, a Jewish policeman in the Olkusz Ghetto (Eastern Upper Silesia) on April 15, July 3, and August 17, 1948. Three witnesses testified that during the years 1940 and 1941 Kiwkowicz had "chased the Jews to labor, beaten them, requisitioned Jewish furniture and valuables on his own initiative for the Germans, exposed the bunkers of hiding Jews, and taken part in raids during the 'resettlement.'" For these "harmful deeds against Jewry" he was condemned as a traitor to the Jewish people. The verdict was announced in the press of the DPs and forwarded to the Jewish Agency, the Jewish Distribution Committee, HIAS, and the local Jewish Committee in Egenfelden, the defendant's residence.[17]

Henryk Frydman, the Jewish Elder and chief of police in the Jewish labor camp in Mielec, was also condemned as a traitor by the Jewish Court of Honor in Munich on January 16, 1949, for "sadistic torture, insults and whipping of inmates, and giving away their food rations to a clique of "prominents."[18]

Josef Włodawski was a Warsaw Ghetto policeman and a member of the notorious "13." Afterward he was leader of the *Arbeitseinsatz* in the concentration camp at Hessental (Schwäbish-Hall county), and assistant block Elder in a München-Allach camp. Włodawski reached an abyss of moral degradation and bestiality. Based on testimony by 21 witnesses, the legal department of the Central Committee in Munich charged him, on February 25, 1949, with bestialities that cried out to heaven, having caused the deaths of a large number of people. His behavior during the "resettlement" in the Warsaw Ghetto and his inhuman sadism toward the wretched camp inmates were no different from those of Nazi henchmen.

He was charged (Point 20) with having "enjoyed seeing Jewish blood spilt and behaved worse than the SS men." The department recommended considering him as a traitor to the Jewish people and transferring his case to a military tribunal.[19] In materials under our scrutiny there is no information about the result of the trial in this atrocious case.

As already mentioned, sentenced defendants had the right to appeal. Two appeal cases are preserved in our documentation.

David Neiman, a policeman in the Ostrowiec Ghetto, was found guilty on May 6, 1948 of chasing out Jews hidden in a bunker during the second "resettlement" in that ghetto on January 10, 1943. As a result 20-odd people were shot by the SS men. In the sentence of the court he was denied the right to take part in Jewish public life or to occupy any position in Jewish organizations. Neiman appealed. The second tribunal, consisting of five new judges, voided the sentence, but found him guilty in that he *indirectly* contributed to the discovery of the bunker, because he accompanied another policeman who had come to take his sister out of the bunker. The hidden people, seeing that the bunker had been discovered and knowing well the role of the Jewish police, tried to disperse but were caught by the SS men. The revised sentence, in fact, changed the character of the indictment, but not the punishment.[20] This trial gives an idea of the deplorable role the Jewish police played during the "resettlement" in some of the ghettos and of the attitudes of the inmates toward them: the mere fact that a bunker became known to a Jewish policeman was enough to scare the hidden Jews and to compel them to scatter.

Another appeal case was that of the block Elder in the Melk camp (Mauthausen *Kommando*), Arnold Einhorn. He was tried by the Court of Honor in Munich on August 2, 1949, and sentenced to supreme punishment. Einhorn appealed, and, on September 14 of the same year, another Court of Honor accepted his appeal, arguing that the first court did not follow a basic procedural regulation by admitting as evidence oral testimony from three witnesses, while not admitting the written testimony of a larger number of former ghetto inmates. At the time of the trial these witnesses resided in Austria, and their testimonies had been deposited with the Jewish Historical Commission in Linz. The appeal court further indicated that the statements of the three witnesses examined by the court were contradictory to a large extent. Moreover, they did not directly substantiate the point so categorically expressed in the explanation of the first court's verdict, that the deaths of the victims followed beatings administered by Einhorn. The fact that the chairman of the first Court of Honor, in a dissenting vote, registered his opposition to the severe punishment also justified the appeal.[21] The final sentence of this case is unknown.

Those accused before Courts of Honor tried to defend themselves in various ways. One, Chaim Aleksandrowicz, a higher official of the Kaunas Ghetto police, and later block Elder in the Kaufering camp (Dachau *Aussenkommando*), argued that he got his job in the ghetto and in the camp against his own will, on orders of the underground Zionist organization. Consequently, as an obedient member of the underground movement, he was not personally responsible for his actions. Hearing the testimony of a large number of witnesses and experts, the court found that recruiting in the Kaunas Ghetto police had been carried out on a volunteer basis. The Council of Elders had not asked political parties to delegate their members for service in the police, and no party had done so. No pressure had been exercised to keep anyone on his job. Whatever the defendant had done, he had done it on his own responsibility and had to bear the consequences. Concluding, the sentence stated: "If the defendant himself did not arrive at the only logical conclusion—i.e., that he should not be active in the leading organs of the displaced persons [Aleksandrowicz was a member of the Central Committee of the Poalei Zion-Hitachdut Party], it was the duty of the Rehabilitation Commission to arrive at such a conclusion."[22]

There were Jewish officials of moral standing and social responsibility in exposed positions who sometimes were able to improve the lot of their coreligionists, even in the Nazi labor camps. The trial of Henryk Gliksman, a foreman of the Częstochowa Ghetto and camp Elder in the Częstochowa-Rakow labor camp, is a case in point. An accusation of harmful acts against Jews had been submitted to the legal department. His trial took place in June and August 1949. The testimony of nine witnesses who were with him in the ghetto and in the camp confirmed none of the accusations. To the contrary, the witnesses testified to positive and even heroic acts by the defendant. It was revealed that Gliksman had been a confidant of the Organization of Jewish Fighters in the Częstochowa Ghetto, and on its orders had accepted exposed positions, so as to be able to help in the underground activities. Among other things he helped to organize an unsuccessful explosion of the railway tracks and was beaten by the Germans until he bled. According to the judgment, "the regime in this camp was unlike a concentration camp. Gliksman did not boss; he acted like a comrade [in time of need]. Food was better than in neighboring camps, as were clothing and medical help. No selections nor roll calls were ordered, and the inmates were given a chance to get food outside the camp. They were also given freedom of movement. Inmates were not assaulted nor were they harassed." The Court did not believe the lone witness who testified that Gliksman had assaulted inmates. Gliksman was found not guilty on all counts.[23]

The Kaunas Jewish policeman Bejnisz Tkacz was also rehabilitated. His trial took place in March and May 1948, and the majority of witnesses testified in his favor.[24]

Similarly the Białystok Jewish policeman Hersz Zlotykamień, later a clerk in the Bliżyn camp, was freed after a number of witnesses had testified about his humane attitude toward the inmates, adding that because he had refused to take part in the "resettlement," he had been demoted in his rank. On the occasion of his trial the Court of Honor took the opportunity to praise the Białystok Ghetto police for their fine attitude, as compared to police in other places; they had refused to collaborate in "resettlements" and sometimes even cooperated with the Jewish underground movement. Three of the prosecution witnesses who had testified before the police in the Landsberg DP camp in February 1946, were punished by the Rehabilitation Commission for willfully abstaining from testifying in court.[25]

Another case of rehabilitation was that of Zajnvel Zelinger, an official of the transient camp at Sosnowiec, who later became Jewish Elder in the Sackenheim labor camp and then foreman in the Blechhammer camp. He had treated Jewish camp inmates well and facilitated religious services for Orthodox Jews.[26] Another documented case is that of an inmate who held no position in the ghetto, yet requested rehabilitation by the Rehabilitation Commission following an accusation by a witness that he betrayed a group of young underground activists to the Gestapo. He was rehabilitated after a public trial.[27]

Because of the constantly fluctuating and insecure conditions of life for the displaced persons, the Courts of Honor encountered difficulties in considering accusations against defendants. Defendants and witnesses had sometimes emigrated. To give only one example: a Court of Honor at Munich considered the case against a Jewish policeman, Leon Mercel, of the Łódź Ghetto. He was accused of "carrying out shameful acts against the Jews." This accusation was based on the deposition of seven eyewitnesses. Only two were actually in court. One could not identify the defendant, and the second refused to testify. The court freed the defendant "for lack of evidence."[28]

The Courts of Honor also experienced difficulties (or perhaps one should say sabotage) caused by individual members of local camp committees and the police, with the result that some defendants did not appear in court. For instance, an accusation against Herman Altbauer, a former policeman in the Rohatyn Ghetto (Eastern Galicia), was submitted to the camp police of the displaced persons camp "Adriatica" (in Milan). The defendant was arrested and his case transferred to the local Court of Honor for trial. However, the chief of the security department, a member of the local committee, refused to transfer the investigation material, withholding it for two months without giving any reason. In the meantime, the defendant left Italy, forfeiting bail in cash, valuables, and a gold watch deposited with the camp police. Ten days after Altbauer left Italy, the police, who had neglected to arrest him, transferred his investigation papers and bail receipt to the court. In a letter dated March 23, 1948, the local court asked the Central Court of Honor in Rome how to act against this committee member who was still in office—whether to publicize the truth about the defendant's personality, what to do with the bail deposit. The answer from Rome is not preserved in the documentation. At a court meeting of May 13, 1948, it was decided to give the bail to the *Haganah* as a gift. The final outcome of the case was that the court secretary acquired the gold wristwatch for 2,000 lire at a public auction.[29]

Some central relief organizations active among displaced persons punished defendants prior to verdicts issued by the Courts of Honor. On March 28, 1949, the Central Committee of the JDC in Germany sent out a letter to its branches in Frankfurt/Main, Stuttgart, Bremen, Belsen, Berlin, and Bamberg informing them that the above-mentioned Leon Mercel, Henryk Gliksman, Henry Friedman, and two other persons were condemned as traitors to the Jewish people by the legal department of the Central Committee in Munich. Subsequently, however, only the condemnation of Friedman was confirmed by the court. Mercel and Gliksman were acquitted, and Gliksman fully rehabilitated.[30]

THE TRIALS IN THE STATE OF ISRAEL

The trials that took place in the State of Israel were conducted in an entirely different manner. They were based on the Knesset's Nazis and Nazi Collaborators (Punishment) Law 5710/1950.[31]

The law consists of 17 paragraphs dealing with crimes against the Jewish people, crimes against humanity, and war crimes. All are precisely outlined in Paragraphs 1 (*b*), 2, 3, 4 (*a*), 5 and 6.

Paragraph 9 states: "(*a*) A person who has committed an offense under this law may be tried in Israel even if he has already been tried abroad, whether before an international tribunal or a tribunal of a foreign State, for the same offense. (*b*) If a person is convicted in Israel of an offense under this law after being tried and convicted for the same act abroad, the Israeli court shall, in determining the punishment, take into consideration the sentence which he has served abroad."

According to Paragraph 10, "if a person has done or omitted to do any act, such act or omission constituting an offense under this law, the court shall release him from criminal responsibility—(a) if he did or omitted to do the act in order to save himself from the danger of immediate death threatening him, and if the court is satisfied that he did his best to avert the consequences of the act or omission; or (b) if he did or omitted to do the act with the intent to avert consequences more serious than those which resulted from the act or omission, and actually averted them; these provisions shall not, however, apply to an act or omission constituting an offense under section 1 [annihilation of the Jewish people] or section 2 (f) [murder for which capital punishment is foreseen]."

Based on this law, the courts in Israel from 1951 to 1964 tried a number of Kapos and ghetto policemen who had entered the country with the wave of mass immigration to Israel. No trials were held against former Council members. We shall here deal, for the most part, with two trials against policemen. Other trials will be discussed only insofar as they shed light on the attitudes of Israeli judges toward the question of the guilt or innocence of persons who, themselves persecuted, committed harmful deeds against their brethren on behalf of the Nazis.

The first trial in Israel against a ghetto policeman based on this law took place in the Tel Aviv criminal court in the winter of 1952. The defendant was the deputy police chief of the Ostrowiec Ghetto, Israel Moshe Puczyc. After the ghetto was liquidated in October 1942 he carried out the functions of a policeman in the Ostrowiec camp situated four kilometers from the town. The survivors of the ghetto were transferred to this camp.

Twenty-one charges were made against Puczyc, such as collaborating with the German authorities during the "resettlement action," handing over partisans to the German police, preventing escapees from other liquidated ghettos to enter the Ostrowiec Ghetto, extorting bribes in cash and valuables, keeping Jews under inhumane conditions in the ghetto jail, and assaulting inmates, first in the ghetto and later in the camp.

A large number of witnesses testified for the prosecution; some others testified for the defense. The accusations were actually based on the testimony of a single witness. The court believed none of the witnesses for the prosecution because they contradicted themselves (some of them had signed a certificate of moral behavior for the benefit of the defendant prior to the trial). A verdict of not guilty was passed on March 10, 1952.

The court found that the defendant could not be held responsible for carrying out the orders of the German authorities because his own life would have been in danger if he had refused—a circumstance which had been anticipated in Paragraph 10 (a) of the law. In the concluding paragraphs of the verdict the court analyzed the reasons that had motivated so many people to come and accuse the defendant of so many grave crimes. It was the court's opinion that the defendant went too far in his eagerness to put an end to base aspects of life in the ghetto, especially the activities of so-called "jumpers,"* who maintained that they were entitled to inherit ownerless Jewish valuables. They could not forgive the defendant for confiscating the goods, cash, and valuables that were carried into the ghetto, and, therefore, had accused him of persecuting them for his own personal profit. The court accepted his statement that the ghetto police had to root out the activities of the "jumpers" so that the authorities would not learn about them. The court also gave credence to the defendant's statement that the confiscated articles were used to buy clothing for the poor or to bribe the Germans, though a considerable amount went to a number of policemen for their own private use. These witnesses had testified out of hatred for the defendant. Because of feuds that had broken out between them and the defendant, they had made serious accusations which proved to be groundless. The court stated that other witnesses were people embittered because of the calamity that had befallen their families. They made a scapegoat of the defendant, a man of higher education and of dynamic personality who had achieved a leading position in the ghetto and in the camp. They also accused him of other incidents, witnessed by themselves or told about by others, without knowledge of the circumstances and all the facts involved.[32]

Hersz Bernblat, deputy chief of the Będzin Ghetto police, was sentenced on February 5, 1954, to a jail term of five years by the district court in Tel Aviv-Jaffa. The Supreme Court quashed the sentence.

---

* These were people who took chances by "jumping" out of the ghetto to bring back some of the valuables abandoned in the "Aryan" parts of town by Jews forced to move into the ghetto. They were paid high prices for their services. Often disputes broke out between the "jumpers" and the owners, who accused them of refusing to return smuggled goods.

In the verdicts of the district court in Tel Aviv and of the Supreme Court in Jerusalem, opinions were given about the situation and attitude of the Jews during the Nazi era in general, and in particular about the problems the Councils and the ghetto police faced. As these opinions are of great importance to the historian, we shall here examine them in some detail, without, however, going into the fine legal points touched upon by the judges.

Bernblat was sentenced on two counts by the district court: (a) for carrying children from the orphan home and handing them over to the Germans during the "action" of August 1942, and (b) for not allowing people destined for deportation, or whose fate was yet undecided, to join the group of people who were to be left in the ghetto or sent to labor places.

The verdict of the district court contains a lengthy analysis of Moshe Merin's rescue strategy, as described by one of the witnesses (see Chap. 16):

It does not seem to us that the Israeli legislator intended, in Paragraph 10 (b) of the law, to justify assistance in handing over thousands of Jews to the Nazis in order to postpone the end of the rest by severing the [gangrened] arm, to use Merin's expression. This is no more than a paraphrase for the sacrifice of thousands of souls, mostly of old people, children, the ill, and the weak, in order to delay the war of destruction against the community, in the hope that part of the people would be lucky enough to see the end of the bloody hunt.

Neither does it seem to us that the legislator intended to justify, in this paragraph, the decision as to what part of the people was to be considered a gangrened arm, requiring severance from the body in order to arrest the spread of the gangrene in the entire body. . . . This is synonymous with the decision as to who is superior to whom, or who is to be killed in order to postpone the end of another, in the hope that the latter will reach the end of the road and will be rescued. There were limits to this "psychology" . . . as long as it did not affect the [interested] person himself and the members of his family. Moreover, insofar as the proponents of this "psychology" are concerned, their honest intention of rescuing a remainder by this method was intermingled with egoistic intentions to preserve themselves, their families, and close friends. In other words, the intention of the legislator was not to justify assistance in sacrificing thousands of Jews in order to forestall grave consequences to thousands of other Jews. . . .

The judges of the district court were cognizant of the fact that not always would the historical and psychological criteria of this case correspond to the legal criteria of the legislator and that, therefore, the study of the character of Moniek Merin, Mołczadski and the Będzin Jewish Council should be left to the historians. "But we, the Judges of Israel, are bound to implement the will of the legislator, which is the will of the people. In our opinion, the defense did not succeed in provin that the policy adopted by Merin and Mołczadski fits the text of Paragraph 10 (*b*)."[33]

But the Supreme Court was of another opinion. After an analysis of various opinions in Jewish society of the problem of the rescue strategy, and after corroborating the opinion of the district court that this is a historical problem and not a legal one, the court's president (Mr. Olshan) issued a verdict that the forced delivery of victims by the Council and the ghetto police in order to save the majority of ghetto inmates from greater immediate danger indeed fell under the provisions of Paragraph 10 (*b*) of the law. He gave an imaginary case as an example to support his opinion: Suppose the Nazis had ordered the delivery of 1,000 forced laborers, threatening immediately to deport 10,000 people if the order was not carried out; if the Council and the police delivered the ordered quota, they would fall under the provision of Paragraph 10 (*b*). The court chairman cautioned, however, that not all of what the Council did is liable to fall under the provision of this paragraph, for the question of "avoiding worse consequences" has to be decided in the context of the circumstances and events of the time. He rejected the interpretation found in the district court's verdict, that the results which the defendant endeavored to avoid (shots fired into a crowd by the German guard) could have been worse than the measures the defendant had applied, for this was not what the legislator had in mind.[34]

Another problem that was considered by both the district court and the Supreme Court was membership in an inimical (in fact, criminal) organization—Paragraph 3 (*a*) of the law—in the sense of Paragraph 9 of the statutes of the International Military Tribunal, as attached to the Agreement of the Big Four of August 8, 1945. Both courts were unanimous that membership in the Jewish Councils or the ghetto police did not fall under this paragraph, for the law had not considered them criminal organizations. (It should be mentioned that they were labeled as such in the indictment, but the prosecutor withdrew this charge in the course of the Court's proceedings.[35]) The Courts of Honor of the displaced persons adopted a similar policy (see p.550).

The third question considered by the courts was the nature of the collaboration of the Councils with the German occupiers. In the verdict issued by the district court the testimonies against the Councils and the strategy of collaboration were stressed. One has the impression that to some extent the court agreed with these witnesses.[36]

The relevant part of the verdict begins with this statement:

... In order to carry out their satanic plan with maximum efficiency they [the Nazis] used camouflaged methods, spreading deceitful information, using methods of psychological warfare, and exploiting human weakness. The Councils, ostensibly established to organize life in the ghettos as a sort of continuation of previous Jewish communities, were subordinated to their [the Nazis'] will. By intimidation, heavy pressure, blackmail, punitive measures, deceitful promises, and lies . . . they were gradually transformed into tools in their hands, so that it was easier [for them] to carry out their shameful activities. They [the Councils] were given authority by the Nazis, a sort of internal autonomy of eternal slaves, which turned them into oppressors of their brethren. And the instrument of this authority was the ghetto police.[37]

On the other hand, the Supreme Court analyzed the problem of collaboration more thoroughly, including the controversial points, but without identifying itself with any. Here is an excerpt from Judge Olshan's analysis:

... The very existence of the Jewish Councils and the Jewish police and the carrying out of their regular functions was of help to the Nazis. Otherwise the Nazis could have had no interest in their establishment and in continuing their existence. . . . They were established in occupied Poland and in other areas of the Holocaust in almost every town. The Councils differed, and it may be assumed that they were far from uniform with respect to resisting the Nazis or preferring suicide to the implementation of Nazi orders. They also differed in personal wisdom and in success at easing persecutions or maneuvering the delay of deportations for exterminations and the like. Jewish society was confused, particularly so during the first years of the Holocaust, before the Nazi methods of deceit became known. The masses relied on these bodies [the Councils] in the hope that they would be able, by legal or illicit means, to rescue, or at least to delay [oppressions]. But when they were unsuccessful and, as certainly happened, the Councils appeared cruel because of the necessity to accept lesser evils, a feeling of bitterness became widespread against them and the police. . . . When the details of the catastrophe became known, a debate started within Jewish society— which is continuous up to now and which apparently will never end— about the right and fitting path for the Jews and their leaders to have taken in the areas of the Holocaust.

Judge Olshan, discussing the opinions expressed by opponents of the Councils, summarized them in this sentence: "According to them, it is perhaps altogether impossible to talk about good or bad Councils, for the very existence of this institution and of the Jewish police . . . should [in advance] be condemned, and they themselves and their very remembrance punished with the pillory."

Judge Olshan had this to say of the defenders of the Jewish Councils:

. . . there are others who maintain that its not possible to think of those days in the abstract. . . . Facing a horrible, tragic situation, the Jewish leaders . . . on whom the terrible burden had been imposed were forced to become obedient to the Nazis while maneuvering, calculating, and hoping to weaken orders [in an effort] to rescue [victims] or to postpone executions. They could not but appear cruel, or perhaps traitors, in the eyes of unfortunates who themselves or members of their families had been shipped to the camps—and this despite the fact that the majority of Councilmen and policemen were murdered too. In any event, even extreme critics advance no accusation that *it was the aim* [italics in the text] of the Councils or the Jewish police to assist the Nazis in the extermination of the Jews.[38]

Another important question was touched upon in both these sentences: the moral criteria necessary to evaluate the deeds of people serving on the Councils and police. The district court disqualified the defendant on moral grounds: able to resign, he did not do so for egoistic reasons, although after the selection in a neighboring ghetto he was aware of the fate of people not included in the privileged groups.

The astonishing fact characteristic of that era is that in the [prevailing] atmosphere of extreme pressure . . . morality and values changed, and petty people, though educated and friendly [as is the defendant], were not loath to use rescue means that incorporated the necessity of handing over their brethren to the Nazi killers. . . . The Israeli legislator did not wish to forgive these petty, friendly people, normal ones for normal times, who out of egoistic reasons sinned against the Jewish people in those anomalous times.[39]

However, the third member of the Supreme Court, Dr. Landau, expressed in his conclusion the opinion that people who had never experienced a situation similar to that of the defendant should not accuse "these 'puny people' because they did not rise to a high moral level at a time when they were being persecuted by an authority whose supreme aim was to deprive them of God's image. We should not interpret the basis of the individual crime, as formulated in the Nazis and Nazi Collaborators (Punishment) Law, by a yardstick of moral behavior of which only a few were capable." For this reason Judge Landau was against the negative evaluation by the judges of the district court of the egoistic reasons for the defendant's decision to join the militia and remain there: "Every one cares for himself and his family, and the prohibitions of criminal law, including the Nazis and Nazi Collaborators (Punishment) Law, were not written for heroes, extraordinary individuals, but for simple mortals with their simple weaknesses."[40]

There were also differences between the opinions of the district court and the Supreme Court in interpreting the meaning of "help in handing over the persecuted to inimical authorities" in relation to the role of the Jewish police during the deportation of Jews for forced labor. In the judgment of the district court this role (catching and dragging people from hiding, according to lists prepared by the Councils, and keeping them in the police jail until they were delivered to collecting camps, etc.) fell under Paragraph 26 (6) 2 of the criminal law, which considers it a crime to help others to commit a crime.[41] But the Supreme Court, in the opinion of Judge Landau, stated that the role of the Jewish police in this instance "should not be considered an act of help in the meaning of criminal law, for he [the defendant] had no criminal intent to force the Jews to labor, and acted under pressure and force."[42]

H. Cohn, another judge of the Supreme Court, in his opinion stated that the role of the Jewish police in sending people to forced labor should be judged in light of its merits, covered in Paragraph

10 (*b*) of the law of 1950, for ". . . had these people not been shipped to labor camps they would have been deported to the death camps."[43]

If it is right to criticize a court sentence, it should be pointed out that this interpretation by Judge Cohn cannot pass the test of historical fact. Sending Jews to camps had begun in 1940, two years prior to the "resettlements" to Auschwitz from Upper Eastern Silesia. At that time the Jewish police could not act *with intent* in the meaning of Paragraph 10 (*b*), e.g., "avoidance of worse results." Nobody then yet knew about them. True, a larger percentage of people sent to the forced-labor camps survived than those who remained in the ghettos. But this is an objective fact after the event, and whether or not it can serve *ex post facto* as a basis for interpretation in accordance with Paragraph 10 (*b*) is open for discussion.

CHAPTER 21

Conclusions

WE HAVE REACHED THE END of our study, and it is time to formulate our conclusions. Two periods can be discerned in the history of the Jewish Councils, with the "resettlement actions" as a borderline. During the initial period, when the authorities requested cooperation in the seizure of Jewish property and delivery of Jewish laborers to places of work or to labor camps, the moral responsibility that weighed on the Councils was still bearable. They could justify their cooperation by reasoning that in carrying out German demands they helped to prolong the life of the ghetto, making it useful to the authorities as a source of material gain, and of slave labor for the Nazi war economy, almost free of charge. The situation became morally unbearable when, during the mass "resettlement actions," the Germans forced the Councils and the Jewish police to carry out the preparatory work and to participate in the initial stages of the actual deportation. The latter task was forced mainly upon the Jewish police. The Councils then faced a tragic dilemma never before experienced by a community respresentative organ. Cooperation then reached the morally dangerous borderline of collaboration. The Councils were called upon to make fateful decisions on the life and death of certain segments of their coreligionists. There were Council chairmen in the large ghettos who even then found justification for cooperating with the authorities. However, there were numerous instances where Council members, including chairmen, resisted this delusive temptation, committing suicide or going to execution in the gas chambers together with their families. Others took the perilous path of resistance.

No historian of the catastrophe era can escape raising the question: Did the Councils in their strategy toward the Germans really exercise some justifiable policy that warranted, at least in their own minds, the hope of a delay or amelioration of the ominous end? Therefore the researcher has also to face up to the question of motivation. He may, after a thorough analysis of the pertinent material, arrive at the conclusion that the Councils had no such policy, or that it was wrong, even criminal. But under no circumstances is the historian free from raising the question, unless he starts from the assumption that the Council members were all scoundrels who, for the price of saving themselves and their relatives, agreed to go into partnership with the SS men in the destruction of their own brethren. We have discussed this problem in detail in Chap. 16.

The nature of the Councils' cooperation with the occupation authorities is another problem. It is frequently defined as collaboration, but it is necessary to consider this definition, however briefly.

Stanley Hoffman, the Harvard University professor of history, delivered a lecture at the American Historical Association in December 1966 entitled "Collaboration in France during World War II." In the course of his lecture he made a distinction between collaboration in general and the collaboration of the Vichy government with the occupation authorities in France, which he labeled *collaboration d'État*. Here is a quotation from his paper:

There was, on the one hand, *collaboration with Germany* for reasons of state, i.e., to safeguard French interests in inter-state relations between the beaten power and the victor. This was to a large extent the necessary if undesired by-product of the existence of a French state in Vichy. Even here, what is most enlightening is not the story of French negotiation with, concessions to, or resistance to German officials, but the contrast between Vichy's theory of [limited] independence and Vichy's practice: a contrast imposed by the realities of France's situation. On the other hand, there was *collaboration with the Nazis* in the sense of an openly desired cooperation with and imitation of the German regime [quite apart from any concern for the interests of France]. We find in collaborationism not so much seduction by or fascination with the Nazis (although there was some) as a means to a variety of internal ends. (Stencil 1, pp. 2-3.)

We think that the Councils' collaboration with the Germans can, *mutatis mutandis,* be defined as *collaboration d'État,* a term which is closer to our definition of "cooperation." Considering their tasks, cooperation with the authorities was unavoidable for the Councils. The very rationale for their existence would have vanished without it.

The Councils had to maintain daily contacts with the Germans in such matters as food, delivery of forced laborers, collection of imposed material *Leistungen,* filling production orders for ghetto industry, permission for import of raw materials, carrying out of some welfare activities—medical or sanitary services, education of children, etc.

It was stated in official German pronouncements that the Councils represented the interests of the Jews. There even was a Council (in Będzin) where this task was mentioned in its title: *Interessenvertretung der jüdischen Kultusgemeinde in Bendsburg.* Thus the Councils were made to believe that they would really be able to protect Jewish interests.

For purposes of comparison, it should be remembered that cooperation between the indigent non-Jewish population and the authorities took place throughout the occupied territories. Hundreds of thousands of officials and workers from among the local population (in the Government General alone their number reached 260,000 persons according to a report by Frank of January 1944) served in the German administrative, economic, judicial, and even police apparatuses. Without their assistance it would have been impossible for the Germans to administer and dominate the occupied lands. No accusations of collaboration were advanced against these people after the war, except in some individual cases of overt criminal acts committed against the population in the occupied territories.

There were, however, basic differences between non-Jewish collaboration and Jewish cooperation.

1. Collaboration of non-Jews was on a *voluntary* basis, either because of sharing the National Socialist ideology, or because of opportunity for personal gain (career, authority, etc.), or in order to let off pentup hatred toward the Jews, or because of a lust to rob and kill. This category includes Jewish Gestapo agents and the demoralized members of the Councils and the ghetto police who served the German authorities in order to gain privileges and material goods for themselves and their families. In contrast, the co-

operation of the Councils with the Germans was forced upon the Jews and was maintained in at atmosphere of ever-present merciless terror.

2. Diametrically different were German aims with regard to non-Jewish collaborationists, as compared to Jewish ones. Toward the former their aims were political and tactical: to infect with propaganda and morally disarm the local population in order to neutralize the anti-Nazi movement. But with respect to the Jews, the imposed cooperation was aimed at accomplishing the special tasks of an instrument for carrying out all anti-Jewish persecution measures, including self-destruction, with the Council members and the Jewish police themselves as the final victims.

3. The non-Jewish collaborationists greatly profited from the fruits of their cooperation, sharing the material privileges of the German authority apparatus. They were considered allies in the future "New Europe," while the Councils, as a rule, acted under conditions of constant physical and spiritual degradation, always on the brink of the abyss, with the threat of being thrown into it hanging over them all the time. They were treated as enemies by the Nazis, as were all Jews.

However, cooperation with the Germans was a threat to spineless Council members. They were in danger of going to the extreme in cooperating with the Nazis, not so much in the illusory belief of interceding for the common good of the Jews as for their own benefit. In an atmosphere of moral nihilism, corruption of Nazi officialdom, and inhuman terror, it was not easy for such Council members to be on guard against crossing the fine demarcation line between cooperation and collaboration. Compelled to adjust themselves to the mentality of their German bosses, some of the Council members were disposed to adopt their methods. They were often forced to do so. There were also Councilmen with a compulsive urge to rule, and participation in the Councils provided them with the opportunity of relieving their lust for authority and honor; for this they felt obligated to the Germans.

Here we come to yet another aspect characteristic of the cooperation of the Jewish Councils with the Germans: the seeming "authority." The Jewish Councils got from the Nazis functions which had not been carried out for ages by Jewish community representatives. Since the Middle Ages, no other Jewish body had exercised so much economic, administrative, judicial, and police authority. This alleged "authority" could corrupt many Council members or chairmen. For the price of continuing in office (and this could happen only at the mercy of the Nazis) they entered into open or covert collaboration.

In this connection the question should be raised whether the Councils were a German or a Jewish institution. In the first place it should be mentioned that the Councils were not established in a social vacuum. There were many instances where the Councils came about on the initiative of prewar community leaders and other people active in civic work. On many occasions these people, who at the beginning of the occupation voluntarily interceded with the occupation authorities (at that time, the military) on behalf of the oppressed Jews, later were nominated to serve on the Councils.

The membership of numerous Councils was, in fact, an extension of the prewar *Kehila* bodies. In other cases, representatives of prewar institutions and organizations with long-time experience were nominated. According to our poll, of 740 Council members 43 percent had been active in *Kehilas* and municipal organs before the war.

The argument that the Councils were a German institution because they were established on German orders is not valid at all. All of the community representatives for hundreds of years in Jewish Diaspora history had been established by orders of various governments. They did not fail to be Jewish institutions for all that.

As to the argument that they served the interests of the state, it should be mentioned that from the earliest times all *Kehila* bodies served to some extent the interests of the state, especially in fiscal matters, and were collectively responsible for Jewish taxes, e.g., in Czarist Russia until the middle of the nineteenth century. The *Vaad Arba Aratzot* (the Council of Four Lands, an autonomous Jewish governing body in Poland from the sixteenth to the eighteenth centuries) was dissolved in 1764 by the Polish Sejm (Parliament) because it had not been effective enough for the fiscal interests of the state treasury. Thus serving the interests of the state was not a new task for the Jewish Councils. The horrible difference between the *Kehila* bodies of the past and the Jewish Councils was that for the first time in Jewish history a Jewish organ was forced to help a foreign, criminal regime to destroy coreligionists. The name of the institution should therefore be *Yidnrat* in Yiddish, as opposed to the German name, *Judenrat*. Incidentally the term *Yidnrat* was used, as already mentioned, in the minutes of meetings of the Białystok Jewish Council.

It follows from our study that the phenomenon of the Jewish Councils should be discussed in the framework of Jewish history, and not as a unique and queer episode. The researcher of the Holocaust is not free from looking for historical analogies between the situations the Councils faced and those the *Kehila* leaders of old dealt with. Despite all the differences of the Nazi era, as compared with other dark times in Jewish history, we believe that a historical comparison between the role of the *Kehilas* during the *Kantonist* era, for instance, in the first half of the nineteenth century in Czarist Russia, may prevent us from considering the Jewish Councils as a one-time phenomenon without any parallel in Jewish history.

Appendix I

ANALYSIS OF THE EVALUATION OF THE BEHAVIOR

OF JEWISH COUNCIL MEMBERS IN OUR POLL AND

IN SOME EYEWITNESS ACCOUNTS

ACCORDING TO THE DATA collected in our poll, almost 62 percent of those questioned evaluated the activities of members of the Jewish Councils positively; 14 percent gave a negative opinion; and 16.4 percent expressed mixed opinions. Over 8 percent gave no answer to this opinion or had no opinion ("hard to say"). In other words, almost one-quarter of the persons polled avoided a clearcut answer. It is clear that the last two categories had inhibitions of moral or social nature.

The attitudes toward the Councils were controversial in the Holocaust literature from the start, with negative evaluations prevailing. Even now the survivors continue to discuss the policies of the Councils heatedly. No doubt the persons polled had been influenced by the controversy and were reluctant to give their own opinions, though they were assured of full discretion. A contributing factor in their reticence was that, with few exceptions, the very Councilmen of whom negative opinions were given perished as martyrs together with the other ghetto inmates (only 12% survived). There certainly were reasons enough for individuals of high moral standards to abstain from giving a negative opinion. *De mortuis aut bene aut nihil*, particularly when speaking about innocent victims. We also have to consider that the attitude toward and the evaluation of a Council by an individual may well be influenced by his personal experience and encounters with a particular Councilman or Council as a whole, and whether the individual got favors or was ill-treated (the objective situation in the ghetto dictated that favors could be given only at the expense of another person, as, for example, in the matters of being sent to forced labor, distribution of food cards, placing of one's name on deportation lists, etc.). All these subjective, collective, and personal circumstances have to be considered while drawing any conclusion about the numerical results of the answers in this column of our questionnaire.

Our task was easier in cases where we could confront the evaluations of two or three persons polled about the same Councilman or policeman. But, as has been indicated above, this could be done only with respect to 57 Councilmen, not enough to draw valid conclusions. About only three persons did we receive contradictory evaluations. We shall try to analyze two of them.

Questionnaire No. 42 contains the following description of the chief of the labor office in Rohatyn: "An honest man, behaved correctly." But in questionnaire No. 664, we read the following about the same man: "He used his office for his own gains, obediently following German orders. From morning to late at night he watched to see how the workers carried out their tasks. He kept an eye on those working for the *Kreishauptmannschaft*. He was an egoist by nature and let people toil for him. As far as I knew, his entire family was egoistic. He was prone to boss people, but was not as coarse as others. He worked conscientiously to the very end. He hoped that he would be able to save himself and his family. Nothing more bothered him."

The two questionnaires also differed with regard to the man's fate: No. 42 relates that he died of typhoid in 1943, but No. 664 says that he perished in the course of the final liquidation of the ghetto in June 1943. Of the two persons polled, No. 42, a woman, maintained personal relations with the chief of the labor department, working as a bookkeeper for him before the war. On the other hand, No. 664 ("a resident of Rohatyn who was an inmate of the ghetto") had no direct relations with him. It is, therefore, possible that the personal relations of No. 42 may have influenced her evaluation, which was not the case with No. 664, though he may have been influenced by other reasons. Generally speaking, No. 664 is better informed than No. 42, who, for instance, could not tell what sort of job the Councilman had held in the Council. Moreover, No. 664 tried to be objective in his opinion. He says, for instance, that "he was not as coarse as others." There emerges from the character drawn by No. 664 a Councilman obediently carrying out German orders to the very last. It is hard now to say whether he did so because of his own intention "to save himself and his family," as the witness implied, particularly as he stated in the next line that "he had his own opinion and nobody could convince him that he was wrong in his judgment of the real circumstances." The witness does not say what the opinion was. We may, however, assume with considerable certainty that he belonged to the supporters of the policy prevalent within the majority of the Councils, that by devotedly working for the Germans the Jews would become useful to them and thus would be able to head off the danger of death, or at least gain time until liberation came. This must have been the reason for his severe treatment of forced laborers, from whom he demanded efficient work.

We shall proceed now to evaluate the second chairman of the Głębokie Jewish Council. No. 375 gives a succinct, clearcut description: "A cruel, obedient, corrupt executioner of Gestapo orders, lived in comfort at the expense of the ghetto inmates, was corrupt, followed in the steps of the former chairman, L." On the other hand, No. 701 states:

> He was a quiet man, no bluffer, with a correct attitude toward people. . . . He did favors for some, but harmed others. People now have various opinions about him. Some say that he was not the worst chairman. As compared to [the first chairman], L., he was a just man. I know of many cases where he kept quiet when, after the liquidation of the Dokszyce Ghetto, some of the Jews illegally came to the Głębokie Ghetto which, under the circumstances, meant to escape death [one such case was cited by the witness]. He was also aware of the fact that the underground movement was active in the ghetto and that some inmates were making preparations to escape. True, he tried to persuade them not to leave because it could result in a disaster for the ghetto.

The witness expresses his understanding for this attitude saying:

> I understand that, as chairman, he was responsible for the ghetto, and no reproach can be made against him for opposing the endeavors of the young people to join the partisans. Happily, they did not listen to him. A large part actually escaped into the forests and many Głębokie residents and nonresidents thus saved themselves.

Comparing those two evaluations we see that No. 375 gives an outright negative verdict which he, however, fails to support with facts, though our poll-takers, according to instructions, always tried to elicit from the witnesses concrete facts. On the other hand, No. 701 bases his evaluation on facts, trying to give a balanced and objective opinion about the second ghetto Council chairman at Głębokie. He tells of the divided opinion among surviving inmates of the Głębokie Ghetto, and that the chairman did favors to some and harmed others, without, however, explicitly mentioning the harmful deeds. He even understands the chairman's opposition to the escape movement from the ghetto, though he, personally, does not agree with this. We may assume that No. 701 gives a more balanced, and, therefore, a more objective evaluation of the second chairman of the Głębokie Council.

Next we shall examine two evaluations (Nos. 679 and 680) regarding the chief of the sanitary department, a physician by profession, in the ghetto of Sokołów Podlaski. Questionnaire No. 679 was answered by the former chief of the welfare department of that ghetto (branch of the JSS?). He states:

> . . . he established the sanitary department of the Council and was its chief. He made it his duty to wipe out the typhus epidemic and to take care of the hygiene of the ghetto inmates. . . . He organized two hospitals in the ghetto and gave medical help to patients who could not find hospital accommodations. But he was greedy and was ready to work day and night to earn more money. His ambition was to thoroughly cure the patient, but for a fee. He made no home calls free of charge. The Council quarreled about this with him, requesting that he help, without exception, the rich and the poor alike, but the doctor wanted the Council to pay for the poor patients. He was a hard man. A good physician, he lacked the understanding one expects from a doctor, was not gentle in his approach to the sick, not given to small talk. . . . In his capacity as chief of the sanitation department of the Council, he used to check the conditions of the homes and backyards. People in the street could hear how he yelled and scolded, threatening to impose penalties upon inmates whose homes he found not clean enough. . . . He used to say: "If I didn't yell, people would drown in filth." Dr. Hermann, the German boss of Sokołów Podlaski, disliked him: he didn't deliver enough death certificates.

Let's now turn to the other Sokołów Podlaski Ghetto resident (No. 680) and see what he says:

> . . . Raised and educated in an assimilationist environment, he could not adjust himself to life among the local Jews [in 1941 the Council had brought him in from the Warsaw Ghetto, where he had lived as a refugee from the town of Łęczyce]. He charged for the treatment of patients according to his own "price list." . . . He had no compassion for the poor. He pretended not to know that poor patients sold their clothing to pay for a visit. He did not stand up to his heavy moral responsibility as the sole physician of such an important community. The Jews of Sokołów Podlaski hated him for his heartless greed. He believed that he would be able to rescue himself if he acquired enough ransom money for the Germans. . . . But I must admit that he was a very diligent man, despite his faults. . . . Despite the ghetto conditions, he established two hospitals and worked on the Sanitation Commission. He was in charge of fighting the typhus epidemic, and keeping Jewish homes clean.

Both these descriptions agree on the activities of the doctor and on his character. Both stress that he was a greedy man. No. 679 explains that the reason why he refused to treat patients free of charge, which is a legitimate request in normal times, was that he requested that the Council, which paid him for his work in the hospital, also pay for the treatment of private indigent patients outside the hospital. No. 680

points out one more reason—the urge to accumulate enough ransom money to pay off the Germans. Both, however, portray him as a man of hard character, without compassion for the sick. No. 680 says that he was heartless, with no pity, and tries to explain the physician's acts as the result of alienation from the Jewish community on the part of one who "was raised in an assimilationist environment." It should be added that because of his character traits he could not adjust himself to life in the, for him, strange circumstances. Both, however, stress his energy, diligence, and integrity in organizing medical services in the ghetto and in taking measures to fight the typhus epidemic. Last but not least, there emerges from both questionnaires a picture of the enormously difficult tasks a Jewish physician (the only one at that) faced amid the inhumanly unsanitary conditions of the ghetto (which were no fault of the inmates). His was a very taxing, almost impossible job, and this most probably was the reason for his stern measures to secure a level of sanitary conditions in the ghetto.

We also have two different descriptions about N.L., the chairman of the Sokołów Podlaski Ghetto Council. It is worthwhile to quote from both. One describes him in the following terms:

To the extent that I knew him, he was not ill-natured, but not sufficiently able to evaluate reality. . . . He was a strong believer in the opinion that the more money the Germans got out of the Jews, the easier it would be to gain concessions from them. And he blindly believed in German promises. Also, he overestimated his possibilities . . . and saw himself as the Messiah of the Jews at Sokołów Podlaski. . . . The office of the chairman made him lose his mental stability, and being a man of erratic behavior people had no great confidence in him. He liked to do favors only to those who always agreed with him, but was merciless toward those whom he disliked. He tried to secure food and medical help for the ghetto . . . to see that the two ghetto hospitals received . . . medicine [which due to his wide contacts he got on the "Aryan" side] (No. 678).

In the other questionnaire (No. 681) we read:

. . . During those fateful days Jews saw in him their sole savior, but he handled his fateful tasks as trivial, frivolous mercantile calculations [meaning bribes]. . . . He succeeded in rescuing some Jews [who were caught smuggling on the highways] by asking for their release and paying ransom money. People believed that he was in a position to get concessions from the Germans [he even brought back some of those seized to work at building the Treblinka camp]. These deals made him rich fast. At a time of hunger in the ghettos he lacked nothing. . . . He was the sole authority in the ghetto. . . . L. extorted money by various means, from the rich and the poor. The Germans considered him "a useful Jew," and for the Jews he was the savior from death.

Both these descriptions give similar portrayals of the chairman of the Sokołów Podlaski Ghetto, but in No. 681 his negative traits of character dominate. The reason may, perhaps, be the fact that the witness himself, his sister-in-law, and her fiancé were mistreated by him: he had placed the witness on the list of forced laborers for Treblinka, though he previously obtained a permit for him to go to Warsaw for an operation; and the fiancé of the sister-in-law was alledgedly shot because of the chairman's greediness.

Both descriptions portray a Council chairman whose sudden, unexpected power "unbalanced him," who was contradictory in his behavior, sure of himself and his policy that by bribing the Germans he would obtain all of what he desired from them, and even stop the deportations. He needed a lot of money for his German bosses and was not too choosy in his dealings. According to Questionnaire No. 681, he himself profited from the dealings. His limited intellectual capacity and self-assurance, coupled with his belief in the magical force of bribes, made it possible for him to feed the ghetto inmates false promises that diminished their alertness. It is symptomatic that when, at the concluding prayers on Yom Kippur 1942, a Jewish policeman learned that the Germans were ready to liquidate the ghetto and accordingly informed the chairman, he invited the inmates to his house for *Kiddush*, appealing to them to stay calm, because "as long as I am among you, you may feel secure." But the liquidation of the ghetto was carried out the same night and "almost nobody could escape" (No. 681).

We shall now examine some of the purely negative evaluations. We shall take as a sample the second chairman of the Będzin Council of Elders, M. The evaluation of his personal characteristics and activities is contained in three questionnaires (Nos. 103, 146, and 689). The evaluation of No. 103 is succinct: "Carried out the German orders with the greatest severity." No. 146 was more explicit: "Obediently and devotedly carried out the orders of the Gestapo and M. Merin regarding Jews deported to Auschwitz. But at the same time he cared for the children in the orphanage, secured food for them with no profit for himself, and also provided food for the Borochov-kibbutz." It is evident that No. 146, who, as he put it, knew M. "from my own personal experiences and contacts during the war," tried to find some positive features in his behavior. He even mentions as a "virtue" the fact that he did not extort money for personal gain. The evaluation of No. 689, a party comrade of M., an official of the Będzin Jewish Council and a member of the Zionist underground movement, takes up four large pages. We shall make here only a few quotations:

. . . Right from the first day he became Merin's right hand, his and the Gestapo's devoted servant. . . . He shared with Merin responsibility for all the bad deeds of the Będzin Jewish Council. Always before a deportation M. tried in various ways to convince the Jews that nothing wrong was going to happen to them. Thus, for instance, on August 11, 1942 [on the eve of the "selection" for deportation], he addressed them in the following words: "Jews, put on your holiday clothing and joyfully proceed to the indicated assembly places. Nobody stay home." He who would not report would not be allowed to remain in Zagłębie thereafter. He ruled in the Jewish Council with a strong arm. . . . As he was a recent newcomer in Będzin [born in Baranowicze, he had been sent to work for the Jewish National Fund in Będzin before the war], he had no sympathy for the Będzin Jews and acted disgracefully during the large-scale deportation of 5,000 Jews in June 1942. He used to say: "I do not debate with the Germans." He proved himself a mean scoundrel, trampling on the heads of people.

The witness was in a delegation of Zionist Labor groups asking to free two Council officials from the duty to serve in the ghetto police: one a member of the Hitachdut and another from the Poalei Zion Left group.

The delegation pointed out that these two men and the underground movement in general were against serving in the police. The chairman's answer was: "I am not a Jewish representative and am acting here on behalf of the Gestapo. I am the boss here and things will happen as I wish." Still, because the men had the support of the party underground, he had to release them as unfit for police duty. . . . He fought everyone who opposed Merin. He used to scream: "Whatever Merin does is good—he is a God-blessed leader." He was also responsible for the misdeeds of the police in the course of carrying out his orders. He behaved as a beast much as the police did in the time of expulsions and actions.

The witness also related that the well-known underground activist Frumka Płotnicka once criticized the chairman for behavior unbecoming a former party member. When he gave her a rude answer, she slapped him in his face, saying that he could now go and report to the Gestapo that she had hit him in the face. The witness concluded that "out of fear of revenge by the underground he kept quiet about the incident."

The conclusions of the three evaluations are clear enough. We have here a representative of a Council who was a follower of the policy in which some other Council members also believed, that by offering the Nazi Moloch hundreds they would be able to save thousands, and that no moral canons were admissible in applying this policy. No. 689 clearly states that M. considered Merin a "God-blessed leader," and he fell under his spell without reservations. Carrying out drastic measures inadmissible from the point of view of moral standards, he evoked a deep negative reaction on the part of those who revolted against them, which in turn influenced the witnesses in their evaluation of the ethical standards of the men responsible for the measures.

We shall now briefly scrutinize three more witness accounts, all relating to the Świsłocz Jewish Council.

I.L., a former resident of that ghetto, gave a lengthy evaluation of the activities of the Świsłocz Ghetto Council. He accused it of enriching itself to the detriment of the ghetto inmates, of committing fraud in the course of sending people to forced labor, and even of "betrayal." But another survivor, B.A., wrote: "Everyone was aware that the Council was not to blame for people's being sent to forced labor. One believed that one would save one's life by working diligently, devotedly." He also related that if one had been assigned to forced-labor duty on one day, the Council secretary, F.K., sent him to do easier work the next day. He portrayed the Council chairman, S., as "a good man," and told how he and the secretary had tried to convince German overseers not to kill Jewish forced laborers. The third witness related that after the ghetto had been established, the Council had to struggle with egoistic people who had always resided in the places now designated as the ghetto, and who refused to share their homes with those unfortunate ones expelled from their former homes. The Council forced them to let these people into their homes.

H.E., the poll-taker in New York, was critical of the first witness. He wrote: "His remarks about the Council were dictated by personal motives, for according to information from other sources, or witnesses, the Council did everything in its power to make [the life] of the Świsłocz Jews easier." The poll-taker did not indicate what reasons motivated the negative attitude of the witness. We may assume that the witness, who had escaped before the "resettlement" and later joined the partisans, was opposed to the Council's policy (intercession, bribery). In retrospect, when, after the war, he returned as a decorated partisan from the Soviet Union, he evaluated the Council's activities along the lines popular with the Jewish partisans. He was not personally abused by the Council. To the contrary, he admits that he was permitted to stay in the ghetto illegally and was spared from forced-labor duty.

The material cited is sufficient to illustrate how complicated the problem of objective evaluation is, both with respect to the behavior of individual members of Councils and of Councils as a whole. The researcher faces grave psychological problems grappling with the analysis, particularly so because it is not easy to perceive now the specific climate of those "times with no precedent" and the spirit of people who lived and acted under unimaginable conditions of stress, on the brink of an abyss that constantly threatened to swallow them up. Considering the behavior and deeds of the Councilmen one has always to bear in mind that they were under the pressure of cynical, merciless terror by the Nazis at all times, that the prospect of being killed sooner or later was a concrete eventuality, and that every step they took was liable to postpone or hasten it (25.5% of all Councilmen mentioned in our poll perished before the "resettlement actions"). Only in the context of this extraordinary situation with its relentless psychological stress is it possible to grasp at all or explain the activities and behavior of the Councils and their members.

Appendix II

ORGANIZATIONAL RULES OF THE WARSAW GHETTO POLICE

CONFIRMED BY THE GERMAN DISTRICT ADMINISTRATION

ON NOVEMBER 29, 1940

PARAGRAPH 2 STATED: "The Order police is an organizational entity with the task of securing peace and public order in the area encompassed by the activities of the Warsaw Jewish Council and its institutions, and in any area where it acts on behalf of the Council."

Paragraph 3: ". . . the Order police is the executive organ of the pertinent community department and is fully subordinated to it."

Paragraph 4: "The personnel of the Order police is subordinated (*a*) to the Council's organs in the execution of their tasks and, in particular, to the commission in charge of [direct] supervision over the ghetto police, which consists of Council members appointed by the Council chairman; (*b*) to the ghetto police chiefs in all organizational and internal matters, particularly with respect to training, discipline, service supervision, and technical matters; and (*c*) to the chairman of the Council in all matters."

Paragraph 6: "The Council organs are responsible for the assignments given to the Order police."

Paragraph 7: "The Order police consists of higher and lower grade personnel. The higher grade personnel are: the chief of the Order police, his deputy, the precinct chiefs, and their deputies. The lower level functionaries are: group chiefs, section chiefs, and the rank-and-file policemen. The chief of the Order police is subordinated to the chairman of the 'supervision commission' [of the Council]."

Paragraph 10: "The personnel of the Order police are subordinated to: (*a*) the Council chairman; (*b*) the chairman of the 'supervision commission'; and (*c*) the chief of the Order police in all matters pertaining to high level and low level personnel."

According to Paragraph 12, candidates for the Order police had to have the following qualifications among others: "(*a*) membership in the

Jewish community, (*b*) an unblemished past, (*c*) the ability to act in accordance with the law."

Paragraph 17 stated that "a functionary of the Order police who oversteps his jurisdiction . . . , thus harming the interests of the community or of an individual, or who betrays official secrets, will be disciplined."

Paragraph 18: "A functionary of the Order police who acts with a view to gaining personal profits, or otherwise obtaining material gains for himself or for someone else, will be dismissed."

Paragraph 21: "Any high- or low-grade employee can be dismissed for the good of the Order police. Immediate disciplinary action must follow dismissal."

Paragraph 22: "Dismissal is ordered by the chief of the Order police, who may delegate this power to the chiefs of local units. . . . Their decisions have to be confirmed by the chief of the Order police. Dismissals by the chief of police require approval by the chairman [of the Jewish Council]."

Paragraph 26 contains regulations about uniforms, hats, armbands, and rank insignia (YaVA, microfilm JM/1113).

NOTES

For key to abbreviations used in Notes, see p. xxxiii

CHAPTER 1

1. *Der Chef der Sicherheitspolizei,* PP (II)–288/39 *geheim* (copy in the YIVO Archives); *Nazi Conspiracy and Aggression,* Vol. VI, pp. 97–101, Doc. 3363–PS; *YIVO-Bletter,* Vol. XXX, No. 2 (1947), pp. 163–168.

2. Frank's decree did not regulate the number of Council members in communities with less than 10,000 souls. Accordingly the number of Council members in these communities varied greatly and was in no relation to the figure of the Jewish population (see Chap. 4).

3. VBlGG, No. 9, Dec. 6, 1939.

4. VBlGG, No. 71 (1941), p. 462.

5. Excerpts from the Diary of Hans Frank, governor general of the occupied Polish territories, selected by Judge Israel Carmel, YaVA (Tel Aviv, 1960), p. 12 (Stencil, original German text).

6. VBlGG, Part II (1940), p. 249.

7. VBlGG, Part II (1940), p. 387. This second executive order was published by *Die Krakauer Zeitung* under the heading: "Orders to the *Judenrat* only through the *Stadthauptmann*" (No. 158, 1940). According to Dr. Michał Weichert this regulation was the outcome of a conference held in Cracow on March 14, 1940, between Jewish representatives from Warsaw with high officials of the department *Innere Verwaltung Bevölkerungswesen und Fürsorge (Alaynhilf,* p. 14).

8. Excerpts from the Diary of Hans Frank, pp. 10–12.

9. VBlGG (1939), p. 231 (Par. 2), p. 246 (Pars. 3, 5).

10. VBlGG, No. 50 (1942), p. 342 (Anlage B). According to M. Weichert "the officials of BuF [*Bevölkerungswesen und Fürsorge*] succeeded in retaining the supervision of the Polish Ukrainian and Jewish organizations of Social Aid for reasons of prestige and in order to avoid frontline service *(Alaynhilf,* p. 18).

11. BC, Doc. Occ E3–18; *Trial of the Major War Criminals before the International Military Tribunal* (Nuremberg, 1948), Vol. XXVII, p. 24.

12. *Trial of the Major War Criminals, op. cit.,* Vol. XXVI, p. 349.

13. From the report of the government in the GG on the situation of the Jewish population until July 1, 1940, published in *Eksterminacja,* p. 88.

14. VBlGG (1941), pp. 211–212.

15. *Amtlicher Anzeiger für das Generalgouvernement* (May 30, 1941), p. 761; G.Ż., No. 41 (May 23, 1941). Both orders were in force starting May 15, 1941. With the last order the ghetto was finally separated from the city of Warsaw in administrative matters.

16. ZC, Doc. 1201.

17. *Ibid.*, Doc. 1202.

18. *Ibid.*, Doc. 1204.

19. *Nowa Gazeta Warszawska*, Oct. 18, 1939.

20. D. Rotenberg, *Dos yidishe Rodem in khurves* (Stuttgart, 1948), p. 51.

21. A copy of the order in YaVA, Ms. No. 0–6/2, pp. 441–442.

22. H. Smolar, *Fun minsker geto* (Moscow, 1946), p. 11.

23. Elimelekh Fajnzylber, *Oyf di khurves fun mayn haym. Khurbn Shedlets* (Tel Aviv, 1952), p. 65; *Pinkos fun finf fartilikte kehiles: Pruzhene, Bereze, Maltch, Shershev, Selts* (Buenos Aires, 1958), p. 621; WaC, Doc. 9/1, pp. 6–7.

24. ABLG, Doc. 419; G. Ż., No. 16 (Sept. 13, 1940).

25. Announcements of the Council in Białystok in MTA.

26. Mordecai Bochner, *Sefer Khzhanev* (München-Regensburg, 1949), p. 300; request by the Jewish Council in Zator to the *Landrat* in Bielitz (O/S) of Dec. 15, 1941 (microfilm JM/1552 in YaVA).

27. *Bericht Krakau*, p. 3.

28. Letter of *Umsiedler-Referat bei der jüdischen Gemeinde in Reichshof* [Rzeszów], of May 11, 1941, in YIA.

29. YaVA, File B/12–4, p. 110. We have, however, a letter of the Security Police and Security Service to the Council of Sept. 6, 1941, in which the old label *das jüdische Komitee* was used (*ibid.*).

30. Authorization by the *Komitet*, No. 235, July 10, 1941, with the signatures of Saul Trocki and Leyzer Kruk, in Su-KC.

31. *Ibid.*, graphic charts of the Jewish Council.

32. *Ibid.*, letterhead of the ghetto chief.

33. Ilya Ehrenburg, *Merder fun felker*, Vol. II, p. 41.

34. Stationery for official correspondence of the *Judenräte* in the GG with the German authorities.

35. *Prestuplenya nemetsko-fashistskikh okupantov v Byelorussi 1941–1944* (Minsk, 1963), pp. 21–22.

36. YaVA, announcements of the Jewish Council in Lublin of June 22 and November 17, 1940. It should be mentioned that part of the Jewish press in prewar Poland used the obsolete spelling *Yuden* instead of *Yidn*.

37. WaC, Doc. 16/1–4: announcements concerning the distribution of food in March–June 1941.

38. Anna Natanblut, "Di shuln in varshever geto," *YIVO Bleter*, Vol. XXX, No. 2 (1947), p. 174.

39. ZC, Doc. 28, p. 9; Doc. 43, p. 1; the Diary of I. Hurwic-Klementynowski, pp. 46–47 (ms. in YIA).

CHAPTER 2

1. *Sefer hazvaot*, Vol. I (Jerusalem, 1945), pp. 8–9 (report by former Senator M. Kerner).

2. *Sprawozdanie*.

3. Testimony No. 1043 in the YIA by the former chairman of the Council in Zamość; M. Garfunkel, *Kovno hayehudit bekhurbana* (Jerusalem, 1959), p. 3.

4. *Belkhatov Yizkor-Bukh* (Buenos Aires, 1949), pp. 192–193.

5. *Sefer Skernevits* (Tel Aviv, 1955), pp. 550, 576.

6. Testimony No. R-102/1665 in YaVA.

7. *Pinkos Bendin* (Tel Aviv, 1959), pp. 348–349.

8. *Baranovitsh, sefer zikaron* (Tel Aviv, 1954), p. 512.

9. *Sefer Borshchiv* (Tel Aviv, 1960), p. 177.

10. *Pinkos Kletsk* (Tel Aviv, 1959), p. 368.

11. *Ostrovtse* (Buenos Aires, 1949), pp. 192–193.

12. Testimony B-86/1101 in YaVA.

13. *Kobryn zamlbukh* (Buenos Aires, 1951), p. 251; M. Bialodworsky, "Der Yudenrat in Grodne," *Grodner Opklangen*, No. 2 (1949); Abe Tarlovsky "Grodner yudenrat," *Kovets Grodno, zamlheft*, No. 1 (Paris, 1947), p. 27; testimony by the council member in Bursztyn (Eastern Galicia), Jehuda Hersh Fishman, p. 4 (YIA).

14. WaC, Doc. 9/1, p. 7.

15. H. Garn-Rozental, "Fun toyzenter eyne," *Der Tog* (Jewish daily paper) of June 18, 1946, p. 12.

16. *Pinkos Bendin*, p. 186; *Sefer Khzhanev*, pp. 254–255, 311, 312; Paweł Wiederman, *Płowa bestia* (Münich, 1948), pp. 115, 207; Ph. Friedman, "Hatasbikh hamshikhi shel takif bgeto hanazi," *Bitzaron*, No. 5 (1953), p. 31 (total number of issues to 1953 = 161).

17. Jan Mavult, "Moje wspomnienia, część II, 'Czyściec' " ("Memoirs, Part II 'Purgatory' "), p. 57 (ms. in YIA).

18. *Lodzher geto*, p. 379.

19. Nakhman Blumental, *Teudot mgeto Lublin* (Jerusalem, 1967), p. 40.

20. *Grodner Opklangen*, No. 2, p. 13.

21. *Eyshyshok. Koroteha vekhurbana* (Jerusalem, 1950), p. 96.

22. Herman Kruk. *Togbukh fun vilner geto* (YIVO; New York, 1961), pp. 10–12; M. Dvozhetsky, *Yerusholaim delite in kamf un umkum* (Paris, 1948), p. 42.

23. MTA, minutes of the meeting on the anniversary of the establishment of the Council (Nakhman Blumental, *Darko shel Yudenrat* [Jerusalem, 1962], pp. 219–221).

24. YaVA, File B/12-4, p. 100; Lejb Garfunkel, *op. cit.*, pp. 37–38; Yakov Goldberg, "Bleter fun kovner eltestnrat," FLKh, No. 7 (May 1948), pp. 33–38; Shmuel Grinhaus, "Khurbn Kovno," *ibid.*, pp. 12–14; A. Golub, "Di letste asyfe fun der kovner kehile," *Litvisher Yid* (New York), No. 7–8 (April–May, 1946), p. 31.

25. Philip Friedman, "Khurban Yehudei Lwów," *Encyclopaedia*, Vol. IV, p. 614.

26. *Sefer Pabianits. Yizkor bukh fun der farpaynikter kehile* (Tel Aviv, 1956), p. 313.

27. M. Weichert ["Memoirs"], excerpts of the ms. from Philip Friedman's private archives, II, p. 109.

28. Moshe Taytelboym, *Bilgoray. Yizkor bukh* (Jerusalem, 1955), p. 108.

29. E. Unger, *Zkhor. Myimey kronot hamavet* (Tel Aviv, 1945), pp. 51–53.

30. *Pinkos fun finf fartilikte kehiles*, p. 420.

31. *Mgilat Gline (Gliniany)*, (1950), p. 251 (offset).

32. T. Bernstein and A. Rutkowski, "Di formirung fun der hitleristisher militerfarwaltung," *Blfg*, Vol. XV, pp. 121–122.

33. Testimony No. 287 in YIA.

34. *Pinkos Khmielnik* (Tel Aviv, 1960), Col. 728.

35. *Bericht Krakau*, pp. 3, 10.

36. L. Brener, *Vidershtand un umkum fun Chenstokhover geto* (Warsaw, 1951), pp. 11–12. Some additional facts (that Ash and two other members of the rabbinate were kept for two days in prison, that Ash received in prison a prepared list of six persons) we find in the testimony by one of them (D. Konitspoler, YIA).

37. *Grayeve. Yizkor-bukh* (New York, 1950), p. 203.

38. Ilya Ehrenburg, *Merder fun felker*, p. 41.

39. *Sefer yizkor Goniondz* (Tel Aviv, 1960), p. 615.

40. I. Sh. Hertz, ed., *Zygielboym-Bukh* (New York, 1947), pp. 120–121. The events were similarly related by A. Hartglas in "Hekhadashim haryshonim bekibush hanazi," *Encyclopaedia*, Vol. II, *Varshah*, pp. 496–497.

41. Israel Dov Itzinger (Alter Shnur), "Hayeshiva haplenarit umehalkha" (from "Min Hameytsar") in *Dapim lekheker hashoa vehamered*, Vol. I (Tel Aviv, April 1951), pp. 120–121; *Sefer Hazvaot*, pp. 64–65.

42. Abraham Ochs, "Tarnopol betkufat milkhemet oylam hashnya," *Encyclopaedia*, Vol. III (1955), p. 386; Z. Margules "Khavayati bgeto Tarnopol," *ibid.*, pp. 416–417.

43. *Pinkos Novoredok* (Tel Aviv, 1963), pp. 251–252.

44. M. Weichert ["Memoirs"], Part I, p. 74.

45. Herman Kruk, *op. cit.*, pp. 8–9; A. Sutzkever, *Vilner geto 1941–1944* (Paris, 1946), pp. 21–22. A different account is related by M. Dvorzhetsky: In the first days of July 1941 the Lithuanian *Kommandant* Kalendra sent for Rabbi Shmuel Fried, who after he suffered a heart attack, was not able to walk. The beadle Gordon took him in a carriage to the *Kommandant*, who gave the rabbi the order to establish a *Judenrat* and direct its affairs (*op. cit.*, p. 41).

46. MTA, Pesakh Kaplan, "Der yidnrat in Białystok" (ms.). Rafal Reisner, *"Der umkum fun białystoker yidntum (1939–1945)"* (Melbourne, 1948), p. 43. Reisner related that beside Rabbi Rosenman, the director of the *Kehila* administration, Ephraim Barash, was also called to the *Kommandant*.

47. Lejb Garfunkel, *op. cit.*, p. 37.

48. *Pinkos Mlave* (New York, 1950), pp. 398–399; *Pinkos Byten* (Buenos Aires, 1954), p. 323.

49. For Warsaw: *Bericht Warschau* (Akta R.Ż. w Warszawie No. 16, microfilm No. PNE 53–78); *Sefer Hazvaot*, p. 9. For Cracow: M. Weichert ["Memoirs"], Vol. I, p. 28. For Vilna and Białystok: material cited in notes 45 and 46. For Radom: *Dos yidishe Rodem in khurves*, pp. 51–52. For Grodno: *Grodner Opklangen*, No. 2, p. 13. For Lublin: Minutes No. 1 of Jan. 7, 1940, of the meeting of the *Kehila* administration and members of the advisory committee. For Brody: *Arim Veyimahot beisrael*, Vol. VI ("Brody"), (Jerusalem, 1955), p. 398.

50. *Sefer Lintchits* (Israel, 1953), p. 181; *Stolin sefer zikaron* (Tel Aviv, 1952), p. 213; Shlomo Grynshpan, *Yidn in Plotsk* (New York, 1960), p. 308; testimony by Harry Berger about Końskie (YIA).

51. *Erreignismeldung U.S.S.R.*, No. 11, July 23, 1941 (Doc. ND–2956 in the Wiener Library).

52. See references in n. 50, above.

53. I. M. Fajgenbojm, *Podlashe in nazi-klem* (Buenos Aires, 1953), p. 180.

54. *Kehilat Rohatyn vehasviva* (Tel Aviv, 1962), p. 291.

55. Shmuel Druk, *Yudnshtat Yavorov, der umkum fun yavorover yidn* (New York, 1950), p. 9.

56. Minutes of the meeting of the Lublin Council No. 5, Jan. 25, 1940; File B/12–4, pp. 31, 100, in YaVA.

57. Blume Gedanken, "Ostrolenker in słonimer geto," *Sefer kehilat Ostrolenka*, p. 361.

58. *Pinkos Byten*, pp. 322–323.

59. H. Smolar, *op. cit.*, p. 11.

60. Ph. Friedman, *op. cit.*, *Bitzaron*, No. 5, p. 30; Paweł Wiederman, *op. cit.*, pp. 45–47.

61. *Pinkos Khmielnik*, Col. 728.

62. *Krasnobrod sefer zikaron* (Tel Aviv, 1956), p. 383.

63. Testimony No. 609 by Meyer Rozenwald in YIA.

64. *Grodner Opklangen*, No. 2 (1949), p. 15; M. Dvozhetsky, *op. cit.*, pp. 134–136.
65. *Drohichin. finf hundred yor yidish lebn* (New York, 1958), p. 349.
66. Jakob Rosen, *Mir viln lebn* (New York, 1949), pp. 34–35.
67. Herman Kruk, *op cit.*, p. 9; cf. n. 45, above, this chap.
68. Eliezer Yerushalmi, *Pinkos Shavli* (Jerusalem, 1958), p. 18.
69. Photostat of the order in ABLG.
70. Eliezer Unger, *op. cit.*, pp. 51–52.
71. Testimonies by Y. H. Fishman, p. 10, and Abraham Kalisher, p. 10 (YIA).
72. Abraham Wajsbrot, *Es shtarbt a shtetl. Mgilat Skałat* (Munich, 1948), p. 28.
73. M. Gildenman, *Khurbn Korets* (Paris, 1949), p. 32; *Sefer Łutsk* (Tel Aviv, 1961), p. 482; the liaison man between the authorities and the council in Łutsk was the Ukrainian physician Bilabron (*ibid.*, p. 501).
74. Testimony by Ignacy Sternbach (YIA).
75. *Ayarati Visotsk* (Haifa, 1964), p. 101.
76. *Mitteilungen des Judenrates in Lemberg für die jüdische Gemeinde*; published by the Jewish Council, from which only three issues appeared in Jan., Feb., and March 1942. The texts of the *Mitteilungen* are preserved in the bulky ms. compiled by Professor Thaddeus Zaderecki concerning the history of the Lwów Ghetto in YaVA (Ms. No. 0–6/2); this fact is related on p. 517 of the ms. (hereafter cited as Zaderecki).
77. G.Ż., No. 16, Sept. 13, 1940.
78. G.Ż., No. 13, Sept. 3, 1940.
79. *Ibid.*
80. Mayer Shlojmo, *Der untergang fun Złoczów* (Munich, 1947), p. 16.
81. N. Blumental, *Darko shel Yudenrat* (Białystok); Orbach, "Vi zaynen umgekumen di yidn in Lazdijai," *Baderekh.* (Milan, Nov. 16, 1945), p. 3; *Pinkos Ludmir* (Tel Aviv, 1962), p. 83; testimony by Y. H. Fishman (YIA).
82. I. Celemenski, *Mitn farshnitenem folk* (New York, 1963), p. 56.
83. In the Polish governmental administration we very seldom find Jews (not baptized) in this capacity; perhaps the person interviewed meant "vice mayor."
84. Compare the memorial books and monographs about Biała Podlaska, Międzyrzec, Łomża, Białystok, Ostrowiec, Skierniewice, Zdzięcioł, Vilna, Radzyń, Sarny, Złoczów, Markuszów, Ożarów, Działoszyce, Kowel, Czortków, Żarki, Krzemieniec, Radoszkowice, Raseiniai, Hrubieszów, Szczekociny, Dobromil, and Kołomyja.

CHAPTER 3

1. *Sefer Khzhanev*, pp. 255–256, 283–285.
2. *Pinkos Bendin*, p. 186.
3. *Sefer Klobuck* (Tel Aviv, 1960), pp. 220–221; questionnaire on the Jewish Councils, No. 294.
4. G.Ż., No. 13 (Sept. 3, 1940).
5. G.Ż., No. 29 (Oct. 29, 1940).
6. Records of the JUS, File No. 254 (Sosnowiec) in AJHI; records of the Joint Distribution Committee (JDC), *ibid.*, File No. 106 (Kutno), pp. 6, 15.
7. Zykhroynes V. III, *Milkhome*, p. 96.
8. G.Ż., No. 20 (Sept. 27, 1940).
9. Related personally by Israel Falk, inspector of the JDC in Poland for the Radom district during the war.
10. *Milkhome*, p. 219.

11. G.Ż., No. 36 (Nov 22, 1940). In the note there is a remark that such regulation regarding Jewish real estate is in force also in other cities (they are not listed) and suggests its general application by all Councils; such measures would alleviate to some extent their financial burden.

12. VBlGG, Part I, No. 10 (1940).

13. G.Ż., No. 38 (Nov. 29, 1940).

14. Microfilm JM/1489, in YaVA.

15. Yakov Kurtz, *Sefer Eydut* (Tel Aviv, 1944), p. 277.

16. G.Ż., No. 27 (Oct. 21, 1940).

17. Emanuel Ringelblum, *Notitsn fun varshever geto* (Warsaw, 1952), p. 213; on the same day 20 members of the Jewish *Ordnungsdienst* were also sent to Auschwitz.

18. U.S. Military Tribunal Documents Staff Evidence Analysis. Office of Chief Counsel for War Crimes, Doc. NO-519; copy of a letter by Arthur Greiser of Feb. 14, 1944, to Oswald Pohl.

19. *Lodzher geto*, pp. 266, 280.

20. ZC, Doc. 26, p. 10; AGV, File 220, pp. 114, 115.

21. Records of the JDC, File 415, p. 130.

22. G.Ż., No. 42 (Dec. 13, 1940).

23. G.Ż., No. 16 (Feb. 23, 1941). Artur Eisenbach, *Hitlerowska polityka eksterminacji Żydów* (Warsaw, 1953), p. 170.

24. H. Garn-Rosental, "Fun toyzenter ayne," *Der Tog*, June 18, 1946, p. 12.

25. Itzhak Levin. *Aliti mispetsia* (Tel Aviv, 1947), p. 100.

26. T. Brustin-Bernstein, "Der protses fun farnikhtn di yidishe yishuvim oyfn shetakh fun azoy gerufenem distrikt Galizien," *Blfg*, Vol. II, No. 3, p. 66; Jacob Littauer, *Aufzeichnungen aus einem Erdloch* (Munich, 1948), pp. 62–63.

27. *Sefer Lantsut* (Tel Aviv, 1963), p. xxxviii.

28. Unger, *op. cit.*, pp. 51–52; Ayzyk Huzen, *Kitever yizkor-bukh* (New York, 1958), p. 129; testimony by the chairman of the Council in Kosóv Huculski (Doc. M/20 in YaVA).

29. *Sefer Borshchiv*, p. 193.

30. *Ibid.*

31. Su-KC, *Geto-yedies*, No. 20 (Jan. 3, 1943).

32. Testimony No. 612 (YIA); H. Kruk, *op. cit.*, pp. 378–380.

33. FLKh, No. 4 (1947), p. 58.

34. J. Kermish, "Khurbn," *Pietrkov Trybunalski* (Tel Aviv, 1966), p. 730.

35. *Kitever yizkor-bukh*, pp. 129–130.

36. Doc. M/20, pp. 12–13 (YaVA).

37. *Sefer Borshchiv*, pp. 192–193.

38. Aron Brandes, *Kets hayehudim bemarev polin* (Merkhavia, 1945), p. 9.

39. I. Lewin, *op. cit.*, pp. 100–102.

CHAPTER 4

1. VBlGG, No. 13 (Dec. 21, 1939), Par. 5; VBlGG, Vol. I, No. 18 (March 13, 1940), Par. 8.

2. VBlGG, Part II (1940), p. 23.

3. VBlGG, No. 1, pp. 6–7; No. 13 (Dec. 21, 1939); No. 14 (Dec. 23, 1939).

4. ZC, Docs. 630, 1002; *Geto-tsaytung*, No. 4 (March 28, 1941).

5. *Bericht Warschau*, p. 7.

6. *Sprawozdanie*, p. 47.

7. *Bericht Krakau*, p. 69.

8. ZC, Doc. 1002, p. 7.

9. *Sprawozdanie*, pp. 10, 15, 39.

10. *Bericht Warschau*, p. 7.

11. *Sprawozdanie*, p. 56.

12. ZC, Doc. 110.

13. Zaderecki, p. 445; testimony by Rabbi David Kahane, pp. 15–16 (YIA); Gerszon Tafet, *Zagłada Żydów żołkiewskich* (Łódź, 1946), pp. 25–26.

14. ZC, Doc. 1207; *Der Älteste der Juden in Getto Litzmannstadt*, Feb. 15, 1941 (chart).

15. ZC, Docs. 1207; 26, p. 12; 33, p. 1; Israel Tabaksblat, *Khurbn Lodzh* (Buenos Aires, 1946), p. 57.

16. "Mitteilungen des Judenrates im Lemberg . . ." No. 1, Jan. 1942 (Zaderecki, pp. 487–489); cf. Ph. Friedman, *Encyclopaedia*, Vol. IV, pp. 614–615; testimony by Rabbi D. Kahane.

17. Su-KC, Doc. 286, Table 1 and Graph 2; Doc. 295.

18. *Rada Starszych, II Rocznik Statystyczny* (Częstochowa, 1940), Tabela 1: szemat organizacji Rady Starszych, 1940 (hereafter cited as *Rocznik* with respective number).

19. *Rocznik* II, pp. 163–165.

20. *Der juedische Wohnbezirk in Warschau und seine Verwaltung (Zahlen und Tatsachen)* (Warsaw, June 1942), pp. 2, 3, 15 (publication of the Council, hereafter cited as *Wohnbezirk*).

21. MTA, minutes of the meeting of Aug. 3, 1941; announcements of the Council, Nos. 138, 149, 161; N. Blumental, *op. cit.*, pp. 7–8, 364, 373, 380.

22. MTA, minutes of the conference of the department chiefs of the Council, Jan. 18, 1942; Blumental, *op. cit.*, p. 108; "Tsu der Geshikhte fun di białystoker yidn in der tsayt fun daytsh-sovietishn krig" (anonymous ms. in MTA).

23. *Pinkos fun finf fartilikte kehiles*, p. 623.

24. *Grodner Opklangen*, No. 2, pp. 13–24.

25. *Sprawozdanie*, pp. 1–74.

26. I. Kurtz, *op. cit.*, pp. 234–239; *Der Aufbau und Aufgabenkreis der jued. Gemeinde in Krakau* (chart in *Bericht Krakau*).

27. *Bericht Warschau*, p. 18; BWS, No. 12ª, 3–9 January 1941.

28. BWS, No. 3 (June 2, 1940), p. 1.

29. *Bericht Warschau*, p. 16.

30. *Lodzher geto*, p. 34.

31. Minutes of the Council of the Lublin Ghetto in YaVA, Nos. 5/129 and 20/149.

32. Rotenberg, *op. cit.*, p. 132; Unger, *op. cit.*, p. 57.

33. See sources cited in n. 22 (Chap. 4).

34. Minutes, No. 31/155 (May 20, 1942).

35. E. Yerushalmi, *op. cit.*, pp. 306–318.

36. Ilya Ehrenburg, *op. cit.*, p. 53.

37. Su-KC, Doc. 279.

38. WaC, Doc. 47/1: letter by Rosen to the chairman, A. Czerniakow, requesting that he not be transferred to a new position as head of the tax department.

39. In a note in G.Ż., No. 18, March 4, 1941, it is stated that the position of the chairman in his relations with the Council members is an internal matter to be decided by the Council itself. Answering an inquiry from Hrubieszów, G.Ż. gave its point of view, that the chairman is bound by a decision of a majority of the Council members; in cases of disagreement he should put the matter in question to the appropriate authorities for a final decision (G.Ż., however, made the reservation that this

is only its suggestion and that is not sure whether the authorities agree with this interpretation. In the same answer G.Ż. expresses the view that the Council shall elect a new chairman only when the incumbent resigns or when he is dismissed by the authorities (*ibid.*, No. 16, Feb. 25, 1941).

40. Minutes of the Council meetings held between Jan. 25 and Sept. 29, 1940. The last provision, which was bound to endanger the incriminated Council member, was apparently intended to avoid attempts by the Councilmen to shirk the grave responsibility which rested on them, and served rather as intimidation against such attempts.

41. *Lodzher geto*, pp. 360–366.

42. P. Wiederman, *op. cit.*, p. 145.

43. Minutes, No. 11/135.

44. Minutes, Nos. 20/81, 46/107, and 49/110.

45. Minutes, No. 49/173.

46. E. Yerushalmi, *op. cit.*, pp. 185–187. Arrested at the beginning of September 1942 for his black market dealings, he was ransomed by the Council, which bribed a German official.

47. Minutes of Sept. 18 and 20, 1941, and June 29, 1942 (Blumental, *op. cit.*, pp. 37, 41, 219).

CHAPTER 5

1. Orders by the chiefs of the civil administration at the military High Command in Cracow (Sept. 16), in Częstochowa (Sept. 12), and in Posen (Poznań) (Oct. 3, 1939), quoted in *Eksterminacja*, p. 158, n. 1; VBlGG, Part II (1939), p. 51.

2. VBlGG, 1939, Part II, p. 141; *ibid.*, 1940, p. 16; G.Ż. no. 67, Aug. 4, 1941.

3. VBlGG, Part II (1940), p. 23.

4. *Ibid.*, p. 31.

5. RGBl, Vol. I (1940), pp. 1270–1273.

6. *Proces Artura Greisera przed Najwyższym Trybunałem Narodowym* (1947), p. 27; on p. 51 we read: This segment of the population [the Jews] in the majority of the cities was concentrated in separate quarters, or resettled into the GG. Their enterprises were closed and put under the managment of commissars.

7. Records of JUS Cracow in AJHI Files 1, 28, 38; AGV XV/30: letter (Nov. 9, 1943) of the *Treuhandstelle-Ost* in Poznań to the *Gettoverwaltung* in Łódź.

8. VBlGG, Part II (1940), p. 593 (Par. 8).

9. G.Ż., No. 8 (Aug. 17, 1940).

10. G.Ż., No. 3 (July 30, 1940).

11. *Mitteilungsblatt der HTO* (1940), p. 168 (stencil).

12. G.Ż., No. 14 (Feb. 18, 1941).

13. G.Ż., No. 8 (Aug. 7, 1940).

14. G.Ż., No. 30 (Nov. 1, 1940).

15. *Ibid.*

16. *Krakauer Zeitung*, Nov. 21, 1940.

17. RA, Part I, No. 1115. Simultaneously the Jews were forced to pay all their debts.

18. T. Brustin-Bernstein, "Di virtshaftlekhe diskriminatsyes legabe yidn in Varshe farn shafn dos geto," *Blfg*, Vol. V, no. 3 (1952), p. 163 (hereafter cited as *Virtshaftlekhe diskriminatsyes*). L. Brener, *op. cit.*, p. 9; Isaiah Trunk "Shtudie tsu der geshikhte fun yidn in Wartheland in der tkufe fun umkum (1939–1944)," *Blfg*, Vol. 2 (1949), p. 105 (hereafter cited as *Shtudie*).

19. RA, I, No. 1108.
20. RA, I, No. 1157.
21. A. Eisenbach, *Getto Łódzkie* (Łódź, 1946), pp. 62–68.
22. AGV, File VIII/24, p. 158.
23. I. Tabaksblat, *op. cit.*, p. 106.
24. To provide hostages as a guarantee of payment of the exuberant, financial sanctions were forced on the communities in Włocławek, Lwów, Słonim, Ostróg, and many others (AJHI testimony, No. 375; J. Kermisz, *Akcje i wysiedlenia* (Łódź, 1946), p. 201; RA, I 1959, pp. 5–6.
25. L. Brener, *op. cit.*, p. 15.
26. A copy of the document in YIA.
27. BC, Doc. OccE3-18: "Vorläufige Richtlinien für die Behandlung der Juden im Gebiet des Reichskommissariats Ostland" (Aug. 18, 1941), pp. 4, 6.
28. "Verordnungsblatt für das Reichskommissariat Ostland" No. 307, p. 158; cf. Yerushalmi, *op. cit.*, pp. 144–145.
29. L. Garfunkel, *op. cit.*, pp. 131–132. In Vilna Ghetto an order of the Security Police of July 6, 1943, limited the amount of money allowed to be kept by a Jew to 30 Reichsmarks, the remaining amount as well as preciosa had to be delivered to the ghetto police under death penalty (Rayzl Korchak, *Lahavot Beeyfer* [Merkhavia, 1946], p. 242).
30. *Shtudie*, p. 80.
31. The order was published in the German *Lodscher Zeitung*, No. 285 (1939).
32. *Eksterminacja*, p. 161.
33. G.Ż., No. 11 (Feb. 7, 1941).
34. G.Ż., No. 49 (June 20, 1941).
35. A copy of such an order in *Alaynhilf*, p. 261.
36. VBlGG, Part II (1940), p. 577.
37. In its clarification the Central Labor Office explains the prohibition against issuing labor cards to Jews with the fact that Jews were already registered in accordance with the decree of Oct. 26, 1939, concerning the duty of forced labor, and had then received their cards; therefore the decree regarding the general labor card did not apply to them.
38. G.Ż., No. 41 (Dec. 10, 1940).
39. WaC, Doc. 34/6.
40. VBlGG (1940), pp. 92, 239; G.Ż., No. 8 (Aug. 17, 1940); in Sept. 1940 the premiums paid by Jews were raised (G.Ż., No. 25, Oct. 14, 1940).
41. G.Ż., No. 37 (Nov. 26, 1940).
42. G.Ż., No. 3 (July 30, 1940).
43. G.Ż., No. 19 (Sept. 24, 1940).
44. VBlGG (1940), p. 288.
45. *Virtshaftlikhe diskriminatsyes*, p. 165.
46. G.Ż., No. 33 (Apr. 25, 1941).
47. I. Tabaksblat, *op. cit.*, p. 38.
48. ZC, Doc. 630, p. 7.
49. Rotenberg, *op. cit.*, p. 151; *Sprawozdanie*, p. 43.
50. Rotenberg, *op. cit.*, p. 152.
51. ZC, Doc. 630, p. 7.
52. Su-KC, Doc. 246ᵇ; minutes of the meeting of the Council in Białystok, March 22, 1942; (Blumental *op. cit.*, p. 151).
53. *Shtudie*, pp. 114–115.
54. I. Trunk, "Yiddishe arbet-lagern in Varteland," *Blfg*, Vol. I, No. 1 (1948), pp. 126–130. The German firms which employed Jewish laborers were henceforth

obliged to reimburse the *Gettoverwaltung* in Łódź 0.70 Reichsmarks for each Jew per day.

55. *Ibid.*, p. 126; E. Ringelblum, *Notitsn fun warshever geto* (Warsaw, 1951), p. 151.
56. On August 24, 1942, Governor General Hans Frank made a note in his Diary quite frankly: ". . . by the way I have to state that we had condemned 1,200,000 Jews to a death from hunger. It is understandable as a matter of course that the fact that the Jews will not die out from hunger will accelerate, let's hope, the issuance of anti-Jewish measures" (BGKBZN(H), Vol. II, p. 33).
57. ZC, Doc. 41G.
58. M. Segalson, "Di groyse varshtatn in Kovner geto," FLKh, No. 8 (June 1948), pp. 50–57.
59. ZC, Docs. 631, 1212.
60. G.Ż., No. 11 (Feb. 7, 1941); No. 14 (Feb. 18, 1941); BWS No. 12, p. 6.
61. Zaderecki, p. 579.
62. G.Ż., No. 66 (Aug. 1, 1941).
63. G.Ż., No. 41 (Dec. 10, 1940).
64. G.Ż., No. 27 (April 4, 1941).
65. M. Weichert, *Yidishe Alaynhilf*, pp. 290–291.
66. Jerzy Winkler, "Dos geto kemft kegn virtshaftlikher farknekhtung"; ms. in RA, published in *Blfg*, Vol. I, No. 3–4 (1968), p. 16.
67. BC, Doc. OccE 2–3: "Zweimonatsbericht des Gouverneurs des Distrikts Warschau v. 15. August für die Monate Juni u Juli 1942."
68. Winkler, *op. cit.*, p. 35.
69. G.Ż., No. 44 (Dec. 20, 1940).
70. WaC, Doc. 34/4: "Naye fakhn in der milkhome tsayt" (July 1941), p. 1; E. Ringelblum, "Stosunki polsko-żydowskie w czasie drugiej wojny światowej," (BŻIH, No. 28 [1958], pp. 28–29).
71. *Ibid.*
72. *Ibid.*, p. 28.
73. G.Ż., No. 63 (July 25, 1941).
74. WaC, Doc. 34/4, p. 2.
75. BC, Doc. Occ E 2–3.
76. E. Ringelblum, *op. cit.*, BŻIH, No. 28, p. 30.
77. ZC, Doc. 30; BKC, July 3, 1942.
78. *Ibid.*
79. MTA, minutes of March 1, 1942; (Blumental, *op. cit.*, p. 141).
80. MTA, minutes of Aug. 28, 1941 (Blumental, *op. cit.*, p. 31).
81. ZC, Doc. 55K.
82. A. Eisenbach, *Getto Łódzkie* (Łódź, 1946), p. 102.
83. *Ibid.*, pp. 114, 116.
84. Doc. NG–5340, quoted by Raul Hilberg, *The Destruction of the European Jews* (Chicago, 1961), pp. 305–306.
85. ZC, Doc. 738, p. 15.
86. ZC, Doc. 199.
87. ZC, Doc. 217.
88. ZC, Doc. 33, BKC, Aug. 27, 1942.
89. G.Ż., No. 61 (Aug. 21, 1941).
90. MTA, announcements issued on the dates mentioned (Blumental, *op. cit.*, pp. 360, 468, 498, 516).
91. MTA, minutes of the meeting (Blumental, *op. cit.*, p. 203).
92. MTA, minutes of June 20, 1942 (Blumental, *op. cit.*, p. 185).
93. MTA, minutes of March 22, 1942 (Blumental, *op. cit.*, p. 147).

94. Su-KC, Docs. 222, 247, 267, 268, 269; *Geto-yedies* (a publication of the Council) of March 28, Apr. 4, and May 2, 1943.
95. Su-KC, Doc. 35.
96. G.Ż., No. 12 (Feb. 11, 1941); No. 32 (Apr. 22, 1941); Ester Goldhar-Mark "Dos yidishe fakh- un hekhere shulvesn in Varshe in der tsayt fun der daytsher okupatsye," *Blfg*, Vol. II (1949), pp. 184, 186.
97. *Lodzher geto*, p. 54.
98. *Ibid.*, pp. 152–153.
99. *Ibid.*, pp. 158–159.
100. ZC, Doc. 58, p. 5.
101. ZC, Doc. 55K.
102. ZC, Doc. 41D.
103. ZC, Doc. 538, p. 4.
104. AGV, No. III/45.
105. *Ibid.*
106. *Proces Artura Greisera przed Najwyższym Trybunałem Narodowym* (stenogram, 1947), p. 157.
107. AGV, Nos. 28/48, 93/42, unpaginated.
108. ZC, Doc. 538, p. 21.
109. ZC, Doc. 738, p. 28.
110. ZC, Doc. 734.
111. ZC, Doc. 738, p. 19.
112. ZC, Doc. 738, p. 4.
113. ZC, Doc. 758A.
114. ZC, Doc. 304.
115. ZC, Doc. 616A; A. Eisenbach, *Getto Łódzkie*, p. 245.
116. ZC, Docs. 758A, 55K.
117. Su-KC, Doc. 286, pp. 2–4.
118. Su-KC, Doc. 286, Table 7.
119. Su-KC, Doc. 218a, p. 21.
120. Su-KC, Doc. 217.
121. Su-KC, Doc. 280.
122. Su-KC, Docs. 216, 217, 218. The whole story is told by the great difference between the output produced by shops on behalf of various departments of the ghetto administration for the benefit of the ghetto inmates, on the one hand, and, on the other hand, the turnover for the various German agencies. In December 1942 the turnover inside the ghetto amounted to 35,930 Reichsmarks, as compared to 5,289 Reichsmarks' worth of merchandise produced on orders received from outside the ghetto; in January 1943 the respective figures were 63,553 and 7,857; in February 76,043 and 8,775.
123. Su-KC, Doc. 217.
124. Su-KC, Docs. 206, 207, 266 (*Geto-yedies* of March 14, 1943).
125. Su-KC, Doc. 222, p. 7.
126. Su-KC, Doc. 280, p. 4.
127. Su-KC, Doc. 271 (*Geto-yedies* of June 6, 1943).
128. MTA, minutes of the meeting (Blumental, *op. cit.*, p. 203).
129. MTA, minutes of March 1, 1942; "Tsu der geshikhte fun di białystoker yidn in der tsayt fun daytsch-sovietishn krig," p. 12.
130. MTA, minutes of May 2, Aug. 15, and Oct. 10, 1942; (Blumental, *op. cit.*, pp. 170, 231, 245).
131. MTA, report to the Gestapo "about the February evacuation and employment in the ghetto" (April 2, 1943).

132. Rafal Reisner, *Der umkum fun białystoker yidntum* (Melbourne, 1948), pp. 92–93; MTA, "Tsu der geshikhte fun die białystoker yidn . . ." p. 8.

133. L. Garfunkel, *op. cit.*, pp. 96–97. In a second memorandum by a group of released political prisoners (arrested during the Soviet occupation) to the chief of the Security Police, dated Sept. 12, 1941, the same proposals were offered; he was requested to accept the memorandum sent by the Council and to receive its representatives (YaVA, File B/12–4, p. 102).

134. Zaderecki, pp. 507–508.

135. *Khurban Sukhovole* (Mexico City, 1947), pp. 26–27.

136. Wacław Jastrzębowski, *Gospodarka niemiecka w Polsce* (Warsaw, 1947), *passim*.

137. *Lodzher geto*, pp. 49, 105, 117.

138. ZC, Doc. 345.

139. ZC, Docs. 137, 210, 211, 225, 310, 320, 339 (announcements July 1940–July 1941); in the announcement of July 18, 1941, the producers of prohibited food items were threatened with prison for three months and confiscation of their merchandise, raw materials, and tools; the same applied to the dealers. Parents would be punished for the transgressions of their children; orphans would be taken to the house of correction.

140. ZC, Docs. 25, p. 10; 28, p. 9.

141. T. Tykochinsky, "Voluvke, altvarg der ayntsiker handl bay yidn in varshe in der geto-tsayt 1940 un 1941" (ms. in RA, I, published in *Blfg*, Vol. I, No. 3–4, pp. 203–210).

142. Dvorzhetsky, *op. cit.*, p. 317; Kruk, *op. cit.*, pp. 158, 222; Yerushalmi, *op. cit.*, pp. 66–67, 72, 104–107; in the Šiauliai Ghetto the Council was forced to issue a warning (Feb. 6, 1942) against smuggling food into the ghetto (*ibid.*, p. 72).

143. There is a rich contemporary and memoir literature about the problem of smuggling into the ghettos; see, e.g., WaC, Doc. 34/4, p. 2; Ringelblum, *op. cit.*, pp. 174, 175, 225; Dvorzhetsky, *op. cit.*, pp. 165–168, and many others.

144. Ringelblum, *op. cit.*, pp. 174, 175, 225.

145. MTA, "Tsu der geshikhte fun die białystoker yidn . . .," p. 6.

146. MTA, minutes of Jan. 18, 1942, and many severe warnings by the Council (announcements, Nos. 61, 206, 281, and others, 1941–1942).

147. MTA, "Tsu der geshikhte fun di białystoker yidn . . .," p. 8.

148. Dvorzhetsky, *op. cit.*, pp. 168–170; Kruk, *op. cit.*, pp. 128–129, 212–213.

149. Testimony No. 1043 in YIA; Yerushalmi, *op. cit.*, p. 22; *Rishonim lamered lakhva, Encyclopaedia* (1957), p. 124.

150. Ration cards for Jews from Warsaw, Łódź, Vilna, Częstochowa, among others, in the YIA.

151. ZC, Doc. 1021, pp. 4–5.

152. A copy of the letter in the archive of the author.

153. ABLG, a copy of the letter, p. 3, s.d. [winter 1940].

154. *Lodzher geto*, p. 107.

155. *Alaynhilf*, p. 180.

156. A. Eisenbach, *Getto Łódzkie*, pp. 241–242.

157. WaC, Doc. 60/11 ("Oyfbroyz," No. 3(18), June 1942, p. 7).

158. Tabaksblat, *op. cit.*, pp. 57–58.

159. Su-KC, Doc. 174; Dvorzhetsky, *op. cit.*, p. 176.

160. ZC, Doc. 750.

161. *Lodzher geto*, pp. 105, 106.

162. A. Eisenbach, *Getto Łódzkie*, p. 120.

163. G.Ż., No. 61 (July 21, 1941).

164. *Geto-tsaytung*, No. 10 (May 11, 1941); ZC, Doc. 313.

165. *Lodzher geto*, p. 43.

166. ZC, Doc. 1021, pp. 14, 25.

167. *Wohnbezirk*, p. 8.

168. WaC, Doc. 46/11.

169. Zaderecki, pp. 488, 505, 506.

170. Rocznik, II, p. 103 (Doc. 06/3 in YaVA).

171. YaVA, File B/12–4, p. 108.

172. Yerushalmi, *op. cit.*, pp. 21–22.

173. RA, I, Doc. 1193.

174. *Lodzher geto*, pp. 116–117; YaVA, File B/12–4, p. 103.

175. *Alaynhilf*, p. 180; RA, I, Doc. 1118.

176. YaVA, microfilm JM/814, p. 3.

177. *Alaynhilf*, p. 181; *Shtudie (Blfg*, Vol. 2 [1949], pp. 108–109).

178. RA, I, No. 1193.

179. YaVA, B/12–4, p. 56: letter (April 7, 1942) by the *Stadtkommissar* in Kaunas to the Council of Elders; ZC, Doc. 1399; In Warsaw *Gettokommissar* Auerswald maintained that food should not be allotted to the refugees, that only working people are entitled to social aid (Ringelblum, *op. cit.*, p. 232).

180. *Lodzher geto*, pp. 110–111.

181. WaC, Doc. 34/4, p. 4.

182. Garfunkel, *op. cit.*, p. 102.

183. *Bericht Warschau*, pp. 9–10.

184. "Materialn vegn arbet-lagern in lubliner voyevodshaft beays der daytsher oku-patsye," *Blfg*, Vol. 2, pp. 254–256.

185. G.Ż., Nos. 33 (Nov. 12), 13 (Sept. 3), 17 (Sept. 17), 19 (Sept. 24), 36 (Nov. 22, 1940); testimony B–182/2012, pp. 2–3 in YaVA.

186. YaVA, microfilm JM/1487: report of the department for forced labor, Dec. 1940.

187. L. Garfunkel, *op. cit.*, pp. 107–108.

188. YaVA, File 0–6/3.

189. AGV, Files: IV/25, pp. 192–193; V/16, p. 108; IX/12, p. 2.

190. *Rocznik, II*, p. 60 (diagram).

191. *Sprawozdanie*, pp. 16–17.

192. *Bericht Krakau*, p. 4.

193. ZC, Docs. 621/68, 92/1, 103, 104. For the Kutno Ghetto the authorities accorded the hall of a ruined and long unused sugar plant comprising an area of 3 hectares; in Włocławek—the suburb Rakotówek, inhabited by a *déclassé* segment of the gentile population. The few streets were not paved and there was no electricity. Żychlin Ghetto was established on a swampy field outside the town with only a few buildings and without a single well; a large number of families, like those in Kutno Ghetto, had no shelter (records of JDC in AJHI, No. 106; *ibid.* testimony No. 375. In Kaunas by the end of August 1941, when the ghetto was established, 700 souls were left without shelter (YaVA, File B/12–4, p. 114(3).

194. ZC, Doc. 621/86; Ringelblum, *op. cit.*, pp. 59–61; J. Turkow, *Azoy iz es geven, Khurbn Varshe* (Buenos Aires, 1948), pp. 95–96.

195. ZC, Doc. 64/68.

196. M. Fenigstein, *Varshever yidisher shpitol beaysn nazi-rezhim* ([Munich], 1948), p. 20; ZC, Doc. 621/141–145, 148, 149; Zaderecki, p. 485.

197. AJHI, a table concerning the density of the population in Warsaw Ghetto in comparison with the "Aryan" section of the city in March 1941: RA, I, No. 83.

198. YIA, Doc. IT, pp. 16, 19, 20.

199. YaVA, B/12–4, p. 13.

200. AJHI. Records of the Council in Lublin, File No. 8: report of the health depart-

ment. In Białystok Ghetto the density amounted to 3 m², in that of Prużana—2 m² per capita (Shimon Datner, "Tsu der geshikhte fun betsirk białystok," *Blfg*, Vol. 5, No. 4 [1952], p. 75).

201. BWS, No. 12ᵇ, p. 7.
202. YaVA, B/12–4, p. 13.
203. Zaderecki, pp. 521–522.
204. *Grodner Opklangen*, No. 2 (1949), p. 21; YIA: "Chart of the Organizational Structure of the Łódź Ghetto Administration" (Feb. 15, 1941).
205. ZC, Docs. 621/56, 621/60–63; 1011.
206. For the Łódź Ghetto: YIA Doc. IT, pp. 24–25; for Warsaw: the correspondence between the ghetto commissar, Auerswald, and Czerniakow of Oct. 1941 (YaVA, microfilm JM/1112); for the Council in Kaunas: L. Garfunkel, *op. cit.*, p. 52.
207. Doc. IT, p. 16; L. Garfunkel, *op. cit.*, pp. 52; the Diary of Czerniakow, entry of Nov. 22, 1940.
208. Zaderecki, p. 520.
209. ZC, Doc. 207.
210. *Bericht Warschau*, p. 16.
211. BWS, No. 9, p. 14. The tenement department of the Council received from the City Housing Division 38 premises for the benefit of the refugees, but they were refused because they were uninhabitable.
212. YIA, Doc. No. 60/11: Oyfbroyz, No. 18/3 (June 22, 1942).
213. AGV, No. 136. Letter No. 10281 by Biebow to Rumkowski (Jan. 2, 1942).
214. "Encyclopedia shel geto Lodzh," YBLG, No. 14–15 (April 1956), p. 67. In Sept. 1941, 37 oxen and 383 peasant carts arrived in the ghetto. By Jan. 1, 1942, there were 143 horses.
215. ZC, Docs. 178, 181, 255, 425, 880–890.
216. MTA, announcements of the Council, Nos. 255 (Apr. 29), 280 (June 5, 1942), (Blumental, *op. cit.*, pp. 436, 438, 450).
217. Josef Gar, *Umkum fun der yidicher Kovne* (Munich, 1948), p. 351; Garfunkel, *op. cit.*, p. 104.
218. G.Ż., No. 22 (March 18, 1941), p. 5.
219. AJHI, records of JUS, File No. 32; RA, I, Nos. 255, 1160; *Kwestjonarjusze Instytutu Pamięci Narodowej*, No. 2 (copies in AJHI).
220. WaC, Doc. 48ᵃ.
221. Sh. Glube, "Di din-toyre," FLKh, No. 6 (1947), pp. 44–47.
222. Czerniakow's Diary, entries of May 11 and August 24, 1940; *Tshenstokhover yidn* (New York, 1947), p. 231.
223. ZC, Doc. 28, pp. 9, 19.

CHAPTER 6

1. RA, I, No. 77; records of JDC, File No. 417.
2. G.Ż., *passim*.
3. ABLG, pp. 1, 3.
4. YaVA, microfilm JM/814, p. 1.
5. *Ibid.*
6. *Sprawozdanie*, pp. 31, 34.
7. *Ibid.*, pp. 18–20, 37–38.
8. Minutes, No. 7/68; at the Council meeting of April 14 an additional 2,000 zlotys were allocated for this purpose (minutes, No. 21/32).

9. *Bericht Krakau*, pp. 13–14, 33, 61, 67, 69–74.

10. Brener, *op. cit.*, pp. 3–4; G.Ż., No. 6 (Aug. 9, 1940).

11. Eisenbach, *Getto Łódzkie*, pp. 77–79.

12. ZC, Docs. 117, 245, 388, 1002, 1470; *Geto-tsaytung*, Nos. 13 and 17 (June 20 and Sept. 14, 1941).

13. There are slight variations between the figures in the introduction and in the report proper.

14. YaVA, File 06/3–4.

15. *Ibid.*, File B/12–4, p. 9.

16. Su-KC, Doc. 288.

17. *Ibid.*, Docs. 159, 160.

18. *Ibid.*

19. *Ibid.*, Doc. 163.

20. Minutes of the general meeting of the Council and the ghetto population, June 21, 1942 (Blumental, *op. cit.*, p. 280).

21. MTA, Pesakh Kaplan, "Der Yudnrat in Białystok" (ms.); minutes of Dec. 20, 1941, and March 1, 1942; Blumental, *op. cit.*, pp. 100, 144; minutes of the meeting of the department chiefs, Aug. 20, 1941 (Blumental, *op. cit.*; p. 19).

22. RA, I, according to a questionnaire circulated in the ghetto in May–July 1941.

23. G.Ż., No. 6 (Aug. 9, 1940); Brener, *op. cit.*, p. 66.

24. G.Ż., No. 2 (July 26, 1940).

25. G.Ż., No. 4 (Aug. 2, 1940).

26. *Alaynhilf*, pp. 83–84; "Materyaln vegn di arbetlagern in lubliner woyewodshaft beays der daytsher okupatsye (1940–1941)," *Blfg*, Vol. II (1949), pp. 242–272.

27. AGV, File IV/28, pp. 65–66: memorandum by Biebow to the *Regierungspräsident* in Łódź, Sept. 1, 1941.

28. Su-KC, Docs. 158, 166, 290, and others.

29. AJHI, mss. concerning various cities in Poland, No. 44 (Kutno); JUS, File No. 31. In 37 ghettos the refugees numbered 16.8% of the total Jewish population (13,496 of 80,073).

30. JUS, No. 31.

31. RA, I, No. 41, p. 4.

32. RA, I, No. 81.

33. T. Brustin-Bernstein, "Gerushim vi an etap in der daytsher farnichtungs-politik," *Blfg*, Vol. III, No. 1–2 (1950), p. 68.

34. A. Rutkowski, "Di yidishe bafelkerung in radomer distrikt beays der hitleristisher okupatsye," *Blfg*, Vol. XII (1959), p. 96.

35. Besides the excerpt quoted, *see also*: Brustin-Bernstein "Di gerushim un die farnikhtung fun di yidishe yishuvim in varshever distrikt," *Blfg*, Vol. IV, No. 2 (1951), pp. 103–122 (with the respective tables) and Trunk, *Shtudie, ibid.*, Vol. II, pp. 76–93.

36. *Sefer hazvaot*, p. 16; a report under the heading "Der Totenmarsch von Lublin" compiled in Cracow on March 14, 1940, by a mixed Polish-Jewish Committee for Aid in the GG was sent to Himmler (copy in YIA).

37. RA, I, No. 1203.

38. G.Ż., *passim*: local reports of scores of communities on their activities on behalf of the local Jews and the refugees and expellees.

39. *Sprawozdanie*, pp. 10–17.

40. Ringelblum, *op. cit.*, p. 23.

41. *Sprawozdanie*, pp. 21–25.

42. *Bericht Krakau*, pp. 69–73; YaVA, File 06/3–1.

43. *Bericht Krakau*, pp. 74–75.

44. Brener, *op. cit.*, pp. 18, 19, 20, 45.
45. G.Ż., No. 10 (Aug. 24, 1940).
46. JUS, File 106, pp. 11, 19, 21, 32, 50–69, 86–88.
47. JDC records, File No. 417, p. 7.
48. Archives of the JDC, New York: File—General & Emergency Poland Reports, 1939/1940, confirmation (Nov., 1939) by the U.S. General Consul George H. Hearing in Warsaw to the German authorities, that the JDC is an American organization, requesting that its rights be respected (hereafter cited as G & EPR with respective dates).
49. AJHI, records of the JDC, File 417: "The Activities of the JDC in Poland for Thitreen Months (September 1939–October 1940)," p. 10.
50. *Ibid.*, File 415.
51. *Ibid.*, File 355, pp. 81–82.
52. *Ibid.*, File 106, p. 7.
53. *Ibid.*, File 417, p. 12.
54. G & EPR 1939/1940: Incoming Cable, Warsaw, July 29, 1940.
55. AJHI, JDC, File 378, pp. 266–269.
56. *Ibid.*, p. 265.
57. *Ibid.*, File 417, on JDC activities in Poland, Sept. 1939–Oct. 1940.
58. G & EPR 1941–1944.
59. Circular letter of the JSS, Jan. 24, 1941 (AJHI, JDC, File 376).
60. AJHI, JDC, File 364, p. 146.
61. G & EPR, 1939 (Nov. 3-4, 1939); "A footnote to History," by Alexander Kahn (G & EPR, 1941–1944).
62. AJHI, JDC, File 378, p. 249; G & EPR, 1941–1944: "Binding a nation's wounds," by Alexander Kahn, pp. 5–6.
63. AGV, No. 117, p. 242. Contradicting this information is a statement in a report of the *Gettoverwaltung* for Oct. 1940 to the effect that the first $20,000 from the JDC were received in Berlin on that month and were exchanged at the rate of 5 Reichsmarks = 1 dollar (AGV, No. 115, p. 10); the matter needs further exploration.
64. G & EPR, Jan. 1941.
65. *Ibid.*, JDC Lisbon, No. 428 (Jan. 25, 1941): "Summary Memorandum of Conversations with our Friends X & Y during the Month of January 1941."
66. G & EPR, 1940: "Division of Work in the Old Reich, German Poland, former German Territories (Sosnowiec, Kattowitz), GG."
67. G & EPR, Jan. 1941; JDC Lisbon, No. 428 (Jan. 25, 1941).

CHAPTER 7

1. Ludwik Hirszfeld, *Historia jednego życia* (Warsaw, 1946), p. 220 (2nd ed., 1951, p. 265).
2. AJHI, testimony by Dr. Jendraszko, a Pole who got from the authorities permission to enter Kutno Ghetto to attend the sick.
3. "Okupacja niemieka w Polsce w świetle dziennika Hansa Franka," *BGKBZN*, Vol. I (1947), p. 38.
4. RA, I, No. 223: report by the manager of the refugee shelter, Eng. Einhorn (Aug. 2, 1941).
5. *Lodzher geto*, pp. 233–234.
6. Isaiah Trunk, "Sanitare farheltenishn un shtarbikayt in geto," *Dos bukh fun Lublin* (Paris, 1952), p. 362.

7. Trunk, "Milkhome kegn yidn durkh farshpraytn krankaytn," *YIVO-Bleter*, Vol. XXXVII (New York, 1953), pp. 64, 65.

8. YIA, Doc. IT, pp. 16, 19, 20.

9. Shimon Datner, "Tsu der geshikhte fun yidn in betsirk białystok," *Blfg*, Vol. V, No. 4 (1952), pp. 75–76.

10. A. Rutkowski, "Di yidishe bafelkerung in rodemer distrikt beays der hitleristisher okupatsye," *Blfg*, Vol. XII (1959), p. 79.

11. *Ibid.*, p. 78.

12. Trunk, "Sanitare farheltenishn . . . ," *op. cit.*, p. 357.

13. BC, Doc. OccE3-18, p. 2, Par. IIIC.

14. Yerushalmi, *op. cit.*, pp. 18, 36, 47, 77.

15. AGV, File VII/11, p. 352.

16. *BGKBZN*(H), Vol. 11, p. 33.

17. AJHI, records of the JSS, File No. 409.

18. RA, I, No. 191.

19. RA, I, No. 1950; Czerniakow's Diary, entry of Feb. 20, 1942, relating two cases of cannibalism on Dec. 15, 1941, and Feb. 1942; the date of the third case is unknown.

20. RA, I, No. 223; *Choroba głodowa. Badania kliniczne nad głodem wykonana w getcie warszawskim w roku 1942* (Warsaw, 1947), p. 113.

21. Libman Hersh, "Yiddishe demografye," *Algemeine entsiklopedie, Yidn*, Vol. I, Col. 367–386.

22. *Lodzher geto*, pp. 222–223.

23. *Ibid.*, pp. 227, 228.

24. BC, Doc. OccE3–18, p. 7, Section Vd.

25. ZC, Doc. 43, p. 1.

26. RA, I, No. 214.

27. *Lodzher geto*, p. 219; Dvorzhetsky, *op. cit.*, p. 191.

28. *Lodzher geto*, pp. 167–168.

29. AGV, File 229, p. 514.

30. BKC, Aug. 2, 1942.

31. *Blfg*, Vol. II, pp. 242–272.

32. I. Trunk, "Yidishe arbet-lagern in Varteland," *Blfg*, Vol. I, No. 1 (1948). pp. 155–165.

33. *Trials of War Criminals before the Nuremberg Military Tribunal*, Vol. IV (Case No. 9), pp. 432–433.

34. RA, I, No. 83.

35. AJHI, "Materiały do dziejów Żydów podczas okupacji niemieckiej" (ms.), File IV/2, p. 498.

36. Luba Bielicka, "Vegn der aktsye in varshever shpitol dem 18tn yanuar 1943," *Blfg*, Vol. I, No. 3–4, pp. 211–213.

37. ZC, Doc. 621/73.

38. *Lodzher geto*, p. 57.

39. G.Ż., No. 6 (Aug. 9, 1940); the reasons for the removal of the hospital are, of course, omitted from the item.

40. *Dos bukh fun Lublin*, pp. 360, 361, 390; *Bericht Krakau*, p. 46.

41. AJHI, testimony, No. 311.

42. *Lodzher geto*, p. 4.

43. G.Ż., No. 9 (Aug. 21, 1940), p. 7 (Mińsk Mazowiecki); No. 21 (Sept. 1940), p. 4 (Bełchatów); No. 36 (Nov. 22, 1940) (Brzesko), and others.

44. AGV, File XI/54, pp. 63–64.

45. AJHI, mss. of cities, No. 44.

46. ZC, Docs. 621/112, 621/115.
47. Tadeusz Pankiewicz, *Apteka w getcie krakowskim* (Cracow, 1947).
48. G.Ż., Nos. 35 (May 2, 1941), 70 (Aug. 11, 1941); furthermore there was in the ghetto a licensed wholesale store, which provided the pharmacies with medicaments.
49. Dvorzhetsky, *op. cit.*, pp. 204–207.
50. BWS, No. 12ª, p. 7; RA, I, No. 85; Fenigstein, *op. cit., passim.*
51. *Wohnbezirk*, p. 6.
52. RA, I, No. 315, pp. 1–2.
53. RA, I, No. 1308.
54. RA, I, Nos. 85, 214, 315.
55. A more detailed account in *Lodzher geto*, pp. 54–57.
56. *Bericht Krakau*, pp. 26–48.
57. Su-KC, Doc. 153; the health department continued to publish the prewar edition of "Folks-gezunt" (mimeographed), of which 18 issues appeared (Dvorzhetsky, *op. cit.*, pp. 215, 216).
58. Su-KC, Doc. 124. During the year from July 1941 to July 1942, 4,227 patients were treated, with an average of 205 a day. The hospital laboratories made 5,847 analyses and 1,480 X rays, and 50,934 prescriptions had been filled by July 15, 1942. Notwithstanding the extreme scarcity of instruments and tools in the ghetto, the hospital succeeded in repairing old equipment and installing new. The clinic opened the day after the ghetto was established and operated with very limited equipment and a few instruments—some borrowed, some donated. In time the inventory grew. The clinic conducted medical research and arranged lectures with demonstrations. In all, 42,231 patients were treated at the hospital during the report period, 7,840 house calls were made by the doctors, and 25,125 patients were treated by the dental clinic. Emergency medical aid was extended in 1,135 cases. The clinic employed 27 doctors, 6 dentists, 8 nurses, 5 sanitary aides, and some other medical personnel. The hospital pharmacy filled prescriptions for both hospital patients and outpatients.
59. Su-KC, Doc. 124.
60. Su-KC, Doc. 128.
61. Su-KC, Doc. 149.
62. Minutes of Aug. 2 and 20, 1941 (Blumental, *op. cit.*, pp. 5, 17, 19).
63. Minutes of Aug. 23, 1941 (Blumental, *op. cit.* p. 22).
64. Announcement No. 177 of Dec. 9, 1941 (Blumental, *op. cit.*, p. 390).
65. Minutes of Aug. 24 and Nov. 5, 1941. Announcement No. 176 of Dec. 8, 1941. Blumental, *op. cit.*, pp. 24, 70, 389, 391. A special meeting of the ghetto population was called by the Council about the danger of typhus (minutes of Nov. 23, 1941 [Blumental, *op. cit.*, pp. 297–299]).
66. Announcement No. 223 of Feb. 20, 1942 (Blumental, *op. cit.*, p. 420).
67. See sources listed in n. 65 (Chap. 7).
68. Announcement No. 145, Nov. 1, 1941 (Blumental, *op. cit.*, p. 368).
69. Announcement No. 245, Apr. 1, 1942 (Blumental, *op. cit.*, p. 430).
70. Announcement No. 278, May 31, 1942 (Blumental, *op. cit.*, p. 450).
71. See sources listed in n. 65 (Chap. 7).
72. Minutes of the meeting (Blumental, *op. cit.*, p. 17).
73. From an announcement of the Council, issued on Sept. 7, 1941, on orders of the authorities, one can infer that contagious diseases had broken out in eight houses on two streets. The inhabitants of these houses were not allowed to leave under death penalty; the kind of ailment was not revealed. (Blumental, *op. cit.*, p. 329).
74. Minutes of May 2, 1942 (Blumental, *op. cit.*, p. 173).
75. Announcement No. 278, May 31, 1942 (Blumental, *op. cit.*, p. 450).

76. RA, I, No. 221.
77. RA, I, Nos. 363, 428.
78. *Bericht Krakau*, p. 31.
79. AJHI, records of the Lublin Council, Files 8 and 98.
80. *Dos bukh fun Lublin*, pp. 357–362.
81. *Sprawozdanie*, pp. 34–36.
82. Minutes, No. 49/110 (Oct. 18, 1941); AJHI, records of Lublin Council, File No. 98.
83. Minutes, Nos. 36/97, 38/99 (July 1941).
84. *Dos bukh fun Lublin*, pp. 359–360.
85. AJHI, records of the Council, File No. 18.
86. Minutes, No. 58/119 (Dec. 7, 1941). The following episode is symptomatic of the "help" the authorities gave the Council in its endeavor to combat the epidemic: In June 1941 the *Treuhandstelle* confiscated the only bathhouse in the ghetto and a Pole was put in charge; for Jews the use of the bath was forbidden. The Council requested the return of the only bath in the ghetto, and the request was granted by the mayor. Suddenly the Council was informed by him of the decision to revoke his previous order and to keep the Pole further in charge. Thus, at the same time the authorities allegedly waged a fight against the epidemic, the ghetto was robbed of its sole bathhouse and the Council was forced to build a new one out of its meager means.
87. Minutes, Nos. 36/97 (July 7, 1941) and 45/106 (Sept. 26, 1941).
88. *Sprawozdanie*, p. 36.
89. Minutes, Nos. 50/111 and 57/118.
90. *Bzhezhin yizkor bukh* (1961), pp. 137–138. Also in the Kaunas Ghetto, those with contagious diseases had to be guarded from the Nazis and kept in a secret hospital (Garfunkel, *op. cit.*, pp. 110–111).
91. In the labor camp Ossowa (Lublin district) almost all inmates (53 persons) were shot in Aug. 1941 by SS men after a few laborers got sick with typhus (Ringelblum, *op. cit.*, pp. 156, 170–171). The Jewish hospital in Kaunas was set on fire in Oct. 1941; over 60 patients and the medical personnel perished in the flames (J. Gar, *op. cit.*, p. 69). More facts of this kind could be quoted.
92. *Pinkos fun di finf fartilikte kehiles*, pp. 603–604.
93. *Pinkos Mlave*, p. 402.

CHAPTER 8

1. BWS, No. 6, p. 11; between July 5 and 20, 1941, the registration and evidence department of the Warsaw Council issued 182 certificates of various kinds.
2. *Sprawozdanie*, p. 54; ZC, Doc. 55.
3. *Ibid.*, p. 51; during the period April 1–15, 1940, the Council collected 11,313 declarations.
4. *Bericht Krakau*, pp. 87–88.
5. BWS, No. 12ᵇ, p. 12.
6. VBlGG, No. 13 (1939).
7. BWS, No. 1, p. 13; No. 9, p. 8 (1940).
8. G.Ż., No. 35 (May 2, 1941).
9. *Bericht Krakau*, p. 111.
10. *Lodzher geto*, pp. 41–43.
11. ZC, Docs. 55ii, 1252.
12. Zaderecki, p. 499.

13. *Bericht Krakau*; BWS of the Warsaw Council; reports of the department of statistics of the Councils in Częstochowa and Vilna, among others.
14. ZC, Docs. 58, 1432, 1464, 1465, 1466, 1470, 1496.
15. Brener, *op. cit.*, pp. 171–173; parts of the yearbook in the YIA and YaVA.
16. Su-KC, Docs. 291, 292ª, 292, 293, 286, 288.
17. YIA, File *Poyln, hitler-tsayt*, letters Kaph-Shin.
18. Su-KC, Docs. 67–71, 93–95.
19. YIA, File *Poyln, hitler-tsayt*: File *Varshever geto*; Diary of Czerniakow, entries of Dec. 9, 1939, and Jan. 10, 1940, among others.
20. YIA, File *Poyln hitler-tsayt*, letters Aleph-Tet.
21. *Ibid.*
22. ZC, Doc. 83.
23. *Ibid.*, Docs. 240, 1436, 1437.
24. ZC, Docs. 1427–1429.
25. *Lodzher geto*, pp. 109–113.
26. ZC, Doc. 789.
27. ABLG, Doc. 1882–3 (a copy).
28. Minutes of the Council for Nov. 29, 1941 (Blumental, *op. cit.*, p. 92).
29. *Sprawozdanie*, p. 69.
30. ZC, Doc. 621/120.
31. BWS, No. 12, p. 12; Ruta Sakowska, "*Łączność pocztowa warszawskiego geta*" ("Postal Service in the ghetto of Warsaw"), BŻIH, No. 45–46 (1963), pp. 94–95.
32. Ruta Sakowska, *op. cit.*, p. 95; G.Ż., No. 55 (July 7, 1941), Bochnia, Otwock; No. 51 (June 27, 1941), Kielce; No. 61 (July 21, 1941), Radomsko; No. 6 (Jan. 14, 1942), Radom; No. 11 (Jan. 25, 1942), Rabka; No. 32 (March 15, 1942), Częstochowa; No. 36 (March 25, 1942), Cracow; No. 44 (Apr. 15, 1942), Jasło.
33. G.Ż., No. 19 (March 7, 1941).
34. Postcards with the stamp of the Council of Warsaw and other towns in YIA; a photocopy of the mail stamp of the Cracow Council in YIA and ABLG.
35. *Ibid.*, postcard dated Aug. 1, 1941, sent to Paris.
36. *Bericht Warschau*, p. 18.
37. Ruta Sakowska, *op. cit.*, p. 97.
38. *Yizkor-bukh fun der Zhelekhover yidisher kehile* (Chicago, 1953), p. 227.
39. *Sprawozdanie*, p. 70.
40. *Alaynhilf*, pp. 151–152.
41. ZC, Docs. 118, 119, 139, 141, 144, 172, 267, 396, 1175.
42. BWS, No. 12, p. 12; Ruta Sakowska, *op. cit.*, pp. 94–95.
43. VBlGG, No. 15 (Dec. 6, 1941).
44. *Yizkor-bukh fun der Zhelekhover* . . . , p. 454; *Bericht Krakau*, pp. 115–116; *Sprawozdanie*, pp. 61–63; G.Ż., No. 12 (Aug. 30, 1940).
45. BWS, No. 11, p. 7 (Nov. 1940); No. 12ᵇ, p. 7 (Jan. 1941).
46. Zaderecki, p. 482.
47. YaVA, File DN/3–4, p. 5.
48. Brener, *op. cit.*, p. 14.
49. Su-KC, Doc. 331.
50. ZC, Doc. 862/A.
51. *Lodzher geto*, pp. 38–39.
52. Announcement No. 82 (Sept. 1941) and minutes of the Jan. 10, 1942, meeting of the chiefs of the Council departments (Blumental *op. cit.*, pp. 325–326, 107).
53. Minutes of the meeting (Blumental, *op. cit.*, p. 183).
54. *Geto-tsaytung*, No. 14 (July 15, 1941), No. 13 (June 20, 1941); ZC, Docs. 18, 279, 322.
55. YaVA, DN/3–4, pp. 5–6.

56. Su-KC, Docs. 323, 325.
57. ZC, Doc. 862/A; DN/3-4, p. 5; Su-KC, Doc. 324 ("Takones fun krimineln protses," Par. 138).
58. ZC, Doc. 45; Doc. 26, p. 19; *Geto-tsaytung* (Sept. 21, 1941, the eve of Rosh Hashanah).
59. Doc. DN/3-4.
60. ZC, Doc. 862/A.
61. MTA, Pesakh Kaplan, "Der yudnrat in białystok," ms. (Feb.–March 1943); the author remarked, however, that the sentences were carried out in accord with the ghetto conditions.
62. Levi Shalit, "Azoy zenen mir geshtorbn," *Yidishe tsaytung*, Landsberg, No. 38/203 (May 21, 1948); the author was an attorney in the ghetto court.
63. Su-KC, Docs. 323, 324.
64. ZC, Doc. 862/A.
65. Yerushalmi, *op. cit.*, p. 147.
66. AGV, File IV/53.
67. ZC, Docs. 26, p. 10; AGV, File 220, pp. 114–115.
68. *Wohnbezirk*, p. 6.
69. Doc. DN/3-4, p. 5.
70. *Geto-tsaytung*, No. 8 (Apr. 25, 1941).
71. Su-KC, Docs. 268ᵃ, 305, 305ᵃ, 326–330.
72. Rotenberg, *op. cit.*, p. 114; *Pinkos Kolomay*, p. 332, among others.
73. Nirenberg, "Geshikhte fun lodzher geto," *In di yorn fun yidishn khurbn, di shtime fun untererdishn bund* (New York, 1948), pp. 233–234; Jakub Poznański, *Pamiętnik z geta łódzkiego* ("A Memoir of the Łódź Ghetto"), (Łódź, 1960), p. 60; we should take into consideration that longer prison terms meant, ultimately, the death penalty for the sentenced, because these prisoners were, as was the case *inter alia* in the Łódź Ghetto, the first to be deported from the ghettos during the "resettlements."
74. Su-KC, Docs. 300ᵃ, 301, 339ᵉ.
75. ZC, Doc. 30: BKC of Dec. 22, 1942; BKC of Apr. 26, 1943; AGV, File IV/14, p. 161.
76. RA, I, No. 41; AJHI: "Mss. of cities." No. 151, p. 218; Alexander Hohenstein, *Wartheländisches Tagebuch aus den Jahren 1941/42* (Stuttgart, 1961), pp. 239–243.

CHAPTER 9

1. VBlGG, No. 1 (Oct. 26, 1939).
2. *Bericht Krakau*, p. 3.
3. I. L. Gersht, *Min hamaytsar* (Jerusalem, 1949), pp. 39–41.
4. G.Ż., No. 23 (Oct. 7, 1940).
5. ABLG, Doc. 1884/32; the announcement contained a warning that severe penalties would be applied against the organizers and the worshipers.
6. Yerushalmi, *op. cit.*, p. 113.
7. ZC, Doc. 185.
8. ZC, Docs. 542, 548.
9. AGV, No. 144 (microfilm JM/828 in YaVA).
10. An address by Rumkowski, Jan. 25, 1942 (JM/1932/44, pp. 3–4); ZC, Docs. 304, 569.
11. ZC, Doc. 1616; Eisenbach, *Getto Łódzkie*, p. 245.
12. BWS, 12ᵇ, p. 3; G.Ż., No. 34 (Apr. 28, 1941); No. 42 (May 27, 1941.)
13. Su-KC, Doc. 295.
14. *Lodzher geto*, p. 403.

15. ZC, Doc. 160.
16. *Lodzher geto*, p. 404.
17. G.Ż., No. 24 (Oct. 11, 1940).
18. G.Ż., No. 32 (Nov. 8, 1940).
19. Czerniakow's Diary; from a note in the G.Ż. (No. 32, Nov. 8, 1940) it is evident that Czerniakow was informed as late as Jan. 26, 1941, about the official order forbidding public service.
20. Shimon Huberband, "Memorial vegn oprateven di reshtlekh fun yidishe kultur-oytsres in poyln," *Blfg*, Vol. I, No. 2 (1948), pp. 105–110.
21. *The Persecution of Jews in German-Occupied Poland*. Free Europe Pamphlet No. 2 (London, no date), p. 18; Tabaksblat, *op. cit.*, p. 24; many cases of this kind are cited in the various memorial books.
22. Kaufmann, *Die Vernichtung der Juden Lettlands* (Munich, 1947), pp. 89, 167, 169.
23. Testimony by Rabbi David Kahane (YIA).
24. *Geto-tsaytung*, announcement, No. 242 (Apr. 3, 1941).
25. *Sprawozdanie*, pp. 71–72.
26. G.Ż., No. 29 (Apr. 11, 1941); this was also the case in Tarnów (*ibid.*).
27. *Pinkos Kobryn*, p. 260: *Podlashe in umkum* (Międzyrzec), p. 179; I. Kurc, *Sefer eydut* (Piotrków), pp. 228–229; the śiauliai Council prohibited the baking of matzoth for Passover 1942, because this "would cause the destruction of the ghetto," but privately matzoth were baked and even the Council members took part in this good deed (Yerushalmi, *op. cit.*, p. 181).
28. G.Ż., No. 29 (Apr. 11, 1941) (Warsaw); L. Brener, *op. cit.*, p. 43 (Częstochowa); *Lodzher geto*, p. 409, n. 254.
29. *Lodzher geto*, pp. 410–411.
30. Testimony by Benjamin Frenkel, "Lodzher marysin geto," in YIA.
31. *Lodzher geto*, p. 408.
32. ZC, Docs. 845; 44, p. 2.
33. G.Ż., No. 10 (Feb. 4, 1941).
34. Information by Dr. Hilel Seidman, former employee in the Community Archives of the *Judenrat*.
35. Testimony by Rabbi David Kahane.
36. For Passover of 1941 the rabbinate permitted the use of canned best margarine and saccharine delivered by the *Gettoverwaltung* (ZC, Doc. 1267; *Geto-tsaytung*, Nos. 4 and 5 of March 28 and Apr. 4, 1941).
37. ZC, Doc. 1268.
38. Ringelblum, *op. cit.*, p. 112.
39. Efraim Oshri, *Sefer shalot utshuvot mimamaakim* (New York, 1959).
40. *Geto-tsaytung*, No. 14 (July 15, 1941).
41. ZC, Doc. 29, p. 1.
42. ZC, Doc. 29A: BKC of June 14 and 18, 1942.
43. *Sefer Borschchiv*, p. 147; Efraim Oshri, *op. cit.*, pp. 115–116; *Pinkos Zamoshch*, p. 1005.
44. G.Ż., No. 35 (May 2, 1941).
45. ZC, Doc. 1192, p. 9; in contrast to Łódź a Catholic school for children of converts was opened in the Warsaw Ghetto by Caritas (cf. Ruta Sakowska, *op. cit.*, p. 226).
46. Ringelblum, *op. cit.*, p. 107.
47. Max Kaufmann, *op. cit.*, p. 169.
48. Anna Natanblut, "Di shuln in varshever geto," *YIVO-Bleter*, Vol. XXX, No. 2 (1947), p. 173.
49. The opening of private schools was contingent upon a permission of the authorities (decree by Frank, March 10, 1940).

50. Sara Neshamit, "Leparshat hakhinukh hameurgan begeto varsha," YBLG, No. 21 (May 1959), pp. 98–100.
51. VBlGG, Part I, No. 51 (Sept. 11, 1940).
52. BWS, No. 12ᶜ, p. 2; G.Ż., No. 7 (Jan. 24, 1941).
53. I. Trunk, "Milkhome kegn yidn durch farshpraytn krankaytn," *YIVO-Bleter*, Vol. XXXVII (1953), p. 61.
54. G.Ż., No. 2 (Jan. 7, 1941).
55. WaC, Doc. 36ª/1.
56. G.Ż., No. 34 (Apr. 29, 1941).
57. G.Ż., No. 66 (Aug. 1, 1941).
58. Anna Natanblut, *op. cit.*, pp. 174–176. Up to June 1942 two more schools were opened. (cf. Ruta Sakowska, "O tajnym nauczaniu w getcie warszawskim." *Warszawa lat wojny i okupacji* (1971), p. 226.
59. Ruta Sakowska, "O tajnym nauczaniu . . . ," *op. cit.*, p. 226.
60. WaC, File 49 (loose documents); cf. A. Berman, "O losie dzieci w getcie warszawskim" (about the fate of children in the Warsaw Ghetto). BŻIH, No. 28 (1958), pp. 67–68.
61. "Korespondentsya pnimit," No. 4 in *Dapim lekheker hashoa vehamered*, Vol. I (1951), p. 156; *In di yorn fun yidishn khurbn*, p. 14. In May 1941 there were in the ghetto some 500 "nooks" with about 15,000 children receiving some instruction (Ruta Sakowska, "O tajnym nauczaniu . . . ," *op. cit.*, p. 238).
62. WaC, File 49.
63. Sara Neshamit, *op. cit.*, pp. 106–107.
64. Natan Eck, "Shnayim shesordu," *Davar* (Tel Aviv), Apr. 28, 1957.
65. "Korespondentsya pnimit," *op. cit.*, pp. 155–156.
66. Ester Goldhar-Mark, "Dos yidishe fakh-un hekhere shulvezn in varshe in der tsayt fun der daytsher okupatsye," *Blfg*, Vol. II, pp. 195–202.
67. Ludwik Hirszfeld, *op. cit.*, pp. 207–215.
68. Anna Natanblut, *op. cit.*, p. 183; Goldhar-Mark, *op. cit.*, p. 201. Natanblut related that the classes were overcrowded.
69. Ringelblum, *op. cit.*, p. 147; G.Ż., No. 52 (June 30, 1941).
70. *Pinkos Zamoshch*, pp. 1155, 1156; Philip Friedman, "Khurban yehudey Lwów," *Encyclopaedia*, Vol. IV, p. 683 (in Lwów a special school department was established, which planned to open two schools in both ghetto parts (see Zaderecki, p. 509).
71. Nakhman Korn, "Dertsiyungs-problemen un kinder-elnt in geto," *Dos bukh fun Lublin*, pp. 503–506.
72. G.Ż., No. 32 (Nov. 8, 1940).
73. *Bericht Krakau*, pp. 113–114; G.Ż., No. 63 (July 27, 1941).
74. G.Ż., No. 42 (Dec. 13, 1940).
75. G.Ż., No. 43 (Dec. 17, 1940).
76. G.Ż., No. 59 (July 16, 1941).
77. G.Ż., No. 42 (Dec. 1940); *Alaynhilf*, p. 318.
78. G.Ż., No. 32 (Nov. 8, 1940); No. 19 (Sept. 24, 1940).
79. G.Ż., No. 63 (July 27, 1941).
80. *Alaynhilf*, p. 318.
81. L. Garfunkel, *op. cit.*, pp. 113–114; I. Kaplan, "Kovner shul un lerershaft in umkum," FLKh, No. 9 (1948), pp. 6–16. In Lublin and Chełm the authorities, with invectives and beatings, dispersed the ghetto schools which were functioning with their permission (see reference in n. 71, above and *Yizkor bukh Khelm*, p. 208).
82. AJHI, testimony, No. 303.

83. The authorities sometimes forced Jewish scholars to carry out the confiscation of Jewish libraries, as was for instance the case with the renowned historian Professor M. Bałaban (Diary of Czerniakow, entry of Jan. 24, 1940).
84. Y. L. Gersht, "Lerer kursn far yiddish in lodzher geto," *YIVO-Bleter*, Vol. XXX, No. 1 (1947), pp. 152–155.
85. L. Brener, *op. cit.*, pp. 51–53.
86. Kermisz, *Akcje i Wysiedlenia* (Łódź, 1946), p. 42.
87. L. Brener, *op. cit.*, p. 56.
88. G.Ż., No. 44 (Dec. 20, 1940).
89. G.Ż., *passim* (in the GG); *Lodzher geto*, pp. 53–54; Dvorzhetsky, *op. cit.*, pp. 235–236, and others.
90. I. Kaplan, "Kovner shul un lerershaft in umkum," and Jacob Oleyski, "Di fakhshul in kovner geto," FLKh, No. 9 (1948). Until Aug. 1942 a private Hebrew kindergarten, private *khedorim*, and a sort of yeshiva were functioning (L. Garfunkel, *op. cit.*, p. 236).
91. ZC, Doc. 1464.
92. ZC, Doc. 931/1.
93. *Ibid.*
94. ZC, Doc. 1464, p. 73; Doc. 933.
95. ZC, Doc. 1464, p. 5.
96. Gersht, *op. cit.*, pp. 152–155.
97. ZC, Doc. 1213.
98. Zvi Shner, "Letoldot hekhayim hatarbutyim begeto lodzh bishnot 1940–1941," *Dapim lekheyker hashoa vehamered*, Vol. 1 (1951), pp. 99–101; YBLG, No. 9–10, p. 35.
99. *Lodzher geto*, pp. 53, 54.
100. ZC, Doc. 940.
101. ZC, Doc. 30: BKC, July 31, 1942.
102. *Ibid.*
103. Dvorzhetsky, *op. cit.*, pp. 226, 227; Sima Leykin, "Strashun-gas 12 in vilner geto," *YIVO Bleter*, Vol. XXX, No. 2 (1947), pp. 317–318; M. Kanishtchiker, "Mir boyen a shul in geto," *Zukunft* (Apr. 1955), pp. 168–169.
104. Su-KC, Docs. 291, 348; Dvorzhetsky, *op. cit.*, pp. 227–228.
105. Su-KC, Doc. 288.
106. Dvorzhetsky, *op. cit.*, p. 228.
107. Su-KC, Doc. 383.
108. Su-KC, Doc. 385; Dvorzhetsky, *op. cit.*, p. 223.
109. Su-KC, Doc. 352.
110. Dvorzhetsky, *op. cit.*, p. 225; he related that a teacher did not interrupt her lesson during an "action" in the ghetto and, not having a *Schein*, was sent to Ponary, where she perished (*ibid.*, p. 226).
111. Su-KC, Doc. 385.
112. Su-KC, Docs. 348, 353.
113. Su-KC, Doc. 350.
114. Su-KC, Doc. 346.
115. Su-KC, Doc. 352.
116. Su-KC, Doc. 533.
117. Dvorzhetsky, *op. cit.*, p. 233.
118. Su-KC, Doc. 281.
119. Yerushalmi, *op. cit.*, pp. 239, 242, 279.
120. MTA, announcements of the Council, Aug. 29 and Sept. 5, 1941 (Blumental, *op. cit.*, pp. 322, 328).

121. Announcement of the Council, Aug. 14, 1942 (Blumental, *op. cit.*, pp. 28 [n. 8], 476).
122. Announcement of Nov. 9, 1941 (Blumental, *op. cit.*, p. 375, n. 195).
123. Announcement of Sept. 18, 1942 (Blumental, *op. cit.*, p. 484); cf. Sara Nomberg-Przytyk, *Kolumny Samsona* (Lublin, 1966), pp. 49–54.
124. Announcements of Aug. 14 and 18, 1942 (Blumental, *op. cit.*, p. 477).
125. WaC, Doc. 1; Natanblut, *op. cit.*, p. 183; Dvorzhetsky, *op. cit.*, pp. 231–232.
126. *Documenta Occupationis*, Vol. 5 (Poznań, 1952), p. 25; RA, I, No. 998.
127. RA, I, 998; G.Ż., No. 27 (Apr. 4, 1941).
128. Su-KC, Docs. 378, 379. The Polish paper *Goniec Codzienny* in 146 copies and the German *Wilnaer Zeitung* in 60 copies.
129. AJHI, testimony, No. 3625.
130. Brener, *op. cit.*, p. 56.
131. Su-KC, Doc. 291; Ringelblum, *op. cit.*, p. 244; ZC, Doc. 29: BKC, June 9, 1942.
132. Answers to a questionnaire of the Ringelblum Archives in the Warsaw Ghetto. *Blfg*, Vol. I, No. 2, pp. 118, 122; No. 3–4, p. 199.
133. Ringelblum, *op. cit.*, p. 148.
134. Answer by Hilel Tseytlin, *Blfg*, Vol. I, No. 2, p. 111; Zelig Kalmanovich, "Der gayst in geto," *YIVO-Bleter*, Vol. XXX, No. 2, p. 172.
135. Answers by Aron Einhorn and Dr. Israel Milejkowski, *Blfg*, Vol. I. No. 2, p. 122; No. 3–4, pp. 189–190.
136. Dvorzhetsky, *op. cit.*, p. 232.
137. Su-KC, Docs. 341, 291.
138. Dvorzhetsky, *op. cit.*, pp. 265, 268–271.
139. See the YIA file on refugees in Vilna in 1939–1940.
140. RA, I, No. 1172, p. 8.
141. G.Ż., No. 46 (June 10, 1941); No. 65 (July 30, 1941).
142. Ringelblum, *op. cit.*, p. 203.
143. *Ibid.*, p. 100; Berman, *op. cit.*, p. 69.
144. Su-KC, Docs. 380, 352.
145. Su-KC, Doc. 353; Rachel Pupko-Krynski, "Mayn arbet unter di daytshn," *YIVO-Bleter*, Vol. XXX, No. 2, pp. 217–220.
146. Su-KC, Doc. 476; Dvorzhetsky, *op. cit.*, p. 241.
147. Su-KC, Doc. 382.
148. Su-KC, Docs. 346, 352, 353.
149. Su-KC, Docs. 375, 376.
150. *Lodzher geto*, p. 400.
151. *Lodzher geto*, p. 401.
152. Ringelblum, *op. cit.*, pp. 93, 112.
153. G.Ż., No. 40 (Nov. 6, 1941).
154. Jonas Turkow, *op. cit.*, pp. 195–204; in the chapter "Theater and Entertainment" Turkow depicted in detail this feature of life in the ghetto; he was chairman of the Show Commission of the JSS.
155. WaC, Doc. 35/1.
156. Anna Natanblut, *op. cit.*, p. 181.
157. Turkow, *op. cit.*, pp. 206–210, 212–213.
158. *Ibid.*, pp. 207–229.
159. Abraham Lewin, "Togbukh fun varshever geto," *Blfg*, Vol. V, No. 4 (1952), pp. 64–65; Ringelblum, *op. cit.*, p. 93.
160. Turkow, *op. cit.*, pp. 236–238.
161. *Lodzher geto*, pp. 393–398.
162. Su-KC, Doc. 424.

163. Su-KC, Doc. 529; for the same reasons a strong opposition against concerts by the newly established symphony orchestra manifested itself in the Kaunas Ghetto (L. Garfunkel, *op. cit.*, pp. 250–251).

164. Su-KC, Doc. 479; Dvorzhetsky, *op. cit.*, pp. 248–249; Kruk, *op. cit.*, pp. 136–139, 146–147.

165. Su-KC, Docs. 349, 406, 459, 460.

166. Su-KC, Doc. 350.

167. Su-KC, Docs. 348–351.

168. Su-KC, Doc. 352; Dvorzhetsky, *op. cit.*, p. 250.

169. Su-KC, Docs. 485, 482, 481.

170. Su-KC, Doc. 488.

171. Su-KC., Doc. 522.

172. Su-KC., Docs. 519, 522.

173. Su-KC., Docs. 445ᵃ, 361, 496–502, 619, 623–625. .

174. Su-KC., Docs. 40–44.

175. Su-KC., Docs. 65–67.

176. The material was hidden in tin cans and buried in so-called bunkers; part of these holdings were found after the war, they are now in the YIVO Archives.

177. *Lodzher geto*, pp. 42–43; in Šiauliai Ghetto one person, inspired by a few important members of the Council, collected pertinent documents, eyewitness accounts and kept a diary of the events in the ghetto from June 1941 until July 1944 (Yerushalmi, *op. cit.*, pp. 13–17).

178. ZC, Docs. 21, 888–890.

179. Zaderecki, pp. 485, 486.

180. G.Ż., No. 41 (Dec. 10, 1940); No. 3 (Jan. 3, 1941); No. 4 (Jan. 14, 1941).

181. Still, during the occupation, the Jewish intelligentsia considered how to save the cultural treasures of the communities from destruction (see, for instance, Rabbi S. Huberbands memorial, cited in n. 20, Chap. 9). About the wanton desecration and destruction of synagogues and prayer houses during the first two months of the occupation, see Tatiana Bernstein and Adam Rutkowski, "Prześladowania ludności żydowskiej w okresie hitlerowskiej administracji wojskowej na okupowanych ziemiach polskich (Sept. 1–Oct. 25, 1939)." ("The Persecution of the Jewish Population during the Military Administration of the Polish Occupied Territories"), BŻIH, No. 38 (1961).

182. Czerniakow's Diary, entries of March 12 and 13, May 25, June 6, 1940; Joshua Starr, "Jewish Cultural Property under Nazi Control," *Jewish Social Studies*, Vol. XII, No. 1 (1950), pp. 27–48.

CHAPTER 10

1. *Bericht Warschau*, p. 1.

2. *Bericht Krakau*, p. 4.

3. *Denkschrift* (a memorandum to the local authorities) of July 29, 1940, p. 2; *Sprawozdanie*, p. 8.

4. Danuta Dąbrowska, "Administracja żydowska w Łodzi i jej agendy w okresie od początku okupacji do zamknięcia geta" ("The Jewish Community Administration in Łódź from the Start of the Occupation till the Closing of the Ghetto"), BŻIH, No. 45–46 (1963), p. 111.

5. "Min hadin vehakheshbon shel hamehandes M. Kerner," *Sefer hazvaot*, p. 9.

6. AGV, File 137, p. 359.

7. A note in the G.Ż. (No. 32, Nov. 8, 1940) which discusses this matter contains an assertion that the one-year experience showed that the authorities were not questioning the right of taxation on the part of the Jewish communities, so that technically all remained unchanged.

8. J. Kermisz, "Der khurbn," *Pietrkow Trybunalski* (Tel Aviv, 1966), p. 722; cf. JUS, File No. 31.

9. BWS, No. 1, p. 8; Czerniakow's Diary, entries of June 16 and 27, 1940.

10. BWS, No. 1, p. 10.

11. BWS, No. 8, p. 14.

12. Czerniakow's Diary, entries of Jan. 9 and June 6, 1940.

13. Dąbrowska, *op. cit.*, p. 111.

14. *Lodzher geto*, p. 44.

15. Niederschrift des Beauftragten des Rechnungshofes des Deutschen Reiches ueber die oertliche Pruefung der Ernaehrungs- und Wirtschaftsstelle Getto des Oberbuergemeisters der Stadt Litzmannstadt, pp. 15–16: AGV, File 115.

16. Minutes, No. 2/63, of the Council meeting of Feb. 5, 1941.

17. BWS, No. 1, p. 6; No. 5 (July 15, 1940); No. 7 (Aug. 15, 1940); No. 11, p. 14.

18. BWS, No. 5, p. 6.

19. BWS, No. 8, p. 9.

20. G.Ż., No. 5 (Aug. 6, 1940).

21. G.Ż., No. 11 (Feb. 7, 1941); the note concerns the indebtedness on the part of Jews to the Agency of Social Security.

22. ZC, Docs. 93–99, all dated Apr. 24, 1940.

23. ZC, Doc. 1141.

24. *Denkschrift* of July 29, 1940.

25. BWS, No. 7, p. 11.

26. *Bericht Warschau*, pp. 20–21.

27. G.Ż., No. 7 (Aug. 14, 1940).

28. *Bericht Krakau*, p. 14.

29. *Ibid.*

30. The Jewish Council in Warsaw interpreted Par. 5 of Frank's decree on the establishment of the Councils to the effect that it gives the right to tax, individually, well-to-do Jews on behalf of the financial sanctions imposed by the authorities on the Jewish population (see memorandum by Czerniakow, July 5, 1940; microfilm JM/1113 in YaVA).

31. Annordnung des Leiters der DPO [Deutsche Post-Ost]. No. 28 (Nov. 24, 1941); cf. Ruta Sakowska, *Łączność pocztowa warszawskiego geta*, p. 95.

32. ZC, Doc. 1202.

33. *Bericht Warschau*, p. 3.

34. Satzung der Steuer zugunsten des Judenrates in Warschau bestätigt durch den Beauftragten des Distriktschefs für den Distrikt Warschau am 26 Juni 1941 (microfilm JM/1113).

35. An das Amt des Chefs des Distrikts Warschau, Abt. Umsiedlung, Transferstelle, 8. Januar 1941; in this memorandum Czerniakow remarked that the 100% surcharge on behalf of the Council on the fees paid by the trade and craft cards was confirmed by the *Transferstelle* on Dec. 5, 1940, but due to the fact that the city government did not receive the appropriate instructions from the plenipotentiary of the governor, the surcharge did not materialize.

36. BWS, No. 5, p. 21; No. 8, p. 6; No. 9, pp. 6, 15.

37. BWS, No. 11, p. 14.

38. An das Amt des Chefs des Distrikts Warschau . . ., p. 6 (microfilm JM/1113).

39. *Ibid.*

40. BWS, No. 12^b, p. 1.
41. *Der Wecker* (underground periodical of the Bund in ghetto), No. 5/29, Feb. 15 and Mar. 15, 1942; Ringelblum, *op. cit.*, p. 199.
42. Ringelblum, *op. cit.*, p. 196.
43. G.Ż., No. 47 (Dec. 31, 1940).
44. RA, I, No. 858.
45. Su-KC, Doc. 568: identification card which contains the text of the order.
46. G.Ż., No. 23 (March 21, 1941).
47. *Lodzher geto*, p. 46.
48. *Sprawozdanie*, p. 5.
49. Minutes, No. 41/165, of the meeting of July 5, 1942.
50. YaVA, testimony, No. K–106/1268, p. 4.
51. Dora Agatstein, "Di Entjudung fun der hoyptshtot fun der general-gubernye," *Blfg*, Vol. I, No. 1, pp. 173–174.
52. *Bericht Krakau*, p. 18.
53. Minutes of the meeting of Nov. 8, 1941 (Blumental, *op. cit.*, p. 73).
54. Minutes of May 31, 1942 (Blumental, *op. cit.*, p. 180).
55. Minutes of Nov. 29, 1941 (Blumental, *op. cit.*, p. 94).
56. Announcement, No. 197, of Jan. 4, 1942; minutes of Dec. 20, 1941 (Blumental, *op. cit.*, pp. 403, 101).
57. Minutes of Apr. 4, 1942 (Blumental, *op. cit.*, p. 159).
58. Announcements, No. 59 of Aug. 18, 1941, and No. 137 of Oct. 21, 1941 (Blumental, *op. cit.*, pp. 313, 365).
59. Minutes of May 2, 1942 (Blumental, *op. cit.*, p. 171).
60. Minutes of the same date (Blumental, *op. cit.*, p. 159).
61. Minutes of the Council, May 25, 1940.
62. BWS, No. 6, p. 5.
63. G.Ż., No. 19 (March 17, 1941) and No. 35 (May 2, 1941).
64. *Eksterminacja*, p. 146.
65. Announcements, No. 116 (Oct. 5, 1941) and No. 146 (Nov. 2, 1941) (Blumental, *op. cit.*, pp. 353, 369).
66. Minutes of Nov. 1, 1941 (Blumental, *op. cit.*, p. 62).
67. BWS, No. 3, p. 8; for this service the Council collected from the taxpayers a fee of 5 zlotys (the quoted memorandum by Czerniakow of July 5, 1940, p. 7).
68. Minutes, No. 5/129, Feb. 3, 1942.
69. Testimony, No. 1043, p. 9 (YIA).
70. ZC, Doc. 150.
71. BWS, No. 2, p. 10; No. 9, p. 15.
72. BWS, No. 12^a, p. 9.
73. Minutes, No. 41/165, July 1, 1942; due to the instability in the new ghetto the taxes were imposed for a period of only three months; for the second quarter of 1942, during which the massive "resettlement" in the Lublin Ghetto took place (March–April), the Finance Commission decided not to collect the taxes altogether (*ibid.*).
74. Su-KC, Doc. 565.
75. Minutes, No. 41/165, July 1, 1942.
76. Su-KC, Doc. 565.
77. BWS, No. 5, p. 21; No. 9, p. 15.
78. An den Beauftragten des Distriktschefs . . . d. 21. Mai. 1940 (microfilm JM/1113); in his request that the authorities recognize the certificates issued by the Council, Czerniakow emphasized the fact that in order to establish a fund on behalf of the forced laborers, he must acquiesce in this procedure.

79. *Pinkos Zamoshch*, p. 934.
80. *Bericht Krakau*, p. 128.
81. VBlGG, No. 13 (1939).
82. *Sprawozdanie*, pp. 43, 45.
83. Paweł Wiederman, *op. cit.*, pp. 275–276.
84. BWS, No. 9, p. 8.
85. BWS, No. 1, p. 11.
86. The Warsaw Council was forced to renovate, at its expense, the residence of the governor in the Brühl Palace and the offices of the *Transferstelle* (Czerniakow's Diary entry of Nov. 20, 1940). The Częstochowa Council had to provide for the German officials and their families apartments with luxurious furniture (Brener, *op. cit.*, p. 15). The Białystok Council was ordered to deliver, in the course of three days, an enormous variety of furnishings and housewares for the German casino (e.g., 30 carpets, 20 pairs of draperies, 10 paintings, and thousands of dishes and pieces of furniture: Council announcement, No. 92, Sept. 10, 1941); in the announcement the Council warned of the dire consequences for the whole community if the entire delivery were not carried out on time. Lwów Council established a special office for the express purpose of delivering goods demanded by the Nazis (Zaderecki, p. 487).
87. Brustin-Bernstein, *op. cit.*, p. 108.
88. J. Kermisz, *op. cit.*, p. 201.
89. Friedman, *Encyclopaedia*, Vol. IV, p. 618.
90. WaC, Doc. 10/2.
91. Minutes of the meeting of the Council and its officials in the hall of *Linat Hatzedek*, Nov. 2, 1942 [1941] (Blumental, *op. cit.*, p. 67).
92. RA, I, No. 1259, pp. 5–6.
93. *Sprawozdanie*, pp. 5–6.
94. BWS, No. 5, pp. 24–25.
95. VBlGG, Nos. 1, 13, 14 (1939).
96. *Eksterminacja*, pp. 212–213.
97. *Ibid.*, pp. 216–219; minutes of the session of the labor department of the GG held on Aug. 6, 1940.
98. Microfilm JM/814 in YaVA.
99. BWS, No. 3, pp. 6–7.
100. *Bericht Warschau*, pp. 18–20.
101. *Wohnbezirk*, p. 6.
102. *Der Wecker*, No. 4/28, Feb. 8, 1942.
103. *Bericht Krakau*, pp. 13–15.
104. YaVA, File 06/3–1; the difference in the terminology in the annual and monthly budgets stems from the difference in the terminology of each source.
105. VBlGG, No. 12 (1939).
106. YaVA, File 06/3–1.
107. *Bericht Krakau*, p. 13.
108. On June 24, 1940, a special "currency," the so-called Mark-Quittungen was instituted in the ghetto and the Polish zloty and the German Mark were withdrawn (ZC, Doc. 130); in the budget quoted the type of currency is not stated.
109. ZC, Doc. 40.
110. *Lodzher geto*, pp. 58–60.
111. *Sprawozdanie*, pp. 5–6.
112. Tatiana Bernstein, "O podłożu gospodarczym sporów między władzami administracyjnymi a politycznymi w Generalnej Gubernii" ("On the Economical Background of the Conflicts between the Civil Administration and the Police Authori-

ties in the Government General"), BŻIH, No. 63 (1965), p. 57. The order of the *Stadthauptmann* was, rather, a consequence of the competition between the governor, Zörner, and the *SS-und Polizeiführer*, Globocnik, of the Lublin district in matters concerning Jews than of an expression of the goodwill on the part of the governor to alleviate the financial burden of the Council (cf. Chap. 11).

113. Minutes of the meeting (Blumental, *op. cit.*, pp. 27, 149–151).

114. JUS, File No. 31. In its letter (Feb. 25, 1940) to the office of JDC, the Council asserted that in order to carry out the budget for March a subsidy in the amount of 70,000 zlotys was required; thus, all told, the budget for March amounted to 136,000 zlotys.

115. Ältestenrat der Juden in Pabianice. Finanzbericht für September 1941 (microfilm JM/837 in YaVA).

116. *Ibid.*, II Anlage zum Finanzbericht für September 1941.

117. For the trial against the Council, see pp. 303–306.

118. Testimony, No. 1043, pp. 15–16 (YIA).

119. G.Ż., No. 2 (July 26, 1940).

120. Records of the JDC, File No. 83, in AJHI.

121. *Ibid.*, File No. 106, pp. 86–88.

122. G.Ż., No. 12 (Aug. 1, 1940).

123. Yerushalmi, *op. cit.*, pp. 207–208.

124. Records of the JDC, File No. 106, pp. 51–55; No. 83, p. 36; No. 321, p. 8.

CHAPTER 11

1. Saul Esch. "Hakamat hayikhud haartsi shel yehudey germania ufeulotav hayi-karyot," *Kovets mekkhkarim befarashat hashoa vehagvura*, Yad Vashem, Vol. VI (1968), p. 18.

2. Doc No. 172 in the police files of the Eichmann trial, pp. 16, 17.

3. *Ibid.*

4. Doc. NO-5156, p. 7.

5. YaVA, microfilm JM/1112.

6. *Lodzher geto*, pp. 376–377.

7. *Das Generalgouvernement Polen* (1940), pp. 141–142.

8. Martin Broszat, *NS-Polenpolitik* (1961), p. 74.

9. Tatiana Bernstein, "Spory administracji z SS w GG," BŻIH, No. 53 (1965), pp. 39–40, n. 26.

10. *Ibid.*, p. 43, n. 43.

11. VBlGG, I, No. 4 (March 2, 1940); "An die Abteilung Innere Verwaltung z. Hd. Landrat Kipke im Hause, 19 Nov. 1940, T-J." In the letter of Nov. 19 the decree of March 2, 1940, is quoted with the remark that the registration of the Jewish population was no longer of interest because in the meantime it had been carried out by Krüger, the *Höhere SS- und Polizeiführer* in GG, as was the question of jurisdiction over the Jewish Councils; cf. "Bericht ueber den Aufbau in General-gouvernement bis 1. Juli 1940, B.I, Referat Judenwesen, S. 190–191," quoted in *Eksterminacja*, pp. 86–88.

12. Abtlg. Innere Verwaltung- Bevölkerungswesen u. Fürsorge, Az VI/2581-40, Krakau, den 6.4.1940 (copy in YIA).

13. The description of the course of the contest between the civil and the police administration is based on the article by T. Bernstein cited in n. 9, above. In a circular letter (June 19, 1940) of the main department of *Innere Verwaltung* to

Zörner, which ordered all official contact with the Councils to be channeled through the offices of the civil administration, the reservation was made that in cases when decisions of a security or political nature, concerning Jews were made, the advice of the Security Police must be taken into consideration.

14. YaVA, File 108/56 (microfilm No. IKY–1 in YIA).

15. YaVA, File B/12–4.

16. AGV, File 117: Notizen für die Besprechung beim Regierungsvizepräsident Dr. Moser . . . (March 22, 1941).

17. Eisenbach, *Getto Łódzkie*, pp. 243–245.

18. AJHI, Rumkowski Archives, File 17, p. 536.

19. *Lodzher geto*, p. 32.

20. Rumkowski Archives, File 18, p. 436; The Forschungsstelle-A in Łódź, took an interest in the *Geto-tsaytung* and had under its surveillance both the *Gettoverwaltung* and the Rumkowski administration (YaVA, File DN/3–4 p. 329).

21. AGV, File 220: letter to Biebow, Dec. 21, 1943, in which Rumkowski informed him of the return of the records of his administration which were taken by the Gestapo.

22. Rumkowski Archives, File 17, p. 30.

23. *Ibid., passim.*

24. AGV, File 117, p. 394.

25. ABLG, Doc. 1881^e(3), No. 2.

26. YaVA, File DN/3–4, pp. 230, 245–246. By the way, Veygand's report disclosed that in March 1942 Heydrich entrusted to Biebow the management of the Theresienstadt Ghetto, that his ambition was to become the "expert on Jewish matters" in Germany and to take over supervision of all ghettos.

27. Doc. 1410 in the police files of the Eichmann trial.

28. YaVA, File DN/3–4.

29. Czerniakow's Diary, entry of Oct. 21, 1940; memorandum of the Jewish Relief Committee to Leist, Oct. 22, 1940 (records of JDC, File 378, pp. 49–53).

30. *Bericht Warschau*, p. 12.

31. Czerniakow's Diary, entry of Feb. 7, 1942.

32. Czerniakow's Diary, entry of June 3, 1942.

33. *Eksterminacja*, pp. 240–241.

34. Heinz Höhne, *Der Orden unter dem Totenkopf* (Gutersloh, 1967), pp. 293–297.

35. Minutes, No. 2 (Jan. 9, 1940).

36. YaVA, microfilm JM/1113.

37. Su-KC, Doc. 246.

38. YaVA, microfilm JM/1113.

39. AGV, Files 115, 137, 226, *passim*; Rumkowski Archives, File No. 5.

40. *Kronika Getta Łódzkiego* (printed text of BKC) Vol. I (Łódź, 1965), pp. 42, 61.

41. YaVA, File DW-3-1, pp. 36–38.

42. AGV, File 137, Biebow's letter to Rumkowski, Apr. 22, 1944.

43. AGV, *Organisations Plan der Getto-Verwaltung* (graph); Alexander Hohenstein, *op. cit.*, p. 261; AGV, Files. VI/15, p. 43; III/21, p. 140.

44. Eisenbach, *Getto Łódzkie*, pp. 102–104.

45. AGV, File 115, p. 35; AGV, Bericht für Dezember 1942, p. 4.

46. YaVA, File DN/3–4.

47. Jakub Poznański, *op. cit.*, pp. 75, 81, 91–92; BKC of July 1943.

48. Niederschrift des Rechnungshofes des Deutschen Reiches über die örtliche Prüfung der Ernährungs- und Wirtschaftsstelle-Getto des Oberbürgermeisters der Stadt Litzmannstadt, pp. 20–21 (microfilm JM/1798 in YaVA). Symptomatic of the hypocritical bookkeeping of the *Gettoverwaltung* is the fact that the comptroller was

confronted with an account showing for the city a loss of 3,299,000 Reichsmarks, the expenses for the establishment of the ghetto and the uncollected taxes from the Jews (*ibid.*, p. 22).

49. AGV, File 117, p. 29.
50. YaVA, microfilms JM/1920, JM/1926, *passim.*
51. A. Eisenbach, *Getto Łódzkie*, pp. 265–268; AGV, File 118, pp. 42, 64, 66, 89, 90; Tabaksblat, *op. cit.*, pp. 163, 147–149.
52. AGV, File 116, pp. 241–243, 248, 256, 258: correspondence and notes about phone calls between Waldemar Schön, chief of the division "resettlement" in the district administration, and Dr. Marder, the chief mayor of Łódź, and his subordinates, from Aug. 30 to Sept. 11, 1940. It is worthwhile to mention that not only the German authorities in Warsaw but the Council of the Warsaw Ghetto were eager to utilize the experiences made in the Łódź Ghetto; on Feb. 8, 1941, Czerniakow requested the *Transferstelle* to grant a permit for a trip to Łódź for six days for three Council members in order "to get directly acquainted with the organization of the economic life in the Jewish ghetto of Litzmannstadt: . . . what may be useful for the organization of manpower and of the appropriate offices [in order] to spare him unnecessary experiments" (photocopy of the letter in ABLG). It is not known whether the request was granted.
53. Minutes of the Council, March 22, 1942.
54. N. Blumental, *Słowa niewinne* (Cracow-Łódź-Warsaw, 1947), pp. 230–231.
55. MTA, File No. 56/108 (microfilm): Pesakh Kaplan, "Der yidnrat in Białystok" (ms), p. 1.
56. YaVA, microfilm JM/1552.
57. YaVA, microfilm JM/1489 (Częstochowa); Gar, *op. cit.*, p. 105 (Kaunas).
58. Aktenvermerk über die Unterredung mit H. Gouverneur Dr. Fischer am 8. Mai 1941 (microfilm JM/1112).
59. T. Bernstein, "Vegn di hitleristishe metodn fun der ekonomischer eksploatatsye fun varshever geto," *Blfg.* Vol. XII (1959), pp. 54–69; Eisenbach, *Getto Łódzkie*, pp. 256–257.
60. VBlGG, Part III (1941), p. 211, Par. 3(1).
61. *Amtsblatt des Distrikts Warschau* (1941), p. 50.
62. An die Regierung des General-Gouvernements, Bericht . . . Feb. 1941 (YaVA, microfilm JM/814).
63. Transferstelle Warschau. Organisations Plan der Transferstelle, Warschau den 2 Juli 1942 (microfilm JM/1112).
64. Reports of the *Transferstelle* for the *Getto-Kommissar* covering the months Sept.–Dec. 1942 (*ibid.*).
65. YaVA microfilm JM/814.
66. YaVA, microfilm JM/1113.
67. YaVA, microfilm JM/1112.
68. *Ibid.* The relationship between Auerswald and Bischof was not friendly. It is impossible to establish whether Auerswald lent a hand to the denunciation of Bischof in favoring Jews (see pp. 292–93).
69. YaVA, microfilm JM/1112.
70. Ringelblum, *op. cit.*, p. 196.
71. Microfilm JM/1112: report for Dec. 1941, p. 3.
72. Microfilm JM/1113: reports of the *Transferstelle* covering the months Sept. 1941–July 1942.
73. *Ibid.*: report for Jan. 1942.
74. Czerniakow's Diary, entry of Oct. 14, 1941.
75. *Ibid.*, entry of May 21, 1941.

76. *Ibid.*, entries of June 17 and 18, 1941.

77. *Ibid.*, entry of Oct. 8, 1941.

78. *Ibid.*, entry of Feb. 13, 1942.

79. Microfilm JM/1112. The note further states that the representative of the supply department of the Council replied to Bischof's charge against Czerniakow with the remark that even the Germans regarded his methods as too harsh; to this Czerniakow said that such expressions on the part of Bischof could destroy his authority among the Jewish population and would certainly impede the implementation by him of the orders of the authorities—an intentional stab at Bischof.

80. Aktennotiz über die Unterredung beim H. Gouverneur Dr. Fischer am 30. April 1941 (microfilm JM/1112).

81. Reinhold SS-Hauptsturmführer. An H. Gouverneur für den Distrikt Warschau, SA-Gruppenführer Dr. Fischer (correspondence between Auerswald and Bischof concerning this matter; *ibid.*).

82. BC, Doc. OccE2–1–8.

83. *Betr.*: Liquidation der Transferstelle Warschau/Dienstvertrag Direktor Bischof (microfilm JM/1112).

84. "Die Juden im Distrikt Warschau" von Heinz W. Auerswald, Kommissar für den jüdischen Wohnbezirk in Warschau, pp. 1–2 [Nov. 1941] (*ibid.*); cf. the above-quoted letter to Medeazza of Nov. 1941 (YaVA, microfilm JM/1112).

85. The above-mentioned article summarizes its conclusion as follows: "Es ist selbst-verständlich dass alle auf diesem Gebiet getroffenen Massnahmen [Gettos] nur Übergangsmassnahmen sind, bis nach dem Kriege die Lösung der Judenfrage für ganz Europa einheitlich erfolgen wird. Bis dahin aber müssen die jüdischen Wohnbezirke als Vorläufer der von Alfred Rosenberg in Aussicht gestellten künftigen 'jüdischen Reservationen' ihren Zweck erfüllen."

86. "Die Juden im Distrikt Warschau," *op. cit.*, p. 6.

87. Czerniakow's Diary, entries of Aug. 22, 1941, and March 3, 1942.

88. Letter of Dr. Hagen to Leist of Sept. 22, 1941, requesting him to join the opposition against Auerswald's plan and to support his view with Governor Fischer (microfilm JM/1112: copy of the letter for Auerswald).

89. "Zweijahresbericht," Sept. 1941, p. 6 (microfilm JM/1113).

90. Ringelblum, *op. cit.*, p. 192.

91. *Eksterminacja*, p. 122; Ringelblum, *op. cit.*, pp. 177–178; according to Ringelblum Auerswald insisted that the O.D. should organize its own execution unit to carry out the sentence (p. 178); he also quoted the fact that when Auerswald was late for the execution he said: "Schade zu spät" (*op. cit.*, p. 193).

92. Ringelblum, *op. cit.*, p. 193.

93. Czerniakow's Diary, entry of Nov. 21, 1941.

94. Ringelblum, *op. cit.*, p. 232.

95. Czerniakow's Diary, entries of Nov. 5 and Dec. 17, 1941.

96. *Ibid.*, entries of Feb. 7 and Apr. 8, 1942; doubtless Auerswald knew then what Treblinka had in store for the Jews.

97. *Ibid.*, entry of Feb. 26, 1942.

98. *Ibid.*, entries of May 29 and 30, 1942.

99. *Ibid.*, entry of Apr. 11, 1942.

100. *Ibid.*, entry of July 8, 1942.

101. Letters: of Auerswald's office to the Council, June 19, 1942; of the Division *Wirtschaft* in the district administration to Auerswald, June 30, Aug. 10, and Oct. 1, 1942 (microfilm JM/1112; pertinent notes in Czerniakow's Diary).

102. Czerniakow's Diary, entry of Feb. 9, 1942.

103. *Ibid.*, entry of May 20, 1942.
104. Ringelblum, *op. cit.*, p. 192.
105. Czerniakow's Diary, entry of Nov. 21, 1941.
106. *Ibid.*, entry of Feb. 26, 1942.
107. *Ibid.*, entry of June 29, 1942.
108. *Ibid.*, entry of July 8, 1942.
109. *Ibid.*, entries of May 20 and 21, 1942.
110. *Betr.*: Abgrenzung der polizeilichen Aufgaben des Kommissars für den jüdischen Wohnbezirk in Warschau u. des Stadthauptmanns in Warschau (microfilm JM/ 1112).
111. YaVA, microfilm JM/1112.
112. For further discussion of this, see Chap. 16.
113. *Milkhome*, pp. 52–55, 61.
114. *Ibid.*, p. 72.
115. AGV, File 115, p. 7.
116. *Lodzher geto*, p. 173.
117. Czerniakow's Diary, entries of Nov. 4 and 5, 1940.
118. Tabaksblat, *op. cit.*, p. 164. A note in BKC of Oct. 13, 1942 (No. 172) under the cautious heading "The chairman healthy again," related that after a 14-day illness Rumkowski resumed work in his office on the Bałuty Ring; the cause of the "illness" was of course omitted in the note.
119. RA, I, No. 1144, pp. 7, 10; the schizophrenic behavior of certain German officials is symptomatic of the fact that the said incident took place shortly after a meeting in the office of the Gestapo chief, during which the Germans behaved themselves correctly toward the Councilmen, and were even friendly.
120. RA, I, No. 1174.
121. Moyshe Zylberg, "Khurbn Lublin," *Dos fraye Wort*, No. 32/33, 1946; quoted from N. Blumental *Teudot mgeto Lublin*, p. 50; minutes, No. 38, Aug. 18, 1940 (*Ibid.*, p. 176).
122. *Sefer Borshchiv*, p. 195.
123. RA, I, No. 1157, p. 13.
124. By that the attorney general meant the decree of Dec. 4, 1941, "Über die Strafrechtspflege gegen Polen und Juden in den eingegliederten Ostgebieten," which introduced drastic penalties, including the death penalty, for the slightest offense, even for hostile expressions.
125. Knowing the investigative procedures of the Gestapo, one can easily assume that Brin died as a result of these methods.
126. The records concerning the trial of the Pabianice Council are preserved in the Governmental Archives in Łódź (sygn. 760/6); a microfilm of the records is available in YaVA.
127. Yoseph Zelkowicz, "In yene koshmarne teg," p. 53 (ZC, Doc. 54); Nirenberg, *op. cit.*, p. 269. Jewish sources have no knowledge of the trial. *Sefer Pabianits* relates only that the Council chairman was arrested and sent to Łódź. By the way, the attitude toward the Council members who were later denounced and arrested is utterly negative in the testimonies of the survivors of the Pabianits (Pabianice) Ghetto (see pp. 316, 318, 332, 334). They belonged presumably to the adversaries of the Council, from whose circle the denunciation against the councilmen emanated.
128. Czerniakow's Diary, entry of May 27, 1940.
129. *Ibid.*, entries under the dates mentioned (p. 407). The above-quoted Polish mayor, Juljan Kulski, gives a positive evaluation of Leist's correct behavior (also in

regard to Jews). In the trial against Governor Fischer and Leist, among other officials of the German district administration in Warsaw in 1946/1947, Kulski, and other witnesses (among them Jews), gave evidence in behalf of Leist; he was sentenced to a prison term of eight years (Fischer to death) not for criminal acts, but for membership in a criminal organization (Sturm-Abteilung). See Julian Kulski, *Zarząd Miejski Warszawy 1939–1944* (Warsaw, 1964), pp. 62–80.

130. *Sefer Borshchiv*, p. 198.
131. Ch. Grosman, *Anshey hamakhteret* (Merkhavia, 1965), pp. 342–375.
132. A. Hohenstein, *op. cit., passim*.
133. YaVA, microfilm JM/1920.
134. YaVA, microfilm JM/814.
135. YaVA, microfilm JM/1113.
136. Kulski, *op. cit.*, pp. 106–109, 113.
137. Wiederman, *op. cit.*, p. 67.
138. Karmi, *op. cit.*, pp. 25–26.
139. Robert M. W. Kempner, *Eichmann und seine Komplizen* (Wien-Zürich, 1962), pp. 14–15 of the original text of the minutes.
140. Quoted in a note prepared by an official of the Lublin district administration on March 17, 1942 (Kermisz, *op. cit.*, pp. 32–33).
141. *Ibid.*, pp. 25–26, 53–55.
142. *Ibid.*, p. 54.
143. Letter by Türk to Hoefle of March 24, 1942 (YaVA, microfilm JM/2609, p. 47). According to the letter, 80 Jews of Wąwolnica were shot in retaliation for the assassination attempt.
144. YaVA, microfilm JM/1209.
145. Kermisz, *op. cit.*, pp. 32–33.
146. YaVA, microfilm JM/2609.
147. YaVA, File DN/3–4, p. 179.
148. Kermisz, *op. cit.*, pp. 40–41; Blumental, *Obozy* (Łódź, 1946), pp. 78–79.
149. YaVA, microfilm JM/2702, pp. 44–45.
150. BC, Doc. OccE 3–28.
151. Secret report by Karl, the *Gebietskommissar* of Slutsk, to Kube, *Generalkommisar* of White Russia, Oct. 30, 1941, *IMT* (Blue Series), Vol. XXVII, Doc. PS–1104 (pp. 4–8).
152. YaVA, microfilm JM/2702, pp. 53–54.
153. BC, Doc. OccE-30: note by Gevecke, Sept. 3, 1941, and his letter to Lohse, Sept. 11, 1941.
154. Hohenstein, *op. cit.*, pp. 251–255; he relates that during the "action" in the town he was on leave in Germany. He was informed of its course by his aide, who was shaken by its atrocities.
155. BC, Docs. OccE3–25, OccE3–22.
156. BC, Doc. OccE3–25.
157. BC, Doc. OccE3–27.
158. Tatiana Bernstein "Vegn di hitleristishe metodn . . . ," *Blfg.* Vol. XII (1959), pp. 77–79.
159. AGV, File V/16, p. 108; File IV/25, p. 193; Eisenbach, *Getto Łódzkie*, pp. 209–210. Sometimes the local authority used to purchase wholesale from the *Gettoverwaltung* the housewares of the deported Jews and sell them later to the local population; AGV, Files 28/48 *passim*, IV/29, p. 171; AJHI, File No. 151 (Bełchatow), p. 246.
160. AGV, File 28/48, Aktenvermerk No. 114/42.
161. AGV, File 28/48 *passim*.

CHAPTER 12

1. *Turne. Kiyum un khurbn fun a yidisher shtot* (Tel Aviv, 1954), pp. 810, 811.
2. *Yilon leinformatsye veyediyot*, No. 4 (1952), p. 113.
3. Testimony No. G–28/328, pp. 11–12 (YaVA).
4. Questionnaire No. 179.
5. Questionnaires Nos. 281, 285, 286, 288, 289; in the first months of the occupation five members left for Warsaw.
6. Questionnaire No. 355.
7. Questionnaire No. 849.
8. RA, I, No. 1155.
9. Questionnaire Nos. 49, 50, 52, 54, 65, 68.
10. Questionnaire No. 191.
11. Questionnaire No. 213.
12. *Pinkos Kremenets*, p. 252.
13. Questionnaire No. 284.
14. Questionnaire No. 244.
15. Testimony by Abraham Kalisher (YIA).
16. *Sefer Ozheran vehasviva, Encyclopaedia* (1959), col. 487.
17. *Yizkor-bukh Chizheve*, pp. 926–927; testimonies Nos. G-53/679, B-48/681, in YaVA.
18. *Sefer Stashev*, p. 418.
19. *Pinkos Khmielnik*, p. 731.
20. Brener, *op. cit.*, p. 15: from a source emanating from the Council (Rocznik, II, p. 11), which listed two different slates of Council members, it is evident that 10 persons left the Council and were replaced by others.
21. *Sefer Burshtyn, Encyclopaedia* (1960); testimony by Abraham Kalisher, p. 10.
22. Kruk, *op. cit.*, pp. 25–28.
23. *Ibid.*, pp. 46–48.
24. *Ibid.*, pp. 69, 71; Dvorzhetsky, *op. cit.*, p. 44.
25. *Lodzher geto*, p. 30.
26. Eisenbach, *Getto Łódzkie*, pp. 21–22.
27. Friedman, *Encyclopaedia*, pp. 674–675; Diary of Zvi Radletsky (File E/37-2-2 in YaVA); testimony by Rabbi David Kahane.
28. *Sefer Horodenko*, p. 287.
29. AJHI, "Mss. about Cities," File No. 151, pp. 29, 31, 105, 127.
30. *Ibid.*, pp. 30, 36. A denunciation against the Council chairman was placed before the Gestapo by the mayor on Nov. 16, 1941, in which the chairman was accused of having contacts with smugglers (on whose behalf he interceded before the authorities) and with persons arrested by the Gestapo for political reasons. One can easily imagine the fate in store for a person so accused.
31. G.Ż., No. 11 (Aug. 28, 1940).
32. Testimony by Haim Wierzba in the YIA.
33. *Pinkos Mlave*, pp. 405–406.
34. *Sefer Kelts*, p. 13; Dr. Peltz was allegedly deported to Auschwitz for refusing to perform lethal injections on sick people in the Jewish hospital.
35. Druk, *op. cit.*, pp. 12–16.
36. *Pinkos Kremenets*, p. 268.
37. *Sefer Lantsut*, pp. 363–364; English section of the book, pp. XXXVI–XXXVII.
38. Minutes of the Council, No. 16/140, of the same date.
39. *Sefer Horodenko*, p. 290.
40. *Krasnobród, sefer zikaron* (Tel Aviv, 1956), pp. 345, 352.
41. Ami Weitz, *Al Khorvotekha Stanislavuv* (Tel Aviv, 1947), pp. 28, 44, 76–78, 95.

42. I. Friedman, Sh. Figer, "Rodem," FLKh, No. 1, pp. 18–20; Rotenberg, *op. cit.*, p. 52.
43. WaC, Doc. 212.
44. *Kehilat Rohatyn vehasviva*, p. 226.
45. *Sefer yizkor lekehilat Shedlets*, p. 663.
46. Sholem Shnadovitch, *Reminiscences of My Experiences in World War II* (no place or date of publication; offset), pp. 17 ff.
47. Michał Grynes. *Ven dos lebn hot geblit* (Buenos Aires, 1954), p. 426.
48. Garfunkel, *op. cit.*, pp. 54, 147–148; Gar, *op. cit.*, pp. 284, 295.
49. Yerushalmi, *op. cit.*, pp. 302, 318.
50. *Pietrkov Trybunalski*, pp. 747–748; *Sefer Skernevits*, p. 504.
51. According to the pointed term coined by the late historian, Dr. Philip Friedman.
52. Moshe Bialodvorsky, *op. cit.*, p. 14.
53. Questionnaire Nos. 150, 155; *Pinkos Ludmir* (Tel Aviv, 1963), pp. 410, 416–417, 438, 478, 479, 504–506; the sources are not unanimous in regard to Weiler's successor. According to the witness, Shatz, this was Bardach (*Pinkos Ludmir*, pp. 435–436), while Questionnaire No. 150 gives the name of Dr. Pass.
54. Diary of Josef Klementynowski, p. 5 (YIA).
55. Tabaksblat, *op. cit.*, p. 90.
56. ZC, Doc. 17, p. 30; Doc. 54, p. 17.
57. Questionnaire No. 682.
58. Questionnaire Nos. 686, 689; *Pinkos Bendin*, pp. 189–190.
59. *Sefer Khzhanev*, p. 285; P. Wiederman, *op. cit.*, pp. 115–117.
60. *Turne, Kiyum un khurbn fun a yidisher shtot*, pp. 820, 842.
61. *Dos Bukh fun Lublin*, pp. 424–425.
62. A. Huzen, *Kitever yizkor-bukh*, pp. 128–130.
63. *Tarnopol, Encyclopaedia* (1955), pp. 389–394, 397.
64. Testimony, No. H-68/1488, pp. 16–23 (YaVA).
65. *Pinkos Kremenets*, pp. 422–425.
66. *Sefer Dembits* (Tel Aviv, 1960), p. 151.
67. *Sefer Pabianits* (Tel Aviv, 1956), p. 332.
68. *Sefer Kroke*, p. 409.
69. Testimony by Ignacy Sternbach, pp. 14–18 (YIA).

CHAPTER 13

1. *Lodzher geto*, p. 30.
2. *Eksterminacja*, pp. 148–149.
3. VBlGG, Part I, No. 48, pp. 225–228; No. 50, pp. 244–246.
4. *Sprawozdanie*, pp. 18–20; *Pinkos Hrubieshov* (Tel Aviv, 1962), p. 600.
5. *Milkhome*, pp. 107–108: cf. note in the G.Ż., No. 51 (June 27, 1941).
6. *Milkhome*, p. 106.
7. G.Ż., 1940, *passim*.
8. G.Ż., Oct. 29, 1940.
9. ABLG, Doc. 1881/c. No. 3; *Sprawozdanie*, p. 64.
10. G.Ż., No. 21 (Oct. 1, 1940).
11. Ringelblum, *op. cit.*, pp. 168, 172.
12. Brener, op. cit., pp. 49–51.
13. M. Weichert relates yet another reason for the friction between the Council and TOZ: both parties were competing for the position of the chairman of the just established local committee of the JSS.

14. *Alaynhilf*, p. 23.
15. *Ibid.*, p. 332.
16. *Ibid.*, p. 27.
17. *Ibid.*, p. 21.
18. *Ibid.*, p. 27.
19. ABLG, Doc. 1882/5.
20. *Alaynhilf*, pp. 51–53.
21. BWS, No. 6, p. 5; G.Ż., No. 9 (Aug. 21, 1940).
22. *Alaynhilf*, p. 23.
23. Zaderecki, p. 504.
24. Ringelblum, *op. cit.*, pp. 120–122; Jonas Turkow, *op. cit.*, p. 69.
25. Turkow, *op. cit.*, p. 238.
26. *Ibid.*, p. 145.
27. Minutes, No. 35/96, of the same date.
28. *Milkhome*, pp. 94–95.
29. *Alaynhilf*, p. 17.
30. *Pinkos Zhirardov, Amshinov un Viskit* (Buenos Aires, 1961), p. 401.
31. *Sefer Lantsut*, English section, p. XXXV.
32. *Yizkor-bukh Khelm* (Johannesburg, 1954), p. 602; *Pinkos Khmielnik*, p. 730; Questionnaire Nos. 636, 637.
33. Questionnaire Nos. 564, 568.
34. A call of the "City Relief Committee" of the JSS of Oct. 18, 1941, to the Jewish population to support its relief action, signed by them.
35. Questionnaire No. 112; *Dos Radomer bukh*, p. 282.
36. Czerniakow's Diary, entry of Aug. 8, 1940; G.Ż., No. 5 (Aug. 6, 1940); a letter by the presidium of the JSS, signed by Dr. Eliahu Tisch, Dec. 20, 1940 (No. 1509), to the Jewish community in Lisbon, says, among other things: "The presidium of the JSS was established in accordance with the Jewish communities [Jewish Councils] in Warsaw, and Cracow, the directors of the 'Joint' and the central committees of TOZ, Centos, ORT, CEKABE [Free Loan Association], JEAS" (copy in YIA).
37. YaVA, microfilm JM/1113.
38. G.Ż., No. 6 (Aug. 9, 1940).
39. Report of the *Stadthauptmann* in Lublin to the government in Cracow for Sept. 1940 (YaVA, microfilm JM/814); *Dos Rodemer bukh*, p. 282.
40. Czerniakow's Diary, entries of March 14, 26, 27, and 28, 1940. The date of the conference given by Dr. Weichert is erroneous (*Milkhome*, pp. 51–52); according to the notes taken down by Czerniakow day by day, the invitation to participate in the Cracow conference arrived indeed on March 14, but on the 17th he noted: "the invitation to Cracow for 27.III." They left Warsaw on the afternoon of March 26 and arrived in Cracow about midnight (entry of March 26); about other trips to Cracow, for instance, to the meetings with Dr. Arlt on March 29 and 30, the Diary is silent (*Milkhome*, p. 61); it is improbable that Czerniakow should have omitted in his Diary such an important event as another trip to Cracow.
41. *Milkhome*, p. 103.
42. *Ibid.*, pp. 223–224; *Yizkor-bukh Khelm*, pp. 602–609: minutes of the conference. Weichert remarked that the representatives of the Councils had no right to vote at the conference in Busk; the minutes of the conference in Khelm don't specify such restrictions.
43. *Alaynhilf*, pp. 42, 311.
44. Circular letter No. 11, Dec. 11, 1940 (ABLG, Doc. 1881/4).
45. *Alaynhilf*, p. 101.
46. *Ibid.*, p. 355.

47. *Ibid.*, p. 120.
48. *Ibid.*, p. 206.
49. YaVA, microfilm JM/1982.
50. Minutes, No. 40/101, of the same date.
51. Minutes, Nos. 9/10 of March 21, 1941, and 53/114 of Nov. 23, 1941. Dr. Adam Wolberg, chief of the health division of the JSS, was present at both meetings.
52. Minutes, No. 8/132, of Feb. 18, 1942.
53. Report of the local JSS committee for July 1940 (ABLG, Doc. 1881/3(4); minutes, No. 35/159, of June 9, 1942.
54. *Yizkor-bukh Khelm*, pp. 617–618; at the suggestion of the chairman a resolution was approved that the Councils should subsidize the "allocations" of the JSS in small localities on a monthly basis, taking into account their budgets for the last six months (*ibid.*, p. 618).
55. Facsimile of the letter in *Pinkos Zamoshch*, pp. 166–167.
56. *Yizkor-bukh Khelm*, pp. 610, 618.
57. Ruta Sakowska, "Komitety Domowe w getcie warszawskim," BŻIH, No. 61 (1967), pp. 65–66.
58. The by-laws of the house committees were the product of a compromise between two tendencies, one of which tended to subject them to the supreme control of the Council chairman as his local executive apparatus, and the other to insist on their subordination to the authority of the JSS, as its organic component (YaVA, drafts of and remarks about the by-laws); cf. B. Mark, "Di vidershtand-bavegung in varshever geto," *Blfg*, Vol. IV, No. 1 (1951), p. 16; G.Ż., No. 28 (Oct. 23, 1940); No. 3 (Jan. 10, 1941); Perec Opoczynski, "Di tragedie fun a hoyz-komitet," *Blfg*, Vol. XIV (1961), pp. 171–179.
59. Czerniakow's Diary, entries of May 6 and June 27, 1940; G.Ż., No. 6 (Aug. 9, 1940).
60. BWS, No. 9, p. 15.
61. Czerniakow's Diary, entry of March 13, 1940. At the beginning of Dec. 1941 the authorities ordered the Council to deliver furniture for 50 bedrooms and 4 studies; in the entry of Dec. 3 Czerniakow expressed his hope that the house committees might share in the expense.
62. *Ibid.*, entry of Jan. 21, 1942.
63. *Ibid.*, entry of June 17, 1942.
64. Mark, *op. cit.*, pp. 16, 17.
65. Ringelblum, *op. cit.*, pp. 121–122.
66. Michel Mazor, *La Cité Engloutie* (Paris, 1955), p. 39.
67. G.Ż., No. 5 (Jan. 17, 1941).
68. *Lodzher geto*, pp. 46, 102–103.
69. Brener, *op. cit.*, p. 48.
70. J. Kermisz, *Pietrkov Trybunalski*, p. 732.
71. WaC, Doc. 34/6; G.Ż., No. 34 (Nov. 15, 1940).
72. ABLG: letter of *Gettokommissar* Auerswald to Czerniakow, received in the office of the Council on June 19, 1942, in which the "Union of the Artisans" was forbidden to use the official stamp, which should be confiscated and destroyed.
73. G.Ż., No. 37 (Nov. 26, 1940).
74. G.Ż., No. 6 (Jan. 21, 1941), and ff. issues.
75. G.Ż., No. 24 (March 25, 1941).
76. G.Ż., No. 60 (July 18, 1941).
77. Zaderecki, p. 486.
78. WaC, Doc. 34/6; G.Ż., No. 34 (Nov. 15, 1940).
79. Su-KC, Docs. 187, 195; Dvorzhetsky, *op. cit.*, pp. 183–184.
80. Su-KC, Docs. 164, 165, Tables 5 and 6.

81. *Ibid.*, Docs. 163, 288; Kruk, *op. cit.*, p. 219.
82. Su-KC, Docs. 169, 185, 189, 199; Kruk, *op. cit.*, pp. 375, 383.
83. Kruk, *op. cit.*, p. 291.
84. Su-KC, Doc. 186.
85. Brener, *op. cit.*, p. 45.
86. YaVA, microfilm JM/1764 (a photostat of the report).
87. After the war a controversy regarding the origins and nature of the *arbeter-sekretariat* and the *arbeter-rat* sprang up among three survivors of the Częstochowa Ghetto in their published books (Brener's review of B. Orenstein's *Khurbn chenstokhov* [Munich, 1948], in *Blfg*, Vol. I, No. 3–4, p. 230; *idem,* "Der emes vegn chenstokhover geto," *Blfg*, Vol. VIII, No. 1–2, pp. 180–183; Zvi Rosenwein, "Vegn arbeter-rat in chenstokhov" in *Chenstokhov, tsugob-materyaln tsum bukh chenstokhover yidn* [New York, 1958], pp. 47–51). Our analysis of the matter is based on the document quoted in n. 86, above, which was apparently unknown to the polemicists, and on the objective facts about the *arbeter-rat* related by the authors themselves.
88. *Lodzher geto*, pp. 386–390.
89. *Ibid.*, pp. 393–395.
90. *Ibid.*, pp. 405–407.

CHAPTER 14

1. Czerniakow's Diary, entry of Feb. 7, 1940; *Wohnbezirk*, pp. 2, 3, 15.
2. Czerniakow's Diary, entry of Jan. 27, 1940; Czerniakow complained about the inefficiency of the clerical apparatus and "the lack of a Jewish bureaucracy."
3. G.Ż., No. 47 (Dec. 31, 1940); No. 1 (Jan. 3, 1941); Paweł Wiederman, *op. cit.*, p. 208.
4. G.Ż., No. 1 (Jan. 3, 1941); No. 3 (Jan. 10, 1941); No. 6 (Jan. 21, 1941); No. 16 (Feb. 25, 1941). By the way, he accused the Councilmen of badly organized, unproductive work; he maintained that they did not measure up to the tasks facing their communities and lacked social responsibility.
5. ZC, Doc. 55, p. 107.
6. Szloyme Mayer, *op. cit.*, p. 6.
7. I. Maltieyl, *Beeyn Nokom* (Tel Aviv, 1947), pp. 32–33.
8. Kurts, *Sefer Eydut*, p. 291.
9. Minutes of the meeting of the department chiefs, Jan. 10, 1942 (Blumental, *op. cit.*, p. 105).
10. Czerniakow's Diary, entry of July 27, 1941.
11. *Blfg*, Vol. I, No. 3–4, p. 193.
12. Mazor, *op. cit.*, p. 49.
13. Turkow, *op. cit.*, p. 49; Czerniakow's Diary, entry of Oct. 27, 1940.
14. Ochs, *op. cit., Encyclopaedia*, p. 392.
15. *Pinkos Bendin*, p. 355.
16. Diary of Y. Klementynowski, p. 23.
17. Kurts, *op. cit.*, p. 290.
18. Minutes of Jan. 27, 1942 (Blumental, *op. cit.*, p. 118).
19. Source for the Kutno Ghetto: testimony, No. 303 (AJHI); for Kaunas Ghetto: Garfunkel, *op. cit.*, p. 241; for Lwów: Maltieyl, *op. cit.*, pp. 32–33.
20. *Der Wecker* (underground periodical of the Bund), in the ghetto, Feb. 8, 1942; Ringelblum, *op. cit.*, pp. 207–208; these additional bread rations stemmed from the flour confiscated by the authorities, which was smuggled into the ghetto

(Czerniakow's Diary, entries of Feb. 26 and March 27 and 29, 1942). Besides bread, vegetables were sometimes distributed among the Council clerks (entry of March 28, 1942).

21. *Lodzher geto*, pp. 109–110; Garfunkel, *op. cit.*, p. 241; Dvorzhetsky, *op. cit.*, p. 157; Kurts, *op. cit.*, pp. 290–291.
22. *Blfg.*, Vol. II, p. 277.
23. Czerniakow's Diary, entry of June 22, 1941.
24. T1395-T1398: Düsseldorfstapostelle archives, sheets 61–64, cf. Jacob Robinson, *The Crooked Shall Be Made Straight*, pp. 166, 329.
25. *Blfg*, Vol. IV, No. 2 (1951), pp. 226–227.
26. Minutes, Nos. 17/141 of March 31, 1942, and 22/146 of April 19, 1942; *Lodzher geto*, pp. 375, 377.
27. A. Rutkowski, "Der umkum fun yidn in rodemer distrikt," *Blfg*, Vol. XII (1959), p. 88.
28. *Lodzher geto*, p. 46.
29. Su-KC, Docs. 21, 113.
30. Minutes, No. 48/172, of Aug. 9, 1942.
31. YaVA, microfilm JM/1837: "Anlage zum Finanzbericht für September, 1941."
32. Minutes of the meeting of the department chiefs, Jan. 18, 1942; "Tsu der geshikhte fun di białystoker yidn in der tsayt fun sovietish-daytshn krig" (anonymous ms.), pp. 12–13 (MTA).
33. Entries of Nov. 2, 1939; June 10, 1940; July 18, 1941; and others.
34. Entries of Aug. 2 and 7, 1941.
35. Minutes, No. 18/142, of the same date.
36. *Sprawozdanie*, pp. 5, 6.
37. YaVA, File 06/3–1.
38. YaVA, microfilm JM/1837.
39. The source, for Lublin: minutes, No. 59 (Dec. 21, 1940); for Warsaw: Ringelblum, *op. cit.*, p. 208; for Vilna: Kruk, *op. cit.*, p. 119.
40. Diary of Czerniakow, entry of July 8, 1940.
41. ZC, Doc. 50A.
42. Minutes, No. 54/115, of the same date.
43. Pesakh Kaplan, "Der yudenrat in białystok," p. 5 (MTA).
44. Ringelblum, *op. cit.*, pp. 204–205.
45. *Der Wecker*, No. 4/28 (Feb. 8, 1942).
46. Ringelblum, *op. cit.*, p. 207; Czerniakow's Diary, entry of Feb. 12, 1942, about the arrest of a fixer, who, together with a clerk of the tenement department, distributed apartments for bribes.
47. Turkow, *op. cit.*, p. 57.
48. Tabaksblat, *op. cit.*, pp. 57, 58, 60, 67.
49. *Pinkos Kolomay*, p. 329.
50. Yerushalmi, *op. cit.*, p. 214.
51. Minutes of Sept. 24, and Oct. 3, 1941.
52. The source, for Kaunas: Garfunkel, *op. cit.*, pp. 239–240; for Lublin: minutes, Nos. 40 of Aug. 31, 1940, and 44/105, Sept. 20, 1941; for Lwów: Szende, *op. cit.*, p. 96, Maltieyl, *op. cit.*, pp. 96–97; for Zamość: *Pinkos Zamoshch*, pp. 942–943; for Bełchatów: *Bełkhatover yizkor-bukh*, p. 414; for Klementów: [L. Zylberberg], *A yid fun Klementów dertsaylt* (Łódź, 1947), pp. 15–17; for Kopyczyńce: testimony, No. 635, of Szmuel Plutsman (YIA).
53. G.Ż., No. 10 (Aug. 24, 1940).
54. Minutes of Nov. 22 and Nov. 29, 1941; announcements, Nos. 77, 160, 332, 334, and

406 of the period between Aug. 1941 and the end of Feb. 1943 (Blumental, *op. cit.*, pp. 85, 95, 322, 381, 483, 485, 527, 529).

55. Minutes, No. 40, Aug. 31, 1940; No. 41, Sept. 7, 1940.
56. Minutes, No. 53, Nov. 9, 1940; No. 59, Dec. 21, 1940; No. 44/105, Sept. 20, 1941; according to the minutes of the meeting of May 24, 1941, the "Personnel Commission was entrusted with the task of reorganizing the office apparatus and of dismissing those officials who are not fit to work."
57. *Lodzher geto*, pp. 36, 366.
58. Diary of Y. Klementynowski, p. 4.
59. ZC, Doc. 28: BKC of May 9, 1942.
60. *Geto-tsaytung* of Apr. 25, 1941; I. Nirenberg, "Geshikhte fun lodzher geto," *In di yorn fun yiddishen khurbn* (New York, 1948), pp. 233–234; Jakub Poznański, *Pamiętnik z getta łódzkiego* (Łódź, 1960), p. 60.
61. Turkow, *op. cit.*, pp. 58–59.
62. Ringelblum, *op. cit.*, p. 252.
63. *Sefer hazvaot*, pp. 178–179.
64. *Sefer yizkor lekehilat shedlets*, p. 655.
65. *Zygelbojm-bukh*, pp. 129–130.
66. Kruk, *op. cit.*, pp. 46, 48.
67. Ringelblum, *op. cit.*, p. 138.
68. Czerniakow's Diary, entry Dec. 9, 1939 (about the employment of Dr. Alfred Nossig, who turned out to be a Gestapo confidant and was shot by the Organization of Jewish Fighters); entries of Apr. 15 and May 15, 1940; entries of May 9 and Nov. 24, 1941, among others.
69. Garfunkel, *op. cit.*, pp. 244–245.
70. Minutes, No. 58/119, Dec. 7, 1941.
71. *Dos bukh fun Lublin*, p. 485; minutes, No. 21/145, Apr. 8, 1942; for obvious reasons, the minutes are silent regarding the cause of his death; they register only the fact and the decision to hire another person in his place.
72. *Turne, Kiyum un khurbn fun der yiddisher shtot*, p. 824.
73. *Pinkos Ludmir*, p. 457.
74. In his entry of May 3, 1942, Czerniakow linked the demand of the *Transferstelle* to furnish a list of working people, including those employed in the offices of the Council, with a suspicion that a "resettlement" of the unemployed was in preparation.
75. *Lodzher geto*, pp. 283–284.
76. Szende, *op. cit.*, p. 113.
77. Kruk, *op. cit.*, p. 562.

CHAPTER 15

1. *Lodzher geto*, p. 347.
2. Dvorzhetsky, *op. cit.*, pp. 151–152.
3. Turkow, *op. cit.*, p. 96.
4. RA, I, Nos. 83, 116, 223; records of the JDC, File No. 373; *Pinkos Kremenets*, p. 428; ZC, "Die erste sieben Monate im Lodzer Ghetto" (ms. in AJHI); *Dos bukh fun Lublin*, pp. 358, 390.
5. *Yizkor-bukh Khelm*, pp. 602–604; Rutkowski, *op. cit.*, p. 85.
6. *Yizkor-bukh Khelm*, p. 604.

7. *Ibid.*
8. ZC, Doc. 27.
9. YaVA, testimony, No. Sh-164/1785.
10. Cf. *Sefer Borshchiv*, p. 181.
11. Trunk, "Maarev-eyropeishe yidn in di mizrekh-europeishe getos," *Goldene Keyt*, No. 15 (Tel Aviv, 1953), pp. 81–82.
12. *Lodzher geto*, pp. 351–352.
13. ZC, Doc. 1220, pp. 9–10; Ringelblum, "Notitsn fun varshever geto," *Blfg*, Vol. I, No. 1, pp. 45–46; Kaufmann, *op. cit.*, pp. 184, 185; *Pinkos Zamoshch*, p. 963.
14. *Pinkos Zamoshch*, p. 951.
15. *Lodzher geto*, p. 356; Max Kaufmann, *op. cit.*, p. 184.
16. *Lodzher geto*, pp. 258, 259.
17. *Pinkos Zamoshch*, p. 1136.
18. *Pinkos Zamoshch*, p. 951; Max Kaufmann, *op. cit.*, pp. 183–184.
19. ZC, Doc. 28, p. 9; *Pinkos Zamoshch*, p. 946.
20. Diary of J. Klementynowski, p. 36; *Pinkos Zamoshch*, p. 947.
21. AJHI, testimony, No. 303.
22. *Sefer Pabianits*, p. 316.
23. *Yizkor-bukh Khelm*, p. 91.
24. ZC, Doc. 1/30, pp. 1–2; ZC, Doc. 38, p. 12; *Dos bukh fun Lublin*, p. 389; *Mezrych zamlbukh*, p. 557, among others. In Lublin and in Międzyrzec (Mezrych) the Council members (in Międzyrzec, only the chairman) had the privilege of living outside the ghetto.
25. Ringelblum, *op. cit.*, pp. 227–228.
26. Dvorzhetsky, *op. cit.*, p. 156.
27. Minutes of Jan. 18, 1942, and the pertinent announcements, Nos. 61, 206, 281 of 1941 and 1942.
28. Garfunkel, *op. cit.*, p. 230.
29. WaC, Doc. 34/4, pp. 3–4; Dvorzhetsky, *op. cit.*, pp. 165, 168–169; Garfunkel, *op. cit.*, p. 91.
30. Ringelblum, *op. cit.*, p. 231; Rachel Auerbach, *Bekhutsot Varshe* (Tel Aviv, 1954), p. 66; ZC, Doc. 1221, pp. 3–4; I. Hiller, "Togbukh fun lodzher geto" (ms. in the Bund Archives in New York); *Dos bukh fun Lublin*, pp. 434–435; Yerushalmi, *op. cit.*, p. 202; etc.
31. Dvorzhetsky, *op. cit.*, pp. 134–136.
32. Michael and Zvi Rayak, *Khurbn Głubok* . . . (Buenos Aires, 1956), pp. 111–112.
33. *Pinkos Novaredok* (Tel Aviv, 1963), pp. 243, 244, 322–326.
34. Tuvie Friedman, *Al maatsaram shel assrot poshim naziim* . . . (Haifa, Jan. 1958), Chap. I, p. 14; *Pinkos Kolomay*, p. 334 (see also the plan of the ghetto on pp. 336–337).
35. WaC, Doc. 31/3, pp. 4–5; additional groups not listed in the document were 2,500 workers in the ghetto shops (in the second half of 1941) and a certain number of people who worked illegally in secret shops, factories, etc. (their exact number cannot be ascertained); the wages of the first group were very meager, the earnings of the second group were, in periods of favorable circumstances, not bad.
36. Ringelblum, *op. cit.*, pp. 120–123; Zylberberg, *op. cit.*, pp. 15–17.
37. Ringelblum, *op. cit.*, pp. 120–123; Turkow, p. 52; Questionnaire No. 787 (Opoczno).
38. *Sefer Stashev*, p. 424.
39. Druk, *op. cit.*, p. 17.
40. *Braynsk—sefer hazikaron* (New York, 1948), p. 266.
41. *Yizkor-bukh fun der zhelekhover yidisher kehile*, p. 228.
42. From an answer to a questionnaire, *Blfg*, Vol. I, No. 3–4, p. 199.

43. *Der Wecker*, No. 12/36, Dec. 1941.
44. Minutes, No. 12/136, March 7, 1942.
45. RA, I, No. 335.
46. Ringelblum, *op. cit.*, pp. 198–199.
47. *Lodzher geto* ("Provisioning the Ghetto," pp. 102–151); "Tsu der geshikhte fun di białystoker yidn . . . ," pp. 6–7; Su-KC, Doc. 274 (*Geto-yedies*, n.d. [1942]); Garfunkel, *op. cit.*, pp. 98, 102; Yerushalmi, *op. cit.*, p. 81.
48. Circular letter of the *Landesernährungsamt* of the *Statthalter* in Wartheland, July 9, 1941, to all administrative offices and the central economic agencies; the circular put the rations for the nonworking Jewish population on a par with those of Polish prisoners and inmates of concentration camps: Trunk, *Shtudie*, pp. 108–109. Similar regulations were in force in all occupation areas.
49. *Blfg*, Vol. II, p. 277.
50. Dvorzhetsky, *op. cit.*, p. 157; MTA, "Tsu der geshikhte fun di białystoker yidn . . . ," p. 5.
51. *Lodzher geto*, pp. 109–111.
52. *Ibid.*, p. 112.
53. Ringelblum, *op. cit.*, p. 232.
54. *Lodzher geto*, p. 378.
55. *Ibid.*, pp. 106, 170.
56. Ringelblum, *op. cit.*, pp. 116, 124; Memoirs, by Jan Mawult, pp. 6–7 (No. 137, YIA).
57. Questionnaire No. 781.
58. Testimony, No. 617, by Moshe Feingold (YIA).
59. Turkow, *op. cit.*, p. 58; Ringelblum, *op. cit.*, p. 111.
60. Tabaksblat, *op. cit.*, p. 165.
61. ZC, Docs. 47; 28, pp. 4–5; 14.
62. *Pinkos Zamoshch*, pp. 942–943.
63. Testimony, No. 331, by Liber Farbiarz (YIA); the expulsion order was later revoked and some expellees returned home (Brustin-Bernstein, in *Blfg*, Vol. III, No. 1–2, p. 69).
64. *Yizkor-bukh fun der zhelekhover yidisher kehile*, p. 219.
65. *Sefer zikaron lekehila kedoysha Zavierche vehasviva* (Tel Aviv, 1958), p. 383.
66. *Mezrych zamlbukh*, p. 545.
67. *Sefer Horodenko*.

CHAPTER 16

1. Shmul Zygelbojm, "In onhoyb fun khurbn," *Zygelbojm-bukh*, pp. 151–153; the statement was delivered by Czerniakow, not in writing but orally. Some Council members called upon representatives of the Polish population and informed them about the whole matter.
2. AJHI, JUS, File 31.
3. ABLG (a photocopy).
4. *Ibid.*; the curfew was extended until 9 P.M. (minutes of the Council, No. 29/30, May 6, 1940).
5. BWS, No. 9, pp. 8–9.
6. Records of JDC, File 378, pp. 20–62.
7. BWS, No. 11, pp. 7–8.
8. BWS, No. 11, pp. 18–19.
9. *Ibid.*

10. Copy in YIA.
11. Minutes of the Council meeting with its officials of Nov. 2, 1941.
12. *Zygelbojm-bukh*, pp. 131, 132, 134, 135; *Sefer hazvaot*, pp. 51–52.
13. *Pinkos Ludmir*, p. 438.
14. *Kehilat Zharki*, p. 241.
15. *Pinkos Byten*, p. 226.
16. Yerushalmi, *op. cit.*, p. 82.
17. Czerniakow's Diary, entries of Jan. 17, Feb. 9 and 27, and March 10 and 11, 1942.
18. *Sefer zikaron Stoypts-Sverzhno* (Tel Aviv, 1964), p. 317.
19. Weisbrod, *op. cit.*, p. 30.
20. Announcement of the *Judenrat*, Sept. 10, 1941.
21. Testimony, No. 1043, pp. 15–17 (YIA).
22. *Kehilat Zharki*, pp. 236, 237, 241.
23. *Pitchayever yizkor-bukh*, pp. 168–169.
24. *Radoshkovits sefer zikaron*, p. 201.
25. *Sefer Stashev*, p. 427.
26. *Sefer hazikaron Braynsk*, pp. 265–266.
27. *Khurbn un gevure fun shtetl Markishev*, p. 201.
28. Kurts, *op. cit.*, p. 139.
29. *Pinkos Khmielnik*, p. 661.
30. *Baranovitsh sefer zikaron* (1953), p. 513.
31. *Megilat Grytse* (1955), pp. 276–277.
32. FLKh, No. 3 (1946), p. 4.
33. *Wolkovysker yizkor-bukh* (1949), Vol. II, p. 629.
34. Testimony, No. 1043 (YIA).
35. YaVA, File DN/3–4, pp. 230, 245.
36. Testimony, No. 1043 (YIA), p. 35.
37. *Sefer Mir*, p. 323.
38. *Pinkos Ludmir*, p. 444.
39. Brener, *op. cit.*, p. 80.
40. Testimony, No. 1043 (YIA), pp. 36–37.
41. YaVA, testimony, No. G–128/1711.
42. *Pinkos Bendin*, p. 191.
43. *Dos bukh fun Lublin*, pp. 484–485.
44. YIA, testimony by Hava Klein.
45. ZC, Doc. 1220.
46. ZC, Doc. 1192, *Lodzher geto*, p. 367, No. 103.
47. Minutes of the general meeting, June 21, 1942.
48. Minutes of the "extraordinary meeting," Oct. 11, 1942.
49. Dvorzhetsky, *op. cit.*, p. 141; *Geto-yedies*, No. 24 (Jan. 31, 1943), mentions a meeting of the Council of foremen addressed by Gens along the same line.
50. *Geto-yedies*, No. 42 (June 6, 1943); cf. Dvorzhetsky, *op. cit.*, p. 141.
51. Su-KC, announcement, No. 153.
52. *Pinkos Bendin*, p. 189.
53. *Sefer Stashev*, pp. 449–450.
54. *Lukover kedoyshim un heldn*, p. 12.
55. B. Ajzensztajn, *Ruch podziemny w ghettach i obozach* ("The Underground in the Ghettos and Camps"), p. 20.
56. *Drohichin* [Memorial book], p. 349.
57. *Megilat Kurenits*, p. 205.
58. *Yizkor-bukh Khelm*, p. 632.
59. Weisbrod, *op. cit.*, p. 73.

60. Testimony, No. 1043 (YIA).
61. YIA, testimony by Hilel Kenigsberg.
62. To the question of the attitude of the *Wehrmacht* to the "Final Solution," the following should be taken into consideration: on the eve of the invasion of Soviet Russia an agreement between General Wagner, the *Oberquartiermeister* of the High Command of the *Wehrmacht*, and Heydrich on the terms of co-operation between the *Einsatzgruppen*, subordinated to Himmler, and the army was concluded. In accordance with this agreement General Walter Brauchitsch, the chief commander of the Eastern Front, issued an order on April 28, 1941, which read in part: "The *Einsatzgruppen* in the front line are entitled to draw auxiliary personnel from the Armed Forces, which are obliged to provide unconditionally on their demand the required people" (*Trial of the War Criminals before the NMT*, Green Series, Vol. X, pp. 1240–1242). Detachments of the army partici-pated in the executions in Kiev ("Babi yar") at the end of Sept. 1941, and in Human on Oct. 20, 1941 (*Erreignismeldungen* of the EG, Nos. 97 and 119); they handed over Jewish POWs of the defeated Soviet Army for executions, as for instance in Winnica (reports of the EG, No. 128, Nov. 3, 1941), in Dniepropetrovsk and Boryspol (report, No. 132, Nov. 12, 1941), etc. At the request of the army 146 Jews were shot in Borysov by a unit of the EG, which operated in the vicinity of Smolensk (report, No. 148, Dec. 19, 1941). But in daily practice the attitude of the army was not uniform; it depended to some degree on the commanders of the local army units. The same reports of the EG which often emphasized the "excellency" or "smoothness" of the collaboration on the part of the army, complained also that "often the *Einsatzkommandos* had to listen to more or less disguised criticism of their consistent attitude to the Jewish ques-tion" (report, No. 126); the commandant of the same POW camp in Winnica, from which Jewish POWs were handed over for execution, put his deputy and two officers under court martial for delivering 362 Jewish POWs to the S.D. (report, No. 128). In Przemyśl an army officer prevented Gestapo men from taking Jewish workers employed by him and threatened by use of force not to allow the transportation of the workers by the railroad (*Sefer Pshemyshl*, p. 512).
63. BC, Doc. OccE3–28.
64. *Ibid.*
65. BC, Doc. OccE3–33.
66. BC, Doc. OccE3–28: letter of Dec. 18, 1941.
67. BC, Doc. OccE3–38.
68. BC, Doc. OccE2–1–8: *Wochenberichte der Distrikte.*
69. *Eksterminacja*, p. 242.
70. AGV, File IV/60, p. 255.
71. BC, Doc. OccE2–1–8: *Wochenberichte der Distrikte.*
72. See, for instance, Himmler's order of Oct. 9, 1942, concerning the concentration of all Jewish workers employed in the armament industry in the concentration camps of the Warsaw and Lublin districts, in which he wrote with disdain of "the so-called armament workers actually employed in the tailor-furrier and cobbler shops" (*Eksterminacja*, pp. 244–245); the same argument was used by the SS representatives in Distrikt Galizien (Friedman, *op. cit.*, pp. 647–648).
73. BC, Doc. OccE3–40.
74. A note by Oswald Pohl, Sept. 3, 1943, concerning the takeover of the Jewish labor camps in the GG under the jurisdiction of the *SS u. Polizei-Führer* by the *Verwaltungs- und Wirtschaftshauptamt SS* (*Eksterminacja*, pp. 254–255).
75. *Dapim min hadleyka*, pp. 85–86.
76. MTA, File No. 56/108.

77. ZC, Doc. 1218, p. IV; ZC, Doc. 27, p. 3.
78. See n. 62, above.
79. *Sefer Borshchiv*, p. 188; Turkow, *op. cit.*, pp. 271–272; *Lukover kedoyshim un heldn*, p. 12, and many others.
80. Wiederman, *op. cit.*, p. 153.
81. Su-KC, Doc. 273: *Geto-yedies*, No. 52 (Aug. 15, 1943).
82. *Lodzher geto*, pp. 296–297.
83. Su-KC, Doc. 267: *Geto-yedies*, No. 30 (March 14, 1943); cf. Kruk, *op. cit.*, p. 472.
84. ZC, Doc. 1218, p. IV; ZC, Doc. 27, p. 3.
85. Layb Rochman, *In dayn blut zolstu lebn. Tog-bukh 1943–1944* (Paris, 1949), p. 50.
86. *Lukover kedoyshim un heldn*, p. 14.
87. WaC, Doc. 6/2.
88. *Sefer-yizkor lekehilat Shedlets*, pp. 650–651.
89. *Sefer-yizkor lekehilat Sarny*, pp. 320–321.
90. I. Feigenboym, *Podlashe in umkum*, pp. 128–130.
91. RA, I, No. 1408.
92. RA, I, No. 469.
93. Władysław Bednarz, *Obóz straceń w Chelmnie nad Nerem* (Warsaw, 1946), p. 14.
94. N. Blumental, J. Kermish, *Hameri vehamered begeto Varshe* (Jerusalem, 1965), pp. 189–191; excerpts of both calls are published in BŻIH, No. 13–14 (1955), pp. 202–203.
95. *Pinkos Zamoshch*, pp. 1005–1006.
96. VBlGG, No. 94 (Nov. 1, 1942), No. 98 (Nov. 14, 1942).
97. *Sefer-yizkor lekehilat Shedlets*, p. 709; Kałuszyn Ghetto lasted approximately that long.
98. T. Brustin-Bernstein, *op. cit.*, *Blfg*, Vol. III, No. 1–2, Table 8.
99. According to Kalmanovich, the speech cited was made by Gens at the meeting of the ghetto police on Oct. 25, 1942 (*YIVO-Bleter*, Vol. XXXV [1951], pp. 39–40). Dvorzhetsky quoted a second speech made by him in a gathering of the police and members of the ghetto administration on Oct. 27 (*op. cit.*, pp. 415–416). The essence of both speeches is identical, but not having at my disposal the complete original text of both speeches I am in no position to determine whether this is the same speech taken down by two persons in two different ways, or whether these represent two different speeches made on two different dates.
100. See n. 99, above. His speech on the occasion of the presentation of the literary awards to Israel Dimentman and Lea Rudnitsky was similar in content, it probably took place before the end of Feb. 1943 (*Geto-yedies*, No. 28, Feb. 28, 1943; Dvorzhetsky, *op. cit.*, p. 308.
101. Dvorzhetsky, *op. cit.*, p. 416.
102. Kalmanovich, *op. cit.*, pp. 39–40.
103. Wiederman, *op. cit.*, p. 25 and *passim*; according to Wiederman, Merin tried to justify his strategy at a meeting with Rumkowski and Czerniakow, held in Warsaw on an unknown date (*ibid.*, pp. 89–90); there is no record left of the meeting.
104. ZC, Doc. 54; excerpts of the speech published in *Lodzher geto*, pp. 311–314.
105. S. Kot, *Khurbn Białystok* (Buenos Aires, 1947), pp. 58–59.
106. Ch. Grosman, *op. cit.*, p. 201; R. Rayzner, *op. cit.*, pp. 118–119; *Dapim min hadleyka*, p. 65.
107. Weisbrod, *op. cit.*, pp. 36–37; an identical way of reasoning was recorded among Jews in the Warsaw Ghetto (Elboym-Dorembus, *Oyf der arisher zayt* [Buenos Aires, 1957], p. 48).
108. Sz. Mayer, *op. cit.*, pp. 20–21.
109. Garfunkel, *op. cit.*, pp. 71–76.

110. Wiederman, *op. cit.*, pp. 86–96.
111. Weisbrod, *op. cit.*, pp. 49–50.
112. AJHI, ms. 99/A, p. 24.
113. *Sefer Lutsk*, p. 502.
114. *Pinkos Bendin*, pp. 188–189.
115. Wiederman, *op. cit.*, p. 98.
116. Dvorzhetsky, *op. cit.*, p. 294.
117. Sh. Glube, "Di din-toyre," FLKh, No. 6 (1947), pp. 44–47; the event took place in the first decade of Dec. 1941, when the annihilation camp in Chełmno had just started to function and there was no certainty about the purpose of the deportation.
118. Kalmanovich, *op. cit.*, p. 42.
119. YIA, photostat of Rumkowski's speech, Jan. 25, 1942.
120. Turkow, *op. cit.*, p. 268.
121. *Dapim min hadleyka*, pp. 67–68; see also the "notes" written by him after the February "action," where he again justified the absence of an organized resistance on the part of the Organization of Jewish Fighters during the "resettlement" (the motive of gaining time, during which "the deliverance may come"); he concludes the "notes" with the sober statement that not one Jew would have remained in the ghetto had there been armed resistance.
122. ZC, Doc. 27, p. 4(18).
123. ZC, Doc. 1220, p. 6.
124. ZC, Doc. 1192, p. 5.
125. Wiederman, *op. cit.*, pp. 85, 180; cf. Friedman, "Hatasbikh hamshikhi shel takif begeto hanazi," *Bitzaron*, Vol. 28, No. 5 (1953), p. 33.
126. YIA, Klementynowski's Diary, p. 23; Nirenberg, *op. cit.*, pp. 236–237.
127. Merin characterized Rumkowski as "a sick man who belongs rather in a mental institution than in the position of reigning over a community numbering two hundred thousand souls" (Wiederman, *op. cit.*, p. 89).
128. YIA, Doc. IT, p. 30; Wiederman, *op. cit.*, p. 85.
129. *Lodzher geto*, pp. 253, 254, 267–273.
130. Report of Nov. 15, 1942, sent to the Polish government in London by the Jewish underground organizations, published in *Blfg*, Vol. IV, No. 2 (1951), pp. 183–207; Jan Galewicz "Wspomnieina o Abramie Gepnerze" ("Recollections about Abraham Gepner"), *Zeszyty Historyczne*, No. 9 (1966), pp. 9–10.
131. YaVA, Doc. 06/1–4; the list contains 47 typed sheets.
132. Benedict Kautsky, *Teufel und Verdammte* (Zurich, 1946), pp. 293–294; Eugen Kogon, *The Theory and Practice of Hell: The German Concentration Camps and the System Behind Them* (New York, 1950), pp. 254–255.
133. S. Ginsburg, *Historishe Verk*, Vol. III (New York, 1937), p. 28.
134. Publication of the Institute of Contemporary Jewry, Shprintzak Division, in association with the Hebrew University (Jerusalem, 1967), pp. 34–35.
135. Questionnaire No. 757; testimony of Rabbi David Kahane; Friedman, *op. cit.*, pp. 613–614.
136. *Pinkos Novaradok*, p. 254; Questionnaire Nos. 304, 306. Light on the type of offenses on the part of the Council is shed by the accusation made against one of the Council members who was shot, namely, that he was responsible for illegal food traffic in the ghetto (Questionnaire No. 325).
137. *Pinkos Novaradok*, p. 254; Questionnaire No. 309.
138. Dora Agatstein, "Hayehudim bekroke betkufat hakibush hanazi," *Sefer Kroke*, p. 390, n. 59; Questionnaire No. 394.
139. Questionnaire Nos. 413, 418.

140. Questionnaire No. 150.
141. Questionnaire No. 157; testimony N–27/1141 (YaVA).
142. Questionnaire No. 749.
143. Questionnaire Nos. 617, 624.
144. Questionnaire No. 267.
145. Questionnaire No. 277.
146. *Sefer zikaron. Ondenk-bukh k.k. Zavierche vehasviva,* pp. 361–362; Questionnaire No. 775.
147. Questionnaire Nos. 354, 361, 363; *Sefer Pshemishl,* p. 383; testimony K–120/1193 (YaVA).
148. Henokh Kazminski, "The Late Dr. Jacob Lemberg," *Landsberger-tsaytung,* No. 40 (Sept. 25, 1946) (in Latin letters); Tabaksblat relates, according to an eye-witness, that before the execution Dr. Lemberg, speaking in a firm voice in-formed the Jews forcibly gathered together that he had been ordered to state the reason why the 10 Jews were being hanged, emphasizing that he was acting under duress (Tabaksblat, *op. cit.*), pp. 137, 149.
149. *Lomzhe ir oyfkum un untergang* (1957), p. 291.
150. *Khurbn Bilgoray* (Tel Aviv, 1956), p. 303; Questionnaire Nos. 221, 222, 223, 224; *Khurbn Bilgoray* mentions only the shooting of H. Janover.
151. *Baranovitsh Sefer Zikaron* (Tel Aviv, 1953), p. 528; Questionnaire No. 463. According to the questionnaire, the sentence, in which they were accused of not handing over Jews, was read to the victims just before their execution.
152. *Sefer Kalushin* (Tel Aviv, 1961), p. 467.
153. Questionnaire No. 484.
154. Tadeusz Pankiewicz, *Apteka w getcie krakowskim* (Cracow, 1947), pp. 44–45.
155. Questionnaire No. 406.
156. Questionnaire No. 106.
157. Yerushalmi, *op. cit.,* p. 305.
158. Questionnaire No. 152.
159. Questionnaire No. 827.
160. Szlome Mayer, *op. cit.,* p. 32.
161. Józef Barski, "O niektórych zagadnieniach warszawskiego getta" ("About Some Problems of the Warsaw Ghetto"), BŻIH, No. 49 (1964), pp. 40–41; Jan Galewicz, *op. cit.,* pp. 10–11.
162. Questionnaire Nos. 611, 618, 623.
163. Questionnaire Nos. 536, 537.
164. Questionnaire No. 172.
165. *Shedletser yizkor-bukh,* p. 653; *Sefer Pshemyshl,* pp. 519, 520. Dr. Leibel was until 1934 a practitioner in Przemyśl.
166. Questionnaire No. 828.
167. Questionnaire No. 707.
168. *Lukover kedoyshim un heldn,* pp. 18–19.
169. Questionnaire No. 462; testimony W–123/2261 (YaVA).
170. Czerniakow's Diary, entry of July 23, 1942. Much was written about Czerniakow's suicide in the *Khurbn* literature, but no new particulars having been discovered, the same version was repeated.
171. Questionnaire No. 242.
172. *Sefer hazikaron lekdoyshey Bolekhov* (1957), pp. 341–342.
173. *Ibid.,* p. 328.
174. *Rovne, sefer zikaron,* pp. 543–544.
175. *Yalkut Volyn,* Vol. II (Tel Aviv, 1949), No. 10, p. 27; testimony, No. 277 (YIA); Questionnaire No. 813; *Mezhrych gadol bebinyana ubekhurbana* (Tel Aviv, 1955),

Cols. 359–360. *Mezhrych gadol* and the questionnaire present two conflicting versions about the circumstances of his suicide; it is now impossible to establish which version is true.

176. Testimony K–169/1939 (YaVA).

177. Reisner, *op. cit.*, p. 119; *Dapim min hadleyka*, p. 63.

178. *Grodner Opklangen*, No. 2 (1949), p. 20.

179. *Yirgun oley Shebreshin. Tsror yediyot* (Haifa), No. 1 (1947), p. 4; No. 4 (1952), pp. 22, 23. Self-sacrificing deeds of two other Jews were there related: one, Shmaria Wertser, threw himself into the flames when the holy scrolls were set afire; the second, Joseph Springer, the representative of the local Bund organization, plunged from a bridge into Wieprz River as he (along with two others) was being led, under guard, to premises in which he would have been forced to compile a list of political activists in the town.

180. Testimony SH–164/1785 (YaVA); *Pinkos Kremeniets*, p. 422. According to another witness he succeeded in taking his life during the next "action" in early Sept. 1942 (*ibid.*, p. 258); during this "action" the physician Khaskelberg and the whole family of the ghetto pharmacist (name unknown) took their lives by poison.

181. *Sefer zikaron leyehadut Lomzha*, p. 64; B. Mark, *Der oyfshtand in białystoker geto* (Warsaw, 1950), p. 84.

182. Testimony K–87/1075, pp. 15–16 (YaVA).

183. Two witnesses, Hanna Weinheber-Haker (*Pinkos Kołomay*, p. 341) and Jacob Higer (Questionnaire No. 543), tell of two suicide attempts; on the other hand, Eliezer Unger (*Zkhor*, pp. 58–59) relates only the suicide attempt together with his sister and places the event in Nov. (not Dec.) 1942. Because Unger left the ghetto in March 1942 we give credibility to the two witnesses.

184. Questionnaire No. 158.

185. *Pinkos fun di finf fartilikte kehiles*, p. 691.

186. *Ibid.*, p. 690.

187. *Ibid.*, pp. 629, 606.

188. Questionnaire No . ʻ ṭ.

189. Szlojme Mayer, *op. cit.*, p. 21.

190. Questionnaire Nos. 374, 700; *Khurbn Głubok*, pp. 71, 155, 160, 161.

191. Questionnaire Nos. 465, 475.

192. Dr. B. Bigil, *Ayarati Berezno, mayn shtetele Berezne* (Tel Aviv, 1954), pp. 91, 92, 96–97, 100 (testimonies of four former ghetto inmates).

193. Questionnaire Nos. 776–780; *Sefer zikaron . . . Zavierche*; pp. 384–385.

194. Questionnaire No. 742. In contradiction the *Shedletser yizkor-bukh* relates that Hersh Eisenberg "was the vice chairman of the Council in the large ghetto" (p. 663); alas, we are in no position to clarify this discrepancy.

195. Weisbrod, *op. cit.*, pp. 56, 59.

CHAPTER 17

1. *Dapim min hadleyka*, pp. 93–94; Brener, *op. cit.*, pp. 64–65.

2. I. Trunk, "Yidisher vidershtand in der nazi-tkufe", *Shtudies in yidisher geshikhte in poyln* (Buenos Aires, 1963), pp. 302–303.

3. Reports on the "Witenberg day" in the Vilna Ghetto by Nusia Długi, Breine As, Shimon Palewski, Zhenie Berkman, and Mark Dvorzhetsky, *YIVO-Bleter*, Vol. XXX, No. 2, pp. 188–213.

4. R. Korczak, *op. cit.*, pp. 167–168; *Dapim min hadleyka*, pp. 97–107 (minutes of the meeting of the members of the kibbutz Dror, in Białystok Feb. 27, 1943); address by Yitzhak Cukierman (Antek) at a meeting held in kibbutz Yagur, published in *Nasze Słowo* (Warsaw, April 1948); *Sefer hapartizanim hayehudim*, Vol. 1 (Merkhavia, 1958), p. 570.

5. Yerushalmi, *op. cit.*, p. 315.

6. *Sefer Lutsk*, pp. 501–502.

7. Dvorzhetsky, *op. cit.*, pp. 446–448.

8. *Geto-yedies*, No. 50, Aug. 1, 1943.

9. MTA, announcements, Nos. 391, 392.

10. Testimony, Sh–133/1436 (YaVA).

11. *Lakhovits sefer zikaron*, p. 321. This fact is related by the initiators of the escape plan.

12. Testimony, I–3/255 (YaVA).

13. *Megilat Kurenits*, pp. 177, 285.

14. *Sefer Kobryn*, p. 305.

15. *Sefer Khmielnik*, p. 774.

16. *Pinkos Kletsk*, p. 371.

17. *Ibid.*, p. 355.

18. *Pinkos Novaredok*, p. 254.

19. *Pinkos Bendin*, pp. 355–357 (facsimile of Merin's letter to the Będzin Council); Fredke Mazia, *Rayim besaar* (Jerusalem, 1964), pp. 112–114.

20. Kaganovich, *Milkhome fun di yidishe partizaner in mizrekh eyrope* (Buenos Aires, 1956), Vol. I, p. 302.

21. *Arim veyimahot beyisrael*, Vol. VI, *Brody* (1959), p. 406, n. 43.

22. Testimony by Bessy Stein (YIA).

23. *Khurbn Głubok*, p. 155.

24. Dvorzhetsky, *op. cit.*, pp. 446–448; Korczak, *op. cit.*, pp. 170–171.

25. Yerushalmi, *op. cit.*, p. 274.

26. FLKh, No. 4, p. 49; *Sefer milkhamot hagetaot*, ed. by Yitzhak Cukierman and Moshe Basok (Eyn-kharod, 1954), pp. 659–660.

27. *Sefer kehilat Sarny*, p. 308.

28. Kaganovich, *Der yidisher ontayl in der partizaner bavegung in Soviet-Rusland*, p. 307. The partisan Hirsh Posesorsky (a refugee from Warsaw and a member of the Bund youth organization Tsukunft) organized the escape of 120 inmates of the camp in Nowe Swierzno in the second half of Jan. 1943 (those who remained behind in the camp were shot the next morning). After enduring many hardships in the woods the escapees joined the Soviet partisan unit of Brigadier Shestopolov (*Sefer hapartizanim*, Vol. I, pp. 581–582); oral testimony by Gita Krysztal-Pik, who escaped with the Posesorsky group.

29. Yitzhak Nimtsovich, "Eyner fun undzere heldn," *Yidisher Kemfer* (New York) Oct. 15, 1954.

30. Questionnaire No. 815.

31. *Pinkos fun di finf fartilikte kehiles*, p. 608.

32. Kurts, *op. cit.*, pp. 176–178; *In diyorn fun yidishn khurbn*, pp. 64, 140; B. Goldstein, *Finf yor in varshever geto* (New York, 1947), p. 128; testimony by David Rosenstein (YIA). Besides the Council members, several members of the Bund in the town were arrested as well as Bundists in Lublin, Radom, Tomaszów Mazowiecki, Częstochowa and Cracow. All perished, most of them in Auschwitz.

33. Questionnaire No. 298.

34. Questionnaire No. 409.

35. Aron Brandes, *Kets hayehudim bemaarav poyln* (1946), pp. 31–32; *Sefer hapartizanim*, Vol. I., p. 100.

36. Józef Barski, *op. cit.*, BŻIH, No. 49 (1964), p. 40.

37. Szlojme Mayer, *op. cit.*, p. 20.

38. Testimony by a person whose name cannot be published at present (YIA).

39. Questionnaire Nos. 691, 694, 696, 698.

40. *Blfg*, Vol. XVII (1969), pp. 78–79.

41. Garfunkel, *op. cit.*, p. 186.

42. *Pinkos fun di finf fartilikte kehiles*, pp. 607–609, 638, 641, 682; Questionnaire No. 629.

43. Konrad Wallenrod, a 14th-century legendary hero of the poem by the Polish poet Adam Mickiewicz, served in disguise the Order of the Knights of the Cross to avenge the subjugated Lithuanians. Shmuel Rufeisen, a member of Hechalutz, born in 1921 in a village near Żywiec (Western Galicia), escaped to Vilna after the outbreak of the German-Soviet war and became an interpreter with the Byelorussian police commandant in Turec under the assumed identity *Volksdeutsche* Josef Oswald. Thanks to the favored attitude toward him on the part of the police commandant he was promoted to the post of police chief of Mir. Here he established contacts with the local Hashomer Hatzair group and helped start an underground resistance group among the remnants of the slaughtered Jewish community (the massacre took place on Nov. 7, 1941). A few days before the intended liquidation of the ghetto he informed his friends about the German design, and a plan of action was adopted: as the police chief he would lead the local police from the town under the pretext of carrying out a round-up of partisans. The Jews would avail themselves of the opportunity to take to the woods. Approximately 180 persons left the town and arrived at an agreed-upon place, where they awaited in vain the arrival of Rufeisen. Rufeisen had been arrested by the gendarme chief following a denunciation that he intentionally removed the police in order to facilitate the flight of the Jews—a charge to which Rufeisen confessed. Imprisoned under lenient conditions he took advantage of the opportunity and escaped to the partisans. There he was tried, and was acquitted thanks to the intervention of his friends from Mir. Disguised as a nun he survived the war in a monastery for women. After the war he became a monk, emigrated to Israel, and joined the Carmelite monastery in Haifa as "Brother Daniel" (*Sefer hapartizanim*, Vol. 1, pp. 468–474).

44. Questionnaire Nos. 721, 725, 727, 729–731; Smolar, *op. cit.*, pp. 63–64; *Sefer hapartizanim*, Vol. I, p. 514; Leizer Kacowich, "In gerangl mitn toyt," *Aynikayt*, Sept. 28, 1944.

45. Questionnaire No. 564.

46. Questionnaire No. 629.

47. Garfunkel, *op. cit.*, pp. 185–186; Questionnaire No. 117.

48. Testimony, No. 272, by Aron Irlicht; see also n. 28, above.

49. Grosman, *op. cit.*, pp. 77, 199.

50. MTA, minutes of the [seventh] general meeting of the ghetto inhabitants, Aug. 16, 1942 (Blumental, *op. cit.*, p. 239).

51. Grosman, *op. cit.*, pp. 77–78; *Dapim min hadleyka*, pp. 85–86; Mark, *Der oyfshtand in białystoker geto*, p. 115. Mark quoted an entry by Tenenboym (Jan. 19, 1943), concerning Barash's handing over to the underground organization a half kilogram of gold and 30 golden watches. This entry was omitted from the *Dapim*.

52. *Dapim min hadleyka*, pp. 32, 39, 43, and others.

53. *Ibid.*, pp. 57, 67.

54. Grosman, *op. cit.*, pp. 306–307; Mark, *op. cit.*, pp. 114–115.

55. R. Korczak, *op. cit.*, (3rd ed., 1965), pp. 218–219.

56. *Ibid.*, pp. 155–156.

57. Kruk, *op. cit.*, p. 571; some of the group were dressed as policemen, allegedly escorting Jewish forced laborers.

58. Dvorzhetsky, *op. cit.*, p. 311.

59. Korczak, *op. cit.*, pp. 175–176 (quoted according to the Hebrew translation of the speech).

60. *Ibid.*, pp. 160–177; "Der tog fun Yitzhak Witenberg," *YIVO-Bleter*, Vol. XXX, No. 2, pp. 188–213. As Korczak relates, Witenberg was poisoned by Gens and the chief of the ghetto police, Dressler, who were afraid that Witenberg might implicate them during the interrogation in the Gestapo.

61. Dvorzhetsky, *op. cit.*, p. 321.

62. *Sefer milkhamot hagetaot*, pp. 479–480: testimony by Sholem Cholawski, who was among the leaders of the resistance group; Kaganovich, *Di milkhome fun di yidishe partizaner in mizrekh eyrope*, Vol. I, pp. 203–204.

63. Testimony by Leon Slutski (YIA); three testimonies by Aron Shverin, Haim Szklar, and Abraham Feinberg in FLKh, No. 3 (1946), pp. 1–11; *Sefer milkhamot hagetaot*, pp. 477–478; B. Ajzenstein, *op. cit.*, p. 98. According to Kaganovich (*op. cit.*, pp. 100–101) the Germans summoned Lopatin on Sept. 2, 1943, and told him that in accordance with a superior order all Jews had to be killed, with the exception of 30 artisans and himself. Lopatin allegedly answered that he was not a master over the life and death of people and that no Jew, including himself, would take advantage of privileged status. He immediately ran into the ghetto, set fire to his house, ordered all Jews to do likewise, and exhorted them to storm the gates. However, this version seems very unlikely. There is no recorded instance of the Germans openly declaring that the Jews were to be killed. The official explanation of "resettlement" was, always, the intention to move the Jews to another working place.

64. Questionnaire Nos. 605, 606; testimony by Sholem Cholawski in *Sefer milkhamot hagetaot*, pp. 478–480; *idem*, "Nesviezh, eyda mitkomemet," *Sefer hapartizanim*, Vol. I, pp. 548–553.

65. Moshe Lakhovitsky, *Khurban Nesviezh (an eyewitness account)*, (1948), pp. 41–45 (mimeographed); Questionnaire Nos. 602, 610.

66. *Pinkos Zhetl* (Tel Aviv, 1957), pp. 369–370; Kaganovich, *op. cit.*, Vol. I, pp. 154–156, 178, 224–225, 339, 340; Vol. II, pp. 241, 264, 265.

67. In the B. Ajzenstein book cited, his name is rendered Gimelfeld (Himelfeld), *ibid.*, p. 101.

68. Kaganovich, *op. cit.*, Vol. I, pp. 100–103, 196; Ajzenstein, *op. cit.*, pp. 95–98; *Yalkut Volyn*, Vol. I, No. 7, p. 22; Vol. II, Nos. 15–17, p. 56; *Sefer milkhamot hagetaot*, pp. 487–489.

69. Leib Koniukhovsky, "Der umkum fun martsinkantzer yidn," *YIVO-Bleter*, Vol. XXXVII (1953), pp. 216–229.

70. Testimony, No. 343, by Shmuel Lerer (YIA).

CHAPTER 18

1. Czerniakow's Diary, entry of Sept. 20, 1940; WaC, Doc. 42/2, pp. 1–2; G.Ż., No. 32 (Nov. 8, 1940).

2. Zaderecki, p. 486.

3. ZC, Doc. 762; *Geto-tsaytung*, No. 2 (March 14, 1941).
4. Rotenberg, *op. cit.*, p. 73.
5. YaVA, testimony R–102/1665, pp. 5–6.
6. *Bericht Krakau*, p. 102; Brener, *op. cit.*, p. 35.
7. *Ibid.*
8. ZC, Doc. 762.
9. *Rocznik*, I (1940), pp. 42–43.
10. WaC, Doc. 42/2, p. 1.
11. Jan Mawult, *op. cit.*, pp. 6, 9.
12. YaVA, File B/12–4, contemporary report, chap. "Di yidishe geto-politsey."
13. Blumental, *Obozy* (Łódź, 1946), p. 136.
14. Mawult, *op. cit.*, pp. 25–26; WaC, Doc. 42/2, p. 2.
15. For organizational regulations, see Appendix II.
16. Mawult, *op. cit.*, p. 27.
17. G.Z., No. 1 (Jan. 3, 1941); the note relates that the duties of the OD were established by Czerniakow.
18. Brener, *op. cit.*, pp. 35–36.
19. YaVA, File B/12–4.
20. WaC, Doc. 42/2, p. 8.
21. *Lodzher geto*, p. 37.
22. *Ibid.*, p. 38.
23. Su-KC: letter of the Council to the police commander, March 17, 1942.
24. Su-KC, Docs. 318, 320, 321, 337.
25. Su-KC, Docs. 303, 304.
26. Yerushalmi, *op. cit.*, p. 198.
27. *Lodzher geto*, pp. 37, 416; W. Gliksman, "Yoman hamishtara hayehudit (makuf 1) begeto chenstokhov bashanim 1941–1942," YaV, *Kovets*, Vol. VI (1967), pp. 287–313.
28. Su-KC, Doc. 339; Kruk, *op. cit.*, pp. 276–280; Dvorzhetsky, *op. cit.*, p. 314.
29. RA, I, Doc. 41; Archives of the "Instytut Historii Najnowszej" (Warsaw), supplement No. 31, pp. 3–4; A. Hohenstein, *op. cit.*, p. 241; P. Kaplan, "Der khurbn białystok" (MTA, ms.), published in Polish translation in BŻIH, No. 60 (1966), p. 79; ZC, BKC (Apr. 26, 1943).
30. Ringelblum, *op. cit.*, p. 138.
31. G.Ż., No. 67 (Aug. 4, 1941).
32. Shlome Waga, *Churbn Chenstekhov* (Buenos Aires, 1949), p. 83; Brener, *op. cit.*, p. 37; Wiederman, *op. cit.*, pp. 127–128; *Milkhome* (III), p. 227; *Min hamoykad, aykh hushmada kehilat Radom*, pp. 35–36; *Pinkos Kolomay*, p. 332.
33. *Yizkor-bukh fun der Zhelekhover yidisher kehile*, p. 217.
34. Minutes, No. 28/89.
35. *Pinkos Zamoshch*, p. 1163 (photostat of the announcement).
36. YIA, File "Poyln, hitler-tkufe, farshidene getos un lagern."
37. *Bet hamishpat hamkhozi, Tel-Aviv-Yaffo* (defendant Hersh Bernblat). T.P. No. 15/63, pp. 16–17.
38. *Pinkos Bendin*, p. 191; Wiederman, *op. cit.*, p. 120; OD units, which were compelled to deliver a certain number of forced laborers under threat of being sent to Auschwitz, raided their apartments at night.
39. *Pinkos zikaron . . . Zavierche*, p. 391.
40. Su-KC, Doc. 274.
41. Announcement, No. 336, Sept. 20, 1942.
42. Announcement, No. 186, of the same date.
43. Kruk, *op. cit.*, pp. 143, 234, 247.

44. BWS, No. 12ª, p. 5.
45. Mawult, *op. cit.*, pp. 33–34.
46. BWS, No. 11, p. 22; *Bericht Warschau*, p. 15.
47. B. Mark, "Naye dokumentn tsu der geshikhte fun der vidershtand bawegung un fun dem oyfshtand in varshever geto," *Blfg*, Vol. VII, No. 1 (1954), pp. 26–27.
48. G.Ż., No. 38 (Nov. 29, 1940).
49. W. Gliksman, *op. cit.*, and his letter to me, Apr. 17, 1967.
50. YaVA, File B/12–4: letters of the chief of the ghetto police of Nov. 30 and Apr. 25, 1943.
51. Minutes, No. 56/117 (Nov. 30, 1941) and No. 52/176 (Sept. 6, 1942).
52. Wiederman, *op. cit.*, pp. 106–107.
53. Su-KC, Doc. 11 (July 15, 1942).
54. YaVA, microfilm JM/837, p. 17.
55. Mark Turkow, *Malka Ovshany dertsaylt* (Buenos Aires, 1948), p. 21.
56. Minutes, No. 7/68.
57. Mawult, *op. cit.*, p. 7 (Warsaw); graph of the organizational structure of the ghetto administration, Feb. 15, 1941 (Łódź); Zaderecki, p. 488 (Lwów); Su-KC, Docs. 283–285, p. 3 (Vilna).
58. *Kehilat Sherpts*, p. 444; testimony, No. G–28/328, p. 3 (YaVA).
59. Testimony, No. 1043, p. 13.
60. Testimony, No. Sh–87/942, pp. 4–5 (YaVA).
61. Zylberberg, *op. cit.*, p. 4.
62. Mark Turkow, *op. cit.*, p. 23.
63. *Sefer Stashev*, p. 452.
64. WaC, Doc. 42/2, pp. 7–8.
65. Mawult, *op. cit.*, pp. 12–13.
66. Ringelblum, *op. cit.*, pp. 116, 124; Jonas Turkow, *op. cit.*, p. 153.
67. Szende, *op. cit.*, p. 96.
68. Jacob Littner, *Aufzeichnungen aus einem Erdloch* (Munich, 1948), p. 90.
69. *Yizkor tsum undenk fun di kedoyshei Krasnystaw*, p. 105.
70. Testimony of Ignacy Sternbach (YIA).
71. *Sefer zikaron . . . Zavierche*, p. 362.
72. *Sefer Stashev*, p. 453.
73. J. Turkow, *op. cit.*, pp. 139, 146.
74. *Lodzher geto*, p. 422.
75. L. Garfunkel, *op. cit.*, p. 244.
76. Friedman, *op. cit.*, p. 618.
77. Pankiewicz, *op. cit.*, pp. 32–33; *Pinkos Novydvor* (1965), p. 329.
78. For the list of memorial books, see above, Chap. 2, n. 84.
79. Mawult, *op. cit.*, pp. 14, 16; J. Turkow, *op. cit.*, pp. 139, 152.
80. Rotenberg, *op. cit.*, p. 73.
81. Testimonies by Rabbi David Kahane and Ignacy Sternbach.
82. *Lodzher geto*, pp. 38, 413; J. Turkow, *op. cit.*, pp. 146–153; *Pinkos Novydvor*, p. 329; *Mezrych-zamlbukh* (1952), p. 559; *Yizkor-bukh Khelm*, p. 566; *Belkhatov-Yizkor-bukh*, pp. 418–419; *Dos bukh fun Lublin*, p. 424; testimony by Aron Grende (YIA); Smolar, *Fun Minsker geto*, pp. 86–87.
83. YaVA, testimony, No. K–87/1075, p. 19.
84. *Yizkor-bukh Khelm*, pp. 90, 91, 566.
85. Testimony by Henry Berger, pp. 4–5 (YIA).
86. Rotenberg, *op. cit.*, p. 73.
87. Benjamin Orenstein, *Otvotsk*, p. 40.
88. Testimony by Yakov Elbirt, pp. 8–9 (YIA).

89. J. Kermisz, *Akcje i Wysiedlenia*, p. 200.

90. Testimony, No. 1043, pp. 13–14. His name was Alvin Lippmann. He served as a pilot with the rank of lieutenant in the *Kaiser* army and was, according to the witness, acquainted with Goering and General Udet. His aide was also a Jew from Czechoslovakia.

91. *Stzhegover Yizkor-bukh*, p. 98.

92. Smolar, *op. cit.*, p. 87.

93. *Bericht Warschau*, p. 15; Mawult, *op. cit.*, p. 50.

94. YaVA, File B/12–4, chap. "Yidishe geto-politsey."

95. Orenstein, *op. cit.*, p. 13.

96. Testimony, No. 1043, p. 13.

97. *Lodzher geto*, p. 353.

98. Kruk, *op. cit.*, pp. 422–423.

99. AGV, File 113: report for Sept. 1940; ZC, BKC No. 94 (Apr. 19, 1943).

100. WaC, Doc. 42/2; *Blfg.*, Vol. IV, No. 2, p. 218.

101. Minutes, No. 17/141, March 31, 1942.

102. *Wohnbezirk*, p. 6 (Warsaw); graph of the Jewish ghetto administration of Feb. 15, 1941 (Łódź); ZC, BKC (Apr. 19, 1943).

103. Zaderecki, p. 488.

104. Su-KC, Docs. 283–285; Dvorzhetsky, *op. cit.*, p. 305.

105. YaVA, File B/12–4, chap. "Yidishe geto-politsey," p. 1.

106. Announcement, No. 292, June 25, 1942.

107. Mawult, *op. cit.*, p. 24; WaC, Doc. 42/2, pp. 5–6.

108. Brener, *op. cit.*, pp. 36–37.

109. Su-KC, Docs. 146, 283–285.

110. BKC, No. 94 (Apr. 19, 1943); No. 74 (March 3, 1943); AGV, File. 117.

111. Kruk, *op. cit.*, p. 156.

112. YaVA, File B/12–4, p. 1; Garfunkel, *op. cit.*, p. 238.

113. Kruk, *op. cit.*, pp. 373, 380.

114. Mawult, *op. cit.*, pp. 26–27.

115. Rotenberg, *op. cit.*, pp. 113–114.

116. Brener, *op. cit.*, p. 36.

117. *Yizkor-bukh Khelm*, p. 550.

118. Testimony by Rabbi David Kahane, pp. 17–18. Zaderecki (p. 486) relates that the badge of the OD was stamped by the mayor. At its inception the OD numbered 500 men.

119. *Sefer hazikaron lekdoyshey Bolekhov*, p. 308.

120. Photographs in YIA; the OD in Ozorków wore unusually high hats, apparently to ridicule them.

121. G.Ż., No. 5 (Jan. 17, 1941).

122. Doc. PS–3658, p. 2, Par. III[a].

123. Testimony by Berl Orlovsky (YIA); a photograph of an armband worn by the ghetto police in Kaunas (Garfunkel, *op. cit.*, Table 20).

124. Kruk, *op. cit.*, p. 380.

125. Minutes, No. 48/172, of Aug. 9, 1942. The salary of the chairman was set at 400 zlotys, that of a Council member at 325 zlotys, and that of a Council employee at 100 to 300 zlotys.

126. Ältestenrat der Juden in Pabianice, III Anlage zum Finanzbericht für September 1941" (microfilm JM/837).

127. Mawult, *op. cit.*, p. 12[a].

128. WaC, Doc. 42/1.

129. Ringelblum, *op. cit.*, pp. 116, 120–122, 231.

130. Garfunkel, *op. cit.*, p. 93; because almost all watches had been confiscated during the "delivery action," the OD used to awaken the workers at dawn with the exclamation: "Get up to the airport." (*ibid.*, p. 89, n. 9).

131. *Pinkos Gostynin* (New York, 1960), p. 253; *Pinkos Bendin*, p. 291; *Sefer zikaron . . . Zavierche*, p. 363; testimony by Leon Unger (YIA); *Khurbn Braynsk* (New York, 1948), p. 271.

132. *Drohichin*, p. 291.

133. *Khurbn Braynsk*, p. 275.

134. *Lukover kedoyshim un heldn*, p. 44.

135. Kruk, *op. cit.*, pp. 107–108.

136. Ringelblum, *op. cit.*, p. 111.

137. *Pinkos Kolomay*, pp. 334–335.

138. *Grodner Opklangen*, No. 2 (1949), p. 18.

139. Kruk, *op. cit.*, pp. 158, 296 ff.; cf. Dvorzhetsky, *op. cit.*, pp. 165, 302–303.

140. Dvorzhetsky, p. 165.

141. Yakov Goldberg, "Bletlekh fun Kovner eltestenrat," FLKh, No. 7, pp. 45–47; Garfunkel, *op. cit.*, pp. 242, 245; Kruk, *op. cit.*, pp. 78–79, 85, 175, 326.

142. There is a proliferation of contemporary and postwar literature about "The 13." To cite only a few: Ringelblum, *op. cit.* (index to Abraham Ganzweich and Sternfeld); Czerniakow's Diary, entries of May 10 and 30, of June 12, 13, and 19, of July 24, and of Aug. 5, all entries 1941; A. Rozenberg "Dos draytsentl", *Blfg*, Vol. 5, No. 1–2, pp. 187–225; No. 3, pp. 116–148; J. Turkow, *op. cit.*, pp. 155–178; Hilel Seidman, *Togbukh*, pp. 217–218; B. Mark, "Shmul Winters togbukh", *Blfg*, Vol. 3, No. 1–2. According to his Diary, Czerniakow's attitude toward Ganzweich was one of contempt. We may assume that Auerswald closed the Office to Fight against Usury and Speculation under his influence, but the so-called "First Aid" continued its existence and his officers participated in the "resettlement" of summer 1942; approximately 200 members of Ganzweich's police were included into the ranks of the regular OD.

143. Minutes of the June 20, 1942, Council meeting, and of the rally on June 21, 1942; Datner, "Khurbn Białystok un umgegnt"; "Fenigstein un Zelkovich–di hyenes fun białystoker geto," *Białystoker Shtime*, No. 255 (Sept.–Oct. 1949), pp. 41–48.; Reisner, *op. cit.*, pp. 94 ff. Grossman, *op. cit.* (1st ed. 1950), p. 77.

144. Pankiewicz, *op. cit.*, pp. 22–24, 32–34. *Sefer Kroke*, pp. 417, 422.

145. *Dos Bukh fun Lublin*, p. 474.

146. Wiederman, *op. cit.*, pp. 58–59.

147. *Lodzher geto*, pp. 38, 422, 475.

148. YaVA, testimony, No. H–55/207; *Grodner Opklangen*, No. 2 (1949), No. 3–4 (1950).

149. *Blfg*, Vol. IV, No. 2, pp. 187, 191, 193.

150. *Lodzher geto*, pp. 270–272.

151. *Ibid.*, pp. 320–321.

152. *Ibid.*, p. 272.

153. *Sefer yizkor lekehilat Shedlets*, p. 670. The OD men tore off the badges and wanted to step into the train together with all the Jews, but were prevented.

154. Minutes, No. 17/141.

155. Ringelblum, *op. cit.*, p. 293; J. Turkow, *op. cit.*, p. 392; Pankiewicz, *op. cit.*, pp. 147–148.

156. *Der Shturm* (underground periodical of the ghetto Bund) of July 5, 1942. It noted that only the 10 policemen knew that they were led away to be shot: "We note respectfully their dignified bearing" the paper concluded the report about this collective murder.

157. Szende, *op. cit.*, p. 157; testimony by Rabbi David Kahane.

158. *Sefer Rypin* (Tel Aviv, 1962), p. 820. *Stzhegove-yizkor-bukh* tells about the hanging in Feb. 1942 of 15 men, among whom were all the Councilmen and the ghetto police (p. 94), but it is not clear whether it is the same fact, or another similar occurrence.

159. *Lodzher geto*, p. 318. The reaction on the part of the victims was in most recorded instances a reverse one: the ghetto population was on the whole shocked by the participation of Jews in the "resettlements," whereby they were delivering to the enemy their own flesh and blood.

160. Ringelblum, *op. cit.*, pp. 270–271; *Oyf der vakh* (an underground paper of the Bund) of Sept. 20, 1942 (The Bund Archives in the name of Franz Kurski, New York).

161. ABLG (photocopy).

162. *Dos bukh fun Lublin*, section "der khurbn," *passim*.

163. Szende, *op. cit.*, p. 108.

164. Vladke (pseudonym), *Fun bayde zaytn fun geto-moyer* (New York, 1948), p. 39.

165. Ringelblum, *op. cit.*, pp. 275–276.

166. *Lodzher geto*, p. 326; Szende, *op. cit.*, p. 109; *Pinkos Kolomay*, p. 350; *Dos bukh fun Lublin*, p. 480.

167. Ringelblum, *op. cit.*, p. 275.

168. Szende, *op. cit.*, p. 143.

169. *Pinkos Kolomay*, p. 400; *Sefer Buchach*, p. 233; Szende, *op. cit.*, p. 108; Weisbrod, *op. cit.*, pp. 56–57; Kruk, *op. cit.*, p. 380; *Sefer Dembits* (Tel Aviv, 1960), p. 154.

170. Ringelblum, *op. cit.*, p. 284; *Sefer Kroke*, pp. 392, 406; Pankiewicz, *op. cit.*, p. 29; *Milkhome*, pp. 323–324; testimony by Moshe Levartov (Cracow); Dvorzhetsky, *op. cit.*, p. 302; *Pinkos Kolomay*, p. 350; testimony, No. 620, by R. Epstein (Buczacz); Weisbrod, *op. cit.*, pp. 56–57; testimony by Max Sokaletsky (Skałat). All cited testimonies are in YIA.

171. *Pinkos Zamoshch*, p. 952; *Pinkos Kolomay*, p. 350; *Pinkos Bendin*, p. 357.

172. YaVA, testimony, No. B–48/681.

173. Druk, *op. cit.*, p. 39; Mayer, *op. cit.*, p. 31; Szende, *op. cit.*, p. 143. Policemen of the Lublin Ghetto were once sent to the Markuszów Ghetto (Lublin district) in order to round up Jews for forced labor (*Khurbn un gevure . . . Markushev*, pp. 355–356).

174. *Bet hamishpat hamkhozi . . . , op. cit.*, p. 6.

175. Kruk, *op. cit.*, pp. 379–381; Z. Kalmanovich, *op. cit.*, pp. 41–42; Lea Rudashevsky, "Durch geto un katsetn," FLKh, No. 6, p. 40; testimony by Rachel Singer (YIA); Dvorzhetsky, *op. cit.*, pp. 414–416. These sources disagree in a number of details (e.g., the number of persons led out for execution and the number actually executed), but all confirm that the ghetto police of Vilna, headed by its commandant, conducted the "selection" and led away the doomed to the execution place. Only Dvorzhetsky relates that "more than 400 Jews were executed *exclusively* [italics added] by the ghetto police" (p. 414).

176. *Sefer Dembits*, p. 154.

177. Ringelblum, *op. cit.*, p. 123.

178. WaC, Doc. 42/2.

179. MTA, microfilm M–II/2–2 (Blumental, *op. cit.*, pp. 309–311).

180. Announcements, Nos. 287 and 288 (June 16 and 17, 1942); minutes of the meeting of the OD men with the leadership of the Council, June 20, 1942 (Blumental, *op. cit.*, pp. 195–201).

181. Ringelblum, *op. cit.*, p. 116.

182. Wiederman, *op. cit.*, pp. 255–256.

183. Mayer, *op. cit.*, p. 16; *Khurbn Głubok*, p. 73; Littner, *op. cit.*, p. 108 (Zbaraż); Questionnaire Nos. 666 (Rohatyn), 848 (Borysław).

184. A. Levin, *Mipinkaso shel hamore meyehudyiah* ("The Ghetto Fighters House" [Israel, 1964]), entry of July 29, 1942, p. 92.

185. Orenstein, *op. cit.*, p. 26.

186. Dr. I. Kanter, "Der Untergang fun Kolomay," *Dos naye lebn*, of Dec. 30, 1947.

187. *Ostrowtse* (1949), pp. 198–199.

188. Dr. Z. Levenbuk, "Di purim-aktsye in Baranovitsh," *Baderekh* (Rome), March 4, 1947.

189. *Sefer Kelts*, pp. 239–240.

190. *Sefer Kobryn*, pp. 317–318.

191. Questionnaire Nos. 348–353.

192. *Sefer Skernevits*, p. 640.

193. Pesakh Kaplan, "Der khurbn Białystok," (YIA, microfilm M–II/2–2).

194. Testimony by a ghetto survivor whose name cannot for the present be published (YIA).

195. *Kehilat Rohatyn vehasviva*, p. 294. The Jews of Rohatyn were alarmed by some OD men on the eve of Rosh Hashanah 1942, before the start of the second "action," and they escaped to the shelters (*ibid.*, p. 310).

196. Questionnaire No. 584.

197. *Sefer hazikaron lekdoyshey Bolekhov*, p. 321.

198. *Pinkos Kovel*, p. 101; *Kehilat Zharki*, p. 235; *Loshits, lezeykher an umgebrakhter kehile* (1963), pp. 260–261; *Grodner Opklangen*, No. 2 (1949), p. 18; *ibid.*, No. 3–4 (1950), p. 15; *Turne, kiyum un khurbn fun a yiddisher shtot* (1954), p. 811; J. Kaplan, "Gever in riger geto," FLKh, No. 1 (1946), p. 4; Kaufman, *op. cit.*, p. 181; Garfunkel, *op. cit.*, pp. 94, 95, 165.

199. *Blfg*, Vol. IV, No. 2, p. 201. Abrasha Blum, one of the leaders of the Bund in the Warsaw Ghetto was able to escape from the crowd brought to the Umschlagplatz, because of the help of a ghetto policeman (Bernard Goldstein, *op. cit.*, p. 280).

200. Ringelblum, *op. cit.*, p. 116.

201. A. Sh. Rosen, "Der umkum fun yiddish'n Sokolov," *Dos naye Lebn*, No. 69/141, p. 8; *Sefer kehilat Ostrolenka*, p. 350; *Sefer zikaron Chizhevo*, p. 1042.

202. *Pinkos Khmielnik*, p. 753.

203. *Sefer yizkor lekehilat Shedlets*, pp. 697–698.

204. Questionnaire No. 733.

205. M. Kaganovich, *Der ontayl fun yidn in der partizaner bawegung in sovietrusland*, p. 8.

206. Questionnaire No. 542.

207. *Baranovitsh, sefer zikaron*, pp. 469–470.

208. Su-KC, Doc. 617.

209. Dvorzhetsky, *op. cit.*, p. 303; Abraham Sutskever, *Vilner geto, 1941–1944* (Paris, 1946), pp. 179–180; Kalmanovich, *op. cit.*, p. 65; Yitzhak Kovalsky, *Di gehayme drukeray fun yidishn untergrunt in lite un waysrusland* (New York, 1953), p. 32; Neomi, "Der I-ter May in vilner geto," *Dror* (Łódź), May 1947, p. 10.

210. Garfunkel, *op. cit.*, p. 174; cf. Zvi A. Braun and Dov Levin, *op. cit.*, pp. 201, 212, 216, 221.

211. Yelin M. un Gelpern D., *Partizaner fun kaunaser geto* (Moscow, 1948), p. 59.

212. Garfunkel, *op. cit.*, pp. 171, 183; Zvi A. Braun and Dov Levin, *Toledoteha shel makhteret* (Jerusalem, 1962), pp. 352–355.

213. Kaplan, *op. cit.*, pp. 4–5; Kaufmann, *op. cit.*, pp. 174–179.
214. Questionnaire Nos. 726–728, 723, 724.
215. *Sefer zikaron lekehilat Stolin* (Tel Aviv, 1952), p. 216.
216. *Kehilat Rohatyn vehasviva*, p. 228; Questionnaire No. 666.
217. Questionnaire No. 771.
218. Tuvie veZushe Bielski, *Yehudey yaar* (Tel Aviv, 1946), p. 58.
219. Arieh Bauminger, "Mordey geto kroke," *Sefer Kroke*, p. 425.
220. J. Turkow, *op. cit.*, p. 154.
221. *Braynsk sefer hazikaron*, p. 271.
222. Questionnaire No. 426.
223. Kermisz, "Khmielniker yidn untern nazi-rezhim," *Pinkos Khmielnik*, p. 683.
224. Questionnaire No. 350.
225. *Kehilat Sarny*, p. 309.
226. J. Turkow, *op. cit.*, pp. 143, 406; Meilech Neustadt, *Khurban umered shel yehudey varshe* (Tel Aviv, 1947), pp. 86, 90. Acts of revenge against particularly hateful policemen were also carried out in other ghettos, as, for instance, in Międzyrzec (H. Rylski, "Mezrych in period fun der hitlerisher okupatsye," *Blfg*, Vol. VIII, No. 3–4 [1955], p. 48).
227. Report by a Polish underground courier ("Lilka") on the situation in the Warsaw ghetto (The Bund Archives, New York); cf. Ringelblum, *op. cit.*, p. 213, in which he argues against this opinion.
228. Bauminger, *op. cit.*, p. 419.
229. *Ibid.*, p. 224.
230. Hanna Wiernik-Shlesinger, "Eydut akhat," *Yalkut Moreshet*, Vol. I (1963), p. 76. The commandant of the OD in the Będzin Ghetto cooperated with the resistance group as the liquidation date of the ghetto approached, when there was no doubt about the coming end (*Bet hamishpat hamkhozi . . . , op. cit.*, p. 12).
231. Rylski, *op. cit.*, p. 48.
232. WaC, Doc. 42/2, p. 6; *Lodzher geto*, p. 38.
233. YaVA, File B/12–4, p. 14 (Kaunas); minutes, No. 50/174, Aug. 26, 1942 (Lublin).
234. AGV, File 220, p. 111. They numbered 522 persons in July 1943, to whom the fire security of 85 objects was assigned.
235. YaVA, File B/12–4, p. 14 (Kaunas): minutes, No. 50/174, Aug. 26, 1942 (Lublin).
236. Minutes, No. 50/174.
237. YaVA, File B/12–4, p. 14 (Kaunas); minutes, No. 50/174, Aug. 26, 1942 (Lublin).
238. *Lodzher geto*, p. 272; *Yizkor-bukh fun der Zhelekhover kehile*, p. 228.

CHAPTER 19

1. B. Mark, *op. cit.*, *Blfg*, Vol. VII, No. 1 (1954), pp. 25–30.
2. Su-KC, Docs. 286ᵃ, 305, 305ᵃ.
3. MTA, announcement, No. 326 (Blumental, *op. cit.*, p. 480).
4. *Ibid.*, p. 461.
5. *Lodzher geto*, pp. 414, 420.
6. Gliksman, *op. cit.*, pp. 299–300.
7. *Ibid.*, pp. 300–303.
8. Yerushalmi, *op. cit.*, p. 116.
9. Minutes of the general meetings of Nov. 9 and 23, 1941, and Apr. 5, 1942.

10. Announcement, No. 253, Apr. 22, 1942; minutes, May 31, 1942.

11. Minutes, Aug. 24 and Nov. 8, 1942, and others.

12. Minutes of the "special meeting" of Oct. 11, 1942 (Blumental, *op. cit.*, p. 253).

13. *Sefer Kolomay*, p. 332; Waga, *op. cit.*, p. 83; *Milkhome*, p. 227; *Min hamoked*, pp. 35–36 (Radom); *Pinkos Bendin, passim*; and others.

14. Su-KC, Docs. 302, 338, 339.

15. Kruk, *op. cit.*, p. 598.

16. Ringelblum, *op. cit.*, pp. 96, 97; apparently the man was apprehended in order to be sent to a labor camp.

17. *Lodzher geto*, pp. 108, 379.

18. *Ibid.*, p. 380.

19. Kurts, *Sefer eydut*, pp. 148, 149.

20. WaC, Docs. 34/1, 34/2.

21. Testimony by Mirka Weis (YIA).

22. Photocopy in ABLG.

23. Blumental, *Teudot mgeto Lublin*, p. 53.

24. Minutes, No. 51, Blumental, *op. cit.*, p. 192.

25. *Pinkos Bendin*, p. 349.

26. Tabaksblat, *op. cit.*, pp. 93–94.

27. During the night of Apr. 18, 1942, the Gestapo dragged over 50 persons from their homes, among them a large number of participants in the underground press, and shot them in the streets.

28. Ringelblum, *op. cit.*, p. 218.

29. [Mordecai W. Bernstein], "Bibliografye fun der bundisher prese in varshever geto," *Historisher zamlbukh* (Warsaw, 1948), pp. 30–32.

30. I. Trunk, *Geshtalten un gesheyenishn* (Buenos Aires, 1962), pp. 139–140; a more detailed account in the chap., "Dos politishe lebn in di getos," *ibid.*, pp. 132–172.

31. Brener, *op. cit.*, pp. 54–55.

32. A few issues are preserved in the Bund Archives in the name of Franz Kurski, File *Lodzher geto*.

33. See, e.g., No. 33 of Sept. 10, 1943, pp. 3–6, 10, 11.

34. *Blfg*, Vol. IV, No. 2, pp. 186–187. Czerniakow refused to sign the Council announcement of July 24, 1942, which called upon the Jews to appear voluntarily at the assembly square, and committed suicide the same day. The announcement is signed, "the Jewish Council in Warsaw."

35. YaVA, File DN/3–4, p. 207. The report tells about "clashes between German officials and Jews."

36. *Lodzher geto*, p. 380.

37. AGV, File 115: "Tätigkeitsbericht der Getto-Verwaltung für 1–30.9.1940."

38. *Lodzher geto*, pp. 380–381.

39. *Ibid.*, pp. 382–385.

40. Zvi Rosenwein, "Der hunger-shtrayk in chenstokhover geto," *Chenstochov* (New York, 1958), pp. 47–49.

41. Ringelblum, *op. cit.*, pp. 165–166.

42. AJHI, testimony, No. 303.

43. *Ibid.*, JUS, File No. 9: memorandum of the local relief-committee to JDC, Jan. 1, 1941.

44. Shmerke Kacherginski, *Lider fun getos un lagern* (New York, 1948), pp. 177–197. Regarding jokes and satires against Czerniakow and other members of the *Judenrat*, see WaC, File 38/2, pp. 19–20, 49, 53, 59–60.

45. ZC, Doc. 26, pp. 8, 51; Doc. 55, p. 35; *Lodzher geto*, p. 392.

CHAPTER 20

1. YIA, ADPC, Germany, File 1532.

2. *Ibid.*, various files.

3. YaVA, microfilm, signature M–21/39–62.

4. YaVA, microfilm, signature M–21/37–32.

5. ADPC, Germany, File 1531: sentence against Mietek Bornstein vel Czapnicki.

6. *Ibid.*, File 1737: sentence in the trial against Szmul Żbik.

7. Interview with the attorney general of Hamburg, Herr Kurt Jegge, published in *Der Stern* (Hamburg), Oct. 20, 1968. This assertion was also confirmed by some defendants in the *Einsatzgruppen* trial before the Nuremberg Military Tribunal (Case No. 9), such as Ohlendorf and Hartel, who testified, that those unwilling to carry out the execution orders of their superiors were sent back to Germany or or were assigned to other tasks (*Trials of War Criminals before the Nuremberg Military Tribunal*, Vol. IV, pp. 481–482). This was also the opinion of Judge Michal E. Musmanno in his testimony in the Eichmann trial in Jerusalem during the session of May 15, 1961 (minutes of Session No. 40, stencil).

8. YaVA, microfilm signature M–21/41–112.

9. YaVA, microfilm, signature M–21/43–145: sentence in the trial against David Najman.

10. YaVA, microfilm, signature M–21/39–54: sentence against Josef Włodawski.

11. Testimony by Moshe Zemel (YIA), *Sefer Kelts*, pp. 239–240. *Sefer Kelts* does not mention the fact of lynching.

12. ADPC, Germany, File 2283.

13. Sentences and lists of executed sentences in N. Blumental and Joseph Kermisz, *Hameri vehamered begeto Varshe* (Jerusalem, 1965), pp. 116, 123–124, 127, 146–147; *Hekhaluts halokhem*, No. 33 (Sept. 19, 1943), pp. 4–6.

14. *Baderekh*, organ of *Merkaz hapleytim beyitalie* of Aug. 27, Sept. 30, Nov. 1, and Nov. 15, 1948: There were also sessions of the court on Oct. 21 and 27, but no accounts on these sessions were available to the author.

15. YIA, ADPC, Italy, File 304.

16. YaVA, microfilm, signature M–21/37–20.

17. YaVA, microfilm, signature M–21/39–71. The sentence charged him with participation in "resettlement action in the years 1940–1941." If the copyist has not made typographical error (i.e., 1942 instead of 1941), the period given is erroneous because the first "resettlement action" in the Olkusz Ghetto took place in July 1942.

18. ADPC, Germany, Files 1531, 1533.

19. YaVA, microfilm, signature M–21/39–54.

20. YaVA, microfilm, signature M–21/43–145.

21. YaVA, microfilm, signature M–21/40–77.

22. YaVA, microfilm, signature M–21/37–32.

23. YaVA, microfilm, signature M–21/39–51.

24. ADPC, Germany, File 1530; YaVA, signature M–21/39–62.

25. YaVA, signature M–21/39–65.

26. YaVA, signature M–21/42–128.

27. YaVA, signature M–21/38–36.

28. YaVA, signature M–21/40–79.

29. ADPC, Italy, Files 309, 318.

30. ADPC, Italy, File 1531. Apparently the juridical department of the Central Committee in Munich used to inform the offices of JDC and HIAS immediately after completing an investigation against a suspect, as a precaution (*ibid.*, letter to the office of JDC, Apr. 10, 1949).

31. *Sefer hakhukim,* 57 (Aug. 9, 1950).

32. Indictment and sentence of the defendant by the Court of Peace in Tel Aviv (photocopy in YIA).

33. *Bet hamishpat hamkhozi, Tel-Aviv-Yaffo, tik plili 15/63, psak din,* pp. 9–10.

34. *Piskey-din shel bet hamishpat haelyon beisrael.* Vol. XVIII (1964/1965), *khelek sheni,* 4, pp. 95–96.

35. *Ibid.,* p. 98. *Bet hamishpat hamkhozi* . . . , *op. cit.,* p. 1.

36. *Bet hamishpat hamkhozi* . . . , *op. cit.,* pp. 8–9.

37. *Ibid.,* p. 11.

38. *Piskey-din shel bet hamishpat* . . . , *op. cit.,* pp. 94–96.

39. *Bet hamishpat hamkhozi* . . . , *op. cit.,* p. 11

40. *Piskey-din shel bet hamishpat* . . . , *op. cit.,* p. 101.

41. *Bet hamishpat hamkhozi* . . . , *op. cit.,* pp. 20–21.

42. *Piskey-din shel bet hamishpat* . . . , *op. cit.,* pp. 107–108.

43. *Ibid.,* p. 89.

Index of Places

Index of Persons, Organizations, Offices

Note: It was not possible to find first names of some persons. In these cases, an attempt was made to identify them by other biographical data. Names of certain individuals appear in the sources only by one or two initials, and these initials are not included in the index. The bibliographical material contained in the notes is not included in the index.